LEARNING Microsoft® WORD 2002

Suzanne Weixel

275 Madison Avenue, New York, NY 10016

Acknowledgements

Thanks to everyone at DDC Publishing, especially Jennifer Frew, Chris Katsaropoulos, James Reidel, and Yvonne Gilchrist. And, of course, to my family, Rick, Nathaniel, and Evan.

Suzanne Weixel

Managing Editor
Jennifer Frew

Technical Editors
Gabrielle Nemes
James Reidel

Design and Layout
Shu Chen
Elviro Padro

Acquisitions Manager
Chris Katsaropoulos

Cover Design
Amy Capuano

Published by DDC Publishing

For information, address DDC Publishing, Inc., 275 Madison Avenue, New York, NY 10016
http://www.ddcpub.com

DDC Publishing Inc. Printing

10 9 8 7 6 5 4 3 2

Printed in the United States of America.

Contents

Introduction vi

Microsoft® Office User Specialist (MOUS) Information x

MOUS Index xi

Directory of Data Files on CD ... xiv

Lesson 1: Getting Started with Word 1

Exercise 1 2
- About Microsoft® Word 2002
- Conventions Used in This book
- Use the Mouse
- Use the keyboard
- Start Word 2002
- The Word Window
- Exit Word

Exercise 2 10
- Execute Commands
- Use Menus
- Use Toolbars
- Use Dialog Box Options
- Use Shortcut Menus
- Use Task Panes

Exercise 3 17
- Use Window Controls
- Use Zoom
- Scroll a Window

Exercise 4 23
- Use the Ask a Question Box
- Use the Help Program
- Use the What's This? Pointer
- Use the Office Assistant
- Microsoft Word on the Web
- Recover a Document

Exercise 5 29
- Critical Thinking

Lesson 2: CREATE, Save, and Print Documents 31

Exercise 6 32
- Create a New Document
- Type in a Document
- Use Click and Type
- Correct Errors
- Use Undo and Redo
- Save a New Document
- Create Folders
- Close a Document

Exercise 7 37
- Preview a Document
- Print

Exercise 8 41
- Insertion Point Movements
- Change the View
- Full Screen View
- Show/Hide Marks
- Rulers

Exercise 9 45
- Use AutoCorrect
- Select Text in a Document
- Replace Selected Text
- Align Text Horizontally
- Save Changes

Exercise 10 53
- Select a Font
- Change Font Size
- Apply Font Styles

Exercise 11 59
- Correct Spelling as You Type
- Correct Grammar as You Type
- Check Spelling
- Check Grammar
- Use the Thesaurus

Exercise 12 65
- Format a Full-block Business Letter
- Insert the Date and Time
- Use Shrink to Fit

Exercise 13 71
- Set Tabs
- Format a Modified-block Business Letter
- Create Envelopes
- Create Labels

Exercise 14 78
- Critical Thinking

Lesson 3: Open and Edit DOCUMENTS 81

Exercise 15 82
- Open a Recently Used Document
- Open Any Stored Document
- Save a Document with a New Name

Exercise 16 86
- Use Proofreaders' Marks
- Insert Text
- Use Overtype Mode
- Use Uppercase Mode
- Change Case

Exercise 17 90
- Move Text in a Document
- Cut and Paste Text
- Use the Clipboard
- Use Drag-and-Drop Editing
- Move Paragraph

Exercise 18 96
- Use Copy and Paste
- Copy Text with Drag-and-Drop

Exercise 19 100
- Critical Thinking

Lesson 4: Text Formatting ... 103

Exercise 20 104
- Apply Font Effects
- Apply Text Effects
- Apply Underlines
- Apply Font Color

Exercise 21 108
- Highlight Text
- Copy Formatting

Exercise 22 112
- Apply Styles
- Create a Style
- Modify a Style
- Reapply Direct Formatting
- Check Formatting
- Select Paste Formatting Options
- Clear Formatting

Exercise 23 118
- Insert Symbols and Special Characters
- Customize Toolbars

Exercise 24 124
- Bulleted Lists
- Numbered Lists
- Sort

Exercise 19 130
- Critical Thinking

Lesson 5: Document Formatting 133

Exercise 26 134
- Vertical Alignment

Exercise 27 138
- Line Spacing
- Paragraph Spacing
- Indent Text

Exercise 28 144
- Format a One-page Report
- Set Margins
- Set Page Orientation

Exercise 29 149
- Create Footnotes and Endnotes

Exercise 30 154
- Create Hyperlinks

Exercise 31 160
- Critical Thinking

Lesson 6: Manage Documents 163

Exercise 32 164
- Open a Document as Read-only
- Open a Document from Windows
- File Types

Exercise 33 169
- Preview a Closed Document
- Print Files without Opening Them

Exercise 34 174
- Document Properties

Exercise 35 177
- Use Basic Search to Find a File

Exercise 36 182
- Critical Thinking

Lesson 7: Creating Tables 185

Exercise 37 186
- Insert a Table
- Move the Insertion Point in a Table
- Enter Data in a Table
- Format a Table

Exercise 38 192
- Select in a Table
- Insert Columns, Rows, or Cells
- Delete Columns, Rows, or Cells

Exercise 39 197
- Set Alignments with Table Cells
- Align Table on the Page
- Column Width and Row Height

Exercise 40 204
- Use the Tables and Borders Toolbar
- Draw a Table
- Merge and Split Cells

Exercise 41 211
- Move and Resize Tables
- Rotate Text
- Wrap Text

Exercise 42 216
- Calculate in a Table
- Number Formats
- Sort Rows

Exercise 43 222
- Cell Borders and Shading

Exercise 44 226
- Critical Thinking

LESSON 8: Merge 229

Exercise 45 230
- Mail Merge Basics
- Use the Mail Merge Wizard
- Create a New Address List
- Use Merge Fields

Exercise 46 238
- Merge with an Existing Address List
- Merge Envelopes

Exercise 47 244
- Edit an Address List
- Customize Merge Fields
- Merge Labels

Exercise 48 250
- Sort Recipients in an Address List
- Select Specific Recipients
- Filter Recipients
- Create a Director with Mail Merge

Exercise 49 257
- Critical Thinking

LESSON 9: Multiple-Page Documents 261

Exercise 50 262
- Create an Outline
- Edit an Outline
- Collapse and Expand Outlines
- Number an Outline

Exercise 51 267
- Insert Hard Page Breaks
- Insert Section Breaks
- Insert Page Numbers
- Control Text Flow
- View the Word Count

Exercise 52 276
- Create Headers/Footers
- Different First Page Headers/Footers
- Different Odd/Even Headers/Footers
- Different Section Headers/Footers

Exercise 53 282
- Use Document Map
- Copy or Move Text from One Page to Another

Exercise 54 291
- Preview Multiple Pages
- Drag and Drop Text from One Page to Another
- Print Specific Pages

Exercise 55 297
- Find and Replace
- Insert bookmarks
- Select Browse Object

Exercise 56 304
- Create a Master Document
- Work with Subdocuments

Exercise 57 312
- Insert a Cross-reference
- Create an Index
- Modify an Index

Exercise 58 320
- Create a Table of Contents
- Update a Table of Contents

Exercise 59 324
- Critical Thinking

LESSON 10: The Internet 331

Exercise 60 332
- Internet Basics
- Use Internet Features in Word
- Save a Web Page Locally
- Work with the Favorites folder

Exercise 61 338
- Search the Internet
- Print Web Page Information
- Copy Data from a Web page to a Word Document

Exercise 62 342
- Create a Web Page Document in Word
- Use Web Layout View
- Preview a Web Page
- Open an HTML Document

Exercise 63 346
- Use Web Page Titles
- Web Page Graphics
- Apply a Background
- Apply a Theme

Exercise 64 350
- Use Tables in HTML Documents
- Use Web Page Templates
- Insert a Link Bar in a Word Document

Exercise 65 355
- Critical Thinking

LESSON 11: Collaboration 357

Exercise 66 358
- Insert Comments
- Track Changes
- Customize Revision Marks
- Compare and Merge Documents
- Accept/Reject Changes

Exercise 67 366
- Create Multiple Versions of a Document
- Protect a Document
- Use Digital Signatures

Exercise 68 372
- Open Multiple Documents
- Arrange Documents On-screen
- Copy/Move Text from One Document to Another

Exercise 69 378
- Send E-mail from Word
- Attach a Word Document to an E-mail Message
- Send a Word Document as E-mail
- Copy Data from a Word Document into an E-mail Message

Exercise 70 385
- Receive E-mail Messages in Outlook or Outlook Express
- Print an E-mail Message
- Save an E-mail Attachment

Exercise 71 388
- Merge to an E-Mail Message

Exercise 72 392
- Critical Thinking

LESSON 12: Desktop Publishing and Automation 395

Exercise 73 396
- Create Newsletter Columns
- Set Column Width
- Insert Column Breaks
- Balance Columns

Exercise 74 402
- Use Dropped Capitals
- Enhance a Document with Borders and Shading

Exercise 75 408
- Templates
- Wizards
- Save a Document as a Template
- Set Default File Location for Workgroup Templates

Exercise 76 414
- Insert a File in a Document
- Use AutoText

Exercise 77 419
- Record a Macro
- Run a Macro

Exercise 78 425
- Create a Form
- Insert Form Fields
- Set Form Field Options
- Fill Out a Form

Exercise 79 433
- Critical Thinking

Lesson 13: Graphics on CD 439

Exercise 80 440
- About Graphics Objects
- Insert Drawing Objects
- Use the Drawing Canvas
- Move Drawing Objects
- Set Text Wrap Options

Exercise 81 448
- Select Objects
- Resize Objects
- Use a Text Box
- Copy an Object
- Align Drawing Objects

Exercise 82 456
- About Clip Art
- Insert Clip Art

Exercise 83 462
- Download Graphics Objects from the Web

Exercise 84 466
- Adjust Objects
- Rotate and Flip Objects

Exercise 85 470
- Line Color and Style
- Fill Color
- Shadows and 3-D Effects

Exercise 86 476
- Group and Ungroup Objects
- Layer Objects and Text

Exercise 87 482
- Create WordArt
- WordArt Text
- WordArt Shapes and Formatting

Exercise 88 488
- Watermarks

Exercise 89 494
- Critical Thinking

Lesson 14: Integration on CD 497

Exercise 90 498
- Microsoft® Office XP
- Run Multiple Programs at the Same Time
- Arrange Multiple Program Windows
- Switch Among Open Programs

Exercise 91 503
- Copy and Move Data from One Office Document to Another

Exercise 92 509
- Link Files
- Edit a Linked Object
- Update Links

Exercise 93 515
- Embed Objects
- Edit Embedded Objects

Exercise 94 521
- Create a Chart
- Modify a Chart
- Import Data into a Chart
- Create Diagrams and Organization Charts

Exercise 95 531
- Use Smart Tags

Exercise 96 537
- Merge a Word Document with an Access Database

Exercise 97 541
- Embed a PowerPoint Slide in a Word Document
- Export PowerPoint Slides and Notes to a Word Document
- Export PowerPoint Text to a Word Document

Exercise 98 549
- Critical Thinking

Lesson 15: Challenge Exercises on CD 555

Exercise 99 556
- Locate Data on the Internet
- Make Web Data Available for use Offline
- Edit and Format a Table in a Word Document
- Send a Word Document via E-mail

Exercise 100 560
- Link a Worksheet into a Word Document
- Locate Data on the Internet
- Edit Excel Worksheet
- Update Linked Object in a Word Document

Exercise 101 563
- Save a Word Document as a Web Page
- Download Clip Art and Insert it on a Web Page
- Link Excel Data with a Web Page
- Update Linked Data

Exercise 102 566
- Create a Home Page Using a Table
- Link the Home Page to a Presentation Web Site
- Link the Home Page to an Internet Site
- Add a Web page to Your Favorites Folder
- Print a Web Page off the Internet

Exercise 103 569
- Use Smart Tags to Locate Financial Data on the Internet
- Copy Data from the Internet into an Excel Worksheet
- Use Excel Worksheet Data to Create a Word Table
- Attach a Word Document to an E-mail Message

Exercise 104 573
- Use an Access Database as a Merge Data Source
- Change the Data Source for a Merge

Exercise 105 575
- Use Graphics Objects to Create a Double-Sided Flyer
- Insert a File
- Apply Newsletter Formatting
- Use Mail Merge to Generate Mailing Labels

Index

Introduction

Microsoft Word 2002 is Microsoft's word processing application. Using Word 2002 you can create business letters, memos, Web pages, newsletters, and more. Using formatting features, such as tables or drawing, you can improve the appearance of your word processing documents.

How We've Organized the Book

Learning Microsoft Word 2002 is made up of fifteen lessons:

- Lesson I: Basics
  This short lesson introduces essential Word 2002 skills—including how to start Word, how to use the mouse and keyboard, screen elements, and an overview of features in the Word application.
- Lesson 2: Create, Save, and Print Documents
  In this lesson, you will create and work with Word documents. You will also learn how to format business letters, envelopes, and labels.
- Lesson 3: Open and Edit Documents
  Essential editing skills are introduced in this lesson.
- Lesson 4: Text Formatting
  For documents to be effective, they must be formatted properly. Formatting skills are introduced in this lesson.
- Lesson 5: Document Formatting
  Work with alignment, line and paragraph spacing, and hyperlinks in this lesson. You will also create and format a one-page report.
- Lesson 6: Manage Documents
  In this lesson, you will preview files and work with document properties. You will also learn to locate a file—even if you're not sure of the file name or exact location.
- Lesson 7: Tables
  Use Word tables to organize information more clearly.
- Lesson 8: Merge
  Merge is used to create form letters, envelopes, and labels. You will learn how to do a mass mailing quickly and easily using Word's Merge feature.
- Lesson 9: Multiple-page Documents
  Work with multiple-page documents, headers and footers, and outlines in this lesson.
- Lesson 10: The Internet
  The Internet is one of the greatest resources for locating information as well as sharing information. In this lesson, Internet basics and Web page creation is covered.
- Leeson 11: Collaboration
  Word 2002 makes it easier to work and share information with others. In this lesson, you will learn to work with document revision features and sending e-mail from Word.
- Lesson 12: Desktop Publishing and Automation
  Learn to use many of Word's desktop publishing features, such as columns, borders and shading, and text boxes. Also included in this lesson are templates and macros.
- Lesson 13: Graphics on CD
  Enhance Word documents with graphics objects, clip art, and AutoShapes. In this lesson, you will also use the Internet simulation to download clip art from the Internet.
- Lesson 14: Integration on CD
  If you are using Word as part of the Office XP suite, it is import to know how to integrate the applications. Learn to copy information between programs, embed an Excel worksheet in a Word document, and merge a Word document with an Access Database
- Lesson 13: Challenge Exercises on CD
  This lesson combines critical thinking, application integration, and Internet skills. In the Challenge Lesson, you will retrieve data from the Internet, send Web documents via e-mail, download clip art, create a Web page, and more. In each exercise, only basic step directions are given—you need to rely on your own skills to complete the exercise.

Each lesson in Learning Microsoft Word 2002 is made up of short exercises designed for using Word 2002 in real-life business settings. Every application exercise is made up of seven key elements:

- On the Job. Each exercise starts with a brief description of how you would use the features of that exercise in the workplace.
- Exercise Scenario. The Word tools are then put into context by setting a scenario. For example, you may be a marketing assistant at a video production company developing documents to send to prospective clients.
- Terms. Key terms are included and defined at the start of each exercise, so you can quickly refer back to them. The terms are then highlighted in the text.
- Notes. Concise notes for learning the computer concepts.
- Procedures. Hands-on mouse and keyboard procedures teach all necessary skills.
- Application Exercise. Step-by-step instructions put your skills to work.
- On Your Own. Each exercise concludes with a critical thinking activity that you can work through on your own. You may have to create a personal Web page or compose a business letter. You are challenged to come up with data and then additionally challenged to use the data in a document. The *On Your Own* sections can be used as additional reinforcement, for practice, or to test skill proficiency.
- In addition, each lesson ends with a Critical Thinking Exercise. As with the *On Your Owns*, you need to rely on your own skills to complete the task.

Working with Data and Solution Files

As you work through the exercises in this book, you'll be creating, opening, and saving files. You should keep the following instructions in mind:

- Many exercises instruct you to open a file from the CD-ROM that comes with this book. The data files are used so that you can focus on the skills being introduced—not on keyboarding lengthy documents. The files are located in the Datafiles folders on the CD-ROM.

  ✓ *See What's on the CD for more information on the data files.*

- When the application exercise includes a file name and a CD icon and a keyboard icon, you can either use your exercise file that you created in a previous exercise or use the data file provided on CD.
- The Directory of Files on CD lists the exercise file (from the CD-ROM) you can open to complete each exercise.
- Unless the book instructs otherwise, use the default settings for text size, margin size, and so on when creating a file. If someone has changed the default software settings for the computer you're using, your exercise files may not look the same as those shown in this book. In addition, the appearance of your files may look different if the system is set to a screen resolution other than 800 x 600.
- All the exercises instruct you to save the files created or to save the exercise files under a new name. You should verify the name of the hard disk or network folder to which files should be saved.

What's on the CD

We've included on the CD:

- Data files for many of the exercises. This way you don't have to type lengthy documents from scratch.
- Internet simulation so that you can go to real Web sites to get information—without an Internet connection or modem. Following the steps in the book, you will experience going "online" to locate facts, data, and clip art. You will then use the information in Word documents.
- Bonus Lesson of advanced skills. The bonus lessons cover graphics, application integration, and challenge exercises. The bonus lesson are provided in .pdf format. You must first install Adobe Acrobat (provided on the CD) before you can open, view, or print the files. Once Adobe Acrobat is installed, you simply double-click the file to open it. Exercises can be printed out and distributed.
- Typing tests with automatic scoring can be used to test typing speed and accuracy.
- Keyboarding course for those who wish to practice and improve their keyboarding skills.
- Computer Literacy Basics include information on computer care, computer basics, and a brief history of computers. Once Adobe Acrobat is installed, these exercises can be printed out and distributed.

To Access the Files Included with This Book

1. Insert the *Learning Word 2002* CD in the CD-ROM drive. A menu of options should automatically appear. If it does not, perform the following steps:
   a. Click Start>Run.
   b. Type D:\CDmain.exe (where D: is the letter of your CD-ROM drive).
2. Move the mouse pointer over a menu item to display information on how to install or access the files.
3. Click a menu item to activate it.

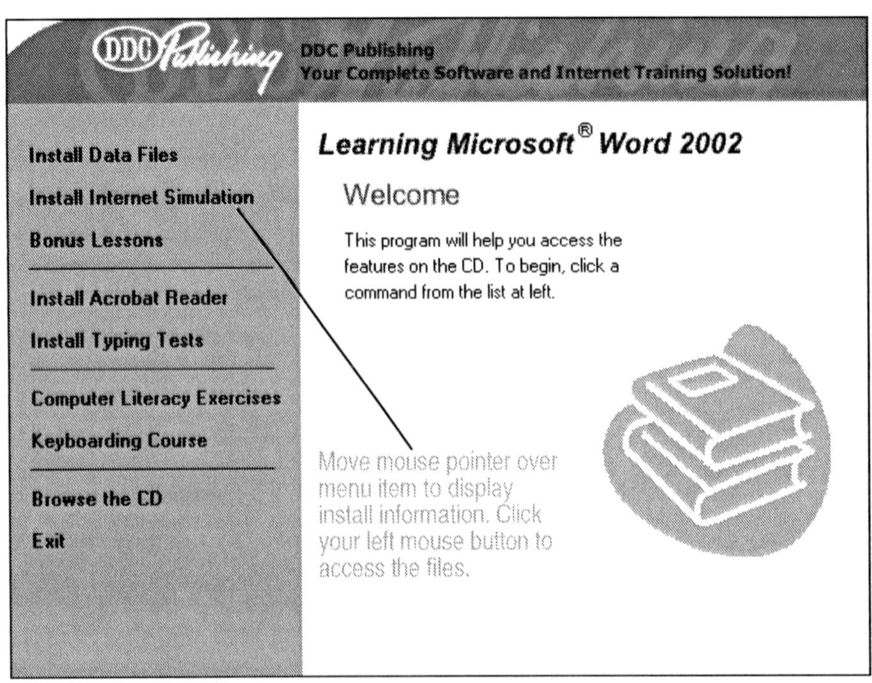

Support Material

A complete instructor support package is available with all the tools teachers need:

- Annotated Instructor's Edition includes entire student book with teacher notes, course curriculum guide, and lesson plans. (Catalog number Z98TE)
- Visual aid on diskette—25 PowerPoint slides. (Catalog number VA98)
- CD of exercise solutions. (Catalog number SL2002)
- Printout of exercise solutions to compare students' printouts with. (Catalog number SLB98)

APPROVED COURSEWARE

What does this logo mean?

It means this courseware has been approved by the Microsoft® Office User Specialist Program to be among the finest available for learning Microsoft Word 2002. It also means that upon completion of this courseware, you may be prepared to become a Microsoft Office User Specialist.

What is a Microsoft Office User Specialist?

A Microsoft Office User Specialist is an individual who has certified his or her skills in one or more of the Microsoft Office desktop applications of Microsoft Word, Microsoft Excel, Microsoft PowerPoint®, Microsoft Outlook® or Microsoft Access, or in Microsoft Project. The Microsoft Office User Specialist Program typically offers certification exams at the "Core" and "Expert" skill levels. * The Microsoft Office User Specialist Program is the only Microsoft approved program in the world for certifying proficiency in Microsoft Office desktop applications and Microsoft Project. This certification can be a valuable asset in any job search or career advancement.

More Information:

To learn more about becoming a Microsoft Office User Specialist, visit www.mous.net

To purchase a Microsoft Office User Specialist certification exam, visit www.DesktopIQ.com

To learn about other Microsoft Office User Specialist approved courseware from DDC Publishing, visit http://ddcpub.com and http://www.trainteachers.com/html/mouscert.html

---

* The availability of Microsoft Office User Specialist certification exams varies by application, application version and language. Visit www.mous.net for exam availability.

Index of MOUS Objectives

Microsoft Office User Specialist (MOUS) is a certification program to help users prove their ability to use Office programs. MOUS offers two levels of Word certification: Core and Expert. All the MOUS objectives are covered in this book.

Skill Sets and Skills Being Measured—Word Core	**Exercise**
Inserting and Modifying Text	
Insert, modify and move text and symbols	9, 16, 17, 23, 55, 68, 69, 81 (on CD), 91 (on CD)
Apply and modify text formats	20, 21, 22
Correct spelling and grammar usage	11
Apply font and text effects	20, 21
Enter and format Date and Time	12
Apply character styles	20, 22
Creating and Modifying Paragraphs	
Modify paragraph formats	26, 27, 74
Set and modify tabs	13
Apply bullet, outline, and numbering format to paragraphs	24, 50
Apply paragraph styles	22
Formatting Documents	
Create and modify a header and footer	52
Apply and modify column settings	9, 73
Modify document layout and Page Setup options	28, 51
Create and modify tables	37, 38, 39, 30, 41, 42, 43
Preview and Print documents, envelopes, and labels	7, 13, 33, 54
Managing Documents	
Manage files and folders for documents	6
Create documents using templates	64, 75
Save documents using different names and file formats	9, 15

Working with Graphics	
Insert images and graphics	80, 81, 82, 87 (all on CD)
Create and modify diagrams and charts	94 (on CD)
Workgroup Collaboration	
Compare and Merge documents	66
Insert, view and edit comments	66
Convert documents into Web pages	62
Skill Sets and Skills Being Measured—Word Expert	**Exercise**
Customizing Paragraphs	
Control Pagination	51
Sort paragraphs in lists and tables	24, 42
Formatting Documents	
Create and format document sections	51
Create and apply character and paragraph styles	22
Create and update document indexes and tables of contents, figures, and authorities	57, 58
Create cross-references	57
Add and revise endnotes and footnotes	29
Create and manage master documents and subdocuments	56
Move within documents	53, 55
Create and modify forms using various form controls	78
Create forms and prepare forms for distribution	78
Customizing Tables	
Use Excel data in tables	100, 101, 103 (all on CD)
Perform calculations in Word tables	40, 42
Creating and Modifying Graphics	
Create, modify, and position graphics	80, 81, 82, 84, 85, 86 (all on CD)
Create and modify charts using data from other applications	94 (on CD)
Align text and graphics	80 (on CD)

Customizing Word	
Create, edit, and run, macros	77
Customize menus and toolbars	23
Workgroup Collaboration	
Track, accept, and reject changes to documents	66
Merge input from several reviewers	66
Insert and modify hyperlinks to other documents and Web pages	30, 102 (on CD)
Create and edit Web documents in Word	62, 63, 64
Create document versions	67
Protect documents	67
Define and modify default file locations for workgroup templates	75
Attach digital signatures to documents	67
Using Mail Merge	
Merge letters with a Word, Excel, or Access data source	45, 96 (on CD), 104 (on CD)
Merge labels with a Word, Excel, or Access data source	47
Use Outlook data as mail merge data source	46, 48

Directory of Data Files on CD

Exercise #	File name	Page #
15	15NEWJOB	84
16	16VACATION	88
17	17POLICY	93
18	18NEWPOLICY	98
19	19FLYER	100
21	21FRIDAYS	109
22	22COURSE	116
23	23CONTEST	121
24	24FIREDRILL	128
26	26FIREDRILL	135
27	27COURSE	141
28	28WAYLAND	146
29	29CARE	151
30	30TRAIN	157
31	31AD1	160
32	32COURSE	166
33	33WAYLAND	170
33	33LETTER	170
34	34LETTER	175
35	35CONTEST	179
36	36CONTEST	182
36	36CONTEST2	182
37	37SCHEDULE	188
38	38SCHEDULE	194
39	39SALE	200
40	40SITES	207
41	41SITES	213
42	42PACKAGE	218
43	43PACKAGE	223
46	46SOURCE	241
47	47SOURCE	247
48	48DOCTORS	253
50	50SCUBA	264
51	51SAFETY	271
52	52SAFETY	278
53	53SAFETY2	284
54	54SAFETY3	293
55	55SUMMARY	300
56	56MODERN	308
56	56SHOES	308
57	57SAFETY4	315

Exercise #	File name	Page #
58	58SAFETY	322
59	59SERVICES	324
59	59SENIORS	324
60	Internet simulation	335
61	Internet simulation	340
62	62ONLINEAD	344
63	63PETESWEB.htm	348
63	63ONLINEAD.htm	348
65	Internet simulation	355
65	65CONTEST3	355
66	66NEWCLASS	364
66	66REVIEW	364
67	67MISSION	370
68	68CLASSMEMO	375
68	68NEWCLASS	375
69	69JUDGES	382
69	69CONGRATS	382
71	71NAMES	390
72	72PROMISE	392
72	72LEGAL	392
72	72MKTG	392
73	73THEBILL	399
74	74HEALTH	405
75	75OPTICAL	411
76	76WINNERS	416
76	76JUDGES	416
77	77WINNERS	422
79	79UPDATE	433
The following exercies are located on the CD		
80	80HEALTH	445
81	81CONTEST2	453
82	82THEBILL	460
82	SCUBA1.wmf	460
82	COOK1.wmf	460
83	83CONTEST3	464
84	LENS1.wmf	468
85	85CONTEST4	474
86	86OGI	479
86	86OPTIMEMO	479
88	88JOBFAIR	491

Exercise #	File name	Page #
88	SOAR.wmf	491
89	SHOE.wmf	495
90	90DATA.xls	501
90	90PRES.ppt	501
90	90MEMO.doc	501
91	91OUTREACH.doc	505
91	91EXPENSE.xls	505
92	92COSTMEMO	512
92	92Q1	512
93	93RETREAT	517
93	93BUDGET.xls	517
94	94CHARTS	526
94	94SURVEY	526
95	95MEETING	534
96	96STUDENTS	538
97	97SLIDES	542
97	97TRAINING.ppt	542
98	98CARIB	549
98	98FINANCE	550
98	98DIVERS	550
99	Internet simulation	556
99	99CAMERA	556
100	Internet simulation	560
100	100COZUMEL	560
100	100LODGING	560
101	101COZUMEL2	563

Exercise #	File name	Page #
101	SUNSET.jpg	563
101	SCUBA.wmf	563
101	101LODGING	563
102	102TRAVEL	566
102	DIVER.wmf	566
102	PELICAN.wmf	566
102	WHALE.wmf	566
102	TRAVEL	566
102	102DIVE.htm	566
102	Internet simulation	567
102	102FISH.htm	567
103	Internet simulation	569
103	103INVEST.doc	569
103	103STOCKS.xls	569
104	104PETESDATA.mdb	573
105	105PETESDATA	575
105	PELICAN.wmf	575
105	105SIDEB	576
105	WHALE.wmf	576
105	DIVER.wmf	576

Lesson 1

Getting Started with Word

Exercise 1

- About Microsoft® Word 2002
- Conventions Used in This book
- Use the Mouse
- Use the keyboard
- Start Word 2002
- The Word Window
- Exit Word

Exercise 2

- Execute Commands
- Use Menus
- Use Toolbars
- Use Dialog Box Options
- Use Shortcut Menus
- Use Task Panes

Exercise 3

- Use Window Controls
- Use Zoom
- Scroll a Window

Exercise 4

- Use the Ask a Question Box
- Use the Help Program
- Use the What's This? Pointer
- Use the Office Assistant
- Microsoft Word on the Web
- Recover a Document

Exercise 5

- Critical Thinking

Exercise 1

Skills Covered:

◆ **About Microsoft® Word 2002** ◆ **Conventions Used in This book**
◆ **Use the Mouse** ◆ **Use the keyboard** ◆ **Start Word 2002**
◆ **The Word Window** ◆ **Exit Word**

On the Job

Microsoft Word 2002 is a word-processing application you can use to prepare many different types of documents. Word 2002 makes it easy to create simple documents such as letters and memos, as well as more complex documents such as newsletters and brochures. You can use Word 2002 with only a keyboard, with only a mouse, or with a combination of the two.

You've just been hired as the assistant to the president of Optical General, Inc., a manufacturing company that produces lenses for medical and high tech equipment. She has asked you to become familiar with Microsoft Word 2002, since the company uses it throughout its business operations. In this exercise, you'll practice using the mouse and the keyboard to start and exit Word 2002 and you will review the screen elements of the Word window so you can use these skills on the job.

Terms

Format Arrange and enhance a document to improve its appearance.

Word processing The act of creating text-based documents.

Internet A global network of computers.

Conventions Consistent organization and use of language that make it easy to understand the material in this book.

Font size The size of the characters typed in a document. Font size is measured in points, with approximately 72 points in an inch.

Mouse A device that allows you to select items on-screen by pointing at them with the mouse pointer.

Mouse pointer A marker on your computer screen that shows you where the next mouse action will occur. The mouse pointer changes shapes depending on the current action.

Toolbar A row of buttons used to select features and commands.

Insertion point The flashing vertical line that indicates where the next action will occur in a document on-screen.

Scroll wheel A wheel on some mouse devices used to navigate through a document on-screen.

I-beam A mouse pointer shape resembling the uppercase letter I.

Hyperlink Text or graphics in a document set up to provide a direct connection with a destination location or document. When you click a hyperlink, the destination is displayed.

Mouse pad A smooth, cushioned surface on which you slide a mouse.

Current File The file currently open and active. Actions and commands will affect the current file.

Window The area on-screen where an application is displayed.

Default A standard setting or mode of operation.

Elements Menus, icons, and other items that are part of Word's on-screen interface.

Keyboard shortcuts Key combinations used to execute a command without using the mouse.

Scroll To page through a document in order to view some part of its contents that is not currently displayed.

Zoom To increase (zoom in) or decrease (zoom out) the displayed size of the document on-screen.

Notes

About Microsoft® Word 2002

- Microsoft Word 2002 is designed to make it easy for you to create, edit, **format**, and distribute **word processing** documents.
- With Word 2002 you can easily include text and graphics in documents.
- You can transfer data between documents and between different applications running under the Windows operating environment.
- Word 2002 also provides tools for accessing the **Internet** and for creating documents for distribution on the Internet.
- If you have used previous versions of Microsoft Word, you will notice many similarities as well as many new features and enhancements.
- If you are using Word 2002 as part of the Microsoft Office XP Suite of applications, you will find it easy to transfer your knowledge of Word 2002 to any of the other Office programs.

Conventions Used in This Book

- **Conventions** are used throughout this book to make it simple for you to understand the concepts and the skills required to use Word 2002 effectively.
  - Definitions of new words are provided in the Terms sections.
  - Concepts are introduced in the Notes sections.
  - Actions are listed in the Procedures sections.
  - Exercise Directions provide step-by-step instructions for applying the new skills.
  - Illustrations are included to provide visual support for the text.
- Documents used to illustrate exercises are created using a 12-point **font size**, unless otherwise noted.

✓ *If the default font size on your computer system is 10 points, your instructor may ask you to change it so your completed documents match the solution files provided with this book. Changing fonts and font sizes are covered in Lesson 2, Exercise 10.*

- This book assumes you have installed all of the features covered. If necessary, run Word 2002 Setup again to install additional options.

Use the Mouse

- Use your **mouse** to point to and select commands and features of Word 2002.
- Traditional mouse devices work by sliding a tracking ball on your desk.
- Newer devices might work using light or a wireless connection.
- When you move the mouse on your desk, the **mouse pointer** moves on-screen. For example, when you move the mouse to the left, the mouse pointer moves to the left.
- When you click a mouse button, Word 2002 executes a command. For example, when you click on the Print **toolbar** button, Word prints the current document.
- Clicking a mouse button can also be used to move the **insertion point** to a new location.
- A mouse may have one, two, or three buttons. Unless otherwise noted, references in this book are to the use of the left mouse button.
- Your mouse might have a **scroll wheel**. Use the scroll wheel to move through the file open on your screen.
- The mouse pointer changes shape depending on the program in use, the object being pointed to, and the action being performed. Common mouse pointer shapes include an arrow, an **I-beam**, which indicates location on-screen, and a hand with a pointing finger, which indicates a **hyperlink**.

- You should use a mouse on a **mouse pad** that is designed specifically to make it easy to slide the mouse.
  - ✓ *You can move the mouse without moving the mouse pointer by picking it up. This is useful if you move the mouse too close to the edge of the mouse pad or desk.*

Use the Keyboard

- Use your keyboard to type characters, including letters, numbers, and symbols. The keyboard can also be used to access Word commands and features.
- In addition to the regular text and number keys, computer keyboards have special keys used for shortcuts or for executing special commands.
  - Function keys (F1-F12) typically appear in a row above the numbers at the top of the keyboard. They can be used as shortcut keys to perform certain tasks.
  - Modifier keys (Shift, Alt, Ctrl) are used in combination with other keys or mouse actions to select certain commands or perform actions. In this book, modifier key combinations are shown as the modifier key followed by a plus sign, then followed by another key or mouse action. For example, Ctrl+S is the key combination for saving the **current file**.
  - The Numeric keys include the 10-key keypad to the right of the main group of keyboard keys on an enhanced keyboard.
    - ✓ *Laptop and notebook computers integrate the numeric keys into the regular keyboard.*
  - When the Num Lock (number lock) feature is on, the keypad can be used to enter numbers. When the feature is off, the keys can be used to move the insertion point in a document.
  - The Escape key (Esc) is used to cancel a command.
  - Use the Enter key to execute a command or to start a new paragraph when typing text.
  - Directional keys are used to move the insertion point.
  - Editing keys (Insert, Delete, and Backspace) are used to insert or delete text.
  - The Windows key is used alone to open the Windows Start menu, or in combination with other keys to execute certain Windows commands.

Start Word 2002

- To use Word 2002 you must first start it so it is running on your computer.
- Use Windows to start Word.
  - You can use the Windows Programs menu to locate and select Word 2002.
  - You can use the New Office Document command on the Windows Start menu.
  - You can use the Microsoft Office Shortcut bar if it is installed on your computer.

Start Word using Windows

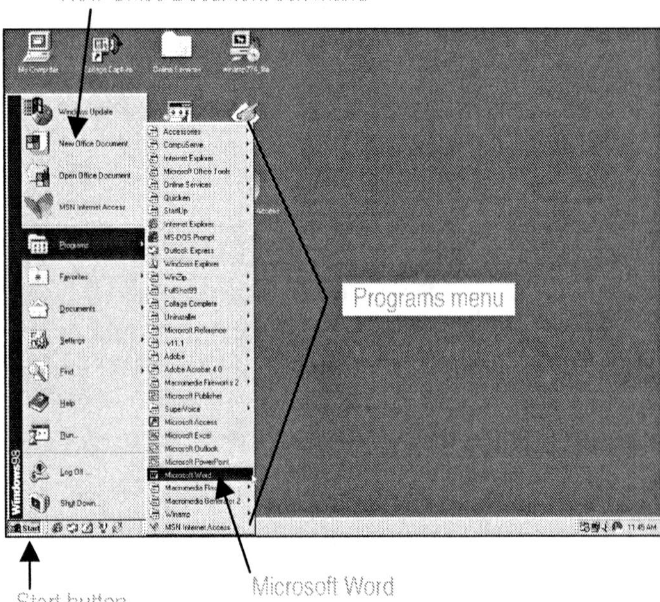

The Office Shortcut Bar

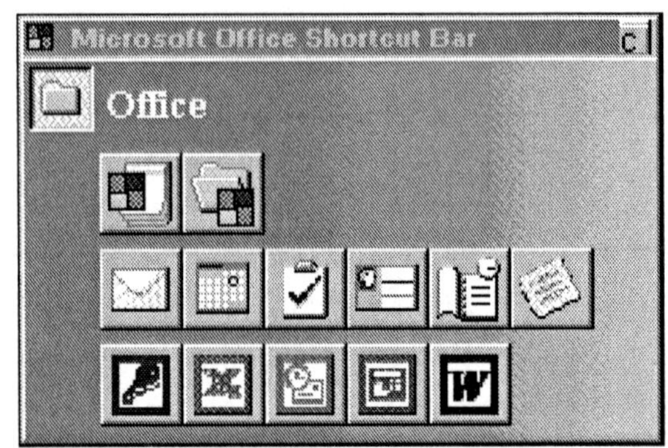

The Word Window

- When Word is running, it is displayed in a **window** on your screen.
- The **default** Word window displays **elements** for creating, editing, formatting, and distributing a document.
- The figure below identifies the default elements of the Word window. The numbers denoting each element correspond to the numbers next to the descriptions.

✓ *There are many ways to customize the appearance of Word. If your Word window does not look exactly the same as the one shown in this book, it may have been customized. You learn more about customizing Word in other exercises.*

Title bar (1)

- Displays the program and document name.

Menu bar (2)

- Displays the names of the main menus. Select a menu name to drop-down a list of commands or options.

Standard toolbar (3)

- Displays buttons for accessing common features and commands like saving, opening, and printing a file.

✓ *Toolbar buttons change depending on the most recent selections. To see additional buttons, click Toolbar Options* ».

Formatting toolbar (4)

- Displays buttons for accessing common formatting features and commands like centering text.

✓ *By default, the Standard and Formatting toolbars are displayed on the same line. In Exercise 2 you learn how to move a toolbar.*

Rulers (5)

- Horizontal ruler measures width of the document page and displays information such as left and right margins, tabs stops, and indents.

The default Word window

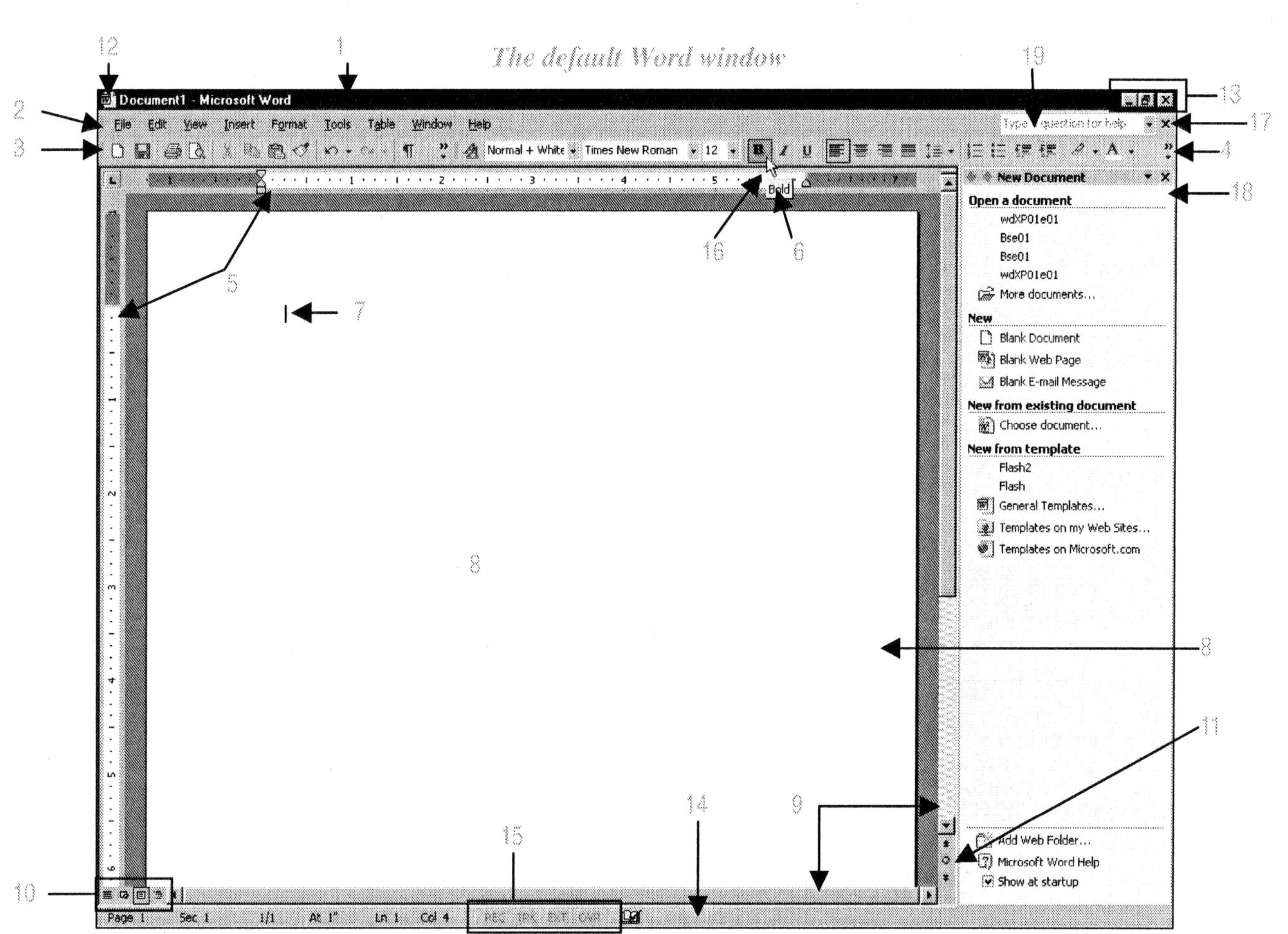

- Vertical ruler measures height of the document page and displays the top and bottom margins.

  ✓ *Vertical ruler is only displayed in Print Layout view and Print Preview.*

ScreenTip (6)

- Displays the name of the element on which the mouse pointer is resting.

Insertion point (7)

- A blinking vertical line displayed to the right of the space where characters are inserted in a document.

Document window (8)

- The area in which you type document text.

Scroll bars (9)

- Used with a mouse to shift the on-screen display up and down or left and right.

View buttons (10)

- Used to change to one of four available document views. These options are also available on the View menu.

Select Browse Object (11)

- Used to shift the on-screen display according to a selected object, such as by page, by picture, or by heading.

Program Control icon (12)

- Used to display a menu with commands to control the Word window.

Control buttons (13)

- Used to control the size and position of the current window. Or to close the current window.

Status bar (14)

- Displays document information, such as which page is displayed, where the insertion point is located, and which mode buttons are active.

Mode buttons (15)

- Used to change the way Word operates to make creating and editing documents easier.

  ✓ *Active mode buttons appear bold.*

Mouse pointer (16)

- Marks the location of the mouse on-screen.

  ✓ *The appearance of the mouse pointer changes depending on the program being used and the current action.*

Document Close button (17)

- Used to close the document window.

Task Pane (18)

- An area on the right side of the program window that can be used to access some common features, such as creating new documents, searching for files, and inserting clip art.

Ask a Question box (19)

- A box at the right end of the menu bar that is used to access Word's Help program.

  ✓ *You learn about getting help in exercise 4.*

Exit Word

- When you are done using Word, you exit the Word program.
- If you try to exit Word without saving your documents, Word prompts you to do so.
- If you exit Word without closing your documents, Word closes them automatically.

Procedures

Conventions Used in This Book

Throughout this book, procedures for completing a task are documented as follows:

- **Keyboard shortcut** keys (if available) are included with the task heading.
- Mouse actions are numbered on the left.
- Keystrokes are listed on the right.

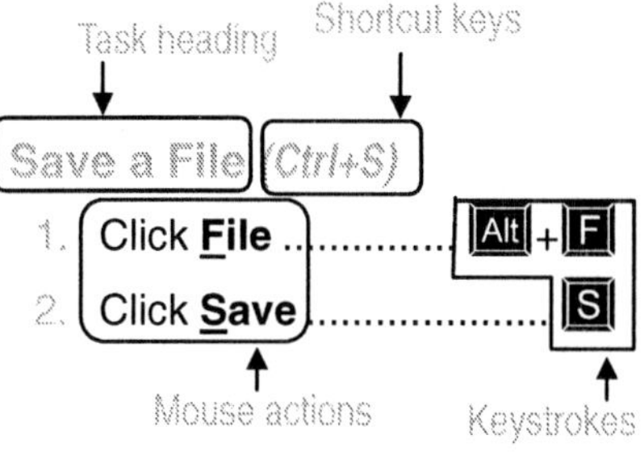

Use the Mouse

Move the mouse pointer:

- Right — Move mouse to right.
- Left — Move mouse to left.
- Up — Move mouse away from you.
- Down — Move mouse toward you.

Mouse actions:

- Point to — Move mouse pointer to touch specified element.
- Click — Point to element then press and release left mouse button.
- Right-click — Point to element then press and release right mouse button.
- Double-click — Point to element then press and release left mouse button twice in rapid succession.
- Drag — Point to element, hold down left mouse button, and then move mouse pointer to new location.

✓ *Element, or icon representing element, moves with mouse pointer.*

- Drop — Drag element to new location, and then release mouse button.

IntelliMouse actions:

- Scroll — Rotate center wheel backward to scroll down or forward to scroll up.
- Pan — Press center wheel and drag up or down.
- Auto Scroll — Click center wheel to scroll down; move pointer up to scroll up.
- Zoom — Hold down Ctrl and rotate center wheel.

Use the Keyboard

- Press specified key.

For key combinations:

1. Press and hold modifier key(s) .... Ctrl, Alt, Shift
2. Press combination key.

   ✓ *Remember, key combinations are written with a plus sign between each key. For example, Ctrl+Esc means to press and hold Ctrl, while you press and release Esc. Then you release the Ctrl key.*

3. Release both keys.

Start Word

1. Click **Start** button Start .... Windows key
2. Click **Programs** .... P
3. Click **Microsoft Word** on Programs menu.

OR

1. Click **Start** button Start .... Windows key
2. Click **New Office Document** .
3. Click **General** tab.
4. Double-click **Blank Document** button .

OR

- Click **Microsoft Word** button on Office Shortcut bar.

Exit Word *(Alt + F4)*

- Click **Program Close** button X.

OR

1. Click **File**..................... Alt + F
2. Click **Exit** X
3. Click **Yes** to save open documents .... Y

   OR

   Click **No** to close without saving .... N

Exercise Directions

1. Start your computer.
2. Move the mouse pointer around the Windows desktop.
3. Point to the Start button.
   ✓ *A ScreenTip is displayed.*
4. Point to the Recycle Bin icon.
5. Click any icon on the desktop.
   ✓ *The icon is selected.*
6. Right-click the Recycle Bin icon.
   ✓ *A menu is displayed.*
7. Press Esc to cancel the menu.
8. Start Microsoft Word 2002.
   a. Click the Start button.
   b. Click Programs on the Start menu.
   c. Click Microsoft Word on the Programs menu.
9. Point to each button on the Standard and Formatting toolbars to see the ScreenTips.
10. Move the mouse pointer over the document window.
    ✓ *It changes from an arrow to an I-beam.*
11. Press Alt+F.
    ✓ *The File menu opens as shown in Illustration A. You learn about using menus in Exercise 2.*
12. Press Esc.
    ✓ *The File menu closes.*
13. Exit Word.
    - Click the Program Close button.
      ✓ *Click No if a box is displayed asking if you want to save the changes.*

Illustration A

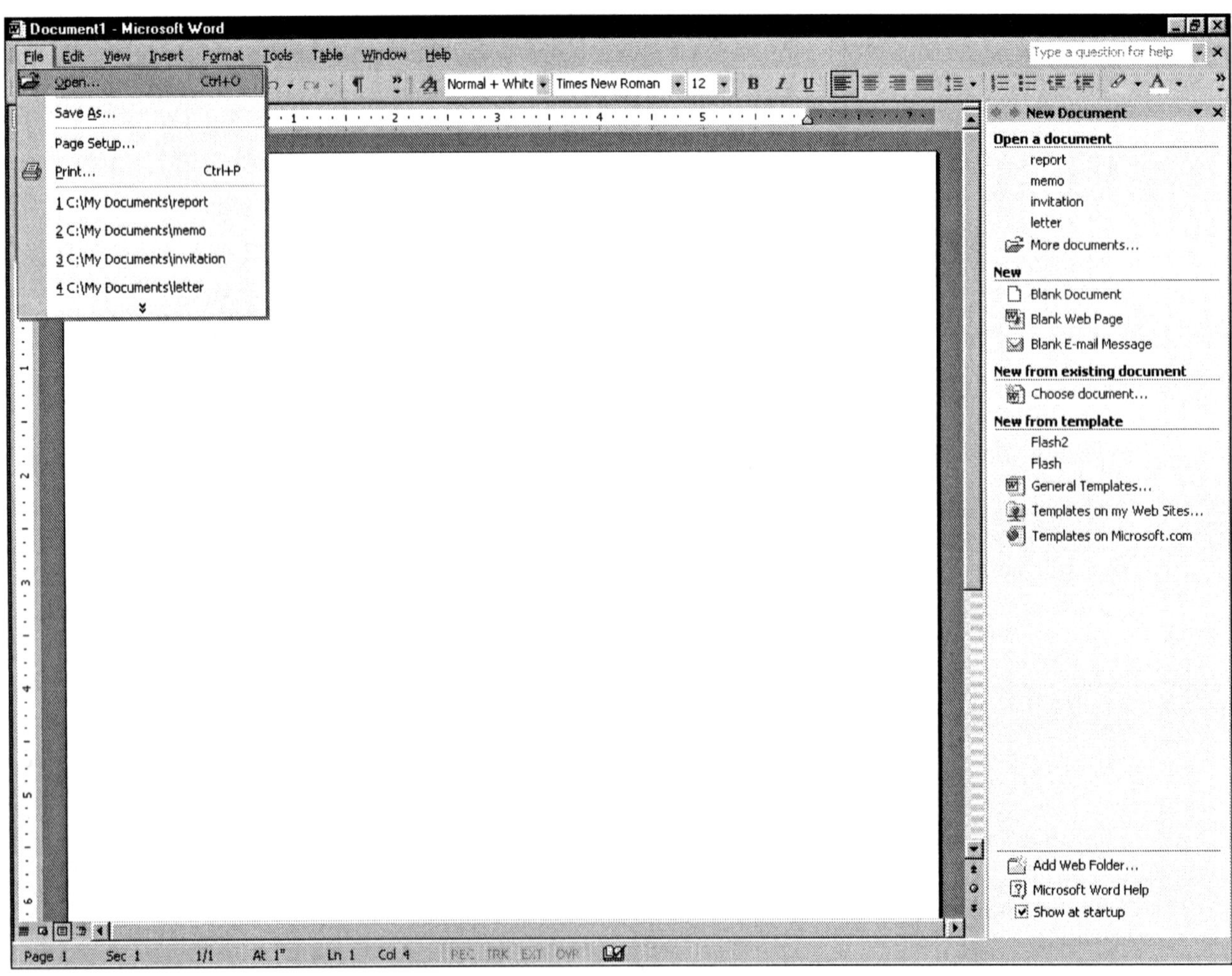

On Your Own

1. Practice starting and exiting Word using the mouse.
2. Practice moving the mouse around the Word window to identify different elements.
3. Point to the View buttons.
4. Point to the Close button.
5. Point to the Mode buttons.
6. Practice starting and exiting Word using the keyboard.

Exercise 2

Skills Covered:

◆ **Execute Commands** ◆ **Use Menus** ◆ **Use Toolbars**
◆ **Use Dialog Box Options** ◆ **Use Shortcut Menus** ◆ **Use Task Panes**

On the Job

To accomplish a task in Word, you must execute a command. You select the commands using menus, toolbars, and dialog boxes. Once you learn to use these tools, you will be able to access the features you need to create documents with Word.

To get up to speed using Word 2002, you want to spend more time exploring the menus, toolbars, and dialog boxes. In this exercise, you will practice using toolbars, selecting menu commands, and choosing options in dialog boxes.

Terms

Command Input that tells the computer which task to execute.

Menu A list of commands.

Toolbar A row of buttons used to execute commands. Each button displays an icon (picture) representing its command.

Dialog box A window in which you select options that affect the way Word executes a command.

Icon A picture used to identify an element on screen, such as a toolbar button.

Toggle A command that can be switched off or on.

Ellipsis A symbol comprised of three periods (...) that indicate more will follow.

Submenu A secondary or subordinate menu that is displayed when you select a command on another menu.

Hotkey The underlined letter in a command name.

ScreenTip A balloon containing information that is displayed when you rest your mouse pointer on certain screen elements.

Shortcut menu A menu of context-appropriate commands that appears when pointing at an item and then right-clicking the mouse. Also called a *context menu.*

Task pane An area on the right side of an Office XP program window in which you can access commands and options for certain program features.

Notes

Execute Commands

- To accomplish a task in Word, you execute **commands**. For example, *Save* is the command for saving a document.
- Commands are accessible in three ways:
  - **Menus**
  - **Toolbars**
  - **Dialog boxes**
- You use the mouse and/or the keyboard to select and execute commands.

Menu bar

The Standard toolbar

Use Menus

- Word groups commands into nine menus, which are listed on the menu bar.
- When you select—or open—a menu, a list of commands you use most often drops down into the window.
- You can expand the menu to see all commands in that group. The menu automatically expands when left open for a few seconds.
- Commands that are not available appear dimmed on the expanded menu.
- Command names are listed on the left side of a drop-down menu.
- If a toolbar button is available for a menu command, the button **icon** is displayed to the left of the command name.
- Some commands are **toggles** that can be either active or inactive. A check mark or bullet to the left of a toggle command means the command is already active.

Tools menu

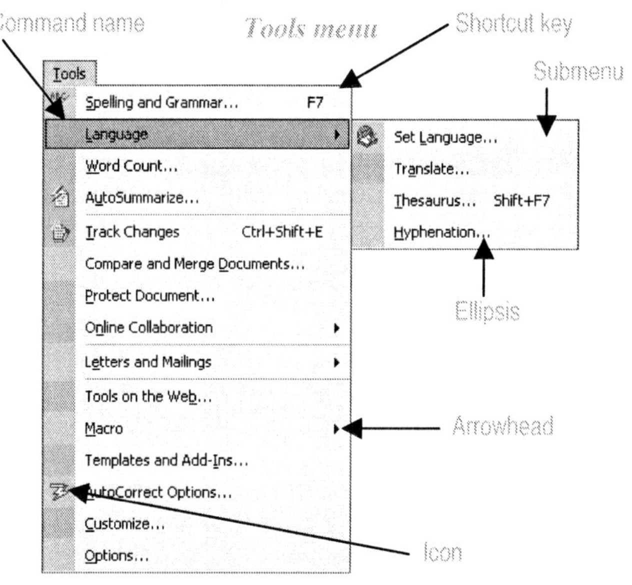

- Shortcut keys and other symbols are listed on the right side of the menu:
  - an **ellipsis** (...) indicates that the command opens a dialog box.
  - an arrowhead indicates that the command opens a **submenu**.
- Each menu and command has an underlined letter called a **hotkey**. Hotkeys are used to select commands with the keyboard.

Use Toolbars

- Word comes with 18 toolbars, which provide quick access to common commands.
- By default, only the Standard and the Formatting toolbars are displayed.
- You can display or hide toolbars as needed.
- When you point to a toolbar button with the mouse, a **ScreenTip** displays the name of the button.
- Some buttons are toggles; they have a dark outline around them when they are active, or "on."
- Buttons representing commands that are not currently available are dimmed.
- Using the toolbar handle, you can drag a toolbar to any side of the Word window, move it above, below, or beside other toolbars, or float it over the document window area.
- All toolbars have a *Toolbar Options* button you can use to select options for displaying buttons.

  ✓ *If there are buttons available that do not fit on the toolbar, the Toolbar Options button will have a right-pointing double-arrow on it ». Click it to select other buttons.*

Use Dialog Box Options

- Word displays a dialog box when you must provide additional information before executing a command. For example, in the Print dialog box, you can specify which pages to print.
- You enter information in a dialog box using a variety of elements. Use the numbers to locate the corresponding element in the figures below.

Font dialog box

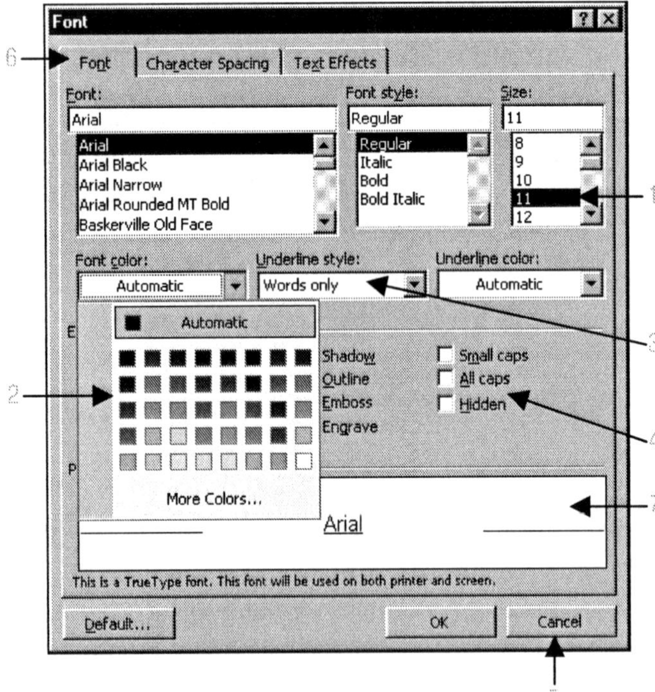

Print dialog box

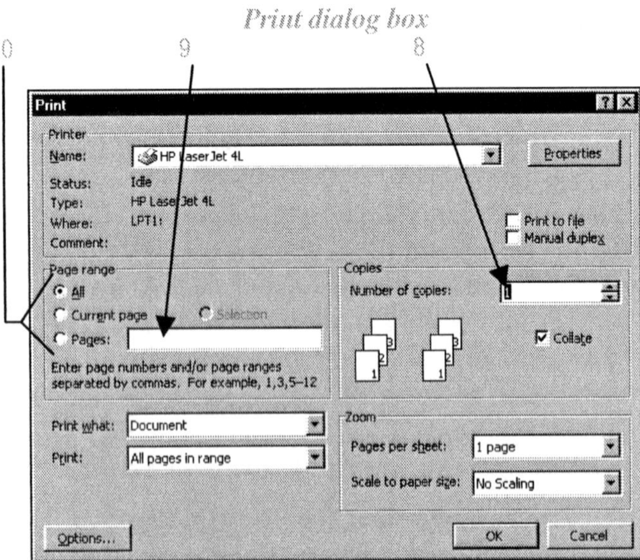

List box (1)

- A list of items from which selections can be made. If more items are available than can fit in the space, a scroll bar is displayed.

Palette (2)

- A display, such as colors or shapes, from which you can select an option.

  ✓ *Some commands (such as Backgrounds on the Format menu) and some toolbar buttons (such as Font Color on the Formatting toolbar) open palettes.*

Drop-down list box (3)

- A combination of text box and list box; type your selection in the box or click the drop-down arrow to display and select the list.

Check box (4)

- A square that you click to select or deselect an option. A check mark in the box indicates that the option is selected.

Command button (5)

- A button used to execute a command. An ellipsis on a command button means that clicking the button opens another dialog box.

Tabs (6)

- Markers across the top of the dialog box that display additional pages of options within the dialog box.

Preview area (7)

- An area where you can preview the results of your selections before executing the commands.

Increment box (8)

- A space where you type a value, such as inches. Increment arrows beside the box are used to increase or decrease the value with a mouse. Also called a spin box.

Text box (9)

- A space where you type variable information, such as a file name.

Option buttons (10)

- A series of circles; only one of which can be selected at a time. Click the circle you want to select one item or one control in the series.

Use Shortcut Menus

- **Shortcut menus** are useful for quickly accessing commands pertaining to the current task using a mouse.
- Shortcut menus are sometimes referred to as *context menus.*
- Commands on shortcut menus vary depending on the action being performed.

Shortcut menu

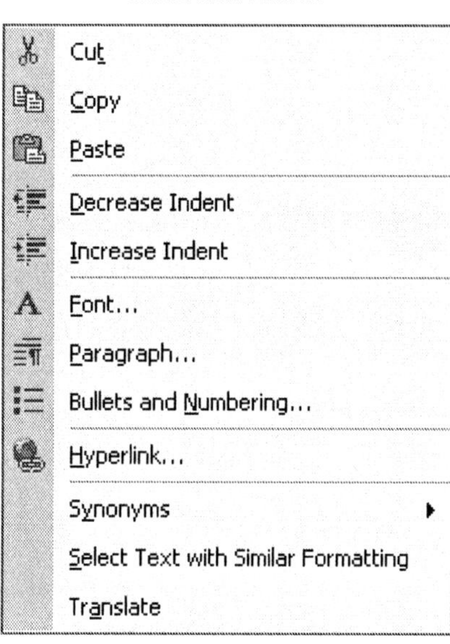

Use Task Panes

- Word 2002 has different **task panes** that you can use to access certain program features.
- For example, you can use the **New Document task pane** to create new files, or open existing files.
- Other features that can be accessed from the task pane include the Office Clipboard, the Media Gallery, Mail Merge, and the Search feature.
- Task panes have some features in common with dialog boxes. For example, some have text boxes in which you type text as well as drop-down list boxes, check boxes, and options buttons.
- You can leave the task pane open while you work, or you can open it only when you need it.

Procedures

Open a Menu with the Mouse

- Click the **menu name**.

Open a Menu with the Keyboard

1. Press and hold .... Alt
2. Press **hotkey** in menu name.

   OR

   a. Press **left** and **right arrow** keys to select menu name ....

   b. Press **Enter**.

Expand a Menu

- Click **expand arrows** at menu bottom .

OR

- Click menu name and wait a few seconds.

Select a Menu Command

1. Click **menu name**... Alt + *hotkey*
2. Click the desired **command** .... *hotkey*

   OR

   a. Press **up** and **down arrows** to highlight command ....

   b. Press **Enter** .... Enter

   ✓ *If a submenu is displayed, select the command from the submenu.*

Close a Menu without Making a Selection

- Click the **menu name** again.

  ✓ *If the menu expands instead of closing, click it again.*

OR

- Click in the document window.

OR

- Press **Esc** .... Esc

Select a Command from a Toolbar

1. Point to a **toolbar button**.
2. **Click**.

   ✓ *If the button you want is not displayed, click the **Toolbar Options** button to display additional buttons, and then click the button.*

Display/Hide Toolbars

1. Click **View**.................... Alt + V
2. Click **Toolbars**..................... T

   OR

   Right-click any **toolbar**.

✓ *A checkmark beside a toolbar name indicates the toolbar is already displayed.*

3. Click **desired toolbar** to display or hide.

Add a Button to a Toolbar

1. Click **Toolbar Options** button [»].
2. Click **Add or Remove Buttons**.............................. A
3. Click **toolbar name**.
4. Click **button** you want to add or remove.

   ✓ *A check mark beside a button indicates the button already exists on the toolbar.*

Show Standard and Formatting Toolbar Buttons on Two Rows

1. Click **Toolbar Options** button [»].
2. Click **Show Buttons on Two Rows**.................... H

   ✓ *Repeat to show buttons on one row again.*

Move a Toolbar

1. Move the mouse pointer so it touches a toolbar handle.

   ✓ *The mouse pointer changes from an arrow to a cross with 4 arrows* ✥.

2. Drag the toolbar to a new location.

Use a Dialog Box

1. Select a **command** followed by an ellipsis (...).
2. Make **selections** or **type text entries** in dialog box.
3. Click **OK** command button.............................. Enter

   ✓ *Sometimes command button displays* Close *or* Yes *in place of* OK.

OR

Click **Cancel** to close dialog box without making changes............................ 

Dialog Box Options

Move from one option to the next:

- Click desired **option**.

OR

- Press **Tab** key.................... Tab

OR

- Press .... Alt+*hotkey*

Select from a list box:

- Click desired **item**.... ↑↓, Enter

Select from a drop-down list box:

1. Click **drop-down arrow**.................... Alt+*hotkey*
2. Click desired **item**.... ↑↓, Enter

Select/deselect check box:

- Click **check box**.... Alt+*hotkey*

  ✓ *A check mark indicates a box is selected. Repeat action to remove check mark and deselect the box.*

Display tabbed pages:

- Click desired **tab** ... Alt+*hotkey*

  ✓ *If no hotkey is displayed, press Ctrl+Tab.*

Use a text box:

1. Click in **text box**.... Alt+*hotkey*
2. Type **data**.

Use an increment box:

1. Click in **increment box**...... Alt+*hotkey*
2. Type **value**.

   OR

   Click **increment arrows** to change value.

Select option button:

- Click **option button**.................. Alt+*hotkey*

  ✓ *A black dot indicates option is selected. Select alternative option button to change setting.*

Select palette option:

1. Click **palette** drop-down arrow ... Alt+*hotkey*

   ✓ *Some palettes are always open. If the palette is open, skip to step 2.*

2. Click desired **option**.................... ↑↓←→, Enter

Use Shortcut Menus

1. Right-click **element** on-screen.
2. Click **command**............ *hotkey*

   ✓ *If no hotkeys are available, use arrow keys to select command, then press Enter.*

Open the Task Pane

1. Click **View**.................... Alt+V
2. Click **Task Pane**.................. K

   ✓ *A check mark indicates the task pane is currently displayed.*

Select a Different Task Pane

1. Click the **Other Task Panes** drop-down arrow [▾] on the task pane title bar.
2. Click desired **task pane**.

   ✓ *Click the* **Back** *arrow on the Task Pane title bar to display the previously open task pane; click the* **Forward** *arrow to display the next task pane that was opened* [⇦ ⇨].

Scroll the Task Pane Display

- Click **Scroll arrow** at bottom of task pane [▾] to scroll down.

OR

- Click **Scroll arrow** at top of task pane [▴] to scroll up.

Hide the Task Pane

1. Click **View**.................... Alt+V
2. Click **Task Pane**.................. K

OR

- Click **Close** button [X] on task pane title bar.

Exercise Directions

Use Menus

1. Start Word.
2. Open the File menu using the mouse.
   - Click the word File on the menu bar.
3. Let the menu expand to show all commands.
4. Note the commands on the File menu.
5. Close the menu.
   - Click the word File on the menu bar, or press Esc.
6. Open the View menu using the mouse.
   - Click the word View on the menu bar.
7. Select the Toolbars commands.
   - Click the word Toolbars, or press the T key.
8. Look at the submenu of available toolbars.
   ✓ *Notice the check marks next to the toolbars that are currently displayed.*
9. Close the menu.
   - Click the word View on the menu bar, or press Esc twice.

Use a Dialog Box

1. Open the Format menu with the keyboard.
   - Press and hold Alt, and then press the O key.
2. Select the Font command.
   - Press the F key, or click the command name.
3. Select Bold in the Font style list box.
4. Select the Superscript check box.
5. Select the Text Effects tab to show another page of options.
6. Select the Font tab.
7. Open the Font Color palette.
   - Click the drop-down arrow, or press Alt+C.
8. Select the color red.
9. Open the Underline style drop-down list.
   - Click the drop-down arrow, or press Alt+U.
10. Cancel the dialog box without making any of the selected changes.
    - Click the Cancel command button, or press Esc twice.

Use the Task Pane

1. Display the task pane if it is not already displayed.
2. Change to the Search task pane.
3. Change to the Clipboard task pane.
4. Change to the New Document task pane.
5. Close the task pane.

Use Toolbar Buttons and Shortcut Menus

1. Click the Bold button on the Formatting toolbar.
   - If the Bold button is not displayed, use the Toolbar Options button to locate it and select it.
   ✓ *Bold is a toggle; it remains on (pressed in) until you turn it off.*
2. Click the Bold button again.
3. Right-click anywhere in the document window.
4. Select the Paragraph command.
   - Click the command.
5. Note that the Paragraph dialog box includes increment boxes, drop-down lists, and a preview area, as shown in Illustration A.
6. Cancel the dialog box without making any changes.
   - Click the Cancel command button or press Esc.
7. Exit Word.
   ✓ *If Word prompts you to save changes, select No.*

Illustration A

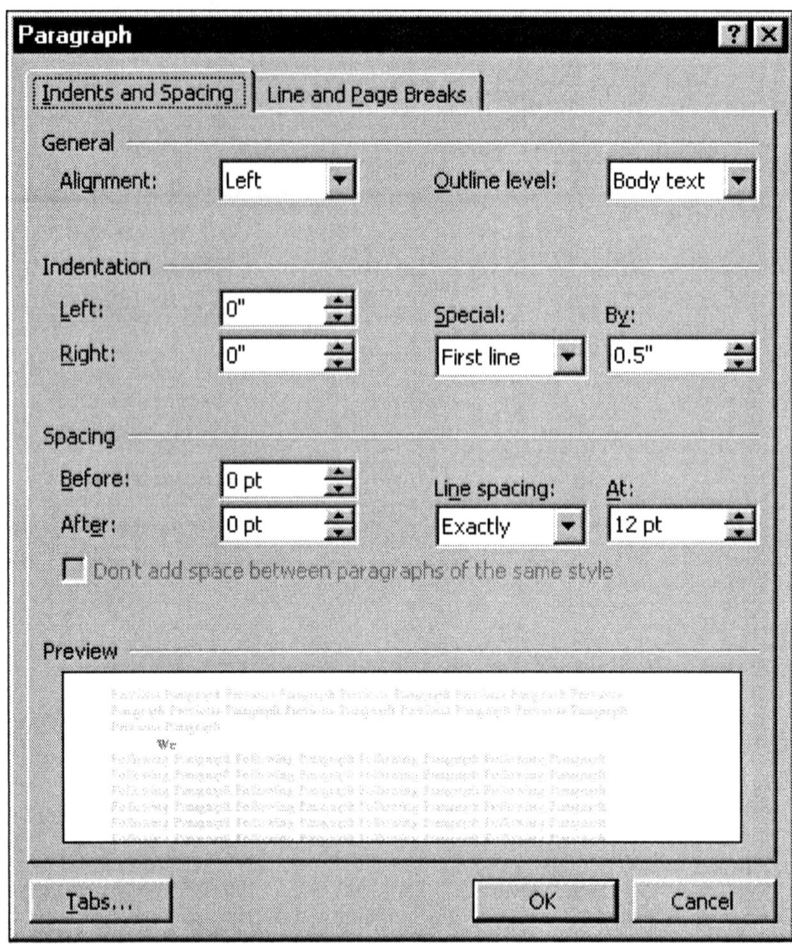

On Your Own

1. Start Word and explore the nine menus.
2. Look to see which commands are on each menu.
3. Notice which ones open dialog boxes, which open submenus, and which have corresponding toolbar buttons.
4. Select a command that opens a dialog box. For example, try opening the Options dialog box from the Tools menu.
5. If the dialog box has multiple pages, check out each page. Note the different options available on each page.
6. Use the Toolbar Options button on the Standard and/or Formatting toolbars to see what other buttons are available.
7. Try moving the toolbars to other locations on the screen.
8. Move them back.
9. Exit Word without saving any changes.

Exercise 3

Skills Covered:

◆ **Use Window Controls** ◆ **Use Zoom** ◆ **Scroll a Window**

On the Job

Controlling the way Word 2002 documents are displayed on your computer is a vital part of using the program successfully. For example, you can control the size and position of the program window on-screen, and you can control the size that a document is displayed.

As you spend more time working with Word 2002, you'll find that there are many tools that help you do your job more efficiently. In this exercise, you will learn how to maximize, minimize, and restore the Word window on your screen, and you will experiment with the zoom level. You'll also practice scrolling through a document.

Terms

Default A standard setting or mode of operation.

Maximize Enlarge a window so it fills the entire screen.

Minimize Hide a window so it only appears as a button on the Windows taskbar.

Restore Return a window to its previous size and position on the screen.

Zoom in Increase the size of the document as it is displayed on-screen. This does not affect the actual size of the printed document.

Zoom out Decrease the size of the document as it is displayed on-screen. This does not affect the actual size of the printed document.

Scroll Shift the displayed area of the document up, down, left, or right.

Notes

Use Window Controls

- When you start Word 2002, it opens in a program window using **default** settings.
  - ✓ *Some default settings control features of a new document, such as the margins, the line spacing, the character font, and the font size. You learn about these features in upcoming exercises.*
- By default, the Word program window opens with a new blank document displayed in Print Layout view.
  - ✓ *You learn more about views in Exercise 8.*
- You can control the size and position of the Word window.
  - You can **maximize** the window to fill the screen.
  - You can **minimize** the window to a taskbar button.
  - You can **restore** the window to its previous size and/or position.
    - ✓ *The Restore button toggles with the Maximize button.*
- There are three ways to control the Word window:
  - With the Control buttons located on the right end of the title bar.

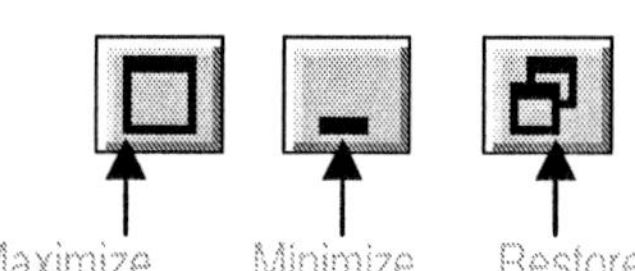

- With the Program Control icon drop-down menu.

Program Control drop-down menu

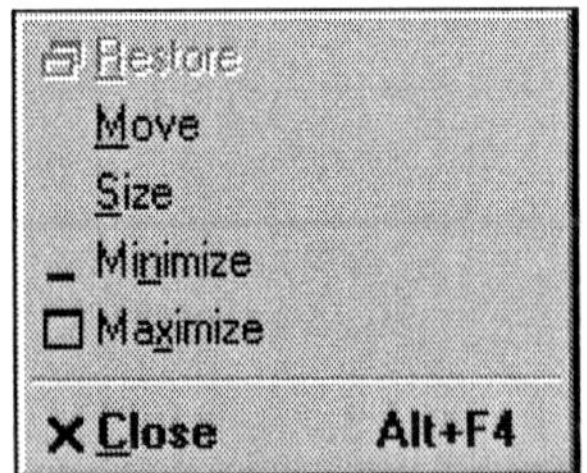

- With the taskbar button shortcut menu.

Taskbar button shortcut menu

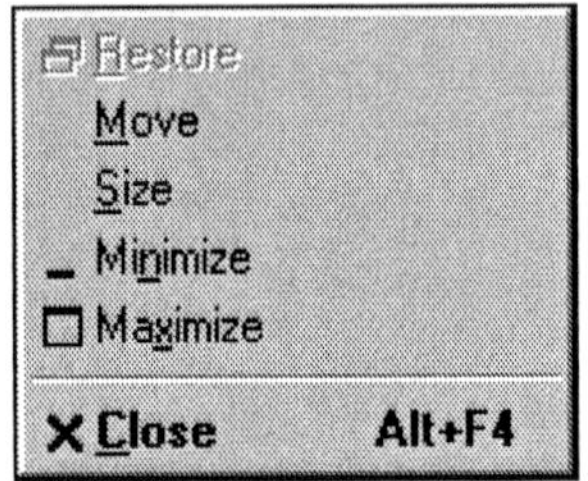

Use Zoom

- You can adjust the zoom magnification setting to increase or decrease the size Word uses to display a document on-screen.
- Set the zoom using the Zoom drop-down list box on the Standard toolbar, or the Zoom dialog box.

Zoom dialog box

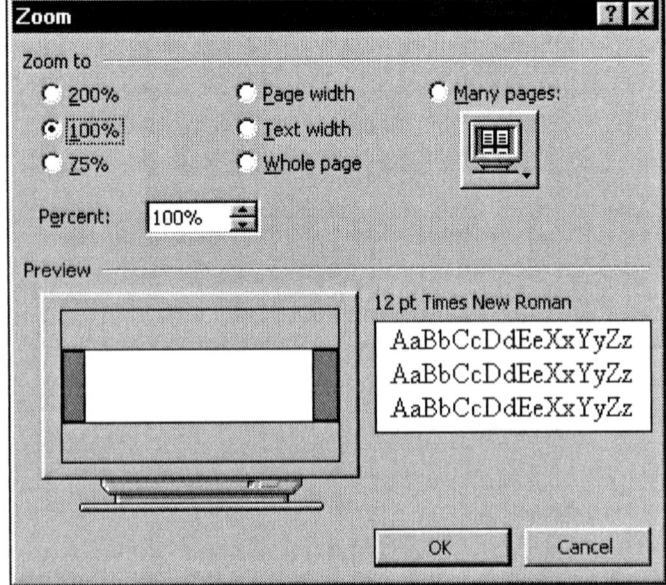

- **Zooming in** makes the document appear larger on-screen. This is useful for getting a close look at text or data.

Zoom in to display the document in a large size

Zoom drop-down list box

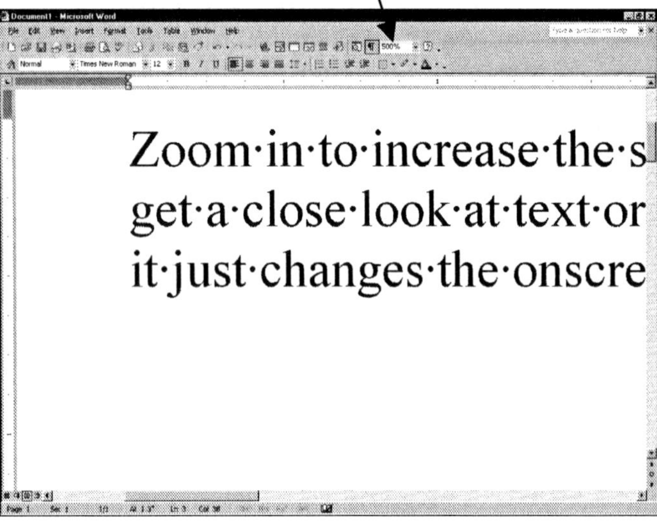

✓ *When you zoom in, only a small portion of the file will be visible on-screen at a time.*

- **Zooming out** makes the document appear smaller on-screen. This is useful for getting an overall look at the document page.

Zoom out to get an overall view of one or more pages

Zoom drop-down list box

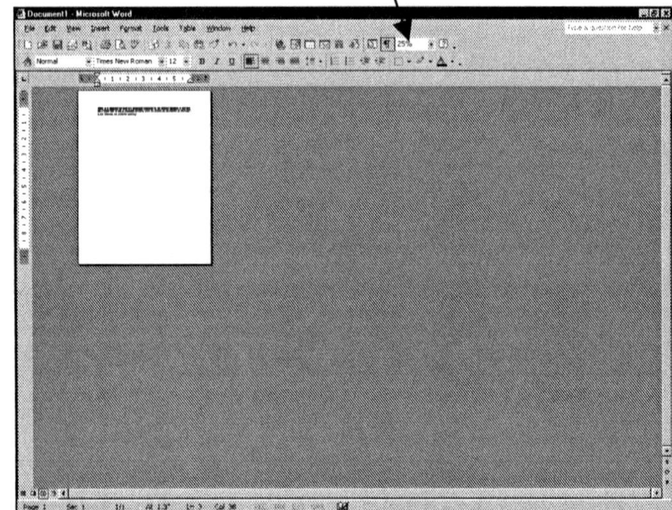

- You can set the zoom magnification as a percentage of a document's actual size. For example, if you set the zoom to 50%, Word displays the document half as large as the actual printed document would appear. If you set the zoom to 200%, Word displays the document twice as large as the actual printed document would appear.
- You can also select from four preset sizes:
  - Page width. Word automatically sizes the document so that the width of the page matches the width of the screen. You see the left and right margins of the page.
  - Text width. Word automatically sizes the document so that the width of the text on the page matches the width of the screen. The left and right margins may be hidden.
  - Whole page. Word automatically sizes the document so that one page is visible on the screen.
  - Many pages. Word automatically sizes the document so that the number of pages you select can all be seen on the screen.

    ✓ *Some options may not be available, depending on the current view. Options that are not available will be dimmed.*

Scroll a Window

- When there is more text in a document or dialog box than can be displayed on-screen at one time, you must **scroll** to see the hidden parts.
- You can scroll up, down, left, or right.
- You can scroll using the directional keys on the keyboard, or using scroll bars in the Word window or in a dialog box.

  ✓ *Some mouse devices have scroll wheels that are used to scroll.*

Tools for scrolling in a document

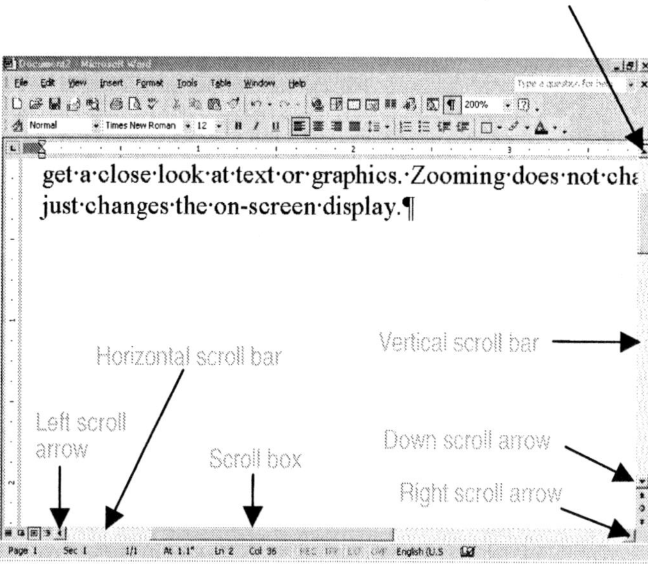

- The size of the scroll boxes change to represent the percentage of the file visible on the screen. For example, in a very long document, the scroll boxes will be small, indicating that a small percentage of the document is visible. In a short document, the scroll boxes will be large, indicating that a large percentage of the document is visible.

Procedures

Control Windows

Minimize a window:

- Click the **Minimize** button.

OR

1. Click the **Program Control** icon.
2. Click **Minimize** .... N

OR

1. Right-click the taskbar button.
2. Click **Minimize** .... N

Maximize a window:

- Click the **Maximize** button.

OR

1. Click the **Program Control** icon.
2. Click **Maximize** X

OR

1. Right-click the taskbar button.
2. Click **Maximize** X

Restore a window:

- Click the **Restore** button.

OR

1. Click the **Program Control** icon.
2. Click **Restore** .... R

OR

1. Right-click the taskbar button.
2. Click **Restore** .... R

Adjust Zoom

Use zoom drop-down list:

1. Click **Zoom** button drop-down arrow 88% on Standard toolbar.
2. Click desired percentage.

   OR

   Click preset option.

   OR

   a. Click in **Zoom** button drop-down list box 88% on Standard toolbar.

   b. Type desired percentage.

   c. Press **Enter** .... Enter

Use Zoom dialog box:

1. Click **View** .... Alt+V
2. Click **Zoom** .... Z
3. Click desired zoom option.

   OR

   a. Click **Percent increment box** .... Alt+E

   b. Type percentage.
4. Click **OK** .... Enter

Scroll

Scroll down:

- Click in **Vertical Scroll Bar** below Scroll box.

OR

- Drag **Scroll Box** down.

OR

- Press **Page Down** .... Page Down

OR

- Spin scroll wheel on mouse toward your palm.

Scroll up:

- Click in **Vertical Scroll Bar** above Scroll Box.

OR

- Drag **Scroll Box** up.

OR

- Press **Page Up** .... Page Up

OR

- Spin scroll wheel on mouse away from your palm.

Scroll left:

- Click **Left Scroll Arrow** .... ←

OR

- Click in **Horizontal Scroll Bar** to left of Scroll Box.

OR

- Drag **Scroll Box** left.

Scroll right:

- Click **Right Scroll Arrow** .... →

OR

- Click in **Horizontal Scroll Bar** to right of Scroll Box.

OR

- Drag **Scroll Box** right.

Exercise Directions

1. Start Word.
2. Minimize the Word window.
3. Maximize the Word window.
4. Restore the Word window.
5. Click in the document window and type your name.
   - ✓ *Do not worry about making errors while you type. This is just a practice exercise and you will not save the document. You learn more about typing and correcting errors in Exercise 6.*
   - ✓ *As you type, smart tags, which look like red-dotted lines, may appear under the text. Ignore these lines. You will learn more about smart tags in Exercise 95.*
6. Press Enter.
7. Type the first line of your address.
8. Press Enter.
9. Type the next line of your address.
10. Press Enter.
11. If necessary, type the next line of your address.
12. Set the Zoom to 25%.
13. Set the Zoom to 500%. It should look similar to the document shown in Illustration A.
14. Scroll down to the bottom of the document.
15. Scroll up to the top of the document.
16. Scroll to the right margin.
17. Scroll to the left margin.
18. Set the Zoom to Page Width.
19. Exit Word.
    - ✓ *When Word prompts you to save the changes, select No.*

Illustration A

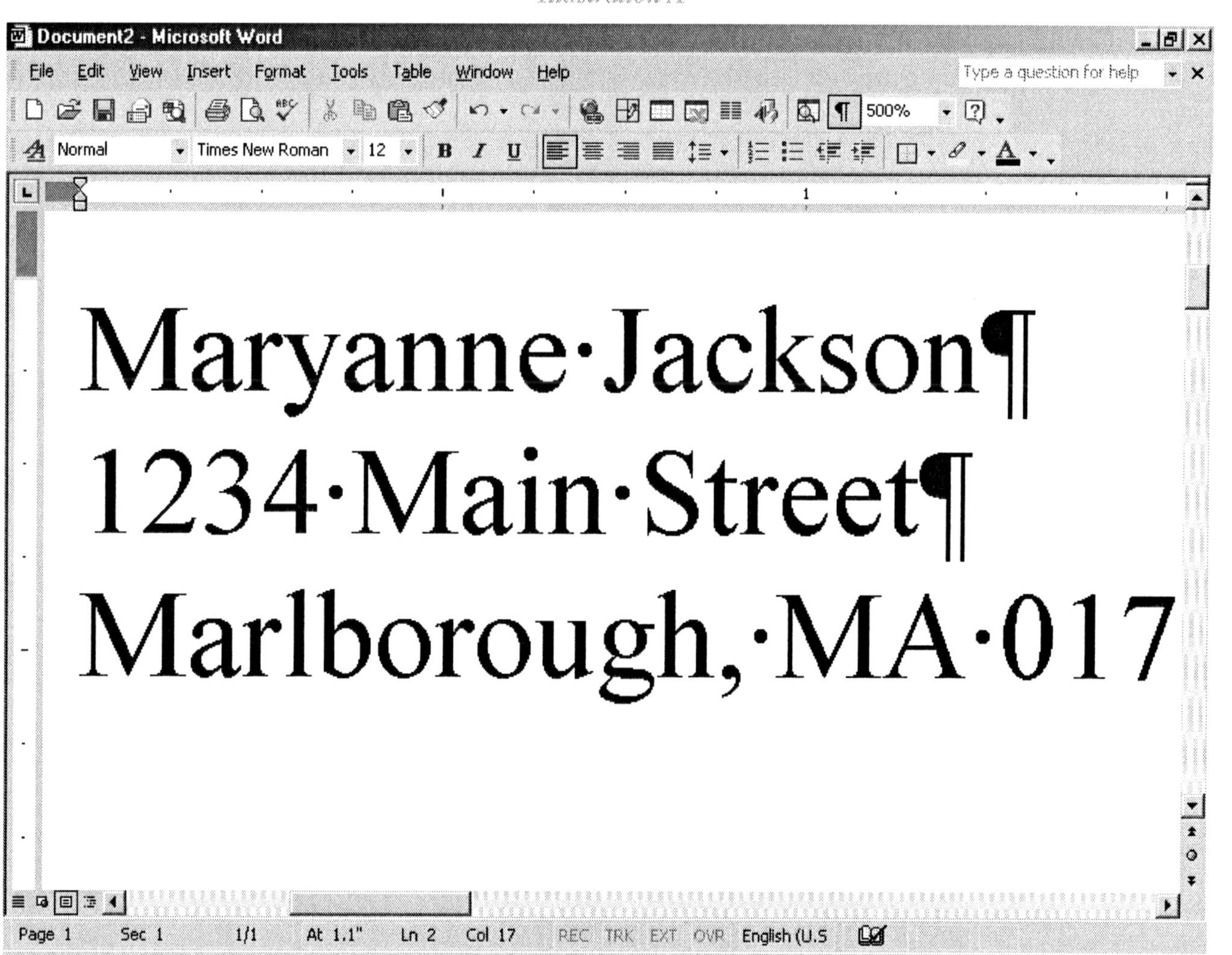

On Your Own

1. Start Word.
2. Practice maximizing, minimizing, and restoring the Word window, using all three available methods.
3. Type some text in the Word document window.
   ✓ *Click the mouse point anywhere in the document window and start typing. You learn more about typing in a Word document in Exercise 6.*
4. Try different zoom magnifications to see how the display is affected.
5. Set the zoom very high so you have to scroll down to see the end of the document.
6. When you are finished, leave the Word window maximized and the zoom set to page width.
7. Exit Word without saving the document.

Exercise 4

Skills Covered:

◆ **Use the Ask a Question Box** ◆ **Use the Help Program**
◆ **Use the What's This? Pointer** ◆ **Use the Office Assistant**
◆ **Microsoft Word on the Web** ◆ **Recover a Document**

On the Job

You can get help regarding any of Word 2002's features while you work using a variety of methods. Type questions in the Ask a Question Box to quickly start a Help program and display specific information. Alternatively, use the Index or Contents in the Help program to locate the information you need. Microsoft also makes information about Word and tips on using it available on the World Wide Web.

As a new employee at Optical General, it's important to learn how to solve problems on your own. In this exercise, you will learn how to use the Help system to answer the questions you may have while working with Word 2002.

Terms

Hyperlinks or links Text or graphics in a document set up to provide a direct connection with a destination location or document. When you click a hyperlink, the destination is displayed.

Tile Position more than one window side by side on the desktop so that they do not overlap.

Office Assistant A feature of Microsoft Office Help program, designed to make it easy to locate helpful information when you need it.

Internet A worldwide network of computers.

World Wide Web A system for finding information on the Internet through the use of linked documents.

Notes

Use the Ask a Question Box

- The *Ask a Question Box* appears at the right end of the menu bar.
- Type a question, keyword, or phrase in the box and press Enter to display a list of related Help topics.
  - ✓ *It is not necessary to type a complete sentence in order to access the list of Help topics.*
- Click the topic to start the Help program and display the associated Help page.

Ask a Question box

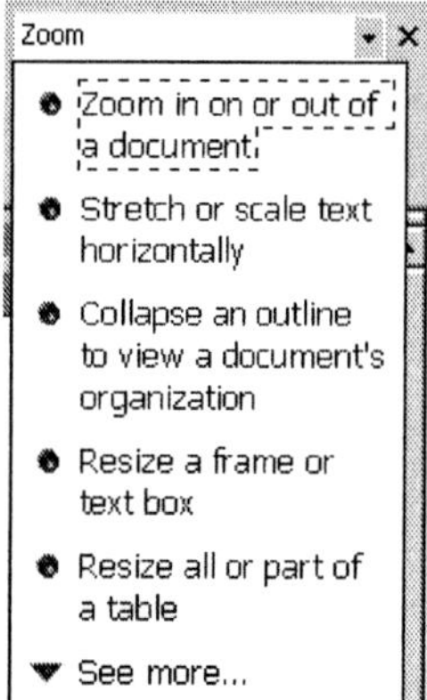

Use the Help Program

- Word comes with a Help program.
- The Help program provides thorough information about how to use Word 2002 features.
- The Help program opens in its own program window, which is split into two panes.
- Pages of information are displayed in the right pane.
- The left pane contains three tabs designed to make it easy for you to locate the help information you need: Contents, Answer Wizard, and Index.
- The Contents tab is like a table of contents in a book.
  - Each topic in the table of contents appears with a small book icon.
  - Open the book to display its subtopics.
  - Close the book to hide its subtopics.
  - Click a subtopic to display the help page.

Select a Topic on the Contents tab

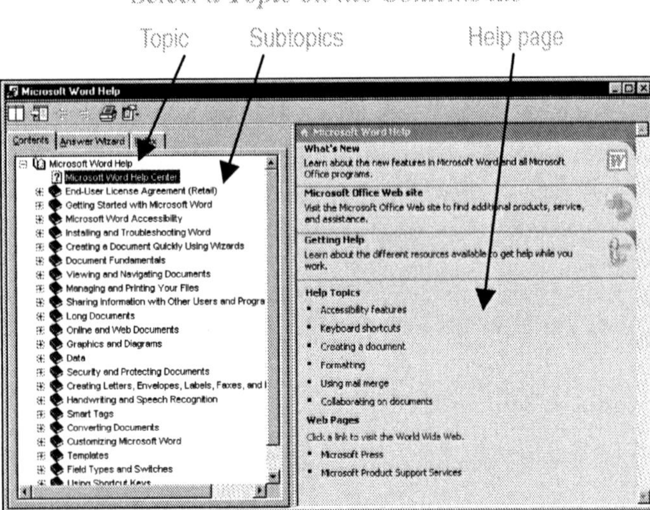

Type a specific question on the Answer Wizard tab

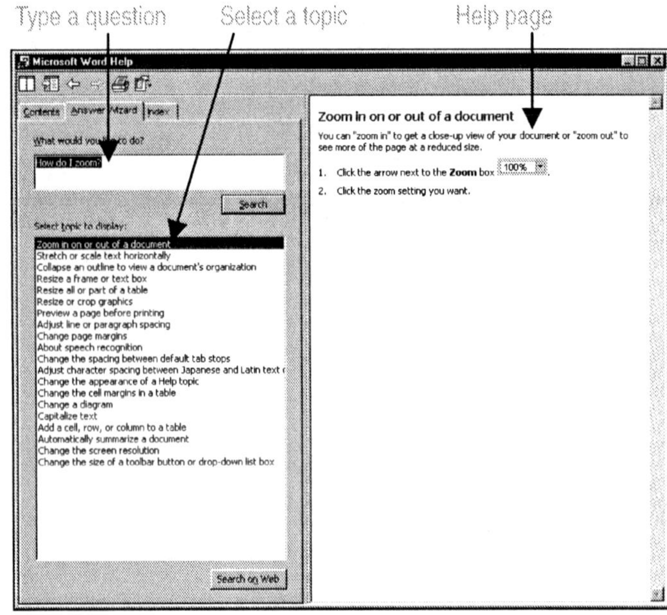

Locate a topic based on a keyword on the Index tab

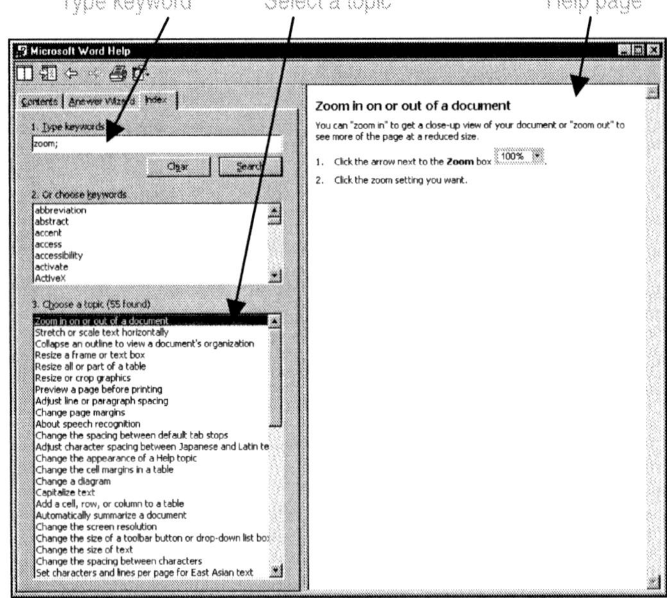

- Help pages use **hyperlinks** to make it easy to move from one topic to another.
- When the mouse pointer touches a hyperlink, it changes to a hand with a pointing finger.
- You can hide the left pane of the Help window to make more room on-screen once you find the information you need.
- You can **tile** the Help window with the program window so you can work in your file and read the Help information at the same time.

Use the What's This? Pointer

- Click a screen element or command with the What's This? pointer to display help information in a ScreenTip.

What's This? pointer

- What's This? can be accessed from the Help menu or from within most dialog boxes.

Use the Office Assistant

- The **Office Assistant** is an animated character that functions much like the Ask a Question box.
- You type a question or keyword in the Office Assistant help bubble, then select from a list of available help pages. The Office Assistant starts the Help program and displays the selected information.

Ask the Office Assistant for help

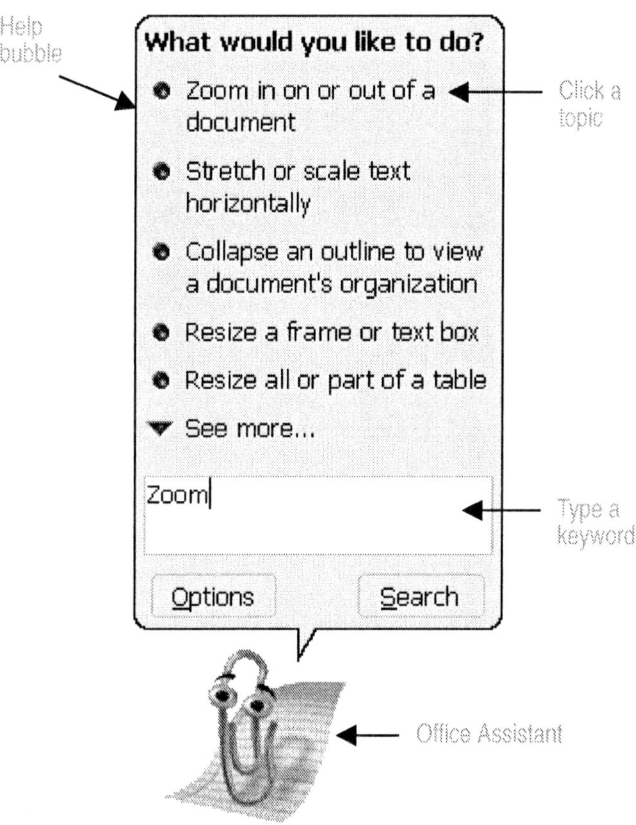

- The Office Assistant is not installed by default. You can install it by running the Word 2002 Setup program.
- You can also set the Office Assistant to display tips or suggestions about current features while you work. For example, if you start typing a letter in Word, the Office Assistant will ask if you need help.
- If a light bulb appears above the Office Assistant, it means a tip is available. Click the light bulb to display the tip.
- By default, the Office Assistant is represented by an animated paper clip, called *Clipit*. You can select a different animated figure.
- You can disable the Office Assistant if you want to be able to access the Help program directly.

Microsoft Word on the Web

- If you have access to the **Internet**, you can connect to Microsoft on the **World Wide Web** and get up-to-date information and support for Word 2002.

Recover a Document

- In the event of a system failure, Word will attempt to save your most recent changes.
- If any damage was done to the document during the crash, Word will attempt to repair it.
- When you open the program again, the Document Recovery task pane will be displayed, listing original files, recovered files, and repaired files (if any).

The Document Recovery pane in Word

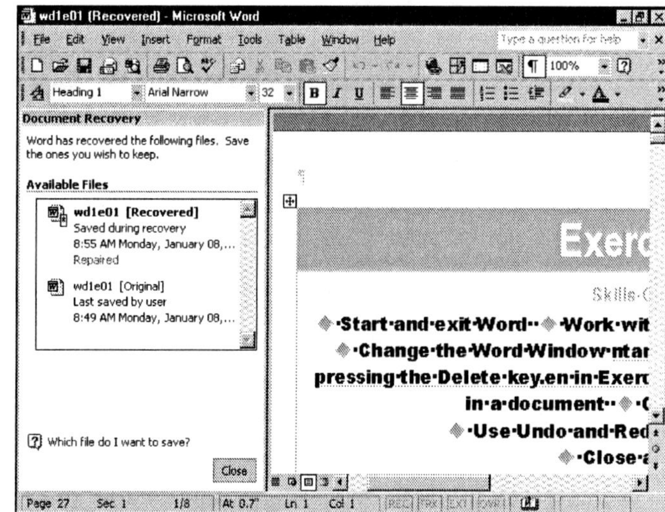

- You can review the documents to see the changes and repairs.
- You have the option of saving one or all of the listed files.

Procedures

Use Ask a Question box

1. Click in **Ask a Question** box.
2. Type question.
3. Press **Enter** .... Enter
4. Click **See more** to see next page of topics if it appears .... Tab, ↑↓, Enter
5. Click **See previous** to see previous page of topics if it appears .... ↑↓, Enter
6. Click desired topic......................... ↑↓, Enter

Start Help Program *(F1)*

1. Turn off Office Assistant
   ✓ *See below for required steps.*
2. Click **Microsoft Word Help** button on Standard toolbar.

   OR

   a. Click **Help** .... Alt+H

   b. Click **Microsoft Word Help** .... H

Control Left Help Pane

- Click **Show** button to display hidden left pane
- Click **Hide** button to hide left pane
- Click **Autotile** button to tile program windows.
- Click **Untile** button to untile program windows.
- Click **Scroll** arrows to display hidden tabs, if necessary.

Use Help Contents

1. Start Help program.
2. Click **Contents** tab...... Alt+C
3. Double-click book to display subtopics..... ↑↓, Enter

   OR

   Click **plus sign (+)** beside topic.
4. Click desired subtopic .... ↑↓, Enter
5. Click hyperlink to see related topic.

Use Answer Wizard

1. Start Help program.
2. Click **Answer Wizard** tab.................. Alt+A
3. Type a question or a keyword .... Alt+W, *text*
4. Click **Search** button Search .... Alt+S
5. Click desired topic.......... Alt+T, ↑↓, Enter
6. Click hyperlink to see related topic.

Use Index:

1. Start Help program.
2. Click **Index** tab. .... Alt+I
3. Type keyword in Step 1 box. ... Alt+T, *keyword*

   OR

   Click keyword in Step 2 box....... Alt+K, ↑↓

   ✓ *To select new keywords, first clear the Step 1 box.*
4. Click **Search**............... Alt+S
5. Click desired topic in Step 3 box....... Alt+H, ↑↓
6. Click hyperlink to see related topic.

Close Help Program

- Click Help window's **Close** button .... Alt+F4

Use What's This? *(Shift+F1)*

1. Click **Help** .... Alt+H
2. Click **What's This?** .... T
3. Click any screen element or command.
4. Click outside ScreenTip to cancel What's This?............ Esc

Display Office Assistant *(F1)*

- Click **Microsoft Word Help** button on Standard toolbar.

OR

1. Click **Help** .... Alt+H
2. Click **Show the Office Assistant**............................ O

   ✓ *If the Office Assistant Help bubble is not displayed, click the Office Assistant.*

   ✓ *If the Office Assistant is covering information you want to see on-screen, drag it out of the way.*

Hide Office Assistant

1. Right-click Office Assistant.
2. Click **Hide** .... H

OR

1. Click **Help** .... Alt+H
2. Click **Hide the Office Assistant**............................ O

Use Office Assistant

1. Display Office Assistant and Help bubble.................. F1
2. Type question in text box.

   ✓ *Replace existing text if necessary.*
3. Click **Search** .... Enter
4. Click **See more** to see next page of topics .... Tab, ↑↓, Enter
5. Click **See previous** to see previous page of topics .... ↑↓, Enter
6. Click desired topic... ↑↓, Enter

Change Office Assistant Animation

1. Right-click Office Assistant.
2. Click **Choose Assistant**.................... Alt+C

3. Click **Next** .... Alt+N
4. Repeat step 4 until desired animation is displayed.
5. Click **OK** .... Tab, Enter

✓ *If selected animation has not been installed, install it, or select a different animation.*

Change Office Assistant Options

1. Right-click Office Assistant.
2. Click **Options** .... Alt+O
3. Select or deselect options as desired.
4. Click **OK** .... Enter

Turn Off Office Assistant

1. Right-click Office Assistant.
2. Click **Options** .... Alt+O
3. Click the **Use Office Assistant** check box .... Alt+U to deselect it.
4. Click **OK** .... Enter

Microsoft Word on the Web

1. Click **Help** .... Alt+H
2. Click **Office on the Web** ..... W
3. Follow steps to connect to Internet.
4. Click hyperlinks to display related topics
5. Follow steps to disconnect from Internet.

✓ *To connect to the Internet you must have a computer with a modem or other Internet connection and an account with an Internet Service Provider. For more information, see Exercise 60*

Recover a File

✓ *If your program was able to recover or repair a file, it will display the Document Recover pane automatically when you restart your programs.*

1. Click desired file in Document Recovery pane.

✓ *You can review each file to see which one you want to keep.*

2. Save desired file.
3. Steps for saving files are covered in Exercise 5.

✓ *If you save a repaired file, the program will prompt you to review the repairs before continuing.*

Exercise Directions

1. Start Word
2. Use the Ask a Question box to locate help topics relating to the Zoom feature.
   a. Type **Zoom** in the Ask a Question box.
   b. Press Enter.
3. Read the list of topics.
4. Select the topic: *Zoom in on or out of a document.*
5. Read the Help topic.
6. Display the Contents tab in the left pane of the Help program.
7. Open the topic: *Managing and Printing Your Files.*
8. Display the Index tab.
9. Search for topics about ScreenTips.
   a. Type **ScreenTip** in the step 1 text box.
   b. Click Search.
10. Select the topic: *About getting help while you work.*
11. Click the Office Assistant link on the help page. The Help program should look similar to Illustration A.
12. Read the Help page.

    ✓ *If necessary, scroll down in the window to see the rest of the information.*
13. Close the Help program.
    - Click the **Close** button in the upper-right corner or press Alt+F4.
14. Turn on the What's This? pointer.
15. Click the Bold button on the Formatting toolbar.
16. Read the ScreenTip.
17. Turn off the What's This? pointer.
    - Click anywhere outside the ScreenTip or press Esc.
18. Display the Office Assistant if it is installed on your computer.

    ✓ *If it is not installed, start the Help program and use any method you want.*
19. Use the Office Assistant to locate information about displaying toolbars.
    a. Type **Toolbars** in the Office Assistant bubble.
    b. Click Search.
    c. Click See More.
    d. Click the topic *About Toolbars.*
20. Hide the Office Assistant.
21. Close the Help program.
22. Exit Word.

    ✓ *If Word prompts you to save changes, click No.*

Illustration A

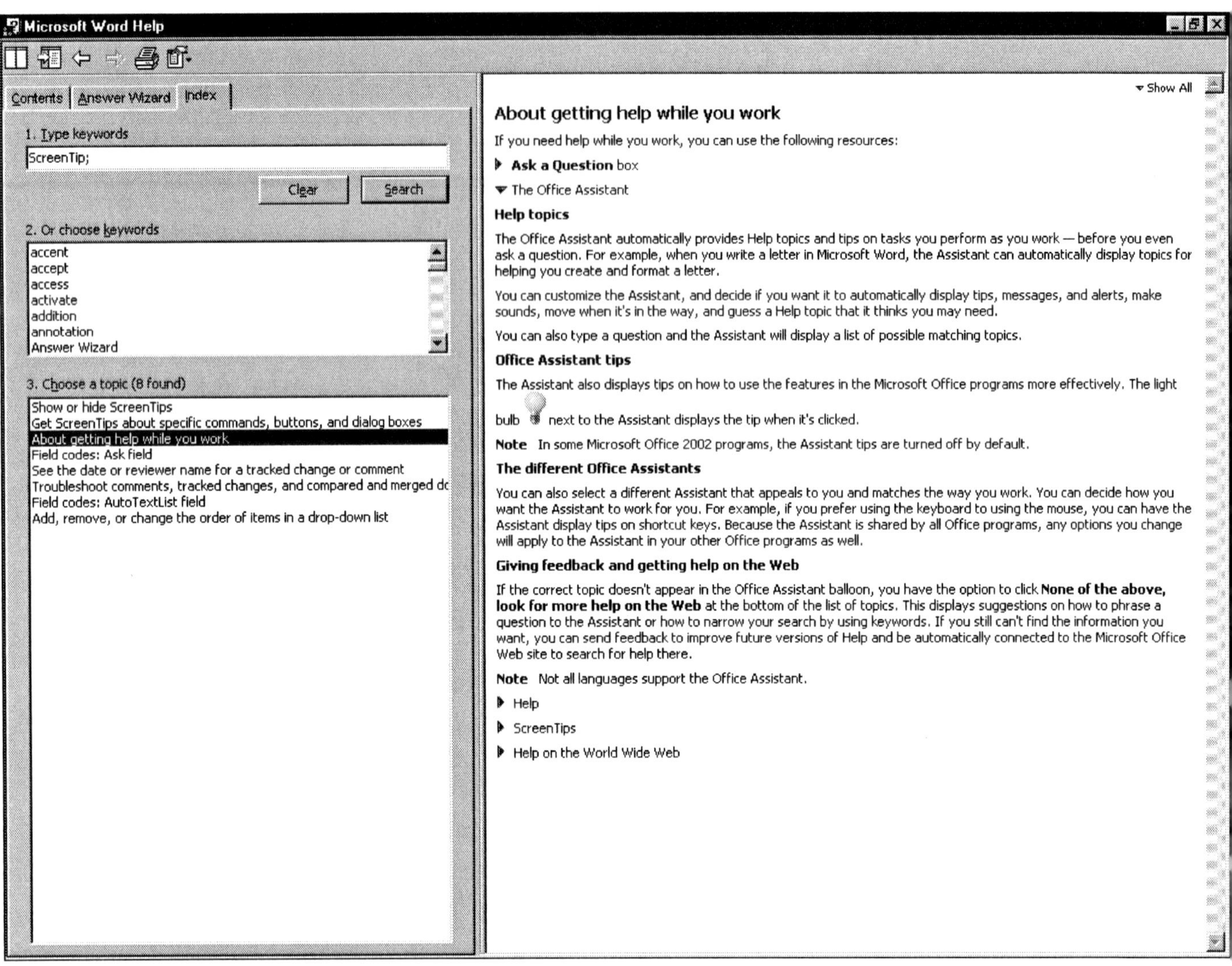

On Your Own

1. Start Word and display the Office Assistant.
   ✓ *If the Office Assistant is not installed on your computer, use the Ask a Question box, or the Answer Wizard in the Help program.*
2. Open the Office Assistant dialog box to see what other animations are available for use as the Office Assistant.
3. If you find one you like, select it.
4. Open the Office Assistant dialog box again to see the options available for controlling the Office Assistant.
5. Close the dialog box without making any changes.
6. Use the Ask a Question box to search for help topics related to menus.
7. Open any topic that sounds interesting.
8. Explore the topics on the Help Contents page.
9. Open any topic that sounds interesting.
10. Continue to explore the help topics as long as you want. When you are done, close the Help program and exit Word. Do not save the document.

Exercise 5

◆ Critical Thinking

The marketing director at Optical General has asked you to write a letter to a client. In this exercise, you will use the basic skills you have learned in this lesson to start Word, use the keyboard and the mouse, execute commands, scroll and zoom in the Word window, and use the Help program.

Exercise Directions

1. Start Word.
2. Exit Word using the keyboard.
3. Start Word again.
4. Open the Office Assistant if it is not already displayed.
   - ✓ *If the Office Assistant is not installed on your system, skip to step 10.*
5. Right-click the Office Assistant to display a shortcut menu.
6. Click Choose Assistant from the shortcut menu to open the Office Assistant dialog box.
7. Click the Options tab.
8. Deselect the Use Office Assistant check box.
9. Click OK.
   - ✓ *This turns off the Office Assistant.*
10. Minimize the Word window.
11. Maximize the Word window.
12. Set the zoom to 200%.
13. Type **Dear Mrs. Jones,**
14. Press Enter.
15. In the Ask a Question box, type **How do I use toolbars?** and then press Enter.
16. Look over the available topics.
17. Click See more.
18. Select the topic *Move a toolbar.*
19. Read the topic.
20. Click the Contents tab in the left pane of the Help window.
    - ✓ *Expand the Help window to show the left pane, if necessary.*
21. Open the topic *Getting Started with Microsoft Office.*
22. Click *Getting Help.*
23. Select the subtopic *Print a Help topic.*
24. Click the hyperlink *Print the current topic.* The Help window should look similar to the one in Illustration A.
25. Close the Help program.
26. Set the zoom to Page width.
27. Exit Word. Do not save any changes when prompted.

Illustration A

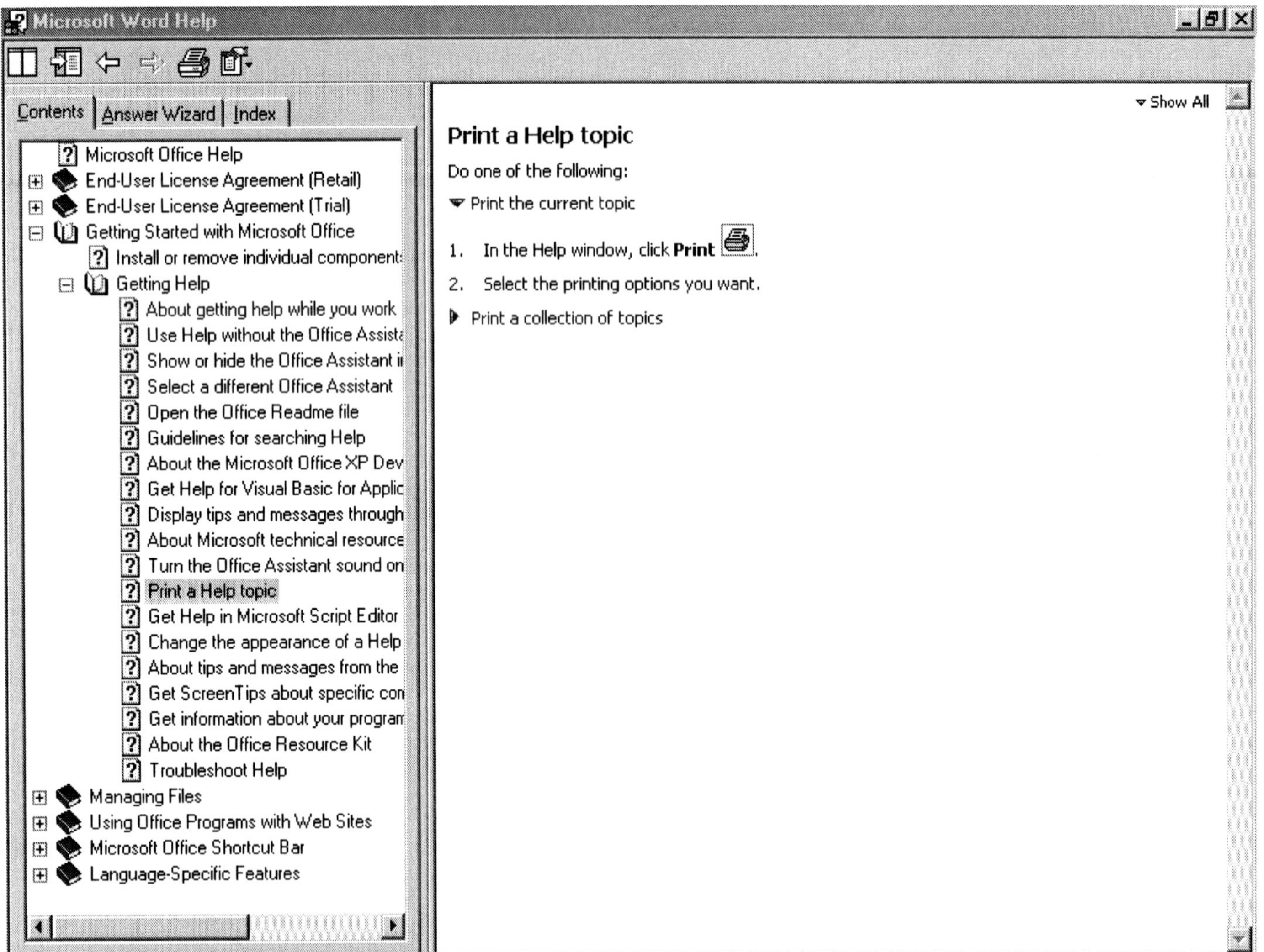

Lesson 2

Create, Save, and Print Documents

Exercise 6

- Create a New Document
- Type in a Document
- Use Click and Type
- Correct Errors
- Use Undo and Redo
- Save a New Document
- Create Folders
- Close a Document

Exercise 7

- Preview a Document
- Print

Exercise 8

- Insertion Point Movements
- Change the View
- Full Screen View
- Show/Hide Marks
- Rulers

Exercise 9

- Use AutoCorrect
- Select Text in a Document
- Replace Selected Text
- Align Text Horizontally
- Save Changes

Exercise 10

- Select a Font
- Change Font Size
- Apply Font Styles

Exercise 11

- Correct Spelling as You Type
- Correct Grammar as You Type
- Check Spelling
- Check Grammar
- Use the Thesaurus

Exercise 12

- Format a Full-block Business Letter
- Insert the Date and Time
- Use Shrink to Fit

Exercise 13

- Set Tabs
- Format a Modified-block Business Letter
- Create Envelopes
- Create Labels

Exercise 14

- Critical Thinking

Exercise 6

Skills Covered:

◆ **Create a New Document** ◆ **Type in a Document**
◆ **Use Click and Type** ◆ **Correct Errors** ◆ **Use Undo and Redo**
◆ **Save a New Document** ◆ **Create Folders** ◆ **Close a Document**

On the Job

You use Word to create text-based documents such as letters, memos, reports, flyers, and newsletters. Now that you know how to get started with Word, the next step is learning how to create, save, and close documents.

You are the office manager at the Wayland Home Health Care Associates, a small company that provides specialized home health care services such as private nursing, elder care, and rehabilitation therapy. A new registered nurse has recently joined the staff, and you must type up a brief biography that will be made available in the office and sent to prospective patients. In this exercise, you will start Word, create and save a document, and then exit Word.

Terms

Word wrap A feature that causes text to move automatically from the end of one line to the beginning of the next line.

Paragraph mark (¶) A nonprinting character inserted in a document to indicate where a paragraph ends.

Horizontal alignment The position of text on a line in relation to the left and right margins.

Undo The command for reversing a previous action.

Redo The command for reversing the Undo command.

Save Store a file on a disk.

File type The format in which a file is saved. Some common file types include graphics files, text files, and word processing files.

Folder Location on a disk where Word and other Windows applications store files.

Notes

Create a New Document

- Word starts with a new blank document open.
- By default the new document is named *Document1* until you save it and give it a new name.
- You can create additional new documents without closing and restarting Word, by using either of the following methods:
  - The New Document task pane
  - The New button on the Standard toolbar.

✓ *Each new document is named using consecutive numbers, so the second document is* Document2, *the third is* Document3, *and so on until you exit Word.*

Type in a Document

- By default, the insertion point is positioned at the beginning (left end) of the first line of a new document.
- You simply begin typing to insert new text.
- Characters you type are inserted to the left of the insertion point.
- **Word wrap** automatically wraps text at the end of a line to the beginning of the next line.
- When you press Enter, Word inserts a **paragraph mark** and starts a new paragraph.
- After you type enough text to fill a page, Word automatically starts a new page.

Use Click and Type

- You can use the Click and Type feature to position the insertion point anywhere in a blank document to begin typing.

  ✓ *Click and Type is only active in Print Layout view and Web Layout view. Changing the view is covered in Exercise 8.*

- With Click and Type, the mouse pointer changes to indicate the **horizontal alignment** of the new text.

  ✓ *You learn more about horizontal alignment in Exercise 9.*

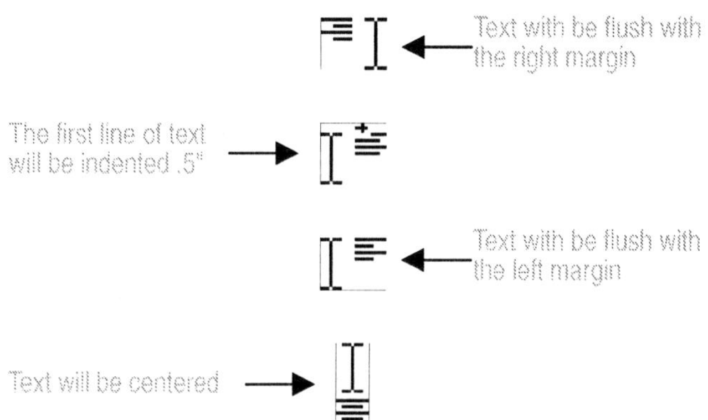

Correct Errors

- You can erase characters to the left of the insertion point by pressing the Backspace key.
- You can delete characters to the right of the insertion point by pressing the Delete key.
- You can cancel commands before you execute them by pressing the Escape key or clicking a Cancel button.

Use Undo and Redo

- Use the **Undo** command to reverse a single action made in error, such as deleting the wrong word.
- The Undo command also lets you change your mind about an entire series of actions used to edit or format a document.
- Use the **Redo** command to reverse actions that you undo.
- If the Undo command and the Undo button are dimmed and entirely gray, there are no actions that can be undone.
- If the Redo button is dimmed, there are no actions that can be redone. However, sometimes when there are no actions to redo, the Repeat command is available from the Edit menu in place of Redo. Use Repeat to repeat the most recent action.

Save a New Document

- If you want to have a file available for future use, you must **save** it on a removable disk, on an internal fixed disk, or on a network drive.
- When you save a new document, you use the Save As dialog box to give it a name and select the location where you want it stored.
- Word automatically adds a period and a three-character file extension to the end of the file name to identify the **file type**. By default, the file extension is *.doc*, which identifies a Word document file.
- To specify a disk for storing the document, you select the disk drive letter from the Save in list. Floppy disk drives are usually drives A: and B:. A hard drive is usually drive C: A Zip drive, network drive, or CD drive may be drive D, or drive E, depending on how many devices your computer system has.

Create Folders

- The first time that you save a file, the file is saved to the My Documents **folder** by default.

  ✓ *Many school and office computers may be set to save files to another folder by default.*

- The My Documents folder is a convenient place to keep your files, since this is where Word and other Office XP applications look first when you go to open or save a file. However, after you have many saved files, you will want to set up new folders in which to store your files.

- You may want to set up folders for different projects, personal documents, budgets, and so on.
- When you save a document, you can also select a different folder in the Places bar or from the Save in list in the Save As dialog box.

Save As dialog box

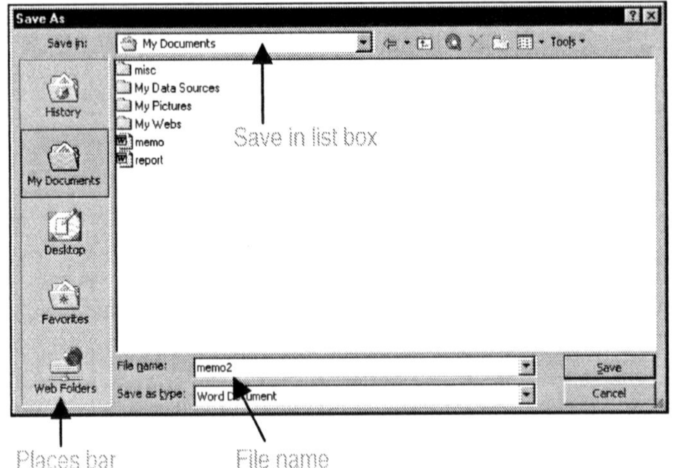

Close a Document

- A document remains open on-screen until you close it.
- Close a document when you are finished working with it.
- If you try to close a document without saving it, Word prompts you to save it.
- You can close a document without saving it if you do not want to keep it for future use or if you are not happy with changes you have made.

Procedures

Create a New Document
(Ctrl+N)

- Click **New** button [New].

OR

1. Click **File** .... Alt+F
2. Click **New** .... N

   ✓ *The New Document task pane opens.*

3. Click **Blank Document** [Blank Document].

OR

1. Click **View** .... Alt+V
2. Click **Task Pane** .... K

   ✓ *If New Document task pane is not displayed, select it from the Other task panes drop-down list.*

3. Click **Blank Document** [Blank Document].

Activate Click and Type

1. Click **Tools** .... Alt+T
2. Click **Options** .... O
3. Click **Edit** tab .... Ctrl+Tab
4. Select **Enable click and type** check box C

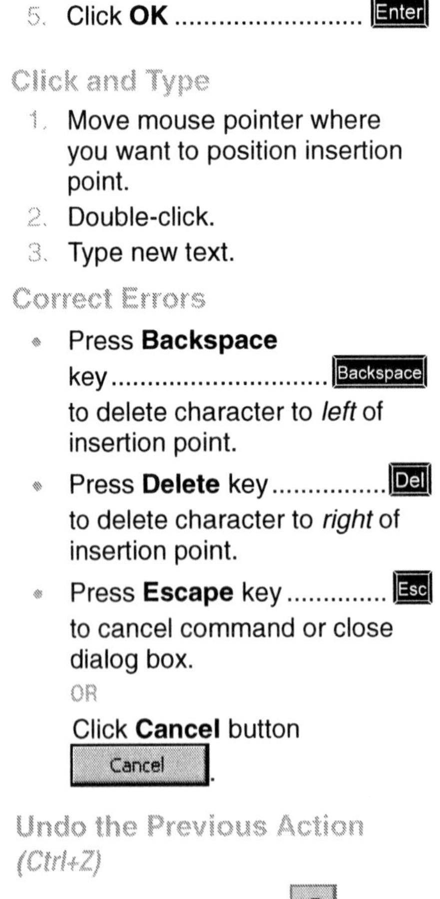

5. Click **OK** .... Enter

Click and Type

1. Move mouse pointer where you want to position insertion point.
2. Double-click.
3. Type new text.

Correct Errors

- Press **Backspace** key .... Backspace to delete character to *left* of insertion point.
- Press **Delete** key .... Del to delete character to *right* of insertion point.
- Press **Escape** key .... Esc to cancel command or close dialog box.

  OR

  Click **Cancel** button [Cancel].

Undo the Previous Action
(Ctrl+Z)

- Click **Undo** button [Undo].

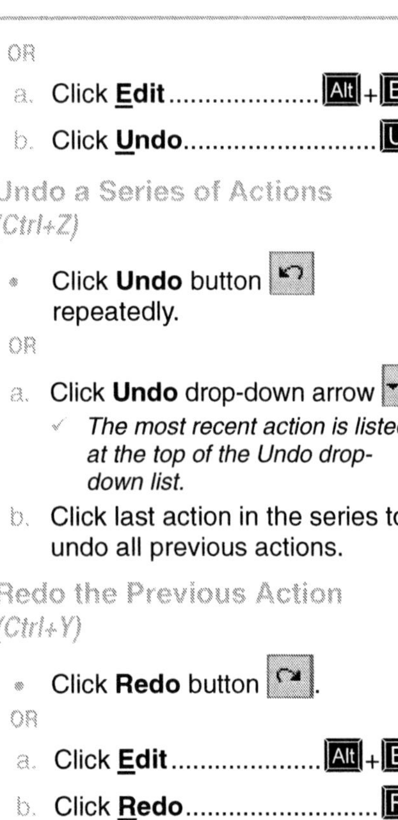

OR

a. Click **Edit** .... Alt+E
b. Click **Undo** .... U

Undo a Series of Actions
(Ctrl+Z)

- Click **Undo** button [Undo] repeatedly.

OR

a. Click **Undo** drop-down arrow [▾].

   ✓ *The most recent action is listed at the top of the Undo drop-down list.*

b. Click last action in the series to undo all previous actions.

Redo the Previous Action
(Ctrl+Y)

- Click **Redo** button [Redo].

OR

a. Click **Edit** .... Alt+E
b. Click **Redo** .... R

Redo a Series of Actions
(Ctrl+Y)

- Click **Redo** button [Redo] repeatedly.

OR

a. Click **Redo** drop-down arrow.
b. Click the last action in the series to redo all previous actions.

Repeat the Previous Action (Ctrl+Y or F4)

1. Click **Edit** .... Alt+E
2. Click **Repeat** .... R

Save a New Document (Ctrl+S)

1. Click **Save** button.

   OR

   a. Click **File** .... Alt+F
   b. Click **Save** .... S
2. Click **Save in** drop-down arrow .... Alt+I
3. Select drive and folder.
4. Double-click **File name** text box .... Alt+N
5. Type file name.
6. Click **Save** button Save .... Alt+S

To create a new folder for storing files:

1. Click **Save** button.

   OR

   a. Click **File** .... Alt+F
   b. Click **Save** .... S
2. Click **Create New Folder** button.
3. Type new folder name.
4. Click **OK** .... Enter

   ✓ *The new folder automatically becomes the current folder.*

Close a Document (Ctrl+W)

1. Click **Close Window** button.

   OR

   a. Click **File** .... Alt+F
   b. Click **Close** C
2. Click **Yes** to save document .... Y

   OR

   Click **No** to close without saving .... N

Exercise Directions

✓ *Note that the Word documents in the illustrations use a 12-point Times New Roman font unless otherwise noted.*

1. Start Word.
2. Type your name on the first line of the document.
3. If you make a typing error, press Backspace to delete it, and then type the correct text.

   ✓ *Word marks suspected spelling errors with a red wavy underline and suspected grammatical errors with a green wavy underline. If you see these lines in the document, proofread for errors. You learn about checking spelling and grammar in Exercise 11.*
4. Close the document without saving it.
5. Create a new document.
6. Save the document with the name NURSE.

   ✓ *Your instructor will tell you where to save the documents you create for use with this book. If necessary, create a new folder.*
7. Use Click and Type to position the insertion point in the center of the first line of the document.

   ✓ *If necessary, activate the Click and Type feature. If, after activating the feature it still does not work, you may not have the document displayed in Print Layout view. In that case, type the document even with the left margin. Changing views is covered in Exercise 8.*

   a. Move the mouse pointer across the first line of the document until it changes to include lines of centered text.
   b. Double-click.
8. Type the headline—the first line of text—as shown in Illustration A.
9. Use Click and Type to leave a blank line and position the insertion point at the left side of the document.
   a. Move the mouse pointer down and to the left until it changes to include lines of left-aligned text.
   b. Double-click.
10. Type the first full paragraph shown in Illustration A.

    ✓ *Remember that you do not have to press Enter at the end of each line. Word wrap automatically moves the text to the next line as necessary.*
11. Press Enter twice to start a new paragraph and insert a blank line between paragraphs.
12. Undo the previous action.
13. Redo the previous action.
14. Type the second paragraph shown in Illustration A.
15. Close the document.
16. When Word prompts you to save the changes, click Yes.
17. Exit Word

Illustration A

Wayland Announces New Hire

Wayland Home Health Care Associates is pleased to announce the hiring of Cynthia Ramirez, RN. Ms. Ramirez received her nursing degree from Framingham State College in 1991. She has extensive experience working with geriatric patients, and she specializes in rehabilitation therapy.

We are certain that Ms. Ramirez will be a valuable addition to our practice. Her skills and experience make her highly qualified, and we are sure you will find her "bedside manner" to be professional and compassionate. Ms. Ramirez is currently accepting new patients. Please contact our office for more information or to make an appointment.

On Your Own

1. Create a new document in Word.
2. Save the document as BIO.
3. Type a brief biography about yourself, using at least two paragraphs.
4. Correct errors as necessary.
5. Close the document, saving all changes, and exit Word when you are finished.

Exercise 7

Skills Covered:

◆ **Preview a Document** ◆ **Print**

On the Job

Unless a document is designed to be read while displayed on-screen, you must print it in order to distribute it. For example, you must print a letter in order to deliver it by mail. Preview a document before you print it to make sure the document is correct and looks good on the page. You save time and paper by correcting errors and adjusting layout before you print.

As a marketing assistant at Northlake Video Links, a video production company, you have been asked to develop documents to send to prospective clients. In this exercise, you will create a document describing the company's background and experience to include in a marketing package. You will include a mission statement at the end of the document. When you have completed the document, you will preview it, and then print it.

Terms

Print Create a hard copy of a document file on paper.

Hard copy A version of a document printed on paper.

Notes

Preview a Document

- Use Print Preview to display a document as it will look when printed.
- By default, Word displays one full page of a document at a time in Print Preview.
- You can change the Zoom setting in Print Preview to zoom in or out on the document.

Print Preview screen

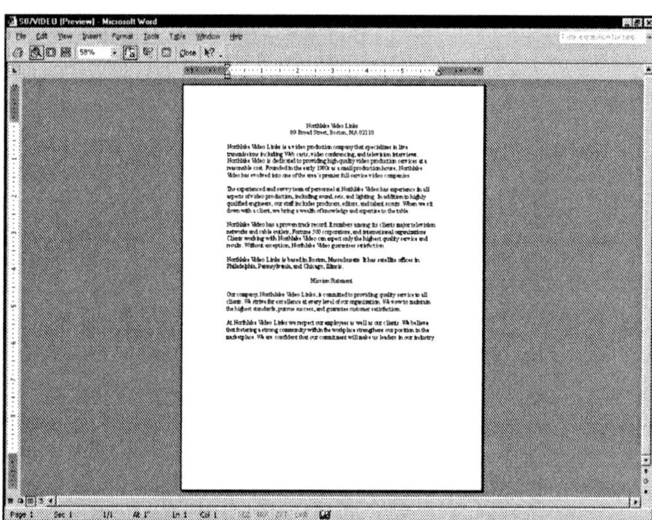

Print

- **Printing** creates a **hard copy** version of a document.
- Your computer must be connected to a printer in order to print.
- You can quickly print a single copy of the current document using the default print settings from the Standard toolbar, or you can use the Print dialog box to select Print options.

Print dialog box

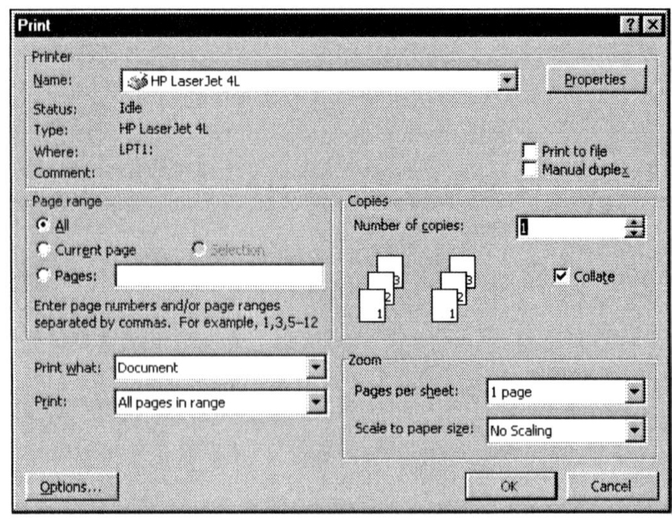

Procedures

Preview Document

1. Click **Print Preview** button.

   OR

   a. Click **File** .... Alt+F
   b. Click **Print Preview** V
2. Press **Page Down** to see next page.
3. Press **Page Up** to see previous page.
4. Click **Close** button Close .... Alt+C

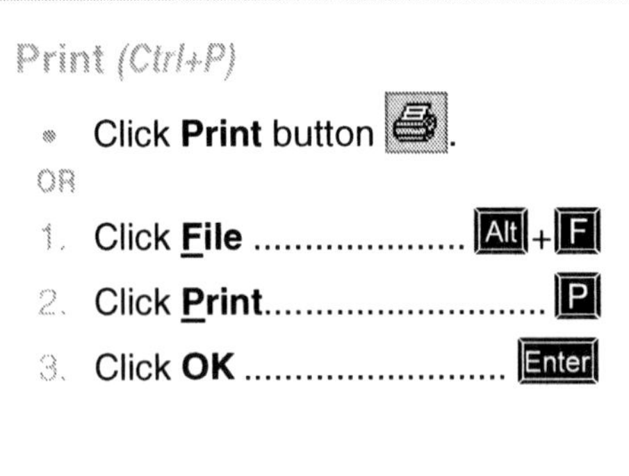

Print *(Ctrl+P)*

- Click **Print** button.

OR

1. Click **File** .... Alt+F
2. Click **Print** .... P
3. Click **OK** .... Enter

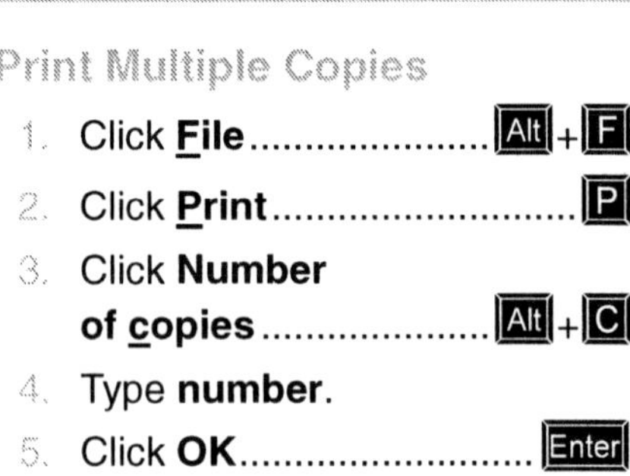

Print Multiple Copies

1. Click **File** .... Alt+F
2. Click **Print** .... P
3. Click **Number of copies** .... Alt+C
4. Type **number**.
5. Click **OK** .... Enter

Exercise Directions

1. Start Word.
2. Create a new document and save it as VIDEO.
3. Type the document shown in Illustration A.
   a. Use Click and Type to center lines as indicated.
   b. Use Click and Type to start paragraphs flush left as indicated.
   c. Press the Enter key twice between each paragraph to leave a blank line.
4. If you make typing errors, use Backspace or Delete to erase them.
5. Display the document in Print Preview. It should look similar to the one shown in Illustration A.
6. Close Print Preview.
7. Print one copy of the document.
8. Close the document, saving all changes.
9. Exit Word.

Illustration A

Northlake Video Links
89 Broad Street, Boston, MA 02110

Northlake Video Links is a video production company that specializes in live transmissions including Web casts, video conferencing, and television interviews. Northlake Video is dedicated to providing high-quality video production services at a reasonable cost. Founded in the early 1980s as a small production house, Northlake Video has evolved into one of the area's premier full-service video companies.

The experienced and savvy team of personnel at Northlake Video has experience in all aspects of video production, including sound, sets, and lighting. In addition to highly qualified engineers, our staff includes producers, editors, and talent scouts. When we sit down with a client, we bring a wealth of knowledge and expertise to the table.

Northlake Video has a proven track record. It numbers among its clients major television networks and cable outlets, Fortune 500 corporations, and international organizations. Clients working with Northlake Video can expect only the highest quality service and results. Without exception, Northlake Video guarantees satisfaction.

Northlake Video Links is based in Boston, Massachusetts. It has satellite offices in Philadelphia, Pennsylvania, and Chicago, Illinois.

Mission Statement

Our company, Northlake Video Links, is committed to providing quality service to all clients. We strive for excellence at every level of our organization. We vow to maintain the highest standards, pursue success, and guarantee customer satisfaction.

At Northlake Video Links we respect our employees as well as our clients. We believe that fostering a strong community within the workplace strengthens our position in the marketplace. We are confident that our commitment will make us leaders in our industry.

On Your Own

1. Create a new document in Word.
2. Save the document as OWDDOCS.
3. Type four or five paragraphs about the different types of documents you can create using Word 2002. For example, you can create letters, memos, reports, newsletters, and schedules.
4. Include information about why you would want to create each type of document, what you would include in each type of document, and whether or not you would need to print each type of document.
5. Preview the document.
6. Print one copy of the document.
7. Save your changes, close the document, and exit Word when you are finished.

Exercise 8

Skills Covered:

◆ **Insertion Point Movements** ◆ **Change the View**
◆ **Full Screen View** ◆ **Show/Hide Marks** ◆ **Rulers**

On the Job

Mastering insertion point movements in Word is necessary to enter and edit text anywhere in a document. Changing the view allows you to see your document in different ways in order to select the view most suitable for the current task. You can also display and hide different screen elements to ensure you have the tools you need when you need them.

As the owner of Pelican Peter's, a dive shop in Naples, Florida, you want to provide your employees with information about a new vacation policy. In this exercise, you will create a document about the policy that you can print and hang in the store.

Terms

Insertion point The flashing vertical line that indicates where the next action will occur.

Web page A document stored on the World Wide Web.

Nonprinting characters Characters, such as paragraph marks and tab symbols, that are not printed in a document but that can be displayed on-screen.

Notes

Insertion Point Movements

- The **insertion point** indicates where text will be inserted or deleted.
- You can move the insertion point anywhere in the existing text with keystrokes or mouse clicks.
  - ✓ *If Click and Type feature is enabled, you can move the insertion point anywhere in a blank document as well.*
- Using scroll bars to shift the document view does not move the insertion point.

Change the View

- By default, Word starts with documents displayed in Print Layout view.
  - You can change the view at any time.

The View buttons

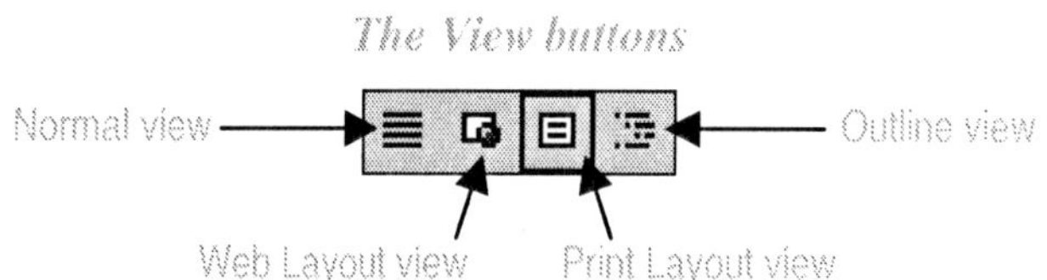

  - Normal view is used for most typing, editing, and formatting.
  - Print Layout view displays a document on-screen the way it will look when it is printed.
  - Web Layout view wraps text to fit the window, the way it would on a **Web page** document.
  - Outline view is used to create and edit outlines.
- The View buttons are located on the bottom left of the Word window.

Full Screen View

- In any view, including Print Preview, use Full Screen view to display a document without the title bar, toolbars, ruler, scroll bars, status bar, or taskbar.
- Full Screen view lets you see more of your document on-screen at one time.

Full Screen view

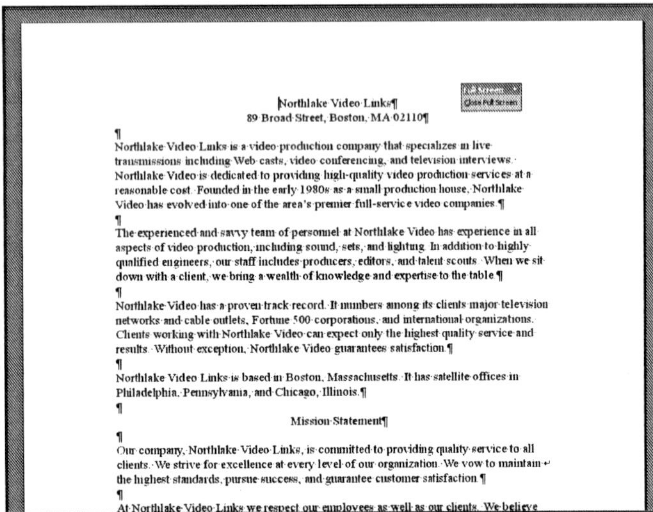

Northlake Video Links
89 Broad Street, Boston, MA 02110

Northlake Video Links is a video production company that specializes in live transmissions including Web casts, video conferencing, and television interviews. Northlake Video is dedicated to providing high-quality video production services at a reasonable cost. Founded in the early 1980s as a small production house, Northlake Video has evolved into one of the area's premier full-service video companies.

The experienced and savvy team of personnel at Northlake Video has experience in all aspects of video production, including sound, sets, and lighting. In addition to highly qualified engineers, our staff includes producers, editors, and talent scouts. When we sit down with a client, we bring a wealth of knowledge and expertise to the table.

Northlake Video has a proven track record. It numbers among its clients major television networks and cable outlets, Fortune 500 corporations, and international organizations. Clients working with Northlake Video can expect only the highest quality service and results. Without exception, Northlake Video guarantees satisfaction.

Northlake Video Links is based in Boston, Massachusetts. It has satellite offices in Philadelphia, Pennsylvania, and Chicago, Illinois.

Mission Statement

Our company, Northlake Video Links, is committed to providing quality service to all clients. We strive for excellence at every level of our organization. We vow to maintain the highest standards, pursue success, and guarantee customer satisfaction.

At Northlake Video Links we respect our employees as well as our clients. We believe

Show/Hide Marks

- When typing, you insert **nonprinting characters** like spaces, tabs, and paragraph marks, along with printing characters like letters and numbers.
- Displaying nonprinting characters on-screen is helpful because you see where each paragraph ends and if there are extra spaces or unwanted tab characters.
- On-screen, the most common nonprinting characters are displayed as follows:
  - Space: dot (•)
  - Paragraph: paragraph symbol (¶)
  - Tab: right arrow (→)
- Other nonprinting characters include optional hyphens and line breaks.

Rulers

- The horizontal ruler measures the width of the document page. It displays information such as margins, tabs stops, and indents.
- The vertical ruler measures the height of the document page.

  ✓ *The vertical ruler is only displayed in Print Layout view and Print Preview.*

Procedures

Insertion Point Movements

With the mouse:

- Click mouse pointer in text where you want to position insertion point.

✓ *If the Click and Type feature is enabled, double-click anywhere in a blank document in Print Layout view to position insertion point.*

With the Keyboard:

To Move	Press
One character left	←
One character right	→
One line up	↑
One line down	↓
Previous word	Ctrl + ←
Next word	Ctrl + →
Top of screen	Alt + Ctrl + Page Up
Bottom of screen	Alt + Ctrl + Page Down
Beginning of document	Ctrl + Home
One screen down	Page Down
One screen up	Page Up
One page down	Ctrl + Page Down
One page up	Ctrl + Page Up
End of document	Ctrl + End
Beginning of line	Home
End of line	End

Change View

- Click desired view button:
  - **Normal**
  - **Web Layout**
  - **Print Layout**
  - **Outline**

OR

1. Click **View** .... Alt + V
2. Click **Normal** .... N

   OR

   Click **Web Layout** .... W

   OR

   Click **Print Layout** .... P

   OR

   Click **Outline** .... O

Full Screen View

1. Click **View** .... Alt + V
2. Click **Full Screen** .... U

To display screen elements again:

- Press **Esc** .... Esc

OR

Click **Close Full Screen** button Close Full Screen .... Alt + C

Show/Hide Marks

(Ctrl + Shift +8)

- Click **Show/Hide ¶** button ¶.

OR

1. Click **Tools** .... Alt + T
2. Click **Options** .... O
3. Click **View** tab .... Ctrl + Tab
4. Select **All** check box .... Alt + L in Formatting marks section.
5. Click **OK** .... Enter

Show or Hide Ruler

1. Click **View** .... Alt + V

   ✓ *Check mark next to ruler indicates ruler is displayed.*

2. Click **Ruler** .... R

Exercise Directions

1. Start Word and create a new document.
2. Save the new document with the name VACATION.
3. Display nonprinting characters.
4. Use Click and Type to position the insertion point in the center of the first line and type the heading, as shown in Illustration A.
5. Use Click and Type to position the insertion point flush left, two lines down, then type the first paragraph shown in Illustration A.
   - Notice the paragraph marks that are inserted automatically in the document.
6. Press Enter twice to start a new paragraph and insert a blank line.
7. Type the second paragraph shown in Illustration A.
8. Change to Web Layout view.
9. Change to Normal view.
10. Change to Print Layout view.
11. Hide the rulers.
12. Show the rulers.
13. Use Print Preview to preview the document.
14. Print one copy of the document.
15. Close the document, saving all changes.
16. Exit Word.

Illustration A

Pelican Peter's Vacation Policy

I would like all employees to be aware of our new vacation policy. As of January 1, vacation time will be directly related to the number of hours worked each month. Specifically, employees will earn 8 hours of vacation time for every 120 hours worked.

The new policy does not affect vacation time you may have already earned. As always, you must clear vacation time with your manager to be sure you are not put on the schedule. Please contact me if you have any questions about this policy.

On Your Own

1. Create a new document in Word.
2. Save the file as OWDCOURSE.
3. Draft a press release of at least two paragraphs announcing that you are taking a course to learn how to use Microsoft Office 2002. Include information such as your instructor's name, the textbook you are using, and when the course will be completed.
4. Using Click and Type, center a headline at the top of the document.
5. Using Click and Type, move the pointer back to the flush left or first line indent position to type the rest of the press release.
6. Change the view.
7. Change to Full screen view.
8. Change to Print Layout view.
9. Display, hide, and then redisplay the ruler.
10. Display the document in Print Preview.
11. Print one copy of the document.
12. Close the document when you are finished, saving all changes.

Exercise 9

Skills Covered:

◆ **Use AutoCorrect** ◆ **Select Text in a Document**
◆ **Replace Selected Text** ◆ **Align Text Horizontally** ◆ **Save Changes**

On the Job

As you type a document, Word's AutoCorrect feature automatically corrects common spelling errors before you even know you've made them. You must select text in a document in order to edit it or format it. Save changes to a document to keep it up to date and accurate and to insure that you don't lose work in the event of a power failure or computer problem. Set horizontal alignment to improve the appearance of a document and make it easier to read.

You work in the personnel department at Ramirez, Johnson, and Gold, an investment-banking firm in New York City. In this exercise, the Personnel Director has as asked you to type a memo to employees about a new policy regarding casual attire on Fridays.

Terms

AutoCorrect A Word feature that automatically corrects common spelling and typing errors as you type.

Caps Lock Keyboard key used to **toggle** uppercase letters with lowercase letters.

Toggle A command that turns a particular mode on and off. Also, to switch back and forth between two modes.

Select Mark text for editing.

Contiguous Next to or adjacent.

Noncontiguous Not next to or adjacent.

Highlight To display text in different colors than the surrounding text.

Horizontal alignment The position of text in relation to the left and right page margins.

Flush Lined up evenly along an edge.

Selection bar A narrow strip along the left margin of a page. When the mouse pointer is in the selection area, it changes to an arrow pointing up and to the right.

Notes

Use AutoCorrect

AutoCorrect dialog box

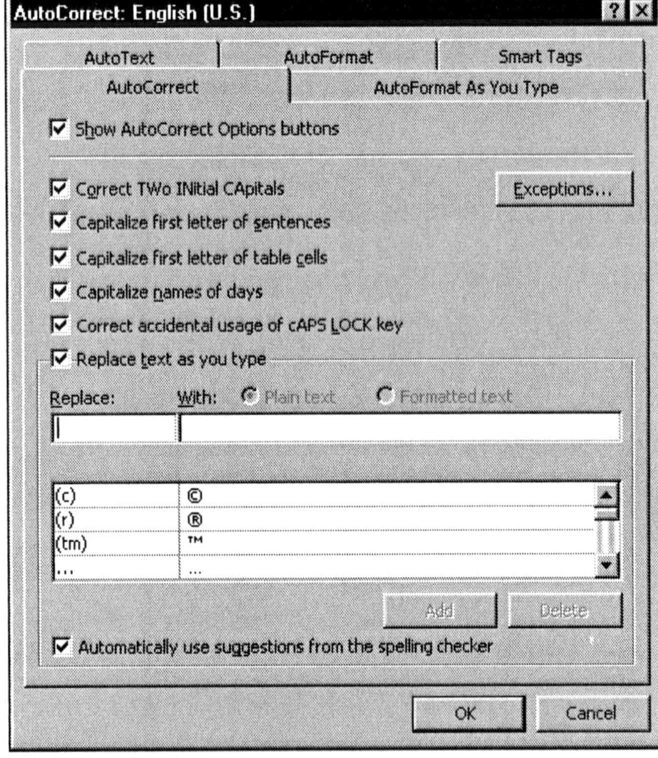

- **AutoCorrect** automatically replaces spelling or common typing errors with the correct text as soon as you press the spacebar.
- Word comes with a built-in list of AutoCorrect entries including common typos like *adn* for *and* and *teh* for *the.*
- AutoCorrect can also replace regular characters with symbols, such as the combination of the letters *T* and *M* with the trademark symbol, ™.
- AutoCorrect also corrects capitalization errors as follows:
  - TWo INitial CApital letters are replaced with one initial capital letter.
  - The first word in a sentence is automatically capitalized.
  - The days of the week are automatically capitalized.
  - Accidental use of the cAPS LOCK feature is corrected if the **Caps Lock** key is set to ON.
- You can add words to the AutoCorrect list. For example if you commonly misspell someone's name, you can add it to the list.
- You can also set Word to use the spelling checker dictionary to determine if a word is misspelled and to correct it automatically.
  - ✓ *You learn how to use Word's spelling checker in Exercise 11.*
- If AutoCorrect changes text that was not incorrect, you can use Undo or the AutoCorrect Options button to reverse the change.
- If you find AutoCorrect distracting, you can disable it.

Select Text in a Document

- You must **select** text already entered in a document in order to edit it or format it.
- You can select any amount of **contiguous** or **noncontiguous** text.
  - ✓ *You can also select nontext characters such as symbols, nonprinting characters such as paragraph marks, and graphics such as pictures.*
- Selected text appears **highlighted** on-screen as white characters on a black background.

Selected text in a document

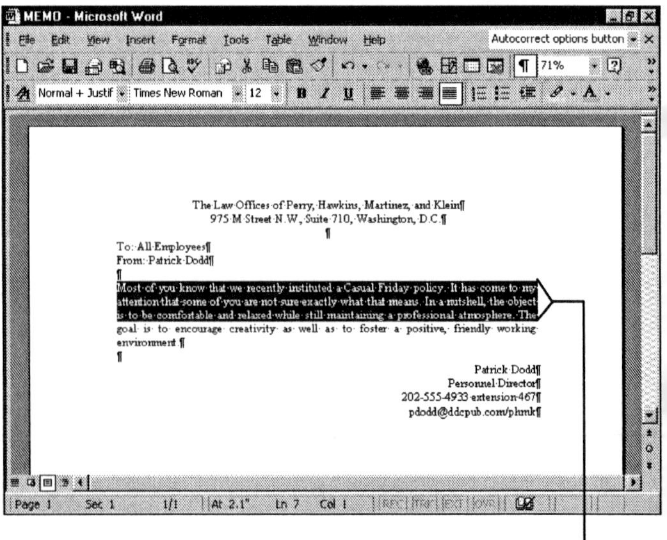

Replace Selected Text

- You can replace selected text simply by typing new text.
- You can delete selected text by pressing the Delete key or the Backspace key.
  - ✓ *If you accidentally replace selected text, use the Undo command to undo the action.*

Align Text Horizontally

- **Horizontal alignment** is used to adjust the position of paragraphs in relation to the left and right margins of a page.
  - ✓ *You have already used Click and Type to align text horizontally in a document.*
- There are four horizontal alignments:
  - *Left.* Text is **flush** with left margin. The right margin is uneven (or ragged). Left is the default horizontal alignment.
  - *Right.* Text is flush with right margin. The left margin is uneven.
  - *Center.* Text is centered between margins.
  - *Justify.* Text is spaced so both left and right margins are even.
- You can use different alignments in a document.

Text aligned in a document

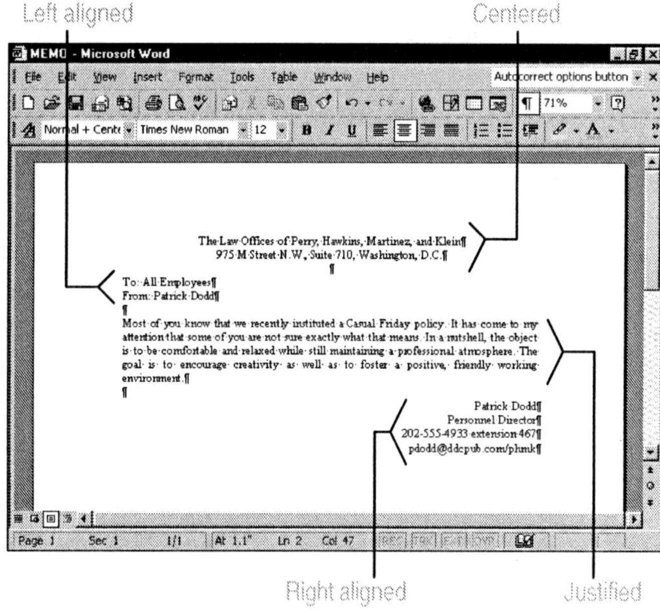

Save Changes

- To keep revisions permanently, you must save the document.
- Saving frequently ensures that no work will be lost if there is a power outage or you experience computer problems.
  - ✓ *The Document Recovery feature also helps insure that you won't lose your work in case of a failure. Refer to Exercise 4 for more information.*
- Saving replaces the previously saved version of the document with any new changes.

Procedures

Use AutoCorrect

Add words to the AutoCorrect list:

1. Click **Tools** .... Alt+T
2. Click **AutoCorrect** .... A
3. Type misspelled word to add.
4. Click in **With** text box ... Alt+W
5. Type correct word.
6. Click **Add** button [Add] .... Alt+A
7. Click **OK** .... Enter

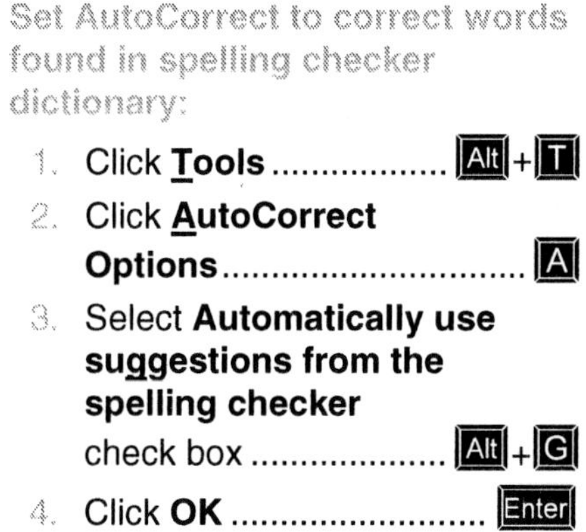

Set AutoCorrect to correct words found in spelling checker dictionary:

1. Click **Tools** .... Alt+T
2. Click **AutoCorrect Options** .... A
3. Select **Automatically use suggestions from the spelling checker** check box .... Alt+G
4. Click **OK** .... Enter

Disable AutoCorrect:

1. Click **Tools** .... Alt+T
2. Click **AutoCorrect Options** .... A
3. Clear **Replace text as you type** check box.................... Alt+T
   - ✓ *Clicking should remove check mark; if not, click check box again.*
4. Click **OK** .... Enter

Use AutoCorrect Options button:

1. Click word that was automatically corrected.
   - ✓ *A small blue box is displayed below the word.*
2. Rest mouse pointer on **blue box**.
   - ✓ *The AutoCorrect Options button is displayed.*
3. Click **AutoCorrect Options** button.
4. Select one of the following:
   - **Change Back** .... H
     to reverse the change.
   - **Stop Automatically Correcting** .... A
     to remove the word from the AutoCorrect list.
   - **Control AutoCorrect Options** C
     to open the AutoCorrect dialog box.

Select Using the Keyboard

1. Position insertion point at the location where you want to start selecting.
2. Use following key combinations:
   - One character right .... Shift+→
   - One character left .... Shift+←
   - One line up........... Shift+↑
   - One line down .... Shift+↓
   - To end of line........ Shift+End
   - To beginning of line .... Shift+Home
   - To end of document ..... Shift+Ctrl+End
   - To beginning of document... Shift+Ctrl+Home
   - Entire document......Ctrl+A
     - ✓ *Pressing the Shift key while using any other insertion point movement key will add the selection function to the movement function.*

Select using the Mouse

1. Position insertion point to the left of first character to select.
2. Hold down left mouse button.
3. Drag to where you want to stop selecting.
4. Release mouse button.

Mouse Selection Shortcuts

One word:

- Double-click word.

One sentence:

1. Press and hold **Ctrl** .... Ctrl
2. Click in sentence.

One line:

- Click in **selection bar** to the left of the line.
  - ✓ *In the selection bar, the mouse pointer changes to an arrow pointing up and to the right.*

One paragraph:

- Double-click in selection bar to the left of the paragraph you want to select.

Document:

- Triple-click in selection bar.

Select noncontiguous blocks:

1. Select first block.
2. Press and hold **Ctrl** .... Ctrl
3. Select additional block(s).

Cancel a Selection

- Click anywhere in document

OR

- Press any arrow key ....

Replace Selected Text

1. Select text to replace.
2. Type new text.

   OR

   Press **Delete** .... Del
   to delete selected text.

Align Horizontally

1. Position insertion point in paragraph to align.

   OR

   Select paragraphs to align.

   OR

   Position insertion point where you intend to type text.
2. Click alignment button:
   - **Center** .... Ctrl+E
   - **Right** .... Ctrl+R
   - **Justify** .... Ctrl+J
   - **Left** .... Ctrl+L

OR

1. Click **Format** .... Alt+O
2. Click **Paragraph**................. P
3. Click **Alignment** drop-down arrow .... Alt+G
4. Click desired alignment option ....
   - **Left**
   - **Centered**
   - **Right**
   - **Justified**
5. Click **OK** .... Enter

Save Changes
(Ctrl+S)

- Click **Save** button.

OR

1. Click **File** .... Alt+F
2. Click **Save** .... S

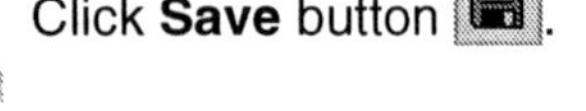

Exercise Directions

1. Start Word, if necessary.
2. Create a new document and save it as CASUAL.
3. Display nonprinting characters, if necessary.
4. Open the AutoCorrect dialog box.
   a. Add the misspelled name **Ramirex** to the AutoCorrect list; Replace it with the correctly spelled **Ramirez**.
   b. Add the misspelled word **personell** to the AutoCorrect list; Replace it with the correctly spelled **personnel**.
   c. Add the misspelled word **casaul** to the AutoCorrect list; Replace it with the correctly spelled **casual**.
   d. Be sure the *Replace text as you type* check box is selected, then close the dialog box.
5. Type the document shown in Illustration A.
   - Type the actual date in place of the text **Today's date**.
   - Type the circled errors exactly as shown in the illustration.
     ✓ *Notice that Word automatically corrects the errors.*
   - Press Enter twice to start new paragraphs and leave blank lines as marked on the illustration.
6. Save the changes to the document.
7. Horizontally align the text in the document as marked on the illustration.
   a. Select the lines marked for centering.
   b. Center the selected text.
   c. Select the three paragraphs marked for justification.
   d. Justify the selected paragraphs.
   e. Select the lines marked for right alignment.
   f. Right align the selected text.
8. Select the text **Personnel Director** on the **From:** line near the top of the document and replace it with the name **Patrick Dodd**.
9. Display the document in Print Preview. It should look similar to Illustration B.
10. Close Print Preview.
11. Print the document.
12. Close the document, saving all changes.
13. Exit Word

Illustration A

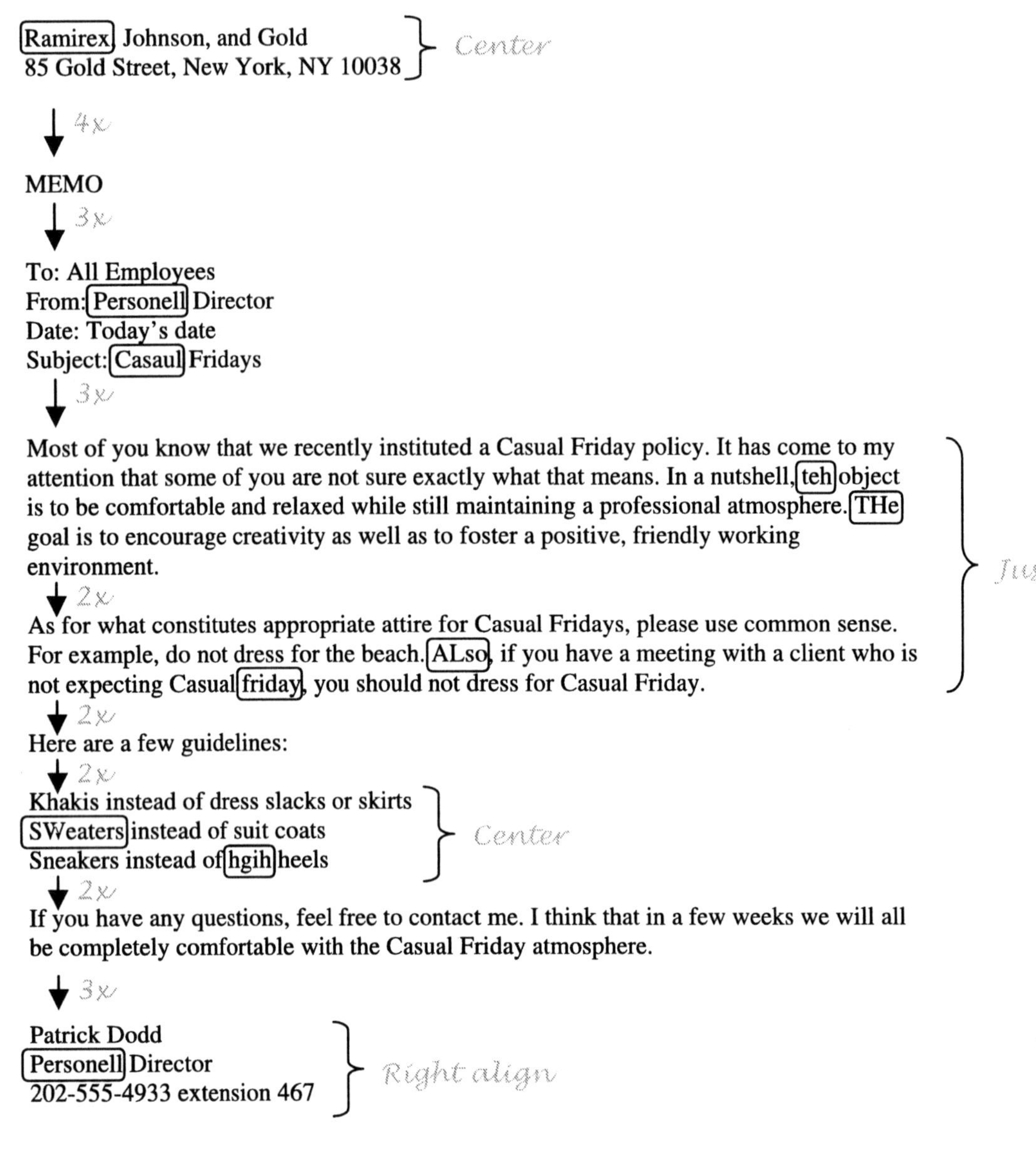

Ramirex Johnson, and Gold
85 Gold Street, New York, NY 10038

MEMO

To: All Employees
From: Personell Director
Date: Today's date
Subject: Casaul Fridays

Most of you know that we recently instituted a Casual Friday policy. It has come to my attention that some of you are not sure exactly what that means. In a nutshell, teh object is to be comfortable and relaxed while still maintaining a professional atmosphere. THe goal is to encourage creativity as well as to foster a positive, friendly working environment.

As for what constitutes appropriate attire for Casual Fridays, please use common sense. For example, do not dress for the beach. ALso, if you have a meeting with a client who is not expecting Casual friday, you should not dress for Casual Friday.

Here are a few guidelines:

Khakis instead of dress slacks or skirts
SWeaters instead of suit coats
Sneakers instead of hgih heels

If you have any questions, feel free to contact me. I think that in a few weeks we will all be completely comfortable with the Casual Friday atmosphere.

Patrick Dodd
Personell Director
202-555-4933 extension 467

Illustration B

Ramirez, Johnson, and Gold
85 Gold Street, New York, NY 10038

MEMO

To: All Employees
From: Patrick Dodd
Date: Today's date
Subject: Casual Fridays

Most of you know that we recently instituted a Casual Friday policy. It has come to my attention that some of you are not sure exactly what that means. In a nutshell, the object is to be comfortable and relaxed while still maintaining a professional atmosphere. The goal is to encourage creativity as well as to foster a positive, friendly working environment.

As for what constitutes appropriate attire for Casual Fridays, please use common sense. For example, do not dress for the beach. Also, if you have a meeting with a client who is not expecting Casual Friday, you should not dress for Casual Friday.

Here are a few guidelines:

Khakis instead of dress slacks or skirts
Sweaters instead of suit coats
Sneakers instead of high heels

If you have any questions, feel free to contact me. I think that in a few weeks we will all be completely comfortable with the Casual Friday atmosphere.

Patrick Dodd
Personnel Director
202-555-4933 extension 467

On Your Own

1. Create a new document in Word.
2. Save the file as OWDNAME.
3. Add your last name to the AutoCorrect list.
4. Add other words that you commonly misspell.
5. Type a memo to your teachers asking them to be sure to spell your name correctly. Include the misspelled version as well as the correct spelling. When AutoCorrect changes the misspelled version, use the AutoCorrect Options button to reverse the change.
6. Change the horizontal alignment of some of the text in the memo.
7. Print the document.
8. Close the document, saving all changes.
9. Exit Word

Exercise 10

Skills Covered:

◆ **Select a Font**

◆ **Change Font Size** ◆ **Apply Font Styles**

On the Job

Use fonts, font sizes, and font styles, to dress up the appearance of a document. Fonts are a basic means of applying formatting to text and characters. They can set a mood, command attention, and convey a message.

The store hours at Pelican Peter's are changing. In this exercise, you will write a memo to employees telling them about the change. You will use fonts, font sizes, and font sizes to affect the appearance of the document and to emphasize certain word.

Terms

Font A complete set of characters in a specific face, style, and size.

Font face The character design of a font set.

Serif A font face that has curved or extended edges.

Sans Serif A font face that has straight edges.

Script A font face that looks like handwriting.

Font size The height of an uppercase letter in a font set.

Font style The slant and weight of characters in a font set.

Notes

Select a Font

- A **font** is a set of characters that all have the same design.
- Each font set includes upper- and lowercase letters, numbers, and punctuation marks.
- There are three basic categories of **font faces**:
  - **Serif** fonts are easy to read and are often used for document text.

    A Serif Font

  - **Sans serif** fonts are often used for headings.

    A Sans Serif Font

  - **Script** face fonts are often used to simulate handwriting on invitations or announcements.

    A Script Font

- The default Word font is Times New Roman, a serif font.
- The current font name is displayed in the Font box on the Formatting toolbar.
- You can select a font from the Font drop-down list, or in the Font dialog box.
- The font list is alphabetical; however, the most recently used fonts are listed at the top of the list.

The Font box and drop-down list

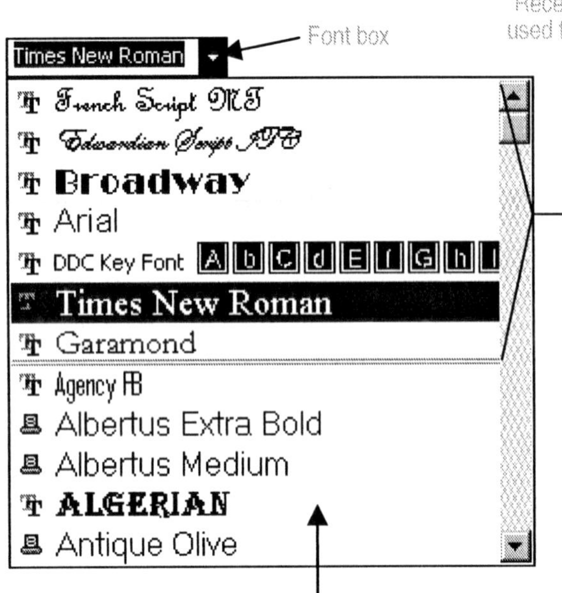

- Both Word and Windows come with built-in fonts; you can install additional fonts.
- Fonts can be changed before or after you enter text in a document.
- You can set the tone of a document by putting thought into the fonts you select.
  - ✓ *More than two or three font faces makes a document look disjointed and unprofessional.*

Change Font Size

- **Font size** is measured in points. There are approximately 72 points in an inch.
- The default Word font size is 12 points.
- The current font size is displayed in the Font Size box on the Formatting toolbar.
- You can select a font size from the Font size drop-down list, or in the Font dialog box.
- You can also type a font size into the Font Size box, and then press Enter to make the change. You can even type half sizes, such as 10.5, 12.5, and so on.

Font Size box and drop-down list

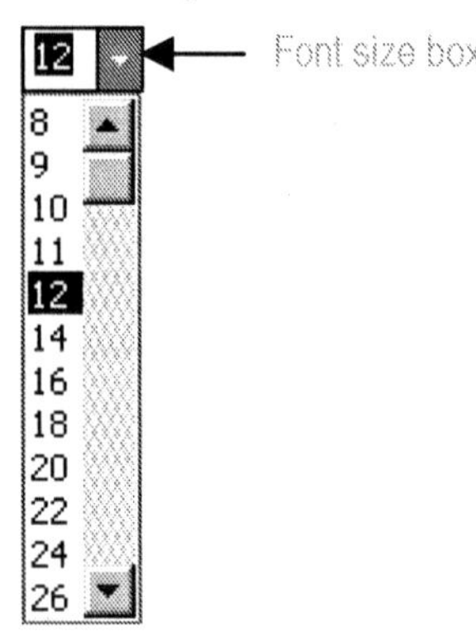

Apply Font Styles

- The most common **font styles** are bold and italic.
- When no style is applied to a font, it is called regular.
- You can combine font styles to achieve different effects, such as ***bold italic***.
- You can apply font styles using toolbar buttons, or by selecting the styles in the Font dialog box.

The Font dialog box

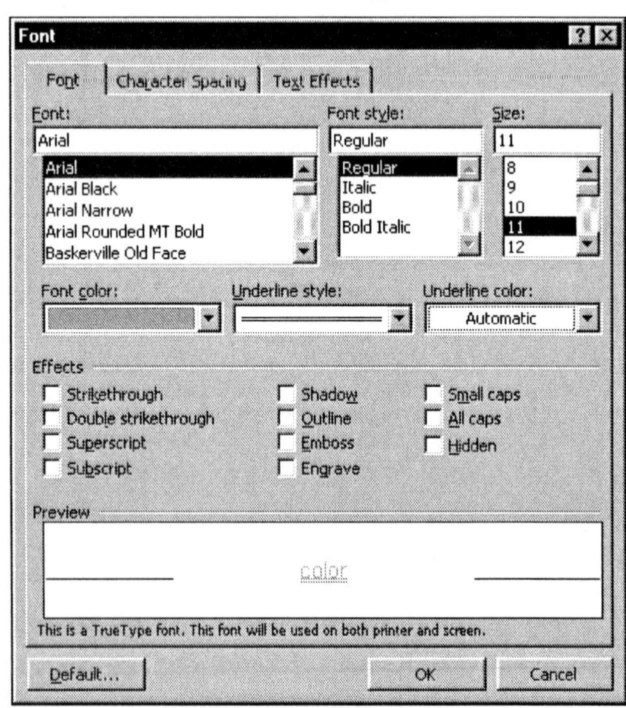

Procedures

Select a Font

(Ctrl + Shift + F)

1. Select text.

   OR

   Position insertion point where new text will be typed.
2. Click **Font** drop-down arrow [Times New Roman ▾].
3. Click font name .... ↓, Enter

OR

1. Select text.

   OR

   Position insertion point where new text will be typed.
2. Click **Format** .... Alt+O
3. Click **Font** .... F
4. Click font name in **Font** list .... Alt+F, ↓
5. Click **OK** .... Enter

Change Font Size

1. Select text.

   OR

   Position insertion point where new text will be typed.
2. Click **Font Size** drop-down arrow [10 ▾].
3. Click font size .... ↓, Enter

OR

1. Select text.

   OR

   Position insertion point where new text will be typed.
2. Click **Format** .... Alt+O
3. Click **Font** .... F
4. Click font size in **Size** list .... Alt+S, ↓
5. Click **OK** .... Enter

Apply Font Styles

1. Select text.

   OR

   Position insertion point where new text will be typed.
2. Click font style button:
   - **Bold** [B] .... Ctrl+B
   - **Italic** [I] .... Ctrl+I

   ✓ *To remove font styles repeat steps 1 and 2.*

OR

1. Select text.

   OR

   Position insertion point where new text will be typed.
2. Click **Format** .... Alt+O
3. Click **Font** .... F
4. Click font style in **Font style** list........ Alt+Y, ↓

   ✓ *To remove font styles click Regular.*
5. Click **OK** .... Enter

Exercise Directions

1. Start Word, if necessary.
2. Create a new document and save it as HOURS.
3. Type the memo shown in Illustration A.

   ✓ *You may select the font formatting before you type the document, or type the document using the default font, and then apply the font formatting as marked on the illustration.*

   ✓ *Notice as you type the days of the week that Word displays a ScreenTip. This is part of a feature called AutoText, which is similar to AutoCorrect. You can ignore the ScreenTip and continue typing, or you can press Enter to insert the text shown in the ScreenTip. You learn more about using AutoText in Exercise 76.*
4. Use the default font except where marked on the illustration.

   ✓ *If the specified font is not available on your computer, select a different, comparable font.*
5. Use the default font size except where marked on the illustration.
6. Apply the specified font styles as marked.
7. Preview the document. It should look similar to Illustration B.
8. Print the document.
9. Close the document, saving all changes.
10. Exit Word.

Illustration A

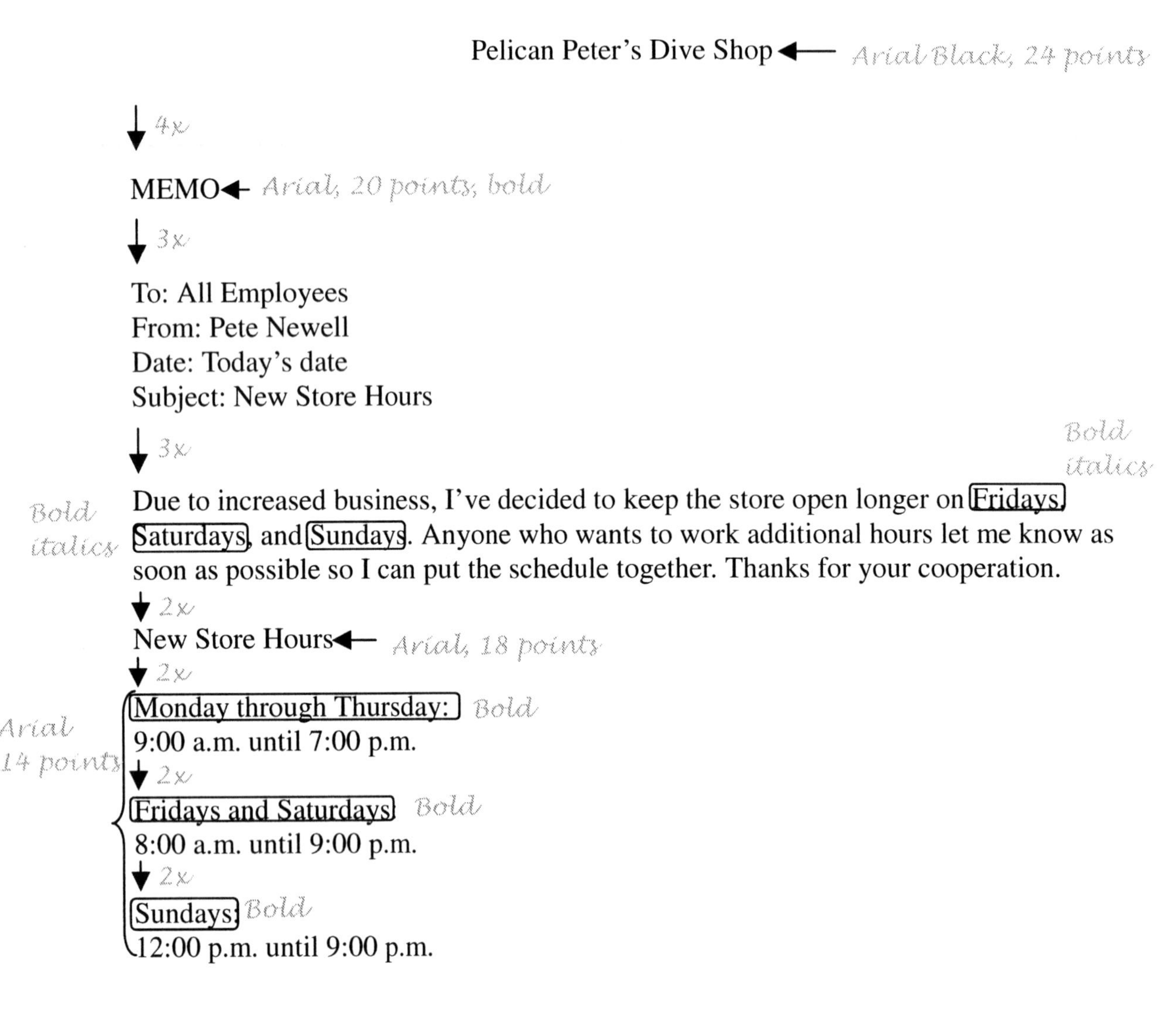

Pelican Peter's Dive Shop ← Arial Black, 24 points

↓ 4x

MEMO ← Arial, 20 points, bold

↓ 3x

To: All Employees
From: Pete Newell
Date: Today's date
Subject: New Store Hours

↓ 3x

Due to increased business, I've decided to keep the store open longer on Fridays, Saturdays, and Sundays. Anyone who wants to work additional hours let me know as soon as possible so I can put the schedule together. Thanks for your cooperation. (Bold italics)

↓ 2x

New Store Hours ← Arial, 18 points

↓ 2x

Monday through Thursday: Bold
9:00 a.m. until 7:00 p.m.

↓ 2x

Fridays and Saturdays: Bold
8:00 a.m. until 9:00 p.m.

↓ 2x

Sundays: Bold
12:00 p.m. until 9:00 p.m.

(Arial 14 points)

Illustration B

Pelican Peter's Dive Shop

MEMO

To: All Employees
From: Pete Newell
Date: Today's date
Subject: New Store Hours

Due to increased business, I've decided to keep the store open longer on ***Fridays***, ***Saturdays***, and ***Sundays***. Anyone who wants to work additional hours let me know as soon as possible so I can put the schedule together. Thanks for your cooperation.

New Store Hours

Monday through Thursday:
9:00 a.m. until 7:00 p.m.

Fridays and Saturdays:
8:00 a.m. until 9:00 p.m.

Sundays:
12:00 p.m. until 9:00 p.m.

On Your Own

1. Create a new document in Word.
2. Save the file as OWDNOTE.
3. Write a note to a friend suggesting plans for the weekend. You might include possible movies to see or rent, a day at the mall, or anything else you like to do together.
4. Use different fonts, font sizes, and font styles in your note.
5. Preview the note, and then print it.
6. Close the document, saving all changes.
7. Exit Word.

Exercise 11

Skills Covered:

◆ **Correct Spelling as You Type** ◆ **Correct Grammar as You Type** ◆ **Check Spelling** ◆ **Check Grammar** ◆ **Use the Thesaurus**

On the Job

A professional document should be free of spelling and grammatical errors. Word can check the spelling and grammar in a document and recommend corrections.

The marketing director at Northlake Video Links has asked you to create a mission statement explaining the goals for the company. In this exercise, you will type the statement, and then improve it by correcting the spelling and grammar.

Terms

Smart tag A feature of Office XP designed to let you perform actions within Word that you would normally have to open another application to accomplish. For example, you can add a person's name and address to an Outlook contact list using a smart tag in Word.

Thesaurus A listing of words with synonyms and antonyms.

Synonyms Words with the same meaning.

Antonyms Words with opposite meanings.

Notes

Correct Spelling as You Type

- By default, Word checks spelling as you type and marks presumed misspelled words with a red, wavy underline.

This·is·an·example·of·a·missspelled·word.¶

- Any word not in the Word dictionary is marked as misspelled, including proper names, words with unique spellings, and many technical terms. Word will also mark double occurrences of words.
- You can ignore the wavy lines and keep typing, correct the spelling, or add the marked word to the dictionary.
- If the wavy underlines distract you from your work, you can turn off the Check spelling as you type feature.

✓ *Word uses a few other underlines to mark text on-screen. For example, blue wavy underlines indicate inconsistent formatting and purple dotted lines indicate **smart tags**. You learn about checking for inconsistent formatting in Exercise 22. You learn about smart tags in Exercise 95.*

Correct Grammar as You Type

- Word can also check grammar as you type, identifying presumed errors such as punctuation, matching case or tense, sentence fragments, and run-on sentences.
- Word marks grammatical errors with a green, wavy underline.

This·is·an·example·of·a·grammatical·errors.¶

- As with the spelling checker, you can ignore the green wavy lines and keep typing, or correct the error.
- If the wavy underlines distract you from your work, you can turn off the Check grammar as you type feature.

Check Spelling

- You can check the spelling in an entire document or in part of a document.
- To check the spelling in part of a document, you must first select the section you want checked.
- The spelling checker identifies any word not in the Word dictionary as misspelled, including proper names, words with unique spellings, and technical terms.
- When Word identifies a misspelled word, you can correct the spelling, ignore the spelling, or add the word to the dictionary.

Correct spelling with Spelling Checker

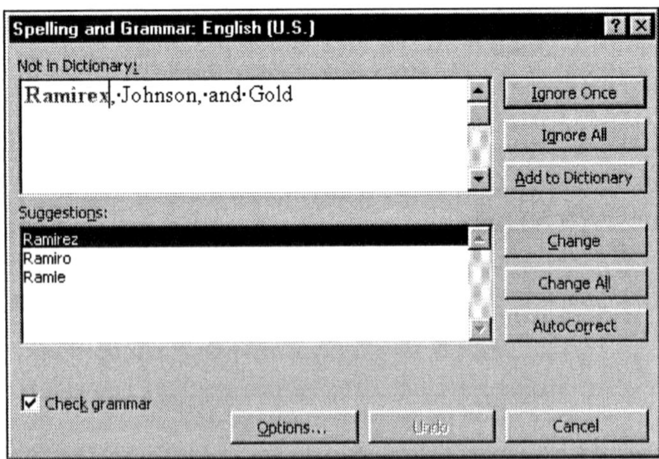

Check Grammar

- By default, Word checks the grammar in a document at the same time that it checks the spelling.
- When Word identifies a grammatical mistake, you can accept the suggestion or ignore it.

Correct grammar with Grammar Checker

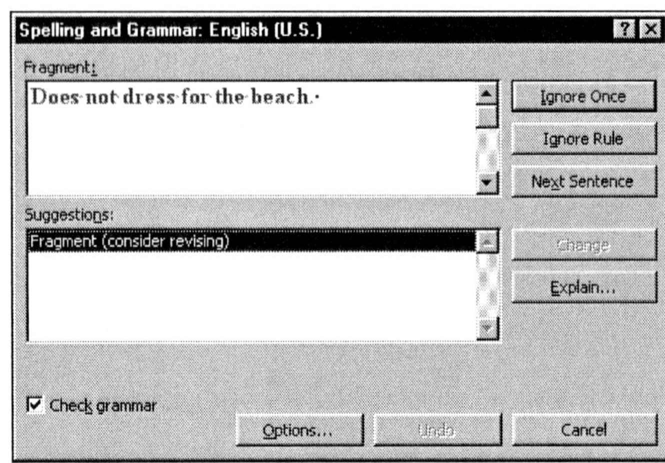

Use the Thesaurus

- Use the **thesaurus** to locate **synonyms**, definitions, and **antonyms** for words typed in a document.
- A thesaurus can improve your writing by helping you eliminate repetitive use of common words and to choose more descriptive words.

Choose synonyms with the Thesaurus

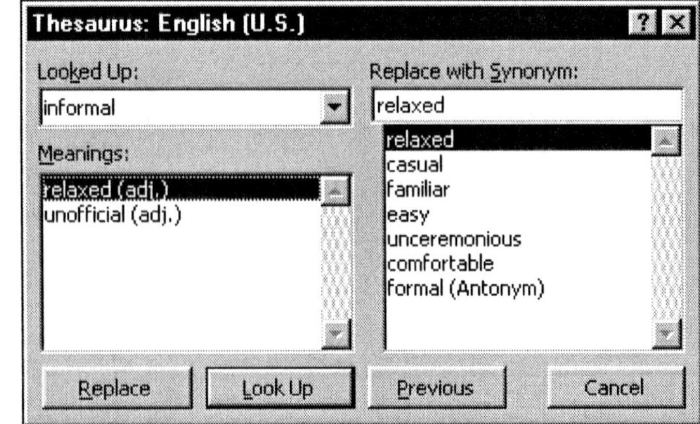

Procedures

Correct Spelling as You Type

1. Right-click red, wavy underline.
2. Click correctly spelled word on shortcut menu.

   OR

   - Click **Ignore All** I
   - Click **Add** to add word to dictionary .... A

To turn off Automatic Spelling Checker:

1. Click **Tools** .... Alt+T
2. Click **Options** .... O
3. Click the **Spelling & Grammar** tab .... Ctrl+Tab
4. Clear **Check spelling as you type** check box .... Alt+P
5. Click **OK** .... Enter

Correct Grammar as You Type

1. Right-click grammatical error marked with green, wavy underline.
2. Click correct grammar option on shortcut menu.

   OR

   Click **Ignore Once** to hide the underline I

To turn off Automatic Grammar Checker:

1. Click **Tools** .... Alt+T
2. Click **Options** .... O
3. Click the **Spelling & Grammar** tab .... Ctrl+Tab
4. Deselect **Check grammar** as you type check box ...... Alt+G
5. Click **OK** .... Enter

Select Grammar Style

1. Click **Tools** .... Alt+T
2. Click **Options** .... O
3. Click the **Spelling & Grammar** tab .... Ctrl+Tab
4. Click **Writing style** drop-down arrow .... Alt+W
5. Click desired style ... ↑↓, Enter
6. Click **OK** .... Enter

Check Spelling *(F7)*

1. Position insertion point where you want to start checking.

   ✓ *Word checks document from the insertion point forward.*

   OR

   Select text you want to check.
2. Click **Spelling and Grammar** button ✓.

   OR

   a. Click **Tools** .... Alt+T
   b. Click **Spelling & Grammar** .... S
3. Choose from the following options:
   - Click correctly spelled word in **Suggestions list** .... Alt+N
   - Change the misspelled word manually in the **Not in Dictionary** text box.
   - Click **Change** .... Alt+C
   - Click **Change All** to change the word everywhere in document .... Alt+L
   - Click **Ignore Once** to continue without changing word .... Alt+I
   - Click **Ignore All** to continue without changing word and without highlighting it anywhere else in document .... Alt+G
   - Click **Add** to add word to dictionary .... Alt+A
   - Click **AutoCorrect** . Alt+R to add the word to the AutoCorrect list.
   - Click **Undo** .... Alt+U to reverse the last change
4. Repeat step 3 options for every misspelled word.
5. Click **OK** when Word completes check. .... Enter

Check Grammar *(F7)*

✓ *The **Check grammar** option must be selected in the Spelling and Grammar display box.*

1. Position insertion point where you want to start checking.

   OR

   Select text you want to check.
2. Click **Spelling and Grammar** button ✓.

   OR

   a. Click **Tools** .... Alt+T
   b. Click **Spelling & Grammar** .... S
3. Choose from the following options:
   - Click the correct grammar in **Suggestions** list ..... Alt+N
   - Edit the error manually in the **Not in Dictionary** box.
   - Click **Change** .... Alt+C
   - Click **Ignore Once** to continue without changing text .... Alt+I
   - Click **Ignore Rule** to continue without changing text and without highlighting error if it occurs anywhere else in document .... Alt+G
   - Click **Next Sentence** to skip highlighted error and continue checking document .... Alt+X
   - Click **Explain** .... Alt+E to display information about grammatical error.
   - Click **Undo** .... Alt+U to reverse the last change
4. Repeat step 3 options for every grammatical error.
5. Click **OK** when Word completes check .... Enter

Use Thesaurus *(Shift+F7)*

1. Click on the word you want to look up.
   ✓ *The insertion point should be positioned within the word.*
2. Click **Tools**.................. Alt+T
3. Click **Language** L
4. Click **Thesaurus** .... T
5. Choose from the following options:
   - Click **Look up** .... Alt+L to display synonyms for word highlighted in Replace with Synonym list.
   - Click a word in the **Meanings list** .... Alt+M to display synonyms for the word.
   - Click **Previous** ...... Alt+P to display the previously displayed list.
6. Click the replacement word you want in the **Replace with Synonym** list. ..... Alt+S, ↑↓
7. Click **Replace**............. Alt+R

Locate a synonym as you type

1. Right-click on the word you want to look up.
2. Click **Synonyms** on shortcut menu .... Y
3. Click desired synonym on submenu .... ↑↓, Enter

   OR

   Click **Thesaurus**.................. T to open the Thesaurus dialog box.

Exercise Directions

1. Start Word, if necessary.
2. Create a new document.
3. Save the file as MISSION.
4. Display paragraph marks.
5. Begin at the top of the screen and type the paragraphs shown in Illustration A, including all the circled errors.
6. As you type, correct the spelling of the word **committed**.
7. As you type, correct the grammar in the first sentence of the second paragraph.
8. Check the spelling and grammar starting at the beginning of the document.
   a. Correct the spelling of the word **clientele**.
   b. Ignore all occurrences of the proper name **Khourie**.
   c. Correct the spelling of the word **guarantee**.
   d. Change the double comma in the middle of the second sentence in the second paragraph to a single comma.
   e. Capitalize the word **we** at the beginning of the last sentence.
9. Use the Thesaurus to replace the word **excellence** in the last sentence.
10. Display the document in Print Preview.
11. Print the document.
12. Close the document, saving all changes.
13. Exit Word.

Illustration A

Northlake Video Links is comitted to excellence. In order to meet the needs of our clientelle, we encourage and support creativity at every level of our organization from our president, Mr. Khourie, to our newest sound technician. We vow to maintain the highest standards, pursue the extraordinary, and guarentee customer satisfaction.

The employees at Northlake Video is encouraged to set personal and professional goals. Following the leadership of Mr. Khourie,, we respect all employees as individuals and believe that fostering a strong community within the workplace strengthens our position in the marketplace. we are confident that our commitment to excellence will make us leaders in our industry.

Replace

On Your Own

1. Create a new document.
2. Save the document as OWDMISSION.
3. Type your own mission statement for this class in the blank document. Include information such as the goals you'd like to achieve and the things you'd like to learn.
4. Check and correct the spelling and grammar.
5. Use the Thesaurus to improve the wording of your document.
6. Print the document.
7. Save your changes, close the document, and exit Word when you are finished.

Exercise 12

Skills Covered:

◆ **Format a Full-block Business Letter**
◆ **Insert the Date and Time** ◆ **Use Shrink to Fit**

On the Job

As a representative of your employer, you write business letters to communicate with other businesses, such as clients or suppliers, or to communicate with individuals, such as prospective employees. For example, you might write a business letter to request a job quote from a supplier, or to inquire about a loan from a bank. You write personal business letters to a business on behalf of an individual. For example, you might write a personal business letter to your insurance company to ask about a claim that needs to be paid, or to a prospective employee asking about job opportunities. The letter serves as a formal record of your inquiry.

You are the assistant to Janice O'Toole, marketing director of Fox Footwear, a company that designs and manufactures shoes for teens and adults. In this exercise, you will create a full-block business letter on behalf of Ms. O'Toole, confirming an appointment with David Marker, an account executive at Northlake Video Links, for the following week.

Terms

Business letter A letter from one business to another business or individual.

Personal business letter A letter from an individual to a business.

Full block A style of letter in which all lines start flush with the left margin.

Modified block A style of letter in which some lines start at the center of the page.

Letterhead stationery Stationery that already has a company's or individual's name and address printed on it.

Salutation The line at the start of a letter including the greeting and the recipient's name, such as *Dear Mr. Doe.*

Computer's clock The clock/calendar built into your computer's main processor to keep track of the current date and time.

Notes

Format a Full-block Business Letter

- A letter written to or from any type of business is considered a **business letter**.
- A business letter written on behalf of an individual is considered a **personal business letter**.
- There are two common styles used for either type of business:
  - In a **full-block** business letter, all lines start flush with the left margin.
  - In a **modified-block** business letter, certain lines start at the center of the page.

✓ *Formatting a modified-block business letter is covered in Exercise 13.*

A Full-block Business Letter

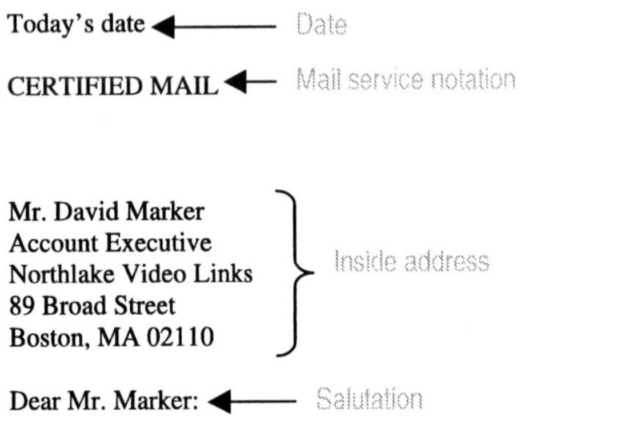

Today's date

CERTIFIED MAIL

Mr. David Marker
Account Executive
Northlake Video Links
89 Broad Street
Boston, MA 02110

Dear Mr. Marker:

Subject: Appointment Confirmation

This letter is to confirm our appointment scheduled for 9:00 a.m. next Monday at my office. I am looking forward to meeting with you to discuss the possibility of using the Internet to broadcast marketing information about Fox Footwear to our clients and suppliers.

As I mentioned on the telephone, we at Fox Footwear are eager to expand our use of Internet technology to include Web broadcasting. Judging from the response we have received from our existing Web site, I believe that the exciting and innovative use of video on the Web will help us forge strong alliances with other companies around the world. We are confident that Northlake Video Links is a partner that can bring insight and experience to us in this new venture.

Enclosed please find our current marketing brochure. Feel free to contact me or my assistant if you have any questions, or if you require any assistance.

Body

Sincerely,

Janice O'Toole
Marketing Director
Fox Footwear, Inc.
4500 Montgomery Street
San Francisco, CA 94111
(415)555-6750
foxfootwear@ddcpub.com

Jo/yo

Enclosure

Copy to: K. Bernstein

- The parts of a business letter are the same regardless of the style.
- Vertical spacing is achieved by inserting blank lines between letter parts.
- Refer to the illustration on the previous page to identify the parts of a business letter.
  - Return address. Indicates from whom the letter is being sent.

    ✓ *Omit the return address if the letter is printed on* ***letterhead stationery****.*

  - Date. The date the letter is written.
  - Inside address. Indicates to whom the letter is being sent.
  - **Salutation.** The greeting.
  - Body. The text that comprises the letter.
  - Closing. The closing sentiment, such as Sincerely, or Best regards.
  - Signature line. The typed name of the letter writer.
  - Title line. The job title of the letter writer.
  - Reference initials, which are the initials of the person who wrote the letter, followed by a slash, followed by the initials of the person who typed the letter.

    ✓ *Whenever you see "yo" as part of the reference initials in an exercise, type your own initials.*

  - Special notations are included when appropriate:
    - Mail service notation indicates a special delivery method. It is typed in all capital letters, two lines below the date. Typical mail service notations include *CERTIFIED MAIL, REGISTERED MAIL,* or *BY HAND.*
    - Subject notation identifies or summarizes the letter topic. The word *Subject* may be typed in all capital letters or with just an initial capital. It is placed two lines below the salutation.

      ✓ *The word* Re *(meaning* with regard to*) is sometimes used in place of the word* Subject.

    - Enclosure or attachment notation indicates whether there are other items in the envelope. It is typed two lines below the reference initials in any of the following styles: *ENC., Enc., Encl., Enclosure, Attachment.*

      ✓ *If there are multiple items, the number may be typed in parentheses following the notation.*

    - Copy notation indicates if any other people are receiving copies of the same letter. It is typed two lines below either the enclosure notation, or reference initials, whichever is last. It may be typed as Copy to:, cc: or pc: (photocopy) with the name(s) of the recipient(s) listed after the colon.

Insert the Date and Time

- Use the Date and Time feature to insert the current date and/or time automatically in a document.
- The inserted date and time are based on your **computer's clock**. A variety of date and time formats are available.

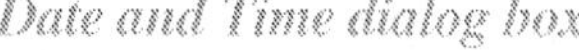
Date and Time dialog box

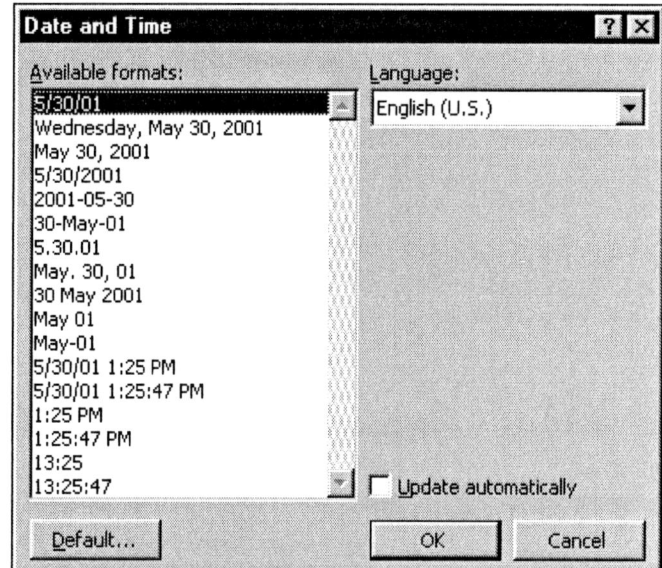

- You can set Word to update the date or time automatically whenever you open or print the document.

Use Shrink to Fit

- Shrink to Fit automatically reduces the font size and spacing in a document just enough to fit the document on one less page.
- Use Shrink to Fit if the last page of a document contains only a small amount of text.
- The Shrink to Fit feature is only available in Print Preview mode.

Procedures

Create a Full-block Business Letter

1. Start 2" from the top of the page .... Enter 4x
   - ✓ *By default, Word leaves a 1" margin between the top of the page and the first line of text. Press Enter four times to move the insertion point down another 1", resulting in 2" of space. If you are using a larger font size, or if the margins are different, you may enter more or fewer blank lines. Use the vertical ruler for reference.*
2. Insert the date.
3. Leave one blank line and type the mail service notation .... Enter 2x
4. Leave three blank lines and type the inside address .... Enter 4x
5. Leave a blank line and type the salutation............... Enter 2x
6. Leave one blank line and type the subject notation .... Enter 2x
7. Leave a blank line and type the letter body..... Enter 2x
8. Leave a blank line and type the closing .... Enter 2x
9. Leave three blank lines and type the signature line .... Enter 4x
10. Type the title line .... Enter
    - ✓ *If you are not using letterhead stationery, type the return address information below the title line.*
11. Leave a blank line and type the reference initials. .. Enter 2x
12. Leave a blank line and type the enclosure notation ...... Enter 2x
13. Leave a blank line and type the copy notation .... Enter 2x

Insert Date and/or Time

1. Position the insertion point.
2. Click **Insert** .... Alt+I
3. Click **Date and Time** .... T
4. Click the desired format
   - ✓ *Select **Update automatically** check box if you want date and/or time to update when you save or print document.*
5. Click **OK**............................ Enter

Use Shrink to Fit

1. Click **Print Preview** button.

   OR

   a. Click **File**................. Alt+F

   b. Click **Print Preview** V
2. Click **Shrink to Fit** button.
3. Click **Close** button

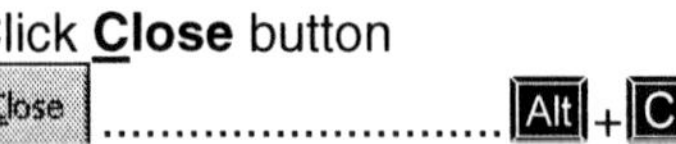

Exercise Directions

1. Start Word, if necessary.
2. Create a new document and save it as MEETING.
3. Type the letter shown in Illustration A.
   - Use the default font and font size (12-point Times New Roman).
     - ✓ *Word may display ScreenTips as you type certain parts of the letter (for example, Subject). Simply ignore them and continue typing.*
   - Press the Enter key to leave blank lines between parts of the letter as indicated.
   - Insert the current date using the MONTH DAY, YEAR format found third from the top in the Date and Time dialog box.
   - Set the date so that it does not update automatically.
4. Check the spelling and grammar in the document.
   - Accept Word's suggestions to correct errors.
   - Ignore all proper names.
5. Display the document in Print Preview.
6. If necessary, use the Shrink to Fit option to ensure that the letter fits on a single page.
7. Print one copy of the document.
8. Close the document, saving all changes.
9. Exit Word.

Illustration A

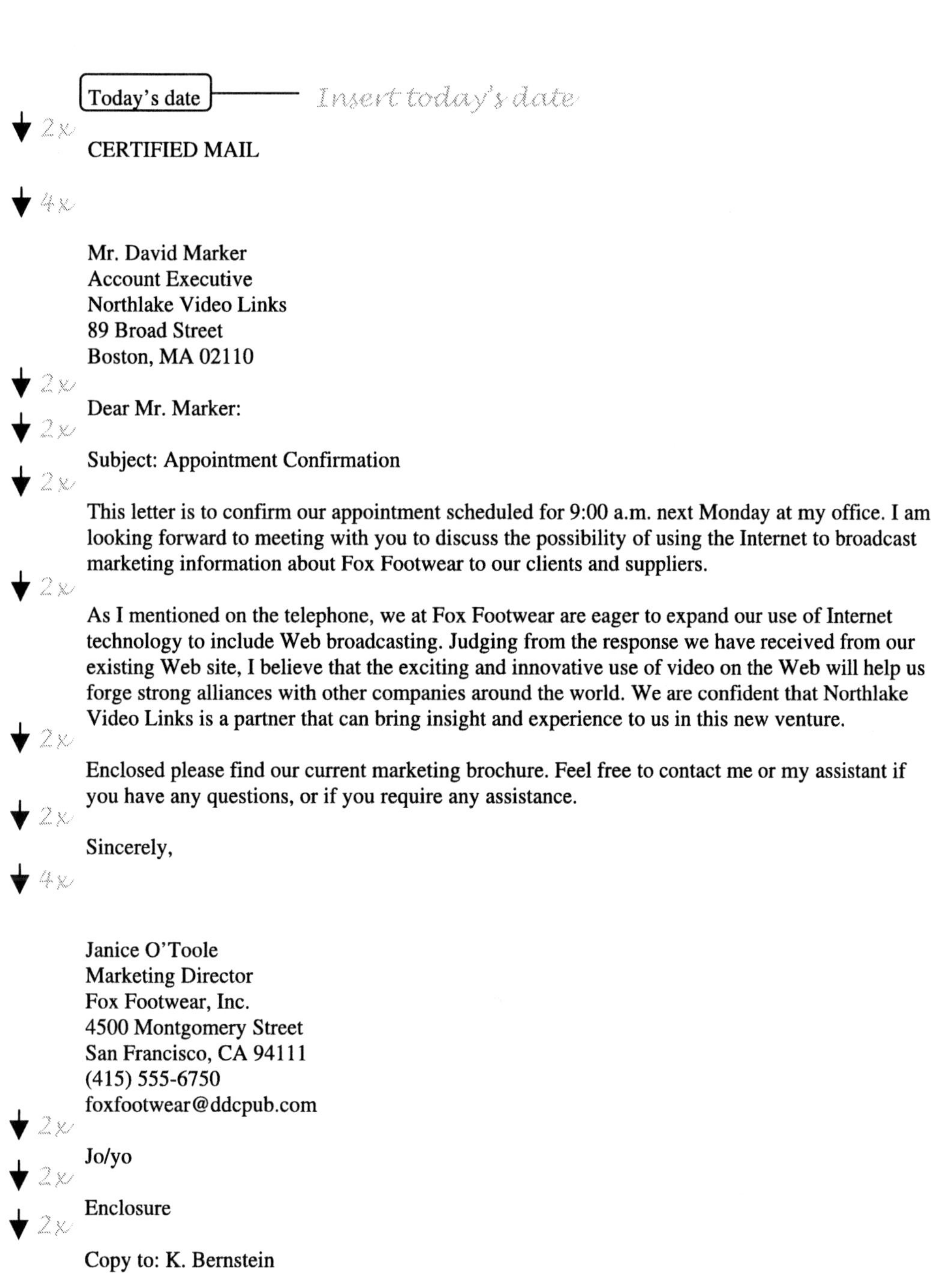

Today's date — *Insert today's date*

↓ 2x

CERTIFIED MAIL

↓ 4x

Mr. David Marker
Account Executive
Northlake Video Links
89 Broad Street
Boston, MA 02110

↓ 2x

Dear Mr. Marker:

↓ 2x

Subject: Appointment Confirmation

↓ 2x

This letter is to confirm our appointment scheduled for 9:00 a.m. next Monday at my office. I am looking forward to meeting with you to discuss the possibility of using the Internet to broadcast marketing information about Fox Footwear to our clients and suppliers.

↓ 2x

As I mentioned on the telephone, we at Fox Footwear are eager to expand our use of Internet technology to include Web broadcasting. Judging from the response we have received from our existing Web site, I believe that the exciting and innovative use of video on the Web will help us forge strong alliances with other companies around the world. We are confident that Northlake Video Links is a partner that can bring insight and experience to us in this new venture.

↓ 2x

Enclosed please find our current marketing brochure. Feel free to contact me or my assistant if you have any questions, or if you require any assistance.

↓ 2x

Sincerely,

↓ 4x

Janice O'Toole
Marketing Director
Fox Footwear, Inc.
4500 Montgomery Street
San Francisco, CA 94111
(415) 555-6750
foxfootwear@ddcpub.com

↓ 2x

Jo/yo

↓ 2x

Enclosure

↓ 2x

Copy to: K. Bernstein

On Your Own

1. Create a new document in Word.
2. Save the document as OWDEVENTS.
3. Representing your school or organization, draft a full-block business letter to a local newspaper asking them to include information about upcoming events in a schedule or calendar listing. School events might include athletic contests such as a homecoming football game, club activities, field trips, band and choir concerts, or vacation days.
4. In the letter, indicate that you have attached the necessary information and that you are sending a copy to your instructor.
5. Save your changes, close the document, and exit Word when you are finished.

Exercise 13

Skills Covered:

◆ **Set Tabs** ◆ **Format a Modified-block Business Letter** ◆ **Create Envelopes** ◆ **Create Labels**

On the Job

You use tabs to align text in a document, such as the date in a modified-block business letter. Handwriting on an envelope looks unprofessional. With Word you can set up and print envelopes to match your letters. You can also create and print mailing labels or return address labels.

You are interested in obtaining a position as a video production assistant. In this exercise, you will create a personal business letter asking about job opportunities at Northlake Video Links. You will also create an envelope to accompany the document. Finally, you will create return address labels and save them in a separate document.

Terms

Tab A location (or measurement) you use to align text.

Tab leader A repeated character, such as a dot or underline, that fills the space between tab stops.

Delivery address The recipient's address printed on the outside of an envelope.

Return address The letter-writer's address, typically appearing at the very top of the letter as well as in the upper-left corner of an envelope.

Notes

Tab stops on the horizontal ruler

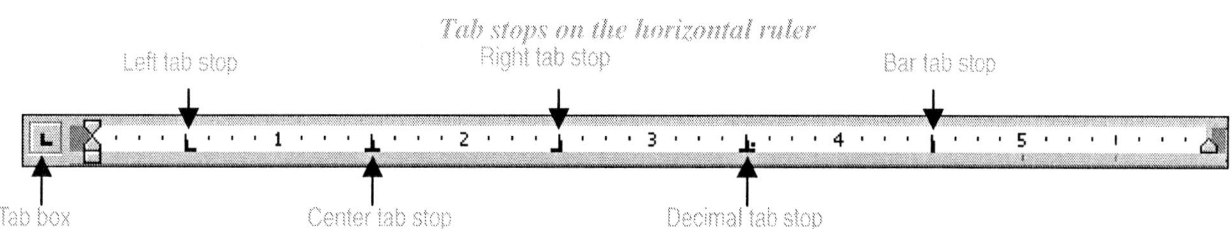

Set Tabs

- **Tabs** are used to indent a single line of text.
- Each time you press the Tab key, the insertion point advances to the next set tab stop.
- There are five types of tab stops:
  - Left: Text starts flush left with the tab stop.
  - Right: Text ends flush right with the tab stop.
  - Center: Text is centered on the tab stop.
  - Decimal: Decimal points are aligned with the tab stop.
  - Bar: A horizontal bar is displayed at the tab stop position. Text starts 1/10" to the right of the bar.
- By default, left tab stops are set every ½" on the horizontal ruler.

- You can set any type of tab stop at any point along the ruler.
- You can use the Tabs dialog box to set precise tab stops.
- Select a **tab leader** in the Tabs dialog box to fill the space between tab stops with a character such as a dot or an underline.
- You can set tabs before you type new text, for the current existing paragraph, or for selected multiple paragraphs.
- Once you set tabs, the formatting will be carried forward each time you press the Enter key to start a new paragraph.

Tabs dialog box

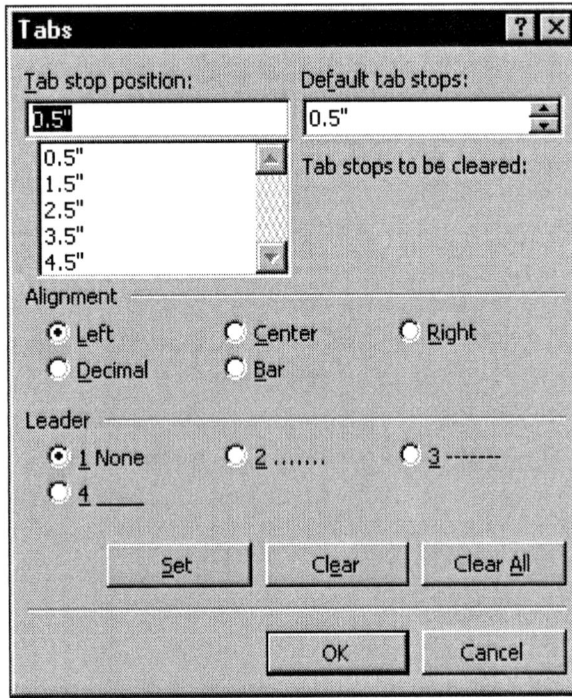

Format a Modified-block Business Letter

- The parts of a modified-block style letter are the same as those of a full-block style letter.
  - ✓ *Refer to Exercise 12 for a list of the parts of a business letter.*
- However, in a modified-block style letter the return address, date, closing, signature, and title lines begin at the center point of the page.
- A left tab stop set at the center point of the page enables you to position the insertion point quickly where you need it.
  - ✓ *Using a center tab stop or centered alignment centers the text; you must use a left tab stop in order to position the text to start at the center point of the page.*
- When you create a modified-block business letter that is not printed on letterhead stationery, type the return address above the date.

A personal business letter in modified-block style

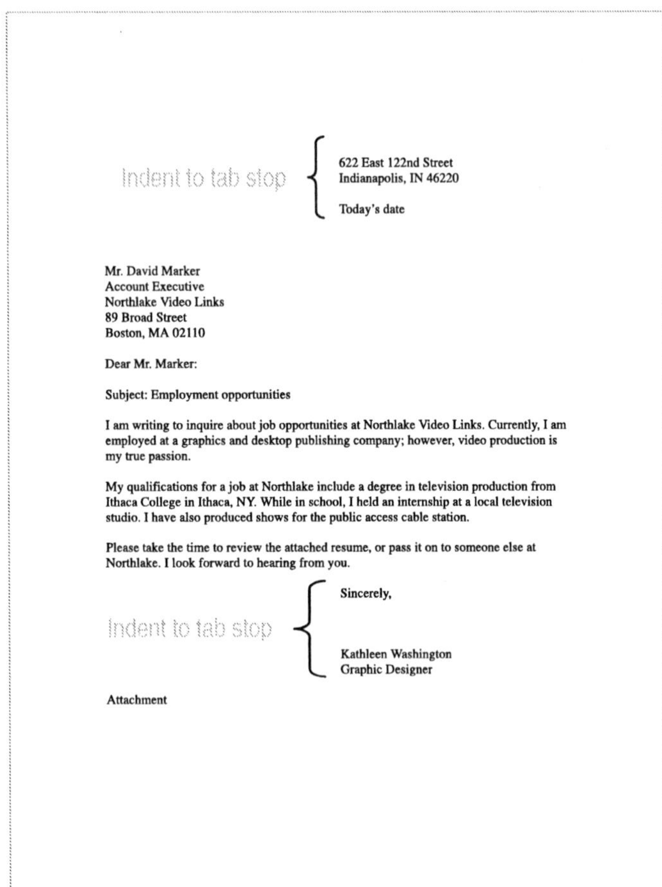

Indent to tab stop

622 East 122nd Street
Indianapolis, IN 46220

Today's date

Mr. David Marker
Account Executive
Northlake Video Links
89 Broad Street
Boston, MA 02110

Dear Mr. Marker:

Subject: Employment opportunities

I am writing to inquire about job opportunities at Northlake Video Links. Currently, I am employed at a graphics and desktop publishing company; however, video production is my true passion.

My qualifications for a job at Northlake include a degree in television production from Ithaca College in Ithaca, NY. While in school, I held an internship at a local television studio. I have also produced shows for the public access cable station.

Please take the time to review the attached resume, or pass it on to someone else at Northlake. I look forward to hearing from you.

Indent to tab stop

Sincerely,

Kathleen Washington
Graphic Designer

Attachment

Create Envelopes

- Word has a feature that automatically sets up an envelope for printing.
- By default, Word creates standard size 10 envelopes ($4^{1}/_{8}$" by 9½").
- If a letter document is open on-screen, Word picks up the inside address for the envelope's **delivery address**.
  - ✓ *You can also select text in the document to use as the delivery address.*
- You can print the envelope directly or add it to the beginning of the open document and save it.

The Envelopes page of the Envelopes and Labels dialog box

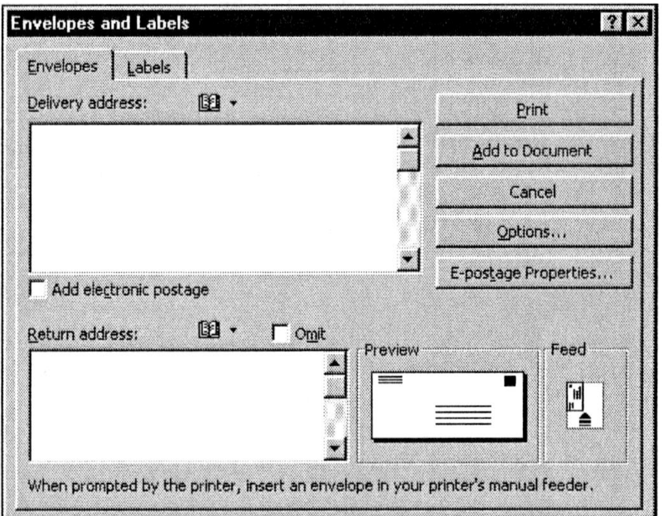

- You select the manufacturer and label type loaded in the printer.
- By default, Word creates a full page of labels using the inside address from the current document, or the selected address.
- You can change the default to create labels using the return address or to create a single label.

The Labels page of the Envelopes and Labels dialog box

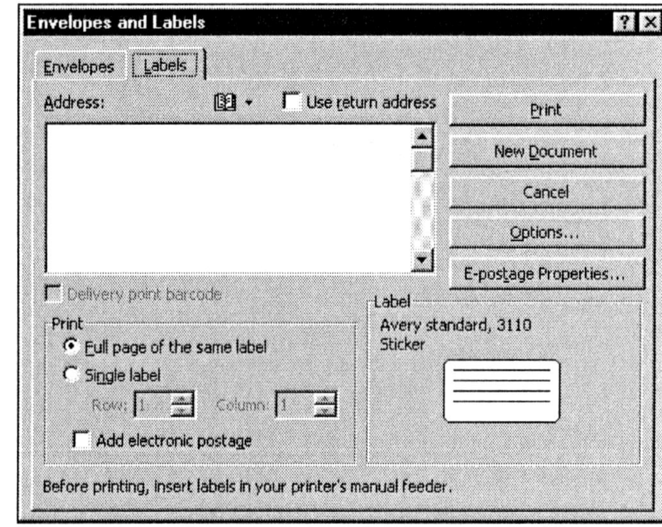

Create Labels

- Use the Label feature to create mailing labels, **return address** labels, file folder labels, or diskette labels.
- The Label feature automatically sets up a document to print on predefined label types.

Procedures

Set Tabs

To set a left tab stop:

1. Position insertion point in paragraph to format.
   OR
   Select paragraphs to format.
2. Click ruler where you want to set tab stop.

To set a different type of tab stop:

1. Position insertion point in paragraph to format
   OR
   Select paragraphs to format
2. Click the **Tab** box.
   ✓ *Each time you click, the tab icon changes. Stop when tab style you want is displayed.*
3. Click ruler where you want to insert new tab stop.

To set a precise tab stop:

1. Position insertion point in paragraph to format.
   OR
   Select paragraphs to format.
2. Click **Format** .... Alt+O
3. Click **Tabs** .... T
4. Select type of tab
   - **Left** .... Alt+L
   - **Center** .... Alt+C
   - **Right** .... Alt+R
   - **Decimal** .... Alt+D
   - **Bar** .... Alt+B
5. Click in the **Tab stop position** box....... Alt+T
6. Type precise position.
7. Select leader, if desired:
   - **1 None** .... Alt+1
   - **2 ....** .... Alt+2
   - **3 -------** .... Alt+3
   - **4 ______** .... Alt+4
8. Click **OK** .... Enter

To clear tab stops:

1. Position insertion point in paragraph to format.
   OR
   Select paragraphs to format.
2. Drag tab stop marker off ruler.

OR

1. Click **Format**................ Alt+O
2. Click **Tabs** .... T
3. Click **Clear All** .... Alt+A
   OR
   a. Select tab stop(s) to clear.
   b. Click **Clear**............. Alt+E
4. Click **OK** .... Enter

Format a Modified-block Business Letter

1. Start 2" from top of page .... Enter 4x
   - ✓ *Press Enter four times to leave 2" of space.*
2. Set left tab stop at 3".
3. Press **Tab** .... Tab
4. Insert date.
5. Leave three blank lines and type inside address .... Enter 4x
6. Leave a blank line and type the salutation .... Enter 2x
7. Leave a blank line and type the letter body .... Enter 2x
8. Leave a blank line .... Enter 2x
9. Press **Tab** .... Tab
   - ✓ *This moves the insertion point to the tab stop you set in step 2.*
10. Type the closing.
11. Leave three blank lines .... Enter 4x
12. Press **Tab** .... Tab
13. Type signature line.
14. Move to next line and press **Tab** .... Enter, Tab
15. Type title line.
16. Leave a blank line and type reference initials .. Enter 2x

Create an Envelope

1. Click **Tools** .... Alt+T
2. Click **Letters and Mailings** .... E
3. Click **Envelopes and Labels** .... E
4. Click **Envelopes** tab ... Alt+E
5. Type **Delivery address** .... Alt+D
   - ✓ *If inside address is already entered, skip step 5.*
6. Type **Return address** ... Alt+R

   OR

   Select **Omit** check box .... Alt+M
   - ✓ *If Omit check box is selected, you cannot type in Return address text box.*
7. Click **Print** button

   Print .... Alt+P
   - ✓ *You are prompted to save the new return address as the default. Click No to leave the address as is.*

   OR

   Select **Add to Document** .... Alt+A

Create a Single Label

1. Click **Tools** .... Alt+T
2. Click **Letters and Mailings** .... E
3. Click **Envelopes and Labels** .... E
4. Click **Labels** tab .... Alt+L
5. Click **Single label** option button .... Alt+N
6. Click **Options** button

   Options... .... O
7. Select label type from **Label products** list .... Alt+P
8. Select label type from **Product number** list .... Alt+U
   - ✓ *Make sure correct printer and tray information is selected.*
9. Click **OK** .... Enter
10. Type label text.
    - ✓ *If inside address is already entered, skip step 10.*
11. Make sure labels are loaded in printer.
12. Click **Print** button

    Print .... Alt+P

Create Return Address Labels

1. Click **Tools** .... Alt+T
2. Click **Letters and Mailings** .... E
3. Click **Envelopes and Labels** .... E
4. Click **Labels** tab .... Alt+L
5. Select **Use return address** check box ...... Alt+R
6. Click **Options** button

   Options... ... Alt+O
7. Select label type from **Label products** list ...... Alt+P
8. Select label type from **Product number** list .... Alt+U
   - ✓ *Make sure the correct printer and tray information is selected.*
9. Click **OK** .... Enter
   - ✓ *Make sure labels are loaded in printer.*
10. Click **Print** button

    Print .... Alt+P

    OR

    a. Click **New Document** .... Alt+D

    b. If prompted to save the return address, click **No** .. N

    c. Click **Save** button to save labels.

Exercise Directions

1. Start Word, if necessary.
2. Create a new document and save it as NEWJOB.
3. Type the letter shown in Illustration A.
   ✓ *You may type the name and address of the letter writer as shown in the illustration, or use your own name and address.*
   - Use the default font and font size (12-point Times New Roman).
     ✓ *If Word displays ScreenTips, ignore them and continue typing.*
   - Press the Enter key to leave blank lines between parts of the letter as indicated.
   - Align the return address, date, closing, signature, and title lines with a left tab stop set at 3" on the horizontal ruler.
   - Insert the current date using the MONTH DAY, YEAR format found third from the top in the Date and Time dialog box.
   - Set the date so that it does not update automatically.
4. Check the spelling and grammar in the document, and correct errors as necessary.
5. Create an envelope for the letter.
   a. Use the inside address for the account executive at Northlake Video.
   b. Enter the return address as it appears in the document you typed—either your own or the one shown in the illustration.
6. Add the envelope to the document.
   - When prompted to save the new return address as the default, choose No.
7. Display the document in Print Preview.
8. Print the document.
9. Create a full page of return address labels using the return address as it appears in the document.
   ✓ *Do not save the return address as the default.*
10. Save the labels in a new document with the name LABELS
11. Preview the new label document. It should look similar to the one in Illustration B depending on the Product # selected.
12. Print the LABELS document.
    ✓ *You can print the labels on standard letter-sized paper if you do not have labels available.*
13. Close the label document, saving all changes.
14. Close the letter document, saving all changes.
15. Exit Word.

Illustration A

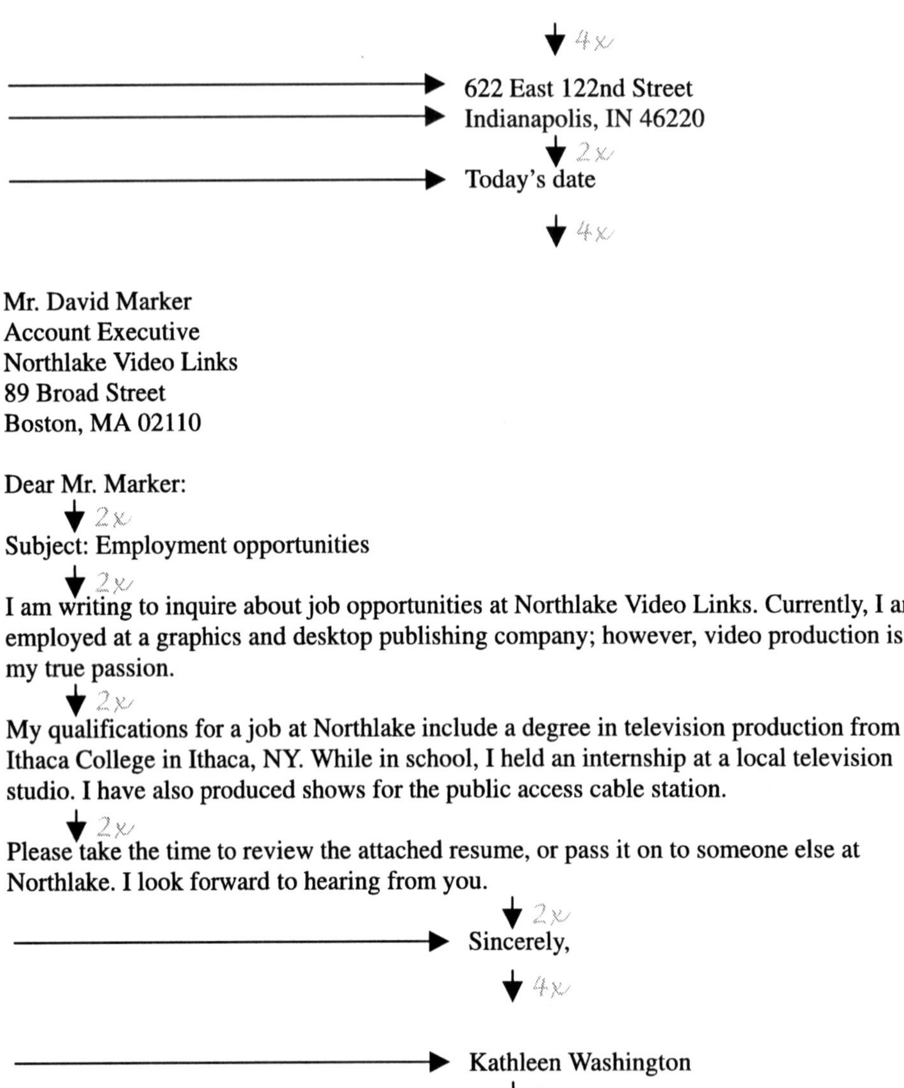

622 East 122nd Street
Indianapolis, IN 46220

Today's date

Mr. David Marker
Account Executive
Northlake Video Links
89 Broad Street
Boston, MA 02110

Dear Mr. Marker:

Subject: Employment opportunities

I am writing to inquire about job opportunities at Northlake Video Links. Currently, I am employed at a graphics and desktop publishing company; however, video production is my true passion.

My qualifications for a job at Northlake include a degree in television production from Ithaca College in Ithaca, NY. While in school, I held an internship at a local television studio. I have also produced shows for the public access cable station.

Please take the time to review the attached resume, or pass it on to someone else at Northlake. I look forward to hearing from you.

Sincerely,

Kathleen Washington

Attachment

Illustration B

Kathleen Washington 622 East 122nd Street Indianapolis, IN 46220	Kathleen Washington 622 East 122nd Street Indianapolis, IN 46220	Kathleen Washington 622 East 122nd Street Indianapolis, IN 46220
Kathleen Washington 622 East 122nd Street Indianapolis, IN 46220	Kathleen Washington 622 East 122nd Street Indianapolis, IN 46220	Kathleen Washington 622 East 122nd Street Indianapolis, IN 46220
Kathleen Washington 622 East 122nd Street Indianapolis, IN 46220	Kathleen Washington 622 East 122nd Street Indianapolis, IN 46220	Kathleen Washington 622 East 122nd Street Indianapolis, IN 46220
Kathleen Washington 622 East 122nd Street Indianapolis, IN 46220	Kathleen Washington 622 East 122nd Street Indianapolis, IN 46220	Kathleen Washington 622 East 122nd Street Indianapolis, IN 46220
Kathleen Washington 622 East 122nd Street Indianapolis, IN 46220	Kathleen Washington 622 East 122nd Street Indianapolis, IN 46220	Kathleen Washington 622 East 122nd Street Indianapolis, IN 46220
Kathleen Washington 622 East 122nd Street Indianapolis, IN 46220	Kathleen Washington 622 East 122nd Street Indianapolis, IN 46220	Kathleen Washington 622 East 122nd Street Indianapolis, IN 46220

On Your Own

1. Create a new document in Word.
2. Save the document as **OWDCDS**.
3. Draft a personal letter to a company with whom you do business asking for a credit on returned merchandise. Record stores, clothing stores, or sporting goods stores are companies you may use.
4. Create an envelope for your letter.
5. Create your own mailing labels using the return address from your letter.
6. Save your changes, close the document, and exit Word when you are finished.

Exercise 14

◆ **Critical Thinking**

You are the owner of Pelican Peter's, a dive shop in Naples, Florida. In this exercise, you will write a letter to a new travel agent in the area, asking her to refer customers to your shop. You will create an envelope to accompany the letter, and a page of return address labels that she can use to send you information about her business. Finally, you will create a flyer about Pelican Peter's that she can hang up in her office, or distribute to customers. You will use alignments and font formatting to make the flyer visually exciting.

Exercise Directions

Type a Business Letter

1. Start Word, if necessary.
2. Create a new document and save it as PROPOSAL.
3. Display nonprinting characters.
4. Make sure AutoCorrect is on.
5. Type the letter in Illustration A exactly as shown, including all circled errors.
6. Insert the date in the Month Date, Year format so that it does not update automatically.
7. Correct spelling and grammatical errors.
   - Ignore all proper names.
   - Correct all other spelling and grammatical errors that AutoCorrect did not automatically change.
8. Use the Thesaurus to find an appropriate replacement for the word wide in the second paragraph.
9. Save the changes you have made to the document.
10. Display the document in Print Preview.
11. Shrink the document to fit on one page. It should look similar to Illustration A.
12. Display the document in Full Screen view.
13. Return the document to Normal view.

Create an Envelope and Label

1. Create an envelope for the letter using the inside address and return address from the letter.
2. Print the document.
3. Close the document, saving all changes.
4. Create a full page of mailing labels using the return address in the document:

   Pete Newell
   Owner
   Pelican Peter's Dive Shop
   2200 Gulfshore Boulevard N.
   Naples, FL 34102
5. Save the label document with the name RETURN
6. Display the RETURN document in Print Preview, and then print it.
   ✓ *If you do not have a labels available, print it on regular paper.*
7. Close the RETURN document, saving all changes.

Create a Flyer

1. Create a new document and save it as FLYER.
2. Display nonprinting characters.
3. Type and format the document shown in Illustration B, using the specified alignments, font formatting, and tabs.
   ✓ *Use the Comic Sans MS font unless otherwise noted. If the font is not available on your system, select a different font.*
4. Check the spelling and grammar in the document.
5. Correct all errors, but leave capitalization as shown in the illustration.
6. Display the document in Print Preview.
7. If the document is longer than one page, shrink it to fit on one page.
8. Print the document.
9. Close the document, saving all changes.

Illustration A

Today's date

Ms. Melissa D'Agastino
Vice President
Gulf Shores Travil Agency
7334 Fifth Avenue
Naples, FL 34102

↓ 2x

Dear Ms. D'Agastino:

↓ 2x

Welcome to Naples! I am the owner of Pelican Peter's, a dive shop located conveniently only three blocks from the marina on Gulfshore Bullevard. Perhaps you have already noticed us. We has the larger-than-life-sized wooden pelican on the sidewalk in front of the shop.

↓ 2x

Pelican Peter's has been in business since 1992. In addition to a full line of SCUBA and snorkeling gear, we offers a wide variety of surfing, boating, and beach ACcessories. We also provide training and certification.

↓ 2x

Ms. D'Agastino, I hope you will consider referring your customers to Pelican Peter's for their boating needs. I have attached a flyers describing our business that you could hang in your office, or copy to distirbute to customers. I would also love to learn more about you and your agency. Please use the enclosed return address labels to send me any information you might have available.

↓ 2x

I look forward to meeting you in the near future.

↓ 2x

Sincerely,

↓ 4x

Pete Newell
Owner
Pelican Peter's Dive Shop
2200 Gulfshore Boulevard N.
Naples, FL 34102
(941) 555-0780
Pelicanpeters@ddcpub.com

↓ 2x

Attachment
Enclosure

Illustration B

Centered

PELICAN PETER'S

36 points

a full-service dive shop

18 points

3x

Bold | Bold

Justified

Pelican **Peter's** offers a full line of **SCUBA** and **snorkeling** equipment including masks, snorkels, fins, wet suits, compressors, hoses, and valves.

20 points

2x

Training and certification are available.
Ask for a schedule of upcoming classes.

16 points, italics, centered

2x

18 points, flush left

At Pelican Peter's you'll also find:

Right tab at 5.5" with a dot leader

Left tab at 1"

Surfer Gear .... boards, clothes
Kayaks .... sea and lake
Clothing .... all types, all sizes
Water Ski Gear .... skis, ropes, etc.
Windsurfers .... all types

And so much more!

Center tab at 3"

2x

Right aligned

Pelican Peter's

22 points

2200 Gulfshore Boulevard N.
Naples, FL 34102
Phone: (941) 555-0780
Online at: pelicanpeters.com

14-point Arial

Lesson 3

Open and Edit Documents

Exercise 15

- Open a Recently Used Document
- Open Any Stored Document
- Save a Document with a New Name

Exercise 16

- Use Proofreaders' Marks
- Insert Text
- Use Overtype Mode
- Use Uppercase Mode
- Change Case

Exercise 17

- Move Text in a Document
- Cut and Paste Text
- Use the Clipboard
- Use Drag-and-Drop Editing
- Move Paragraph

Exercise 18

- Use Copy and Paste
- Copy Text with Drag-and-Drop

Exercise 19

- Critical Thinking

Exercise 15

Skills Covered:

◆ **Open a Recently Used Document** ◆ **Open Any Stored Document**
◆ **Save a Document with a New Name**

On the Job

When you are ready to revise and improve a document that you've already created and saved, open it again in Word. When you save changes, Word updates the document stored on the disk. Use the Save As command when you want to leave the original document unchanged, and save a copy of the document with a new name or in a new location. For example, you can save a letter with a new name, and then change the inside address to send it to someone else.

The letter you sent to an account executive at Northlake Video Links asking about employment opportunities resulted in a job interview. You want to write another letter thanking the account executive for his time. Since you are writing to the same person at the same address, you can save time by revising the existing letter. In this exercise, you will open the existing letter document and save it with a new name. You will then revise the document and save the changes. Finally, you will print the document.

Terms

Revise Edit, change, or update a document.

Places bar A strip of buttons on the left side of certain dialog boxes used to open common folders quickly.

Notes

Open a Recently Used Document

- To **revise** a document that has been saved and closed, open it in Word.
- By default, the four most recently used documents are listed at the bottom of the File menu and at the top of the New Document task pane.
  - ✓ *The listed file names may also include the complete path to the file, which means the folder and/or disk where the file is stored. Since you can have a file with the same name stored in different locations, be sure you select the one you really want to open.*

Open saved documents from the File menu

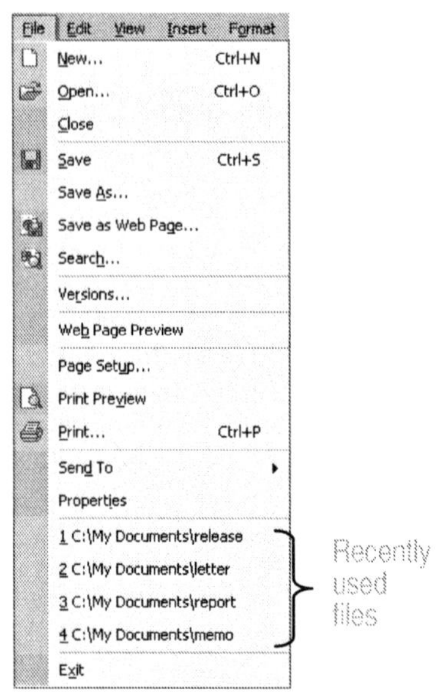

Open saved documents from the task pane

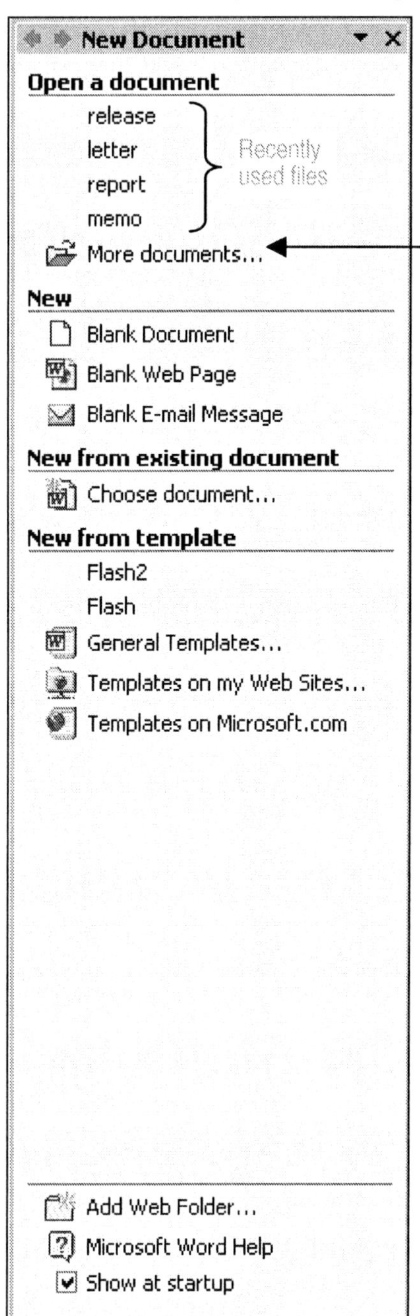

- Click a document name to open it.

Open Any Stored Document

- Any document stored on disk can be opened from Word, no matter when it was last used.
- Use the Open dialog box to locate and open stored files.

Open dialog box

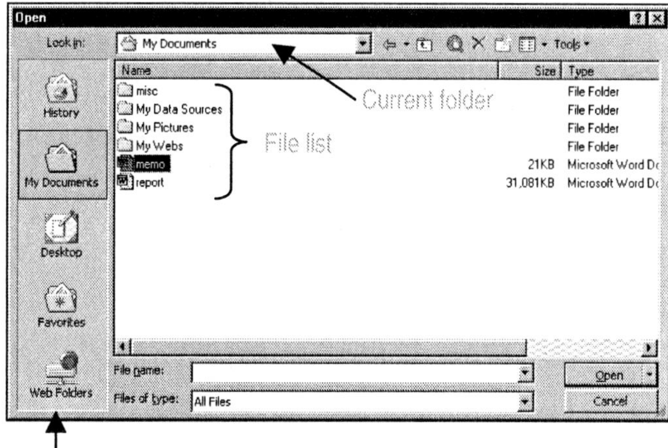

Save a Document with a New Name

- The Save As feature lets you save a copy of a document in a different location or with a different file name.
- Use the Save As command to leave the original document unchanged while you edit the new copy.

Save As dialog box

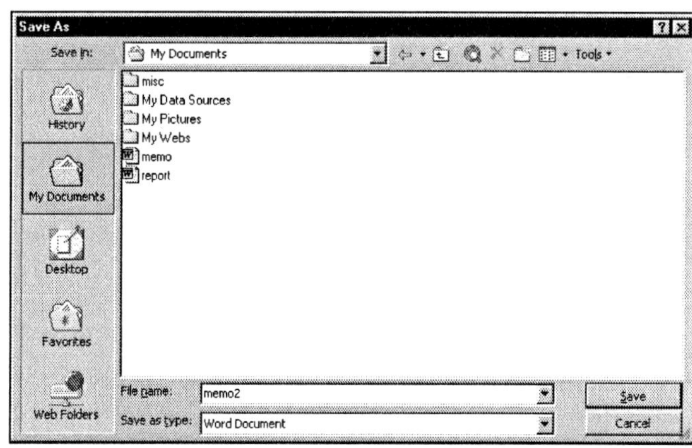

Procedures

Open a Recently Used Document

1. Click **File** .... Alt+F
2. Click document name at bottom of menu .... 1 – 4 (number of document).

OR

1. Click **View** .... Alt+V
2. Click **Task Pane** .... K
   ✓ *If the New Document task pane is not displayed, select it from the Other Task Panes drop-down list.*
3. Click document name at top of task pane.

Open any Stored Document (Ctrl+O)

1. Click **Open** button .

   OR

   a. Click **File** .... Alt+F
   b. Click **Open** .... O
2. Click **Look in** drop-down arrow .... Alt+I
3. Select drive or folder.
   ✓ *If necessary double-click folder name.*

   OR

   Click folder in Places bar to open it.
4. Double-click document name.

   OR

   a. Click document name.
   b. Click **Open** button

   .... O

Save a Document with a New Name

1. Click **File** .... Alt+F
2. Click **Save As** .... A
3. Type new file name.
4. Select new drive and/or folder.
5. Click **Save** button
   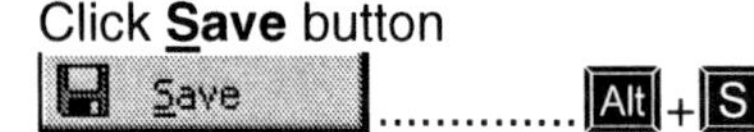

   .... Alt+S

Exercise Directions

1. Start Word, if necessary.
2. Open NEWJOB or open 15NEWJOB.
   ✓ *If necessary ask your instructor where this file is located.*
3. Save the document as THANKS.
4. Revise the document according to the following steps, to create the document shown in the Illustration.
   ✓ *For a refresher on selecting and replacing text, refer to Exercise 8.*
5. Leave the envelope at the top of the document unchanged.
6. Replace the date in the letter with the current date.
7. Replace the Subject notation text with the text shown in Illustration A.
8. Replace the three paragraphs that comprise the body of the letter with the three paragraphs shown in Illustration A.
9. Delete the Attachment notation.
10. Check the spelling and grammar, correcting all errors.
11. Save the changes.
12. Display the document in Print Preview. It should look similar to Illustration A.
13. Print the document.
14. Close the document, saving all changes.
15. Exit Word.

On Your Own

1. Open OWDEVENTS, the letter you created in the On Your Own section of Exercise 12, or open 15OWDEVENTS.
2. Save the document as OWDNEWEVENTS.
3. Edit the letter so that you can send it to a different newspaper. For example, replace the date with the current date and replace the name and address of the recipient.
4. Check the spelling and grammar in the document.
5. Save your changes, close the document, and exit Word when you are finished.

Illustration A

622 East 122nd Street
Indianapolis, IN 46220

Today's date

Mr. David Marker
Account Executive
Northlake Video Links
89 Broad Street
Boston, MA 02110

Dear Mr. Marker:

Subject: Interview follow-up

Thank you very much for taking the time to meet with me this morning regarding job opportunities at Northlake Video Links. I enjoyed the tour of the offices and studios and I appreciated the chance to meet some of the employees.

Since our meeting, I am more certain than ever that I would be a valuable asset to Northlake Video. I believe that my qualifications make me uniquely suited for the position of assistant video producer, which is currently available. I am sure that I would fit very well and that I would be able to meet the challenges and responsibilities.

Again, thank you for meeting with me. I look forward to hearing from you about the possibility of my employment.

Sincerely,

Kathleen Washington

Exercise 16

Skills Covered:

◆ **Use Proofreaders' Marks** ◆ **Insert Text**
◆ **Use Overtype Mode** ◆ **Use Uppercase Mode** ◆ **Change Case**

On the Job

Making changes to existing documents is a key benefit of using Word 2002. Some of the most important revisions can be made using simple features. For example, you can insert new text to add to a document, you can type over existing text to change a document, and you can change the case of text in order to improve a document.

Many employees of Pelican Peter's dive shop have expressed concern over the new vacation policy. You have decided to issue a new notice regarding the policy. In this exercise, you will open the vacation policy document and save it with a new name. You will then revise the document and save the changes. Finally, you will print the document so you can post it in the shop.

Terms

Proofreaders' marks Symbols written on a printed document to indicate where revisions are required.

Insert mode The method of operation used for inserting new text within existing text in a document. Insert mode is the default.

Overtype mode A method of operation used to replace existing text in a document with new text.

Case The specific use of upper- or lowercase letters.

Notes

Use Proofreaders' Marks

- Often you may need to revise a Word document based on a marked-up printed copy of the document. **Proofreaders' marks** on printed documents are written symbols that indicate where to make revisions.
- Following is a list of common proofreaders' marks:
  - ~~~~~ is used to mark text to be bold.
  - ∧ is used to mark where new text should be inserted.
  - ___ is used to mark text to be deleted.
  - ¶ is used to mark where a new paragraph should be inserted.
  - ≡ is used to mark a letter that should be capitalized.
  - ________ or (ital) is used to mark text to be italicized.
  - (highlight) is used to mark text to highlight.
  -] [is used to mark text to center.

✓ *There are many other common proofreading symbols. You can find a list in reference books such as* Webster's Collegiate Dictionary, *or* The Chicago Manual of Style.

Insert Text

- By default, you type new text in a document in **Insert mode**. Existing text moves to the right as you type to make room for new text.
- You can insert text anywhere in a document.
- You can also insert nonprinting characters, such as paragraph marks to start a new paragraph, tabs, and spaces.

Use Overtype Mode

- To replace text as you type, use **Overtype mode**.
- In Overtype mode, existing characters do not shift right to make room for new characters. Instead, new characters replace existing characters as you type, deleting existing characters.
- When Overtype mode is active, the OVR indicator on the Status bar is displayed in bold OVR. When Overtype mode is off, the OVR indicator is dimmed, and the default Insert mode is active.
- Overtype mode is useful when you have to replace an entire block of text.
- However, most editing should be done in Insert mode so you do not accidentally type over text that you need.

Use Uppercase Mode

- Use Uppercase mode to type all capital letters without pressing the Shift key.
- Uppercase mode affects only letter characters.
- When Uppercase mode is on, the Caps Lock indicator on your keyboard is lit.

Change Case

- You can automatically change the **case** of text in a document.
- There are five case options:
  - Sentence case: First character in sentence is uppercase.
  - lowercase: All characters are lowercase.
  - UPPERCASE: All characters are uppercase.
  - Title Case: First character in each word is uppercase.
  - tOGGLE cASE: Case is reversed for all characters.

Change Case dialog box

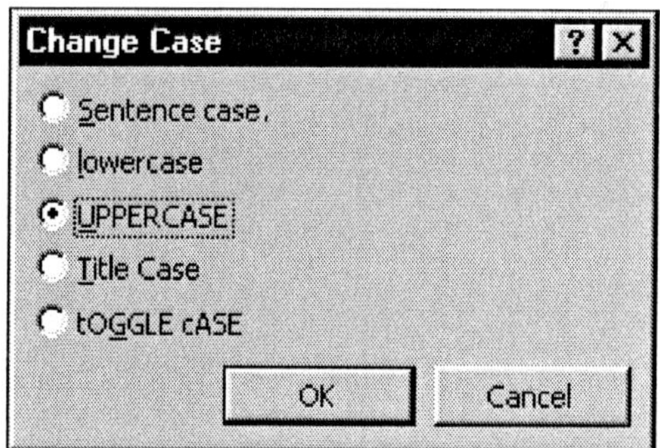

Procedures

Insert Text

1. Position insertion point to right of character where you want to insert new text.
2. Type new text.

Use Overtype Mode

1. Position insertion point to left of first character you want to replace.
2. Press **Insert** key.................. Ins

   OR

   Double-click **OVR** indicator OVR on status bar.

   ✓ *OVR indicator appears in bold when active.*
3. Type new text.

Turn off Overtype mode:

- Press **Insert** key again .... Ins

OR

- Double-click **OVR** indicator 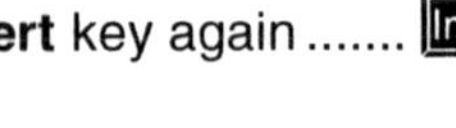 again.

  ✓ *OVR indicator appears dimmed when inactive.*

Use Uppercase Mode

1. Press **Caps Lock** key .... Caps Lock
2. Type text.

To turn off Uppercase mode:

- Press **Caps Lock** key .... Caps Lock

Change Case

1. Select text.

   OR

   Position insertion point where new text will begin.
2. Click **Format**................ Alt+O
3. Click **Change Case** .... E
4. Click the case you want:
   - **Sentence case**............... S
   - **lowercase** L
   - **UPPERCASE** .... U
   - **Title Case**....................... T
   - **tOGGLE cASE** .... G
5. Click **OK**........................... Enter

   ✓ *You can also select text and then press **Shift+F3** to toggle through sentence case, lowercase, and uppercase. Release the keys when the desired case is in effect.*

Exercise Directions

1. Start Word, if necessary.
2. Open VACATION or open 16VACATION.

   ✓ *If necessary, ask your instructor where this file is located.*
3. Save the document as NEWVACATION.
4. Make the revisions as marked in Illustration A.
   - Insert new text and paragraphs as marked.
   - Use Overtype mode to replace text as necessary.
   - Change case as marked.
   - Apply font formatting as marked.
5. Check the spelling and grammar and make necessary corrections.
6. Display the document in Print Preview.
7. Print the document.
8. Close the document, saving all changes.
9. Exit Word.

Illustration A

I hope that this notice will clear up all questions regarding

Pelican Peter's Vacation Policy

~~I would like all employees to be aware of~~ our new vacation policy. As of January 1, vacation time will be directly related to the number of hours worked each month. Specifically, employees will earn 8 hours of vacation time for every 120 hours worked.

eight

The new policy does not affect vacation time you may have already earned. As always, you must clear vacation time with your manager to be sure you are not put on the schedule. Please contact me if you have any questions about this policy.

This means that if you regularly work 40 hours per week, you will earn one vacation day every three weeks. TO EARN FIVE VACATION DAYS, YOU MUST WORK 600 HOURS.

On Your Own

1. Open OWDCDS, the document you created in the On Your Own section of Exercise 13, or open 16OWDCDS.
2. Save the document as OWDREVCDS.
3. Print the document, and then have a classmate read it and use proofreaders' marks to suggest insertions, deletions, case changes, and formatting changes.
4. Make the revisions.
5. Save your changes, close the document, and exit Word when you are finished.

Exercise 17

Skills Covered:

◆ **Move Text in a Document** ◆ **Cut and Paste Text**
◆ **Use the Clipboard** ◆ **Use Drag-and-Drop Editing**
◆ **Move a Paragraph**

On the Job

Move text to rearrange a document quickly without retyping existing information. You can move any amount of text, from a single character to an entire page.

The employees at the investment banking firm of Ramirez, Johnson, and Gold have been asking a lot of questions regarding Casual Fridays. The personnel director has asked you to edit a document that lists guidelines for the new policy. In this exercise, you will open an existing document, edit and format the text, and rearrange the guidelines into a more suitable order.

Terms

Cut To delete a selection from its original location and move it to the Clipboard.

Paste To insert a selection from the Clipboard into a document.

Clipboard A temporary storage area that can hold up to 24 selections at a time.

Drag-and-drop editing The action of using a mouse to drag a selection from its original location and drop it in a new location.

Notes

Move Text in a Document

- While editing, you may decide you need to move text that is already typed in a document to a new location.
- Word's move commands can save you from deleting and retyping text.
- Be sure to consider nonprinting characters when you select text to move:
  - Select the space following a word or sentence to move along with text.
  - Select the paragraph mark following a paragraph or line to move paragraph formatting with text.
- Use Undo to reverse a move that you made unintentionally.

✓ *When you paste text into a new location, Word may display the Paste Options button, which allows you to select the way formatting is pasted along with the text. For now, ignore the Paste Options button. It is explained in Exercise 22. You can turn off the display of the Paste Options button if you want. Click Tools, Options, Edit. Deselect the Show Paste Options button check box, then click OK.*

Cut and Paste Text

- Use the **Cut** and **Paste** commands to move text in a document.
- The Cut command deletes selected text from its original location and moves it to the **Clipboard**.
- The Paste command copies the selection from the Clipboard to the insertion point location.
- Up to 24 selections can remain in the Clipboard at one time.
- You can access the Cut and Paste commands from the Edit menu, from the Standard toolbar, or from a shortcut menu.

Use the Clipboard

- Use the Clipboard task pane to access selections for pasting.
- The last 24 items cut or copied are displayed in the Clipboard.
- You can paste or delete one or all of the items.
- You can turn the following Clipboard options off or on:
  - Show Office Clipboard Automatically. Sets the Clipboard task pane to open automatically when you cut or copy a selection.
  - Collect Without Showing Office Clipboard. Sets the Clipboard task pane so it does not open automatically when you cut or copy data.
  - Show Office Clipboard Icon on Taskbar. Displays a Clipboard icon at the right end of the taskbar if there are selections on the Clipboard. Double-click the icon to open the task pane.
  - Show Status Near Taskbar When Copying. Displays a ScreenTip with the number of items on the Clipboard when you cut or copy a selection.

Clipboard task pane

Use Drag-and-Drop Editing

- Use **drag-and-drop editing** to move text with the mouse.
- Drag-and-drop editing is convenient when you can see the text to move and the new location on the screen at the same time.

Move a Paragraph

- You can use keyboard shortcuts to quickly move an entire paragraph up or down in a document.

Procedures

Move Text

1. Select text to move.
2. Press **F2** key F2
3. Position insertion point at new location.
4. Press **Enter** .... Enter

Use Cut and Paste to Move Text *(Ctrl+X, Cltr+V)*

1. Select text to move.
2. Click **Cut** button.

   OR

   a. Click **Edit** .... Alt+E
   b. Click **Cut** .... T

   OR

   a. Right-click selection.
   b. Click **Cut** .... T
3. Position insertion point in new location.
4. Click **Paste** button.

   OR

   a. Click **Edit** .... Alt+E
   b. Click **Paste** .... P

   OR

   a. Right-click new location.
   b. Click **Paste** .... P

Paste a Selection from the Clipboard Task Pane

1. Click **View** .... Alt+V
2. Click **Task Pane** .... K
3. Click **Other Task Panes** drop-down arrow
4. Click **Clipboard**.
5. Click item to paste.

   OR

   Click **Paste All** button Paste All to paste all selections from the Clipboard.

Set Clipboard Options

1. Display Clipboard task pane.
2. Click **Options** drop-down button Options.
3. Click desired options:
   - **Show Office Clipboard Automatically** .... A
   - **Collect Without Showing Office Clipboard** C
   - **Show Office Clipboard Icon on Taskbar** .... T
   - **Show Status Near Taskbar When Copying** .... S

   ✓ *A checkmark indicates the option is selected.*

Delete Selections from the Clipboard

1. Right-click selection to delete.
2. Click **Delete** .... D on context menu.

   OR

   - Click **Clear All** button Clear All to delete all selections from the Clipboard.

Use Drag-and-Drop Editing to Move Text

1. Select text to move.
2. Move mouse pointer anywhere over selected text and press and hold down the left mouse button.
3. Drag selection to new location.

   ✓ *As you drag, mouse pointer changes to a box with a dotted shadow attached to an arrow; selection does not move until you drop it in step 4.*
4. Release mouse button when insertion point is in new location.

Move a Paragraph

1. Position insertion point anywhere within paragraph to move.
2. Press .... Alt+Shift+↑

   OR

   Press .... Alt+Shift+↓
3. Repeat step 2 until paragraph is in desired location.

Exercise Directions

1. Start Word, if necessary.
2. Open 17POLICY.
3. Save the file as NEWPOLICY
4. Rearrange the text in the document as marked in Illustration A.
   - Move the last paragraph in the document up so that it becomes the last sentence of the paragraph beginning **As of September 1**.
   - Move the first sentence in the document so that it becomes the last sentence in the document.
   - Move the item **Boat shoes** to the end of the list of appropriate casual attire.
   - Move the entire list of appropriate attire—including the heading—so that it follows the list of inappropriate attire.
5. Check the spelling and grammar in the document and make all necessary corrections.
6. Display the document in Print Preview. It should look similar to Illustration B.
7. Print the document.
8. Close the document, saving all changes.

On Your Own

1. Create a new document in Word.
2. Save the file as OWDLIST.
3. Create a list of things you have accomplished in the past year. For each item in the list, describe what you accomplished, how you accomplished it, and when it was done. List the items in chronological order.
4. Rearrange the listed items into order of importance. Use cut-and-paste and drag-and-drop techniques.
5. Print the document.
6. Close the document, saving all changes.

Illustration A

Ramirez, Johnson, and Gold

85 Gold Street, New York, NY 10038

Casual Fridays Policy

If you have any questions regarding this policy, please contact me at extension 234.

Move

As of September 1, employees are encouraged to wear casual clothing to work on Fridays. This is by no means a mandatory policy. If you are more comfortable in your regular business attire, feel free to continue wearing it. However, if you choose to participate in Casual Fridays, use the following guidelines to help you determine which articles of clothing are appropriate and which are not.

Move

ITEMS CONSIDERED APPROPRIATE CASUAL ATTIRE

Boat shoes
Slacks, such as khakis or corduroys
Open-necked shirts
Sweaters
Golf shirts
Polo shirts
Sneakers

Move

Move

ITEMS CONSIDERED INAPPROPRIATE CASUAL ATTIRE

Shorts
Belly-baring t-shirts
Undershirts of any kind
Flip-flops
Jeans
Ties

Remember, if you have a meeting with a client who is not expecting Casual Friday, you should wear your regular work attire.

Illustration B

Ramirez, Johnson, and Gold

85 Gold Street, New York, NY 10038

Casual Fridays Policy

As of September 1, employees are encouraged to wear casual clothing to work on Fridays. This is by no means a mandatory policy. If you are more comfortable in your regular business attire, feel free to continue wearing it. However, if you choose to participate in Casual Fridays, use the following guidelines to help you determine which articles of clothing are appropriate and which are not. Remember, if you have a meeting with a client who is not expecting Casual Friday, you should wear your regular work attire.

ITEMS CONSIDERED INAPPROPRIATE CASUAL ATTIRE

Shorts
Belly-baring t-shirts
Undershirts of any kind
Flip-flops
Jeans
Ties

ITEMS CONSIDERED APPROPRIATE CASUAL ATTIRE

Slacks, such as khakis or corduroys
Open-necked shirts
Sweaters
Golf shirts
Polo shirts
Sneakers
Boat shoes

If you have any questions regarding this policy, please contact me at extension 234.

Exercise 18

Skills Covered:

- **Use Copy and Paste**
- **Copy Text with Drag-and-Drop**

On the Job

Copy or move text from one location to another to speed up your work and avoid repetitive typing. You can copy or move any amount of text, from a single character to an entire document.

The personnel director of Ramirez, Johnson, and Gold wants you to enhance the Casual Fridays policy document. In this exercise, you will revise the guidelines using some of the editing and formatting techniques you have learned so far in this book.

Terms

Copy To create a duplicate of a selection and move it to the Clipboard.

Notes

Use Copy and Paste

- Use the Copy and Paste feature to copy existing text from one location in a document and paste it to another location.
- The **Copy** command stores a duplicate of selected text on the Clipboard, leaving the original selection unchanged.
- The Paste command pastes the selection from the Clipboard to the insertion point location.
- You can access the Copy and Paste commands from the Edit menu, the Standard toolbar, or from a context menu.
- You can store up to 24 selections on the Clipboard at one time.
- Use the Clipboard task pane to choose which selection to paste into the document.
  - ✓ *The same Clipboard used for moving is used for copying. For more information, refer to Exercise 17.*

Copy Text with Drag-and-Drop

- Use drag-and-drop editing to copy text with the mouse.
- The Drag-and-Drop feature is convenient when you can see the text to copy and the new location on the screen at the same time.

Procedures

Use Copy and Paste
(Ctrl+C, Ctrl+V)

1. Select the text to copy.
2. Click **Copy** button.

   OR

   a. Click **Edit** .... Alt+E
   b. Click **Copy** C

   OR

   a. Right-click selection.
   b. Click **Copy** C
3. Position insertion point in new location.
4. Click **Paste** button.

   OR

   a. Click **Edit** .... Alt+E
   b. Click **Paste** .... P

   OR

   a. Right-click new location.
   b. Click **Paste** .... P

   ✓ *To paste the text more than once, repeat steps 3 and 4.*

Paste a Selection from the Clipboard Task Pane

1. Click **View** .... Alt+V
2. Click **Task Pane** .... K
3. Click **Other Task Panes** drop-down arrow.
4. Click **Clipboard**.
5. Click item to paste.

   OR

   Click **Paste All** button Paste All to paste all selections from the Clipboard.

   ✓ *The actions for pasting a copied item from the task pane are the same as for pasting a cut item. For more information on using the Clipboard task pane, refer to Exercise 17.*

Use Drag-and-Drop to Copy Text

1. Select text to copy.
2. Move mouse pointer anywhere over selected text and press and hold down the left mouse button.
3. Press and hold the **Ctrl** key .... Ctrl
4. Drag selection to new location.

   ✓ *As you drag, the mouse pointer changes to a box with a dotted shadow and a plus sign attached to an arrow; the selection does not move until you drop it in step 5.*
5. Release mouse button.
6. Release the **Ctrl** key .... Ctrl

Exercise Directions

1. Start Word, if necessary.
2. Open NEWPOLICY or open 18NEWPOLICY.
3. Save the file as FRIDAYS.
4. Use the following steps to revise the document to create the document shown in Illustration A.
5. Delete one blank line from above the heading **Casual Fridays Policy** and one blank line from below the head **Casual Fridays Policy**.
6. Delete one blank line from above the heading **ITEMS CONSIDERED INAPPROPRIATE CASUAL ATTIRE**.
7. Position the insertion point at the end of the last sentence in the document and type: **Use the following as a quick reference guide**.
8. Start a new paragraph at the end of the document, leaving one blank line.
9. Type the heading **Dos**, in bold and then press Enter.
10. Copy the list of appropriate attire to the new line under the heading **Dos**.
11. Select all lines from the heading **Dos** to the end of the document.
12. Set a Left tab stop at 3" on the horizontal ruler.
13. Position the insertion point at the end of the word **Dos**, press tab, and type the heading **Don'ts**, in bold.
14. One by one, copy the items from the list of inappropriate attire and paste them in a list under the heading **Don'ts**, aligned with the left tab stop.
    a. Copy the text to the Clipboard being sure not to copy the paragraph mark with it.
       ✓ *If you copy the paragraph mark, the paragraph formatting is copied as well, including the default tab stops.*
    b. Position the insertion point at the end of the appropriate line.
    c. Press Tab.
    d. Paste the item at the tab stop location.
15. Check the spelling and grammar in the document.
16. Display the document in Print Preview. It should look similar to the one in the Illustration.
    ✓ *If necessary, use Shrink to Fit to fit the document on a single page.*
17. Print the document.
18. Close the document, saving all changes.
19. Exit Word

On Your Own

1. Open OWDLIST, the file you created in the On Your Own section of Exercise 17, or open 18OWDLIST.
2. Save the file as OWDLIST2.
3. At the end of the document write a sentence or two explaining that you are going to list the accomplishments of which you are the most proud.
4. Copy the three items of which you are the most proud to create a new list at the end of the document.
5. Display the document in Print Preview. Make editing or formatting changes as necessary.
6. Print the document.
7. Close the document, saving all changes.

Illustration A

Ramirez, Johnson, and Gold

85 Gold Street, New York, NY10038

Casual Fridays Policy

↓ 2x

As of September 1, employees are encouraged to wear casual clothing to work on Fridays. This is by no means a mandatory policy. If you are more comfortable in your regular business attire, feel free to continue wearing it. However, if you choose to participate in Casual Fridays, use the following guidelines to help you determine which articles of clothing are appropriate and which are not. Remember, if you have a meeting with a client who is not expecting Casual Friday, you should wear your regular work attire.

↓ 2x

ITEMS CONSIDERED INAPPROPRIATE CASUAL ATTIRE

Shorts
Belly-baring t-shirts
Undershirts of any kind
Flip-flops
Jeans
Ties

ITEMS CONSIDERED APPROPRIATE CASUAL ATTIRE

Slacks, such as khakis or corduroys
Open-necked shirts
Sweaters
Golf shirts
Polo shirts
Sneakers
Boat shoes

If you have any questions regarding this policy, please contact me at extension 234. Use the following as a quick reference guide:

Tab to 3" · Copy · Copy

Dos	**Don'ts**
Slacks, such as khakis or corduroys	Shorts
Open-necked shirts	Belly-baring t-shirts
Sweaters	Undershirts of any kind
Golf shirts	Flip-flops
Polo shirts	Jeans
Sneakers	Ties
Boat shoes	

Exercise 19

◆ Critical Thinking

Pelican Peter's is having a sale. In this exercise, you will use the skills you have learned to create a flyer advertising the sale. You will start by opening an existing document that you can modify to create the flyer. You will save the document with a new name. You will insert and replace text. You will use different cases in the document, and you will copy and move text to improve the flyer. Finally, you will print the flyer.

Exercise Directions

1. Start Word, if necessary.
2. Open the document FLYER, or open 19FLYER.
3. Save the document as SALE.
4. Make the insertions and deletions marked on Illustration A.
5. Copy and move text as marked on Illustration A.
6. Change case as marked on Illustration A.
7. Adjust spacing by inserting or deleting blank lines.
8. Check the spelling and grammar in the document.
9. Correct all errors, but leave capitalization as shown in the illustration.
10. Display the document in Print Preview. It should look similar to Illustration B.
11. Print the document.
12. Close the document, saving all changes.
13. Exit Word

Illustration A

PELICAN PETER'S

Title case ⟨ a full-service dive shop ⟩ Copy and paste at end of document

Announcing Pelican Peter's Super Spring Sale. Huge savings on our

~~Pelican Peter's offers a~~ full line of **SCUBA** and **snorkeling** equipment including masks, snorkels, fins, wet suits, compressors, hoses, and valves.

↓ 2x ~~Training and certification are available.~~
~~Ask for a schedule of upcoming classes.~~

~~At Pelican Peter's you'll also find:~~ Additional savings on:

¶ Surfer Gear ....boards, clothes
Kayaks..................................sea and lake
Clothing ....all types, all sizes
Water Ski Gear........... skis, ropes, etc.
Windsurfers...............................all types

Rearrange items into alphabetical order

~~And so much more!~~ ↓ 2x

~~Pelican Peter's~~
2200 Gulfshore Boulevard N.
Naples, FL 34102
Phone: (941) 555-0780
Online at: pelicanpeters.com

Move

Illustration B

PELICAN PETER'S

A Full-Service Dive Shop

2200 Gulfshore Boulevard N.
Naples, FL 34102
Phone: (941) 555-0780
Online at: pelicanpeters.com

Announcing Pelican Peter's Super Spring Sale. Huge savings on our full line of **SCUBA** and **snorkeling** equipment including masks, snorkels, fins, wet suits, compressors, hoses, and valves.

Additional savings on:

CLOTHING................all types, all sizes
KAYAKS ....sea and lake
SURFER GEAR..............boards, clothes
WATER SKI GEAR...... skis, ropes, etc.
WINDSURFERS........................all types

PELICAN PETER'S

A Full-Service Dive Shop

Lesson 4

Text Formatting

Exercise 20

- Apply Font Effects
- Apply Text Effects
- Apply Underlines
- Apply Font Color

Exercise 21

- Highlight Text
- Copy Formatting

Exercise 22

- Apply Styles
- Create a Style
- Modify a Style
- Reapply Direct Formatting
- Check Formatting
- Select Paste Formatting Options
- Clear Formatting

Exercise 23

- Insert Symbols and Special Characters
- Customize Toolbars

Exercise 24

- Bulleted Lists
- Numbered Lists
- Sort

Exercise 19

- Critical Thinking

Exercise 20

Skills Covered:

◆ **Apply Font Effects** ◆ **Apply Text Effects**
◆ **Apply Underlines** ◆ **Apply Font Color**

On the Job

You can enhance text using font effects, text effects, underlines, and colors. These techniques are useful for printed documents or documents you intend to post on the World Wide Web. Some of these formatting features, such as text effects, color, shadow, and fancy underline styles, are useful for creating exciting documents in which the text jumps out to capture a reader's attention. Alternatively, some formatting features are useful for adding subtle description to text, such as a single underline or superscript.

Fox Footwear, Inc. is sponsoring an essay writing contest for teens. You have been asked to design a document advertising the contest. If the company approves of the document, it will be made available at retail stores and posted as a Web page on the company Web site. In this exercise, you will create the document using font effects, text effects, and color.

Terms

Font effects Formatting features used to enhance or emphasize text.

Text effects Effects used to animate text on-screen.

Notes

Apply Font Effects

- Word includes numerous **font effects** for enhancing and emphasizing text, including the ones available in the Font dialog box:
  - ~~Strikethrough~~
  - ~~Double strikethrough~~
  - Superscript
  - Subscript
  - Shadow
  - Outline
  - Emboss
  - Engrave
  - SMALL CAPS
  - ALL CAPS

Font dialog box—Font tab

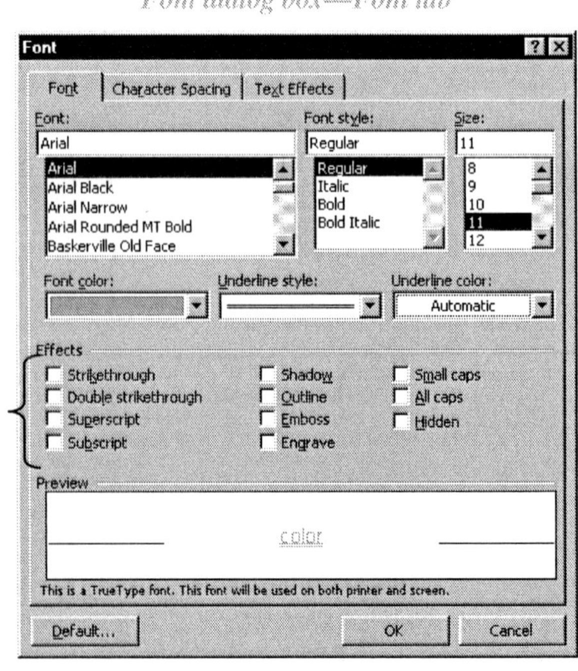

Apply Text Effects

- Word has six **text effects** you can apply to text for viewing on-screen.
- Text effects are animations used in documents that will be viewed on-screen. They cannot be printed.
- Select text effects in the Font dialog box.

Font dialog box—Text Effects tab

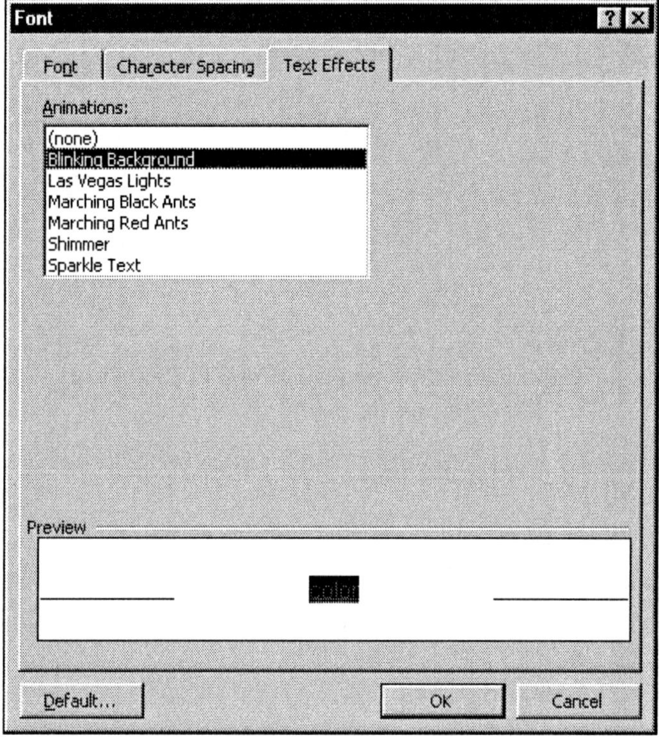

Apply Underlines

- There are nine types of underlines available in Word:
  - Single (underlines all characters, including nonprinting characters, such as spaces and tabs)
  - Words only
  - Double
  - Dotted
  - Thick
  - Dash
  - Dot dash
  - dot dot dash
  - Wave

Apply Font Color

- Use color to enhance text in documents that will be viewed on-screen or printed on a color printer.
- You select a font color using the Font Color button A on the Formatting toolbar, or from the Color palette in the Font dialog box.
- You can change the color of an underline independently from the color of the font.

Procedures

Apply Font Effects

1. Select text.

   OR

   Position insertion point where new text will be typed.
2. Click **Format** .... Alt+O
3. Click **Font** .... F
4. Select check box for desired effect(s).

   ✓ *Clear checkmark to remove effect.*
5. Click **OK** .... Enter

   ✓ *Select text and press Ctrl+Spacebar to remove all character formatting.*

Apply Text Effects

1. Select text.

   OR

   Position insertion point where new text will be typed.
2. Click **Format** .... Alt+O
3. Click **Font** .... F
4. Click **Text Effects** tab ... Alt+X
5. Click desired

   Animation .... Alt+A, ↕

   ✓ *View a sample of the effect in the Preview area.*
6. Click **OK** .... Enter

Apply Underlines (Ctrl+U)

1. Select text.

   OR

   Position insertion point where new text will be typed.
2. Click **Underline** button U.

   ✓ *Repeat steps to remove underline.*

OR

1. Select text.

   OR

   Position insertion point where new text will be typed.
2. Click **Format** .... Alt+O
3. Click **Font** .... F

4. Click **Underline style** drop-down arrow .... Alt+U
5. Click desired underline type.
   ✓ *Click (None) to remove underline*
6. Click **OK** .... Enter

Apply Font Color

1. Select text.

   OR

   Position insertion point where new text will be typed.
2. Click **Format** .... Alt+O
3. Click **Font**.......................... F
4. Click **Font color** drop-down arrow .... Alt+C
5. Click desired color ... ↑↓, Enter
   ✓ *Click Automatic to select default color.*
6. Click **OK** .... Enter

OR

1. Select text.

   OR

   Position insertion point where new text will be typed.
2. Click **Font Color** button to apply color displayed on button.

   OR

   a. Click **Font Color** drop-down arrow.

   b. Click desired color.

Apply Color to Underlines

1. Select underlined text.

   OR

   Position insertion point where new underlined text will be typed.
2. Click **Format**................ Alt+O
3. Click **Font** .... F
4. Click **Underline color** drop-down arrow.......... Alt+I
5. Click desired color .. ↑↓, Enter
   ✓ *Click Automatic to select default color.*
6. Click **OK**.......................... Enter

Exercise Directions

1. Start Word, if necessary.
2. Open 20CONTEST.
3. Save the document as CONTEST.
4. Apply the formatting shown in the illustration.
   a. Change the font and font size as marked.
      ✓ *If the specified font is not available on your computer, select a different font.*
   b. Set horizontal alignments as marked.
   c. Apply font and text effects as marked.
   d. Change font color as marked
   e. Apply underlines and underline colors as marked.
5. Check the spelling and grammar.
6. Display the document in Print Preview. It should look similar to the illustration.
   ✓ *The animated effects do not appear in Print Preview or in a printed document.*
   ✓ *If the document is longer or shorter than the one shown, check to see if you inadvertently formatted the blank lines between paragraphs. In the illustration, all blank lines have the default 12-pt. Times New Roman formatting.*
7. Save the changes.
8. Print the document.
9. Close the document, saving all changes.
10. Exit Word

On Your Own

1. Open the document OWDLIST2, or open 20OWDLIST2.
2. Save the document as OWDEFFECTS.
3. Apply font effects to highlight some of the document text.
4. Change the font color for some text.
5. Try some text effects.
6. Try different underline styles.
7. Preview the document.
8. Save your changes, close the document, and exit Word.

Illustration A

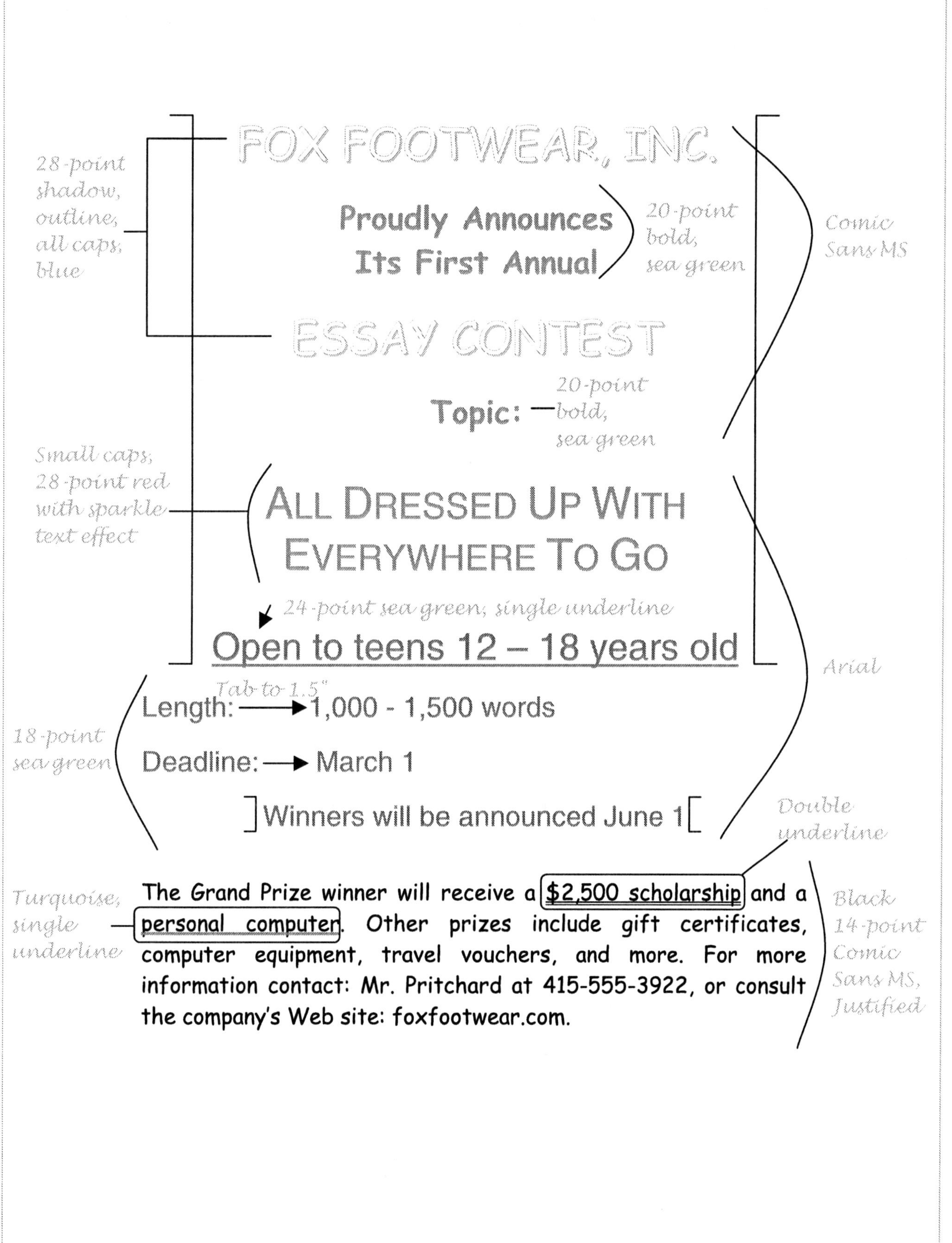

Exercise 21

Skills Covered:

◆ **Highlight Text** ◆ **Copy Formatting**

On the Job

You can highlight text to change the color around the text without changing the font color. Highlighting is useful for calling attention to text and for making text stand out on the page. Use the Format Painter to quickly copy formatting from one location to another. The Format Painter saves you time and makes it easy to duplicate formatting throughout a document.

To complete the Casual Fridays Policy document for Ramirez, Johnson, and Gold, you want to apply highlights and additional formatting. In this exercise, you will open the existing document, save it with a new name. You will then apply highlights to call attention to specific text, and you will use the Format Painter to copy formatting from one location to another.

Terms

Highlight formatting Change the color around text in a document.

Notes

Highlight Text

- Highlighting calls attention to text by placing a color background on the text just like using a highlighter pen on paper.
- Yellow is the default highlight color, but you can change **highlight formatting**.
  - ✓ *Color highlighting will print in color when printed on a color printer and print in gray when printed on a black and white printer.*

Copy Formatting

- Use the Format Painter to copy formatting from existing formatted text to existing unformatted text.
- You can copy character formatting, such as fonts and font effects as well as paragraph formatting, such as horizontal alignments.
  - ✓ *The Format Painter will not copy case changes.*

Procedures

Apply Highlights

Highlight existing text:

1. Select text.
2. Click **Highlight** button.

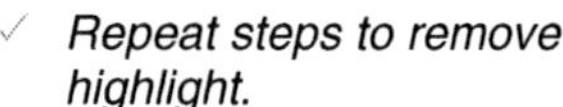

   ✓ *Repeat steps to remove highlight.*

OR

1. Click **Highlight** button.
   ✓ *Mouse pointer changes to look like an I-beam with a highlighter pen attached to it.*
2. Drag across text to highlight.
3. Click **Highlight** button again to turn off Highlight feature.

Change highlight color:

1. Click **Highlight** button drop-down arrow.
2. Click new color.
   ✓ *Click None to select the automatic background color.*

Copy Formatting

Copy formatting once;

1. Select formatted text.
2. Click **Format Painter** button.
   ✓ *The mouse pointer looks like an I-beam with a paintbrush.*

3. Select text to format.
   ✓ *Click a word to quickly copy character formatting to that word.*
   ✓ *Click in a paragraph to quickly copy paragraph formatting to the entire paragraph.*

Copy formatting repeatedly:

1. Select formatted text.
2. Double-click **Format Painter** button.
3. Select text to format.
4. Repeat step 3 until all text is formatted.
5. Click **Format Painter** button to turn off Format Painter.

Exercise Directions

1. Start Word, if necessary.
2. Open FRIDAYS or open 21FRIDAYS.
3. Save the document as FRIDAYSREV.
4. Change the heading **Casual Fridays Policy** to 22-point Arial with a Small Caps font effect.
5. Use the Format painter to copy the formatting from the heading to the company name on the first line of the document.
6. Format the color of the word **Dos** to turquoise, and change the font to 14-point Arial, with an All Caps font effect, and a single line underline.
7. Copy the formatting to the word **Don'ts**.
8. Apply a yellow highlight to the heading **Items Considered Inappropriate Casual Attire**.
9. Apply a green highlight to the heading **Items Considered Appropriate Casual Attire**.
10. Check the spelling and grammar.
11. Preview the document. It should look similar to the one in the Illustration.
12. Print the document.
13. Close the document, saving all changes.
14. Exit Word

Illustration A

RAMIREZ, JOHNSON, AND GOLD

85 Gold Street, New York, NY 10038

22-point Arial, small caps

CASUAL FRIDAYS POLICY

As of September 1, employees are encouraged to wear casual clothing to work on Fridays. This is by no means a mandatory policy. If you are more comfortable in your regular business attire, feel free to continue wearing it. However, if you choose to participate in Casual Fridays, use the following guidelines to help you determine which articles of clothing are appropriate and which are not. Remember, if you have a meeting with a client who is not expecting Casual Friday, you should wear your regular work attire.

ITEMS CONSIDERED INAPPROPRIATE CASUAL ATTIRE ← Yellow highlight

Shorts
Belly-baring t-shirts
Undershirts of any kind
Flip-flops
Jeans
Ties

ITEMS CONSIDERED APPROPRIATE CASUAL ATTIRE ← Green highlight

Slacks, such as khakis or corduroys
Open-necked shirts
Sweaters
Golf shirts
Polo shirts
Sneakers
Boat shoes

If you have any questions regarding this policy, please contact me at extension 234. Use the following as a quick reference guide:

DOS	DON'TS
Slacks, such as khakis or corduroys	Shorts
Open-necked shirts	Belly-baring t-shirts
Sweaters	Undershirts of any kind
Golf shirts	Flip-flops
Polo shirts	Jeans
Sneakers	Ties
Boat shoes	

Turquoise
14-point Arial,
all caps,
single underline

On Your Own

1. Start Word and create a new document
2. Save the document as OWDINVITE.
3. Design an invitation to an upcoming event in your life, such as a graduation, a school play, or a birthday party.
4. Use font formatting to enhance the appearance of the document. For example, make important information stand out in a different font and increase the size.
5. Apply underlines where appropriate.
6. Change some font colors to enhance the document.
7. Use the Format Painter to copy existing formatting to unformatted text.
8. Use highlighting to call attention to the items you think are the most important.
9. Preview the document.
10. Save your changes, close the document, and exit Word.

Exercise 22

Skills Covered:

◆ **Apply Styles** ◆ **Create a Style** ◆ **Modify a Style**
◆ **Reapply Direct Formatting** ◆ **Check Formatting**
◆ **Select Paste Formatting Options** ◆ **Clear Formatting**

On the Job

Word provides many ways to apply and remove formatting in documents. Use styles to apply a collection of formatting settings to characters or paragraphs. Styles help ensure continuity in formatting throughout a document. You can also set Word to check for formatting inconsistencies in much the same way it checks for spelling and grammatical errors.

Highland Property Management Company has contracted with a training service to provide computer training for employees. You have been asked to prepare a document listing the courses that will be available for the first three months of the year. In this exercise, you will use styles and direct formatting to apply consistent formatting to the document.

Terms

Style A collection of formatting settings that can be applied to characters or paragraphs.

Style sheet A list of available styles.

Direct formatting Individual font or paragraph formatting settings applied directly to text, as opposed to a collection of settings applied with a style.

Notes

Apply Styles

- **Styles** make it easy to apply a collection of formatting settings to characters or paragraphs all at once.
- Word includes built-in styles for formatting body text, headings, lists, and other parts of documents.
- Different Word templates have different **style sheets** depending on formatting required for the document. For example, the default Normal template uses only five styles, while the Resume template includes 25 styles.

The Style list for the Normal template style sheet

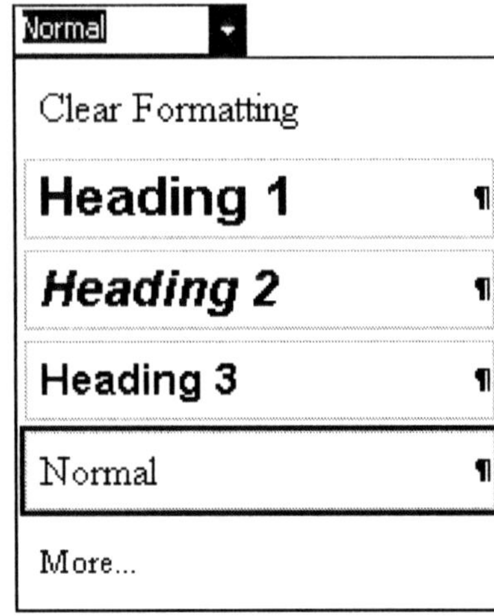

- You can apply a style to existing text, or select a style before you type new text.
- You can select a style from the drop-down style list on the Formatting toolbar or from the Styles and Formatting task pane.
- By default, the Styles and Formatting task pane displays a list of styles in use in the current document. You can select to display all available styles (styles attached to the style sheet even if they are not in use), or all styles attached to all style sheets. You can also customize the style list if you want.

The Styles and Formatting task pane

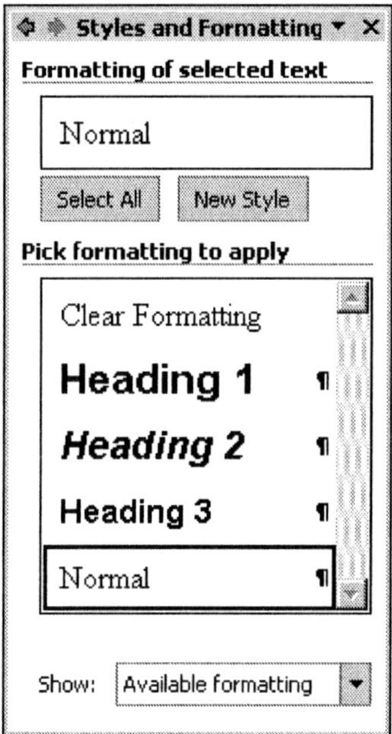

Create a Style

- You can create new styles for formatting your documents.
- Styles can contain font and/or paragraph formatting.
- Style names should be short and descriptive.
- The style will be added to the style sheet for the current document.

Modify a Style

- You can modify an existing style.
- When you modify a style that has already been applied to text in the document, the formatted text automatically changes to the new style.
- If you modify a style and give it a new name, it becomes a new style; the original style remains unchanged.

Reapply Direct Formatting

- By default, Word keeps track of **direct formatting** that you apply to text or paragraphs, and displays information about the formatting in the style box and in the Styles and Formatting task pane.

  ✓ *To disable the track formatting option, click Tools, Options, Edit, deselect the Keep track of Formatting check box, and then click OK.*

- For example, if you apply italics to text formatted with the Normal style, Word displays a plus sign followed by the word Bold in the Style list box and the Styles and Formatting task pane.
- You can use the Styles and Formatting task pane or the Style list to reapply direct formatting that you have already used in a document to selected text.
- This feature is similar to the Format Painter, but you do not have to scroll through the document from the formatted text to the text you want to format.

Check Formatting

- Use Word's Format Checker to ensure consistent formatting throughout a document.
- As with the spelling checker and the grammar checker, you can have Word check formatting while you work. Word underlines formatting inconsistencies with a wavy blue underline.

Check formatting

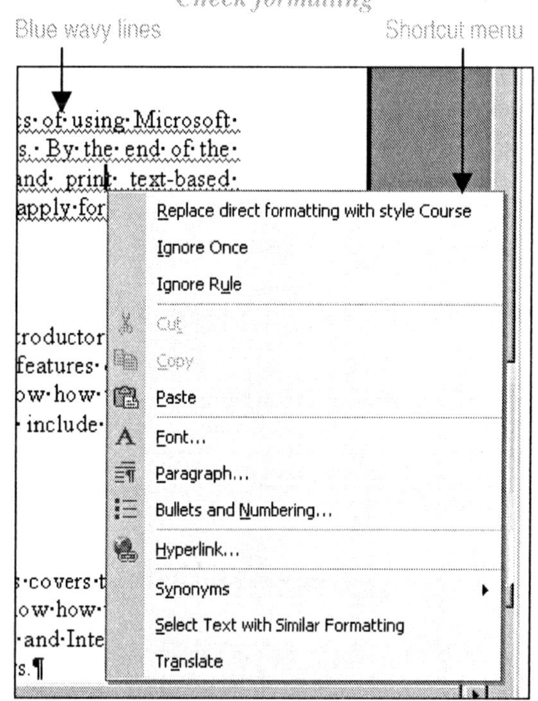

- You can ignore the blue lines and keep typing, or you can use a shortcut menu to correct the error.
- The automatic format checker is off by default; you must turn it on to use it.
- If the wavy underlines distract you from your work, you can turn off the automatic formatting checker.

Select Paste Formatting Options

- When you use the Clipboard to paste text from one location to another, Word automatically displays the Paste Options button.
- Click the Paste Options button to display a list of options for formatting the text in the new location.

Paste Options button

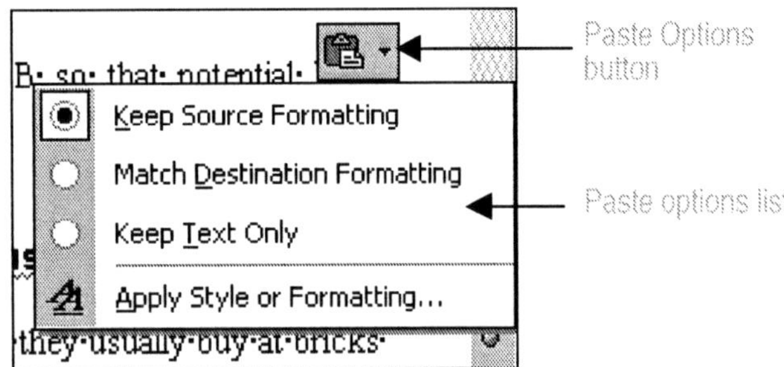

Clear Formatting

- You can quickly remove all formatting from selected text.
- Clearing the formatting from text removes both direct formatting and styles.
  - ✓ *To quickly remove direct character formatting from selected text, press Ctrl+Spacebar; to remove direct paragraph formatting, press Ctrl+Q.*
- You can clear formatting using the Style list, or the Styles and Formatting task pane.
- After you clear the formatting, text is displayed in the default normal style for the current document. For the default document, that means single spaced 12-point Times New Roman, flush left.

Procedures

Apply a Style

1. Click in the paragraph.

   OR

   Select the text.
2. Click the **Style** drop-down arrow [Normal ▾] on the Formatting toolbar.
3. Select style to apply .... [↕], [Enter]

Open the Styles and Formatting Task Pane

- Click the **Styles and Formatting** button on the Formatting toolbar.

OR

1. Click **Format** .... [Alt]+[O]
2. Click **Styles and Formatting** .... [S]

Apply a Style Using the Task Pane

1. Click in the paragraph.

   OR

   Select the text.
2. Open the Styles and Formatting task pane.
3. Click style to apply in **Pick formatting to apply** list.
   - ✓ *The styles are listed alphabetically in the Pick formatting to apply list; however, the most recently used styles are listed above the alphabetical list. If necessary, scroll through the list to find the desired formatting.*

Change the list of Displayed Styles

1. Open the Styles and Formatting task pane.
2. Click **Show**: drop-down arrow
3. Click desired list:
   - **Available formatting** to display all direct formatting in the current style sheet.
   - **Formatting in use** to display all direct formatting currently in use in the document.
   - **Available styles** to display all styles in the current style sheet.
   - **All styles** to display all existing styles
   - **Custom** to open the Format Settings dialog box.
     - ✓ *Use the options in the Format Settings dialog box to select specific styles and formatting to display.*

Create a Style

Use the Style drop-down list:

1. Format text or paragraph.
2. Select formatted text or paragraph.
3. Click in the **Style** box [Normal] on the Formatting toolbar.
4. Type style name.
5. Press **Enter**...................... Enter

Use the Styles and Formatting task pane:

1. Format text or paragraph.
2. Select formatted text or paragraph.
3. Open the Styles and Formatting task pane.
4. Click the **New Style** button [New Style].
5. Type style name.
6. Select formatting options as desired.

   ✓ *Use options displayed in New Style dialog box just as you would use regular formatting options. Click the Format button for more formatting options.*
7. Click **OK**.......................... Enter

Modify a Style

1. Change formatting of text or paragraph formatted with the style.
2. Select modified text or paragraph.
3. Open the Styles and Formatting task pane.
4. Click style to modify.
5. Click **Update to match selection**.......... Alt+U

   OR

   a. Click **Modify** .... Alt+M

   b. Select formatting options as desired.

   ✓ *Use options displayed in Modify Style dialog box just as you would use regular formatting options. Click the Format button for more formatting options.*

   c. Click **OK**..................... Enter

Reapply Direct Formatting

1. Click in the paragraph.

   OR

   Select the text.
2. Click the **Style** drop-down arrow [Normal] on the Formatting toolbar.

   OR

   Open the Styles and Formatting task pane.
3. Click direct formatting to apply.

   ✓ *If necessary, scroll through the list to find the desired formatting.*

Turn on Automatic Format Checking

1. Click **Tools**................. Alt+T
2. Click **Options**...................... O
3. Click the **Edit** tab........ Ctrl+Tab
4. Select **Keep track of formatting** check box. .... Alt+K

   ✓ *This is usually selected by default.*
5. Select **Mark formatting inconsistencies** check box................... Alt+F
6. Click **OK**........................... Enter

Check Formatting as You Type

1. Right-click formatting inconsistency marked with blue, wavy underline.
2. Click desired correct formatting option on context menu.

   OR

   Click **Ignore Once** to hide this occurrence I

   OR

   Click **Ignore Rule** to hide all occurrences .... U

Select Paste Formatting Options

1. Paste text at new location.

   ✓ *Refer to Exercises 17and 18 for information on pasting.*
2. Click **Paste Options** button [Paste Options]
3. Select one of the following:
   - **Keep Source Formatting**..................... K

     to maintain formatting from original location.
   - **Match Destination Formatting**..................... D

     to apply existing formatting to pasted text.
   - **Keep Text Only** .... T

     to remove all existing formatting.
   - **Apply Styles or Formatting**..................... A

     to open Styles and Formatting task pane.

If Paste Options button is not displayed:

1. Click **Tools** .... Alt+T
2. Click **Options** .... O
3. Click the **Edit** tab .... Ctrl+Tab
4. Select **Show Paste Options buttons** check box .... Alt+O
5. Click **OK** .... Enter

Clear Formatting

1. Select text.
2. Click the **Style** drop-down arrow [Normal] on the Formatting toolbar.

   OR

   Open the Styles and Formatting task pane.
3. Select **Clear Formatting**.............. ↑↓, Enter

   ✓ *Clear Formatting is usually found at the top of the drop-down style list or at the top of the alphabetical list of styles in the Pick formatting to apply list.*

Exercise Directions

1. Start Word, if necessary.
2. Open 22COURSE.
3. Save the document as COURSE.
4. Turn on the formatting checker.
5. Apply the Heading 1 style to the company name.
6. Apply the Heading 3 style to the names of the months.
7. Increase the font size of the company name to 24 points and center it.
   - ✓ *Notice the direct formatting is displayed in the Style box and the Styles and Formatting task pane.*
8. Modify the Heading 1 style to include the changes.
   a. Select the company name.
   b. Click the Heading 1 style in the task pane.
   c. Click Update to match selection.
9. Apply the new Heading 1 style to the text **Training Schedule**.
10. Format the address in 14-point italic, centered horizontally.
11. Reapply the formatting you have just applied to the company address to the names of the three courses.
12. Format the paragraph describing the Word 1 in 16-point Arial, justified.
13. Create a style named **Course** based on the formatting of the course description.
    - ✓ *Notice that the formatting checker underlines the entire Word 1 description.*
14. Right-click the paragraph describing the Word 1 course to see what the formatting checker suggests.
15. Select the option to replace the direct formatting with the style formatting.
16. Apply the Course style to the paragraphs describing the Word 2 and Word 3 courses.
17. Move the insertion point to the end of the document and press Enter twice to leave a blank line.
18. Clear all formatting from the new line, then type **For more information, call:**.
19. Copy the phone number from the company address line near the top of the document and paste it at the end of the new last line of the document.
20. Select to paste only the text, without any formatting.
21. Complete the line by typing **ext. 343** after the pasted phone number.
22. Check the spelling and grammar in the document.
23. Display the document in Print Preview. It should look similar to the one in the Illustration.
24. Print the document.
25. Close the file saving all changes.
26. Exit Word.

On Your Own

1. Start Word and create a new document.
2. Save the document as OWDSCHEDULE.
3. Create a document outlining a schedule for an event. It might be the event to which you previously created an invitation, or it might be something else. For example, it might cover the schedule of a birthday party, a weekend, or a school event.
4. Use heading styles to format headings for each part of the schedule. For example, if you are scheduling a weekend, use headings for each day. You can use other heading styles for parts of the day, such as morning and afternoon.
5. Modify the heading styles if you want.
6. Create your own body text style named **mytext** and apply it to text in your document.
7. Apply some direct formatting for emphasis, and then reapply the formatting to other text in the document.
8. If you want, try pasting text and selecting different Paste Options for formatting.
9. Check the spelling and grammar in the document.
10. Close the document, saving all changes

Illustration A

Highland Property Management Co.

575 W. Osborne Street, Phoenix, AZ 85013 602-555-4326

Training Schedule

January

Microsoft Word 1

This introductory course will cover the basics of using Microsoft Word to create common business documents. By the end of the course you will know how to: create and print text-based documents such as letters and envelopes, and apply formatting.

February

Microsoft Word 2

A continuation of the Word I course, this introductory level class will delve into some of the more intriguing features of Microsoft Word. By the end of the course you will know how to conduct a mail merge, set up a document in columns, include headers and footers, and insert pictures.

March

Microsoft Word 3

This final course in the Microsoft Word series covers the advanced features. By the end of this course you will know how to work with tables, create and modify outlines, use e-mail and Internet features in Word, and share documents with other users.

For more information, call: 602-555-4326 ext. 343.

Exercise 23

Skills Covered:

◆ **Insert Symbols and Special Characters**

◆ **Customize Toolbars**

On the Job

Use symbols to supplement the standard characters available on the keyboard and to add visual interest to documents. For example, you can insert shapes such as hearts and stars into documents as borders or separators. You can also insert special characters such as paragraph marks and hyphens. Word's toolbars provide quick access to commonly used features. If the default buttons don't include the features you need, you can easily customize any toolbar. You can even create a new toolbar all your own.

The owner of Fox Footwear asked you to create a flyer announcing the essay contest. In this exercise, you will create the flyer using the formatting techniques you have learned so far. You will also insert symbols to enhance the flyer.

Terms

Symbol A character that is not included on the keyboard.

Special characters Characters that are not included on the keyboard.

Notes

Insert Symbols and Special Characters

- **Symbols** are characters that cannot be typed from the keyboard, such as hearts, stars, and other shapes as well as foreign alphabet characters.
- Several symbol fonts come with Office and others are available through vendors and shareware.
- Many regular character fonts also include some symbol characters.
- You select a font, and then select the desired symbol in the Symbol dialog box.
- You can also select from a list of recently used symbols.
- Most symbols have a character code which is displayed in the Character code box in the Symbol dialog box. If you happen to know a symbol's character code, you can type it in the box to select the desired symbol.
- Symbols can be selected, edited, and formatted in a document just like regular text characters. For example, you can change the font size of an inserted symbol, or cut, copy, and paste inserted symbols.

Symbol dialog box

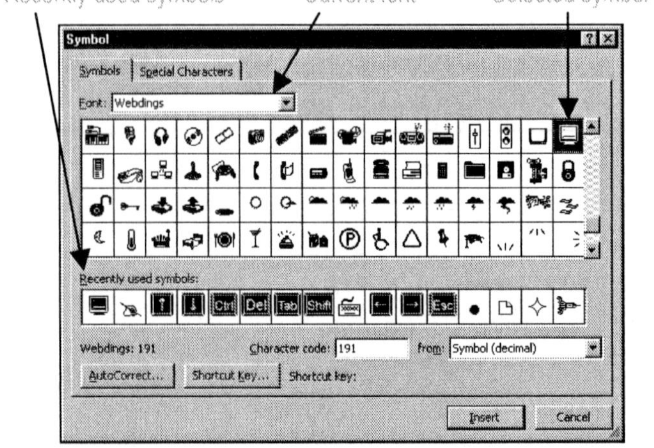

Recently used symbols   Current font   Selected symbol

- The Symbol dialog box also includes a list of **special characters** that you can insert in a document.
- For example, you can insert a paragraph mark character, or an ellipsis.

Symbol dialog box—Special Characters tab

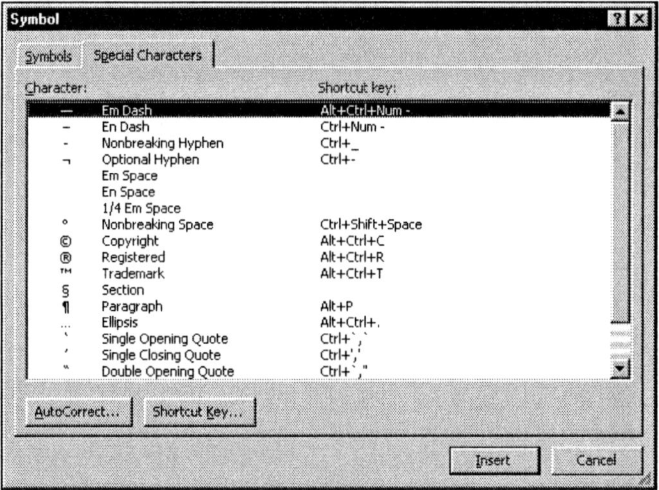

Customize Toolbars

- By default, Word's toolbars include buttons for accessing the most commonly used tasks.
- Use the Customize dialog box to customize toolbars to display buttons for accessing the tasks that you perform most frequently and to remove buttons you do not use.
- For example, by default, the Formatting toolbar includes buttons for applying bold, italic, and continuous underline effects. However, if you frequently apply the small caps effect, or the double underline effect, you can add those buttons to the Formatting toolbar.
- You can also create a new toolbar.

Customize dialog box—Commands tab

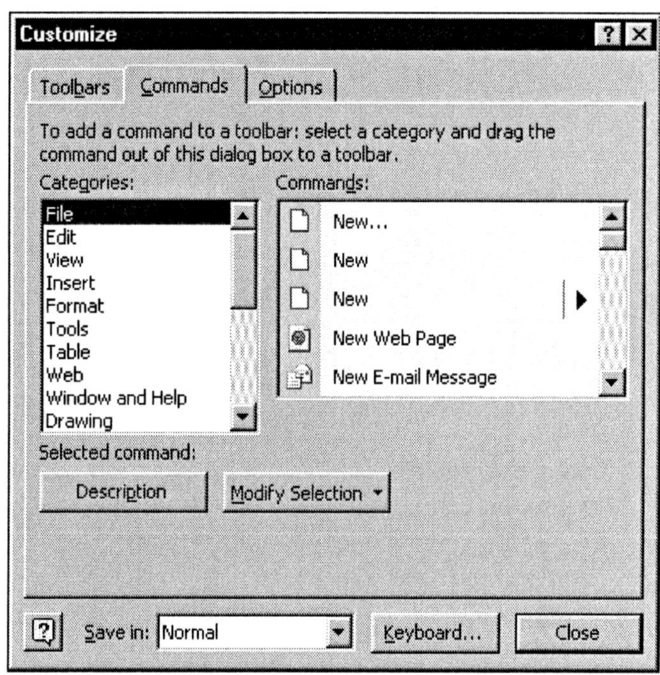

Procedures

Insert Symbols

1. Position insertion point where you want to insert a symbol.
2. Click **Insert** .... Alt+I
3. Click **Symbol**. .... S
4. Click **Font** drop-down arrow .... Alt+F
5. Select any symbol font................ ↓, Enter

   ✓ *You can scroll through the font list, or start typing the name of the desired font in the Font box. Word will jump through the alphabetical list to get the character(s) you type.*

6. Click desired symbol ... Tab, →
7. Click **Insert**.................. Alt+I

   ✓ *Repeat the steps to insert additional symbols without closing the Symbol dialog box.*

8. Click **Close**....................... Enter

Insert Special Characters

1. Position insertion point where you want to insert a special character.
2. Click **Insert**.................. Alt+I
3. Click **Symbol**....................... S
4. Click **Special Characters** tab .... Alt+P
5. Click desired character .... ↓
6. Click **Insert** .... Alt+I

   ✓ *Repeat the steps to insert additional characters without closing the Symbol dialog box.*

7. Click **Close** .... Esc

Customize Toolbars

Add a toolbar button:

1. Display the toolbar to which you want to add a button.
2. Click **Tools** .... Alt+T

OR

Right-click any toolbar.

OR

a. Click **View** .... Alt+V

b. Click **Toolbars** .... T

OR

a. Click **Toolbar Options** button on any toolbar.

b. Select **Add or Remove Buttons** .... A

3. Click **Customize** C

✓ *If necessary drag the Customize dialog box to move it away from the toolbar.*

4. Click the **Commands** tab........... Alt+C

5. In the **Categories** list box, select the category that contains the desired button .... Alt+G, ↑↓

6. In the **Commands** list, click the desired button ..... Alt+D, ↑↓

7. Drag the desired button out of the Customize dialog box and onto the desired toolbar.

✓ *A thick I-beam indicates the location where the button will be placed on the toolbar.*

8. Release the mouse button.

9. Click **Close** to close the Customize dialog box....... Enter

Remove a toolbar button:

1. Display the toolbar from which you want to remove a button.

2. Click **Tools** .... Alt+T

OR

Right-click any toolbar.

OR

a. Click **View** .... Alt+V

b. Click **Toolbars** .... T

OR

a. Click **Toolbar Options** button on any toolbar.

b. Select **Add or Remove Buttons** .... A

3. Click **Customize** C

✓ *If necessary drag the Customize dialog box to move it away from the toolbars.*

4. Click the **Commands** tab........... Alt+C

5. Drag the desired button off of the toolbar where it is currently located.

✓ *The mouse pointer resembles a button attached to an arrow with an X.*

6. Release the mouse button.

7. Click **Close** to close the Customize dialog box. ..... Enter

Change toolbar button size:

1. Click **Tools** .... Alt+T

OR

Right-click any toolbar.

OR

a. Click **View** .... Alt+V

b. Click **Toolbars** .... T

OR

a. Click **Toolbar Options** button on any toolbar.

b. Select **Add or Remove Buttons** .... A

2. Click **Customize** C

3. Click **Options** tab .... Alt+O

4. Select **Large Icons** check box..................... Alt+L

✓ *Icons size changes immediately on-screen.*

5. Click **Close** to close dialog box, leaving icons large ... Enter

OR

a. Deselect **Large Icons** check box .... Alt+L

b. Click **Close** .... Enter

Create a new toolbar:

1. Click **Tools** .... Alt+T

OR

Right-click any toolbar.

OR

a. Click **View** .... Alt+V

b. Click **Toolbars** .... T

OR

a. Click **Toolbar Options** button on any toolbar.

b. Select **Add or Remove Buttons** .... A

2. Click **Customize** C

3. Click **Toolbars** tab .... Alt+B

4. Click **New** .... Alt+N

5. Type toolbar name.

6. Click **OK** .... Enter

✓ *New toolbar is displayed as floating palette on-screen.*

7. Follow steps to add buttons to a toolbar.

Exercise Directions

1. Start Word, if necessary.
2. Open CONTEST or open 23CONTEST.
3. Save the document as CONTEST2.
4. Add a button for opening the Symbol dialog box to the Standard toolbar.
   a. Open the Customize dialog box.
   b. Click the Commands tab.
   c. Select the Insert category
   d. Drag the Insert Symbol button Ω on to the Standard toolbar.
5. Create a new toolbar named **Font Effects**.
6. Add buttons for applying Subscript, Superscript, Strikethrough, Double Strikethrough, Small Caps, and All Caps to the new toolbar.
7. Dock the toolbar at the top of your screen.
8. Use the new toolbar to apply Small Caps formatting to the following three lines:

   Proudly announces

   Its first annual

   Topic:
9. Use the new Insert Symbol toolbar button to open the Symbol dialog box.
10. Use the Wingdings font and Webdings font to insert symbols as marked in the Illustration.
    - Insert the Wingding symbol of a hand holding a pen (#64) at the beginning and end of the line **ESSAY CONTEST** (leave a space between the symbol and the text).
    - Insert ten of the Webding symbol of a computer monitor (#191) on the line above the last paragraph in the document. Size the symbols to 36 points, leave a space between each symbol, and center the line horizontally.

    ✓ *Remember, you can use Copy and Paste to copy a symbol from one location to another, or use the Repeat command (Ctrl+Y) to repeat the insertion.*
11. Remove the Insert Symbol button from the Standard toolbar.
12. Hide the Font Effects toolbar.
13. Check the spelling and grammar in the document.
14. Display the document in Print Preview. It should look similar to the illustration.
15. Print the document.
16. Close the document, saving the changes.
17. Exit Word.

Illustration A

FOX FOOTWEAR, INC.

PROUDLY ANNOUNCES
ITS FIRST ANNUAL

ESSAY CONTEST

TOPIC:

ALL DRESSED UP WITH EVERYWHERE TO GO

<u>Open to teens 12 – 18 years old</u>

Length: 1,000 - 1,500 words

Deadline: March 1

Winners will be announced June 1

The Grand Prize winner will receive a <u>$2,500 scholarship</u> and a <u>personal computer</u>. Other prizes include gift certificates, computer equipment, travel vouchers, and more. For more information contact: Mr. Pritchard at 415-555-3922, or consult the company's Web site: foxfootwear.com.

On Your Own

1. Open the document OWDINVITE, the document you created in Exercise 21, or open 23OWDINVITE.
2. Save the document as OWDINVITE2.
3. Use symbols to enhance the document. For example, use symbols as separators between words or paragraphs, or use them to decorate or emphasize the document.
4. Try different symbol fonts.
5. Try changing the font size for a symbol inserted in a document.
6. Try repeating a symbol to create a line across the page.
7. Create a new custom toolbar that you can use to format documents. For example, create an Underlining toolbar that includes buttons for applying different types of underlines.
8. Use the buttons on the toolbar to format the document.
9. Preview and print the document.
10. Close the document, saving all changes.

Exercise 24

Skills Covered:

◆ **Bulleted Lists** ◆ **Numbered Lists** ◆ **Sort**

On the Job

Lists are an effective way to present items of information. Use a bulleted list when the items do not have to be in any particular order, like a grocery list or a list of objectives. Use a numbered list when the order of the items is important, such as directions or instructions. Use Sort to organize a list into alphabetical or numerical order.

As a personnel assistant at Optical General, Inc., a manufacturer of lenses for medical industries, you have been asked to issue a memo about a change in emergency procedures. In this exercise, you will edit and format a memo document using a bulleted list and a numbered list. You will also sort the bulleted list into alphabetical order.

Terms

Bullet A dot or symbol that marks an important line of information or designates items in a list.

Sort To organize items into a specified order.

Notes

Bulleted Lists

- Use **bullets** to mark lists when the order of items does not matter.
- Word has seven built-in bullet symbols, but uses a simple black dot by default.
- A variety of bullet styles are available in the Bullets and Numbering dialog box, or you can create a customized bullet using a symbol.
- Word automatically carries bullet formatting forward to new paragraphs in a list.

Select a bullet style in the Bullets and Numbering dialog box

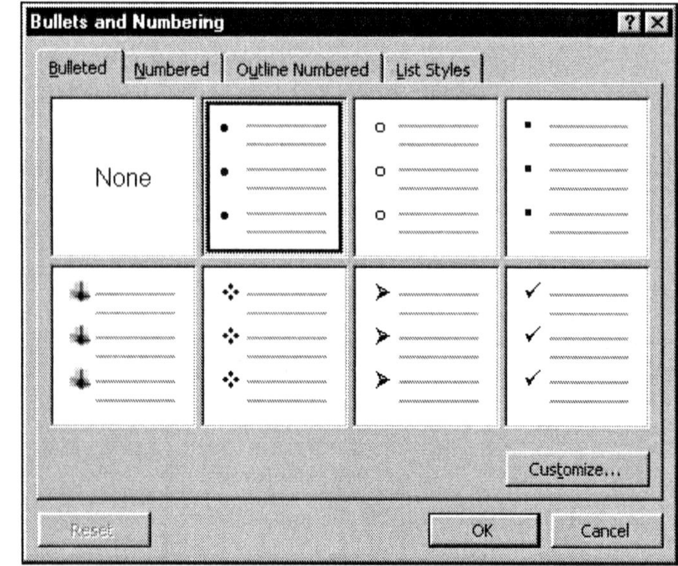

Numbered Lists

- Use numbers to mark lists when the order of items matters, such as with directions or how-to steps.
- Word automatically renumbers a list when you add or delete items.
- Word comes with seven numbering styles, but the default numbering style is an arabic numeral followed by a period.
- You can select a different number style in the Bullets and Numbering dialog box.
- Word automatically carries number formatting forward to new paragraphs in a list.

Select a number style in the Bullets and Numbering dialog box

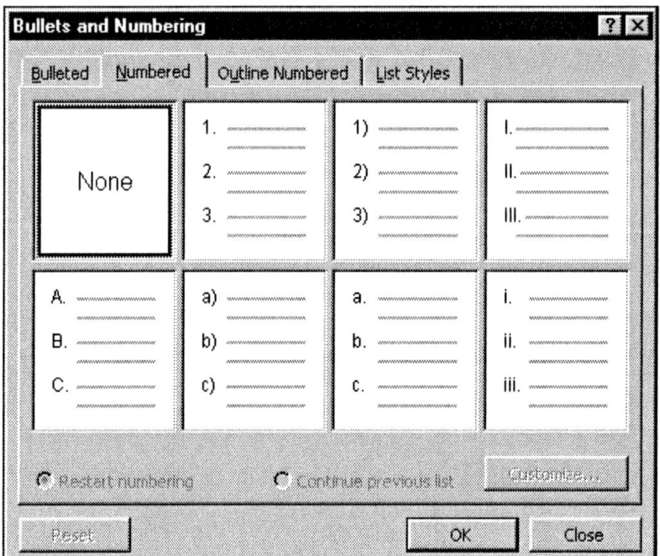

Sort

- Word can automatically **sort** items into alphabetical, numerical, or chronological order.
- A sort can be ascending (A to Z or 0 to 9) or descending (Z to A or 9 to 0).
- The default sort order is alphabetical ascending.
- Although the Sort command is on the Table menu, sorting is useful for arranging lists, paragraphs, or rows of regular text as well as in a table.

Options for a default sort

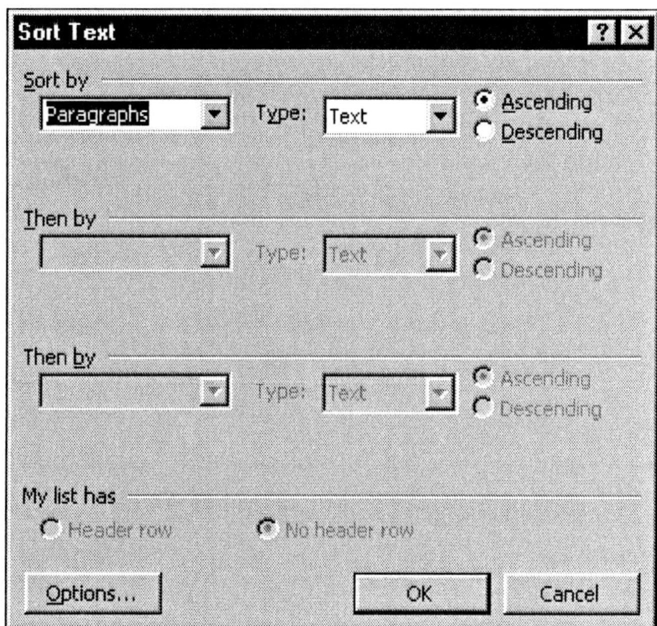

Procedures

Create Bulleted List

Use the default bullet:

1. Position insertion point where you want to start list.
   OR
   Select paragraphs you want in the list.
2. Click **Bullets** button.

Select a different bullet:

1. Position insertion point where you want to start list.
   OR
   Select paragraphs you want in the list.
2. Click **Format** .... Alt+O
3. Click **Bullets and Numbering** .... N
4. Click **Bulleted** tab .... Alt+B
5. Click desired bullet style.... ↕↔
6. Click **OK** .... Enter

Customize bullet:

1. Position insertion point where you want to start list.
   OR
   Select paragraphs you want in list.
2. Click **Format** .... Alt+O
3. Click **Bullets and Numbering** .... N
4. Click **Bulleted** page tab .... Alt+B
5. Click desired bullet style .... ↕↔
6. Click **Customize** .... Alt+T
7. Click desired **Bullet** character .... Alt+U, ↕↔
8. Click **Font** .... Alt+F
9. Select desired font options.
10. Click **OK** .... Enter
11. Set additional bullet list options as desired:
    - Click **Indent at** .... Alt+A
      to enter an indent setting for bullet.
    - Click **Tab space after** .... Alt+B
      to enter a tab stop setting between the bullet and the text.
    - Click **Indent at** .... Alt+I
      to enter an indent setting for text.
12. Click **OK** .... Enter
13. Click **OK** .... Enter

Use a symbol as a bullet:

1. Position insertion point where you want to start list.
   OR
   Select paragraphs you want in list.
2. Click **Format** .... Alt+O
3. Click **Bullets and Numbering** .... N
4. Click **Bulleted** tab .... Alt+B
5. Click desired bullet style .... ↕↔
6. Click **Customize** .... Alt+T
7. Click **Character** C
8. Click desired symbol .... Tab, ↕↔

   ✓ *You may select any symbol from any font set. Refer to Exercise 23 for more information.*
9. Click **OK** .... Enter
10. Click **OK** .... Enter

Use a picture as a bullet:

1. Position insertion point where you want to start list.
   OR
   Select paragraphs you want in list.
2. Click **Format** .... Alt+O
3. Click **Bullets and Numbering** .... N
4. Click **Bulleted** page tab .... Alt+B
5. Click desired bullet style ..... ↕↔
6. Click **Customize** .... Alt+T
7. Click **Picture** .... P
8. Click desired picture .... Tab, ↕↔
9. Click **OK** .... Enter
10. Click **OK** .... Enter

Turn off bullets:

- Click **Bullets** button.

  ✓ *To remove existing bullets, select bulleted list then click Bullets button.*

Create Numbered List

Use default number style:

1. Position insertion point where you want to start list.
   OR
   Select paragraphs you want in list.
2. Click **Numbering** button.

Select different number style:

1. Position insertion point where you want to start list.
   OR
   Select paragraphs you want in list.
2. Click **Format** .... Alt+O
3. Click **Bullets and Numbering** .... N
4. Click **Numbered** tab .... Alt+N
5. Click **Number style** .... ↕↔
6. Click **OK** .... Enter

Turn off numbering:

- Click **Numbering** button.

  ✓ *To remove numbers, select numbered list, then click Numbering button.*

Customize a numbered list:

1. Position insertion point where you want to start list.
   OR
   Select paragraphs you want in list.
2. Click **Format** .... Alt+O
3. Click **Bullets and Numbering** .... N
4. Click **Numbered** tab .... Alt+N
5. Click number style............ ↑↓←→
6. Click **Customize** .... Alt+T
7. Set desired options:
   - Click **Number format**.................... Alt+O
     to type a different character.
   - Click **Font** .... Alt+F
     to change font formatting
   - Click **Number style**...................... Alt+N
     to select a different style from drop-down list.
   - Click **Start at**........... Alt+S
     to enter the number to start at.
   - Click **Number position**.................. Alt+U
     to select location of the number in relation to the text.
   - Click **Aligned at**...... Alt+A
     to enter the horizontal location at which to align the number.
   - Click **Tab space after** .... Alt+B
     to enter the tab stop setting between the number and the text.
   - Click **Indent at** .... Alt+I
     to enter an indent setting for text.

Restart numbering in a list:

1. Right-click number in list.
2. Click **Restart Numbering** ... R

OR

1. Position insertion point in numbered paragraph.
2. Click **Format** .... Alt+O
3. Click **Bullets and Numbering** .... N
4. Click **Numbered** tab.... Alt+N
5. Click **Restart Numbering** option button .... Alt+R
6. Click **OK** .... Enter

Continue a previous list:

1. Right-click number.
2. Click **Continue Numbering** C

OR

1. Position insertion point in numbered paragraph.
2. Click **Format** .... Alt+O
3. Click **Bullets and Numbering** .... N
4. Click **Numbered** tab.... Alt+N
5. Click **Continue Numbering** option button .... Alt+C
6. Click **OK** .... Enter

Quickly Change Formatting of Number or Bullets in a List

1. Click first number or bullet.
   ✓ *All numbers or bullets appear shaded.*
2. Select desired formatting.
   ✓ *For example, select a new color or size.*

Sort a List

Use default sort order:

1. Select the paragraphs you want sorted.
2. Click **Table** .... Alt+A
3. Click **Sort**............................ S
4. Click **OK** .... Enter

Use a numerical or chronological sort:

1. Select the paragraphs you want sorted.
2. Click **Table** .... Alt+A
3. Click **Sort**............................ S
4. Click **Type** drop-down arrow.......... Alt+Y
5. Click **Number** .... ↓, Enter
   OR
   Click **Date** .... ↓, Enter
6. Click **OK** .... Enter

Reverse the sort order:

1. Select the paragraphs you want sorted.
2. Click **Table** .... Alt+A
3. Click **Sort**............................ S
4. Click **Descending** .... Alt+D
5. Click **OK** .... Enter

Exercise Directions

1. Start Word, if necessary.
2. Open 24FIREDRILL.
3. Save the document as FIREDRILL.
4. Edit and format the document as shown in Illustration A.
   a. Set fonts, font sizes, and alignments as shown.
   b. Insert symbols as shown.
5. Use the default bullet style to turn the five guidelines into a bulleted list.
6. Select a different bullet style.
7. Use the default number style to turn the four steps for evacuation into a numbered list.
8. Select a different number style.
9. Change back to the default number style
10. Sort the bulleted list into ascending alphabetical order.
11. Check the spelling and grammar.
12. Display the document in Print Preview. It should look similar to the one in the illustration, depending on the bullet style you selected.
13. Print the document.
14. Close the document, saving all changes.
15. Exit Word.

On Your Own

1. Create a new document in Word.
2. Save the file as OWDGOALS.
3. Type a bulleted list of five things you'd like to accomplish in the next year. These can be goals for school, work, or personal development. Examples might include earning a better grade in math, completing a project on the job, or getting in better shape by exercising and eating right.
4. Sort the list in alphabetical order.
5. Type a numbered list that includes at least five steps describing how you expect to accomplish one of the items in the bulleted list.
6. Change the sort order of the bulleted list to descending order.
7. Save your changes, close the document, and exit Word.

Illustration A

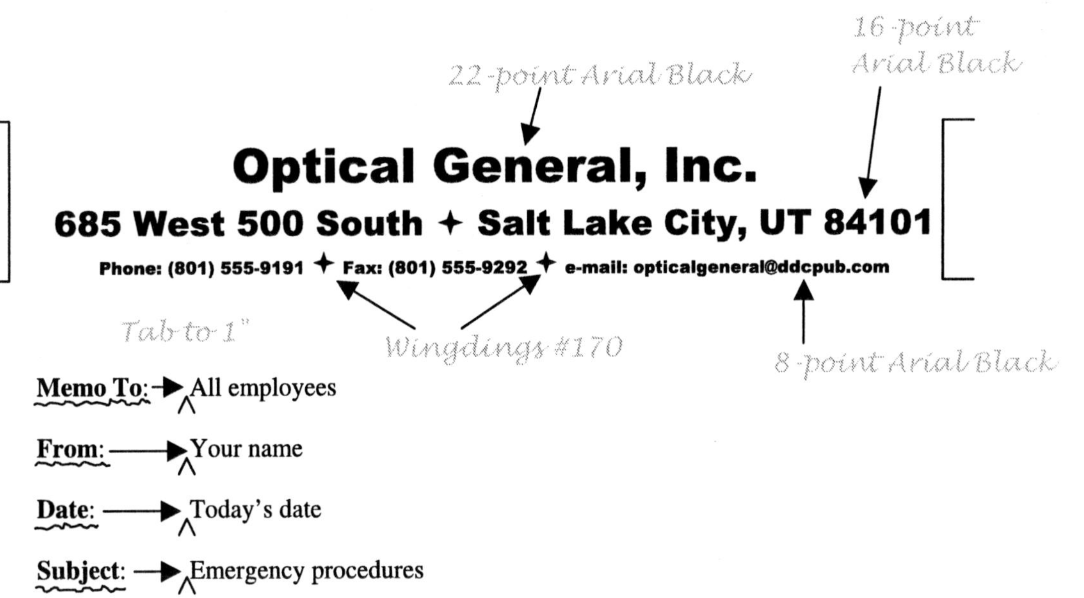

Memo To: All employees

From: Your name

Date: Today's date

Subject: Emergency procedures

Recently, we invited professionals in the field of emergency evacuations to evaluate our emergency procedure policies. While most of our policies received high marks, we have made some changes to our fire emergency procedure. Please review the following information, and then post this memo within clear sight of your desk. We will have a drill sometime in the near future.

1. Alarm sounds.
2. Proceed calmly to one of the fire exits.
3. Walk out of the building.
4. Convene with your department in the designated meeting area.

Numbered list

Adhere to the following guidelines:

- ✓ Avoid the elevators.
- ✓ Do not ignore the alarm.
- ✓ Leave personal belongings behind.
- ✓ Use the closest fire exit.
- ✓ Walk! Do not run.

Bulleted list, sorted ascending alphabetical order

If you have any questions about the new procedures, please contact me in the Personnel Department at ext. 344. Thank you for your cooperation.

Exercise 25

◆ Critical Thinking

Now that you have learned more about how to format document text, you can create a more elaborate flyer advertising the sale at Pelican Peter's. In this exercise, you will type and format a new flyer, including font effects, text effects, underlines, color, highlights, styles, symbols, and lists.

Exercise Directions

1. Start Word, if necessary.
2. Create a new document.
3. Save the document as PETESAD.
4. Use the following steps to type and format the document shown in Illustration A.
5. Center the first line and type the word **Announcing** in red, 16-point Jokerman font, or a font that is similar to Jokerman.
6. Select the text and create a style named **Pelican Subtitle**.
7. On the second line, also centered, type **Pelican Peter's** using the same font in turquoise, 36 points.
8. Select the text and create a style named **Pelican Title**.
9. On the third line, apply the Pelican Subtitle style and type **Super Spring Sale!**.
10. Select the text and apply a wave underline.
11. On the fourth line, flush left in black 12-point Comic Sans MS or a similar font, type **Huge savings on our full line of SCUBA and snorkeling equipment including:**.
12. Highlight the line in yellow.
13. Create the bullet list shown in the illustration, using 12-point Comic Sans MS in turquoise: **Masks, Snorkels, Fins, Wet suits, Compressors, Hoses**.
14. Customize the bullet marker using an appropriate symbol (Webdings #74 is used in the illustration).
15. Increase the size of the bullet so it is clearly visible in the document, and change the font color to Bright Green.
16. Sort the list into ascending alphabetical order.
17. Leave a blank line and then, using the same formatting as in step 11, type **Additional savings on:**.
18. Create the second bullet list shown in the illustration, using a right tab with dot leaders to align the text at the end of each line.
    - ✓ *Use the same formatting as the previous list, or copy the formatting from the previous list to the new list.*
19. Leave a blank line and then type **SUBSCRIBE TO OUR MAILING LIST!**.
20. Copy the formatting from the third line of the document to the new text.
21. Type the numbered list shown in the illustration, using 12-point Comic Sans MS in Bright Green.
22. On the next line, use the Pelican Title style to format the text **Pelican Peter's**.
23. Use the Pelican Subtitle style to type the last five lines in the document.
24. Modify the font size of the last four lines in the document to 12 points.
25. Preview the document. It should look similar to Illustration A.
26. Print the document.
27. Save the document and close it.
28. Exit Word.

Illustration A

Announcing

Pelican Peter's

Super Spring Sale!

Huge savings on our full line of SCUBA and snorkeling equipment including:

- Compressors
- Fins
- Hoses
- Masks
- Snorkels
- Wet suits

Additional savings on:

- CLOTHING .... all types, all sizes
- KAYAKS .... sea and lake
- WINDSURFERS .... all types

SUBSCRIBE TO OUR MAILING LIST!

1) Stop in.
2) Sign our guest register.
3) Receive notification of special savings and promotions via e-mail or snail mail.

Pelican Peter's

A Full-Service Dive Shop

2200 Gulfshore Boulevard N.
Naples, FL 34102
Phone: (941) 555-0780
Online at: pelicanpetes.com

Lesson 5

Document Formatting

Exercise 26

- Vertical Alignment

Exercise 27

- Line Spacing
- Paragraph Spacing
- Indent Text

Exercise 28

- Format a One-page Report
- Set Margins
- Set Page Orientation

Exercise 29

- Create Footnotes and Endnotes

Exercise 30

- Create Hyperlinks

Exercise 31

- Critical Thinking

Exercise 26

Skills Covered:

- **Vertical Alignment**

On the Job

Align text vertically to make the best use of white space and to improve readability.

In this exercise you will enhance the document describing changes in the fire emergency procedures for Optical General by applying font formatting. You will then vertically align the document on the page.

Terms

Vertical alignment The position of text in relation to the top and bottom page margins.

Notes

Vertical Alignment

- **Vertical alignment** is used to adjust the position of all text on a page in relation to the top and bottom margins.
- There are four vertical alignments:
  - *Top:* Text begins below the top margin. Top is the default vertical alignment.
  - *Center:* Text is centered between the top and bottom margins.
  - *Justified:* Paragraphs are spaced to fill the page between the top and bottom margins.
  - *Bottom:* The last line of text begins just above the bottom margin.
- Centering vertically can improve the appearance of some one-page documents, such as flyers or invitations.
- Vertical justification improves the appearance of documents that contain nearly full pages of text.

Procedures

Align Vertically

1. Click **File** .... Alt+F
2. Click **Page Setup** .... U
3. Click **Layout** tab......... Ctrl+Tab
4. Click **Vertical alignment** ..... Alt+V drop-down arrow.
5. Select **Vertical alignment** option: ... ↑↓, Enter
   - **Top**................................ T
   - **Center**............................ C
   - **Justified** .... J
   - **Bottom**........................... B
6. Click **OK** .... Enter

Exercise Directions

1. Start Word, if necessary.
2. Open the document FIREDRILL or open 26FIREDRILL.
3. Save the file as FIREDRILL2.
4. Delete all blank lines in the document.
5. Increase to 14 points the font size of all text from the fourth line (starting with **Memo To**) to the end of the document.
6. If necessary, delete one of the tabs from the **Your Name** line so that the text aligns with the other heading information.
7. Apply a yellow highlight to the last sentence in the first paragraph, and to the sentence **Adhere to the following guidelines**.
8. Preview the document.
9. Center the document vertically.
10. Preview the document again.
11. Align the document vertically with the bottom of the page.
12. Preview the document again.
13. Justify the document vertically.
14. Preview the document one more time. It should look similar to the one in the illustration.
15. Print the document.
16. Close the document, saving all changes.
17. Exit Word.

Optical General, Inc.

685 West 500 South ✦ Salt Lake City, UT 84101

Phone: (801) 555-9191 ✦ Fax: (801) 555-9292 ✦ e-mail: opticalgeneral@ddcpub.com

Memo To: All employees

From: Your name

Date: Today's date

Subject: Emergency procedures

Recently, we invited professionals in the field of emergency evacuations to evaluate our emergency procedure policies. While most of our policies received high marks, we have made some changes to our fire emergency procedure. Please review the following information, and then post this memo within clear sight of your desk. We will have a drill sometime in the near future.

1. Alarm sounds.
2. Proceed calmly to one of the fire exits.
3. Walk out of the building.
4. Convene with your department in the designated meeting area.

Adhere to the following guidelines:

- ✓ Avoid the elevators.
- ✓ Do not ignore the alarm.
- ✓ Leave personal belongings behind.
- ✓ Use the closest fire exit.
- ✓ Walk! Do not run.

If you have any questions about the new procedures, please contact me in the Personnel Department at ext. 344. Thank you for your cooperation.

On Your Own

1. In Word, open the document OWDEFFECTS, the document you created in the On Your Own Section of Exercise 20, or open 26OWDEFFECTS.
2. Save the file as OWDACCOMPLISH.
3. Try different vertical alignments until you settle on the one that makes the document look the best.
4. Save the changes, close the document, and exit Word.

Exercise 27

Skills Covered:

◆ **Line Spacing** ◆ **Paragraph Spacing** ◆ **Indent Text**

On the Job

Format documents using the right amount of space between lines, paragraphs, and words to make the pages look better and the text easier to read. Use indents to call attention to a paragraph, to achieve a particular visual effect, or to leave white space along the margins for notes or illustrations.

You want to improve the appearance of the training course list you created for Highland Property Management Co. In this exercise, you will reapply formatting to a version of the document. You will use line spacing, paragraph spacing, and indents to format the course list.

Terms

Line spacing The amount of white space between lines of text in a paragraph.

Leading Line spacing measured in points.

Paragraph spacing The amount of white space between paragraphs.

Indent A temporary left and/or right margin for lines or paragraphs.

Notes

Line Spacing

- **Line spacing** sets the amount of vertical space between lines. By default line spacing in Word is set to single space. Line spacing can be measured in either lines (single, double, etc.) or in points.
- When line spacing is measured in points, it is sometimes called **leading** (pronounced *ledding*).

By default, Word uses leading that is 120% of the current font size. For a 10-point font, that means 12-point leading. This paragraph is formatted with the default leading for a 12-point font (14.4 pts.).

Increase leading to make text easier to read. In this paragraph, the font is still 12 points, but the leading has been increased to exactly 16 points.

Decrease leading to fit more lines on a page. In this paragraph, the leading has been set to exactly 10 points, while the font size is still 12 points. Keep in mind that decreasing leading makes text harder to read.

- Line spacing measured in lines can be set to single spaced, 1.5 spaced, or double spaced.

Paragraph Spacing

- **Paragraph spacing** can affect space before or after paragraphs.
- The amount of space can be specified in lines or in points. The default is points.
- Use increased paragraph spacing in place of extra returns or blank lines.

Indent Text

- There are five types of **indents**:
  - *Left* indents text from the left margin.
  - *Right* indents text from the right margin.
  - *Double* indents text from both the left and right margins.
  - *First line* indents just the first line of a paragraph from the left margin.
  - *Hanging* indents all lines but the first line from the left margin.
- Indent markers on the horizontal ruler show where current indents are set.

Indents in a document

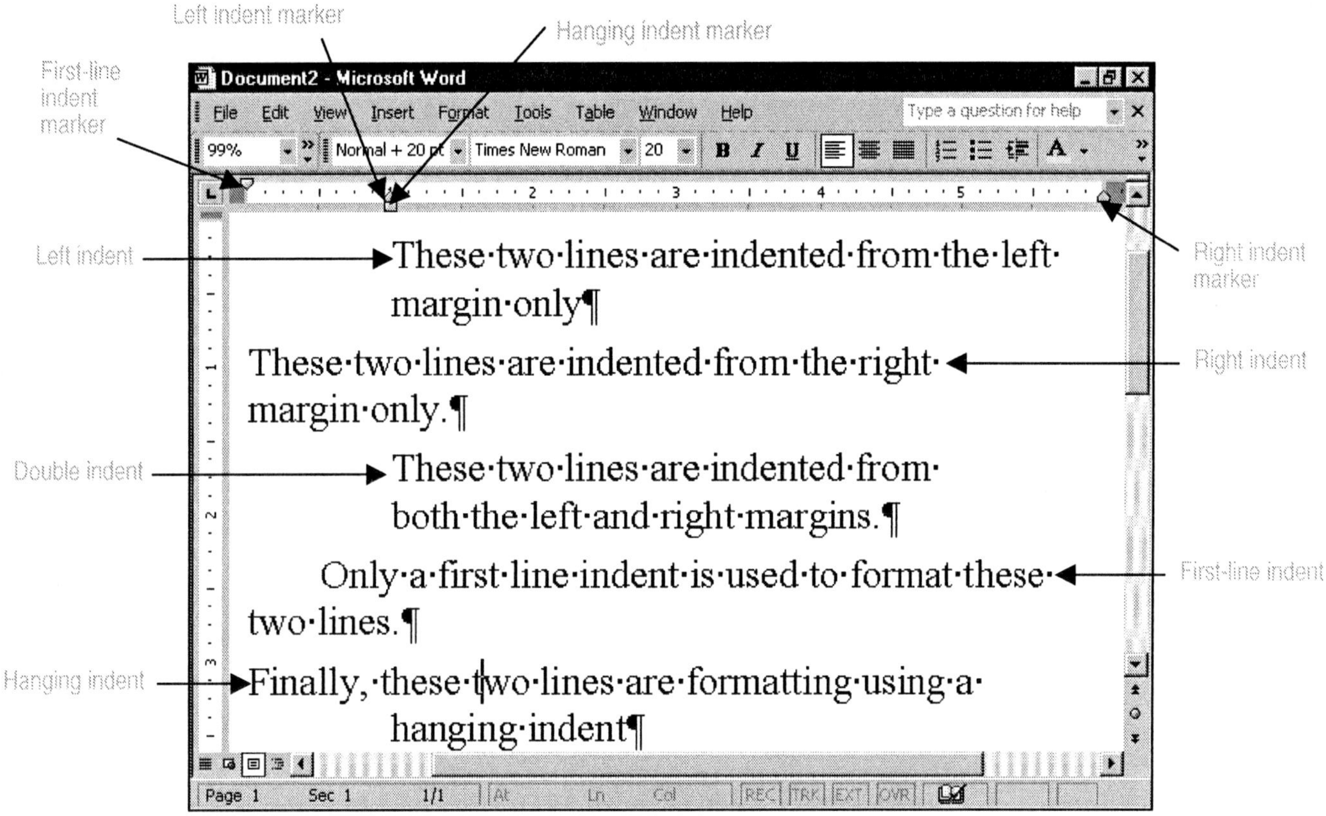

Procedures

Set Line Spacing
(Ctrl+1, Ctrl+2, Ctrl+5)

1. Position insertion point where text will be typed.

   OR

   Position insertion point in paragraph to change.

   OR

   Select paragraphs to change.
2. Click **F<u>o</u>rmat** .... Alt+O
3. Click **<u>P</u>aragraph** .... P
4. Click **<u>I</u>ndents and Spacing** tab .... Alt+I
5. Click **Li<u>n</u>e spacing** ...... Alt+N
6. Select a line spacing option: .... ↓, Enter
   - Single

   - 1.5 lines
   - Double

   OR

   a. Select leading option .... ↓, Enter
      - **At least** to set a minimum leading.
      - **Exactly** to set an exact leading.
      - **Multiple** to specify a number of times to increase leading.

   b. Click **<u>A</u>t** box .... Alt+A

   c. Type value in points.
7. Click **OK** .... Enter

Set Paragraph Spacing

1. Position insertion point where text will be typed.

   OR

   Position insertion point in paragraph to change.

   OR

Select paragraphs to change.

2. Click **Format** .... Alt+O
3. Click **Paragraph**.................. P

   ✓ *To open the Paragraph dialog box quickly, right-click paragraph to format, then click Paragraph.*

4. Click **Indents and Spacing** tab .... Alt+I
5. Click **Before** text box .. Alt+B

   OR

   Click **After** text box ..... Alt+E
6. Type amount of space to leave.

   ✓ *Type* li *after value to specify lines.*

7. Click **OK** .... Enter

Indent Text

Indent from the left:

1. Position insertion point where text will be typed.

   OR

   Position insertion point in paragraph to change.

   OR

   Select paragraphs to change.
2. Click **Increase Indent** button.

   OR

   Click **Decrease Indent** button.

   OR

   Drag **Left-indent** marker on ruler.

Indent from the left and/or right:

1. Position insertion point where text will be typed.

   OR

   Position insertion point in paragraph to change.

   OR

   Select paragraphs to change.
2. Drag **Left-indent** marker on ruler.

   AND/OR

   Drag **Right-indent** marker on ruler.

Set precise left and/or right indents:

1. Click **Format**................ Alt+O
2. Click **Paragraph**.................. P
3. Click **Indents and Spacing** tab .... Alt+I
4. Click **Left** text box........ Alt+L
5. Type distance from left margin.
6. Click **Right** text box..... Alt+R
7. Type distance from right margin.
8. Click **OK** .... Enter

Indent first line only *(Tab)*:

1. Position insertion point where text will be typed.

   OR

   Position insertion point in paragraph to change.

   OR

   Select paragraphs to change.
2. Drag **First Line indent** marker.

   OR

   a. Click **Format** .... Alt+O

   b. Click **Paragraph**............. P

   c. Click **Indents and Spacing** tab .... Alt+I

   d. Click **Special** drop-down arrow .... Alt+S

   e. Click **First line**..... ↓, Enter

   f. Click **By** text box .... Alt+Y

   g. Type amount to indent.

   h. Click **OK** .... Enter

Hanging indent *(Ctrl+T)*:

1. Position insertion point where text will be typed.

   OR

   Position insertion point in paragraph to change.

   OR

   Select paragraphs to change.
2. Drag **Hanging indent** marker.

   OR

   a. Click **Format**........... Alt+O

   b. Click **Paragraph** .... P

   c. Click **Indents and Spacing** tab........................... Alt+I

   d. Click **Special** drop-down arrow..... Alt+S

   e. Click **Hanging** ..... ↓, Enter

   f. Click **By** text box..... Alt+Y

   g. Type amount to indent.

   h. Click **OK** .... Enter

Exercise Directions

1. Start Word, if necessary.
2. Create a new document, or open 27COURSE.
3. Save the document as COURSE2.
4. Format the first four lines as follows.
   - Line 1: Centered, 24-point Arial, bold.
   - Line 2. Centered, 14-point Arial, italics.
   - Line 3. Centered, 18-point Arial, 6 pts. of space before and after.
   - Line 4. 13-point Arial, bold, flush left. Right tab set at right margin.
5. Justify the description of the Word 1 course, and indent it .5" from both the left and right margins. Leave 3 pts. of space before the paragraph and 6 pts. of space after the paragraph.
6. Copy the formatting from line 4 to the other lines with the months and course names.
7. Copy the formatting of the Word 1 course description to the other two course descriptions.
8. Copy the formatting from the third line in the document to the heading **Instructors**.
9. Format the list of instructors as follows:
   - Make the course names 16 points and bold.
   - Use 1.5 line spacing.
   - Align the paragraphs flush left with a hanging indent of .75".
10. Format the final paragraph as follows:
    - Use a first line indent of .5".
    - Double-space the lines.
    - Leave 12 points of space before the paragraph.
11. Change the last line of the document to a 10 point, centered.
12. Check the spelling and grammar in the document.
13. Preview the document. It should look similar to the illustration.
14. Print the document.
15. Close the document, saving all changes.
16. Exit Word.

Highland Property Management Co.

575 W. Osborne Street, Phoenix, AZ 85013 602-555-4326

Training Schedule

January **Microsoft Word 1**

This introductory course will cover the basics of using Microsoft Word to create common business documents. By the end of the course you will know how to: create and print text-based documents such as letters and envelopes, and apply formatting.

February **Microsoft Word 2**

A continuation of the Word I course, this introductory level class will delve into some of the more intriguing features of Microsoft Word. By the end of the course you will know how to conduct a mail merge, set up a document in columns, include headers and footers, and insert pictures.

March **Microsoft Word 3**

This final course in the Microsoft Word series covers the advanced features. By the end of this course you will know how to work with tables, create and modify outlines, use e-mail and Internet features in Word, and share documents with other users.

Instructors

Word 1 The instructor for the introductory Word class is Cathy Bennett. Ms. Bennett has ten years of experience in computer training.

Word 2 Joseph Castaldy is the instructor for the intermediate Word class. Mr. Castaldy has been involved in computer training for eight years.

Word 3 Mary Rose Jarvis will be teaching the advanced Word class. Ms. Jarvis is one of the most highly regarded corporate trainers in Arizona. She has more than twelve years of corporate training experience.

We have hired the most qualified corporate trainers available in the state of Arizona to teach these classes. Class size is limited in order to maximize the amount of instruction delivered to each student, so please reserve your space as soon as possible. All classes will be held at corporate headquarters.

For more information call: 602-555-4326 ext. 343.

On Your Own

1. Create a new document in Word.
2. Save the file as OWDRESUME.
3. Think of some documents that could benefit from line spacing, paragraph spacing, and indent formatting. For example, many instructors require reports and papers to be double spaced. First drafts of documents that will be read by others should be double spaced so reviewers can jot notes or make corrections. A resume can be set up neatly using spacing and indent features, as can a reference list.
4. Create a resume describing your school experience, outside activities such as clubs or athletic teams, and any work experience.
5. Use spacing and indent features to format the resume.
6. Use alignments and font formatting to enhance the text and to call attention to important items.
7. Use lists and symbols if appropriate.
8. Save your changes, close the document, and exit Word.

Exercise 28

Skills Covered:

◆ **Format a One-page Report** ◆ **Set Margins** ◆ **Set Page Orientation**

On the Job

Format a one-page report so that when you print the report it looks good on the page. Set margins to meet expected requirements and to improve the document's appearance and readability. For example, leave a wider margin in a report if you expect a reader to make notes or comments; leave a narrower margin to fit more text on a page.

New clients may want to know the history of a company. In this exercise, you'll create a one-page report providing background information about Wayland Home Health Care Associates, Inc. The report will be used as part of an information package sent to prospective clients.

Terms

Gutter Space added to the margin to leave room for binding.

Margins The amount of white space between the text and the edge of the page on all four sides.

Section In Word, a segment of a document defined by a section break. A section may have different page formatting from the rest of the document.

Portrait orientation The default position for displaying and printing text horizontally across the shorter side of a page.

Landscape orientation Rotating document text so it displays and prints horizontally across the longer side of a page.

Notes

Format a One-page Report

- Traditionally, a one-page report is set up as follows:
  - Text starts 2" from the top of the page.
  - Text is justified.
  - Lines are double spaced.
  - First-line indents are .5" or 1".
  - The report title is centered and all uppercase.
  - Spacing following the title ranges from ¾" (54 pts.) to 1" (72 pts.).
  - Unbound reports have left and right margins of 1".
  - A **gutter** on bound reports makes the left margin wider than right margin.

✓ *Use the Mirror margins option to set gutter width on inside margin of each page.*

Set Margins

- **Margins** are measured in inches.
- Default margins are 1.25" on the left and right and 1" on the top and bottom.
- Margin settings affect an entire document, or the current **section**.

✓ *To set margins for a paragraph that are different from the page margins, use indents as described in Exercise 27.*

- On the rulers, areas outside the margins are shaded gray, while areas inside the margins are white.

  ✓ *To see both vertical and horizontal rulers, use Print Layout view.*

- Light gray bars mark the margins on the rulers.

Set Page Orientation

- There are two page orientations available:
  - **Portrait**
  - **Landscape**

- Portrait is the default orientation, and is used for most documents, including letters, memos, and reports.
- Use landscape orientation to display a document across the wider length of the page. For example, if a document contains a table that is wider than the standard 8.5" page, Word will split it across two pages. When you change to landscape orientation, the table will fit on the 11" page.

Procedures

Set Margins in Print Layout View

1. Move the mouse pointer over the margin marker on the ruler.

   ✓ *The mouse pointer changes to a double-headed arrow ⟷, and the ScreenTip identifies the margin.*

2. Drag the margin marker to new location.

   ✓ *Press and hold the Alt key while you drag to see the margin width.*

Set Margins in Any View

1. Click **File** .... Alt+F
2. Click **Page Setup** .... U
3. Click **Margins** tab........ Alt+M
4. Click **Top** text box .... Alt+T
5. Type top margin width.
6. Click **Bottom** text box .... Alt+B
7. Type bottom margin width.
8. Click **Left** text box .... Alt+F
9. Type left margin width.
10. Click **Right** text box .... Alt+H
11. Type right margin width.
12. Click the **Apply to** drop-down arrow .... Alt+Y
13. Select **This point forward.**

    OR

    Select **Whole document.**
14. Click **OK** .... Enter

Set Page Orientation

1. Click **File**...................... Alt+F
2. Click **Page Setup** .... U
3. Click **Margins** tab .... Alt+M
4. Click **Portrait** .... P

   OR

   Click **Landscape**................. S
5. Click **OK** .... Enter

Exercise Directions

1. Start Word, if necessary.
2. Type the document shown in Illustration A, or open 28WAYLAND.
3. Save the file as WAYLAND.
4. Use the following steps to format the document as shown in the illustration.
5. Set 1" margins on all sides.
6. Apply the Heading 1 style to the title, and then center it.
7. Change the spacing to leave 1" (72 pts.)of space before the title and .75" (54 pts.) of space after the title.
8. Justify and double space all body text paragraphs, and apply a .5" first line indent.
9. Apply the Heading 3 style to the subheadings.
10. Format the list of services as a bulleted list, and single space it.
11. Leave 12 pts. of space before the first item in the list and after the last item in the list.
12. If the document extends onto a second page, change the bottom margin to .75".
13. Check the spelling and grammar.
14. Change the page orientation to Landscape.
15. Display the document in Print Preview. It should extend on to two pages.
16. Print the document.
17. Change the page orientation back to Portrait.
18. Preview the document the again. It should look similar to Illustration A.
19. Print the document.
20. Close the document, saving all changes.
21. Exit Word.

Illustration A

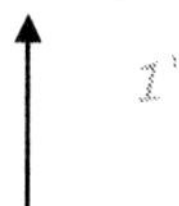

Heading 1

Wayland Home Health Care

72 pts, space before
54 pts, space after

Justified, Double-spaced, 1" line indent

Wayland Home Health Care has been providing quality nursing and rehabilitative care for over twenty years. Based in St. Louis, Missouri, the company was started by Marie Wayland, a Registered Nurse Practitioner. She recognized a need in the community for a full-service home health care company staffed with trained professionals who respect and care for their clients.

Staff

Heading 3

At Wayland Home Health Care, we recognize that trusting your caregiver is a vital part of any recuperation process. All of our staff are thoroughly screened, checked, and insured. In addition to registered nurses, we employ nurses' aides, home health aides, clinical nurse specialists, therapists, and clinical social workers. We offer an affordable, reliable, and convenient solution to all of your home health care needs.

1" ← → *1"*

Services

Heading 3

Call Wayland Home Health Care for any of the following:

12 pts.

- Elder care
- Sick child care
- Rehabilitation therapy
- Respite care
- Counseling
- Hospice care
- Homemakers

Bullet list, single spaced

12 pts.

Wayland Home Health care can provide daily or long-term care in either a live-in or live-out situation. Call us for more information, or to arrange a free, confidential in-home consultation. When you call Wayland, you can rest assured.

.75"

On Your Own

1. Create a new document in Word.
2. Save the file as 28OWDABOUT.
3. In the third person, draft a one-page report about yourself. For example, draft a document that you could include in a directory for an organization of which you are a member. Think of the *About the Author* paragraphs found in books and magazines, or the *About the Performers* paragraphs found in a theater program.
4. Double space the report.
5. Use correct document formatting for a one-page report.
6. Use other formatting effects, including fonts, lists, and symbols.
7. Change the orientation to Landscape.
8. Preview and then print the report.
9. Change back to Portrait orientation.
10. Close the document, saving all changes.
11. Exit Word.

Exercise 29

Skills Covered:

◆ **Create Footnotes and Endnotes**

On the Job

Include footnotes or endnotes in documents to provide information about the source of quoted material, or to supplement the main text.

You have been working to complete a report for Wayland Home Health Care Associates, Inc. In this exercise, you will insert footnotes and endnotes into a version of the report you created in Exercise 28.

Terms

Footnote An explanation or reference to other material printed at the bottom of a page.

Endnote An explanation or reference to other material printed at the end of a document.

Citation A reference to the source of quoted material.

Note reference mark A number or character inserted in the document to refer to footnote or endnote text.

Note text The text of the footnote or endnote citation.

Notes

Create Footnotes and Endnotes

- **Footnotes** or **endnotes** are required in documents that include quoted source material, such as research papers.
- Standard footnotes and endnotes include the following **citation** information:
  - The author of the quoted material (first name first) followed by a comma.
  - The title of the book (in italics) or the article (in quotation marks), followed by a comma.
  - The name of the publication if a magazine or journal (in italics).
  - The publication volume, number and/or date (the date in parentheses) followed by a colon.
  - The page number(s) where the material is located, followed by a period.
  - If the source is a Web page, the citation should also include the URL address, enclosed in angle brackets <>.

    ✓ *Word may automatically format the URL address as a hyperlink, and remove the angle brackets. If so, use the Undo command to remove the automatic formatting. Alternatively, right-click the hyperlink text and choose Remove Hyperlink from the shortcut menu, then retype the brackets.*

    ✓ *There are other styles used for footnotes and endnotes. For example, some use periods between parts instead of commas. If you are unsure which style to use, ask your instructor for more information.*
- Footnotes or endnotes can also provide explanations or supplement text. For example, an asterisk footnote might provide information about where to purchase a product mentioned in the text.

- When you insert a footnote, Word first inserts a **note reference mark** in the text, then a separator line following the last line of text on the page, and finally inserts the note number corresponding to the note mark below the separator line. You then type and format the **note text**.

Footnotes at the bottom of a page

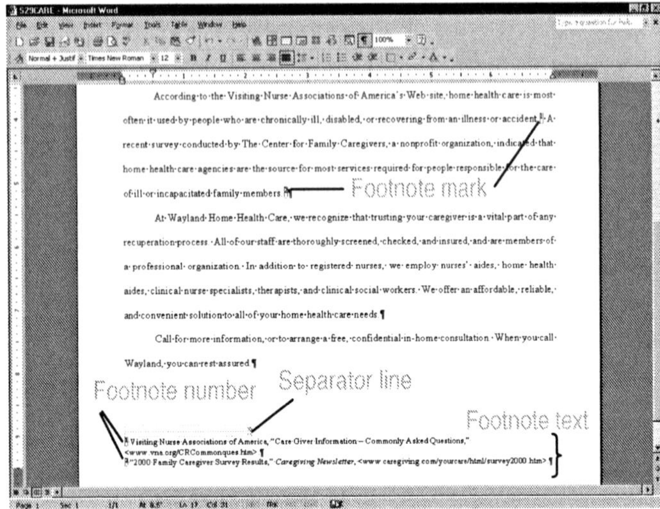

- Endnotes include the same parts as footnotes but are printed on the last page of a document.
- In a one-page document, the endnotes are printed at the end of the text, and the footnotes are printed at the bottom of the page. If you want your endnotes to begin on a separate page, you can insert a page break at the end of the document.
- Footnotes and endnotes are not displayed in Normal view; to see them, use Print Preview or Print Layout view.
- Notes can be displayed in a ScreenTip by resting the mouse pointer on the note reference mark.
- It is easiest to insert footnotes or endnotes in Print Layout view.
- Word uses arabic numerals for footnote marks; if endnotes are used in the same document, the marks are roman numerals.
- You can select a different number format or a symbol for the note mark.
  - ✓ *By default, numbering is consecutive from the beginning of the document. You can set Word to restart numbering on each page or each section. You can also change the starting number if you want.*
- Word automatically updates numbering if you add or delete footnotes or endnotes, or rearrange the document text.

Footnote and Endnote dialog box

Procedures

Footnotes and Endnotes

To insert footnotes in Print Layout view:

1. Position insertion point after text to footnote.
2. Click **Insert** .... Alt+I
3. Click **Reference** .... N
4. Click **Footnote** .... N
5. Click the **Footnote** option button .... Alt+F
6. Click **Insert** .... Alt+I
7. Type note text.
8. Click in document text .... Shift+F5

To insert endnotes in Print Layout view:

1. Position insertion point after text to endnote.
2. Click **Insert** .... Alt+I
3. Click **Reference** .... N
4. Click **Footnote** .... N

5. Click the **Endnote** option button .... Alt+E
6. Click **Insert** .... Alt+I
7. Type note text.
8. Click in document text .... Shift+F5

Display Note Text in ScreenTip

1. Click **Tools**.................. Alt+T
2. Click **Options**....................... O
3. Click **View** tab .... Ctrl+Tab
4. Select **ScreenTips** check box..................... Alt+N
5. Click **OK**.......................... Enter
6. Rest mouse pointer on note reference mark in text.

Edit a Footnote or Endnote

1. Double-click note reference mark in text.
   - ✓ *The insertion point automatically moves to the note text.*
2. Edit footnote or endnote text.
3. Click in document text .. Shift+F5

Delete a Footnote or Endnote

1. Position insertion point to the right of note reference mark in text.
2. Press **Backspace** ...... Backspace
   - ✓ *Mark is selected.*
3. Press **Backspace** ...... Backspace
   - ✓ *Note is deleted.*

Change the Footnote or Endnote Mark in Print Layout View

1. Position insertion point after text to footnote.
2. Click **Insert** .... Alt+I
3. Click **Reference** .... N
4. Click **Footnote** .... N
5. Click the **Footnote** ...... Alt+F or **Endnote** .... Alt+E option button.
6. Click the **Custom Mark** option button................ Alt+C
7. Type character in text box.

   OR

   a. Click **Symbol**.......... Alt+S
   b. Select desired font ...... Alt+F, ↓, Enter
   c. Click symbol to use.
   d. Click **OK** .... Enter
8. Click **Insert** .... Alt+I
9. Type note text.
10. Click in document text............................. Shift+F5

Exercise Directions

1. Start Word, if necessary.
2. Open 29CARE.
3. Save the file as CARE.
4. Position the insertion point after the first sentence in the second paragraph and insert a footnote as follows:

   Visiting Nurse Associations of America, "Care Giver Information - Commonly Asked Questions," <www.vna.org/CRCommonques.htm>.

   - Remove the hyperlink and retype the angle brackets, if necessary.
5. At the end of the of the second paragraph, insert the following footnote:

   "2000 Family Caregiver Survey Results," *Caregiving Newsletter*, <www.caregiving.com/yourcare/html/survey2000.htm>.
6. After the second sentence in the third paragraph, insert the following endnote:

   For more information, contact the American Home Care Association at www.amercanhca.org.

   - Again, remove the hyperlink and retype the angle brackets, if necessary.
7. Change the left and right margins to .75".
8. Check the spelling and grammar in the document and correct errors as necessary.
9. Display the document in Print Preview. It should look similar to the one in the illustration.
10. Close Print Preview.
11. Delete the endnote.
12. Print the document.
13. Close the document, saving all changes.

Wayland Home Health Care

Wayland Home Health Care has been providing quality nursing and rehabilitative care for over twenty years. Based in St. Louis, Missouri, the company was started by Marie Wayland, a registered nurse practitioner. She recognized a need in the community for a full-service home health care company staffed with trained professionals who respect and care for their clients.

According to the Visiting Nurse Associations of America's Web site, home health care is most often it used by people who are chronically ill, disabled, or recovering from an illness or accident.[1] A recent survey conducted by The Center for Family Caregivers, a nonprofit organization, indicated that home health care agencies are the source for most services required for people responsible for the care of ill or incapacitated family members.[2]

At Wayland Home Health Care, we recognize that trusting your caregiver is a vital part of any recuperation process. All of our staff are thoroughly screened, checked, and insured, and are members of a professional organization.[i] In addition to registered nurses, we employ nurses' aides, home health aides, clinical nurse specialists, therapists, and clinical social workers. We offer an affordable, reliable, and convenient solution to all of your home health care needs.

Call for more information, or to arrange a free, confidential in-home consultation. When you call Wayland, you can rest assured.

---

[i] For more information, contact the American Home Care Association at www.amercanhca.org.

---

[1] Visiting Nurse Associations of America, "Care Giver Information – Commonly Asked Questions," <www.vna.org/CRCommonques.htm>.

[2] "2000 Family Caregiver Survey Results," *Caregiving Newsletter*, <www.caregiving.com/yourcare/html/survey2000.htm>.

On Your Own

1. Open the document 28OWDABOUT that you used in the On Your Own section of Exercise 28, or open 29OWDABOUT.
2. Save the document as 29OWDABOUT2.
3. Insert at least two footnotes or endnotes to provide citations or to supplement text with additional information.
4. If necessary, adjust the margins so the document still fits on one page.
5. Print the document.
6. Close the document, saving all changes.

Exercise 30

Skills Covered:

◆ **Create Hyperlinks**

On the Job

Create a hyperlink to connect related documents to each other, to connect a Word document to a Web site, or to connect one location in a document to another location in the same document. For example, create hyperlinks from a table of contents in a report to each chapter heading or from a report topic to an Internet site where more information can be found. Hyperlinks let you expand the boundaries among documents and among computers because, in effect, you can link to information stored anywhere on the Internet.

In this exercise, you will work with a variation of the training course document you created for Highland Property Management Co. You will insert hyperlinks to help readers navigate through the document. You will also insert a hyperlink to an existing Word document describing what employees should expect from in-house training.

Terms

Hyperlink Text or graphics linked to a destination file or location. Click the link to jump to the destination.

Hyperlink destination The location displayed when the hyperlink is clicked.

HTML The file format used to store documents on the World Wide Web.

Hyperlink source The document where the hyperlink is inserted.

Bookmark A nonprinting character that you insert and name so that you can quickly find a particular location in a document.

Notes

Create Hyperlinks

- **Hyperlinks** can be used to link locations within a single document, to link two documents, or to link a document to an e-mail address.
- The **hyperlink destination** can be a file stored on your computer, on your company intranet, or a site on the Internet.
- Hyperlinks can be created in any Word document including Word documents saved as **HTML** files.

  ✓ *You learn how to save a Word document as an HTML file in Exercise 60.*

- You can change existing text to a hyperlink or type new text to create a hyperlink.
- A hyperlink destination does not have to be in the same file format as the **hyperlink source** document. For example, you can link a Word document file to an HTML file or to an Excel file.
- When you click a hyperlink to an e-mail address, Word starts your e-mail program and displays a new e-mail message. The address and subject are filled in with the hyperlink information.

  ✓ *You learn about using e-mail in Word in Exercise 69.*

- You can create a hyperlink within a document for moving to the top of the document, to a specific heading, or to a **bookmark**.
  - ✓ *Bookmarks are covered in Exercise 55.*

The Insert Hyperlink dialog box

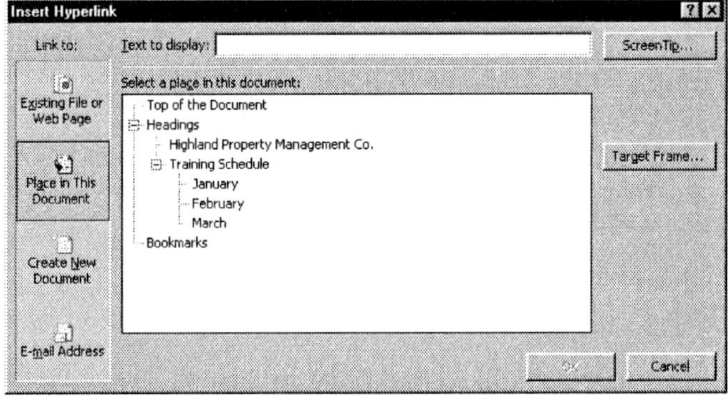

- Word uses its AutoFormat feature to format URLs typed in a document as hyperlinks.
- By default, in Word documents (including those saved in HTML) you must press Ctrl and click the hyperlink in order to go to the hyperlink destination.
- You can change the setting so that you don't have to press Ctrl.
- You can edit and format hyperlink text the same way you edit and format regular text.
  - ✓ *If you change the setting so that you don't have to press Ctrl to click to follow a hyperlink, you must select the hyperlink before you can edit it or format it.*
- You can change a hyperlink destination.
- You can remove a hyperlink completely.

Procedures

Insert a Hyperlink Within a Document

1. Position insertion point where you want to insert hyperlink.

   OR

   Select text to change to a hyperlink.
2. Click **Insert Hyperlink** button .

   OR

   a. Click **Insert** .... Alt+I

   b. Click **Hyperlink**.............. I
3. Click **Place in this document** in Link to bar .... Alt+A
4. In the **Select a place in this document list**, click hyperlink destination............ Alt+C, ↓
   - ✓ *If necessary click the expand symbol + to expand the list to show additional headings and/or bookmarks.*
5. Click **OK**.......................... Enter
   - ✓ *If existing text is not selected, Word uses the destination name as the hyperlink text.*

Insert a Hyperlink to a Different Document

1. Position insertion point where you want to insert hyperlink.

   OR

   Select text to change to a hyperlink.
2. Click **Insert Hyperlink** button .

   OR

   a. Click **Insert**............ Alt+I

   b. Click **Hyperlink**............. I
3. Click **Existing File or Web Page** in the Link to bar .... Alt+X
4. In the **Address** text box, type the hyperlink destination file name..................... Alt+E
   - ✓ *Word automatically completes the file name as you type based on recently used file names; stop typing to accept the entry or keep typing to enter the name you want.*

   OR

   a. Click **Current Folder** .... Alt+U to display a list of files stored in the current folder.

   b. Click the file name in the list of files.

   OR

   a. Click **Recent Files** . Alt+C to display a list of recently used files.

   b. Click the file name in the list of files.

   OR

   a. Click **Browse for File** button .

   b. Locate and click file name.

   c. Click **OK** .... Enter
5. Edit **Text to display** .... Alt+T
   - ✓ *Word displays this text as the hyperlink in the document.*
6. Click **OK** .... Enter

Insert a Hyperlink to a Web Page

1. Position insertion point where you want to insert the hyperlink.

   OR

   Select text to change to a hyperlink.
2. Click **Insert Hyperlink** button .

   OR

a. Click **Insert** .... Alt+I

b. Click **Hyperlink**.............. I

3. Click **Existing File or Web Page** in Link to bar...... Alt+X

4. In the **Address** text box, type the hyperlink destination URL............ Alt+E, *type URL*

   ✓ *Word automatically completes the URL as you type based on other URLs you have typed in the past. Stop typing to accept the entry, or keep typing to enter the URL you want.*

   OR

   a. Click **Browsed Pages** .... Alt+B to display a list of Web pages you have recently accessed.

   b. Click the URL or site name you want in the list of files.

5. Edit **Text to display**........................ Alt+T

   ✓ *Type the text you want displayed for the hyperlink. Word displays this text as the hyperlink.*

6. Click **OK**........................... Enter

Insert a Hyperlink to an E-Mail Address

1. Position insertion point where you want to insert the hyperlink.

   OR

   Select text to change to a hyperlink.

2. Click **Insert Hyperlink** button .

   OR

   a. Click **Insert**............. Alt+I

   b. Click **Hyperlink**.............. I

3. Click **E-mail address** in Look in bar .... Alt+M

4. In the **E-mail address** text box, type the e-mail address........................ Alt+E

   ✓ *This address will be inserted in the To line of the e-mail message.*

   OR

   a. Click the address in the **Recently** used e-mail addresses list........ Alt+C, ↓, Enter

   b. In the **Subject** text box, type the text you want displayed in the e-mail Subject text box... Alt+U, *type text*

5. Click **OK**.......................... Enter

Remove a Hyperlink

1. Right-click hyperlink text.
2. Click **Remove Hyperlink**..... R

   ✓ *This removes hyperlink, not the text.*

Change a Hyperlink Destination

1. Right-click hyperlink text.
2. Click **Edit Hyperlink**............ H
3. Select new destination.
4. Click **OK**........................... Enter

Set Word to Follow Hyperlink On Click

1. Click **Tools** .... Alt+T
2. Click **Options** .... O
3. Click **Edit** tab .... Ctrl+Tab
4. Deselect **Use CTRL+Click to follow hyperlink** check box....................................... H
5. Click **OK**........................... Enter

Select a Hyperlink

1. Right-click hyperlink text.
2. Click **Select Hyperlink**........ S

Exercise Directions

1. Start Word, if necessary.
2. Open 30TRAIN.
3. Save the file as TRAIN.
4. Insert a new line at the top of the document and clear all formatting from it.
5. Increase the font size to 16 points and type the text **RETURN**, and then press Enter.
6. Close the document, saving all changes.
7. Open the file 30COURSE.
8. Save the file as INHOUSE.
9. Edit and format the document as follows.
   ✓ *Refer to Illustration A to see the completed document.*
10. Position the insertion point at the end of the heading **Training Schedule** and press Enter.
11. Type **January** and press Enter.
12. Type **February** and press Enter.
13. Type **March** and press Enter twice.
14. Type **Click here to read about in-house training**. and press Enter.
15. Insert a hyperlink from the text **January** that you typed in step 11 to the heading **January**.
16. Insert a hyperlink from the text **February** that you typed in step 12 to the heading **February**.
17. Insert a hyperlink from the text **March** that you typed in step 13 to the heading **March**.
18. At the end of each course description paragraph, press Enter and type **Return to Top.** (Include the ending period, as shown in the illustration.)
19. Insert hyperlinks from each occurrence of **Return to Top** to the top of the document.
20. Insert a hyperlink from the text you typed in step 14 to the TRAIN document.
21. Increase the font size of all hyperlink text to 16 points.
22. Test the hyperlinks to navigate through the INHOUSE document.
    ✓ *Word's Web toolbar may be displayed.*
23. Test the hyperlink to go to the TRAIN document.
24. Insert a hyperlink from the text **RETURN** at the top of the document, back to the INHOUSE document.
25. Test the hyperlink to return to the INHOUSE document.
26. Close all open documents, saving all changes.

Illustration A

Highland Property Management Co.

575 W. Osborne Street, Phoenix, AZ 85013 602-555-4326

Training Schedule

January
February
March

Click here to learn about in-house training.

January

Microsoft Word 1

This introductory course will cover the basics of using Microsoft Word to create common business documents. By the end of the course you will know how to: create and print text-based documents such as letters and envelopes, and apply formatting.

Return to Top.

February

Microsoft Word 2

A continuation of the Word I course, this introductory level class will delve into some of the more intriguing features of Microsoft Word. By the end of the course you will know how to conduct a mail merge, set up a document in columns, include headers and footers, and insert pictures.

Return to Top.

March

Microsoft Word 3

This final course in the Microsoft Word series covers the advanced features. By the end of this course you will know how to work with tables, create and modify outlines, use e-mail and Internet features in Word, and share documents with other users.

Return to Top.

For more information call: 602-555-4326 ext. 343.

On Your Own

1. Open the document OWDABOUT2, the one-page report about yourself that you used in the On Your Own section of Exercise 29, or open 30OWDABOUT2.
2. Save the file as OWDABOUT3.
3. Open the document 27OWDRESUME, the resume you created in the On Your Own section of Exercise 27, or open 30OWDRESUME.
4. Save the file as OWDRESUME2, and then close it.
5. Create a hyperlink from the OWDABOUT3 report document to the OWDRESUME2 resume document.
6. Create a link back to the report from the resume.
7. Create a link from the bottom of the OWDABOUT3 document to the top of the document.

   ✓ *If you have access to the Internet, you might want to try linking the report to a Web site that you like.*
8. Test the links.
9. Close all open documents, saving all changes.

Exercise 31

◆ Critical Thinking

You have applied for a job as a marketing assistant at Pelican Peter's dive shop. To get an idea about the quality of your work, the owner has asked you to provide two documents. The first is a one-page report detailing ways you think you could increase his business. The second is an advertisement. In this exercise, you will create the report, as well as a sample advertisement. You will include a footnote, and you will link the two documents together.

Exercise Directions

1. Start Word, if necessary.
2. Open 31AD1.
3. Save the document as AD1.
4. Follow steps 5 through 13 to edit and format the document to achieve the result shown in Illustration A.
5. Change the left and right margins to 1".
6. Change the top margin to .5" and the bottom margin to .75".
7. Apply the heading 1 style to the two lines of the title, and then modify the spacing to leave 1" (72 pts.) of space above the title, no space between the lines, and .75" (54 pts.) of space after the title.
8. Center the title.
9. Format all body text paragraphs as follows:
   - 14-point sans serif font
   - Justified
   - Double spaced
   - First line indented by .5"
   - Leave 6 points of space after
10. Apply the Heading 3 style to the two headings.
11. Format the five ad outlets as follows:
    - Numbered list
    - Single spaced
    - No space between items
    - Leave 6 points of space after the fifth item
12. Format the three benefits of using the Web as follows:
    - Bulleted list
    - Single spaced
    - No space between.
    - Double indent 1" from the left and the right margins
13. Justify the document vertically on the page.
14. Create the footnote shown in the illustration.
15. Preview the document. It should look similar to the document in Illustration A.
16. Print the document.
17. Save the document and close it.
18. Create a new document in Word and save it as AD2.
19. Type and format the document shown in Illustration B.
20. Create a hyperlink from the text **CLICK HERE** on the last line of the AD2 to the AD1 document.
21. Test the hyperlink.
22. Create a hyperlink from the first item in the numbered list on the AD1 document to the AD2 document.
23. Test the hyperlink.
24. Close all open documents, saving all changes.

Illustration A

Pelican Peter's Dive Shop
Business Improvement Plan

In today's highly competitive marketplace, there are many steps a small business can take to increase profits. The following report outlines two actions that the owner of Pelican Peter's Dive Shop can take to quickly improve business.

ADVERTISING

The fastest method of increasing visibility is to increase the store's advertising in the local arena.[1] This will provide a way to reach tourists as well as to local residents. Pelican Peter's should consider the following advertising outlets:

1. <u>Print ads in all local newspapers</u>
2. Radio spots
3. T.V. spots on local cable
4. Flyers
5. Direct mail advertising

WEB SITE DEVELOPMENT

The second method recommended for increasing both visibility and business is to develop a presence on the World Wide Web. A web site could provide the following benefits:

- ✓ Provide communication with customers via e-mail
- ✓ Advertise special events and sales
- ✓ Provide an additional retail outlet

---

[1] Based on personal experience.

Illustration B

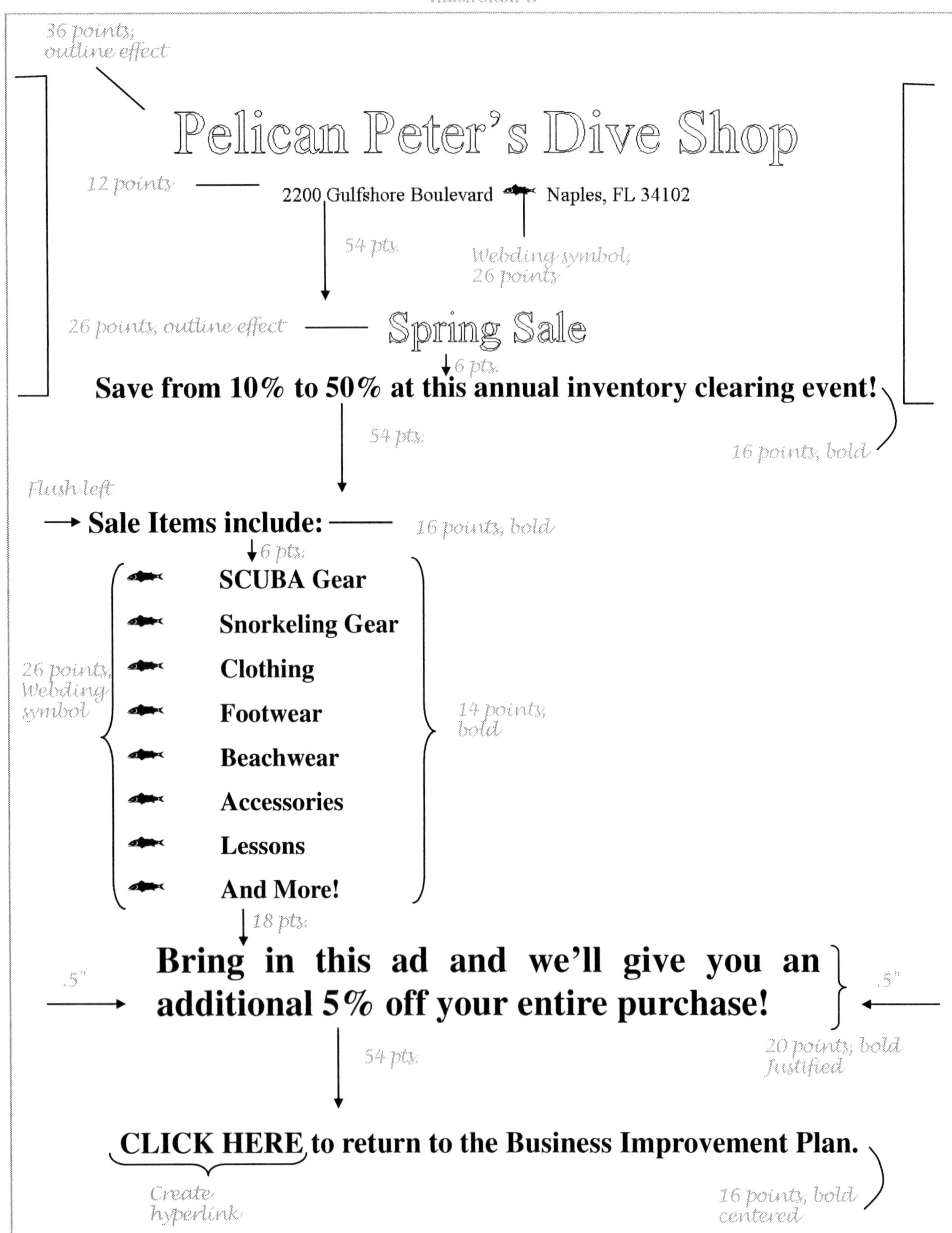

Lesson 6

Manage Documents

Exercise 32

- Open a Document as Read-only
- Open a Document from Windows
- File Types

Exercise 33

- Preview a Closed Document
- Print Files without Opening Them

Exercise 34

- Document Properties

Exercise 35

- Use Basic Search to Find a File

Exercise 36

- Critical Thinking

Exercise 32

Skills Covered:

◆ **Open a Document as Read-only**

◆ **Open a Document from Windows** ◆ **File Types**

On the Job

Word offers many options for opening a document. For example, open a document as read-only when you do not want revisions to affect the original file. (You must save the file with a new name in order to save changes.) You can use Windows features to open a document and start Word at the same time, and you can use Word to open files created with different programs.

The Director of Training at Highland Property Management Co. has asked you to update the current course list for the spring. In addition to making the changes she has requested, you want to propose changing the course names. In this exercise, you will open the document using Windows. You will make the required changes, and then close the document. You will then open the document as read-only, so that you cannot make changes accidentally. You will modify the file, and then save it in text only format so it can be opened using a different program.

Terms

Read-only A mode of operation in which revisions cannot be saved in the original document.

File type The format in which the file is stored. Usually, the file type corresponds to the program used to create the file.

File extension A dot followed by three or four characters attached to a file name, used to indicate the file type. For example, a *.doc* file extension indicates a Word document file.

File icon The icon used to represent a file in a file list, such as Windows Explorer or Word's Open dialog box.

Compatible file type A file type that Word can open, even though it was created and saved using a different program.

Notes

Open a Document as Read-only

- Opening a document as **read-only** is a safeguard against accidentally making changes.
- Word prompts you to use Save As to save revisions made to a document opened as read-only in a new document with a different file name.
- The words *Read-Only* appear in the title bar of a document opened as read-only.

Open a Document from Windows

- Use the Windows Start Menu to open a document and start Word at the same time.
  - Click Documents on the Start menu to select from a list of recently used files.
  - Locate and open any document using Windows Explorer.
  - Open a document using the Open Office Document command.

File Types

- Files are saved in different **file types**, depending on the application used to create, save, and open the file.
- In Windows and Windows applications, file types can be identified by the **file extension** and by the **file icon**.
- Word can open documents saved in **compatible file types**. For example, Word can open text files, Web page files, and files created with other versions of Word.
- You can save a compatible file in its original file type or as a Word document file.
- Some common file types include the following:
  - Word document files .doc
  - Word template files .dot
  - Text files .txt
  - Web pages .htm
  - Excel workbooks .xls
  - Access databases .mdb
  - PowerPoint presentations .ppt
- Word can also open many other types of files depending on the file conversion features you have installed. For example, you may be able to open WordPerfect files (.wpd) and rich text format files (.rtf).

  ✓ *File conversion features are installed during setup.*

Procedures

Open a Document as Read-only *(Ctrl+O)*

1. Click **Open** button.

   OR

   a. Click **File** .... Alt+F
   b. Click **Open** .... O
2. Click document name.
3. Click **Open** drop-down arrow.
4. Click **Open Read-Only** .... R

Open a Word Document from the Documents Menu

1. Click **Start** button ....
2. Select **Documents** .... D
3. Click document name.

Open a Word Document From Windows Explorer (⊞+E)

1. Right-click **Start** button.
2. Click **Explore** X
3. Select drive where folder/file is located.
4. Open folder.
5. Double-click document name that you want to open.

Open a Word Document from the Open Office Document Dialog Box

1. Click **Start** button ....
2. Click **Open Office Document** .... ↑↓, Enter
3. Locate and select desired file.
4. Click **Open** button .... Alt+O

Open a Compatible File Type *(Ctrl+O)*

1. Click **File** .... Alt+F
2. Click **Open** .... O
3. Click the **Look in** drop-down arrow .... Alt+I
4. Select the disk or folder.

   ✓ *Alternatively, click the folder you want to open in the Places bar.*
5. Click the **Files of type** drop-down arrow .... Alt+T
6. Click the file type.
7. Click the desired file name.
8. Click **Open** .... Alt+O

   ✓ *If the File Conversion dialog box is displayed, click OK.*

Save a Compatible File *(Ctrl+S)*

1. Open the compatible file.
2. Click **File** .... Alt+F
3. Click **Save** .... S
4. Click **Yes** .... Y

   to save the file in its original format.

   OR

   Click **No** .... N

   to save the file as a Word document.

Save a Compatible File as a New File in Word Format

1. Open the compatible file.
2. Click **File** .... Alt+F
3. Click **Save As** .... A
4. Click the **Files of type** drop-down arrow .... Alt+T
5. Click **Word document (*.doc)**.
6. Click the **File name** text box .... Alt+N
7. Type the new file name.
8. Click **Save** .... Alt+S

Exercise Directions

1. Without starting Word, open the document 32COURSE.
2. Save the file as NEWCOURSE1.
3. Edit the months **January**, **February**, and **March** to **April**, **May**, and **June**.
4. Close the document, saving all changes.
5. Open the document as read-only.
6. Change the April course title to **Beginning Word**.
7. Change the May course title to **Intermediate Word**.
8. Change the June course title to **Advanced Word**.
9. Try to save the changes.
   - ✓ *Word will display the Save As dialog box.*
10. Cancel the dialog box.
11. Save the document in plain text format, with the name NEWCOURSE2.
    - ✓ *If Word displays a warning or a file conversion dialog box, click OK.*
12. Close the document, saving all changes. If prompted, remember to save the file in text format, not Word format.
13. Open the NEWCOURSE2.TXT document in Word. The text file should look similar to the one in the illustration.
14. Close the file, saving all changes.

Illustration A

Highland Property Management Co.
575 W. Osborne Street, Phoenix, AZ 85013 602-555-4326
Training Schedule
April
Beginning Word

This introductory course will cover the basics of using Microsoft Word to create common business documents. By the end of the course you will know how to: create and print text-based documents such as letters and envelopes, and apply formatting.
May
Intermediate Word

A continuation of the Word I course, this introductory level class will delve into some of the more intriguing features of Microsoft Word. By the end of the course you will know how to conduct a mail merge, set up a document in columns, include headers and footers, and insert pictures.
June
Advanced Word

This final course in the Microsoft Word series covers the advanced features. By the end of this course you will know how to work with tables, create and modify outlines, use e-mail and Internet features in Word, and share documents with other users.

For more information call: 602-555-4326 ext. 343.

On Your Own

1. Open OWDACCOMPLISH, the file you created in the On Your Own section of Exercise 26, or open 32OWDACCOMPLISH.
2. Change some formatting in the document.
3. Save the document as OWDACCOMPLISH2, and then close it.
4. Open the file as read-only.
5. Make some changes to the document
6. Try saving the document.
7. Save the file in text format as OWDACCOMPLISH3.
8. Print the file.
9. Close the document, saving all changes.
10. Open the text file in Word.
11. Close the file.

Exercise 33

Skills Covered:

◆ **Preview a Closed Document**

◆ **Print Files without Opening Them**

On the Job

Preview a document before opening it or printing it to make sure it is the correct file. Print files without opening them to save time or to print more than one document at once.

You are the human resources assistant at Wayland Home Health Care Associates. The director of human resources has asked you to type a letter to a prospective employee confirming a job offer. In this exercise, you will preview, open and revise a one-page report about the company, and then you will create a letter to the applicant. Finally, you will print both documents.

Notes

Preview a Closed Document

- By default, Word displays a simple list of files in the Open dialog box.
- You can change the display in the dialog box to show a preview of the document selected in the file list.
- Previewing is useful for making sure a document is the one you want before you open it or print it.
- Most documents are too large to be displayed completely in the dialog box; use the scroll arrows in the preview area to scroll up and down.
- If you don't want to display a preview, you can set the Open dialog box to display large or small file icons, the default file list, file details, such as size, type, and date last saved, or document properties.

Preview a document in the Open dialog box

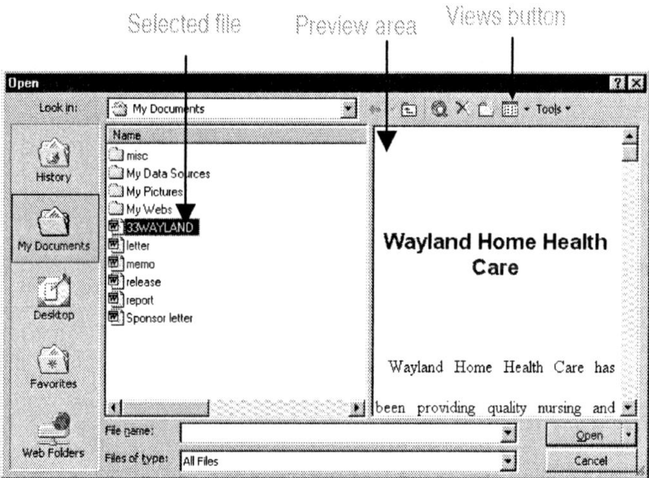

Print Files without Opening Them

- To save time, you can print a document from the Open dialog box without opening it.
- Print without opening when you are certain the document is ready for printing.

  ✓ *You can also print a document without opening it from the Open Office dialog box or from Windows Explorer.*

- You can select more than one file at a time for printing in the Open dialog box.
- Selecting multiple files for printing sends them all to the printer, where they will be printed one after the other.
- All selected files must be in the same folder.

Procedures

Preview a Closed Document

1. Click **File** .... Alt+F
2. Click **Open** .... O
3. Click **Views** button drop-down arrow.
4. Click **Preview** V
5. Click document name to preview.
   ✓ *If necessary, select drive and/or folder to locate document.*

To turn Preview off:

1. Click **File** .... Alt+F
2. Click **Open** .... O
3. Click **Views** button drop-down arrow.
4. Select another view:
   - Click **Large Icons** ... G
   - Click **Small Icons** ... M
   - Click **List** L
   - Click **Details** .... D
   - Click **Properties** .... R

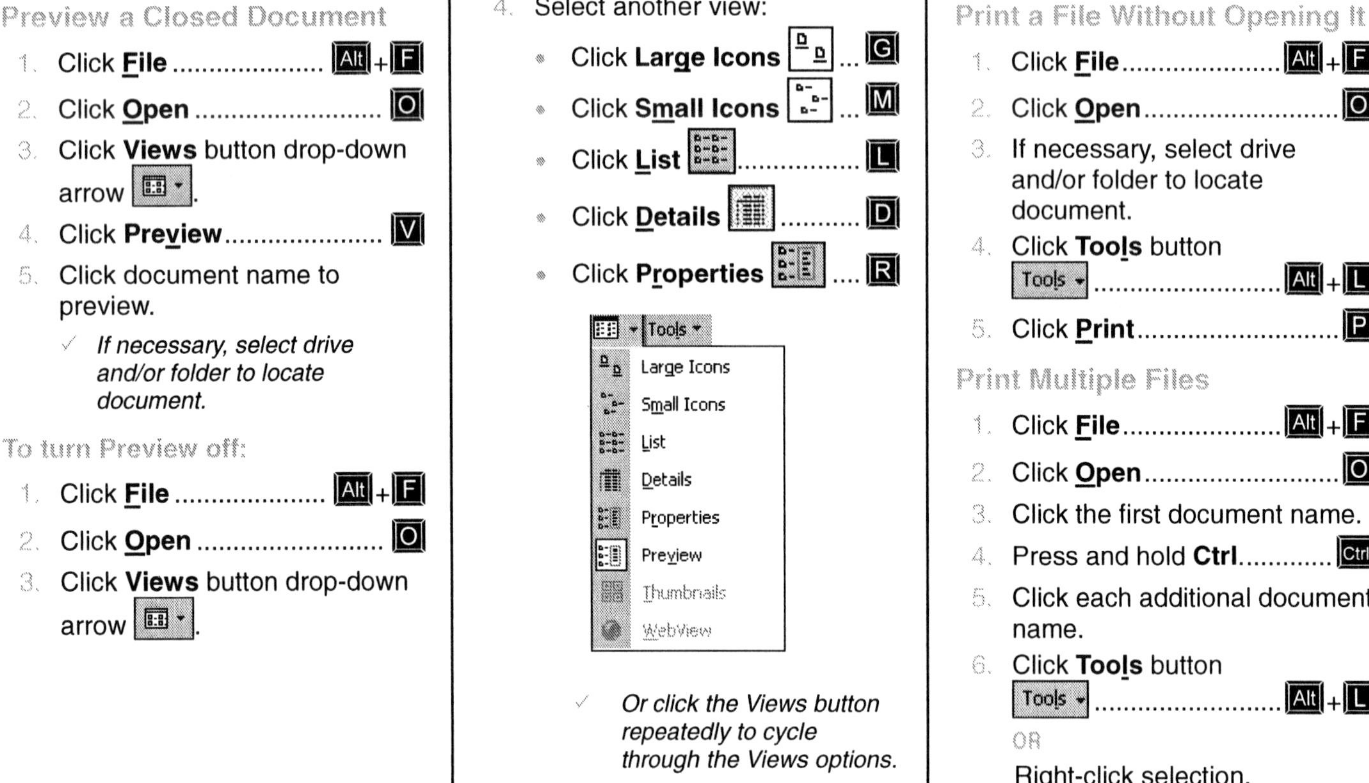

✓ *Or click the Views button repeatedly to cycle through the Views options.*

Print a File Without Opening It

1. Click **File** .... Alt+F
2. Click **Open** .... O
3. If necessary, select drive and/or folder to locate document.
4. Click **Tools** button Tools .... Alt+L
5. Click **Print** .... P

Print Multiple Files

1. Click **File** .... Alt+F
2. Click **Open** .... O
3. Click the first document name.
4. Press and hold **Ctrl**............ Ctrl
5. Click each additional document name.
6. Click **Tools** button Tools .... Alt+L

   OR

   Right-click selection.
7. Click **Print** .... P

Exercise Directions

1. Start Word, if necessary.
2. In the Open dialog box, preview WAYLAND, the document you created in Exercise 28, or preview 33WAYLAND.
3. This should be a one-page report about Wayland Home Health Care.
4. Change the Open dialog box to display details instead of the preview.
5. Open the document and save it as INFO.
6. Make revisions as indicated in Illustration A.
7. If necessary, shrink the document so it fits on one page.
8. Check the spelling and grammar in the document.
9. Close the document, saving all changes.
10. Create a new document and type the letter shown in Illustration B, or open 33LETTER.
11. Save the document as LETTER, and then close it.
12. Preview the document LETTER in the Open dialog box.
13. Print both the INFO and LETTER documents without opening them.

Illustration A

Associates, Inc.

Wayland Home Health Care

Associates

Wayland Home Health Care has been providing quality nursing and rehabilitative care for over twenty years. Based in St. Louis, Missouri, the company was started by Marie Wayland, a Registered Nurse Practitioner. She recognized a need in the community for a full-service home health care company staffed with trained professionals who respect and care for their clients.

Staff

At Wayland Home Health Care, we recognize that trusting your caregiver is a vital part of any recuperation process. All of our staff are thoroughly screened, checked, and insured. In addition to registered nurses, we employ nurses' aides, home health aides, clinical nurse specialists, therapists, and clinical social workers. We offer an affordable, reliable, and convenient solution to all of your home health care needs.

We only hire the best.

Services

Call Wayland Home Health Care for any of the following:

- Elder care
- ~~Sick child care~~
- Rehabilitation therapy
- Respite care
- Counseling
- Hospice care
- Homemakers

Wayland Home Health care can provide daily or long-term care in either a live-in or live-out situation. Call us for more information, or to arrange a free, confidential in-home consultation. When you call Wayland, you can rest assured.

Today's Date

Ms. Lillian Frankel, R.N.
6733 51st Street
St. Louis, MO 63101

Dear Ms. Frankel,

This letter is to confirm the offer of employment that I made to you this morning. Wayland Home Health Care Associates only hires the most qualified candidates, and I hope that you will join our staff. Your credentials seem impeccable, and your references all gave you glowing reports.

I have enclosed a brief report about Wayland Home Health Care. If you have any additional questions, please feel free to call me at any time, or to set up a meeting to discuss salary and benefits. I am confident that we can put together a package that you will find suitable.

Again, I hope you will accept our offer. Thank you very much for considering Wayland Home Health Care.

Sincerely,

Janice Lufton
Director of Human Resources

jl/yo

Enclosure

On Your Own

1. Start Word.
2. Preview some of the documents that you have created for the On Your Own sections of previous exercises, or preview 33OWDRESUME, 33OWDABOUT, and 33OWDGOALS.
3. Display details instead of the preview.
4. Display small icons.
5. Display the preview again.
6. Print at least two of the documents without opening them.
7. When you are finished, exit Word.

Exercise 34

Skills Covered:

◆ **Document Properties**

On the Job

Use document properties to identify important information about a file, such as the name of the author and the main topic.

The director of human resources at Wayland Health Care Associates has asked you to send an employment offer confirmation letter to another applicant. In this exercise, you will open the confirmation letter you wrote to a previous applicant as read-only, save it with a new name, and then modify it to send to the second applicant. You will enter document properties to help differentiate the letters.

Terms

Document Properties Categories of information about a document.

Keywords Important words found in a document. Keywords can be used to classify a document.

Notes

Document Properties

- With the **Document Properties** feature you can save information that is unique to a particular document.
- Using document properties can help you identify a document, or differentiate it from another similar document.
- Document Properties lets you enter information in five categories:
  - *General properties.* Allows you to view the type of document, its size, its location, when it was created, last accessed, and last modified. Use General properties to check file storage and access information.
  - *Summary properties.* Allows you to enter a document title, subject, author, **keywords**, and comments. Use Summary properties to save summary information with a document.
  - *Statistics properties.* Word automatically updates statistical information including the number of pages, paragraphs, lines, words, characters, and bytes in the document. Use Statistics properties to check the size length, or word count in a document.
  - *Contents properties.* Displays the headings in a document if the Save preview picture check box is selected on the Summary tab of the Document properties dialog box.
  - *Custom properties.* Allows you to specify a name, type and value which you can use to find and link files.
- You can set Word to display the Properties dialog box automatically the first time you save a document.

Procedures

Use Document Properties

1. Click **File** .... Alt+F
2. Click **Properties** I
   - Select desired tab .... Ctrl+Tab
3. Click **OK** .... Enter

Automatically Display Properties Dialog Box

1. Click **Tools** .... Alt+T
2. Click **Options** .... O
3. Click **Save** tab .... Ctrl+Tab
4. Select **Prompt for document properties** check box .... Alt+I
5. Click **OK** .... Enter

Exercise Directions

1. Start Word, if necessary.
2. Open LETTER or open 34LETTER as read-only.
3. Save the document as LETTER2.
4. Make the revisions indicated in Illustration A.
5. Save the file.
6. Use the Properties dialog box to check the number of words in the document.
7. Enter the following summary information:

   Title: **Letter to Ms. Nancy Valchois**

   Subject: **Employment offer**

   Author: **Your name**

   Manager: **Janice Lufton**

   Company: **Wayland Health Care Associates**

   Category: **Human Resources**

   Keywords: **licensed nurse practitioner, L.P.N., employment offer, personnel**

   Comments: **Follow up to verbal offer.**
8. Check the spelling and grammar in the document.
9. Print the document.
10. Close the document, saving all changes.

On Your Own

1. Open OWDACCOMPLISH2, the document you used in the On Your Own section of Exercise 32, as read-only, or open 34OWDACCOMPLISH2 as read-only.
2. Check the number of words in the document.
3. Note the file size, date created, and date last modified.
4. Enter document properties, including Title, Subject, Manager, Company, Category, Keywords, and Comments.
5. Try saving the document.
6. Save the document as OWDACCOMPLISH4.
7. Close the document and exit Word.

Illustration A

Today's Date

Ms. ~~Lillian Frankel, R.N.~~ Nancy Valchois, L.N.P.
~~6733 51st Street~~ 786 Montclair Avenue
St. Louis, MO 63101

Dear Ms. ~~Frankel,~~ Valchois,

This letter is to confirm the offer of employment that I made to you this morning. Wayland Home Health Care Associates only hires the most qualified candidates, and I hope that you will join our staff. Your credentials seem impeccable, and your references all gave you glowing reports.

I have enclosed a brief report about Wayland Home Health Care. If you have any additional questions, please feel free to call me at any time, or to set up a meeting to discuss salary and benefits. I am confident that we can put together a package that you will find suitable.

Again, I hope you will accept our offer. Thank you very much for considering Wayland Home Health Care.

Sincerely,

Janice Lufton
Director of Human Resources

jl/yo

Enclosure

Exercise 35

Skills Covered:

◆ **Use Basic Search to Find a File**

On the Job

Use Word's Search feature to locate and open a file stored anywhere on your computer system. You can even locate a file when you don't know the file name.

Fox Footwear, Inc., a maker of shoes, sneakers, and other footwear for teenagers and young adults, is getting ready to announce its second annual essay contest. The marketing director wants you to find a flyer created for last year's contest and modify it for the new contest. In this exercise, you will search for the file, open it, modify it, and print it.

Terms

Wildcard characters Typed characters that represent one or more other characters. For example, an asterisk (*) is used to represent any other character or string of characters.

Notes

Use Basic Search to Find a File

- Word has a Search feature that can help you find a file stored anywhere on your computer system, even if you can't remember the file name.
- Use a basic search to locate a file that contains specified text in its title, contents, or properties.
- Enter text in the Search text box to locate files containing that text. The text may be in the body of the file, or in the document properties.
  - Word finds files containing various forms of the search text. For example, if you enter *run*, Word finds documents containing *run*, *running*, or *ran*.
  - You can use **wildcard characters** in the search text.
    - * represents one or more characters.
    - ? Represents any single character.
- Before starting a search, select the disks or folders to search, as well as the types of files to search for. These can be on your hard drive or on a network.
  - If you know the folder to search, type it in the Search in box.
  - Alternatively, select the check box beside the folder(s) to search.
- In the Results should be box, select the types of files to find:
  - Anything. Finds all file types.
  - Office Files. Finds all files created with Microsoft Office programs. You can select the specific program type.
  - Outlook Items. Finds only files created with Microsoft Outlook.
  - Web Pages. Finds only Web page files.

- You can search using the Search task pane, or by opening the Search dialog box from the Open dialog box. Both methods offer you the same options.

Search task pane

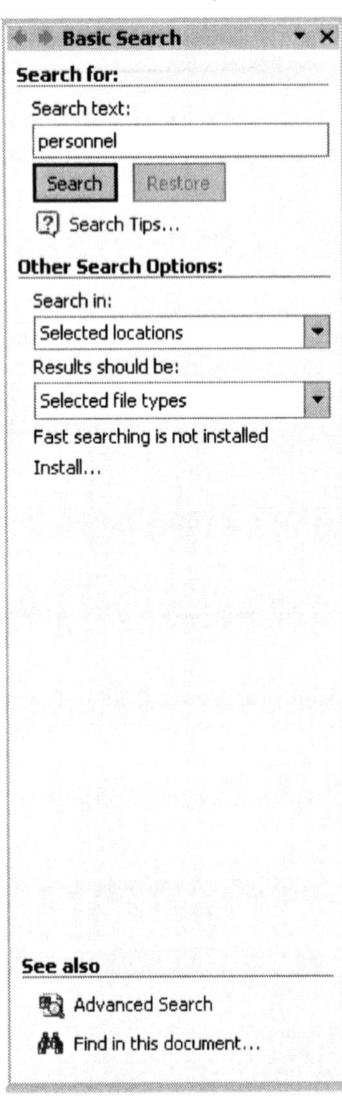

- Word displays files matching your criteria in the Search Results list.

Search Results in task pane

Procedures

Open the Basic Search Task Pane

1. Click **File** .... Alt+F
2. Click **Search** .... H

   OR

   Click **Search** button 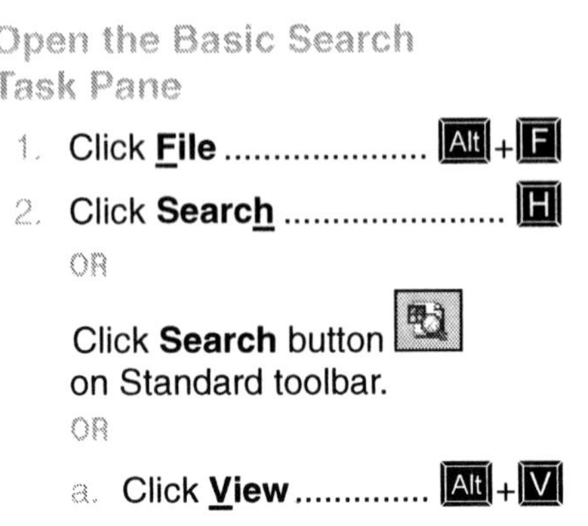 on Standard toolbar.

   OR

   a. Click **View** .... Alt+V
   b. Click **Task Pane** .... K
   c. Click **Other Task Panes** drop-down arrow .... Ctrl+↓
   d. Click **Search** .... ↓, Enter
3. If necessary, click **Basic Search** near bottom of task pane.

Search for Files from the Search Task Pane

1. Open Basic Search task pane.
2. Type search text in **Search text** box.
   - ✓ *If necessary, delete existing text, first.*
3. Click **Search in**: drop-down arrow to open list.
4. Select folders as follows:

- Click plus sign to expand list .... →
- Click check box to select folder .... Space
- Click check box twice to select folder and all subfolders .... Space **2x**
- Click check box three times to select only subfolders .... Space **3x**
- Click check box four times to deselect subfolders .... Space **4x**

5. Click **Search in**: drop-down arrow to close list.
6. Click **Results should be:** .... Tab, Space
7. Click plus sign to expand list .... ↓, →
8. Click desired file type(s) .... ↕, Space
9. Click **Results should be** drop-down arrow to close it.
10. Click **Search** button Search.
11. Click file to open.

    OR

    - Click **Modify** button Modify to display Basic Search Task Pane again.

✓ *To interrupt a search before it is complete, click the Stop button* Stop.

Search for Files from the Open Dialog Box

1. Click **File** .... Alt+F
2. Click **Open** .... O
3. Click the **Look in** drop-down arrow .... Alt+I
4. Select the disk, folder, or network.

   ✓ *Alternatively, click the folder you want to open in the Places bar.*
5. Click **Tools** drop-down arrow Tools ▾ .... Alt+L
6. Click **Search** .... S
7. Click **Basic** tab, if necessary .... Ctrl+Tab
8. Type search text in **Search text** box .... Alt+T

   ✓ *If necessary, delete existing text, first.*
9. Click **Search in**: drop-down arrow .... Alt+I
10. Select folders as follows:
    - Click plus sign to expand list .... →
    - Click check box to select folder .... ↕, Space
    - Click check box twice to select folder and all subfolders .... Space **2x**
    - Click check box three times to select only subfolders .... Space **3x**
    - Click check box four times to deselect subfolders . Space **4x**
11. Click **Results should be:** drop-down arrow .... Alt+B
12. Click plus sign to expand list .... ↓, →
13. Click desired file type(s) .... ↕, Space, Enter
14. Click **Search** .... Alt+S
15. Double-click file to open.

    OR

    a. Click file to open.

    b. Click **OK** .... Enter

    c. Word displays Open dialog box.

    d. Click **Open** .... Alt+O

Exercise Directions

✓ *Before beginning this exercise, make sure that the 35CONTEST.doc file is stored somewhere on your computer system. Ask your instructor for more information.*

1. Start Word, if necessary.
2. Search your computer for the file about the essay contest using the following steps:

   a. Open the Search task pane or the Search dialog box.

   b. Enter the Search text **Annual Contest**.

   c. Select the folder(s) to search. For example, if the file is stored locally, choose to search drive C, or My Computer. If the file is stored on a network, choose the network drive. The more you can narrow down the location, the faster the search will be.

   d. Select Word Files in the Files Should be list.

   e. Start the search.
3. Open the 35CONTEST.doc document from the Search Results list.

   ✓ *Word might find more than one document. If you open the wrong one, close it and try another.*
4. Save the file as CONTEST3.
5. Close the task pane.
6. Make the edits marked in Illustration A to the CONTEST3 document.
7. Check the spelling and grammar in the document.
8. Display the document in Print Preview.
9. Print the document.
10. Close the file, saving all changes.

Illustration A

FOX FOOTWEAR, INC.

Proudly Announces

Its ~~First~~ Annual
Second

ESSAY CONTEST

Topic:

~~ALL DRESSED UP WITH EVERYWHERE TO GO~~
Put Your Best Foot Forward

Open to teens 12 – 18 years old

Length: 1,000 - 1,500 words

Deadline: March 1

Winners will be announced June 1

The Grand Prize winner will receive a $2,500 scholarship and a personal computer. Other prizes include gift certificates, computer equipment, travel vouchers, and more. For more information contact: Mr. Pritchard at 415-555-3922, or consult the company's Web site: foxfootwear.com.

On Your Own

1. Search for one of the resume documents you have used in previous exercises.
2. Open the file as read-only.
3. Check the number of words in the document.
4. Note the file size, date created, and date last modified.
5. Enter document properties.
6. Try saving the document.
7. Save the file as OWDRESUME3.
8. Print the file.
9. Close the document, saving all changes.

Exercise 36

◆ Critical Thinking

Steven Johansson, the marketing director at Fox Footwear, has asked you to locate the press release used to announce the first annual essay contest and modify it for the new contest. He also wants you to save a copy of it in text format so he can take it home and use it with a different computer program. Finally, he wants you to print copies of the new press release and the flyer you created in the previous exercise.

Exercise Directions

1. Start Word, if necessary.
2. Search for and open the file 36CONTEST using the search text **Johansson**.
3. Save the file as FOXPRESS.
4. Make changes to the document as marked on Illustration A.
5. In the Document Properties summary tab, change the title to **Put Your Best Foot Forward**, and edit the comments from **First Annual** to **Second Annual**.
6. Check the spelling and grammar.
7. Save the changes.
8. Save the document in rich text format with the name RTFPRESS.
   ✓ *Unlike Plain Text format, Rich Text Format preserves some font formatting. It has an .rtf file extension.*
9. Close the document.
10. In the Open dialog box, locate and preview the file CONTEST2 or the file 36CONTEST2 to be sure it is the flyer for the second annual essay contest.
11. Locate and preview the rich text format RTFPRESS document and the Word FOXPRESS document.
    ✓ *Remember, to display the RTFPRESS document in the Open dialog box you will have to select to display all file types.*
12. Print all three documents without opening them.
13. Exit Word.

Illustration A

Fox Footwear, Inc. Sponsors ^ Essay Contest for Teens
Second Annual

San Francisco, CA – Fox Footwear, Inc., a maker of shoes, sneakers, and other footwear for teenagers and young adults, has announced that ^ it is sponsoring an essay contest. Prizes include scholarship money, trips, computers, and gift certificates. for the second year in a row

second "Put Your Best Foot Forward"
The topic of the company's ~~first~~ annual essay contest is "~~All Dressed Up with Everywhere to Go.~~" According to Fox Footwear's Marketing Director, Steven Johansson, the object of the contest is to get teens thinking about the ~~opportunities available to them in the 21st century.~~
positive impact they can have on their communities.

"We live in an exciting time. We want to encourage teens to explore their own potential," said Mr. Johansson.

The rules for the contest are as follows:

Students aged 12 through 18 are eligible.
Essays must be between 1,000 and 1,500 words.
Essays may be typed or handwritten.
Original copies will not be returned, and will become the property of Fox Footwear, Inc.
All entries must be postmarked by March 1. Winners will be announced on June 1.

The essays will be judged based on originality, creativity, grammar, and spelling. The judges will be employees of Fox Footwear, Inc.

For more information, contact Mr. Johansson at 415-555-3922, or consult the company's Web site: foxfootwear.com.

Lesson 7

Creating Tables

Exercise 37

- Insert a Table
- Move the Insertion Point in a Table
- Enter Data in a Table
- Format a Table

Exercise 38

- Select in a Table
- Insert Columns, Rows, or Cells
- Delete Columns, Rows, or Cells

Exercise 39

- Set Alignments with Table Cells
- Align Table on the Page
- Column Width and Row Height

Exercise 40

- Use the Tables and Borders Toolbar
- Draw a Table
- Merge and Split Cells

Exercise 41

- Move and Resize Tables
- Rotate Text
- Wrap Text

Exercise 42

- Calculate in a Table
- Number Formats
- Sort Rows

Exercise 43

- Cell Borders and Shading

Exercise 44

- Critical Thinking

Exercise 37

Skills Covered:

◆ **Insert a Table** ◆ **Move the Insertion Point in a Table**
◆ **Enter Data in a Table** ◆ **Format a Table**

On the Job

Create tables to organize data into columns and rows. Any information that needs to be presented in side-by-side columns can be set up in a table. For example, a price list, an invoice, a resume, and a script are all types of documents for which you should use a table. The table format lets you align information side by side and across the page so the information is easy to read.

Highland Property Management Co. is offering the staff training courses. In this exercise, you will create a memo that includes a list of courses being offered. You will set up the course list in a table.

Terms

Table A grid comprised of horizontal rows and vertical columns into which you can enter data.

Column A vertical series of cells in a table.

Row A horizontal series of cells in a table.

Column markers Markers on the horizontal ruler that indicate column borders.

Dividers The lines that indicate the edges of cells in a table. Dividers do not print, although they are indicated on-screen by either gridlines or borders.

Border A line drawn around the edges of an element, such as a table or a table cell. Borders can also be drawn around paragraphs and pages.

Gridline A nonprinting line that indicates the boundaries of cells in a table.

End of row/cell marks Nonprinting characters used to mark the end of a cell or a row in a table.

Cell The rectangular area at the intersection of a column and a row in a table, into which you enter data.

Notes

Insert a Table

- **Tables** are easier to use than tabbed columns when setting up and organizing data in **columns** and **rows**.
- You can insert a table in any Word document using either of the following methods:
  - The Insert Table button on the Standard toolbar
  - The Insert, Table command on the Table menu

✓ *You can also draw a table using the Draw Table tool on the Tables and Borders toolbar. The Draw Table button is covered in Exercise 40.*

- With either method, you specify the number of columns and rows you want in the table.
- Word inserts the table at the insertion point location.
- By default, Word sizes the columns equally across the width of the page.
- **Column markers** on the horizontal ruler show the location of the right **divider** of each column.

- By default, Word places a ½-pt. **border** around all **cells** in a table.

A table with four columns and four rows

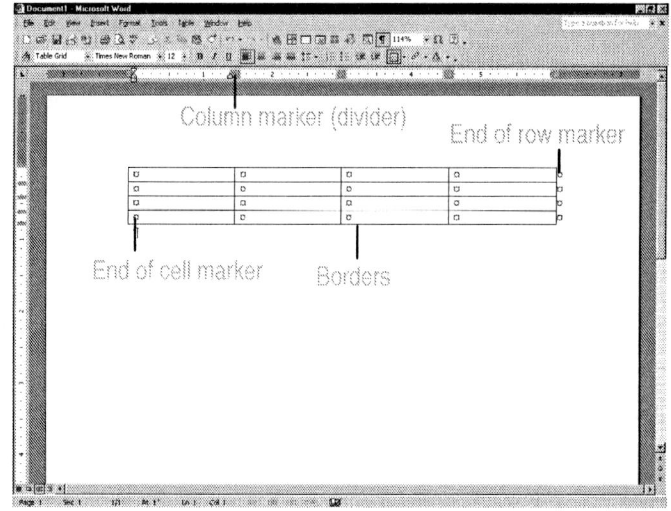

- Tables have three unique nonprinting elements:
  - **Gridlines**
  - **End of cell markers**
  - **End of row markers**

Move the Insertion Point in a Table

- You must position the insertion point in the table cell where you want characters to be entered.
- You can move the insertion point with the keyboard or mouse.

Enter Data in a Table

- You enter data in the cells of a table.
- Row height increases automatically to accommodate as much data as you type.
- Column width does not change automatically. Text wraps at the right margin of a cell the same way it wraps at the right margin of a page.
- When you press Enter in a cell, Word starts a new paragraph within the cell.
- You can edit and format text within a cell the same way you do outside a table.

Format a Table

- You can format text within a table using standard Word formatting techniques. For example, use font formatting, alignments, spacing, and indents to enhance text in a table.
- You can apply formatting to new text, selected text, or to selected cells, columns, or rows.

  ✓ *You select text in a cell using the same techniques you use to select text outside a table. Learn about selecting table components such as cells, rows, and columns in Exercise 38.*

- Select a table AutoFormat style to quickly apply formatting effects to an entire table.
- AutoFormat styles include border lines, shading, color, fonts, and other formatting.

The Table AutoFormat dialog box

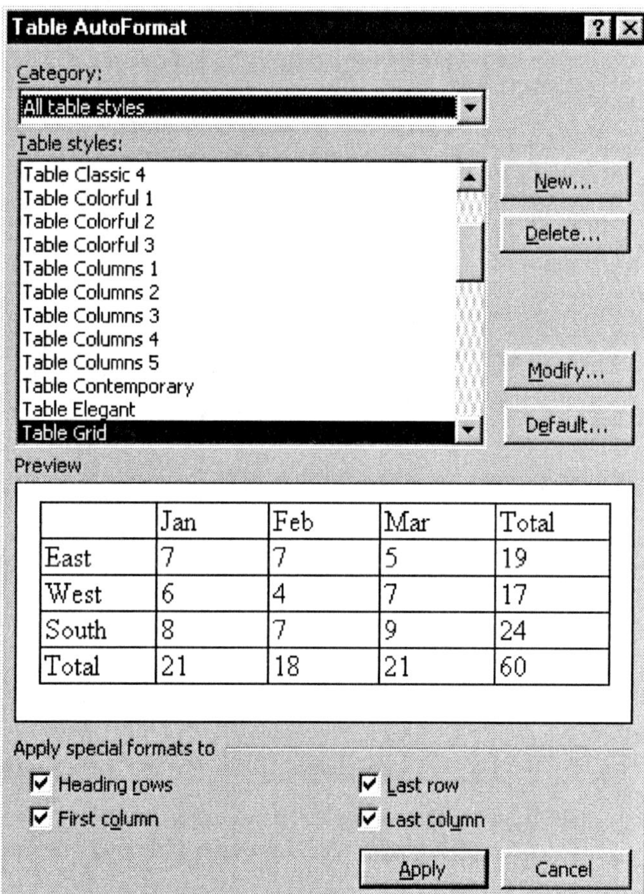

- AutoFormat overrides existing formatting. Therefore, you should apply AutoFormat first, then apply additional formatting as needed.

Procedures

Insert a Table

Use the toolbar button:

1. Position insertion point.
2. Click **Insert Table** button.
3. Drag the mouse pointer across the grid to select desired number of columns and rows.
4. Release the mouse button.

Use menu commands:

1. Position the insertion point.
2. Click **Table** .... Alt+A
3. Select **Insert** I
4. Click **Table** .... T
5. Type **number of columns** .... Alt+C, *number*
6. Press **Tab** .... Tab
7. Type **number of rows** .... Alt+R, *number*
8. Click **OK** .... Enter

Show/Hide gridlines:

1. Click **Table** .... Alt+A
2. Click **Show Gridlines** .... G

   OR

   Click **Hide Gridlines** .... G

Move the Insertion Point in a Table

With the mouse:

- Click mouse pointer in cell where you want to position insertion point.

With the keyboard:

- One cell left .... Shift+Tab

  or Ctrl+↑

  or ←

  when insertion point is at beginning of cell.
- One cell right .... Tab

  or Ctrl+↓

  or →

  when insertion point is at beginning of cell.
- One cell up .... ↑

  when insertion point is on first line of cell.
- One cell down .... ↓

  when insertion point is on last line of cell.
- First cell in column ..... Alt+Page Up
- Last cell in column ..... Alt+Page Down
- First cell in row .... Alt+Home
- Last cell in row .... Alt+End

Enter Data in a Table

1. Click in desired cell.
2. Type data.
3. Move to next cell.
4. Type data.
5. Repeat until all data is entered.

Format a Table AutoFormat

1. Click **Table** .... Alt+A
2. Click **Table AutoFormat** ..... F
3. Select **Table style** .... Alt+T, ↓
4. Click **Apply** .... Alt+A or Enter

Format text in a table

1. Select text to format.
2. Apply formatting as with regular document text.

Exercise Directions

1. Start Word, if necessary.
2. Using a 12-point serif font, type the document shown in Illustration A, or open 37SCHEDULE.
3. Save the document as SCHEDULE.
4. Move the insertion point to the last line of the document and create the table shown in Illustration B.
   a. Insert a table with three columns and five rows.
   b. Enter the data as shown.
   c. Apply the Table Contemporary AutoFormat style to the table.
   d. Apply bold italics to all of the course names.
5. Check the spelling and grammar in the document.
6. Preview the document. It should look similar to Illustration B.
7. Print the document.
8. Close the document, saving all changes.

Illustration A

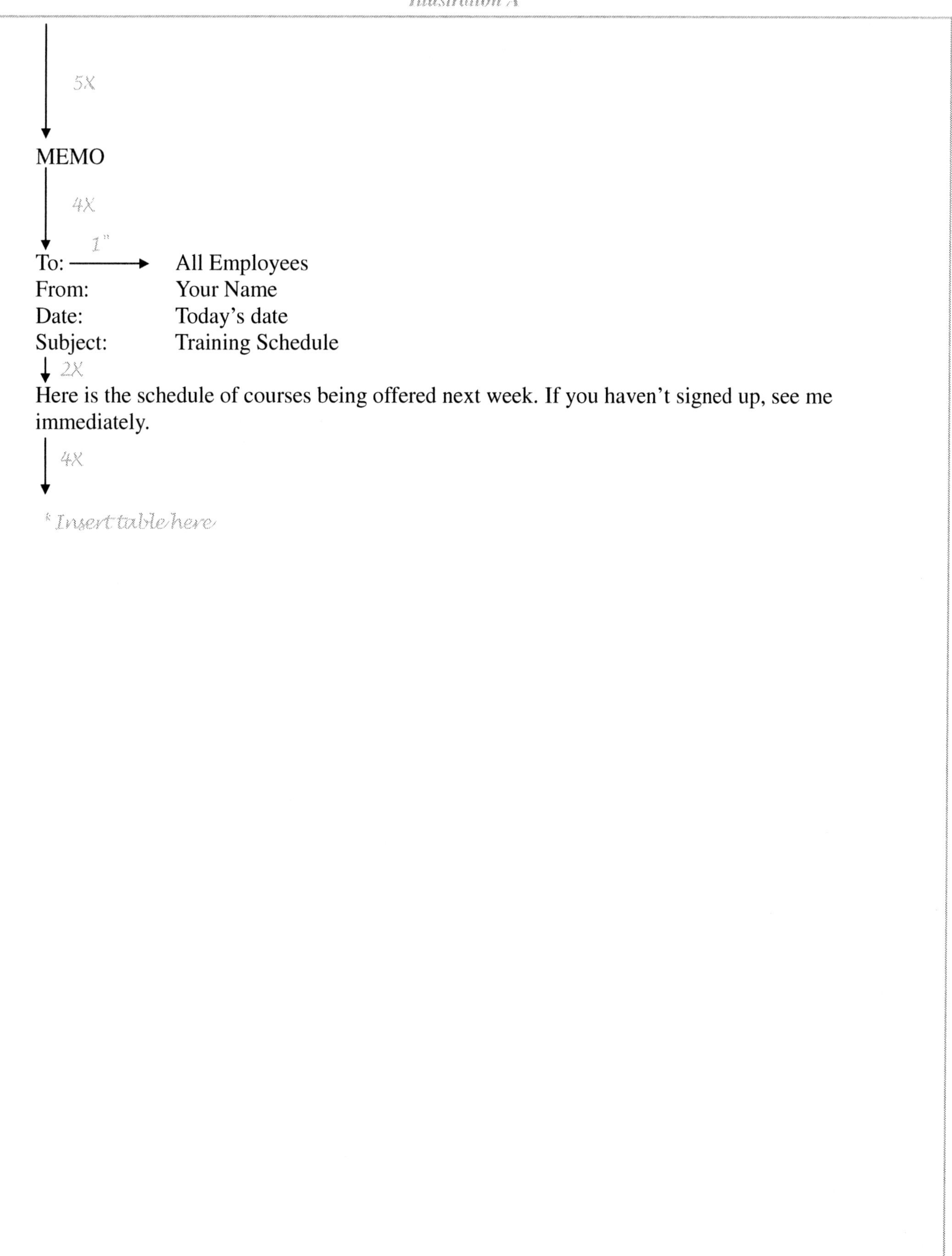

MEMO

To: All Employees
From: Your Name
Date: Today's date
Subject: Training Schedule

Here is the schedule of courses being offered next week. If you haven't signed up, see me immediately.

Illustration B

MEMO

To: All Employees
From: Your Name
Date: Today's date
Subject: Training Schedule

Here is the schedule of courses being offered next week. If you haven't signed up, see me immediately.

Course Name	Location	Time
Word 1	Conference Room A	8:30 – 11:45
Word 2	Conference Room A	1:30 – 3:30
Excel 3	Conference Room B	8:30 – 11:45
Intro to the Internet	Media Lab	1:30 – 3:30

On Your Own

1. Think of documents that would benefit from table formatting. Some examples include a weekly schedule, meeting agenda, travel itinerary, sales report, telephone/address list, and roster.
2. Create a new document in Word.
3. Save the file as OWDTABLE.
4. Use a table to set up the document as a telephone list. The list could include friends, family members, or members of a club or organization to which you belong.
5. Use at least two columns—one for the name and one for the telephone number. You may use more columns if you want to include mailing addresses, e-mail addresses, cell phone numbers, or other information.
6. Include at least five names in the list.
7. Apply an AutoFormat to the table. If you are not satisfied with the results, try a different AutoFormat.
8. Save the changes, close the document, and exit Word.

Exercise 38

Skills Covered:

Select in a Table   Insert Columns, Rows, or Cells
Delete Columns, Rows, or Cells

On the Job

You can change the structure of a table to add or delete columns, rows, or cells. You can even delete the entire table. In order to make changes affecting the table structure, you must first select the elements you want to change.

The training director at Highland Property Management Co. wants you to change the training course schedule. In this exercise, you add a column to the schedule table and add and delete rows.

Terms

Table components Parts of a table, including columns, rows, and cells.

Notes

Select in a Table

- As with other Word features, you must select **table components** before you can affect them with commands.
- You select text within a cell using the standard selection commands.
  - ✓ *Selecting text is covered in Exercise 9.*
- You can select one or more columns, one or more rows, one or more cells, or the entire table.
- Selected table components appear highlighted.

A table with the third row selected

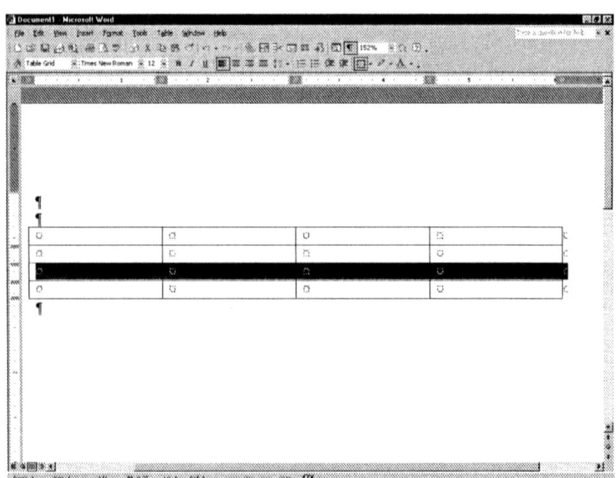

Insert Columns, Rows, or Cells

- You can insert columns, rows, or cells anywhere in a table.
- If necessary, you specify where to insert the new component—above, below, to the left, or to the right of the current component.

Delete Columns, Rows, or Cells

- You can delete any column, row, or cell.
- If necessary, you specify how to shift remaining components to fill in the area left by the deletion.
- You can delete an entire table.
- Data entered in a deleted column, row, or cell is deleted as well.

Procedures

Select in a Table

1. Position insertion point within table component to select.
   ✓ *For example, click in cell if selecting cell; click anywhere in row if selecting row, etc.*
2. Click **Table** .... Alt + A
3. Click **Select** C
4. Click one of the following:
   - **Table** .... T
   - **Column** C
   - **Row** .... R
   - **Cell** .... E

Select with the Mouse

Column:

1. Position mouse pointer at top of column until pointer resembles a down-pointing arrow ⬇ .
2. Click.

Row:

1. Position mouse pointer to left of row until pointer resembles a right-pointing arrow .
2. Click.

Cell:

1. Position mouse pointer to right of left cell border until pointer resembles a right-pointing arrow .
2. Click.

Select adjacent components:

1. Select first components.
2. Press and hold **Shift** .... Shift
3. Click in last component to select.
   ✓ *This method enables you to select adjacent columns, adjacent rows, or adjacent cells.*

Select nonadjacent components:

1. Select first components.
2. Press and hold **Ctrl** .... Ctrl
3. Click in next component to select.
4. Repeat until all desired components are selected.

Insert Columns, Rows, or Cells

1. Position insertion point within table.
   ✓ *To insert more than one component, select as many as you want to insert. For example, to insert two columns, select two columns.*
2. Click **Table** .... Alt + A
3. Click **Insert** I
4. Click one of the following:
   - **Columns to the Left** L
   - **Columns to the Right**... R
   - **Rows Above** .... A
   - **Rows Below** .... B
   - **Cells** .... E

   ✓ *Select option for shifting existing cells to make room for new cells, then click OK.*

Delete Columns, Rows, or Cells

1. Select cells, or click in the row or column to delete.
2. Click **Table** .... Alt + A
3. Click **Delete** .... D
4. Click one of the following:
   - **Columns** C
   - **Rows** .... R
   - **Cells** .... E

   ✓ *Select option for shifting existing cells to fill in deleted cell area, then click OK.*

Delete Entire Table

1. Click anywhere in table.
2. Click **Table** .... Alt + A
3. Click **Delete** .... D
4. Click **Table** .... T

Exercise Directions

1. Start Word, if necessary.
2. Open SCHEDULE or open 38SCHEDULE.
3. Save the document as SCHEDULE2.
4. Select the last two rows in the table.
5. Insert two new rows above the selected rows.
6. Enter the following data in the new rows:

Word 3	**Conference Room A**	**8:30-11:45**
Excel 2	**Conference Room B**	**3:00-4:30**

7. Insert another new row between the Word 3 and Excel 2 rows, and enter the following data:

Excel 1	**Conference Room B**	**1:30-3:30**

8. Insert a new column between the Location column and the Time Column.
9. Enter the following data in the new column:

   Days
   Monday, Wednesday
   Monday, Wednesday
   Tuesday, Thursday
   Tuesday, Thursday
   Tuesday, Thursday
   Monday, Wednesday
   Friday

10. Delete the row for the Word 1 course.
11. Apply the Table 3D effects 2 AutoFormat style to the table.
12. Check the spelling and grammar in the document.
13. Preview the document. It should look similar to the one in Illustration A.
14. Print the document
15. Close the document, saving all changes.
16. Exit Word.

Illustration A

MEMO

To: All Employees
From: Your Name
Date: Today's date
Subject: Training Schedule

Here is the schedule of courses being offered next week. If you haven't signed up, see me immediately.

Course Name	Location	Days	Time
Word 2	Conference Room A	Monday, Wednesday	1:30 – 3:30
Word 3	Conference Room A	Tuesday, Thursday	8:30 – 11:45
Excel 1	Conference Room B	Tuesday, Thursday	1:30 – 3:30
Excel 2	Conference Room B	Tuesday, Thursday	3:00 – 4:30
Excel 3	Conference Room B	Monday, Wednesday	8:30 – 11:45
Intro to the Internet	Media Lab	Friday	1:30 – 3:30

On Your Own

1. Open OWDTABLE, the document you created in the On Your Own section of Exercise 37, or open 38OWDTABLE.
2. Save the document as OWDTABLE2.
3. Add two new rows to the table.
4. Add a new column.
5. Fill in the data for the new rows and column.
6. Delete one row.
7. Apply a different AutoFormat to the table.
8. Save the document, close it, and exit Word.

Exercise 39

Skills Covered:

◆ **Set Alignments within Table Cells** ◆ **Align Table on the Page**
◆ **Column Width and Row Height**

On the Job

Use alignment options and tabs to make tables easy to read. Numbers are usually aligned flush right in a cell, while text can be flush left, centered, or justified. You can vertically align data in a cell as well. Decimal tabs are especially useful in tables for aligning dollar values. Other ways to improve the appearance of a table include aligning the table horizontally on the page, and adjusting column width and row height.

Pete Newell, the owner of Pelican Peter's Dive Shop, has asked you to create a flyer announcing clearance sale prices. In this exercise, you will create a document listing sale price information. You will use different alignment options to set up the data in the table. You will also set **row heights** and **column widths**, and you will align the table horizontally on the page.

Terms

Row height The height of a row in a table, measured in inches.

Column width The width of a column in a table, measured in inches.

Notes

Set Alignments within Table Cells

- You can set horizontal alignment within a cell the same way you set alignment in a document by using paragraph formatting and tabs.
- In a table, numbers are usually right aligned, and text is either left aligned or centered.
- All tab stops can be used within a table cell, but the most useful is the decimal tab stop.
- Decimal tab stops automatically align numbers such as dollar values within a cell or a column.
- You can vertically align data at the top of the cell, centered in the cell, or at the bottom of the cell. The default is at the top.

Aligned text in a table

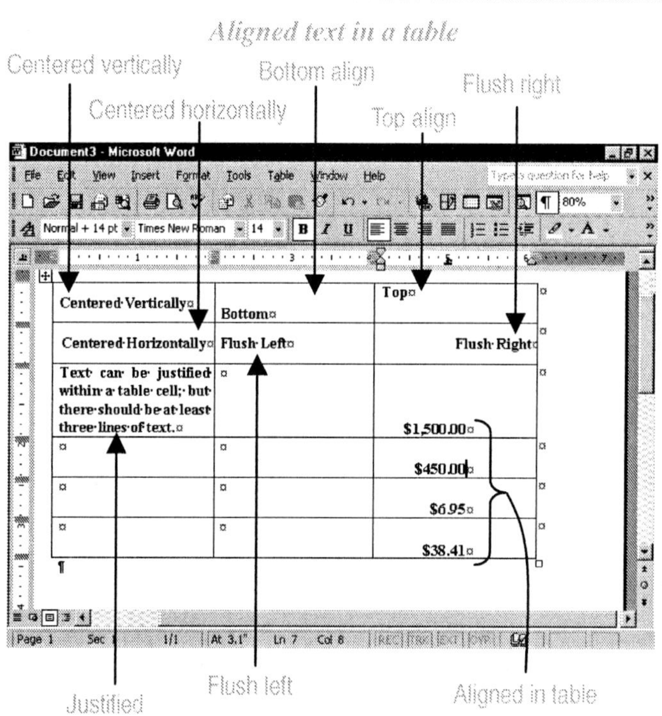

Align Table on the Page

- You can left align, right align, or center a table on the page.

Table tab of the Table Properties dialog box

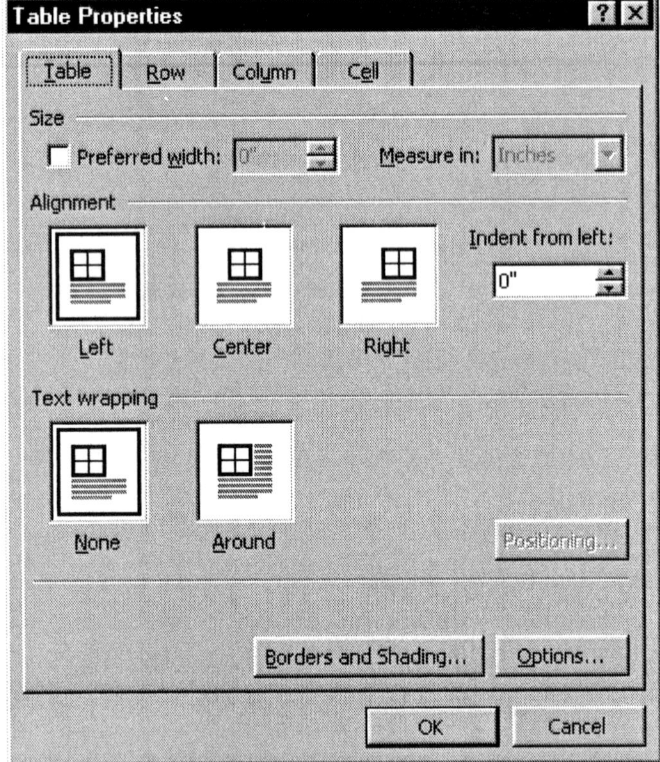

Column Width and Row Height

- By default, Word creates columns of equal width, sized so the table extends from the left margin to the right margin.
- Rows are sized according to the current line spacing.
- By default, row height automatically increases to accommodate lines of text typed in a cell.
- You can drag column dividers to increase or decrease column width.
  - ✓ *Press and hold the* Alt *key as you drag to see the column width measurements displayed on the ruler.*
- In Print Layout view, you can drag row dividers to increase or decrease row height.
  - ✓ *You cannot drag row dividers In Normal view.*
- You can set precise measurements for columns, rows, cells, and entire tables in the Table Properties dialog box.

The Column tab of the Table Properties dialog box

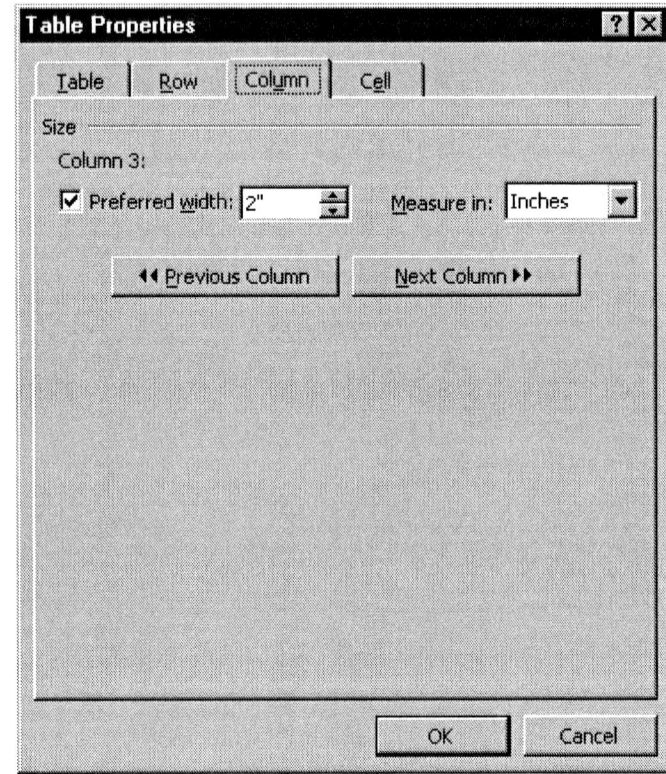

Procedures

Set Horizontal Alignment in a Cell

1. Position insertion point in cell.
   OR
   Select component(s) to format.
2. Click desired alignment button on Formatting toolbar:
   - **Align Left**
   - **Align Right**
   - **Center**
   - **Justify**

Set Tabs in a Cell

1. Position insertion point in cell.
   OR
   Select component(s) to format.
2. Click Tab box at left end of horizontal ruler to select tab stop type.
3. Click desired position on horizontal ruler.
4. For more information on tabs, refer to Exercise 13.

Advance insertion point one tab stop:

- Press **Ctrl+Tab** .... Ctrl+Tab

Set Vertical Alignment in a Cell

1. Position insertion point in cell.
   OR
   Select component(s) to format.
2. Click **Table** .... Alt+A
3. Click **Table Properties** .... R
4. Click the **Cell** tab.......... Alt+E
5. Click desired Vertical Alignment option:
   - **Top** .... Alt+P
   - **Center** .... Alt+C
   - **Bottom** .... Alt+B
6. Click **OK** .... Enter

Align a Table Horizontally

1. Select table.
2. Click desired alignment button on Formatting toolbar:
   - **Center**
   - **Align Right**
   - **Align Left**

OR

1. Click anywhere in table.
2. Click **Table** .... Alt+A
3. Click **Table Properties** .... R
4. Click the **Table** tab ...... Alt+T
5. Click desired Alignment option:
   - **Left** .... Alt+L
   - **Center** .... Alt+C
   - **Right** .... Alt+H
6. Click **OK** .... Enter

Change Column Width

1. Position mouse pointer on column divider.
   ✓ *Pointer changes to a double-vertical line with arrows pointing left and right.*
2. Drag divider left or right.
   ✓ *Press Alt at the same time that you drag the divider to see the width displayed on the horizontal ruler.*

OR

1. Click in column.
2. Click **Table** .... Alt+A
3. Click **Table Properties**........ R
4. Click **Column** tab .... Alt+U
5. Select **Preferred Width** check box .... Alt+W
6. Press **Tab** .... Tab
7. Type column width in inches.
   ✓ *Select Measure in to choose Percent if desired.*
8. Click **OK** .... Enter

   OR

   Click **Next Column** [Next Column] .... Alt+N

   OR

   Click Previous Column [Previous Column] .... Alt+P
9. Repeat steps 1-8 to set additional column widths.

Change Row Height

1. Click **Print Layout View** button.
2. Position mouse pointer on row divider.
   ✓ *Pointer changes to a double-vertical line with arrows pointing up and down.*
3. Drag divider up or down.
   ✓ *Press Alt at the same time that you drag the divider to see the height displayed on the vertical ruler.*

OR

1. Click in row.
2. Click **Table** .... Alt+A
3. Click **Table Properties**........ R
4. Click **Row** tab.............................. Alt+R
5. Select **Specify Height** check box.............................. Alt+S
6. Press **Tab** .... Tab
7. Type row height in inches.
   ✓ *Select Exactly in Row height is box to fix row height at specified size.*
8. Click **OK** .... Enter

   OR

   Click **Next Row** [Next Row] .... Alt+N

   OR

   Click **Previous Row** [Previous Row] .... Alt+P
9. Repeat steps 1-8 to set additional column widths.

Exercise Directions

1. Start Word, if necessary.
2. Type the document shown in Illustration A, or open 39SALE.
3. Save the file as SALE2.

   ✓ *If you type the document, remember to clear the formatting before inserting the table. For example, there should be no extra space before or after the current line, the alignment should be flush left, and the font should be the default 12-pt. Times New Roman. If you do not clear the formatting, the text in the table will have the current font formatting, and the table itself will have the current paragraph formatting.*

4. Format the table as follows:
   a. Set column 1 to be 1.5" wide.
   b. Set the other columns to be 1" wide.
   c. Set row 1 to be at least .75" high.
   d. Set all remaining rows to be exactly .5" high.
   e. Make the text in the first row bold, italic, and 18 points.
5. Set alignment in the table as follows:
   a. Center the data in the first row vertically and horizontally.
   b. Vertically align all other rows with the bottom of the cells.
   c. Right align the data in the Size column.
   d. Use decimal tabs to align the prices in both the Regular Price and the Sale Price columns.
6. Center the entire table on the page.
7. Check the spelling and grammar in the document.
8. Preview the document. It should look similar to Illustration B.
9. Print the document.
10. Close the document, saving all changes.

Illustration A

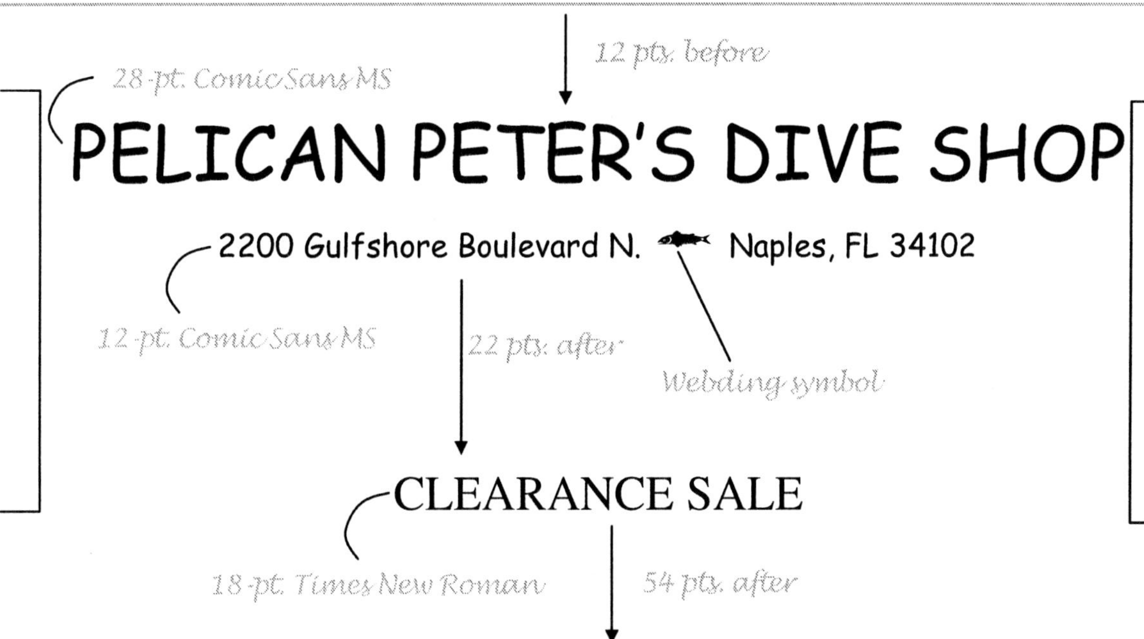

Item	Size	Regular Price	Sale Price
Fins	S, M, L	$19.99	$14.99
Swim goggles	One size	$9.99	$5.99
Men's suits	Assorted	$14.99	$9.99
Women's suits	Assorted	$29.99	$21.99
Wet suits	Assorted	$125.99	$99.99
Boogie boards	One size	$24.99	$12.99
Sea Kayaks	One size	$355.00	$299.00
Sun block	8 ounces	$15.99	$9.99

Illustration B

PELICAN PETER'S DIVE SHOP

2200 Gulfshore Boulevard N. Naples, FL 34102

CLEARANCE SALE

Item	***Size***	***Regular Price***	***Sale Price***
Fins	S, M, L	$19.99	$14.99
Swim goggles	One size	$9.99	$5.99
Men's suits	Assorted	$14.99	$9.99
Women's suits	Assorted	$29.99	$21.99
Wet suits	Assorted	$125.99	$99.99
Boogie boards	One size	$24.99	$12.99
Sea Kayaks	One size	$355.00	$299.00
Sun block	8 ounces	$15.99	$9.99

On Your Own

1. Open OWDTABLE2, the document you used in the On Your Own section of Exercise 38, or open 38OWDTABLE2.
2. Save the document as OWDTABLE3.
3. Adjust the column widths and row heights by dragging the table borders.
4. Set precise column widths and row heights.
5. Use different alignments in the table.
6. Center the table on the page.
7. Save the changes, close the document, and exit Word.

Exercise 40

Skills Covered:

◆ **Use the Tables and Borders Toolbar** ◆ **Draw a Table**
◆ **Merge and Split Cells**

On the Job

Word's Draw Table tool gives you great flexibility to organize tables the way you want them, not necessarily in rigid columns and rows. You can lay out the table cells exactly as you want them in order to organize text and data. You can then merge and split cells, if necessary.

Ramirez, Johnson, and Gold, an investment banking firm, is planning an executive retreat. As the assistant to the senior partner, you have been asked to research and recommend locations for the off-site meeting. In this exercise, you will create a memo to the president and include a table in which you can enter information about possible locations. To complete the table you will use the Draw Table tool, and you will merge and split cells. You will also use different alignments and formatting to improve the appearance of the table.

Terms

Merge Combine multiple adjacent cells together to create one large cell.

Split Divide one cell into multiple cells, either vertically to create columns or horizontally to create rows.

Notes

Tables and Borders toolbar

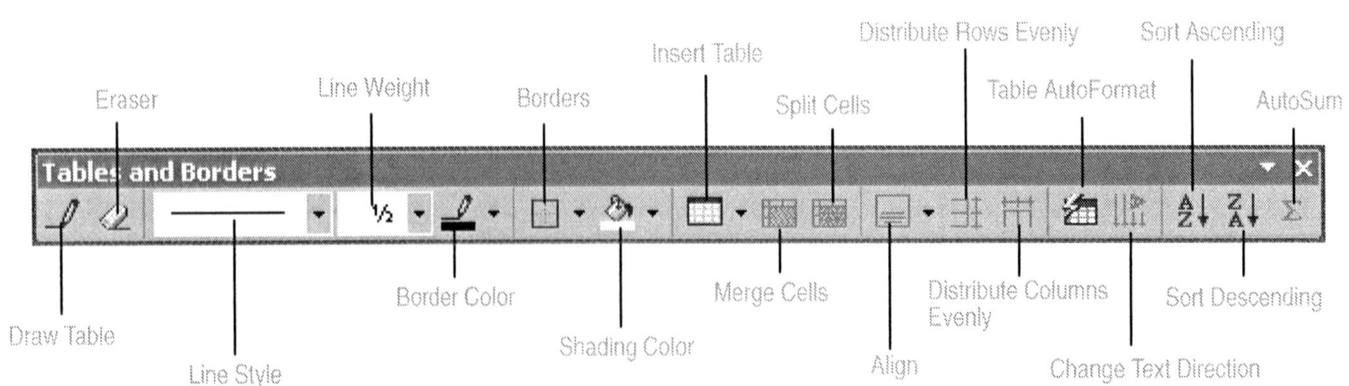

Use the Tables and Borders Toolbar

- Use the Tables and Borders toolbar to create and format tables.
- Many of the commands in the Table Properties dialog box can be accessed quickly using toolbar buttons.
- For example, you can select both horizontal and vertical text alignment from the Align drop-down palette.

Align drop-down palette

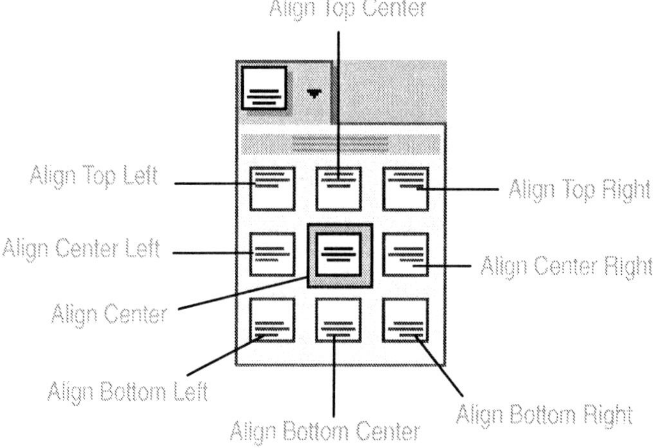

✓ *If the toolbar is in your way while working, move it or dock it across the top of the document window.*

Draw a Table

- Word's Draw Table feature lets you create tables with uneven or irregular columns and rows.

A table drawn with uneven columns and rows

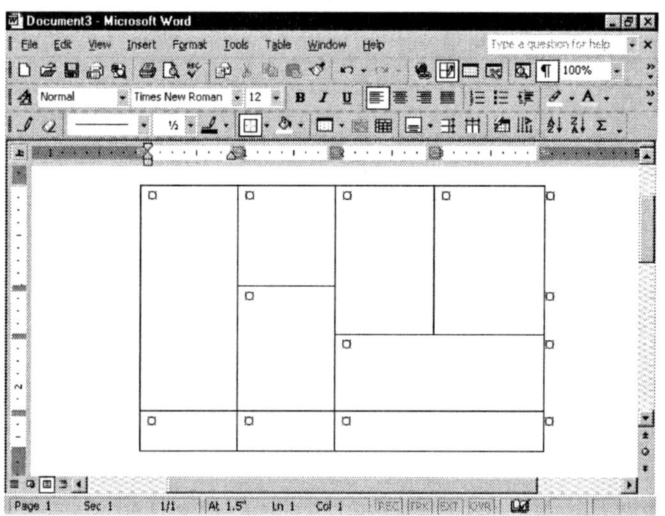

- You must use Print Layout view to draw a table.
- When you draw a table, the mouse pointer functions as a pencil.

- You drag the pointer to draw lines vertically or horizontally to create cell dividers.

  ✓ *Word creates straight lines at 90 degree angles to existing table borders, even if you do not drag in a straight line.*

- You can draw a diagonal line across a cell as a visual element or border, not to split the cell diagonally.
- New cells can be drawn anywhere. Rows and columns do not have to extend across the entire table.
- You can combine the Insert Table command with the Draw Table command to customize any table.

Merge and Split Cells

- You can **merge** adjacent cells horizontally or adjacent cells vertically.
- Among other things, merging is useful for creating a header row across a table.
- You can merge cells using a menu command, a toolbar button, or by using the eraser tool to erase dividers between cells.

  ✓ *If you erase a divider on the outer edge of the table, you simply erase the border line, not the divider itself.*

- **Split** a cell to insert dividers to create additional rows or columns.

Procedures

Display Tables and Borders Toolbar

- Click **Tables and Borders** button on the Standard toolbar.

OR

1. Click **View** .... Alt+V
2. Click **Toolbars** .... T
3. Click **Tables and Borders.**

OR

1. Right-click any toolbar.
2. Click **Tables and Borders**.

Draw a Table

1. Click **Table** .... Alt+A
2. Click **Draw Table** .... W

   OR

   Click **Draw Table** button on Tables and Borders toolbar.

   ✓ *The mouse pointer resembles a pencil.*

3. Click where you want to position the upper-left corner of the table.
4. Drag diagonally down and to the right.
5. Release mouse button where you want to position the lower-right corner of the table.

   ✓ *This draws one cell.*

6. Click and drag the mouse pointer to draw horizontal borders and vertical borders.

   ✓ *As you drag, Word displays a dotted line where the border will be. Once you drag far enough, Word completes the line when you release the mouse button..*

7. Click **Esc** .... Esc

   to turn off Draw Table.

   OR

   Click **Draw Table** button.

Merge Cells

1. Select cells to merge.
2. Click **Merge Cells** button.

   OR

   a. Click **Table** .... Alt+A

   b. Click **Merge Cells** .... M

Merge Cells and Erase Table Dividers

1. Click **Eraser** button on the Tables and Borders toolbar.
2. Drag over borders to erase.
3. Click **Esc**............................ Esc

   to turn off Eraser.

   OR

   Click **Eraser** button .

Split Cells

1. Select cell to split.
2. Click **Split Cells** button.

   OR

   a. Click **Table** .... Alt+A

   b. Click **Split Cells** .... P

3. Enter **Number of columns** to create.......................... Alt+C
4. Enter **Number of rows** to create.......................... Alt+R
5. Click **OK**.......................... Enter

Exercise Directions

1. Start Word, if necessary.
2. Type the document shown in Illustration A, or open 40SITES.
3. Save the document as SITES.
4. Move the insertion point to the last line of the document.
5. Use the Draw Table tool to draw a cell approximately 4" wide and 4" high.
   ✓ *Use the rulers as guides to measure the height and width of cells as you draw, but don't worry if the table components are not sized exactly. You can adjust column width and row height as necessary.*
6. Divide the cell into two columns by drawing a vertical line through the cell. Try to size the columns as follows:
   Column 1 – 1.5" wide
   Column 2 – 2.5" wide
7. Divide the table into four rows, about 1" high each.
8. Merge the cells in the top row to create one cell the width of the table.
9. Leaving the top row intact, use the Split Cells tool to divide each of the cells in the right column into two rows (refer to Illustration B to see the desired result).
   ✓ *Split each cell into one column and two rows.*
10. Enter the text shown in Illustration B, using the following formatting and alignments to achieve the desired result:
    a. Row 1 (Table title): 18-point sans serif, bold. Centered both horizontally and vertically.
    b. City names: 14-point serif, bold, aligned left and centered vertically.
    c. Attractions: 14-point serif, centered horizontally and aligned vertically with the cell bottom.
11. Center the entire table horizontally on the page.
12. Check the spelling and grammar in the document.
13. Preview the document. It should look similar to the one in the Illustration B.
14. Print the document.
15. Close the document, saving all changes.

Illustration A

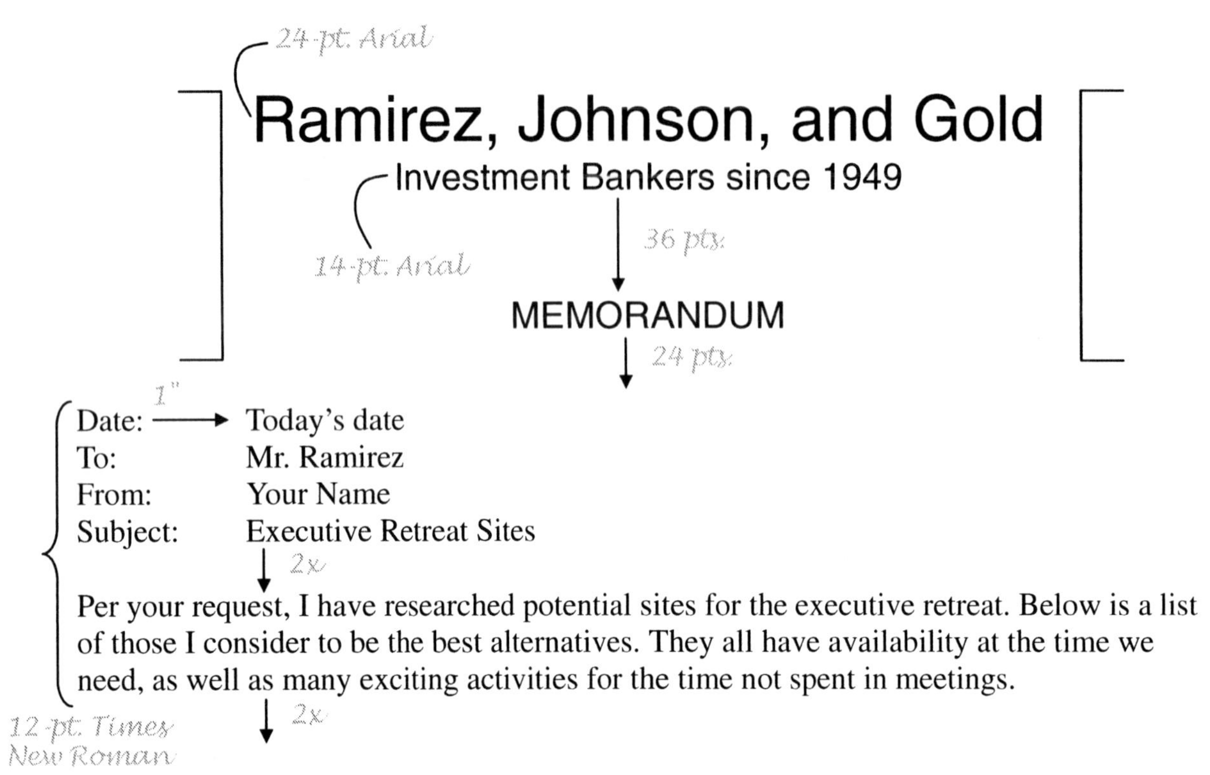

Illustration B

Ramirez, Johnson, and Gold

Investment Bankers since 1949

MEMORANDUM

Date: Today's date
To: Mr. Ramirez
From: Your Name
Subject: Executive Retreat Sites

Per your request, I have researched potential sites for the executive retreat. Below is a list of those I consider to be the best alternatives. They all have availability at the time we need, as well as many exciting activities for the time not spent in meetings.

Potential Sites for Executive Retreat	
San Diego, CA	Great Climate!
	Sea World
Cleveland, OH	Rock and Roll Hall of Fame
	Jacob's Field
Orlando, FL	Disney
	Universal Studios

On Your Own

1. Create a new document and save it as OWDWEEKLY.
2. Create a weekly schedule for yourself by drawing a table. For example, the first column may be time periods, and the first row may be the days of the week.
3. Fill in the schedule using uneven columns and rows.
4. If necessary, merge and split cells to create the schedule correctly.
5. Use different alignments in the table.
6. Center the table on the page.
7. Save the document, close it, and exit Word.

Exercise 41

Skills Covered:

◆ **Move and Resize Tables** ◆ **Rotate Text** ◆ **Wrap Text**

On the Job

You can position and format a table in a text document so it complements the document text. Once a table is in place in a document, you can easily move it and resize it. You can set Word to wrap document text around the table, and you can rotate text in table cells to achieve the exact effect you need.

You want to convince Mr. Ramirez to trust your judgment on the site selection for the executive retreat. To make sure he notices your suggestions, you want to improve the appearance of the table. In this exercise, you will add a column to the table and change the size of the table. You will also move the table on the page and set the document text to wrap around the table.

Terms

Table anchor A rectangle with a four-headed arrow in it, displayed at the upper-left corner of a table, and used to move the table.

Sizing handle A rectangle displayed somewhere along the sides of an object, used to resize the **object**. A table's sizing handle is displayed at the lower-right corner of the table.

Object An element such as a picture or a chart, which can be inserted in a Word document.

Rotate text Shift the position of text so it runs top to bottom or bottom to top, instead of left to right.

Wrap Control the way text flows around an object, such as a table.

Notes

Move and Resize Tables

- You can drag the **table anchor** to move the table anywhere on the page.
- You can drag the **sizing handle** to change the table size.

Move and resize tables

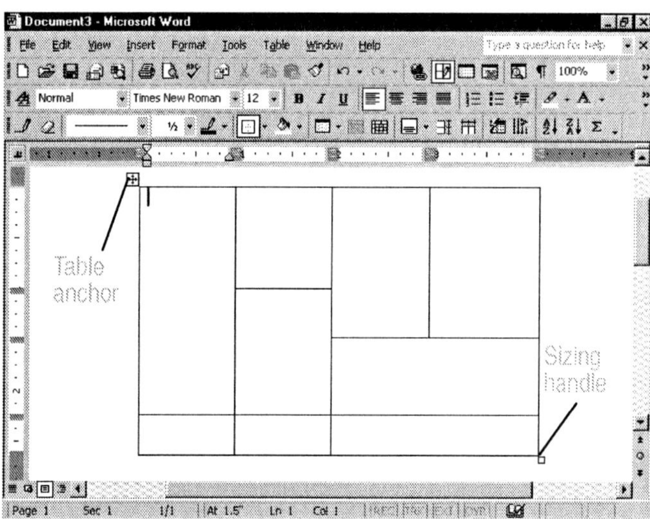

Rotate Text

- **Rotate text** direction within a cell so text runs from left to right, from top to bottom, or from bottom to top.

Rotated text in a table

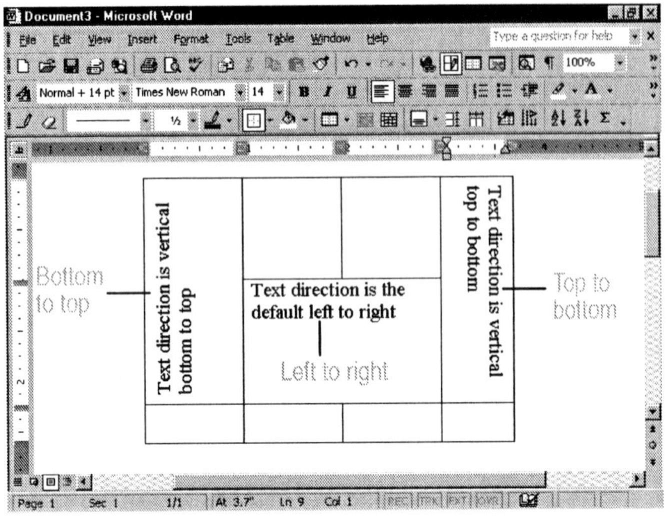

Wrap Text

- By default, tables are inserted on a blank line above or below existing text.
- You can set Word to **wrap** text around the table.
- Wrapping text around a table integrates the table object into the text so text appears above, below, or on either side of the table.

Wrap text around a table

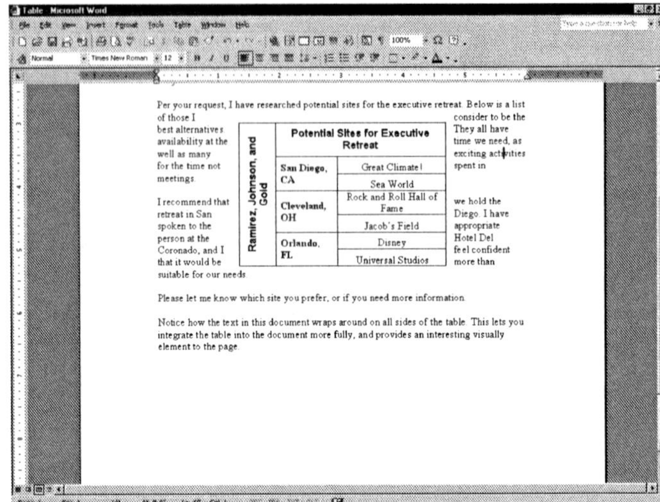

Per your request, I have researched potential sites for the executive retreat. Below is a list of those I consider to be the best alternatives. They all have availability at the time we need, as well as many exciting activities for the time not spent in meetings.

Ramirez, Johnson, and Gold	Potential Sites for Executive Retreat	
	San Diego, CA	Great Climate!
		Sea World
	Cleveland, OH	Rock and Roll Hall of Fame
		Jacob's Field
	Orlando, FL	Disney
		Universal Studios

I recommend that we hold the retreat in San Diego. I have spoken to the appropriate person at the Hotel Del Coronado, and I feel confident that it would be more than suitable for our needs.

Please let me know which site you prefer, or if you need more information.

Notice how the text in this document wraps around on all sides of the table. This lets you integrate the table into the document more fully, and provides an interesting visually element to the page.

Procedures

Move a Table

1. Rest mouse pointer on table so handles are displayed.
   - ✓ *You must be in Print Layout view for the sizing handle and table anchor to be available.*
2. Click and drag table anchor to new location.
   - ✓ *A dotted outline moves with the mouse pointer to show new location.*
3. Release mouse button to drop table in new location.

Resize a Table

1. Rest mouse pointer on table so handles are displayed.
2. Click and drag sizing handle to increase or decrease table size.
   - ✓ *A dotted outline moves with the mouse pointer to show new size.*
3. Release mouse button to resize table.

Rotate Text

1. Click in cell to format.

   OR

   Select components to format.
2. Click **Change Text Direction** button .
   - ✓ *Click the button to toggle through the three available directions.*

Wrap Text

1. Click in table.
2. Click **Table**.................. Alt+A
3. Click **Table Properties**........ R
4. Click **Table** tab.................... T
5. Click **Around** .... A
6. Click **OK**.......................... Enter

Exercise Directions

1. Start Word, if necessary.
2. Open SITES or open 41SITES.
3. Save the document as SITES2.
4. Add the following paragraphs to the memo:

   I recommend that we hold the retreat in San Diego. I have spoken to the appropriate person at the Hotel Del Coronado, and I feel confident that it would be more than suitable for our needs.

   Please let me know which site you prefer, or if you need more information.
5. Use the Draw Table tool to draw a new cell on the left side of the table. Size the new cell to the full height of the table and approximately .75" wide.
6. In the new cell, set the text to run vertically bottom to top.
7. Type the company name, **Ramirez, Johnson, and Gold**, in a bold, turquoise, 18-point sans serif font.
8. Center the company name horizontally and vertically.
9. Align the table on the right side of the page.
10. Set text to wrap around the table.
11. Move the table up so the text wraps around it (refer to Illustration A).
12. Resize the table to set its width to about 4.5".
13. Check the spelling and grammar in the document.
14. Display the document in Print Preview. It should look similar to the one in Illustration A.
15. Print the document.
16. Close the document, saving all changes.

Illustration A

Ramirez, Johnson, and Gold

Investment Bankers since 1949

MEMORANDUM

Date: Today's date
To: Mr. Ramirez
From: Your Name
Subject: Executive Retreat Sites

Per your request, I have researched potential sites for the executive retreat. Below is a list of those I consider to be the best alternatives. They all have availability at the time we need, as well as many exciting activities for the time not spent in meetings.

I recommend that we hold the retreat in San Diego. I have spoken to the appropriate person at the Hotel Del Coronado, and I feel confident that it would be more than suitable for our needs.

Ramirez, Johnson, and Gold	Potential Sites for Executive Retreat	
	San Diego, CA	Great Climate!
		Sea World
	Cleveland, OH	Rock and Roll Hall of Fame
		Jacob's Field
	Orlando, FL	Disney
		Universal Studios

Please let me know which site you prefer, or if you need more information.

On Your Own

1. Create a new document in Word.
2. Save the file as OWDTABLE4.
3. Type a personal business letter to an employer or to your parents explaining why you need a raise. Write at least two paragraphs about why you deserve the raise and what you plan to do with the additional funds. Include information about how you spend the money you receive now.
4. To illustrate your point, draw a table in the letter and list items that you have purchased in the past two weeks. For example, include CDs, books, meals, movie tickets, and other expenses. The table should have at least three columns—the date, the item, and the cost. List at least four items.
5. Merge a row across the top of the table and type in a title.
6. Try rotating text in some of the cells.
7. Use different alignments in the table cells.
8. Set the text in the letter to wrap around the table.
9. Try moving and resizing the table to improve the appearance of the letter.
10. When you are satisfied with the appearance of the table and the letter, save the changes, close the document, and exit Word.

Exercise 42

Skills Covered:

◆ **Calculate in a Table** ◆ **Number Formats** ◆ **Sort Rows**

On the Job

Perform basic calculations in tables to total values in a column or row. If the values change, you can update the result without redoing the math! At the same time, you can format the calculation results with one of Word's built-in number formats. Sorting rows, like sorting paragraphs or lists, helps you keep your tables in order.

Pelican Peter's Dive Shop is offering a special package excursion. In this exercise, you will create a document to advertise the package. You will use a table to organize the information and to calculate costs. Finally, you will sort the data in the table.

Terms

Spreadsheet An application, such as Microsoft's Excel, used for setting up mathematical calculations.

Function A built-in **formula** for performing calculations, such as addition in a table

Formula A mathematical equation.

Field A placeholder used to insert information that changes, such as the date, the time, a page number, or the results of a calculation.

Header row A row that contains a title or column headings.

Notes

Calculate in a Table

- Word tables include basic **spreadsheet functions** so you can perform calculations on data entered in tables.
- By default, Word assumes you want to add the values entered in the column above the current cell, or in the row beside the current cell.
- Word enters the calculation result in a **field** so it can be updated if the values in the table change.
- For anything other than basic calculations, use an Excel worksheet, not a Word table.

The Formula dialog box set up to total a row

Formula

Formula:

=SUM(ABOVE)

Number format:

Paste function: Paste bookmark:

OK Cancel

Number Formats

- When you set up a calculation in a table you can select a number format to use for the result.
- Number formats include features such as dollar signs, commas, percent signs, and decimal points.

The Number format list

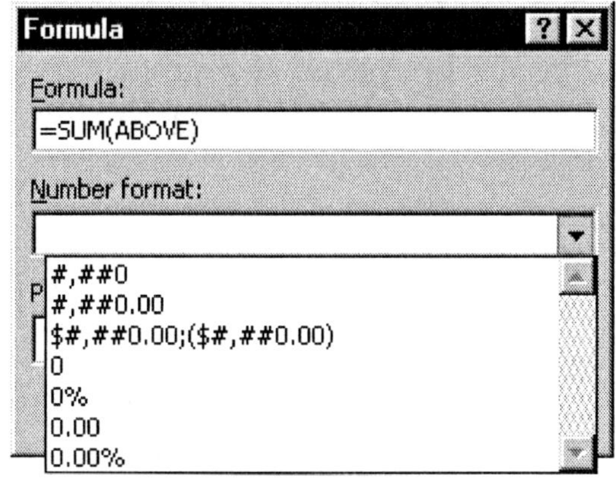

Sort Rows

- Sort rows in a table the same way you sort lists or paragraphs.

  ✓ *See Exercise 24.*
- Rows can be sorted according to the data in any column.
- You can sort by more than one column if you want.
- For example, in a table of names and addresses, rows can be sorted alphabetically by name, by city, or numerically by ZIP Code, or they can be sorted by all three.
- If a table includes a **header row**, you can exclude it from the sort.
- Word rearranges the rows in the table but does not rearrange the columns.

Procedures

Total Values in a Column or Row

1. Click in cell where you want the total to be displayed.
2. Click **Table** .... Alt+A
3. Click **Formula** .... O

   ✓ *By default, Word enters the formula for totaling the values in the cells in the column above or the row to the left.*
4. Click **Number format** drop-down arrow .... Alt+N
5. Click desired format .... ↑↓
6. Click **OK** .... Enter

Update the Total

1. Select the cell where the total is displayed.
2. Press **F9** F9

OR

1. Right-click cell where the total is displayed.
2. Click **Update Field** .... U

✓ *You must update the total each time one of the values used in the formula is changed. The total is not updated automatically.*

Sort Rows

1. Display the Tables and Borders toolbar.
2. Select the data in the column by which you want to sort.
3. Click Sort **Ascending** button on the Tables and Borders toolbar to sort from A to Z or from 0 to 9.

   OR

   Click sort **Descending** button on the Tables and Borders toolbar to sort from Z to A or from 9 to 0.

   ✓ *If the sort does not include the first row, click Table, Sort and select the No header row option button, then click OK.*

Sort by Multiple Columns

1. Click **Table** .... Alt+A
2. Click **Sort** .... S
3. Click **Sort by** .... Alt+S
4. Click desired column.
5. Click **Type** .... Alt+Y
6. Click either:
   - **Text**
   - **Number**
   - **Date**
7. Click either:
   - **Ascending** .... Alt+A
   - **Descending** .... Alt+D
8. Click **Then by** .... Alt+T
9. Click desired column.
10. Click **Type** .... Alt+P
11. Click either:
    - **Text**
    - **Number**
    - **Date**

12. Click either:
    - **Ascending**............ Alt+C
    - **Descending**........... Alt+N
13. Click **Then by**............ Alt+B
14. Click desired column
15. Click **Type**.................. Alt+E
16. Click either:
    - **Text**
    - **Number**
    - **Date**
17. Click either:
    - **Ascending**............ Alt+I
    - **Descending**........... Alt+G

    ✓ *If the sort should not include the first row, make sure the My list has Header row option button is selected*
18. Click **OK**.......................... Enter

Exercise Directions

1. Start Word, if necessary.
2. Type the document shown in Illustration A, or open 42PACKAGE.
3. Save the document as PACKAGE.
4. Move the insertion point to the end of the document and insert a table that has two columns and six rows.
5. Enter the table data as follows:

Item	Package Price
Training	**$225.00**
Equipment Rental	**$159.00**
Boat Fee	**$99.00**
Meals	**$50.00**
Guide Fee	**$75.00**

6. Format all data in an 18-point serif font.
7. Format row 1 in bold, centered horizontally and vertically.
8. Align rows 2 through 6 on the bottom vertically and flush left horizontally.
9. Use a decimal tab to align the dollar values in column 2.
10. Set all rows to be at least .5" high.
11. Sort the table rows—excluding the header row—into descending alphabetical order based on the data in the Item column.
12. Resort the table rows into ascending numerical order based on the data in the Package Price column.
13. In the Item column of the new row, enter **Total Package Price**.
14. In the Package Price column of the new row, calculate the total of the items already entered in the table, using the dollar value format.
15. Edit the price of meals from $50.00 to **$40.00**.
16. Update the calculation result in the table.
17. Resize the table so it is approximately 4" wide.
18. Adjust the column width so column 1 is approximately 2.25" wide and column 2 is approximately 1.75" wide.
19. Center the table horizontally on the page.
20. Check the spelling and grammar in the document.
21. Preview the document. It should look similar to the one in Illustration B.
22. Print the document.
23. Close the document, saving all changes.

Illustration A

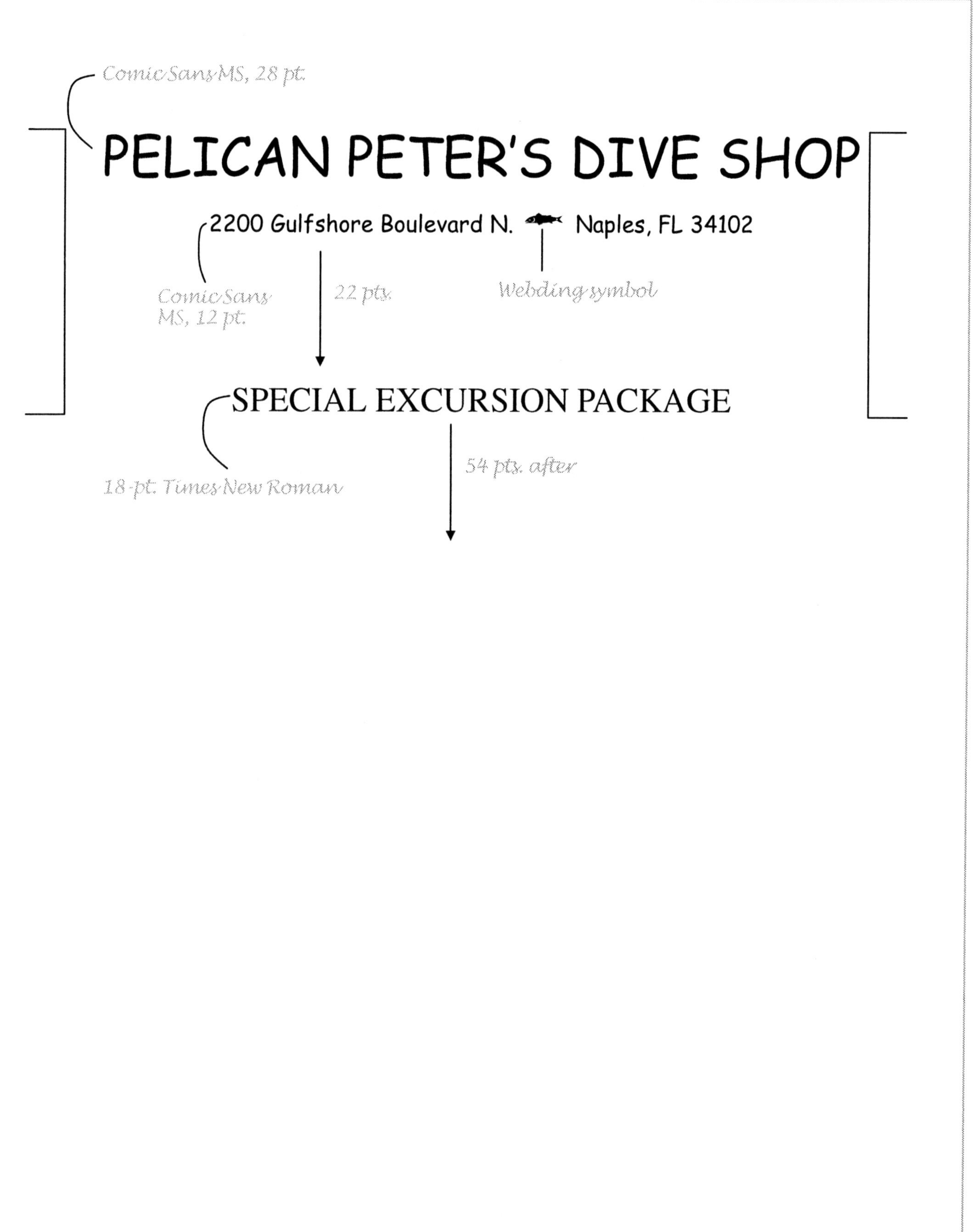

PELICAN PETER'S DIVE SHOP

2200 Gulfshore Boulevard N. Naples, FL 34102

SPECIAL EXCURSION PACKAGE

Item	Package Price
Meals	$40.00
Guide Fee	$75.00
Boat Fee	$99.00
Equipment Rental	$159.00
Training	$225.00
Total Package Price	$598.00

On Your Own

1. Open the document OWDTABLE4, the letter that you wrote in the On Your Own section of exercise 41, or open 42OWDTABLE4.
2. Save the file as OWDTABLE5.
3. Sort the rows in the table into descending numerical order, according to the amount of the expenses.
4. Add a row to the bottom of the table.
5. Label the row **Total**.
6. Calculate the total amount of expenses in the table. Make sure the result is displayed in dollar format.
7. Change one or more of the values in the table.
8. Update the calculation.
9. Apply an AutoFormat to the table.
10. Save the changes, close the document, and exit Word.

Exercise 43

Skills Covered:

◆ **Cell Borders and Shading**

On the Job

Cell borders and shading let you dress up your tables to make them look good, as well as to highlight important information.

Pete Newell of Pelican Peter's Dive Shop likes the flyer you have created advertising the excursion package, but he wants you to add some visual enhancements. In this exercise, you will use cell borders and shading to format the table.

Terms

Line style The appearance of a line.

Line weight The thickness of a line.

Shading A color or pattern used to fill the background of a cell.

Notes

Cell Borders and Shading

- By default, Word applies a ½-pt. black solid line border around all table cells.
- Use the Tables and Borders toolbar buttons to change the borders and shading of table cells.
- You can select borders and shading before you draw new cells, or apply them to selected cells.
  - Select a different **line style**.
  - Select a different **line weight**. 1/4
  - Change the border color.
  - Remove or add border lines.
  - Add color or **shading**. 
- Selected border and shading formatting remains in effect until new formatting is selected.

✓ *When table borders are removed, you can see table dividers on-screen by displaying gridlines.*

Procedures

Apply Cell Borders

1. Position insertion point in cell to format.

   OR

   Select component(s) to format.
2. Click **Borders** drop-down arrow.
3. Click border style.
   - ✓ *Border buttons are toggles—click to display border; click again to hide border.*

Apply Line Styles

1. Click **Line Style** drop-down arrow.
2. Click desired line style.
   - ✓ *Click No Border to remove border lines.*
3. Click cell to format.

   OR

   Select component(s) to format.
4. Apply cell border(s) as desired.

Apply Line Weight

1. Click **Line Weight** drop-down arrow ¼.
2. Click desired line weight.
3. Click cell to format.

   OR

   Select component(s) to format.
4. Apply cell border(s) as desired.

Apply Line Color

1. Click **Border Color** button.
2. Click desired color.
3. Click cell to format.

   OR

   Select component(s) to format.
4. Apply cell border(s) as desired.

Apply Cell Shading

1. Position insertion point in cell to format.

   OR

   Select component(s) to format.
2. Click **Shading Color** drop-down arrow.
3. Click desired color.
4. Click **No Fill** to remove shading or color.

Exercise Directions

1. Start Word, if necessary.
2. Open PACKAGE or open 43PACKAGE.
3. Save the document as PACKAGE2.
4. Apply a turquoise double-line 1½" border around the outside of the table.
5. Apply the same border across the bottom of all cells in the first row.
6. Remove the border line between the cells in the first row.
   - ✓ *Do not merge the cells; simply remove the border line.*
7. Apply a 20% gray shade fill to the cells in the first row.
8. Apply a 12.5% gray shading to the cells in the bottom row.
9. Apply a solid line, black, 3-pt. border above the last row.
10. Change the text in the bottom row to boldface.
11. Check the spelling and grammar in the document.
12. Preview the document. It should look similar to Illustration A.
13. Print the document.
14. Close the document, saving all changes.

Illustration A

PELICAN PETER'S DIVE SHOP

2200 Gulfshore Boulevard N. Naples, FL 34102

SPECIAL EXCURSION PACKAGE

Item	Package Price
Training	$225.00
Equipment Rental	$159.00
Boat Fee	$99.00
Guide Fee	$75.00
Meals	$40.00
Total Package Price	**$ 598.00**

On Your Own

1. Open OWDTABLE5, the document you used in the On Your Own section of Exercise 42, or open 43OWDTABLE5.
2. Save the document as OWDTABLE6.
3. Customize the formatting of the table by applying cell borders and cell shading.
4. Preview the document.
5. Save the document, close it, and exit Word.

Exercise 44

◆ Critical Thinking

You work in the Accounts Payable department at Northlake Video Links. You have been asked to design an invoice to send to a client. You've decided that this is a great opportunity to use your table skills.

Exercise Directions

1. Start Word and create a new blank document.
2. Save the document as INVOICE.
3. Using either the Draw Table tool or the Insert Table command, create the table shown in Illustration A.
   - Size the cells as closely as possible to the sizes indicated on Illustration A.
   - ✓ *If you use the Insert Table command, you will have to merge and split cells to achieve the desired results.*
4. Remove all borderlines from the table.
5. Display gridlines, if necessary, so you can see the cells on-screen.
6. Center the table horizontally on the page.
7. Enter the text shown in Illustration B, using the specified formatting and alignment.
8. In the right cell of the row labeled Total, use a formula to calculate the total amount owed. Format the result using the dollar number format.
9. Apply border lines as shown in Illustration B.
10. Check the spelling and grammar in the document.
11. Preview the document. It should look similar to the one in Illustration B.
12. Print the document.
13. Close the document, saving all changes.

Illustration A

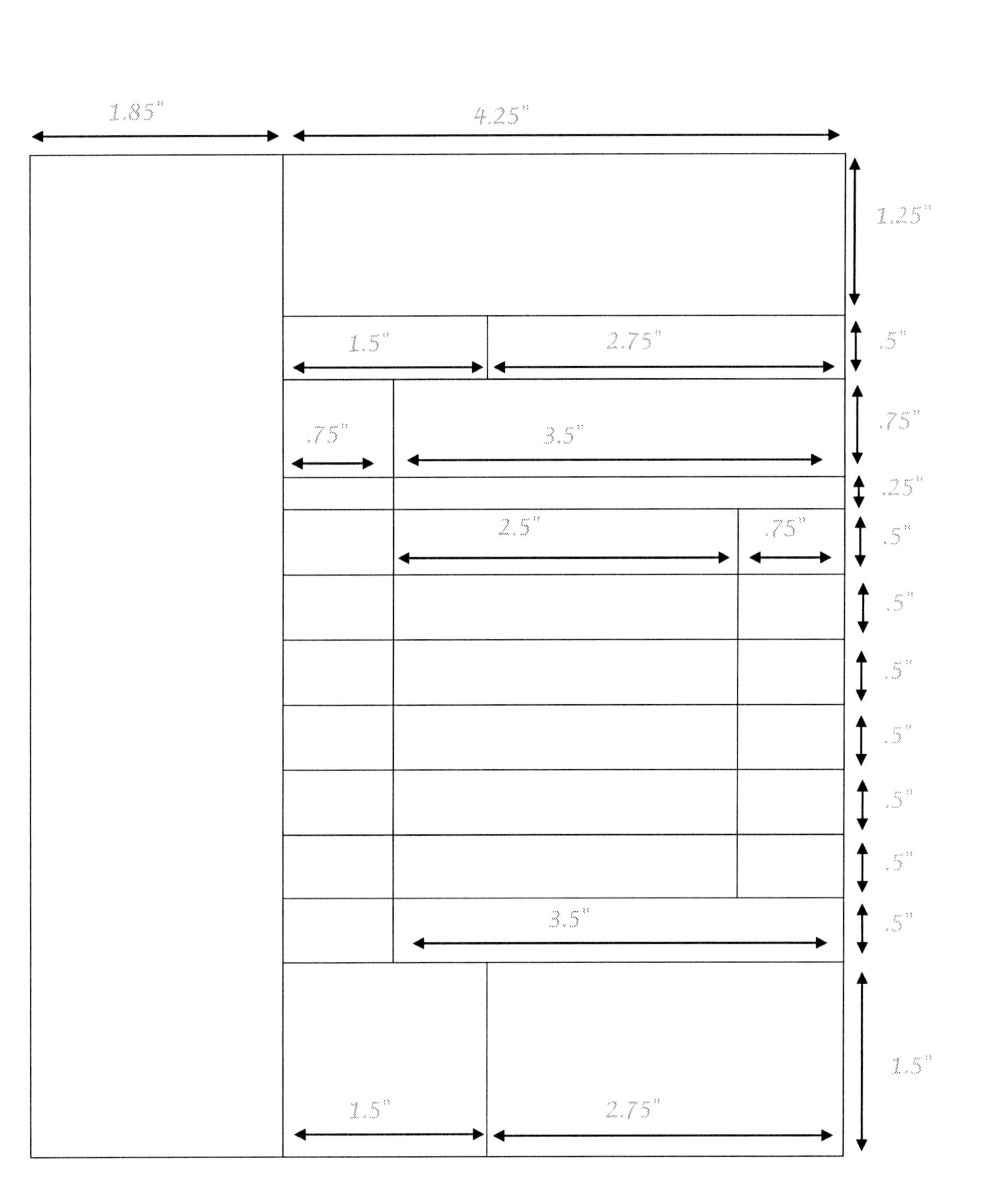

Illustration B

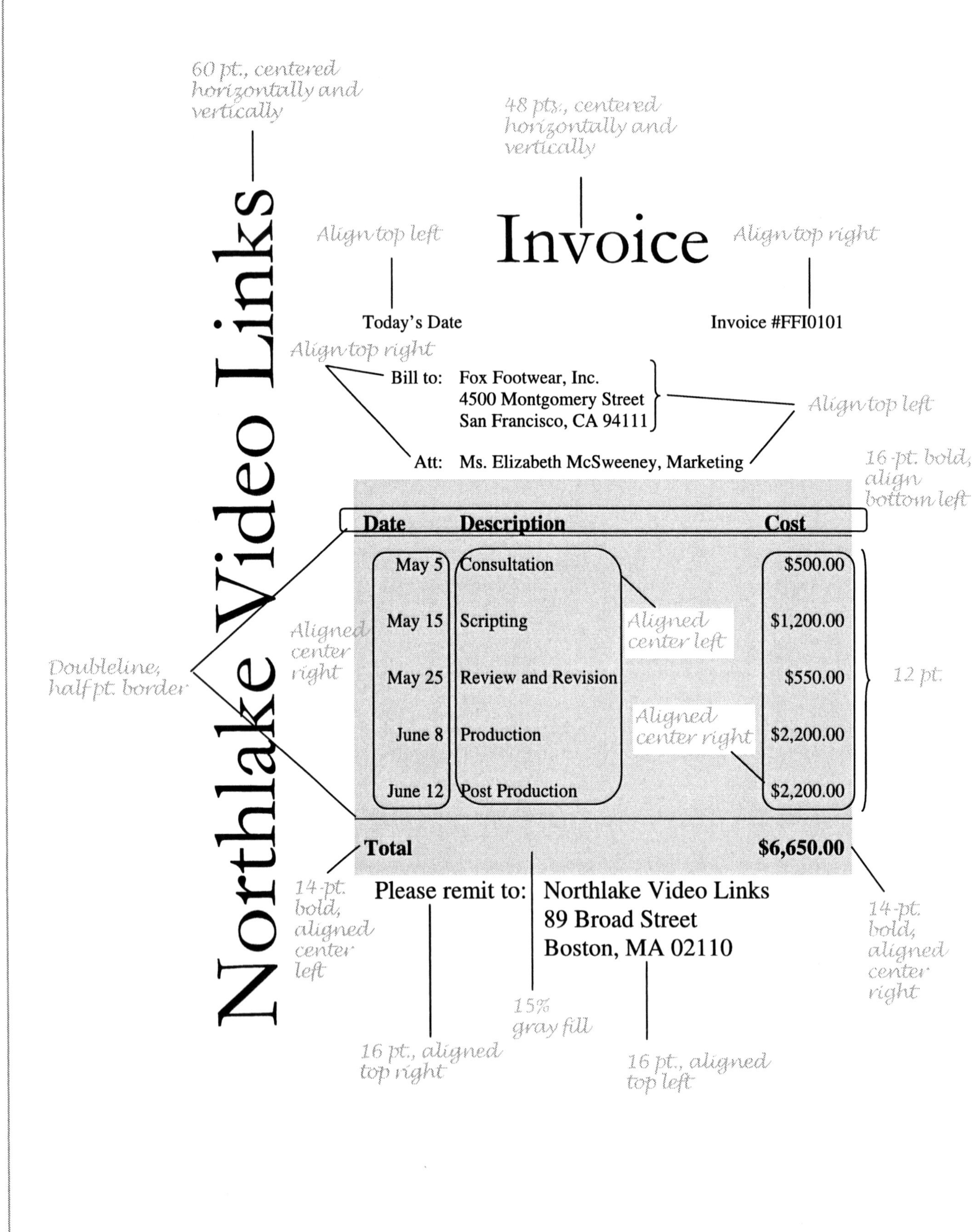

Lesson 8

Merge

Exercise 45

- Mail Merge Basics
- Use the Mail Merge Wizard
- Create a New Address List
- Use Merge Fields

Exercise 46

- Merge with an Existing Address List
- Merge Envelopes

Exercise 47

- Edit an Address List
- Customize Merge Fields
- Merge Labels

Exercise 48

- Sort Recipients in an Address List
- Select Specific Recipients
- Filter Recipients
- Create a Director with Mail Merge

Exercise 49

- Critical Thinking

Exercise 45

Skills Covered:

◆ **Mail Merge Basics** ◆ **Use the Mail Merge Wizard**
◆ **Create a New Address List** ◆ **Use Merge Fields**

On the Job

Use Mail Merge to customize mass mailings. For example, with Mail Merge you can store a document with standard text, such as a form letter, and then insert personalized names and addresses on each copy that you generate or print. You can also use Mail Merge to generate envelopes, labels, e-mail messages, and directories, such as a telephone list.

A letter thanking those people who submitted essays to Fox Footwear's contest becomes a simple task using the Mail Merge feature. The form letter will be personalized with each person's name and address. In this exercise, you will create the letter document and the data source address list, and you will merge them to generate the letters.

Terms

Mail merge A process that inserts variable information into a standardized document to produce a personalized or customized document.

Main document The document containing the standardized text that will be printed on all documents.

Merge field A placeholder in the main document that marks where and what will be inserted from the data source document.

Merge block A set of merge fields stored as one unit. For example, the Address block contains all of the name and address information.

Data source The document containing the variable data that will be inserted during the merge.

Office address list A simple data source file stored in Access file format that includes the information needed for an address list, such as first name, last name, street, city, state, and so on.

Outlook contact list Names, address, and other information stored as contacts for use in the Microsoft Outlook personal information manager program.

Microsoft Access database A file created with the Microsoft Access program used for storing information.

Merge document The customized document resulting from a merge.

Field One item of variable data, such as a first name, a last name, or a ZIP Code.

Record A collection of variable data about one person or thing. In a form letter merge for example, each record contains variable data for each person receiving the letter: first name, last name, address, city, state, and ZIP Code.

Address list form A dialog box used to enter mailing list information for a data source file.

Notes

Mail Merge Basics

- Use **Mail Merge** to create mass mailings, envelopes, labels, or directories.
- To create a mail merge, you must have two important files:
  - A **main document**, which contains information that won't change, as well as **merge fields** and **merge blocks**, which act as placeholders for variable information. For example, you might have a form letter that has merge fields where the address and greeting should be.
  - A **data source** file, which contains variable information such as names and addresses. Word lets you use many types of data source files for a merge, including an **Office address list**, an **Outlook contact list**, or a **Microsoft Access database**.
- During the merge, Word generates a series of **merge documents** in which the variable information from the data source replaces the merge fields entered in the main document.
- You can print the merge documents or save them in a file for future use.
- You can use the Mail Merge Wizard or the buttons on the Mail Merge toolbar to access Mail Merge features and command.

A main document

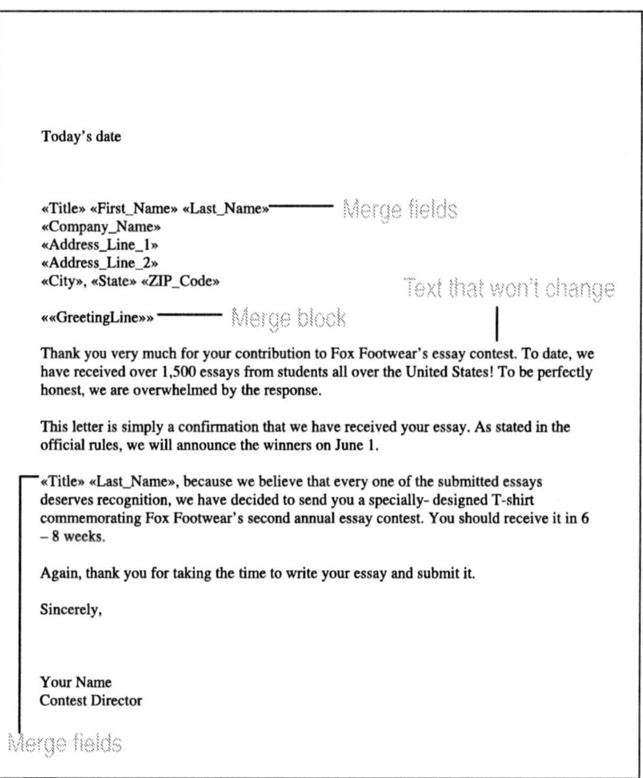
Today's date

«Title» «First_Name» «Last_Name»
«Company_Name»
«Address_Line_1»
«Address_Line_2»
«City», «State» «ZIP_Code»

««GreetingLine»»

Thank you very much for your contribution to Fox Footwear's essay contest. To date, we have received over 1,500 essays from students all over the United States! To be perfectly honest, we are overwhelmed by the response.

This letter is simply a confirmation that we have received your essay. As stated in the official rules, we will announce the winners on June 1.

«Title» «Last_Name», because we believe that every one of the submitted essays deserves recognition, we have decided to send you a specially- designed T-shirt commemorating Fox Footwear's second annual essay contest. You should receive it in 6 – 8 weeks.

Again, thank you for taking the time to write your essay and submit it.

Sincerely,

Your Name
Contest Director

Mail Merge toolbar

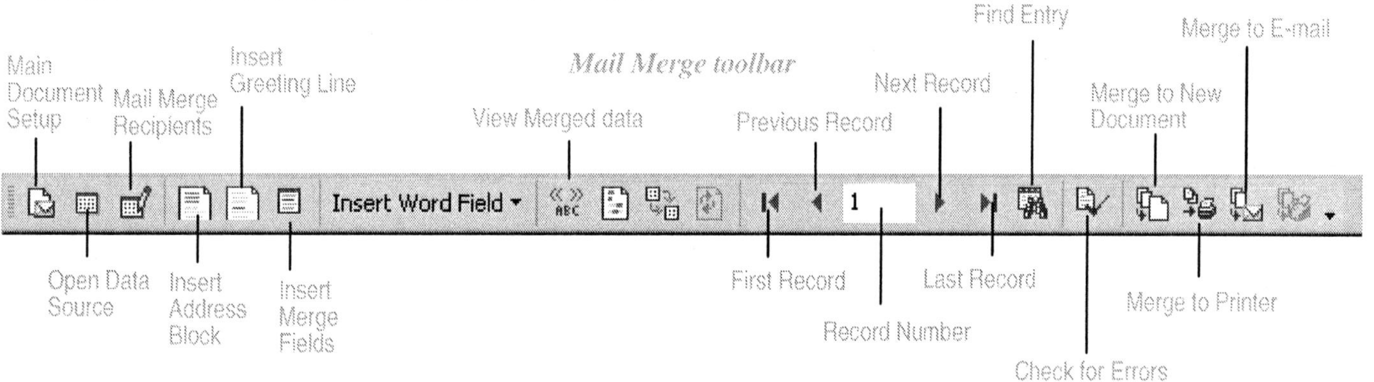

A series of merge documents

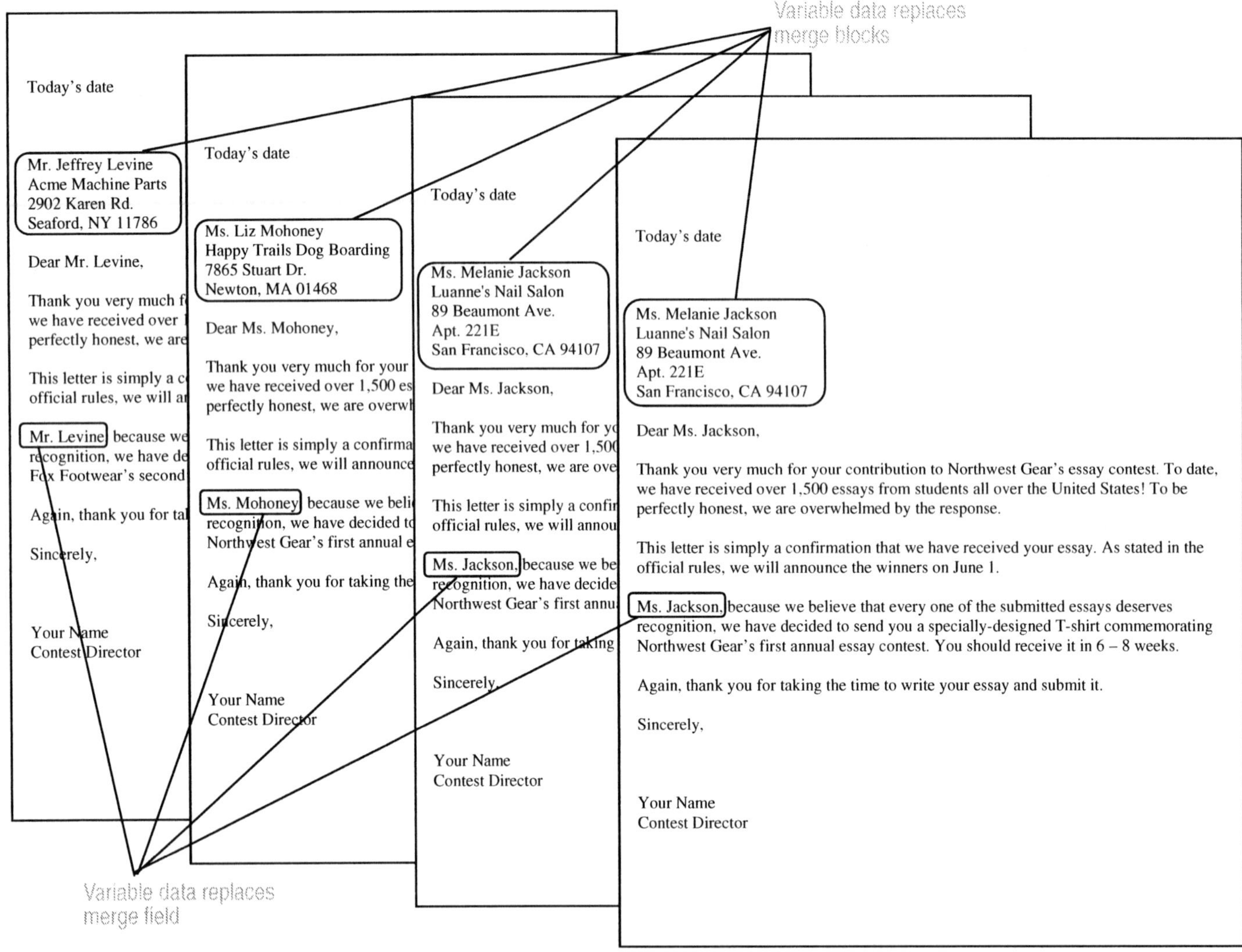

Use the Mail Merge Wizard

- The Mail Merge Wizard steps you through the process of conducting a merge.
- There are six steps in the Mail Merge Wizard:
  - The first step is to select the type of main document you want to create:

Letter	Used for letters or other regular Word documents such as reports, flyers, or memos.
E-mail messages	Used to create messages to send via e-mail.
Envelopes	Used to create personalized envelopes.
Labels	Used to create personalized labels.
Directory	Used for lists such as rosters or telephone lists.

  - The second step is to select a starting document. You may select to start from the current document, an existing document, or a new document based on a template.
  - The third step in the Mail Merge Wizard is to select recipients. In this step, you locate or create the data source file, and then select the individual recipients to include in the merge.

    ✓ *If you select to create a new list, the Mail Merge Wizard prompts you through the steps for creating the data source file by entering the variable data for each recipient.*

  - The fourth step is to create the main document. In this step, you type and format the data you want included in each merge document, and you insert the merge fields or merge blocks where Word will insert the variable data.

Step 4 of the Mail Merge Wizard

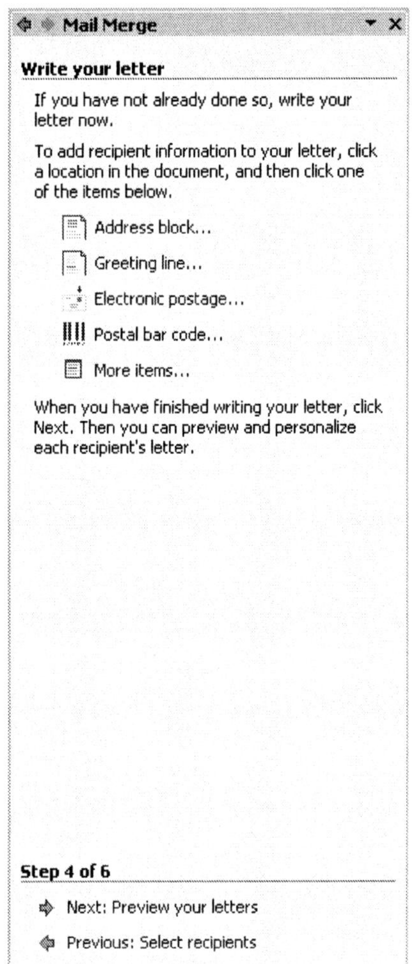

- The fifth step is to preview the merge documents. In this step you have the opportunity to see the merge documents before you print them.
- The final step is to complete the merge. You have the option of printing the merge documents, or saving them in a new file for later use.

Create a New Address List

- An Office address list is a simple data source file used to store all of the variable information required to complete a mail merge.
- The data is stored in a table format, with each column containing one **field** of information, and each row containing the **record** for one recipient.
- One merge document is created for each record in the data source document.

The list of recipients stored in an address list

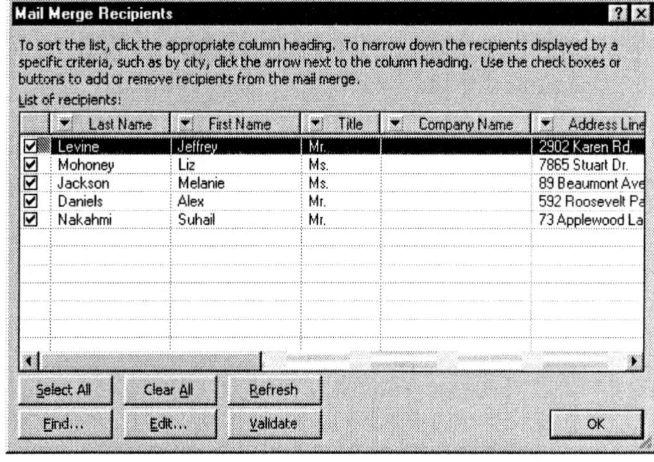

- You enter the data in an **address list form** that has already been set up to include the necessary fields.
- You must save the file the same way you save any Office file—by giving it a name and selecting a storage location.
- By default, Word stores the file in the My Data Sources folder, which is a subfolder of My Documents.
- If a field in the data source is blank, the information is left out of the merge document for that record.
- You can use an address list file many times, with different main documents.
- You can sort the list, and you can select the specific recipients you want to include in the merge.

An address list form

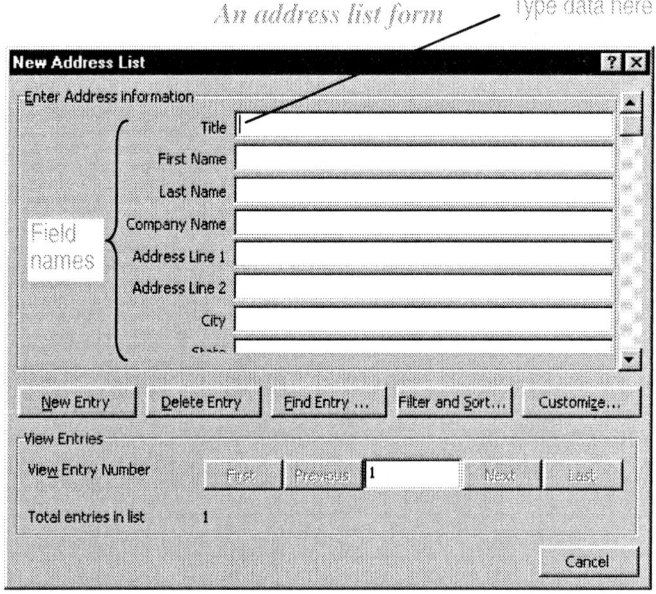

Use Merge Fields

- Word has a preset list of merge fields that correspond to variable information typically used in a mail merge.
- It also creates merge blocks combining several fields so that you can insert one merge block instead of inserting numerous merge fields.
- You insert the merge fields or blocks in the main document at the location where you want the corresponding variable data to print.
- You must type all spaces and punctuation between merge fields. Merge blocks, however, include standard punctuation and spacing, such as a comma following the city.
- By default, when you insert a merge field, you see the field name enclosed in merge field characters (<< >>). The field may be shaded, depending on your system's field code option settings.
  - ✓ *The field code option settings are found on the View tab in the Options dialog box. Select Options from the Tools menu, and then click the View tab.*
- You may insert merge fields more than once in a document. For example, you can insert the name merge field in multiple locations in order to personalize a letter.

Procedures

Use the Mail Merge Wizard to Generate a Form Letter Using a New Address List Data Source File

Select the main document:

1. Open a new blank document.
2. Click **Tools** .... Alt+T
3. Select **Letters and Mailings** .... E
4. Click **Mail Merge Wizard** .... M
5. Click the **Letters** options button.
6. Click **Next: Starting document**.
7. Click the **Use the current document** option button.
8. Click **Next: Select recipients**.

Create an address list data source file:

1. Click the **Type a new list** option button.
2. Click **Create** .
3. Type the title for the first person you want to add to the address list.
4. Press **Enter** .... Enter
   or **Tab** .... Tab
   - ✓ *Press Shift+Tab to move to previous field.*
5. Type the person's first name.
6. Press **Enter** .... Enter
   or **Tab** .... Tab
7. Continue typing variable data until record is complete.
   - ✓ *You may leave blank any fields for which information is not available or necessary.*
8. Click **New Entry** .... Alt+N
   - ✓ *Word displays next blank address form.*
9. Repeat steps 3–8 until you have entered the information for all recipients.
   - ✓ *You can edit the data source file in the future. For example, you can add and delete records. For more information, refer to exercise 40.*
10. Click **Close** .... 
    - ✓ *Word displays the Save Address List dialog box.*
11. Type file name.
12. Click **Save** button Save.
    - ✓ *Word displays the Mail Merge Recipients dialog box. By default, all recipients are selected. For information on selecting specific recipients, refer to Exercise 48.*
13. Click **OK** .... 
14. Click **Next: Write your letter**.
    - ✓ *Word displays the starting document, and a list of available merge blocks.*

Create a form letter document:

1. Begin typing the letter, including all text and formatting as you want it to appear on each merge document. For example, insert the date and move the insertion point down four lines.
2. At the location where you want the recipient's address displayed, click **Address block** .

   OR

   Click **Insert Address Block** button on Mail Merge toolbar.
   - ✓ *Word displays the Insert Address Block dialog box.*
3. Select desired options.
4. Click **OK** .... Enter

   OR

   a. Click **More items** in the task pane.

   OR

   - Click **Insert Merge Fields** button on Mail Merge toolbar.
     - ✓ *Word displays the Insert Merge Field dialog box.*

b. Click field to insert......... [icon]
c. Click **Insert** .... Alt+I
d. Click **Close** .... Esc

5. Continue typing and formatting letter, repeating steps to insert merge fields or merge blocks at desired location(s).
6. Save the document.
7. Click **Next: Preview your letters**.
   ✓ *Word displays the first merge document.*

Preview merge documents:

1. Click the **Next recipient** button [>>] in the Mail Merge Wizard task pane.

   OR

   Click the **Next recipient** button [▶] on the Mail Merge toolbar.

   OR

   Click the **Previous recipient** button [<<] in the Mail Merge Wizard task pane.

   OR

   Click the **Previous recipient** button [◀] on the Mail Merge toolbar.
2. Click **Next: Complete the Merge.**

Complete the merge:

- Click **Print** [icon] to open the Print dialog box to print the merge documents

OR

1. Click **Edit individual letters** [icon] to create a new file containing all merged letters.
   ✓ *Word displays the Merge to File dialog box.*
2. Click **OK** .... Enter to merge all letters to a new file.
   ✓ *You can make changes to individual letters, and/or save the document to print later.*

Exercise Directions

1. Start Word, if necessary.
2. Create a new blank document.
3. Save the file as FORMLET.
4. Start the Mail Merge Wizard.
5. Select to create a letter, using the current document.
6. Create a new address list to use as a data source document.
7. Enter the recipients from Illustration A into the data source file.
8. Save the data source file as SOURCE.
9. Select to use all recipients in the merge, then close the Mail Merge Recipients dialog box.
10. Type the document shown in Illustration B, inserting the merge fields and merge blocks as marked.
11. Check the spelling and grammar in the document.
12. Complete the merge by generating a file containing all of the individual records.
13. Preview the merged documents.
14. Save the file as LETTERS.
15. Print the file.
16. Close all open documents, saving all changes.

Illustration A

Title	First Name	Last Name	Address Line 1	Address Line 2	City	State	ZIP Code
Mr.	Jeffrey	Levine	2902 Karen Road		Seaford	NY	11786
Ms.	Liz	Mohoney	7865 Stuart Drive		Newton	MA	01468
Ms.	Melanie	Jackson	89 Beaumont Avenue	Apt 221E	San Francisco	CA	94107
Mr.	Alex	Daniels	592 Roosevelt Parkway		Auburn	ME	04210
Mr.	Suhail	Nakahmi	73 Applewood Lane		Jenkintown	PA	19046

Illustration B

Today's date

««AddressBlock»»

««GreetingLine»»

Insert Merge blocks

Thank you very much for your contribution to Fox Footwear's essay contest. To date, we have received over 1,500 essays from students all over the United States! To be perfectly honest, we are overwhelmed by the response.

This letter is simply a confirmation that we have received your essay. As stated in the official rules, we will announce the winners on June 1.

Insert Merge fields

«Title» «Last_Name», because we believe that every one of the submitted essays deserves recognition, we have decided to send you a specially designed T-shirt commemorating Fox Footwear's second annual essay contest. You should receive it in 6 – 8 weeks.

Again, thank you for taking the time to write your essay and submit it.

Sincerely,

Your Name
Contest Director

On Your Own

1. Think of ways Mail Merge would be useful to you. For example, are you involved in any clubs or organizations that send out mass mailings? Do you send out "Holiday Letters" every year? Are you responsible for regular reports that contain variable data, such as sales reports or forecasts?
2. Use the Mail Merge Wizard to create a form letter.
3. Save the main document as OWDMERGE1.
4. Create an address list data source file that includes at least five records.
5. Save the data source file as OWDSOURCE1.
6. Type the letter, inserting merge fields and merge blocks as necessary.
7. Check the spelling and grammar in the document.
8. Merge the documents into a new file.
9. Save the merge document file as OWDMERGE2.
10. Print the letters.
11. Close all open documents, saving all changes.

Exercise 46

Skills Covered:

◆ **Merge with an Existing Address List**

◆ **Merge Envelopes**

On the Job

If you have an existing data source document, you can merge it with any main document to create new merge documents. This saves you from retyping repetitive data. For example, using an existing Address List data source makes it easy to create envelopes to accompany a form letter merge that you previously created.

To mail out the form letters for Fox Footwear, you need to print envelopes. In this exercise, you create an envelope main document and merge it with the same Address List file you used in Exercise 45.

Terms

There is no new vocabulary in this exercise.

Notes

Merge with an Existing Address List

- Once you create and save an Office Address List data source file, you can use it with different main documents.
- In Step 3 of the Mail Merge Wizard, you can locate and open the data source file you want to use.
- Alternatively, click the Open Data Source button on the Mail Merge toolbar to display the Select Data Source dialog box.

The Select Data Source dialog box

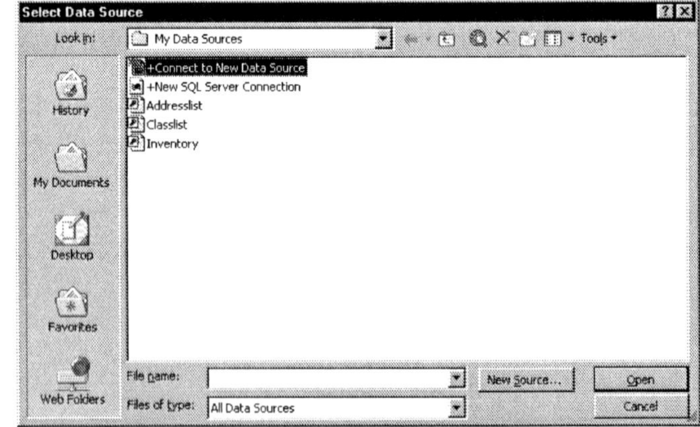

- You can also use existing data source files created with other applications, including Microsoft Access.
  - ✓ *If you select a data source created with Access, you must specify which table or query to use, and the merge fields inserted in the Word document must match the fields used in the Access file.*

- Using an existing data source saves you the time and trouble of retyping existing data.

Merge Envelopes

- To create envelopes using Mail Merge, select Envelopes as the main document type.
- The Mail Merge Wizard prompts you to select envelope options so that the main document is laid out just like the actual paper envelopes on which you will print.

The Envelope Options dialog box

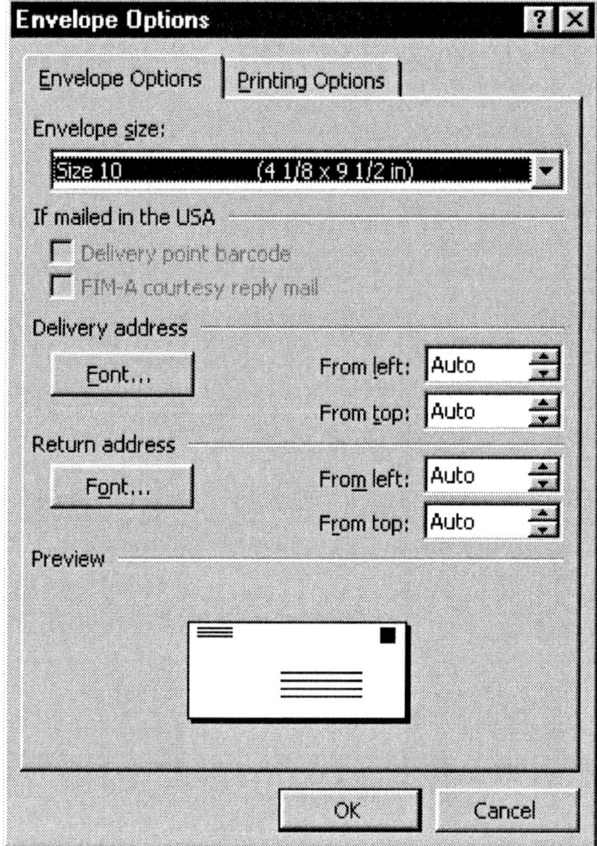

- When you select the size and format of the envelopes, Word changes the layout of the current document to match. Any existing data in the document is deleted.
- To generate the envelopes, you can create a new data source file (see Exercise 45) or use an existing data source file (as covered in this exercise).
- You can merge the envelopes to a printer or to a new document to save, edit, or use at a later time.

Procedures

Use the Mail Merge Wizard to Generate Envelopes using an Existing Address List Data Source File

Select the main document:

1. Open a new blank document.
2. Click **Tools** .... Alt+T
3. Select **Letters and Mailings** .... E
4. Click **Mail Merge Wizard** .... M
5. Click the **Envelopes** option button.
6. Click **Next: Starting document**.

To select envelope options:

1. Click the **Change Document Layout** option button.
2. Click **Envelope Options** .
   ✓ *Word displays the Envelope Options dialog box.*
3. Click **Envelope size**.... Alt+S
4. Click desired size......................... , Enter
5. Click **OK** .... Enter
   ✓ *Word changes the layout of the current document. If a warning is displayed, click OK to continue or Cancel to cancel the change.*
6. Click **Next: Select recipients**.

Select an existing Address List data source file:

1. Click the **Use an existing list** option button.
2. Click **Browse** 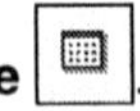.
   ✓ *Word opens the Select Data Source dialog box.*
3. Locate and select the desired data source file.
4. Click **Open** .... 
   ✓ *Word displays the Mail Merge Recipients dialog box. By default, all recipients are selected. For information on selecting specific recipients, refer to Exercise 48.*
5. Click **OK** .... 
6. Click **Next: Arrange your envelope**.
   ✓ *Word displays the starting document and a list of available merge blocks.*

Arrange the envelope:

1. Type any text you want to appear on each printed envelope. For example, type a return address in the upper-left corner.
2. Position the insertion point at the location where you want the recipient's address displayed.
   ✓ *By default, Word creates a text box on the envelope document where the address should print. If necessary, click the Show/Hide ¶ to display non-printing characters so you can see where the text box is located.*
3. Click **Address block** 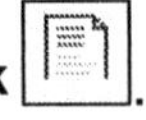.

   OR

   Click **Insert Address Block** button on Mail Merge toolbar.
   ✓ *Word displays the Insert Address Block dialog box.*
4. Select desired options.
5. Click **OK** .... Enter

   OR

   a. Click **More items** in the task pane.

      OR

      - Click **Insert Merge Fields** button on Mail Merge toolbar.

      ✓ *Word displays the Insert Merge Field dialog box.*

   b. Click field to insert .... 
   c. Click **Insert**............. Alt+I
   d. Click **Close**.................... Esc
6. Type any other standard text required on the envelope.
7. Insert additional fields or blocks as necessary.
8. Save the document.
9. Click **Next: Preview your envelopes**.
   ✓ *Word displays the first merge document.*

Preview merge documents:

1. Click the **Next recipient** button in the Mail Merge Wizard task pane.

   OR

   Click the **Next recipient** button on the Mail Merge toolbar.

   OR

   Click the **Previous recipient** button in the Mail Merge Wizard task pane.

   OR

   Click the **Previous recipient** button on the Mail Merge toolbar.
2. Click **Next: Complete the merge.**

Complete the merge:

- Click **Print** to open the Print dialog box and print the merged documents.

OR

1. Click **Edit individual envelopes** to create a new file containing all merged envelopes.
   ✓ *Word displays the Merge to File dialog box.*
2. Click **OK**.......................... Enter to complete the merge.
   ✓ *You can make changes to individual envelopes, and/or save the document to print later.*

Exercise Directions

✓ *In this exercise you will use SOURCE the Office Address List file you created in Exercise 45. If that file is not available on your system, prior to starting the exercise copy the file 46SOURCE and save the copy as SOURCE.*

✓ *To copy the file, right-click the file name and select Copy. Right-click the destination folder and select Paste. Right-click the copied file name and select Rename. Type the new file name and press Enter.*

1. Start Word, if necessary.
2. Create a new blank document.
3. Save the document as MAINENV.
4. Start the Mail Merge Wizard.
5. Select to create envelopes, using the current document.
6. Select envelope size 10.
7. Select to use an existing address list file as a data source document.
8. Locate and open the SOURCE data source file.
9. Close the Mail Merge Recipients dialog box.
10. Set up the envelope main document as shown in Illustration A.
    a. Type the return address.
    b. Insert the Address merge block.
11. Check the spelling and grammar in the document.
12. Preview the merged documents.
13. Complete the merge by generating a file containing all of the individual envelopes.
14. Save the file as ENVELOPES.
15. If requested by your instructor, print the merge documents.

    ✓ *If you do not have actual envelopes, you can print the merge documents on regular paper.*
16. Close all open files, saving all changes.

Illustration A

Fox Footwear, Inc.
4500 Montgomery Street
San Francisco, CA 94111

««AddressBlock»»

On Your Own

1. Create a new document in Word.
2. Save it as OWDENV1.
3. Use the Mail Merge Wizard to create envelopes using OWDMERGE2 (the data source document you used in exercise 45) as the data source.

   ✓ *If* OWDMERGE2 *is not available, use* 46OWDMERGE2.

4. Merge the envelopes to a new document.
5. Save the merge document as OWDENV2.
6. Close all open documents, saving all changes.

Exercise 47

Skills Covered:

◆ **Edit an Address List** ◆ **Customize Merge Fields**
◆ **Merge Labels**

On the Job

You can easily edit a data source document to add or remove records, or to customize merge fields to include specialized information not included in the default Address List data source file. You can also use mail merge to generate mailing labels.

The T-shirts that you promised to the people who submitted essays for Fox Footwear's contest have arrived. In this exercise, you edit the address list data source and customize the merge fields. Finally, you use the Address List to print labels to use on the packages containing the T-shirts.

Terms

There is no new vocabulary in this exercise.

Notes

Edit an Address List

- You can easily edit an existing Address List.
- You can change information that is already entered.
- You can add or delete information, including entire records.

Customize Merge Fields

- Customize merge fields to change field names, delete unused fields, or add fields specific to your needs. For example, you might want to add a field for entering a job title.
- You can also move fields up or down in the field list.

The Customize Address List dialog box

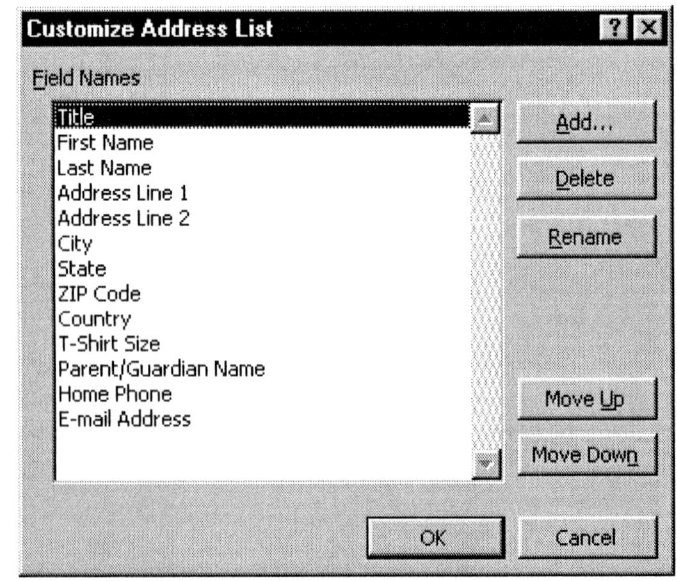

Merge Labels

- To create labels using Mail Merge, select Labels as the main document type.
- The Mail Merge Wizard prompts you to select label options so that the main document is laid out just like the actual paper labels on which you will print.
- When you select the size and format of the labels, Word changes the layout of the current document to match. Any existing data in the document is deleted.
- You can create a new data source file as covered in Exercise 45, or use an existing data source file as covered in Exercise 46.
- You can merge the labels to a printer or to a new document to save, edit, or use at a later time.

The Label Options dialog box

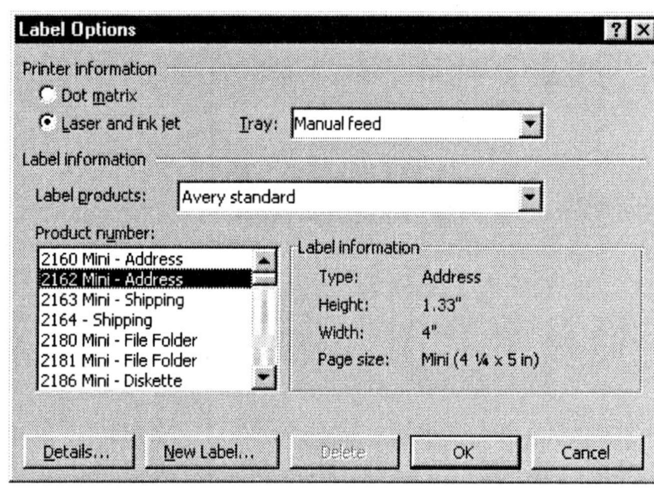

Procedures

Use the Mail Merge Wizard to Generate Labels Using an Existing Address List Data Source File

Select the main document:

1. Open a new blank document.
2. Click **Tools** .... Alt+T
3. Select **Letters and Mailings** .... E
4. Click **Mail Merge Wizard** ..... M
5. Click the **Labels** option button.
6. Click **Next: Starting document**.

To select label options:

1. Click the **Change Document Layout** option button.
2. Click **Label Options** .
   - ✓ *Word displays the Label Options dialog box.*
3. Select label options.
4. Click **OK** .... Enter
   - ✓ *Word changes the layout of the current document. If a warning is displayed, click OK to continue or Cancel to cancel the change.*
5. Click **Next: Select recipients**.

Select an Address List data source file:

1. Click the **Use an existing list** option button and follow steps in Exercise 46 to locate and select desired list.

   OR

   Click the **Type a new list** option button and follow steps in Exercise 45 to create a new list.
2. When list is complete click **OK** .... Enter
3. Click **Next: Arrange your labels**.
   - ✓ *Word displays the starting document, and a list of available merge blocks.*

Arrange the labels:

1. In the first label, position the insertion point at the location where you want the recipient's address displayed.
2. Click **Address block** 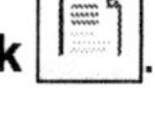.

   OR

   Click **Insert Address Block** button on Mail Merge toolbar.
   - ✓ *Word displays the Insert Address Block dialog box.*
3. Select desired options.
4. Click **OK** .... Enter

   OR

   Click **More items** in the task pane.

   OR

   Click **Insert Merge Fields** button on Mail Merge toolbar.
   - ✓ *Word displays the Insert Merge Field dialog box.*

   a. Click field to insert .... ↑↓

   b. Click **Insert** .... Alt+I

   c. Click **Close** .... Esc
5. Type any other standard text and/or punctuation required on the label.
6. Insert additional fields or blocks as necessary.
7. Click **Update all labels** button Update all labels in the task pane to copy the layout from the first label to all other labels.
   - ✓ *Alternatively, click **Propagate Labels** button on the Mail Merge toolbar.*
8. Save the document.
9. Click **Next: Preview your labels**.
   - ✓ *Word displays the first merge document.*

Preview merge documents:

1. Click the **Next recipient** button [>>] in the Mail Merge Wizard task pane.

   OR

   Click the **Next recipient** button on the Mail Merge toolbar.

   OR

   Click the **Previous recipient** button [<<] in the Mail Merge Wizard task pane.

   OR

   Click the **Previous recipient** button on the Mail Merge toolbar.
2. Click **Next: Complete the merge**.

Complete the merge:

- Click **Print** to open the Print dialog box and print the merged documents

OR

1. Click **Edit individual labels** to create a new file containing all merged labels.
   - ✓ *Word displays the Merge to File dialog box.*
2. Click **OK** .... Enter
   to complete the merge.
   - ✓ *You can make changes to individual labels, and/or save the document to print later.*

Edit an Existing Address List

1. Click **Mail Merge Recipients** button on Mail Merge Toolbar

   OR

   In Step 3 or Step 5 of Mail Merge Wizard, click **Edit recipient list**.
2. Click **Edit**.................... Alt+E
   - ✓ *Word displays the Address List dialog box, with the record for the first recipient displayed.*
3. Do any the following.

To add a new record:

a. Click **New Entry**..... Alt+N

b. Enter variable information as covered in Exercise 45.

To delete a record:

a. Click **Delete Entry** . Alt+D
   to delete the entry currently displayed.

b. Click **Yes** .... Alt+Y
   to delete the entry.

   OR

   - Click **No** .... Alt+N
     to cancel the deletion.

   ✓ *You cannot undo an entry deletion.*

To edit a record:

a. Display record to edit.

   ✓ *Use the Next, Previous, First, and Last buttons to scroll through the records.*

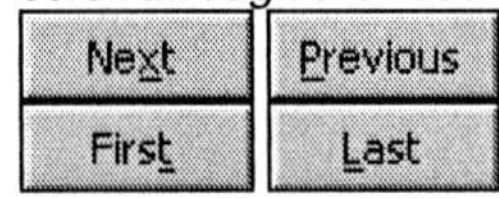

b. Edit variable data as desired.

4. Click **Close** .... Enter
5. Click **OK** .... Enter

Customize Merge Fields

1. Click **Mail Merge Recipients** button on Mail Merge toolbar.

   OR

   In Step 3 or Step 5 of Mail Merge Wizard, click **Edit recipient list**.
2. Click **Edit**.................... Alt+E
   - ✓ *Word displays the Address List dialog box, with the record for the first recipient displayed.*
3. Click **Customize** .... Alt+Z
   - ✓ *Word displays the Customize Address List dialog box.*
4. Do any of the following.

To add a field:

a. Click **Add**................ Alt+A

b. Type field name.

c. Click **OK** .... Enter

To delete a field:

a. Click field to delete................. ↑↓, Enter

b. Click **Delete**........... Alt+D

c. Click **Yes** .... Alt+Y
   to delete the field and all data entered in the field.

   OR

   - Click **No**............ Alt+N
     to cancel the deletion.

To change the order of fields in the field list:

a. Click field to move................. ↑↓, Enter

b. Click **Move Up**........ Alt+U
   to move the field up one line in list.

   OR

   - Click **Move Down** .... Alt+N
     to move field down one line in list.

5. Click **OK**.......................... Enter
6. Click **Close** .... Enter
7. Click **OK**.......................... Enter

Exercise Directions

- ✓ *Prior to starting the exercise, copy the file SOURCE or the file 47SOURCE and save the copy as SOURCE2.*
- ✓ *To copy the file, right-click the file name and select Copy. Right-click the destination folder and select Paste. Right-click the copied file name and select Rename. Type the new file name and press Enter.*

1. Start Word, if necessary.
2. Create a new blank document.
3. Save the file as MAINLABEL.
4. Start the Mail Merge Wizard.
5. Select to create labels, using the current document.
6. Select Avery standard number 2163 mini – shipping labels.
7. Select to use an existing address list file as a data source document.
8. Locate and open SOURCE2.
9. Customize the merge fields as follows:
   a. Delete the Company Name field
   b. Delete the Work Phone field.
   c. Add a T-Shirt Size field.
   d. Move the new field down between the Country and the Home Phone fields.
   e. Add a Parent/Guardian Name field.
   f. Move the new field down between the T-Shirt Size and the Home Phone fields.
10. Add a new record to the address list using the following information:

    Ms. Janine Flaherty
    39621 Gardendale Drive
    Tampa, FL 33624
    T-Shirt Size: **L**
    Parents: **Mr. and Mrs. Jake Flaherty**

11. Fill in the new fields for all existing records using the information in the following table:

	Size	Parent/Guardian
Jeffrey Levine	**XL**	**Mr. and Mrs. Keith Levine**
Liz Mohoney	**S**	**Mrs. Delia Smith**
Melanie Jackson	**M**	**Mr. and Mrs. Ronald Jackson**
Alex Daniels	**M**	**Mr. and Mrs. Robert Daniels**
Suhail Nakhami	**L**	**Mr. Sam Nakhami**

12. Close the Mail Merge Recipients dialog box.
13. Set up the labels main document as shown in Illustration A.
    a. Insert the individual merge fields as shown.
       ✓ *Don't worry if the field names wrap onto multiple lines.*
    b. Type text, punctuation, and spacing as shown, including line breaks,
    c. Once you set up the first label, use Update all labels to set up the other labels.
14. Check the spelling and grammar in the document.
15. Preview the merged documents.
16. Complete the merge by generating a file containing all of the individual labels.
17. Save the file as LABELS.
18. Close all open files, saving all changes.

Illustration A

«Title» «First_Name» «Last_Name» or
«ParentGuardian_Name»
«Address_Line_1»
«Address_Line_2»
«City», «State» «ZIP_Code»

Enclosed shirt size: «TShirt_Size»

«Next Record»«Title» «First_Name» «Last_Name» or
«ParentGuardian_Name»
«Address_Line_1»
«Address_Line_2»
«City», «State» «ZIP_Code»

Enclosed shirt size: «TShirt_Size»

On Your Own

1. Create a new document in Word.
2. Save it as OWDLABELS1.
3. Use the Mail Merge Wizard to create labels using OWDMERGE2 (the data source document you used in exercises 45 and 46) as the data source.
   ✓ *If* OWDMERGE2 *is not available, use* 47OWDDATA2.
4. Add at least one new record to the data source.
5. Delete at least one field.
6. Add at least one field.
7. Fill in all missing information for the existing records.
8. Merge the labels to a new document.
9. Save the merge document as OWDLABELS2.
10. Close all open documents, saving all changes.

Exercise 48

Skills Covered:

◆ **Sort Recipients in an Address List** ◆ **Select Specific Recipients** ◆ **Filter Recipients** ◆ **Create a Directory with Mail Merge**

On the Job

You can use Mail Merge to create a directory, such as a telephone directory, an address list, or a customer directory. Mail Merge makes it easy to select records in your data source file so you can include only specific recipients in a merge. You can also sort the data source file so that the merge documents are generated in alphabetical or numerical order.

As a service to clients, Wayland Home Health Care Associates wants to provide a list of doctors in the area with whom it often consults. You have an existing Office Address List file that includes both doctors and nurses. In this exercise, you will use the existing address list data source file, which you will filter in order to select the records you need. You will also sort the list before generating the directory.

Terms

Column heading The label displayed at the top of a column.

Filter To display records based on whether or not they match specified criteria.

Criteria Specific data used to match a record or entry in a data source file or list.

Directory A single document listing data source file entries.

Notes

Sort Recipients in an Address List

- You can quickly change the order of records in an address list using the data entered in any column in the list.
- Simply click any **column heading** in the Mail Merge Recipients dialog box to sort the records into ascending order.
- Click the column heading again to sort the records into descending order.

Select Specific Recipients

- By default, all recipients in an address list are selected to be included in a merge.
- You can select the specific recipients you want to include. For example, you might want to send letters only to the people who live in a specific town.
- To indicate that a recipient is selected, Word displays a check in the check box at the left end of the recipient's row in the Mail Merge Recipients dialog box.
- You click the check box to clear the check, or click the empty box to select the recipient again.

An address list with only some recipients selected

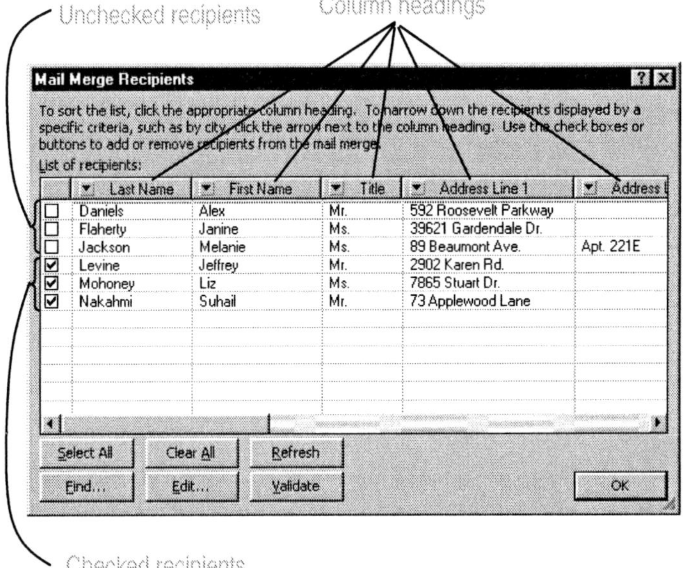

Filter Recipients

- You can **filter** the records in an address list in order to display records that match specific **criteria**.
- The records that match the criteria are displayed, while those that don't match are hidden.
- Filtering can help make it easier to select the specific records you want to include in a merge. For example, if you want to include only the people who live in the state of California, you can deselect all records, filter the list to display only those that have CA entered in the State field, and then select the displayed records.

A list filtered to show entries with the Title Ms.

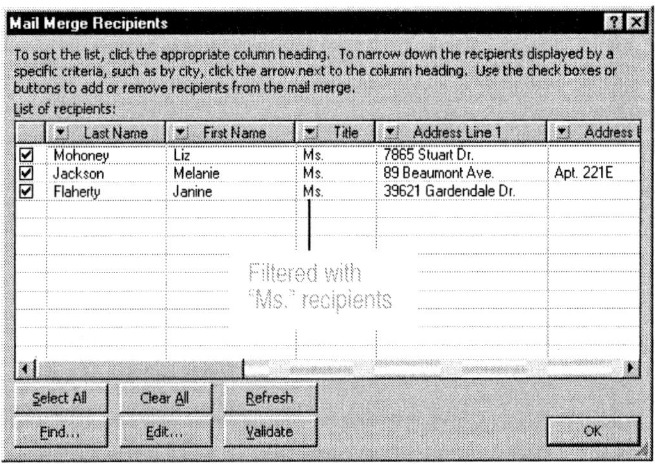

Create a Directory with Mail Merge

- Use Mail Merge to create a **directory**, such as a catalog, an inventory list, or a membership address list.
- When you merge to a directory, Word creates a single document that includes the variable data for all selected recipients.
- You arrange the layout for the first entry in the directory; Mail Merge uses that layout for all entries.

  ✓ *When you preview the directory document you will see each entry on a single page. Once you complete the merge, all entries are listed on one page.*

- You may type text, spacing, and punctuation, and you can include formatting. For example, you might want to include labels such as *Name:*, *Home Phone:*, and *E-Mail:*.
- The Mail Merge Wizard does not give you the option of printing the directory in step 6; however, you may print the merged document the same way you would print any document.

The layout for a directory

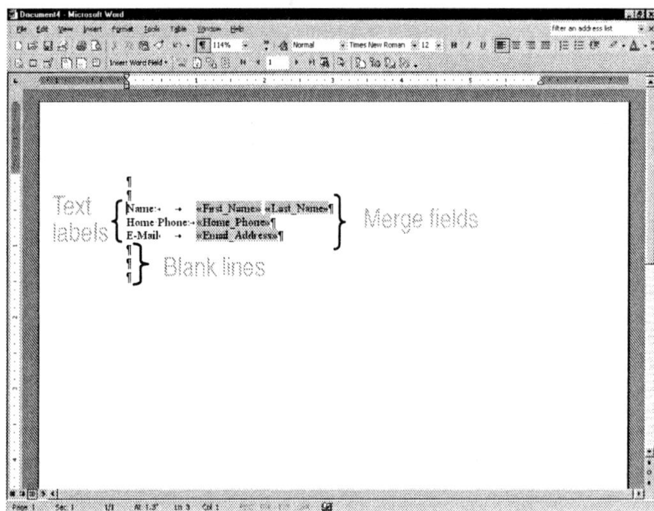

The merged directory

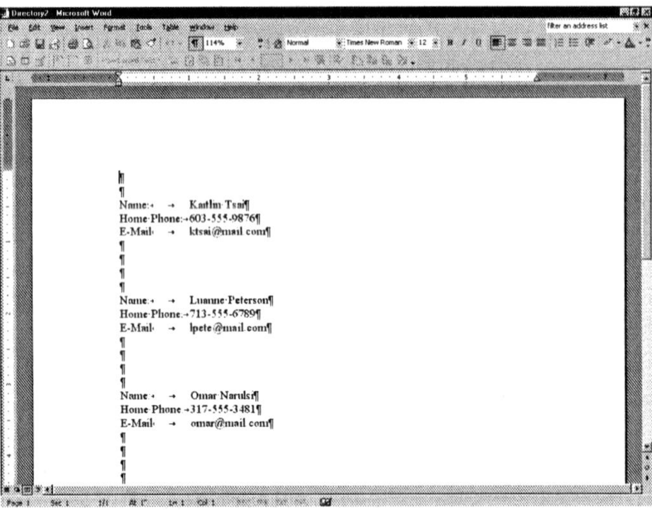

Procedures

Use the Mail Merge Wizard to Generate a Directory Using an Existing Address List Data Source File

Select the main document:

1. Open a new blank document.
2. Click **Tools** .... Alt+T
3. Select **Letters and Mailings** .... E
4. Click **Mail Merge Wizard** .... M
5. Click the **Directory** option button.
6. Click **Next: Starting document**.
7. Click the **Use the current document** option button.
8. Click **Next: Select recipients**.

Select an existing Address List data source file:

1. Click the **Use an existing list** option button.
2. Click **Browse** .
   - ✓ *Word opens the Select Data Source dialog box.*
3. Locate and select the desired data source file.
4. Click **Open** button

    .... Alt+O

   - ✓ *Word displays the Mail Merge Recipients dialog box.*
5. Click **OK** .... Enter
6. Click **Next: Arrange your directory**.

   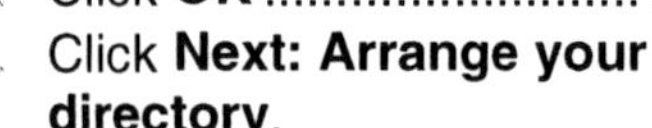

   - ✓ *Word displays the starting document and a list of available merge blocks.*

Arrange the directory:

1. In the current document, position the insertion point at the location where you want the first entry in the directory displayed.
2. Insert the merge fields or merge blocks as necessary to set up the first entry.
3. Type any additional text, spacing, or punctuation you want in the first entry.
   - ✓ *Typed data will be repeated as part of each entry in the directory.*
4. Save the document.
5. Click **Next: Preview your directory**.
   - ✓ *Word displays the first entry in the document.*

Preview merge documents:

1. Click the **Next recipient** button >> in the Mail Merge Wizard task pane.

   OR

   Click the **Next recipient** button on the Mail Merge toolbar.

   OR

   Click the **Previous recipient** button << in the Mail Merge Wizard task pane.

   OR

   Click the **Previous recipient** button on the Mail Merge toolbar.
2. Click **Next: Complete the merge**.

Complete the merge:

1. Click **To New Document** to create the directory document.
   - ✓ *Word displays the Merge to File dialog box.*
2. Click **OK**.......................... Enter
   - ✓ *You can make changes to the document and/or save the document to print later.*

Sort Recipients in an Address List

1. Click **Mail Merge Recipients** button on Mail Merge toolbar.

   OR

   In Step 3 or Step 5 of Mail Merge Wizard, click **Edit recipient list** .
2. Click column heading by which you want to sort.

✓ *To sort in descending order, click column heading again.*

3. Click **OK** .... Enter
   ✓ *Records will be merged in current sort order.*

Select Specific Recipients

1. Click **Mail Merge Recipients** button on Mail Merge toolbar.

   OR

   In Step 3 or Step 5 of Mail Merge Wizard, click **Edit recipient list**.
2. Do one of the following:
   - Click check box at right end of row to deselect recipient ☑.
   - Click blank check box to select recipient ☐.
   - Click **Clear All** .... Alt+A to deselect all recipients.
   - Click **Select All** ...... Alt+S to select all recipients.
3. Click **OK** .... Enter

Filter Recipients

1. Click **Mail Merge Recipients** button on Mail Merge toolbar.

   OR

   In Step 3 or Step 5 of Mail Merge Wizard, click **Edit recipient list**.
2. Click filter arrow on column heading by which you want to filter.
   ✓ *Word displays a list of data.*
3. Select data to filter by.
   ✓ *Word displays only those entries that match the selected data.*

   OR

   Select one of the following:
   - **(All)** to display all entries.
     ✓ *Use this option to remove an existing filter.*
   - **(Blanks)** to display entries in which the current field is blank.
   - **(Nonblanks)** to display entries in which the current field is not blank.

   ✓ *The filter arrow on the column heading changes to blue so you know which column is used for the filter.*
4. Click **OK** .... Enter

Exercise Directions

1. Make a copy of the Office Address List file 48DOCTORS, and name the copy DOCTORS.
   ✓ *To copy the file, right-click the file name and select Copy. Right-click the destination folder and select Paste. Right-click the copied file name and select Rename. Type the new file name and press Enter.*
2. Start Word, if necessary.
3. Create a new blank document.
4. Save the document as MAINDIR.
5. Start the Mail Merge Wizard.
6. Select to create a directory, using the current document.
7. Select to use an existing address list file as a data source document.
8. Locate and open DOCTORS.
9. Filter the list to display only the nurses.
   a. Click the filter arrow on the Title column heading.
   b. Click *Nurse*.
10. Deselect all of the nurses.
11. Remove the filter.
    a. Click the filter arrow on the Title column heading.
    b. Click (All).
12. Sort the list in ascending order by Last Name.
13. Close the Mail Merge Recipients dialog box.
14. Set up the directory main document as shown in Illustration A.
15. Preview the directory.
16. Complete the merge by generating a new directory document.
17. Save the directory document in a new file, named DIRECTORY.
18. Edit the file as shown in Illustration B.
    a. Insert five new lines at the beginning of the document.
    b. Centered on line 1, type **Wayland Home Health Care Associates, Inc.** in a 24-point serif font.
    c. Centered on line 2, type the address as shown in a 12-point serif font.
    d. Leave line 3 blank.
    e. Centered on line 4, type **Directory of Physicians** in a 20-point serif font.
    f. Leave line 5 blank.
19. Check the spelling and grammar in the document.
20. Display the document in Print Preview. It should look similar to the one shown in Illustration B.
21. Print the directory.
22. Close all open files, saving all changes.

Illustration A

Type text 14-pt. serif font

Tab to 1.5"

Insert merge fields

Name:	**«Title» «First_Name» «Last_Name»**
Phone:	**«Work_Phone»**
E-Mail:	**«Email_Address»**
Specialty:	**«Specialty»**

Illustration B

Wayland Home Health Care Associates, Inc.

954 St. Charles Street, St. Louis, MA 63101

Directory of Physicians

Name: Dr. Finn Broderbund
Phone: 314-555-2928
E-Mail: finn@waylandhhca.com
Specialty: Geriatrics

Name: Dr. Francis Dorsky
Phone: 314-555-2924
E-Mail: dorsky@waylandhhca.com
Specialty: Cardiovascular Disease

Name: Dr. William Doyle
Phone: 314-555-2927
E-Mail: wdoyle@waylandhhca.com
Specialty: Infectious Diseases

Name: Dr. Amanda Josephson
Phone: 314-555-2923
E-Mail: josephson@waylandhhca.com
Specialty: Geriatric Care

Name: Dr. Clarissa Joubert
Phone: 314-555-2929
E-Mail: cjoubert@waylandhhca.com
Specialty: Geriatrics

On Your Own

1. Create a new document in Word.
2. Save it as OWDDIRECT1.
3. Use the Mail Merge Wizard to create a directory using OWDDATA2 (the data source document you used in previous merge exercises) as the data source.

   ✓ *If* OWDDATA2 *is not available, use* 48OWD0DATA2.

4. Filter the list.
5. Select to include only certain entries.
6. Sort the list.
7. Merge the directory to a new document.
8. Save the directory as OWDDIRECT2.
9. Edit the directory document to include a title.
10. Check the spelling and grammar.
11. Print the directory.
12. Close all open documents, saving all changes.

Exercise 49

◆ Critical Thinking

Highland Property Management Co. wants you to create class lists for three upcoming in-house training courses so the instructors know how many people to expect. In addition, you need to send out memos to all enrollees confirming their course selection. In this exercise, you will use Mail Merge to create the memos and the directories. You will create a new data source file that you can use for all merges. The file will need to be customized to include fields specific to your needs. It will also need to be filtered and sorted to complete each merge.

Exercise Directions

Generate a Memo with Mail Merge

1. Start Word, if necessary.
2. Create a new blank document.
3. Save the file as CONFIRM.
4. Start the Mail Merge Wizard.
5. Select to create a letter, using the current document.
6. Create a new address list to use as a data source document.
7. Customize the address list as follows:
    a. Rename the Company field to **Department**.
    b. Delete all of the fields pertaining to address (Address Line 1, Address Line 2, City, State, ZIP Code, and Country)
    c. Add a field named **Course**
    d. Delete the Home Phone field.
8. Enter the recipients from the table on the following page into the data source file.
9. Save the data source file as NAMES.
10. Sort the data source file into ascending order by Department.
11. Select to use all recipients in the merge, then close the Mail Merge Recipients dialog box.
12. Type the document shown in Illustration B, inserting the merge fields as marked.
13. Check the spelling and grammar in the document.
14. Preview the merged documents.
15. Complete the merge by generating a new file containing all merged records.
16. Save the file as MEMOS.
17. Print the file.
18. Close all open documents, saving all changes.

Create a Directory with Mail Merge

1. Create a new blank document.
2. Save the file as ENROLLED.
3. Start the Mail Merge Wizard.
4. Select to create a directory, using the current document.
5. Use the NAMES address list as the data source file.
6. Sort the list alphabetically by last name.
7. Filter the list to display only the people enrolled in the Word 1 course.
8. Set up the directory as shown in Illustration C.
9. Preview the directory.
10. Generate the directory and save it in a new file named Word 1.
11. Add the title **Word 1 Class List** in a 24-point sans serif font at the top of the Word 1 directory.
12. Check the spelling and grammar in the document.

13. Print the document.
14. Close the document, saving all changes.
    ✓ *The Enrolled document should still be open on-screen, with the Mail Merge Wizard displaying Step 6.*
15. Go back through the Mail Merge Wizard to step 5.
16. Edit the Recipient list to change the filter from Word 1 to Word 2.
17. Preview the directory.
18. Generate the directory and save it in a new file named Word 2.
19. Add the title **Word 2 Class List** in a 24-point sans serif font at the top of the Word 2 directory.
20. Check the spelling and grammar in the document.
21. Print the document.
22. Close the document, saving all changes.
23. Repeat steps 15–22 to create a directory for the Word 3 class.
24. Close the ENROLLED document, saving all changes.

Illustration A

Mr. Gary Dubin	Human Resources	Word 3	555-3232	gdubin@highlandpmc.com
Ms. Elizabeth Doone	On-site Management	Word 1	555-3233	lizdoone@ highlandpmc.com
Ms. Janice Loring	Accounting	Word 2	555-3234	jloring@ highlandpmc.com
Mr. Antonio DiBuono	Marketing	Word 1	555-3235	antonio@ highlandpmc.com
Ms. Katharine Peterson	Human Resources	Word 2	555-3236	kpeterson@ highlandpmc.com
Ms. Marianne Flagg	On-site Management	Word 3	555-3237	mflagg@ highlandpmc.com
Mr. Howard Jefferson	Customer Support	Word 2	555-3238	hjefferson@ highlandpmc.com
Mr. Julian Lovett	On-site Management	Word 3	555-3239	jullovett@ highlandpmc.com
Ms. Christina Bottecelli	Accounting	Word 1	555-3240	chrisbott@ highlandpmc.com
Ms. Rose Mekalian	Marketing	Word 3	555-3241	rosemekalian@ highlandpmc.com
Mr. Dana Teng	On-site Management	Word 2	555-3242	dteng@ highlandpmc.com
Mr. Luis Martinez	Accounting	Word 1	555-3243	lmartinez@ highlandpmc.com

Illustration B

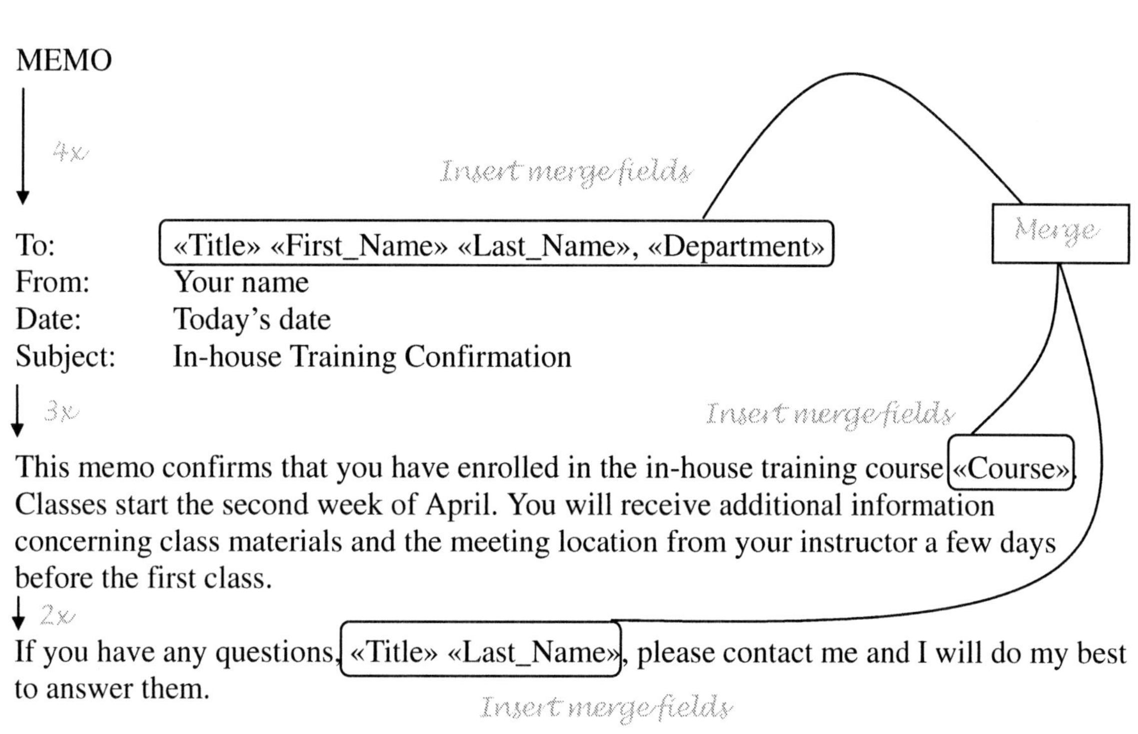

Illustration C

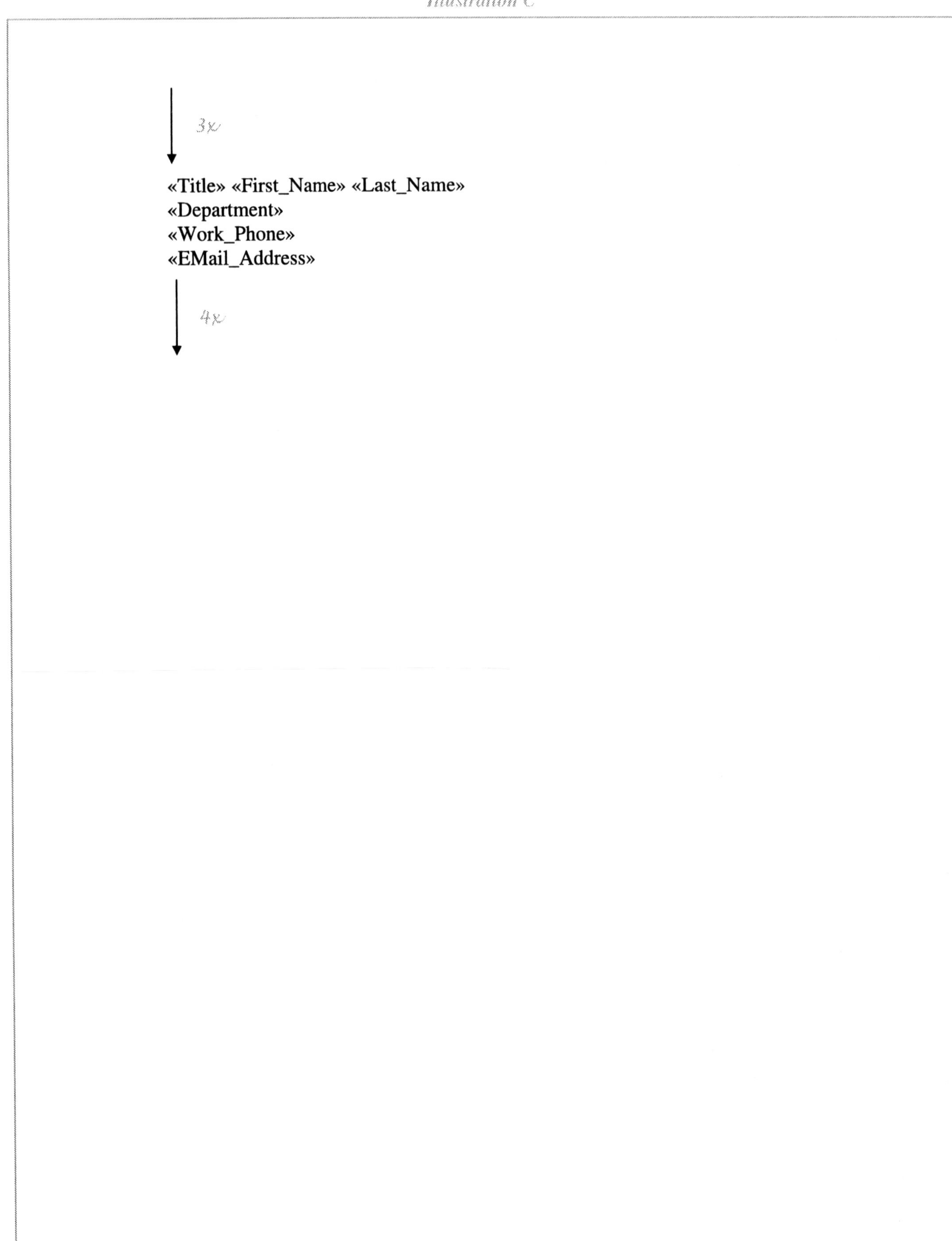

3x

«Title» «First_Name» «Last_Name»
«Department»
«Work_Phone»
«EMail_Address»

4x

Lesson 9

Multiple-page Documents

Exercise 50

- Create an Outline
- Edit an Outline
- Collapse and Expand Outlines
- Number an Outline

Exercise 51

- Insert Hard Page Breaks
- Insert Section Breaks
- Insert Page Numbers
- Control Text Flow
- View the Word Count

Exercise 52

- Create Headers/Footers
- Different First Page Headers/Footers
- Different Odd/Even Headers/Footers
- Different Section Headers/Footers

Exercise 53

- Use Document Map
- Copy or Move Text from One Page to Another

Exercise 54

- Preview Multiple Pages
- Drag and Drop Text from One Page to Another
- Print Specific Pages

Exercise 55

- Find and Replace
- Insert bookmarks
- Select Browse Object

Exercise 56

- Create a Master Document
- Work with Subdocuments

Exercise 57

- Insert a Cross-reference
- Create an Index
- Modify an Index

Exercise 58

- Create a Table of Contents
- Update a Table of Contents

Exercise 59

- Critical Thinking

Exercise 50

Skills Covered:

◆ **Create an Outline** ◆ **Edit an Outline**
◆ **Collapse and Expand Outlines** ◆ **Number an Outline**

On the Job

Create an outline to organize ideas for any document that covers more than one topic, such as an article, a report, a presentation, or a speech. For example, you might create an outline to list the chapters or headings in a report or to arrange main subjects for a presentation. The outline serves as a map you can follow as you complete the entire document.

Pelican Peter's Dive Shop wants to publish a document about safe SCUBA diving. In this exercise, you will create an outline for that document.

Terms

Outline A document that lists levels of topics.

Promote To move up one level in an outline.

Demote To move down one level in an outline.

Collapse To hide subtopics in an outline.

Expand To show subtopics in an outline.

Notes

Outline toolbar

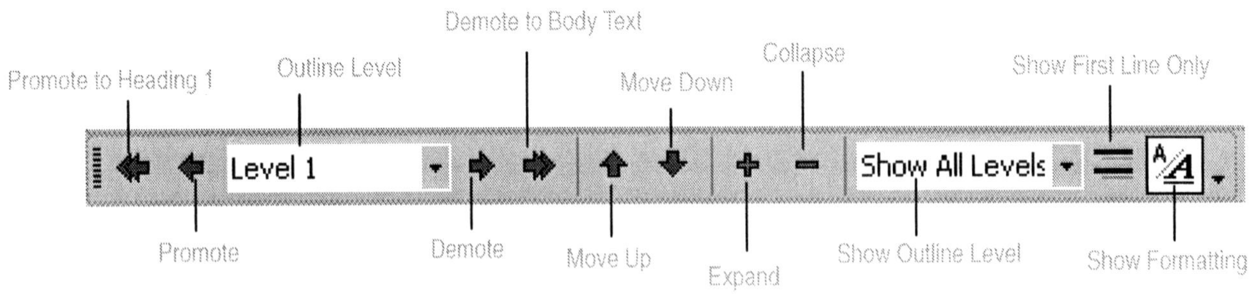

Promote to Heading 1 | Promote | Outline Level | Level 1 | Demote | Demote to Body Text | Move Up | Move Down | Expand | Collapse | Show All Levels | Show Outline Level | Show First Line Only | Show Formatting

Create an Outline

- Use Outline view to create and edit **outlines**.
- Outline topics are set up in levels, which are sometimes called *headings*: Level 1 is a main heading, Level 2 is a subheading, Level 3 is a sub-subheading, and so on up to 9 heading levels.
- Word automatically applies different styles to different levels in an outline.
- Levels that have sublevels under them are preceded by an Expand Outline symbol ✜.
- Levels that do not have sublevels are preceded by a Collapse Outline symbol ▭.
- Regular document text is called *Body text.*

- When you display an unnumbered outline in Normal view, Print Layout view, or Print Preview, it retains its style formatting, but not the indented levels.
- To print an unnumbered outline with the indented levels, it must be displayed in Outline view when you select the Print command.

Edit an Outline

- You can edit an outline using the same techniques you use to edit regular document text. For example, you can insert and delete text at any location.
- To reorganize an outline, you can **promote** or **demote** headings levels. For example, you can demote a Level 1 paragraph to a Level 2 paragraph.
- You can also move headings and subheadings up or down the outline to reorganize the outline.

Collapse and Expand Outlines

- When you want to work with only some heading levels at a time you can **collapse** the outline using the Collapse button [−].
- Collapsing an outline hides some heading levels.
- To see hidden or collapsed levels, you can **expand** the outline using the Expand button [+].

Number an Outline

- Traditional outlines are numbered using a multilevel numbering scheme, with different number and letter styles used to represent different levels.
- Word comes with seven built-in outline numbering styles.
- You can select a numbering style before or after typing the outline.
- Once an outline is numbered, it retains its indented levels in any view.

Select an outline numbering style in the Bullets and Numbering dialog box

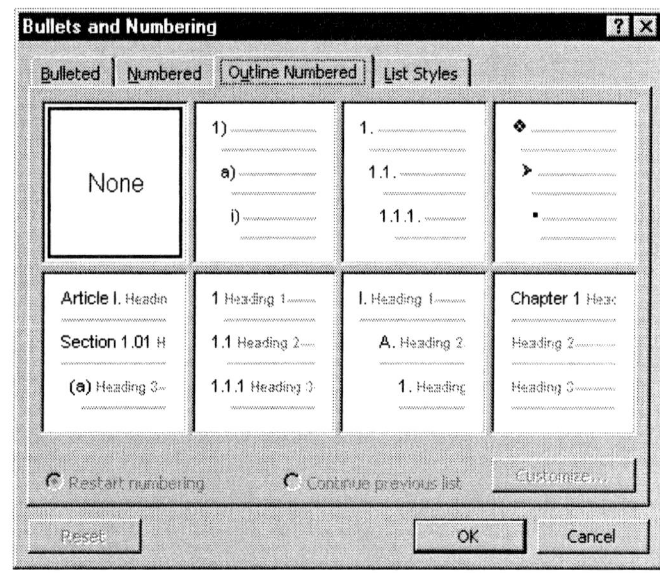

Procedures

Create an Outline

1. Click the **Outline View** button [icon].

   OR

   a. Click **View** .... Alt+V

   b. Click **Outline** .... O

2. Type Heading 1 text.
3. Press **Enter** .... Enter

   ✓ *Heading level is carried forward to the new paragraph.*

4. Type more Heading 1 text.

   OR

   a. Click the **Demote** button [→] .... Tab

   b. Type Heading 2 text.

5. Press **Enter** .... Enter
6. Type Heading 2 text.

   OR

   Click the **Demote** button [→] to type text for the next lower level .... Tab

   OR

   Click the **Promote** button [←] to type text for the next higher level .... Shift+Tab

7. Press **Enter** .... Enter
8. Continue until outline is complete.

Type body text:

1. Position insertion point where you want to type Body text.
2. Click **Demote to Body Text** button [⇒] .... Ctrl+Shift+N
3. Type text.

Edit an Outline

Select headings:

1. Click outline symbol preceding the heading ([+] or [−]).

   ✓ *The heading and all subheadings are selected.*

2. Make desired changes.

Change heading levels:

1. Position insertion point anywhere on heading line.

   OR

   Select heading.
2. Click **Promote** button .... Shift + Tab

   to promote heading one level.

   OR

   - Click **Demote** button .... Tab

     to demote heading one level.

   OR

   a. Click **Outline Level** drop-down arrow Level 1.

   b. Click desired level.

Move headings:

1. Position insertion point anywhere on the heading line.

   OR

   Select heading to move.
2. Drag outline symbol (+ or −) up or down to a new location.

   OR

   Click **Move Up** to move heading up one line.

   OR

   Click **Move Down** to move heading down one line.

Collapse and expand an outline:

1. Click **Show Level** drop-down arrow Show All Levels.
2. Click desired level.

OR

- Double-click **outline symbol** + or − preceding heading.

Number an Outline

1. Position the insertion point where the outline will begin.

   OR

   Select headings to number.
2. Click **Format** .... Alt + O
3. Click **Bullets and Numbering** .... N
4. Click **Outline Numbered** page tab .... Alt + U
5. Select numbering style.

   ✓ *Select None to remove numbering.*
6. Click **OK** .... Enter

Exercise Directions

1. Start Word, if necessary.
2. Open 50SCUBA or create a new document.
3. Save the document as SCUBA.
4. Change to Outline view.
5. Select the Numbering style used in the illustration.
6. Type the outline shown in Illustration A.

   ✓ *If you are using the existing file, format the text as shown in the illustration.*

   a. Press Tab or click Demote to demote a level.

   b. Press Shift+Tab, or click Promote to promote a level.

   c. Press Ctrl+Shift+N or click Demote to Body Text to type regular text.
7. Collapse the outline to show only levels 1 and 2.
8. Display all levels.
9. Move the heading **Certification** and its subheadings up so it is becomes heading B.

   ✓ *Notice that Word renumbers the outline automatically.*
10. Promote the subheading **The Ascent** to level 3.
11. Demote the subheading **30 hours** to level 5.
12. Check the spelling in the document.
13. Print the document.
14. Close the document, saving all changes.

Illustration A

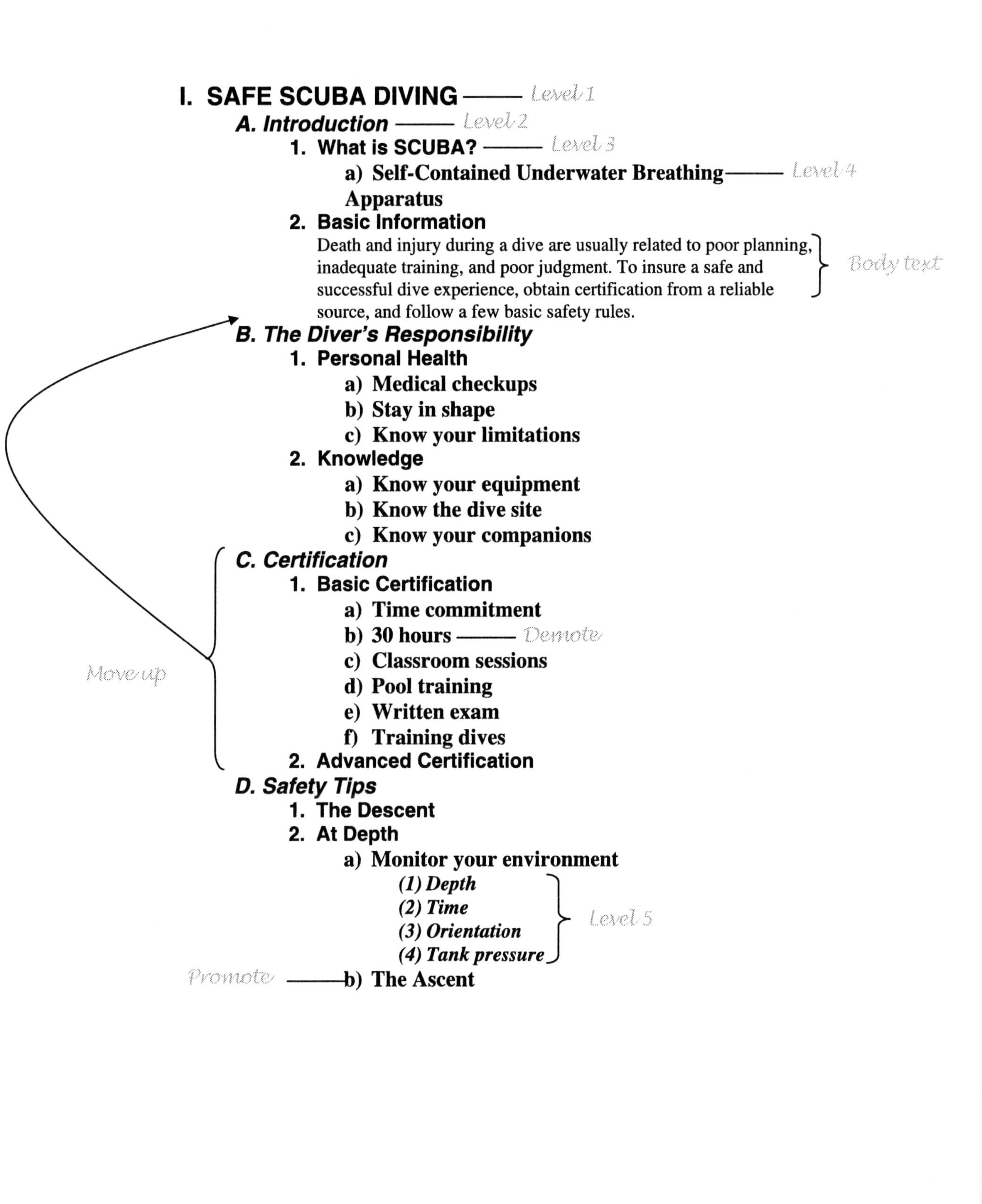

On Your Own

1. Create a new document in Word.
2. Save the file as OWD27.
3. Draft an outline for a speech or presentation you'd like to give. Include at least three levels. For example, draft an outline for a presentation you have to give to a class, to an organization, or for a speech to a family member about a household issue that has been on your mind.
4. Examine the outline and make sure all headings are at the correct level. Change the levels if necessary.
5. Try rearranging the headings to see if you can improve the organization.
6. Close the document, saving all changes.

Exercise 51

Skills Covered:

◆ **Insert Hard Page Breaks** ◆ **Insert Section Breaks**
◆ **Insert Page Numbers**
◆ **Control Text Flow** ◆ **View the Word Count**

On the Job

Make a long document easier to read and work in by inserting page breaks, section breaks, and page numbers. Page breaks let you control where a new page should start, avoiding page layout problems such as headings at the bottom of a page. Section breaks let you change page formatting in the middle of a document. View the Word Count to find out if your document meets length requirements.

Pete Newell has given you the first two pages of a report about SCUBA diving safety. In this exercise, you will format the document using page breaks and section breaks. You will also insert page numbers.

Terms

Soft page break The place where Word automatically starts a new page when the current page is filled with text.

Hard page break A nonprinting character that tells Word to start a new page, even if the current page is not filled with text.

Section A portion of a document.

Section break A nonprinting character that tells Word to start a new section within a document. For example, a section break can separate a one-column from a two-column format.

Widow line The last line of a paragraph printed alone at the top of a page.

Orphan line The first line of a paragraph printed alone at the bottom of a page.

Notes

Insert Hard Page Breaks

- A standard 8.5" by 11" sheet of paper with 1" top and bottom margins has 9" of vertical space for entering text.

  ✓ *The number of lines depends on the font size and line spacing settings.*

- Word inserts a **soft page break** to start a new page when the current page is full.
- Soft page breaks adjust automatically if text is inserted or deleted, so a break always occurs when the current page is full.
- Insert a **hard page break** to start a new page before the current page is full. For example, insert a hard page break before a heading that falls at the bottom of a page; the break forces the heading to the top of the next page.
- Breaks move like characters when you insert and delete text. Therefore, you should insert hard page breaks after all editing is complete to avoid having a break occur at an awkward position on the page.
- In Normal view, a soft page break is marked by a dotted line across the page.

- By default, in Print Layout view page breaks are indicated by a space between the bottom of one page and the top of the next page; if you have nonprinting characters displayed, the space where you insert a hard page break is marked by a dotted line with the words *Page Break* centered in it.

  ✓ *You can hide the space between pages in Print Layout view. If you do, page breaks are marked by a solid black line. Simply click on the space between pages to hide it, or click on the solid line between pages to show the space again.*

- In Normal view, a hard page break is marked by a dotted line with the words Page Break centered in it.

Page breaks in a document

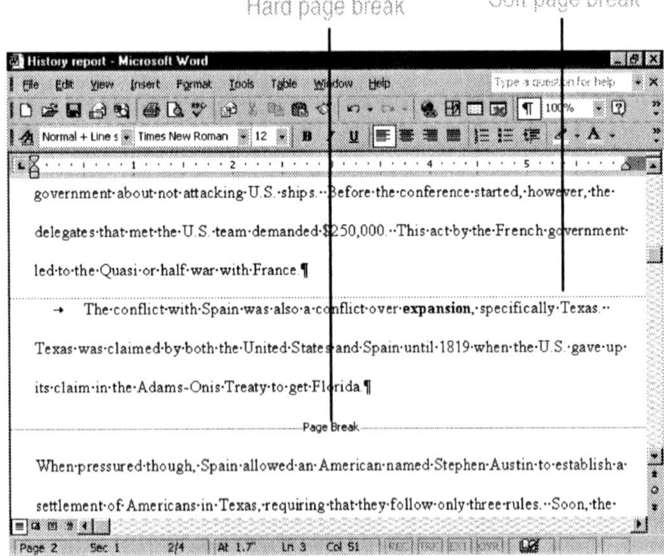

- In Print Layout view, all page breaks look like the space between sheets of paper.

Page breaks in Print Layout view

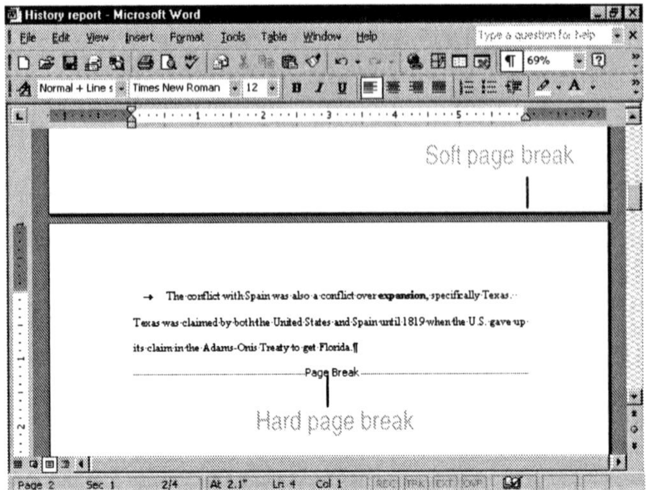

Insert Section Breaks

- A default Word document contains one **section**.
- You can divide a document into multiple sections to apply different formatting to each section. For example, you can set different margins, headers, or footers for each section.
- There are four types of **section breaks**:
  - *Next page* inserts a section break and a page break so that the new section will start on the next page.
  - *Continuous* inserts a section break so that the new section will start at the insertion point.
  - *Even page* inserts a section break and page breaks so the new section will start on the next even-numbered page.
  - *Odd page* inserts a section break and page breaks so the new section will start on the next odd-numbered page.

Break dialog box

Break
Break types
Page break
Column break
Text wrapping break
Section break types
Next page
Continuous
Even page
Odd page
OK
Cancel

- In Normal view, section breaks are displayed as dotted double lines across the width of the page with the words Section Break in the middle, followed by the type of break in parentheses.

  ✓ *In Print Layout view section breaks are displayed only if nonprinting characters are displayed.*

Section breaks in a document

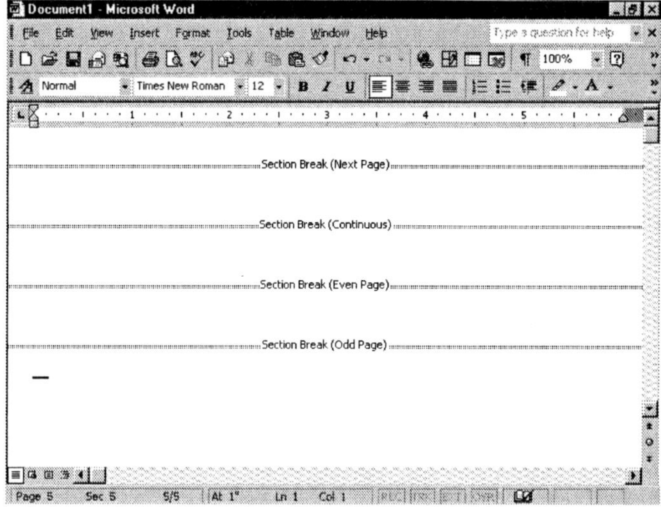

Insert Page Numbers

- You can insert page numbers in a Word document using either the Header and Footer toolbar, or the Insert, Page Numbers command.
  - ✓ *Headers and footers are covered in Exercise 52.*
- Use the Insert, Page Numbers command when you don't want to create an entire header or footer, and to use the options for formatting and positioning the page numbers on the page.
- By default, page numbers print on the bottom right of each page.
- Set options to control page number placement:

Page Numbers dialog box

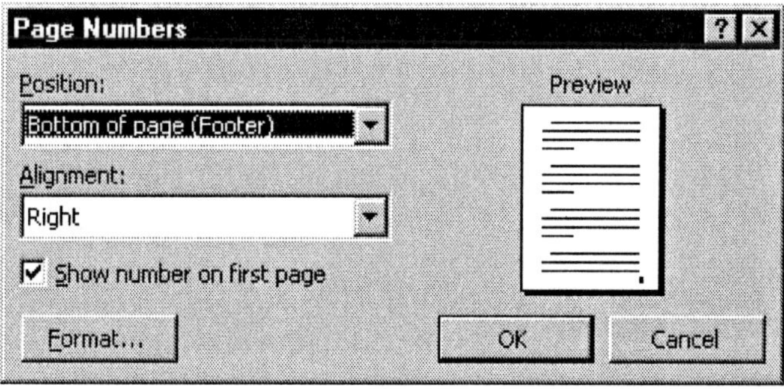

  - *Position* sets numbers at the top or bottom of page.
  - *Alignment* sets numbers left, right, centered, inside (along binding), or outside (along outer edge) of the page.
  - *Show number on first page* shows or suppresses the page number on the first page.

- You can change the page number format to select a different number style, to include chapter numbers, or to restart numbering in a new section.
- Restarting the numbering is useful when your document has a title page that you do not want numbered. Insert a Next Page section break between the title page and the first page of the document. That makes the title page the first section. Then, click the Format button in the Page Numbers dialog box to display the Page Number Format dialog box. Select the option to restart the page numbers for the second section, then click OK to return to the Page Numbers dialog box.

Page Number Format dialog box

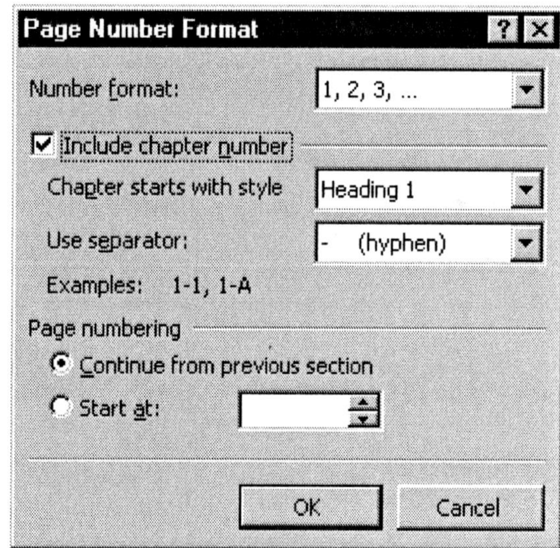

Control Text Flow

- Use text flow options to control the way Word breaks paragraphs and lines at the end of a page. For example, you can control whether or not a heading stays on the same page as the paragraph that follows it.
- You can access the following text flow options in the Paragraph dialog box:
  - **Widow/Orphan** control, for preventing either the first or last line of a paragraph from printing on a different page.
  - Keep lines together, for preventing a page break within a paragraph.
  - Keep with next, for preventing a page break between the current paragraph and the following paragraph.

- Page break before, for forcing a page break before the current paragraph.

View the Word Count

- Word keeps track of statistics such as how many words you have typed in a document.
- There are three ways to view the word count:
  - Use the Word Count command on the Tools menu to check the document statistics.

Word Count dialog box

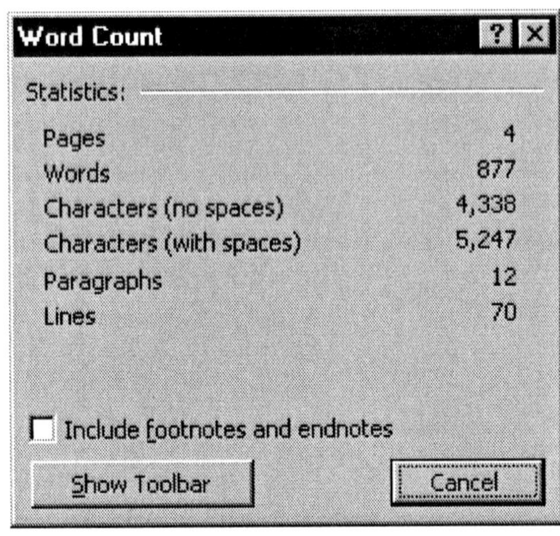

  - Use the Word Count toolbar to have access to the current word count while you work.

Word Count toolbar

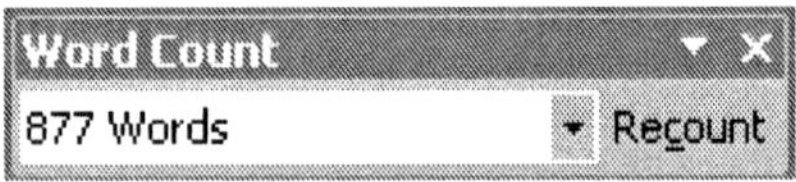

  - Use the Statistics page of the Properties dialog box.

✓ *See Exercise 34 for information about Document Properties.*

Procedures

Insert a Hard Page Break (Ctrl+Enter)

1. Click **Insert** .... Alt+I
2. Click **Break** .... B
3. Click the **Page break** option button .... Alt+P
4. Click **OK** .... Enter

Delete a Hard Page Break

1. In Normal view, position insertion point on hard page break.
2. Press **Delete** .... Del

Insert a Section Break

1. Click **Insert** .... Alt+I
2. Click **Break** .... B
3. Click the option button for desired break:
   - **Next page** .... Alt+N
   - **Continuous** .... Alt+T
   - **Even page** .... Alt+E
   - **Odd page** .... Alt+O
4. Click **OK** .... Enter

Delete a Section Break

1. In Normal view, position insertion point on section break.
2. Press **Delete** key .... Del

Insert Page Numbers

1. Click **Insert** .... Alt+I
2. Click **Page Numbers** .... U
3. Click the **Position** drop-down arrow .... Alt+P
4. Select **Bottom of page (Footer)** .... Enter

   OR

   Top of page (Header) .... ↑, Enter
5. Click the **Alignment** drop-down arrow .... Alt+A
6. Select alignment option: .... ↑, Enter
   - **Right**
   - **Left**
   - **Center**
   - **Inside**
   - **Outside**
7. Select **Show number on first page** if desired .... Alt+S
8. Click **OK** .... Enter

Change Page Number Formatting

1. Click **Insert** .... Alt+I
2. Click **Page Numbers** .... U
3. Click **Format** button Format... .... Alt+F
4. Click the **Number format** drop-down arrow .... Alt+F
5. Select **format** .... ↓, Enter

- **Arabic numerals**...1, 2, 3, 4, 5, etc.
- **Arabic numerals with dashes**..-1-, -2-, -3-, -4-, etc.
- **Lowercase letters**..... a, b, c, d, e, f, etc.
- **Uppercase letters** .A, B, C, D, E, F, etc.
- **Lowercase Roman numerals**.... i, ii, iii, iv, v, etc.
- **Uppercase Roman numerals**..I, II, III, IV, V, etc.

6. Click **OK**.......................... Enter
   to close Page Number Format dialog box.
7. Click **OK**.......................... Enter
   to close Page Numbers dialog box and insert page numbers.

Control Text Flow

1. Click **Format** .... Alt+O
2. Click **Paragraph**.................. P
3. Click **Line and Page Breaks** tab .... Alt+P
4. Select or deselect desired option(s):
   - **Widow/Orphan control**.................. Alt+W
   - **Keep lines together**................ Alt+K
   - **Keep with next**...... Alt+X
   - **Page break before**.................... Alt+B
5. Click **OK**.......................... Enter

View Word Count

1. Click **Tools** .... Alt+T
2. Click **Word Count** .... W
3. Click **Close** button Close to close dialog box when done .... Esc

OR

1. Click **View**.................... Alt+V
2. Click **Toolbars**..................... T
3. Click **Word Count**.
4. Click drop-down arrow to select **Recount to view**.
5. Click **Recount** button Recount .... Alt+C
   to update word count calculation.

Exercise Directions

1. Start Word, if necessary.
2. Open 51SAFETY.
3. Save the document as SAFETY.
4. Insert a page number flush right on the top of all pages in the document.
5. Display the document in Print Preview. Notice that there is a page break in the middle of the numbered list at the bottom of page 1.
6. Close Print Preview.
7. Select the first three items in the numbered list at the bottom of page 1.
8. Select the Keep with next option to set Word so that it won't insert a page break in the middle of the list. Notice that Word moves the entire list to the top of page two.
9. Insert a continuous section break at the beginning of the heading **Preparation**.
10. Change the margins in section 1 to 1.5" on the left and right and .75" on the top.
11. Change the margins in section 2 to 1" on the left and right and .75" on the top and bottom.
    ✓ *Notice that with the change in margins, the numbered list moves back on to page 1.*
12. Insert a page break at the beginning of the heading **Risks**. This moves the heading to the top of page 3.
13. Open the Word Count dialog box to check the number of words in the document.
14. Display the Word Count toolbar and close the dialog box.
15. Delete the word **However**, from the beginning of the second sentence under the heading **Safety Recommendations**. Correct the capitalization.
16. Update the word count.
17. Check the spelling and grammar in the document.
18. Preview the document. It should look similar to the one in Illustration A.
19. Print the document.
20. Close the document, saving all changes.

1

Safe Scuba Diving

Prepared by
Pete Newell, Owner
Pelican Peter's Dive Shop
2200 Gulfshore Blvd. N., Naples, FL 34102

Introduction

The acronym SCUBA stands for Self-Contained Underwater Breathing Apparatus. In other words, SCUBA divers use an apparatus that is completely carried by the diver and not connected to the surface. It is estimated that more than 3.5 million Americans participate in recreational SCUBA diving. Another 500 thousand become certified each year in the United States. The experience of SCUBA diving can be exciting, exhilarating, and empowering. However, without the proper planning, SCUBA diving can also be dangerous.

This report provides a look at the steps divers can take to maximize the pleasure of a dive while minimizing the risks.

Preparation

Preparation is the key to a successful and safe dive. With proper training and common sense diving is a very safe sport. In fact, statistics show that diving is considerably safer than skiing, rock climbing, sky diving, and trail biking. Death and injury during a dive are usually related to shoddy planning, inadequate training, and poor judgment. There are four basic steps to insuring a safe and successful dive experience:

1. Obtain certification from a reliable source.
2. Use the right equipment.
3. Be aware of the risks.
4. Follow the rules.

Illustration A (Page 2 of 3)

Basic Certification

An entry-level SCUBA certification course takes approximately 32 hours to complete. The course includes classroom sessions as well as practical training of essential diving skills in a pool. Successful completion of the course requires passing a written exam and demonstrating your ability to use the skills you have learned during open water training dives. Once certified you may rent equipment, participate in advanced training classes, and take part in actual dives.

Equipment

A prepared diver understands that having the proper equipment in excellent condition will significantly reduce risk. Basic equipment includes the following:

- A tank of compressed air carried on the diver's back.
- A first stage regulator attached to the tank to lower air pressure delivered to the diver.
- A second stage demand regulator and mouthpiece, that delivers air on inhalation and closes on exhalation.
- A face mask that covers the diver's eyes and nose.
- An extra second stage regulator and mouthpiece, carried by the diver in case of emergency.
- Two submersible gauges, one to display an accurate depth and the other to show how much air remains in the tank.
- An inflatable vest worn to provide a means of establishing positive buoyancy.
- A weight belt and weights, worn to compensate for positive buoyancy.
- Fins to facilitate self-propulsion in the water.
- A wet suit or other type of body protection to prevent hypothermia.

Optional equipment such as a snorkel, dive knife, small tank of extra air, dive computer, compass, dive lights, writing slate, whistle, and inflatable signaling device may also be carried.

Risks

About 40% of all SCUBA deaths are determined to be coincidental medical events such as heart attacks. The next most common causes of fatal accidents are panic, exhaustion, and pulmonary overpressure. Environmental causes such as cave dives, rough surf, and strong currents account for 25-30% of fatalities. Equipment related accidents such as running out of air or carrying too much weight account for less than 20% of fatal accidents. Deaths caused by encounters with fish or other marine life are rare.

However, there are potential hazards inherent in every dive. All divers should be aware of the possibility of danger at all times, and should act accordingly. Some common hazards that may be encountered on any dive include the following:

- De-compression sickness
- Air embolism
- Hypothermia
- Physical exhaustion
- Injuries from marine life
- Boating accidents
- Sunburn
- Running out of air

Safety Recommendations

As mentioned earlier, diving can be a safe and rewarding experience. It only takes a momentary lapse of caution for a situation to go from fun to fatal. Follow these basic safety rules to minimize your risk:

- Have all equipment maintained regularly by a professional.
- Check equipment before every dive.
- Be sure you are mentally and physically prepared for a dive.
- Check the weather and water conditions prior to a dive.
- Never dive alone.
- Don't drink alcohol before diving.
- Don't handle unfamiliar marine life.
- Consult a doctor before diving.

On Your Own

1. Start Word.
2. Draft and format a multiple page document, or open 51OWDGUIDES. The document might be a letter, a report, a short story, an outline, or an autobiography. Try to include at least three pages. If necessary, double-space the document and increase the width of the margins.
3. Save the file as OWDGUIDES.
4. Insert page breaks if necessary so that headings or paragraphs start at the top of a page instead of at the bottom of one.
5. Insert at least one section break. Change the margins for section 2.
6. Insert page numbers.
7. Check the word count.
8. Print the document.
9. Close the document, saving all changes.

Exercise 52

Skills Covered:

◆ **Create Headers/Footers** ◆ **Different First Page Headers/Footers**
◆ **Different Odd/Even Headers/Footers**
◆ **Different Section Headers/Footers**

On the Job

Use headers and footers when you need to print information on the top or bottom of every page. You can customize documents by creating different headers and footers on the first page, on odd and even pages, and for different sections. Using different headers and footers helps readers identify different sections of a document.

In this exercise, you will work with a version of the SCUBA safety document. The document provided has been lengthened. It has footnotes and multiple sections. You will create headers and footers for the different sections in the document.

Terms

Header Repetitive text or graphics printed at the top of pages in a document.

Footer Repetitive text or graphics printed at the bottom of pages in a document.

Notes

Create Headers/Footers

- Create a **header** and/or **footer** to print repetitive information such as page numbers, dates, author, or subject on every page of a document.
- Headers and footers are not displayed in Normal view. Use Print preview or Print Layout view to see them on the screen.
- By default, headers print .5" from the top of page, and footers print .5" from the bottom of page.
- You can apply headers and footers to the entire document or to the current section.
- Use Header/Footer toolbar buttons to customize headers and footers.
- For example, you can insert the date or the page number.

✓ *If you insert the page numbers using the Insert Header/Footer command, you can still use the Insert Page Numbers dialog box to select a different number style, to include chapter numbers, or to restart numbering in a new section. Refer to Exercise 51 for more information.*

Different First Page Headers/Footers

- Set Word to print a different header/footer on the first page of a document or section.
- Leave the first page header/footer blank to omit the header/footer from the first page.

Different Odd/Even Headers/Footers

- Print different headers on odd and even pages.
- Using different headers/footers on odd and even pages gives you an opportunity to include information such as a chapter or section name and number, and to customize the appearance of a document.

Header and Footer toolbar

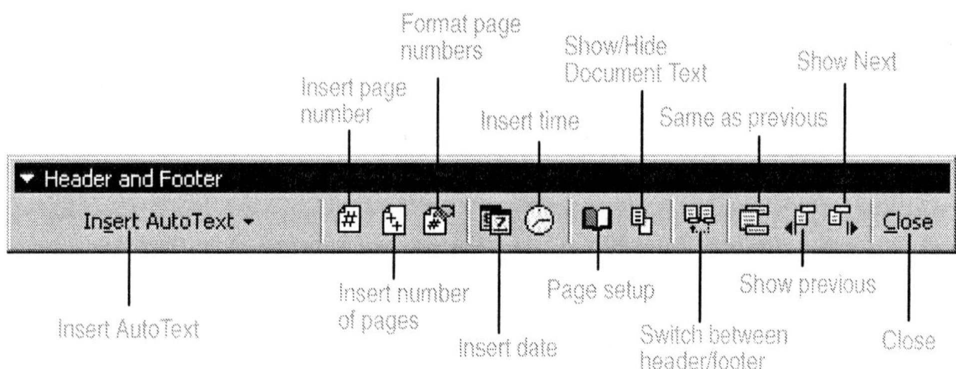

Different Section Headers/Footers

- By default, new sections have the same header/footer as the previous section.
- You can change the header/footer for every section in a document.

Procedures

Create Headers/Footers

Create a header on every page:

1. Click **View** .... Alt+V
2. Click **Header and Footer** .... H
3. In the Header box, type header text.
   - ✓ *Use formatting options as desired, including fonts, font effects, alignment, tabs, and spacing.*
4. Click **Close** button Close .... Alt+C on the Header/Footer toolbar.

Create a footer on every page:

1. Click **View** .... Alt+V
2. Click **Header and Footer** .... H
3. Click the **Switch Between Header and Footer** button.
4. In the Footer box, type footer text.
   - ✓ *Use formatting options as desired, including fonts, font effects, alignment, and tabs.*
5. Click **Close** button Close .... Alt+C on the Header/Footer toolbar.

Insert page numbers, date, and/or time in a header/footer:

1. Click **View** .... Alt+V
2. Click **Header and Footer**.... H
3. Click the **Switch Between Header and Footer** button as needed.
4. Click desired toolbar button(s):
   - **Insert Page Number**
   - **Insert Date**
   - **Insert Time**
5. Click **Close** button Close .... Alt+C on the Header/Footer toolbar.
   - ✓ *Combine text and page numbers, date, or time to achieve different effects. For example, type* Page, *press the spacebar once to leave a space, then insert page number.*

Create first page header/footer:

1. Click **View** .... Alt+V
2. Click **Header and Footer**.... H
3. Click the **Page Setup** button.
4. Select the **Different first page** check box .... Alt+F
5. Click **OK** .... Enter
6. In First Page Header box, type first page header text.
   - ✓ *Leave blank to suppress header on first page.*
7. Click **Switch Between Header and Footer** button.
8. In First Page Footer box, type first page footer text.
   - ✓ *Leave blank to suppress footer on first page.*
9. Click **Show Next** button.
10. In the Footer box, type text for other footers.
11. Click **Switch Between Header and Footer** button.
12. In the Header box, type other header text.
13. Click **Close** button Close .... Alt+C on Header/Footer toolbar.

Create different odd and even headers/footers:

1. Click **View** .... Alt+V
2. Click **Header and Footer**.... H
3. Click the **Page Setup** button.
4. Click the **Different odd and even** check box........... Alt+O
5. Click **OK**.......................... Enter
6. In Even Page Header box, type even page header text.
   ✓ *If Odd Page Header box displays first, click Show Next button to display Even Page Header.*
7. Click the **Switch Between Header and Footer** button.
8. In Even Page Footer box, type even page footer text.
9. Click the **Show Next** button or **Show Previous** button.
10. In Odd Page Footer box, type odd page footer text.
11. Click the **Switch Between Header and Footer** button.
12. In Odd Page Header box, type odd page header text.
13. Click **Close** button Close .... Alt+C on Header/Footer toolbar.

Create different headers/footers in sections:

1. Create sections.
2. Position insertion point in section where you want header/footer.
3. Click **View** .... Alt+V
4. Click **Header and Footer** .... H
5. Click the **Switch Between Header and Footer** button as necessary.
6. Click **Same as Previous** button.
   ✓ *By default, Same as Previous button is toggled on. Click it to toggle it off. If button is already toggled off, skip step 6.*
7. Enter header/footer information.
8. Click **Close** button Close .... Alt+C on Header/Footer toolbar.

Exercise Directions

1. Start Word, if necessary.
2. Open 52SAFETY.
3. Save the file as SAFETY2.
4. Make sure the document is displayed in Print Layout view and that Show/Hide Paragraph marks is turned on, so you can see where page breaks occur.
5. Create a footer for the entire document that includes the page number, centered. Precede the page number with the word **Page**.
6. Create different headers for the odd and even pages in each section as follows:
   - Page 1 – no header
   - Page 2 – the company name flush left (**Pelican Peter's Dive Shop**) and your name flush right
   - Page 3 – the section title flush left (**Equipment**) and the date flush right
   - Page 4 – same as section 2 even pages
   - Page 5 – the section title flush left (**Medical Conditions**) and the date flush right
7. Check the spelling and grammar in the document.
8. Preview the document. The Illustration shows the way the headers and footers on pages 2 and 3 should look.
9. Print the document.
10. Close the document, saving all changes.

Illustration A (Page 2 of 5)

Pelican Peter's Dive Shop Your Name

Basic Certification

An entry-level SCUBA certification course takes approximately 32 hours to complete. The course includes classroom sessions as well as practical training of essential diving skills in a pool. Successful completion of the course requires passing a written exam and demonstrating your ability to use the skills you have learned during open water training dives. Once certified you may rent equipment, participate in advanced training classes, and take part in actual dives.

Safety Recommendations

Diving can be a safe and rewarding experience. It only takes a momentary lapse of caution for a situation to go from fun to fatal. These safety rules can minimize your risk:

- Have all equipment maintained regularly by a professional.
- Check equipment before every dive.
- Be sure you are mentally and physically prepared for a dive.
- Check the weather and water conditions prior to a dive.
- Never dive alone.
- Don't drink alcohol before diving.
- Don't handle unfamiliar marine life.
- Consult a doctor before diving.

The buddy rule cannot be emphasized enough. Any reputable diving organization will insist each diver be accompanied under water by a buddy who can share air or provide other assistance. A SCUBA apparatus is designed to carry an extra demand regulator. This is required in case one diver runs out of air and has to share a single tank with his or her buddy. Ideally, the buddies should have similar training and skill levels; it does no good to have a buddy who dives deeper or stays down longer than you do. Buddies should stay close together and always be aware of each other's location.

Page 2

Equipment

A prepared diver understands that having the proper equipment in excellent condition will significantly reduce risk. Basic equipment includes the following[1]:

- A tank of compressed air carried on the diver's back.
- A first stage regulator attached to the tank to lower air pressure delivered to the diver.
- A second stage demand regulator and mouthpiece, that delivers air on inhalation and closes on exhalation.
- A face mask that covers the diver's eyes and nose.
- An extra second stage regulator and mouthpiece, carried by the diver in case of emergency.
- Two submersible gauges, one to display an accurate depth and the other to show how much air remains in the tank.
- An inflatable vest worn to provide a means of establishing positive buoyancy.
- A weight belt and weights, worn to compensate for positive buoyancy.
- Fins to facilitate self-propulsion in the water.
- A wet suit or other type of body protection to prevent hypothermia.

Optional equipment such as a snorkel, dive knife, small tank of extra air, dive computer, compass, dive lights, writing slate, whistle, and inflatable signaling device may also be carried.

Specialized Safety Equipment

The following special safety equipment can also help minimize risk[2]:

Dive Computers. Dive computers are designed to calculate remaining no-decompression limits while you are diving.
Flares. Waterproof flares are designed to help dive boats find you if you become disoriented and surface in the wrong location.
Rescue Sausages. These devices also help dive boats find you.
Sound Alerts. These devices produce a loud noise at the surface which can alert others that you're in trouble.
Spare Air/Pony Bottle. These systems are designed to give you an alternate air source that is not dependent on air from your tank.
Strobe Lights. This is essential equipment for night dives and drift dives. They produce a very bright light which can be seen from a great distance.

---

1 Lawrence Martin, M.D., "Scuba Diving Explained", 1997, http://www.reefscuba.com/safetytips.htm.
2 http://www.mtsinai.org/pulmonary/books/scuba/sectionb.htm.

On Your Own

1. Open OWDGUIDES, the document you created in the On Your Own section of Exercise 51, or Open 52OWDGUIDES.
2. Save the document as OWDGUIDES2.
3. Create headers and footers for the document.
4. Use different odd and even or different section headers and footers so that you can include more information. For example, include the page numbers and the date on even pages and your name and the title of the document on odd pages
5. Preview the document.
6. Save the document, close it, and exit Word.

Exercise 53

Skills Covered:

◆ **Use Document Map** ◆ **Copy or Move Text from One Page to Another**

On the Job

The Document Map helps you quickly locate sections of a long document without spending time scrolling through pages. Use cut, copy, and paste to copy or move data from one page in a document to another.

Pete Newell has suggested some ways to improve the SCUBA safety document. In this exercise, you will use the Document Map to navigate through a version of the document to locate text you need to rearrange. You will also copy and move text within the document.

Terms

Document Map A vertical pane that opens on the left side of the document window to show the major headings and sections in a document; click a topic in the pane to go to it.

Notes

Use Document Map

- **Document Map** is useful for navigating through long documents.
- Word displays the Document Map in a pane on the left side of the document window.
- The Document Map shows headings and major topics in an outline format.
  - ✓ *Outlines are covered in Exercise 50.*
- If there are no headings or major topics, the Document Map is empty.
- You can expand and collapse the Document Map as you would an outline to show the headings you need.

The Document Map

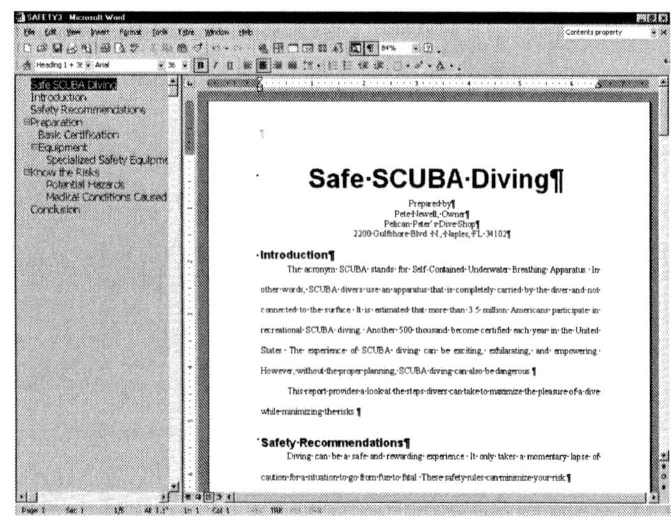

Copy or Move Text from One Page to Another

- Use standard copy and move techniques to copy or move text from one page in a document to another page.
  - ✓ *Moving text is covered in Exercise 17; Copying text is covered in Exercise 18.*
- Use Cut and Paste to move text.
- Use Copy and Paste to copy text.
- Copying and/or moving text may affect hard page breaks or section breaks already inserted in a document. For example, if you cut text before a hard page break, the break may occur high up on the page.

Procedures

Use Document Map

Display Document Map:

1. Click **View** .... Alt+V
2. Click **Document Map** .... D

OR

- Click **Document Map** button on the Standard toolbar.

Hide Document Map:

1. Click **View** .... Alt+V
2. Click **Document Map** .... D

OR

- Click **Document Map** button on the Standard toolbar.

Move insertion point to a heading:

- Click desired heading in Document Map.

Expand/collapse headings:

1. Right-click anywhere in Document Map.
2. Click level of heading to Expand/Collapse.

   OR

   Click **Expand** + or **Collapse** − button next to headings in Document Map.

Use Copy and Paste to Copy Text from One Page to Another *(Ctrl+C, Ctrl+V)*

1. Select the text to copy.
2. Click **Copy** button.

   OR

   a. Click **Edit**................ Alt+E

   b. Click **Copy** C
3. Display other page and position insertion point in new location.
4. Click **Paste** button.

   OR

   a. Click **Edit**................ Alt+E

   b. Click **Paste**..................... P

Move Text from One Page to Another

1. Select text to move.
2. Press **F2**............................. F2
3. Display other page and position insertion point at new location.
4. Press **Enter**...................... Enter

Use Cut and Paste to Move Text *(Ctrl+X, Cltr+V)*

1. Select text to move.
2. Click **Cut** button.

   OR

   a. Click **Edit**................ Alt+E

   b. Click **Cut**......................... T
3. Display other page and position insertion point at new location.
4. Click **Paste** button.

   OR

   a. Click **Edit**................ Alt+E

   b. Click **Paste** .... P

Exercise Directions

1. Start Word, if necessary.
2. Open 53SAFETY2.
3. Save the document as SAFETY3.
4. Display the Document Map.
5. Click the heading **Introduction** in the Document Map.
6. Cut the second paragraph in the Introduction and the numbered list that follows it to the Clipboard.
7. Click the heading **Preparation** in the Document Map.
8. Paste the text from the Clipboard on the line under the heading **Preparation**.
9. Move the insertion point to the end of the document and type the heading **Conclusion**.
10. Format the new heading with the Heading 1 style.
11. Click the heading **Introduction** in the Document Map again.
12. Copy the last two sentences of the first paragraph to the Clipboard.
13. Click the heading **Conclusion** in the Document Map.
14. Paste the copied text on a new line under the heading **Conclusion**.
15. Edit the pasted sentence as shown on Illustration A (Page 5 of 5).
16. Use the Document Map to move the insertion point to the section on Safety Recommendations.
17. Insert a hard page break at the end of the bulleted list.
18. Use the Document Map to move the insertion point to the heading **Know the Risks**.
19. Insert a hard page break.
20. Hide the Document Map.
21. Create a header for all pages but the first. Include the report title, **Safe SCUBA Diving**, flush left and the current date flush right.
22. Create a centered footer for all pages with the word **Page**, followed by the page number.
23. Check the spelling and grammar in the document.
24. Preview the document. It should look similar to the document shown in Illustration A.
25. Close the document, saving all changes.

Illustration A (Page 1 of 5)

Safe SCUBA Diving

Prepared by
Pete Newell, Owner
Pelican Peter's Dive Shop
2200 Gulfshore Blvd. N., Naples, FL 34102

Introduction

The acronym SCUBA stands for Self-Contained Underwater Breathing Apparatus. In other words, SCUBA divers use an apparatus that is completely carried by the diver and not connected to the surface. It is estimated that more than 3.5 million Americans participate in recreational SCUBA diving. Another 500 thousand become certified each year in the United States. The experience of SCUBA diving can be exciting, exhilarating, and empowering. However, without the proper planning, SCUBA diving can also be dangerous.

This report provides a look at the steps divers can take to maximize the pleasure of a dive while minimizing the risks.

Safety Recommendations

Diving can be a safe and rewarding experience. It only takes a momentary lapse of caution for a situation to go from fun to fatal. These safety rules can minimize your risk:

- Have all equipment maintained regularly by a professional.
- Check equipment before every dive.
- Be sure you are mentally and physically prepared for a dive.
- Check the weather and water conditions prior to a dive.
- Never dive alone.
- Don't drink alcohol before diving.
- Don't handle unfamiliar marine life.
- Consult a doctor before diving.

The buddy rule cannot be emphasized enough. Any reputable diving organization will insist each diver be accompanied under water by a buddy who can share air or provide other assistance. A SCUBA apparatus is designed to carry an extra demand regulator. This is required in case one diver runs out of air and has to share a single tank with his or her buddy. Ideally, the buddies should have similar training and skill levels; it does no good to have a buddy who dives deeper or stays down longer than you do. Buddies should stay close together and always be aware of each other's location.

Preparation

Preparation is the key to a successful and safe dive. With proper training and common sense diving is a very safe sport. In fact, statistics show that diving is considerably safer than skiing, rock climbing, sky diving, and trail biking. Death and injury during a dive are usually related to shoddy planning, inadequate training, and poor judgment. There are four basic steps to insuring a safe and successful dive experience:

1. Be aware of the risks.
2. Follow the rules.
3. Obtain certification from a reliable source.
4. Use the right equipment.

Basic Certification

An entry-level SCUBA certification course takes approximately 32 hours to complete. The course includes classroom sessions as well as practical training of essential diving skills in a pool. Successful completion of the course requires passing a written exam and demonstrating your ability to use the skills you have learned during open water training dives. Once certified you may rent equipment, participate in advanced training classes, and take part in actual dives.

Illustration A (Page 3 of 5)

Safe SCUBA Diving Today's Date

Equipment

A prepared diver understands that having the proper equipment in excellent condition will significantly reduce risk. Basic equipment includes the following[1]:

- A tank of compressed air carried on the diver's back.
- A first stage regulator attached to the tank to lower air pressure delivered to the diver.
- A second stage demand regulator and mouthpiece, that delivers air on inhalation and closes on exhalation.
- A face mask that covers the diver's eyes and nose.
- An extra second stage regulator and mouthpiece, carried by the diver in case of emergency.
- Two submersible gauges, one to display an accurate depth and the other to show how much air remains in the tank.
- An inflatable vest worn to provide a means of establishing positive buoyancy.
- A weight belt and weights, worn to compensate for positive buoyancy.
- Fins to facilitate self-propulsion in the water.
- A wet suit or other type of body protection to prevent hypothermia.

Optional equipment such as a snorkel, dive knife, small tank of extra air, dive computer, compass, dive lights, writing slate, whistle, and inflatable signaling device may also be carried.

Specialized Safety Equipment

The following special safety equipment can also help minimize risk:[2]:

Dive Computers. Dive computers are designed to calculate remaining no-decompression limits while you are diving.
Flares. Waterproof flares are designed to help dive boats find you if you become disoriented and surface in the wrong location.
Rescue Sausages. These devices also help dive boats find you.
Sound Alerts. These devices produce a loud noise at the surface which can alert others that you're in trouble.
Spare Air/Pony Bottle. These systems are designed to give you an alternate air source that is not dependent on air from your tank.
Strobe Lights. This is essential equipment for night dives and drift dives. They produce a very bright light which can be seen from a great distance.

---

1 Lawrence Martin, M.D., "Scuba Diving Explained", 1997, http://www.reefscuba.com/safetytips.htm.
2 http://www.mtsinai.org/pulmonary/books/scuba/sectionb.htm.

Page 3

Know the Risks

SCUBA diving is a risky activity. You can help yourself if you know ahead of time the types of hazards you might encounter.

Potential Hazards

About 40% of all SCUBA deaths are determined to be coincidental medical events such as heart attacks. The next most common causes of fatal accidents are panic, exhaustion, and pulmonary overpressure. Environmental causes such as cave dives, rough surf, and strong currents account for 25-30% of fatalities. Equipment related accidents such as running out of air or carrying too much weight account for less than 20% of fatal accidents. Deaths caused by encounters with fish or other marine life are rare.[3]

However, there are potential hazards inherent in every dive. All divers should be aware of the possibility of danger at all times, and should act accordingly. Some common hazards that may be encountered on any dive include the following:

- De-compression sickness
- Air embolism
- Hypothermia
- Physical exhaustion
- Injuries from marine life
- Boating accidents
- Sunburn
- Running out of air

Medical Conditions Caused by Diving

The possibility of suffering a debilitating medical condition while diving is very real. If you experience any of the symptoms on the following list during a dive or after a dive, you should seek professional medical care immediately.[4]

3 Ernest S Campbell, MD, *Diving Medicine Online*, "Diving Safety," http://www.gulftel.com/~scubadoc/divsfe.htm.
4 *Scuba Diving Safety*, http://familydoctor.org/handouts/156.html.

Illustration A (Page 5 of 5)

Arterial gas embolism (AGE). One of the most serious conditions, AGE results in symptoms such as numbness or tingling of the skin, weakness, paralysis, and possibly loss of consciousness. AGE is a type of pulmonary barotrauma in which bubbles enter the circulation and travel to the brain.

Decompression sickness ("the bends"). One of the most well-known conditions, the bends occurs when your body absorbs too much nitrogen, which then forms into bubbles in your body tissue. The bends results from exceeding the no-decompression dive limits. Symptoms include joint pain, fatigue, numbness or tingling of the skin, and even weakness or paralysis.

Inner ear barotrauma. If you experience dizziness or hearing loss after a dive, you may be suffering from this condition.

Middle ear squeeze. This condition commonly occurs if you dive while suffering from a cold or allergies. It causes pain in the ears, which can be severe.

Pulmonary barotrauma. Symptoms of this condition include chest pain, shortness of breath, and hoarseness. The condition results from improper breathing during the ascent to the surface.

Conclusion

As mentioned above, the experience of SCUBA diving can be exciting, exhilarating, and empowering. However, without the proper planning, SCUBA diving can also be dangerous. It is imperative that anyone seriously considering exploring the underwater world of SCUBA diving obtain training from certified professionals. Information about classes, equipment, and organized excursions can be found at most reputable dive shops. The most successful dives are the safest.

On Your Own

1. Open the document OWDGUIDES2 that you used in the On Your Own section of Exercise 52, or open 53OWDGUIDES2.
2. Save the document as OWDGUIDES3.
3. Use the Document Map to navigate through the document.
4. Move text from one page in the document to another. (You can always use Undo to revert back, if necessary.)
5. Copy text from one page in the document to another.
6. If necessary, adjust page breaks.
7. Save the document, close it, and exit Word.

Exercise 54

Skills Covered:

◆ **Preview Multiple Pages**

◆ **Drag and Drop Text from One Page to Another**

◆ **Print Specific Pages**

On the Job

Preview multiple pages to see how an entire multipage document will look when it is printed. For example, when you preview more than one page at a time you can see headers and footers on every page and determine whether the text flow from one page to the next looks professional. Printing specific pages or selected text is an option that can save paper and time if you find that you only need hard copies of parts of a document. Also, when you can see more than one page on-screen, you can easily use drag-and-drop editing to reorganize document text.

The head of marketing for Cornerstone Graphics has asked you to prepare a sample of a lengthy document to show to the company president. In this exercise, you will preview the entire document to determine which sections you need to include in the sample. You will then print selected pages.

Terms

Magnifier The mouse pointer used to zoom in or out on a page in Print Preview.

Notes

Preview Multiple Pages

- By default, Print preview displays one page at a time.
- You can change the Print preview display to show multiple pages at one time.
- Preview multiple pages to get an overall view of the document, not to edit or format text.
  - ✓ *You can edit in Print Preview, but it is difficult if the pages are small.*
- You can select the number of pages you want to display using the Multiple Pages button on the print Preview toolbar.
  - ✓ *You can also select a setting from the Zoom drop down list. For more on the Zoom feature, refer to Exercise 3.*
- The more pages displayed, the smaller the pages appear on the screen, so the harder it is to read the text.
- Click the **Magnifier** tool anywhere on a page in Print Preview to zoom in to get a better look.
- When the page is zoomed, the Magnifier tool includes a minus sign instead of a plus sign. Click the page again to zoom back out.

A five-page document in Print preview

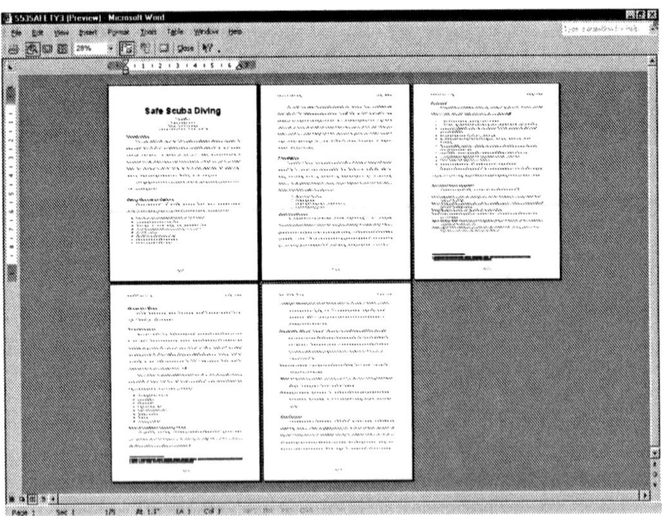

Drag and Drop Text from One Page to Another

- If you can see both locations on the screen at the same time, you can use the drag-and-drop methods for copying or moving text from one page to another.

Print Specific Pages

- Select Print options to print a specific page, several pages, selected text, or the current page.
- In the Print dialog box, you can specify consecutive pages or nonconsecutive pages. You can also specify pages to print by page number.

Set print options in the Print dialog box

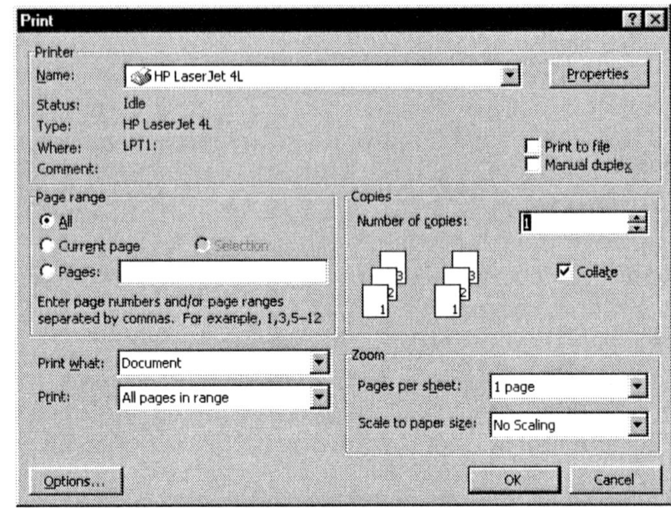

Procedures

Preview Multiple Pages

1. Click **Print Preview** button.

   OR

   a. Click **File** .... Alt+F

   b. Click **Print Preview** V
2. Click **Multiple Pages** button.
3. Drag across number of rows and pages to display.
4. Release mouse button.

Change Back to One-Page Preview

- Click **One Page** button .

Zoom In in Print Preview

1. If necessary, click in document to position the insertion point.
2. Position the magnifier mouse pointer over the area to enlarge.

   ✓ *The magnifier is selected by default. If the magnifier pointer is not displayed, click Magnifier button on Print Preview toolbar to toggle the option on.*
3. Click mouse once.
4. Click again to zoom out.

   ✓ *To cancel the magnifier so you can edit a document, click the Magnifier button on Print Preview toolbar to toggle the option off.*

Use Drag-and-Drop Editing to Copy Text

1. Display multiple pages on-screen in Print Preview or Page Layout view.

   ✓ *If necessary, click the magnifier button to turn off zoom feature.*
2. Select text to copy.
3. Move mouse pointer anywhere over selected text.
4. Press and hold **Ctrl** .... Ctrl
5. Drag selection to new location.
6. Release mouse button.
7. Release **Ctrl** .... Ctrl

Use Drag-and-Drop Editing to Move Text

1. Display multiple pages on-screen in Print Preview or Print Layout view.
2. Select text to move.

   ✓ *If necessary, click the magnifier button to turn off zoom feature.*
3. Move mouse pointer anywhere over selected text.
4. Drag selection to new location.
5. Release mouse button when the insertion point is in new location.

Print Specified Pages *(Ctrl+P)*

Print single page:

1. Click **File** .... Alt+F
2. Click **Print** .... P
3. Click **Pages** .... Alt+G
4. Type page number.
5. Click **OK** .... Enter

Print consecutive pages:

1. Click **File** .... Alt+F
2. Click **Print** .... P
3. Click **Pages** .... Alt+G
4. Type page range as follows: first page number, hyphen, last page number. For example: 3-5
   ✓ *Do not type spaces.*
5. Click **OK** .... Enter

Print nonconsecutive pages:

1. Click **File** .... Alt+F
2. Click **Print** .... P
3. Click **Pages** .... Alt+G
4. Type each page number separated by commas. For example: 3,5,7
   ✓ *Do not type spaces.*
5. Click **OK** .... Enter
   ✓ *You can combine consecutive and nonconsecutive pages. For example, 2-5,7,10.*

Print current page:

1. Click **File** .... Alt+F
2. Click **Print** .... P
3. Click **Current Page** ..... Alt+E
4. Click **OK** .... Enter

Print selected text:

1. Select text to print.
2. Click **File** .... Alt+F
3. Click **Print** .... P
4. Click **Selection** .... Alt+S
5. Click **OK** .... Enter

Exercise Directions

1. Start Word, if necessary.
2. Open SAFETY3 or open 54SAFETY3.
3. Save the document as SAFETY4.
4. Use Print Preview to preview all pages of the document at once.
5. Change the display to show two pages at a time.
6. Zoom in on the top of page 2.
7. Zoom back out.
8. Use drag-and-drop to move the first paragraph on page 2 to page 1, as the first paragraph under the heading **Safety Recommendations**.
9. Close Print Preview.
10. Insert a hard page break between the first and second paragraphs under the heading **Safety Recommendations**.
11. Delete the hard page break after the list of recommendations (now at the top of page 2).
12. Pages 1 and 2 should look similar to those shown in Illustration A.
13. Print pages 1 and 2.
14. Display the Document Map.
15. Use the Document Map to go to the heading **Equipment**.
16. Print the current page.
17. Use the Document Map to go to the heading **Medical Conditions Caused by Diving**.
18. Select the heading and the list of medical conditions and print the selection.
19. Close the document, saving all changes.

Safe SCUBA Diving

Prepared by
Pete Newell, Owner
Pelican Peter's Dive Shop
2200 Gulfshore Blvd. N., Naples, FL 34102

Introduction

The acronym SCUBA stands for Self-Contained Underwater Breathing Apparatus. In other words, SCUBA divers use an apparatus that is completely carried by the diver and not connected to the surface. It is estimated that more than 3.5 million Americans participate in recreational SCUBA diving. Another 500 thousand become certified each year in the United States. The experience of SCUBA diving can be exciting, exhilarating, and empowering. However, without the proper planning, SCUBA diving can also be dangerous.

This report provides a look at the steps divers can take to maximize the pleasure of a dive while minimizing the risks.

Safety Recommendations

The buddy rule cannot be emphasized enough. Any reputable diving organization will insist each diver be accompanied under water by a buddy who can share air or provide other assistance. A SCUBA apparatus is designed to carry an extra demand regulator. This is required in case one diver runs out of air and has to share a single tank with his or her buddy. Ideally, the buddies should have similar training and skill levels; it does no good to have a buddy who dives deeper or stays down longer than you do. Buddies should stay close together and always be aware of each other's location.

Illustration A (Page 2 of 2)

Safe SCUBA Diving Today's Date

Diving can be a safe and rewarding experience. It only takes a momentary lapse of caution for a situation to go from fun to fatal. These safety rules can minimize your risk:

- Have all equipment maintained regularly by a professional.
- Check equipment before every dive.
- Be sure you are mentally and physically prepared for a dive.
- Check the weather and water conditions prior to a dive.
- Never dive alone.
- Don't drink alcohol before diving.
- Don't handle unfamiliar marine life.
- Consult a doctor before diving.

Preparation

Preparation is the key to a successful and safe dive. With proper training and common sense diving is a very safe sport. In fact, statistics show that diving is considerably safer than skiing, rock climbing, sky diving, and trail biking. Death and injury during a dive are usually related to shoddy planning, inadequate training, and poor judgment. There are four basic steps to insuring a safe and successful dive experience:

1. Be aware of the risks.
2. Follow the rules.
3. Obtain certification from a reliable source.
4. Use the right equipment.

Basic Certification

An entry-level SCUBA certification course takes approximately 32 hours to complete. The course includes classroom sessions as well as practical training of essential diving skills in a pool. Successful completion of the course requires passing a written exam and demonstrating your ability to use the skills you have learned during open water training dives. Once certified you may rent equipment, participate in advanced training classes, and take part in actual dives.

Page 2

On Your Own

1. Open the document OWDGUIDES3, the document you used in the On Your Own section of Exercise 53, or open 54OWDGUIDES3.
2. Save the document as OWDGUIDES4.
3. Preview multiple pages of the document at one time.
4. Use drag-and-drop editing to copy or move text from one page in the document to another.
5. Print the last page of the document.
6. Print the first paragraph of the document.
7. Save and close the document, and exit Word.

Exercise 55

Skills Covered:

◆ **Find and Replace**

◆ **Insert bookmarks** ◆ **Select Browse Object**

On the Job

Use the Find, Bookmark, and Browse Object features to locate specific parts of a document, including text, graphics, paragraph marks, etc. Use Find and Replace when you want to automatically replace existing text or formatting with something different.

Pete Newell has asked you to complete a shorter version of the SCUBA safety document that contains information about equipment and certification classes only. In this exercise, you will edit an existing document using the Find and Replace commands. You will also insert bookmarks into the document and use different browse objects to move through the document.

Terms

Bookmark A nonprinting character that you insert and name so that you can quickly find a particular location in a document.

Browse object A specified element that Word locates and displays when you scroll through a document.

Notes

Find and Replace

- Use Word's Find command to locate specific text, nonprinting characters, formatting, graphics, objects, and other items in a document.
- You can use Find to scroll one by one through each occurrence of the Find text, or you can find and select all occurrences at once.

Find tab of the Find and Replace dialog box

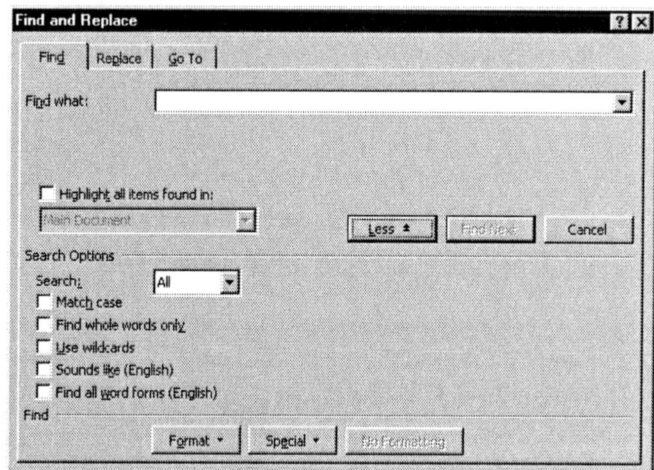

- Combine Find with Replace to replace items.
- The Find and Replace commands are useful for correcting errors that occur several times in a document, such as a misspelled name.
- In addition to text, you can find and replace formatting, symbols, and special characters such as paragraph marks.

Replace tab of the Find and Replace dialog box

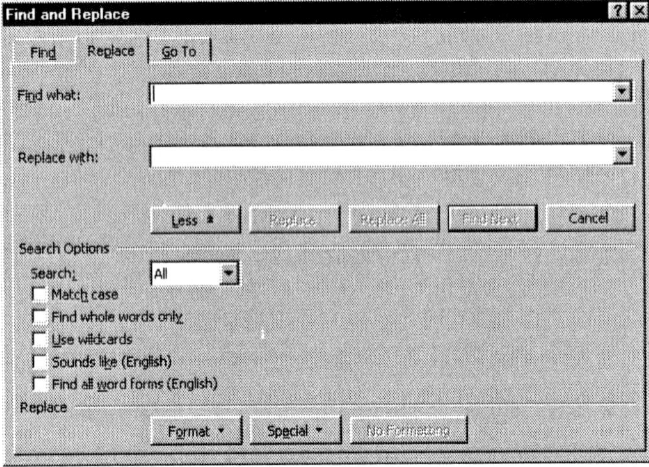

Insert Bookmarks

- Use a **bookmark** to mark a specific location in a document, such as where you stopped working or where you need to insert information.
- You can use many bookmarks in one document.
- Use descriptive bookmark names to make it easier to find the bookmark location that you want.
- Use the Go To feature to go directly to a bookmark.

Go To tab of Find and Replace dialog box

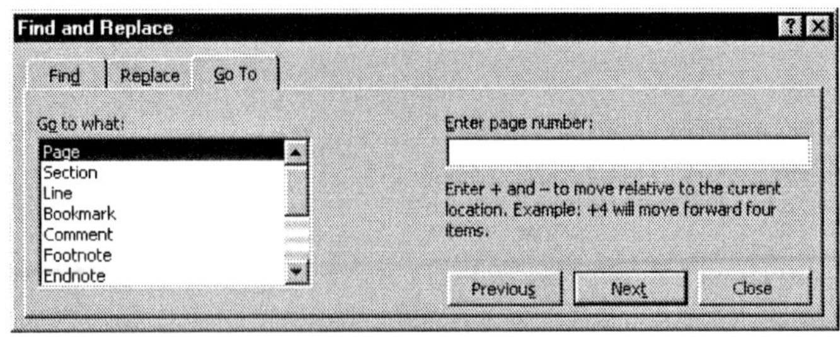

Select Browse Object

- Use **browse object** to scroll to specific points in a document.
- There are twelve browse objects from which to choose; rest the mouse pointer on an object to see its name across the top of the object palette.
- When you choose the Go To browse object, you must specify the object to go to.
- When you choose the Find browse object, you must enter text to Find and/or Replace.

The browse object palette

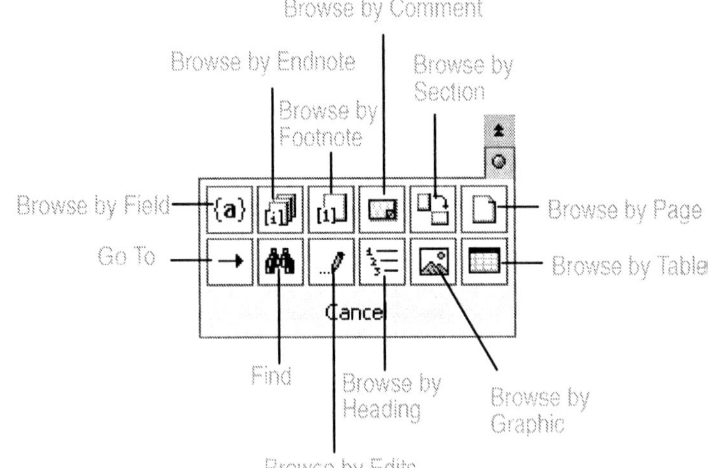

Procedures

Find Text *(Ctrl+F)*

1. Position the insertion point at the beginning of the document .... Ctrl+Home

   ✓ *You may start searching at any point in the document, or you may search selected text. However, to be sure to search the entire document, start at the top.*

2. Click **Edit** .... Alt+E
3. Click **Find** .... F
4. Click **Find what** .... Alt+N
5. Type text to find.
6. Click **More** button [More] (if necessary) .... Alt+M
7. Select options:
   - **Match case** .... Alt+H
     to find only words in same case as text to find.
   - **Find whole words only** .... Alt+Y
     to find text as a whole word, not as part of a longer word.
   - **Use wildcards** ...... Alt+U
     to find words specified with wildcard characters.

- **Sounds like**............Alt+K to find homonyms.
- **Find all word forms** ....Alt+W to find all grammatical forms of text.

8. Click **Find Next** button
   Find Next ....Alt+F
   ✓ *Word highlights first occurrence of text in document. You can click in the document to edit or format the text, while leaving the Find and Replace dialog box open.*
9. Repeat step 8 until finished.
   ✓ *Click Cancel at any time to close the dialog box.*
10. Click **OK**...........................Enter
11. Click **Cancel** button
    Cancel ....Esc

Find and Select Text

1. Click **Edit** ....Alt+E
2. Click **Find**.............................F
3. Click **Find what** ....Alt+N
4. Type text to find.
5. Click **Highlight all items found in:**......................Alt+T
   ✓ *Default is to highlight items in main document only; you may select Headers and Footers from the drop-down list if desired.*
6. Click **Find All** button
   Find All ....Alt+F
   ✓ *Word finds and selects all occurrences of the specified text.*
7. Click **Close** button
   Close ....Esc

Replace Text *(Ctrl+H)*

1. Click **Edit** ....Alt+E
2. Click **Replace** ....E
3. Click **Find what** ....Alt+N
4. Type text to find.
5. Press **Tab**...........................Tab
   OR
   Click **Replace with**......Alt+I
   ✓ *To replace with nothing (delete), leave the Replace with text box blank.*
6. Type replacement text.
7. Click **More** button More (if necessary)...............Alt+M
8. Select options.
9. Click **Find Next** ....Alt+F
10. Click **Replace**.............Alt+R
    OR
    Click **Replace All**........Alt+A
11. Repeat steps 9–10 until done.
    ✓ *Click Cancel at any time to close the dialog box.*
12. Click **OK**...........................Enter
13. Click **Close** button
    Close ....Esc

Find and Replace Special Characters *(Ctrl +H)*

1. Click **Edit**....................Alt+E
2. Click **Replace**......................R
3. Click **Find what**...........Alt+N
4. Click **Special**..............Alt+E
5. Select special character.
6. Press **Tab** ....Tab
   OR
   Click **Replace with** .....Alt+I
   ✓ *To replace with nothing (delete), leave Replace with text box blank.*
7. Click **More**..................Alt+M
8. Click **Special**..............Alt+E
9. Select special character.
10. Click **Find Next** ....Alt+F
11. Click **Replace**......................R
    OR
    Click **Replace All**........Alt+A
12. Repeat steps 10–11 until done.
    ✓ *Click Cancel at any time to close the dialog box.*
13. Click **OK**...........................Enter
14. Click **Close** button
    Close ....Esc

Create a Bookmark

1. Position the insertion point where you want the bookmark.
2. Click **Insert**.................Alt+I
3. Click **Bookmark**.................K
4. Click in the **Bookmark name** text box........................Alt+B
5. Type bookmark name.
6. Click **Add** button
   Add ....Alt+A

Go To Bookmark *(Ctrl+G)*

1. Press **F5** F5
   OR
   a. Click **Edit**...............Alt+E
   b. Click **Go To**.....................G
2. Click Bookmark in the **Go to what** list.............Alt+O
   ✓ *Select any object in the Go to what list to browse directly to that object.*
3. Click **Enter bookmark name** ....Alt+E
4. Type bookmark name.
   OR
   Select bookmark name from drop-down list.
5. Click **Go To** ....Alt+T
6. Click **Close** button
   Close ....Esc

Browse by Object *(Alt + Ctrl + Home)*

1. Click the **Select Browse Object** button.
2. Click the desired browse object.
   ✓ *If you select Find or Go To, the Find and Replace dialog box is displayed.*
3. Click the **Previous** button to scroll up to the previous browse object.
   OR
   Click the **Next** button to scroll down to the next browse object.

Exercise Directions

1. Start Word, if necessary.
2. Open the document 55SUMMARY.
3. Save the file as SUMMARY.
4. Starting with the insertion point at the beginning of the document, use the Find command to locate the first occurrence of the word **dive**.
   - ✓ *Word should highlight the word* Dive *in Pelican Peter's Dive Shop.*
5. Locate the next occurrence of the word.
   - ✓ *Word should highlight the letters* dive *within the word* divers *in the second sentence of the document.*
6. Move the insertion point back to the beginning of the document.
7. Set the Find command to use the Whole Words Only and Match Case options so that it finds whole words in lowercase letters.
8. Locate the first occurrence of the word **dive**.
9. This time, Word should highlight the word **dive** in the first sentence of the second paragraph.
10. Use the Replace command to replace the highlighted word **dive** with the phrase **SCUBA dive**.
11. Replace the next occurrence of the word **dive** as well.
12. Move the insertion point back to the beginning of the document and use the Find command to select all occurrences of the word **training** and format it with bold italics.
   - ✓ *Cancel the Whole Words and Match Case options before starting the Find command.*
13. Use the Browse by Heading browse object to move the insertion point to the heading **Basic Certification** and insert a bookmark named **basiccert**.
14. Use the Browse by Heading browse object to move the insertion point to the heading **Specialized Safety Equipment** and insert a bookmark named **SSE**.
15. Use Go To browse object to go to the **basiccert** bookmark.
16. Use the Go To browse object to go to the **SSE** bookmark.
17. Check the spelling and grammar in the document and correct errors as necessary.
18. Display the document in Print Preview. It should look similar to the one in the illustration.
19. Close Print Preview.
20. Print the document.
21. Close the document, saving all changes.

Illustration A (page 1 of 2)

Safe Scuba Diving

Prepared by
Pete Newell, Owner
Pelican Peter's Dive Shop
2200 Gulfshore Blvd. N., Naples, FL 34102

The acronym SCUBA stands for Self-Contained Underwater Breathing Apparatus. In other words, SCUBA divers use apparatus that is completely carried by the diver and not connected to the surface. It is estimated that more than 3.5 million Americans participate in recreational SCUBA diving. Another 500 thousand become certified each year in the United States. The experience of SCUBA diving can be exciting, exhilarating, and empowering. However, without the proper planning, SCUBA diving can also be dangerous.

Preparation is the key to a successful and safe SCUBA dive. With proper ***training*** and common sense diving is a very safe sport. In fact, statistics show that diving is considerably safer than skiing, rock climbing, sky diving, and trail biking. Death and injury during a SCUBA dive are usually related to shoddy planning, inadequate ***training***, and poor judgment.

Basic Certification

An entry-level SCUBA certification course takes approximately 32 hours to complete. The course includes classroom sessions as well as practical ***training*** of essential diving skills in a pool. Successful completion of the course requires passing a written exam and demonstrating your ability to use the skills you have learned during open water ***training*** dives. Once certified you may rent equipment, participate in advanced ***training*** classes, and take part in actual dives.

Page 1

Safe SCUBA Diving Today's Date

Equipment

A prepared diver understands that having the proper equipment in excellent condition will significantly reduce risk. Basic equipment includes the following[1]:

- A tank of compressed air carried on the diver's back.
- A first stage regulator attached to the tank to lower air pressure delivered to the diver.
- A second stage demand regulator and mouthpiece, that delivers air on inhalation and closes on exhalation.
- A face mask that covers the diver's eyes and nose.
- An extra second stage regulator and mouthpiece, carried by the diver in case of emergency.
- Two submersible gauges, one to display an accurate depth and the other to show how much air remains in the tank.
- An inflatable vest worn to provide a means of establishing positive buoyancy.
- A weight belt and weights, worn to compensate for positive buoyancy.
- Fins to facilitate self-propulsion in the water.
- A wet suit or other type of body protection to prevent hypothermia.

Optional equipment such as a snorkel, dive knife, small tank of extra air, dive computer, compass, dive lights, writing slate, whistle, and inflatable signaling device may also be carried.

Specialized Safety Equipment

The following special safety equipment can also help minimize risk:[2]

Dive Computers Dive computers are designed to calculate remaining no-decompression limits while you are diving.
Flares. Waterproof flares are designed to help dive boats find you if you become disoriented and surface in the wrong location.
Rescue Sausages. These devices also help dive boats find you.
Sound Alerts. These devices produce a loud noise at the surface which can alert others that you're in trouble.
Spare Air/Pony Bottle These systems are designed to give you an alternate air source that is not dependent on air from your tank.
Strobe Lights This is essential equipment for night dives and drift dives. They produce a very bright light which can be seen from a great distance.

---

1 Lawrence Martin, M.D., "Scuba Diving Explained", 1997, http://www.reefscuba.com/safetytips.htm.
2 http://www.mtsinai.org/pulmonary/books/scuba/sectionb.htm.

Page 2

On Your Own

1. Open the document OWDGUIDES4 that you used in the On Your Own section of Exercise 54, or open 55OWDGUIDE54.
2. Save the document as OWDGUIDES5.
3. Insert at least three footnotes to provide citations, or to supplement text with additional information.

   ✓ *For a refresher on footnotes and endnotes, refer to Exercise 29.*

4. Insert at least three endnotes.
5. Browse to the footnotes.
6. Browse to the endnotes.
7. Use Find to locate specific text, such as your own name.
8. Use Find and Replace to locate and replace specific text, such as an abbreviation or acronym.
9. Print the document.
10. Close the document, saving all changes.

Exercise 56

Skills Covered:

- **Create a Master Document**
- **Work with Subdocuments**

On the Job

When you need to organize and manage long documents, you can create a master document with subdocuments. For example, use a master document to manage a book that has multiple chapters, or a report that has many sections.

The marketing director at Fox Footwear has asked you to write a lengthy report about the history of footwear. You are just getting started on the project and have decided that using a master document will help you stay organized. In this exercise, you will create a master document from an existing outline, insert an additional subdocument into the master document, and edit a subdocument. Finally, you will print the master document.

Terms

Master document A document that contains a set of related documents.

Subdocument A document contained in a master document.

Notes

Create a Master Document

- Use a **master document** to organize and manage a long document by dividing it into **subdocuments**.
- For example, you can use subdocuments to renumber pages, footnotes, or endnotes, in a manuscript that contains multiple chapters.
- To create a master document, simply designate headings in an outline as subdocuments.

  ✓ *For information about working with outlines, see Exercise 50.*
- Word automatically saves each designated heading, its subheadings, and its body text as a separate document.
- Word inserts sections breaks between subdocuments in a master document and displays a gray border around each subdocument.
- You can view and edit the subdocuments in the master document, or you can open a subdocument separately.
- Once you create subdocuments, the master document outline is displayed in Master Document view.
- In Master Document view, Word displays additional buttons on the Outlining toolbar.
- A subdocument icon is displayed to the left of each subdocument in Master Document view.
  - Click the subdocument icon to select the entire subdocument.
  - Double-click the subdocument icon to quickly open the subdocument. The subdocument opens in a separate window.
- You can create a master document from a new document, or convert an existing document into a master document.

- You can also insert an existing document into an existing master document as a subdocument.
- You can expand, collapse, and rearrange a master document or the contents of a subdocument using Outline view just as you would a regular Word outline.

Work with Subdocuments

- You can edit and format subdocuments the same way you do any Word document.
- In Master Document view, you can expand and collapse subdocuments using buttons on the Outlining toolbar.
- Collapsed subdocuments are displayed as hyperlinks in the master document outline. When you Ctrl+Click the hyperlink, the subdocument opens.
- When subdocuments are collapsed, a lock icon is displayed under the subdocument icon.
- Word automatically names subdocument files based on the first text in the subdocument heading. You can rename subdocument files.
- You can rearrange subdocuments by rearranging the master document outline.
- You can remove a subdocument from a master document. Removing the subdocument does not delete the contents of the file.
- When you print an expanded master document, all subdocuments are printed as well.

Expanded Master Document

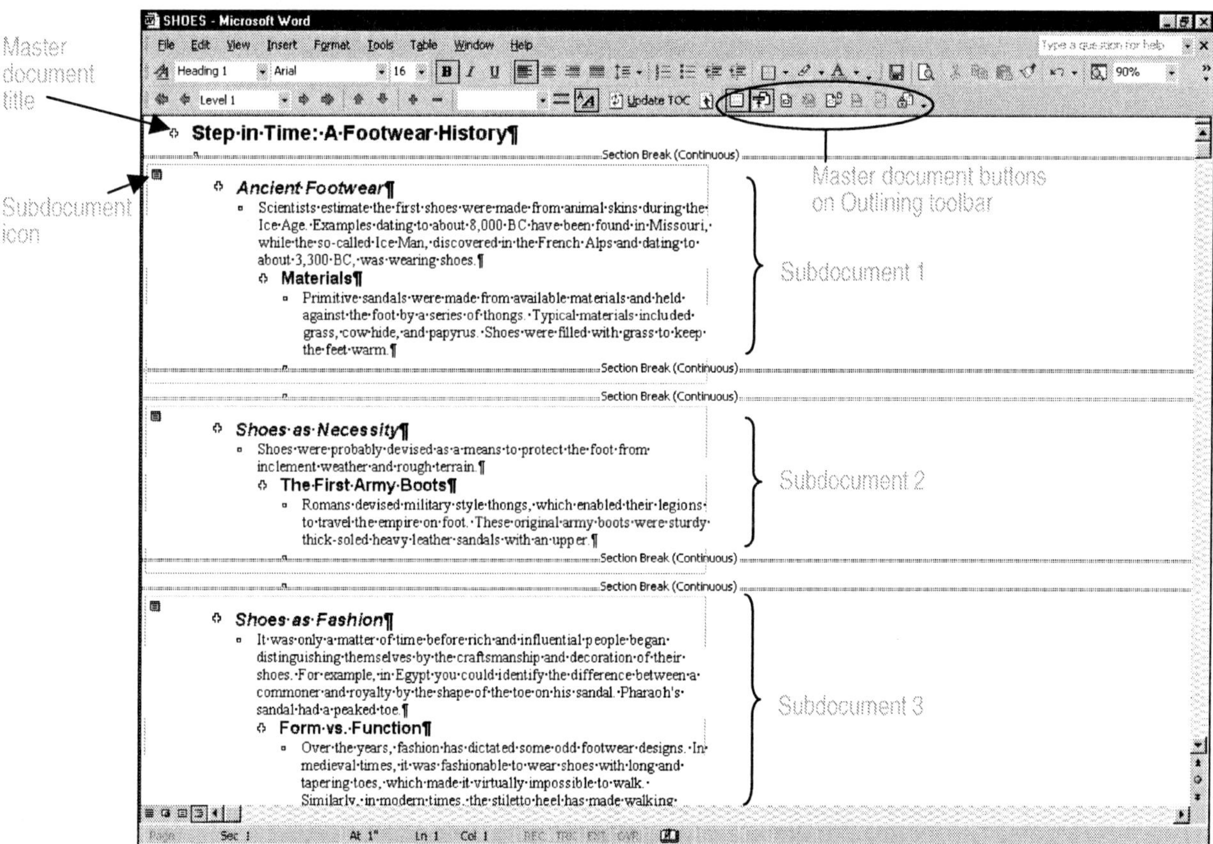

Collapsed Master document

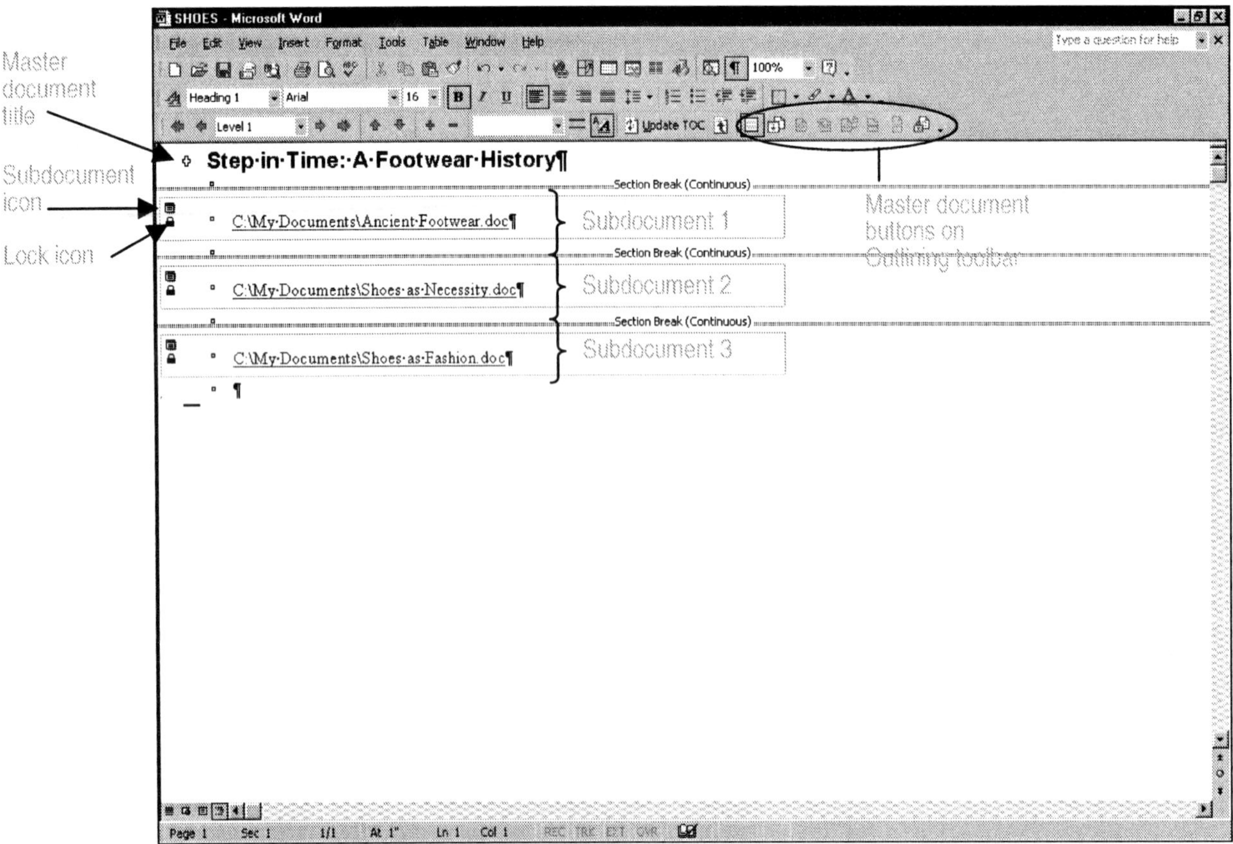

Procedures

Create a Master Document

Use a new document:

1. Create a new Word document.
2. Click **Outline View** button.
   OR
   a. Click **View** .... Alt+V
   b. Click **Outline** .... O
3. Type document title in heading 1 style.
4. Type all subdocument titles in heading 2 style.
5. Type any additional text or headings.
6. Select all subdocuments.
7. Click **Create Subdocument** button.

Use an existing document:

1. Open existing document.
2. Click **Outline View** button.
   OR

   a. Click **View** .... Alt+V

   b. Click **Outline** .... O
3. Apply same heading level to all subdocument titles.
4. Select each subdocument.
5. Click **Create Subdocument** button.

Work with Subdocuments

Insert subdocument in master document:

1. Open master document.
2. Click **Outline View** button.
   OR

   a. Click **View** .... Alt+V

   b. Click **Outline** .... O
3. Position insertion point on blank line in master document.
   ✓ *Be sure that the insertion point is not within the box defining an existing subdocument. If it is, you will end up creating a subdocument of the existing subdocument.*
4. Click **Insert Subdocument** button.
5. Select file to insert from **Look in** drop-down list .... Alt+I, ↕, Enter
6. Click **Open** button

   Open .... Alt+O

Remove subdocument from master document:

1. Open master document.
2. Click **Outline View** button.
   OR
   a. Click **View** .... Alt+V
   b. Click **Outline** .... O
3. Click anywhere in subdocument to be removed.
4. Click **Remove Subdocument** button.

Collapse/expand subdocuments:

1. Open master document.
2. Click **Collapse Subdocument** button.
   OR
   Click **Expand Subdocument** button.

Open subdocument in a new window:

1. Open master document.
2. Click **Outline View** button.
   OR
   a. Click **View** .... Alt+V
   b. Click **Outline** .... O
3. Double-click subdocument icon.
   OR
   a. Collapse master document.
   b. **Ctrl**+click subdocument hyperlink.

Rename a subdocument file:

1. Open subdocument.
2. Click **File** .... Alt+F
3. Click **Save As** .... A
4. If necessary, select storage location from **Save in** drop-down list... Alt+I, ↕, Enter
5. Type new file name.
6. Click **Save** button
   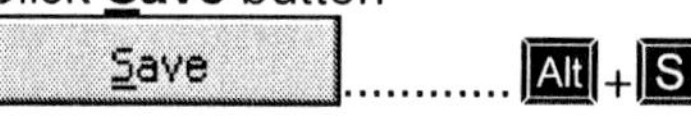
   Save .... Alt+S
   ✓ *Renaming a subdocument does not automatically update the link to the master document.*

Exercise Directions

1. Start Word, if necessary.
2. Open the document 56MODERN, save it as MODERN and close it. Later in this exercise, you will insert this file as a subdocument in a master document.
3. Open 56SHOES and save it as SHOES.
4. Change to Outline view.
5. Format the first line in the document—**Step in Time: A Footwear History**—as Heading 1. This will be the Master Document title.
   - ✓ *You may format the headings using the Style drop-down list on the Formatting toolbar or by promoting them using the Outline toolbar buttons.*
6. Apply Heading 2 to the **Ancient Footwear**, **Shoes as Necessity** and **Shoes as Fashion** headings. These will be the subdocuments.
7. Apply Heading 3 to the following:

   Materials
   The First Army Boots
   Form vs. Function
   - ✓ *All remaining text paragraphs should be at the body text level.*
8. Select Show Level 3 from the Show Level drop-down list to collapse the outline so only the headings are displayed (the body text paragraphs will be hidden).
9. Select all of the heading 2 and 3 levels (all but the first heading in the document).
10. Click the Create Subdocument button on the Outlining toolbar. Word creates the three subdocuments in the master document and displays them in Master Document view.
11. The document on-screen should look similar to the one in Illustration A.
12. Select Show All Levels from the Show Levels drop-down list to display the entire contents of the Master document.
13. Click the Collapse Subdocuments button to collapse the subdocuments. (Click OK if Word prompts you to save the master document.)
14. Open the second subdocument, Shoes as Necessity.doc, by resting the mouse pointer on the hyperlink and pressing Ctrl+Click.
    - ✓ *The document opens in Print Layout view.*
15. Move the insertion point to the end of the last paragraph before the section break (display paragraph marks if necessary), insert a new paragraph formatted as Heading 3, and type the following: **Specialized Shoes**.
16. Following the new heading, insert a paragraph formatted as body text in the Normal style as follows:

    Footwear designed for a specific purpose is a relatively new concept, sparked in large part by the sports industry. Beginning in the 1800s, shoes were developed specifically for use in running and croquet. Now, there are shoes designed for all manner of athletics ranging from baseball to fencing.
17. The Shoes as Necessity document should look similar to Illustration B.
18. Save the file and close it. The master document should still be open on-screen.
19. Click the Expand Subdocuments button on the Outlining toolbar to expand the subdocuments in the master document.
20. Move the insertion point to the blank line at the end of the master document, after the last section break, and insert the file MODERN as a subdocument.
21. Collapse the subdocuments, saving changes as prompted. The master document on-screen should look similar to Illustration C.
22. Expand the subdocuments.
23. Check the spelling and grammar in the master document.
24. Print the master document.
25. Close the master document, saving all changes.
26. Exit Word.

Illustration A

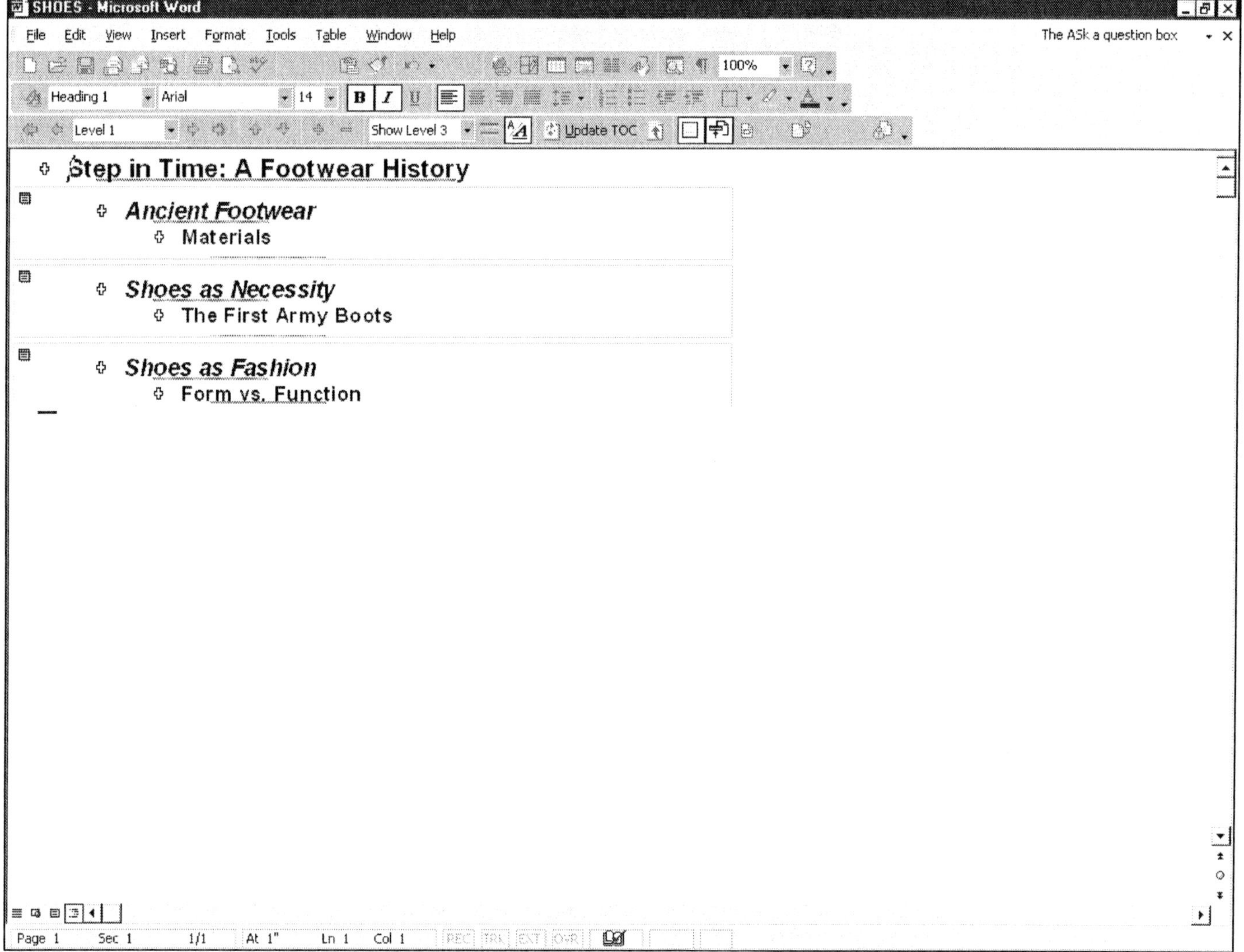

Shoes as Necessity

Shoes were probably devised as a means to protect the foot from inclement weather and rough terrain.

The First Army Boots

Romans devised military style footwear which enabled their legions to travel the empire on foot. These original army boots were sturdy thick-soled heavy leather sandals with an upper.

Specialized Shoes

Footwear designed for a specific purpose is a relatively new concept, sparked in large part by the sports industry. Beginning in the 1800s, shoes were developed specifically for use in running and croquet. Now, there are shoes designed for all manner of athletics ranging from baseball to fencing.

Illustration C

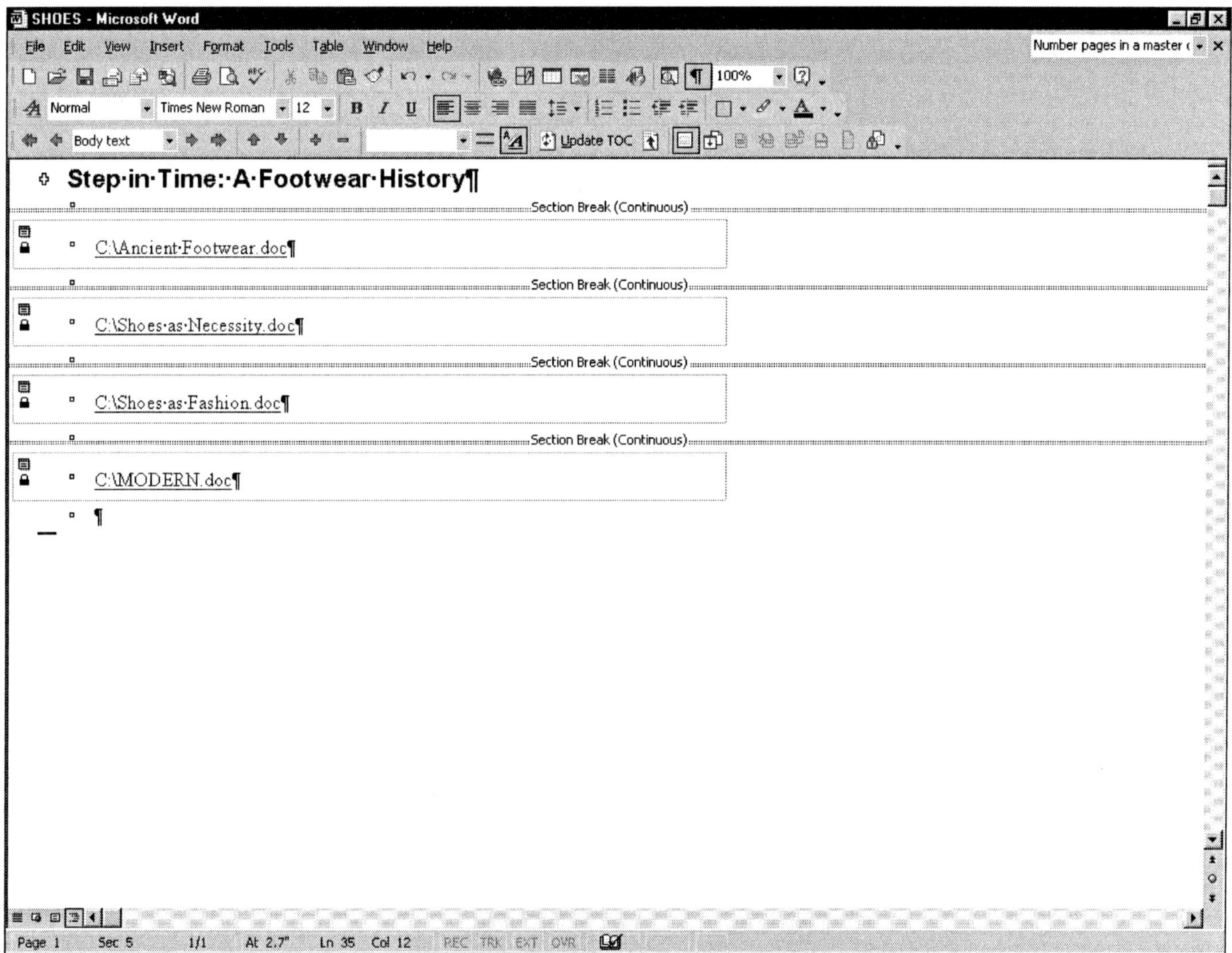

On Your Own

1. Start Word if necessary and open OWDOUTLINE, the outline you created in the On Your Own section of Exercise 50, or open the document 56OWDOUTLINE.
2. Save the document as OWDMASTER.
3. Go through the document and make sure that only headings you want to become subdocuments are formatted in the heading 2 style. If necessary, promote or demote other headings in the document.
4. Create subdocuments from the headings formatted in the Heading 2 style.
5. Save the master document.
6. Collapse the subdocuments.
7. Open one subdocument and enter two or three new paragraphs of information.
8. Save the subdocument and close it.
9. Insert the document OWDRESUME as a subdocument, or insert the document 56OWDRESUME.
10. Save the changes to the master document.
11. Display the entire contents of the master document.
12. Print the master document.
13. Close the document and exit Word.

Exercise 57

Skills Covered:

◆ **Insert a Cross-reference** ◆ **Create an Index** ◆ **Modify an Index**

On the Job

Sometimes it may be difficult for readers to locate the specific information they need in long or complex documents. To quickly refer a reader from one location to another related location, you can create a cross-reference. To help readers find the page containing specific information, you can create an index in which topics and subtopics are listed; Word automatically fills in the correct page number.

You have almost completed the SCUBA Safety report for Pelican Peter's Dive Shop. In this exercise, you will create cross-references in the report. You will also generate an index to help readers locate specific topics in the report quickly and easily.

Terms

Cross-reference Text that refers a reader to a different location in a document.

Cross-reference text The information entered in a document to introduce a cross-reference.

Cross-reference type The type of object which is being referred to, such as a bookmark or heading.

Field code The instructions inserted in a field that tell Word what results to display.

Field results The information displayed in a field.

Index An alphabetical list of topics and/or subtopics in a document along with the page numbers where they appear.

Tab leaders Characters inserted to the left of text aligned with a tab stop, such as page numbers in an index.

Notes

Insert a Cross-reference

- A **cross-reference** is text that directs a reader to another location in the same document for more information. For example, "*For more information, see page 22*" is a cross-reference.
  - ✓ *To reference a location in a different document, make both documents subdocuments of a master document. For information on creating master documents and subdocuments, see Exercise 56.*
- You can create cross-references to existing headings, footnotes, bookmarks, captions, numbered paragraphs, tables, and figures.
- When you create a cross-reference with Word, you enter the **cross-reference text**, and then select the **cross-reference type**.
- After you select the reference type, you select whether you want Word to reference the item by page number, text, or paragraph. This is the information Word will automatically insert in the document.

The Cross-reference dialog box

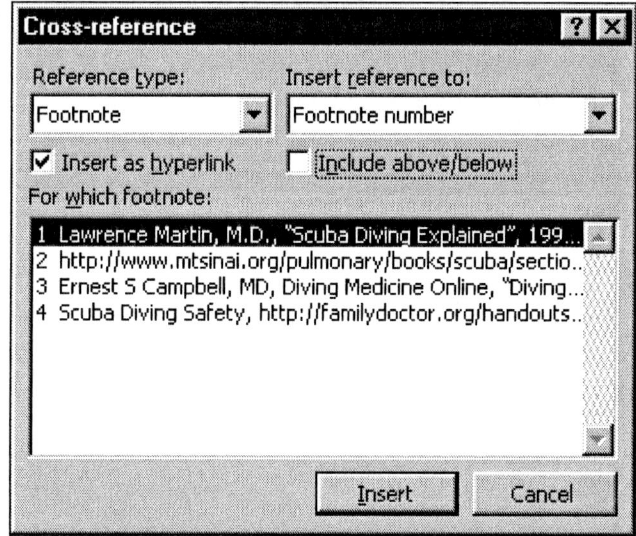

- Word enters the reference as a field, so it can be updated if necessary. This means that if you reference a heading and then move the heading to another location in the document, you can update the cross-reference to reflect the change.
- By default Word will insert a cross-reference as a hyperlink. Ctrl+click the cross-reference to jump to the specified destination.
- You can change the setting if you do not want the cross-reference inserted as a hyperlink.

  ✓ *See Exercise 30 for more information on hyperlinks.*

- If the cross-reference **field code** is displayed in your document instead of the **field results**, you must deselect the Field Codes check box on the View tab of the Tools, Options dialog box.

Create an Index

- An **index** lists topics and subtopics contained in a document, along with the page numbers where they appear.
- Word automatically generates an alphabetical index based on index entries you mark in the document text.
- Word comes with a selection of index formats.
- Other index layout options include the number of columns in the index and whether subtopics should be run in on the same line or if each subtopic should be indented. The default setting is for two columns and indented subtopics.
- You can also choose to right-align page numbers and to precede page numbers with **tab leaders**.

Select options for creating an index

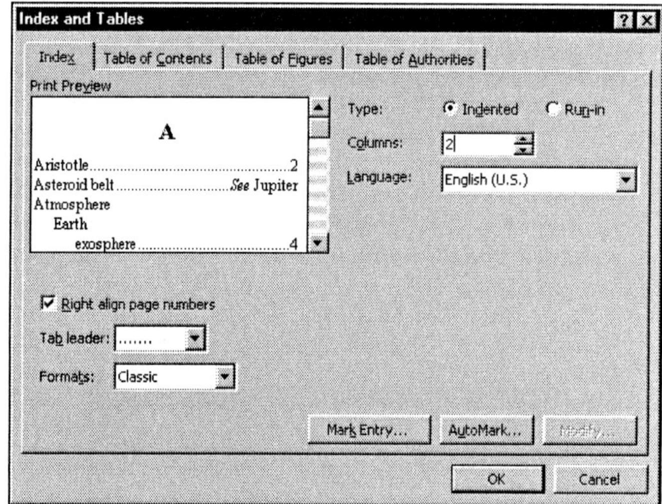

- You can index a single character, a word, a phrase, or a topic that spans multiple pages.
- You can mark all occurrences of the same text, or mark a single occurrence. Keep in mind that Word only marks all occurrences of *exactly* the same text. That means that the formatting, capitalization, tense, etc. must be exactly the same.
- Index entries can cross-reference a different index entry. For example, *Cats, see Pets* is a cross-referenced index entry.
- If you index many subtopics, you can use a multi-level index. For example, *Pets* may be the main index topic, with *Cats, Dogs*, and *Goldfish* as subtopics.
- To mark entries for an index, you select an item you want marked for inclusion in the index, then type the entry text as you want it displayed in the index.
- You can type the entry text using any formatting; it does not have to match the selected text in the document. However, if you are marking all items, only the items that appear exactly as the *selected text* will be marked. It doesn't matter what you type in the mark entry text box.
- If the selected item is exactly as you want it to appear in the index, you do not have to retype the entry text.

- If the entry is for a subtopic, you type the main entry topic under which the subtopic should be listed, then the subentry text as you want it displayed.
- Word automatically inserts an Index Entry field in the document following the selected item.
  - ✓ *Inserting Index Entry fields makes the body of the document appear longer than it will be when printed. For example, page breaks may seem to fall at the wrong place. However, since the fields are not printed in the document, the length is not affected at all. To see the document as it will print, change to Print Preview.*

Keep the Mark Index Entry dialog box open while marking multiple entries

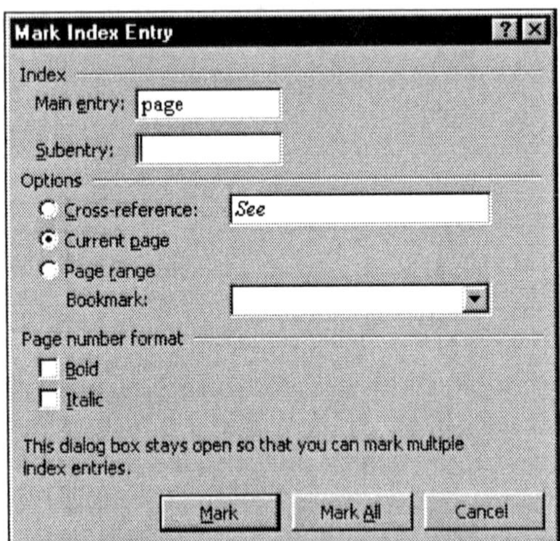

Modify an Index

- You can edit existing index entries by editing the text in the Index Entry field.
- If you add, delete, or move indexed items in the document, you must update the index so that Word changes the page numbers.

Procedures

Insert a Cross-Reference

✓ *Before inserting a cross-reference, make sure that the item which is being referenced – such as the heading, bookmark, or footnote – already exists.*

1. Position insertion point where you want cross-reference to appear.
2. Type cross-reference text, followed by a space and any necessary punctuation.
   - ✓ *For example, type the text: For more information see .*
3. Click **Insert**.................. Alt+I
4. Click **Reference**.................. N
5. Click **Cross-reference**........ R
6. Click **Reference type:** drop-down arrow .... Alt+T
7. Click desired reference type.......................... ↑↓, Enter
8. Click **Insert reference to:** drop-down arrow .... Alt+R
9. Click desired reference option....................... ↑↓, Enter
10. Select specific item in **For which** list..... Alt+W, ↑↓
    - ✓ *If you do not want cross-reference inserted as a hyperlink, deselect the **Insert as hyperlink** check box.*
11. Click **Insert**.................. Alt+I
12. Click **Close** button [Close].

Update a Cross-reference

1. Select cross reference to update.
2. Press **F9**.

   OR

   a. Right-click cross-reference to update.
   b. Click **Update Field** .... U

Create an Index

Mark index entries:

1. Click **Insert** .... Alt+I
2. Click **Reference**.................. N
3. Click **Index and Tables** .... D
4. Click **Index** tab............. Alt+X

5. Click **Mark Entry** button Mark Entry... .... Alt+K
6. In document, select text to mark.
   - ✓ *Mark Entry dialog box remains open while you select text to mark. If necessary, move Mark Entry dialog box out of the way.*
7. Click **Main entry** text box .... Alt+E
8. Type main index entry text.
9. Click **Subentry** text box .... Alt+S
10. Type subentry text if necessary.
11. Click **Mark** button Mark .... Alt+M to mark selected occurrence only.

    OR

    Click **Mark All** button Mark All .... Alt+A to mark all occurrences of selected text in document.
12. Repeat steps 6-11 until all entries are marked.
13. Click **Close**.

Mark a cross-references entry:

1. Click **Insert** .... Alt+I
2. Click **Reference** .... N
3. Click **Index and Tables** .... D
4. Click **Index** tab .... Alt+X
5. Click **Mark Entry** button Mark Entry... .... K
6. In document, select text to mark.
   - ✓ *Mark Entry dialog box remains open while you select text to mark. If necessary, move Mark Entry dialog box out of the way.*
7. Click **Main entry** text box .... Alt+E
8. Type main index entry text.
9. Click **Cross-reference** option button .... Alt+C
10. Type desired main entry text to refer to.
11. Click **Mark** button Mark .... Alt+M
12. Repeat steps 6–11 until all entries are marked.
13. Click **Close**.

Generate index:

1. Position insertion point in document where you want index displayed.
2. Click **Insert** .... Alt+I
3. Click **Reference** .... N
4. Click **Index and Tables** .... D
5. Click **Index** tab .... Alt+X
6. Click **Formats** drop-down arrow .... Alt+T
7. Click desired format .... ↑↓, Enter
8. Select any other desired options.
9. Click **OK** .... Enter

Update index:

1. Click in Index.
2. Press **F9** F9

   OR

   a. Right-click index.

   b. Click **Update Field** .... U

Exercise Directions

1. Start Word, if necessary.
2. Open the document SAFETY4, or open 57SAFETY4.
3. Save the document as SAFETY5.
4. At the end of the first paragraph in the introduction, type the following cross-reference text: (**For more information about risks associated with SCUBA diving, see the section .**) Be sure to leave a space between the last word and the period.
5. Position the insertion point to the left of the period you just typed, and insert a hyperlinked cross-reference to the heading text **Know the Risks**.
6. Preview the first page of the report. It should look similar to Illustration A.
   - ✓ *If you have the Field shading option set to Always on the View page of the Tools, Options dialog box, the cross-reference text will be shaded with gray.*
7. Select the bulleted list of safety rules near the top of page 2 and convert it to a numbered list.
8. Scroll down to the heading **Know the Risks** at the top of page 4 (or use the cross-reference hyperlink you inserted in step 5).
9. At the end of the first paragraph under the heading **Know the Risks**, type the following cross-reference text: *(***For a list of recommended safety rules, refer to page .***)*
10. Position the insertion point to the left of the period you just typed, and insert a hyperlinked cross-reference to the page on which the numbered item **Have all equipment maintained regularly by a professional** appears.
11. Ctrl+click the page number to go to the list.
12. Press Ctrl+Home to move the insertion point to the beginning of the document.

13. Mark entries for an index as follows:

   ✓ *You might want to use the Find command to locate the specified text.*

   a. Select the text **SCUBA** in the first sentence of the introduction, open the Mark Index Entry dialog box and mark all entries of the text **SCUBA**.

   b. Select the text **Self-Contained Underwater Breathing Apparatus**, enter the Cross-reference text **SCUBA**, and then select to mark the one selected item only.

      ✓ *This will create an entry for Self-Contained Underwater Breathing Apparatus, with a cross reference to the index entry SCUBA.*

   c. Select the text **risks** in the last sentence of the first paragraph. Edit the text in the Main entry box so the word begins with an uppercase **R**, and mark all occurrences as a main entry.

   d. Select the text **buddy rule** under the heading **Safety Recommendations**, and mark is as a main entry, Edit the main entry text so it starts with an uppercase **B**.

   e. Mark the first occurrence of the text **safety rules**. Make sure that the main entry text begins with an uppercase **S**. Add the subentry text: **List of**.

   f. Mark all entries of the text **alcohol**, using an uppercase **A**.

   g. Mark the text **successful dive experience**. Edit the main entry to **Successful dive**, and add the subentry **Steps to insure**.

   h. Select the text **certification** and mark all entries using an uppercase **C**.

   i. Select the text **classroom sessions** and create a subentry to the main entry **Certification**. (Edit the main entry text to **Certification**, enter the subentry text **Classroom training**, and then click Mark.)

   j. Repeat the steps above to create subentries for **Practical training** and **Written exam**.

   k. Select the text **equipment**, and mark all entries, using an uppercase **E**.

   l. Select the text **equipment** preceding the list of equipment, edit the main entry text to **Equipment** and include the subentry text: **List of**.

   m. Mark the text **safety equipment** as a subentry to **Equipment**.

   n. Mark the text **basic equipment** as a subentry to **Equipment**.

   o. Make the text **optional equipment** as a subentry to **Equipment**.

   p. Mark the word **hazards** before the list of hazards as a Main entry, with the subentry **List of**. Make sure the main entry text begins with an uppercase **H**.

   q. Mark **medical condition** as a main entry, with the subentry **Symptoms of**. Make sure the main entry text begins with an uppercase **M**.

   r. Mark the text **fatal accidents** with a subentry **Causes of**. Again, make sure the main entry starts with an uppercase letter.

   s. Mark the first occurrence of the word **death** with a cross-reference to the entry **Fatal accidents**.

   t. When you have finished marking the necessary entries, close the Mark Index Entry dialog box.

14. Press Ctrl+End to move the insertion point to the end of the document.
15. Insert a page break.
16. At the top of the new page, type **Index**, and format it with the Heading 1 style.
17. Press Enter to move the insertion point to a blank line.
18. Generate the index as follows:
    a. Select the Classic style.
    b. Right align page numbers.
    c. Use a dotted tab leader.
    d. Use two columns.
    e. Indent the subtopics.
19. When the index is inserted in the document, save the changes.
20. Check the spelling and grammar in the document.
21. Preview the document.
22. Insert a page break before the heading **Medical Conditions Caused by Diving**.
23. Update the index to reflect the page changes.
24. Preview the index page. It should look similar to Illustration B.
25. Close the document, saving all changes.

Illustration A

Safe SCUBA Diving

Prepared by
Pete Newell, Owner
Pelican Peter's Dive Shop
2200 Gulfshore Blvd. N., Naples, FL 34102

Introduction

The acronym SCUBA stands for Self-Contained Underwater Breathing Apparatus. In other words, SCUBA divers use an apparatus that is completely carried by the diver and not connected to the surface. It is estimated that more than 3.5 million Americans participate in recreational SCUBA diving. Another 500 thousand become certified each year in the United States. The experience of SCUBA diving can be exciting, exhilarating, and empowering. However, without the proper planning, SCUBA diving can also be dangerous. (For more information about risks associated with SCUBA diving, see the section Know the Risks.)

This report provides a look at the steps divers can take to maximize the pleasure of a dive while minimizing the risks.

Safety Recommendations

The buddy rule cannot be emphasized enough. Any reputable diving organization will insist each diver be accompanied under water by a buddy who can share air or provide other assistance. A SCUBA apparatus is designed to carry an extra demand regulator. This is required in case one diver runs out of air and has to share a single tank with his or her buddy. Ideally, the buddies should have similar training and skill levels; it does no good to have a buddy who dives deeper or stays down longer than you do. Buddies should stay close together and always be aware of each other's location.

Page 1

Illustration B

Safe SCUBA Diving | Today's Date

Index

A

Alcohol 3

B

Buddy rule 1

C

Certification 3
  Classroom training 3
  Practical training 3
  Written exam 3

D

Death .... *See* Fatal accidents

E

Equipment 3, 4, 5, 8
  Basic 4
  List of 4
  Optional 4
  Safety equipment 4

F

Fatal accidents
  Causes of 6

H

Hazards
  List of 6

M

Medical condition
  Symptoms of 7

R

Risks 1, 3

S

Safety rules
  list of 3
SCUBA 1, 3, 6, 8
Self-Contained Underwater Breathing Apparatus .... *See* SCUBA
Successful dive
  Steps to insure 3

Page 7

On Your Own

1. Start Word and open OWDGUIDES5, the multi-page report you have been working on, or open 57OWDGUIDES5.
2. Save the document as OWDGUIDES6.
3. Insert at least two cross-references in the document. Try using different cross-reference types. For example, select a heading for one cross-reference and a footnote or endnote for another.
   ✓ *If necessary, format the document to include items which can be cross-referenced, such as headings, bookmarks, or lists.*
4. Create an index for the document. Mark main entries and subentries.
5. Insert the index on a new page at the end of the document. Try different formatting options, such as the fancy format with dashed tab leaders.
6. Preview the document and insert page breaks as necessary.
7. Update the index and the cross-references if necessary.
8. Close the document, saving all changes.

Exercise 58

Skills Covered:

◆ **Create a Table of Contents** ◆ **Update a Table of Contents**

On the Job

A table of contents helps readers locate information they need in a long document by listing headings and the page numbers where each heading starts. Word can automatically generate a table of contents using paragraphs formatted with the built-in heading styles. If the page numbers where the headings are located change, you can update the table.

You have just about completed the SCUBA safety report for Pelican Peter's Dive Shop. The final touch is to add a table of contents to help readers locate the sections they need. In this exercise, you will check that all topics you want included in the table of contents are formatted with heading styles. Then, you will generate the table of contents. Finally, you will make some editing changes to the report, and update the table of contents to reflect the changes.

Terms

Table of contents A list of topics and subtopics in a document, usually accompanied by the page numbers where the topics begin and placed before the main body of the document.

Notes

Create a Table of Contents

- Word generates a **table of contents** based on paragraphs formatted with the built-in heading styles.
- You can create a table of contents using as many levels as you want, depending on how many levels of headings are used in the document.
- You do not have to include all heading levels in the table of contents. For example, you may have paragraphs formatted with up to four heading levels, but select to include only two heading levels in the table of contents.
- Paragraphs formatted with the same level of heading style will be listed at the same level in the table of contents.
- Word comes with a selection of table of contents formats which you can preview in the Index and Tables dialog box.
- You can also select whether to include page numbers and whether to right-align them.
- If you right-align page numbers, you can select a tab leader.
- By default, Word formats the headings in a table of contents as hyperlinks. Ctrl+click the heading in the table to jump to the destination.
- If you don't want to use hyperlinks in your table of contents, deselect the Use hyperlinks instead of page numbers check box on the Table of Contents tab of the Index and Tables dialog box.

Table of Contents tab of the Index and Tables dialog box

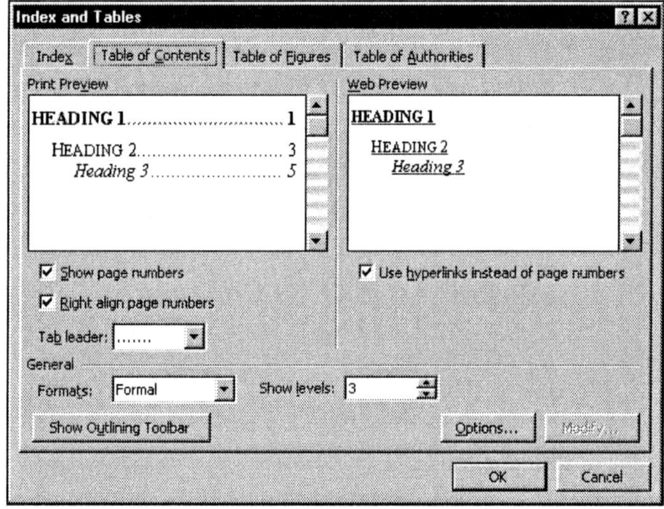

Update a Table of Contents

- Word creates a table of contents using fields, so if the headings change, or the page numbers where the headings are located change, you can automatically update the fields.
- If heading text changes, you can update the entire table to reflect the changes.
- If no heading text changes, but page numbers do, you can select to update page numbers only.

Procedures

Create a Table of Contents

1. Apply heading styles to all paragraphs you want in table of contents.
2. Position insertion point where you want table of contents to appear.
3. Click **Insert** .... Alt+I
4. Click **Reference** .... N
5. Click **Index and Tables** .... D
6. Click **Table of Contents** tab .... Alt+C
7. Click **Formats**: list box .... Alt+T
8. Select desired format .... ↑↓
9. Click **Show levels** text box .... Alt+L
10. Enter number of heading levels to include.
11. Select or deselect **Show page numbers** .... Alt+S
12. Select or deselect **Right align page numbers** .. Alt+R

    ✓ *If you select to right-align page numbers, select a tab leader option from* ***Tab leader*** *drop-down list.*
13. Select or deselect **Use hyperlinks instead of page numbers** .... Alt+H
14. Click **OK** .... Enter

Update a Table of Contents

1. Position insertion point anywhere in table.
2. Press **F9**.

   OR

   a. Right-click anywhere in table of contents.

   b. Click **Update Field** .... U
3. Select **Update page numbers only** .... Alt+P

   OR

   Select **Update entire table** .... Alt+E
4. Click **OK** .... Enter

Exercise Directions

1. Start Word, if necessary.
2. Open the document 58SAFETY, a version of the SCUBA safety report you have used in earlier exercises.
3. Save it as SAFETY6.
4. Move the insertion point through the document to verify that all headings are formatted with heading styles.
5. Press Ctrl+Home to move the insertion point to the beginning of the document.
6. Insert two blank lines before the heading **Introduction**.
7. Clear all formatting from the new blank lines.
8. On the first blank line type **Table of Contents**, then apply the following formatting:
   - 20-point Arial
   - Centered
   - Leave 12 points of space before
9. Position the insertion point on the second blank line.
10. Create a table of contents using the following options:
    - Formal format
    - 3 heading levels
    - Right-aligned page numbers
    - Dot tab leader
    - Use page numbers instead of hyperlinks
11. Preview the first page of the document. It should look similar to Illustration A.

    ✓ *You can control when fields in the table of contents are shaded by using the Field shading: drop-down list on the View tab of the Tools, Options dialog box.*
12. Change the style of the heading **Medical Conditions Caused by Diving** from Heading 3 to Heading 2
13. Update the entire table of contents.
14. Preview the document.
15. Insert a page break before the heading **Specialized Safety Equipment**.
16. Update the table of contents to reflect the changes of the page numbers.
17. Update the index to reflect the changes.
18. Check the spelling and grammar in the document.
19. Close the document, saving all changes.

On Your Own

1. Start Word and open OWDGUIDES6, the multi-page report you have been working with, or open 58OWDGUIDES6.
2. Save the document as OWDGUIDES7.
3. Apply heading styles to the paragraphs you want to include in the table of contents. Use as many heading levels as you want.
4. Create a table of contents at the beginning of the document. Preview different formats to find one you like. See how it looks with the page numbers in different positions and using different tab leaders.
5. After inserting the table of contents in the document, insert a page break after it.
6. Insert any other page breaks necessary to improve the appearance of the document.
7. Update the page numbers in the table of contents.
8. Edit one or more of the headings.
9. Update the entire table of contents.
10. Update the index.
11. Close the document, saving all changes.

Illustration A

Safe SCUBA Diving

Prepared by
Pete Newell, Owner
Pelican Peter's Dive Shop
2200 Gulfshore Blvd. N., Naples, FL 34102

Table of Contents

SAFE SCUBA DIVING **1**
INTRODUCTION **1**
SAFETY RECOMMENDATIONS **2**
SAFETY RULES 3
PREPARATION **3**
BASIC CERTIFICATION 3
EQUIPMENT 4
Optional Equipment *4*
Specialized Safety Equipment *4*
KNOW THE RISKS **5**
POTENTIAL HAZARDS 5
Common Hazards *5*
Medical Conditions Caused by Diving *6*
CONCLUSION **7**
INDEX **8**

Introduction

The acronym SCUBA stands for Self-Contained Underwater Breathing Apparatus. In other words, SCUBA divers use an apparatus that is completely carried by the diver and not connected to the surface. It is estimated that more than 3.5 million Americans participate in recreational SCUBA diving. Another 500 thousand become certified each year in the United States. The experience of SCUBA diving can be exciting, exhilarating, and empowering. However, without the proper planning, SCUBA diving can also be dangerous. (For more information about risks associated with SCUBA diving, see the section Know the Risks.)

Page 1

Exercise 59

◆ Critical Thinking

You have been working on a report about nutrition for the elderly for Wayland Home Health Care Associates. Your supervisor has decided the company should develop a directory that describes the different services the company offers and that your nutrition report should be included. She has an outline of the directory and has asked you to organize the project.

In this exercise, you will take an outline of the directory and convert it into a master document. You will insert an existing document about nutrition as a subdocument in the master document. You will edit and format the subdocument. You will use the find and replace feature, create bookmarks, headers and footers, and cross-references. You will insert section and page breaks, control text flow as necessary, and insert cross-references. Finally, you will create an index and a table of contents.

Exercise Directions

1. Start Word, if necessary.
2. Open 59SERVICES, and save it as SERVICES.
3. Change to Outline view.
4. Format the document title as Heading 1.
5. Format the remaining headings as Heading 2:
   - Directory of Services
   - Elder Care
   - Sick Child Care
   - Rehabilitation Therapy
   - Respite Care
   - Counseling
   - Hospice Care
   - Homemakers
   - List of Resources
6. Select all text in the document except the title and create subdocuments.
7. Open 59SENIORS, save it as SENIORS, and then close it.
8. Insert the SENIORS document as a subdocument into the SERVICES master document between the Elder Care subdocument and the Sick Child Care subdocument.
9. Save the master document.
10. Open the SENIORS document.
11. Find and replace all occurrences of the text **the elderly** with the text **seniors**. Use the match case option.
12. Find and replace all occurrences of the text **the Elderly** with the text **Seniors**. Use the match case option.
13. Insert a header on all pages that has your name flush left and the company name (**Wayland Home Health Care Associates**) flush right.
14. Insert a footer that has today's date flush left and the page number in the format of **Page X of N** flush right.
15. Display the Document Map.
16. Go to the heading **Solutions**.
17. Insert a bookmark named **Solutions**.
18. Go to the heading **Diet Counts**.
19. Move the second paragraph under the heading **Diet Counts** (it begins with the text *The* **National Nutritional Screening Initiative**) and the list that follows it to the end of the section **Identifying Seniors at Risk**.
20. Close the Document Map.
21. Preview all four pages of the document at once.
22. Use the Keep with Next text flow option to keep all items in the numbered list at the bottom of page 2 together.

23. At the end of the first paragraph in the section **A Nutritional Overview**, insert a hyperlinked cross-reference to the section **Solutions**. (You may insert the cross-reference to the bookmark or to the heading).
24. Check the word count in the document.
25. Mark items to create an index for the document. Use your judgment as to which words to include. Include at least ten words. Include at least two cross-references. Include at least three subentries.
    - ✓ *Refer to Illustration B to see suggested index entries.*
26. Insert a page break at the end of the document.
27. At the top of the last page, type the heading **Index** using the Heading 1 style, centered.
28. Below the new heading, create the index, using the Classic format, with page numbers right-aligned, using dot tab leaders, indented in two columns.
29. Insert a blank line before the heading **Nutritional Overview** near the beginning of the document, and clear all formatting from it.
30. Generate a table of contents in the Classic format, with page numbers right-aligned, using dot tab leaders, with no hyperlinks.
31. Insert a next page section break between the table of contents and the heading **A Nutritional Overview**.
32. Set the margins in the first section to be 1.5" on the left and right.
33. Check the spelling and grammar in the document.
    - ✓ *Ignore all errors in the marked index entries.*
34. Display the document in Print Preview. It should look similar to Illustration B.
35. Close the file, saving all changes.
36. Close the master document, saving all changes.

Your Name | Wayland Home Health Care Associates

Nutrition for Seniors

How Aging Affects Our Nutritional Needs

Prepared by
Wayland Home Health Care Associates

A NUTRITIONAL OVERVIEW **2**

Diet Counts 2

RISK FACTORS **2**

Identifying Seniors at Risk 3

Foods to Avoid 4

SOLUTIONS **4**

INDEX **5**

Illustration A, Page 2 of 5

A Nutritional Overview

As people age there are a number of factors that influence their nutritional needs. Physical changes as well as socioeconomic changes have a serious impact on nutrition for seniors. And yet, successful nutrition may have the most positive impact on a senior's ability to enjoy life to its fullest. (For more information see the section Solutions.)

This report takes a look at some of the unique nutritional challenges facing seniors, as well as actions they and their caregivers can take to insure proper nutritional health.

Diet Counts

Nutritionists agree that a healthful diet includes a variety of foods. Food choices also can help reduce the risk for chronic diseases, such as heart disease, cancers, diabetes, stroke, and osteoporosis that are the leading cause of death and disability among Americans.

The U.S Department of Agriculture states that the basic checklist for insuring proper nutrition is the same for all people, no matter what their age[1]:

- Eat a variety of foods
- Balance food intake physical activity in order to maintain or improve weight
- Choose a diet high in grain products, vegetables, and fruits
- Choose a diet low in fat, saturated fat, and cholesterol
- Choose a diet moderate in sugars
- Choose a diet moderate in salt and sodium
- Drink alcohol only in moderation

Risk Factors

The elderly face unique nutritional challenges. According to the American Dietetic Association, the need for calories decreases by 25% as people age, despite the fact that

---

[1] "Nutrition and Your Health: Dietary Guidelines for Americans," Fourth Edition, 1995, <http://www.nalusda.gov/fnic/dga/dga95/cover.html>.

vitamin and mineral requirements do not decline.[2] This means that seniors must monitor their diets carefully to be sure to take in foods with the highest nutritional content.

Factors that influence the nutritional status of seniors include the following:

- Physical activity
- Lifestyle
- Family and social networks
- Intellectual activity
- Disease
- Economics

Identifying Seniors at Risk

Often, seniors who are most at risk nutritionally are those who have physical or chronic health problems that keep them from shopping, preparing meals, and feeding themselves. In addition, those who also have lower incomes, the very old, minorities, and those living alone are seen at higher risk. Also food insecurity, which includes having inadequate income to buy food and other necessities, is a serious concern for seniors.

The National Nutritional Screening Initiative, sponsored by the American Academy of Family Physicians, The American Dietetic Association, and the National Council on the Aging, uses the following ten warning signs to determine the risk of poor nutritional health among seniors[3]:

1. Eats alone
2. Has three or more alcoholic drinks per day
3. Eats fewer than two meals per day
4. Doesn't have enough money to buy food
5. Has tooth or mouth problems
6. Has lost or gained 10 pounds in last six months without trying

---

[2] The American Dietetic Association, 1999, <http://www.eatright.org/olderamericans/foodneeds.html>.
[3] David L. Sutton and Paula Blizniak, "Nutritional Health of Elderly New Yorkers," February 1995.

Illustration A, Page 4 of 5

7. Is not always physically able to shop, cook, and feed himself
8. Takes three or more different medications per day
9. Has had to change foods due to illness or condition
10. Eats few fruits or vegetables or milk products

Foods to Avoid

Certain foods may pose a significant health hazard for seniors because of the level of bacteria present in the product's raw or uncooked state. According to the Food and Drug Administration seniors should avoid the following products[4]:

- Raw fish
- Raw shellfish, including oysters, clams, mussels, and scallops
- Raw or unpasteurized milk or cheese
- Soft cheeses such as feta, Brie, Camembert, blue-veined, and Mexican-style cheese
- Raw or lightly cooked egg or egg products including salad dressings, cookie or cake batter, sauces, and beverages such as eggnog
- Raw meat or poultry
- Raw alfalfa sprouts
- Unpasteurized or untreated fruit or vegetable juice

Solutions

Families, friends, caregivers, and seniors themselves can take proactive steps to make sure all nutritional requirements are met. Preventing health problems due to poor nutrition may be as simple as three balanced meals a day.

When caregivers are unavailable, or inadequate, seniors may find assistance from home health care associations or from government-sponsored programs. These sources may provide meal delivery as well as nutrition counseling and shopping assistance.

[4] "What's a Senior to Eat?", May, 1999, <http://vm.cfsan.fda.gov/~dms/seniorsc.html>.

INDEX

A

Aging ... 1
American Academy of Family Physicians ... 4
American Dietetic Association ... 3

C

Caregivers ... 2, 5
Chronic diseases
- cancer ... 2
- diabetes ... 2
- heart disease ... 2
- osteoporosis ... 2
- stroke ... 2

D

Diet
- healthy ... 2

E

Elderly ... See Seniors

F

Factors
- Disease ... *See* Chronic Disease
- Economics ... 3
- Family and social networks ... 3
- Intellectual activity ... 3
- Lifestyle ... 3
- Physical activity ... 3

Food and Drug Administration ... 4
Food insecurity ... 4
Foods
- Harmful ... 4
- to avoid ... 4

G

Government-sponsored programs ... 5

H

Home health care associations ... 5

N

National Council on the Aging ... 4
Nutrition ... 1, 2, 5
- An Overview ... 2
- Basic checklist ... 2

Nutritionists ... 2

R

Risk
- Identifying ... 3
- Warning Signs ... 4

S

Senior ... 2
Seniors ... 2, 3, 4, 5
Solutions ... 5

T

The American Dietetic Association ... 3, 4
The National Nutritional Screening Initiative ... 4

U

U.S Department of Agriculture ... 2

W

Wayland Home Health Care Associates ... 1

Lesson 10

The Internet

Exercise 60

- Internet Basics
- Use Internet Features in Word
- Save a Web Page Locally
- Work with the Favorites folder

Exercise 61

- Search the Internet
- Print Web Page Information
- Copy Data from a Web page to a Word Document

Exercise 62

- Create a Web Page Document in Word
- Use Web Layout View
- Preview a Web Page
- Open an HTML Document

Exercise 63

- Use Web Page Titles
- Web Page Graphics
- Apply a Background
- Apply a Theme

Exercise 64

- Use Tables in HTML Documents
- Use Web Page Templates
- Insert a Link Bar in a Word Document

Exercise 65

- Critical Thinking

Exercise 60

Skills Covered:

◆ **Internet Basics** ◆ **Use Internet Features in Word**
◆ **Save a Web Page Locally** ◆ **Work with the Favorites folder**

On the Job

Log on to the Internet to access information on any subject and to communicate with other people. Use Word's Internet features to make using the Internet easy and familiar.

Your supervisor at Optical General, Inc. has to travel to Alaska on business. She will have one free day and has heard that the train ride up the White Pass is spectacular. She has asked you to locate some basic information, such as the schedule and prices. In this exercise, you will use the Internet to locate information about the White Pass Railroad site. You will add the site to your Favorites folder and save the page that has the information you need locally so you can read it offline in Word.

Terms

Internet A worldwide network of computers.

World Wide Web A system for finding information on the Internet through the use of linked documents.

Modem A device that enables a computer to transmit data over telephone lines. Cable modems transmit data over cable television lines.

Internet Service Provider (ISP) A company that provides access to the Internet for a fee.

Web browser Software that makes it easy to locate and view information stored on the Internet. Common browsers include Microsoft Internet Explorer and Netscape Navigator.

Web site A set of linked Web pages.

Web page A document stored on the World Wide Web.

Uniform Resource Locator (URL) A Web site's address on the Internet.

Hyperlinks or links Text or graphics in a document set up to provide a direct connection with a destination location or document. When you click a hyperlink, the destination displays.

Notes

Internet Basics

- The minimum requirements to access the **Internet** and the **World Wide Web** are a computer, a **modem**, communications software, and a standard phone line.
- Most networks and even home computers may use high speed data transmission lines or cables, making it faster and more convenient than ever before.
- For a fee, **Internet Service Providers (ISP)** provide you with an e-mail account, **Web browser** software, and Internet access.

- Microsoft Office XP comes with the Internet Explorer Web browser, although your computer may be set up to use a different browser.
  - ✓ *This exercise assumes you are using Internet Explorer. If your computer is set up to use a different browser, ask your instructor for directions.*
- Some things available via the Internet and the World Wide Web include e-mail communication, multimedia downloads such as MP3 music files, product information and support, reference material, shopping, stock quotes, travel arrangements, and games.

Use Internet Features in Word

- If you have a connection to the Internet and Web browser software, you can use Word's Web toolbar (shown at the bottom of the page) to access the Internet.
- Word remains running while you use the Internet, so you can go back and forth from Word to the Internet sites that you have opened on your browser.
- To locate a **Web site**, **Web page**, or document, you enter its Internet address, or **Uniform Resource Locator (URL)**.
- Most sites provide **hyperlinks**, also called **links**, to related pages or sites. Text links are usually a different color and underlined to stand out from the surrounding text. Graphics may also be links.
- When the mouse pointer rests on a link, the pointer changes to a hand with a pointing finger, and a ScreenTip shows the destination.
- Word tracks the Web sites you have visited during the current Internet session so you can move back and forth through them.

Save a Web Page Locally

- You use your browser's Save As command to save a Web page on your computer.
- Once you save a Web page, you can access it while you are working offline.
  - ✓ *Even though you can save a Web page, you still must consider copyright laws before you reuse the information.*
- When you save a Web page you can select from four file types:
  - Web page, complete. This saves all of the associated files needed to display the Web page, including graphics.
  - Web Archive. Saves a snapshot of the current Web page in a single file.
  - Web Page, HTML only. Saves the information on the Web page but does not save the associated files.
  - Text Only. Saves the information in plain text format.

Work with the Favorites Folder

- Use the Favorites folder on your computer to store the URLs of Web sites you like to access frequently.
- You can also add locally stored files and folders to your Favorites folder.
- The easiest way to add a URL to the Favorites folder is by using your Web browser.
- Access the Favorites folder from Word or from Windows when you want to go directly to one of your favorite sites.

The Favorites Folder

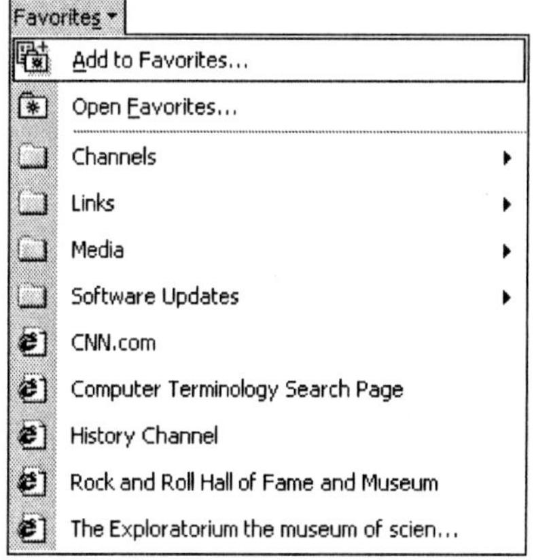

The Web toolbar

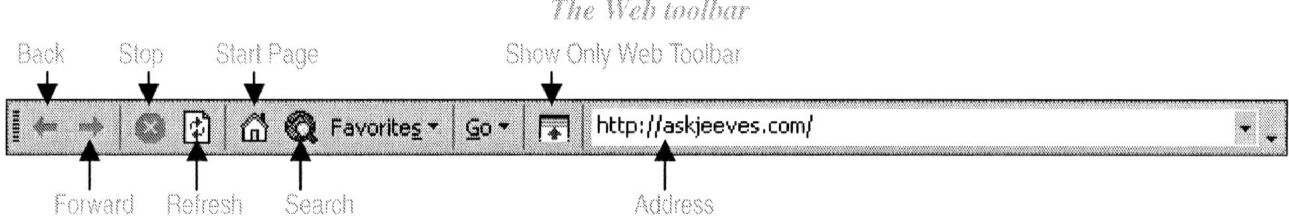

Procedures

Use Internet Features in Word

To display the Web toolbar:

1. Click **View** .... Alt+V
2. Select **Toolbars** .... T
3. Click **Web** .... ↕, Enter

OR

- Right-click on any toolbar and select **Web**.
  - ✓ *Be sure to select the Web toolbar and not the Web Tools toolbar.*

To go to a specific URL:

1. Type URL in Address drop-down list box on Web toolbar
2. Press **Enter** .... Enter

OR

1. Click **Go** button Go ▾ .. Alt+G
2. Click **Open Hyperlink** button Open Hyperlink ..... O
3. Type the URL in the **Address** list box.
4. Click **OK** .... Enter

To go to a previously visited URL:

1. Click Address list drop-down arrow on Web toolbar.
2. Click URL.

To use a hyperlink:

1. Move mouse pointer to touch link.
2. Click left mouse button.

To display the previously displayed page or document:

- Click **Back** button Back on the Browser's toolbar.

OR

- Click **Back** button ⇦ on the Web toolbar

OR

1. Click **Go** button Go ▾ .. Alt+G on the Web toolbar.
2. Click **Back** .... B

To display the next Web page:

- Click **Forward** button Forward on the Browser's toolbar.
  - ✓ *If the Back or Forward button is dimmed on the toolbar, there is no page to go to.*

OR

- Click **Forward** button ➡ on Web toolbar.

OR

1. Click **Go** .... Alt+G on the Web toolbar.
2. Click **Forward** .... F

Save a Web page locally:

1. Open Web page in browser.
2. Click **File** .... Alt+F
3. Click **Save As** .... A
4. Type file name.
5. Select disk or folder.
6. Click **Save as type** .... T drop-down arrow.
7. Click desired file type.
8. Click **Save** .... Alt+S

The Favorites Folder

To use Internet Explorer to add a site to your Favorites folder:

1. Open Internet site to add to Favorites.
2. Click **Favorites** .... Alt+A
3. Click **Add to Favorites** .... A
4. Type site name if necessary .... Alt+N
   - ✓ *Your browser automatically enters a site name; you can edit it if you want.*
5. Click **OK** .... Enter

To use Word to add a file to your Favorites folder:

1. Open file to add to Favorites.
2. Click **Favorites** button Favorites ▾ .... Alt+S on Web toolbar.
3. Click **Add to Favorites** .... A
   - ✓ *The Add to Favorites dialog box is similar to the Save As dialog box.*
4. Type a name.
5. Click **Add** button Add .... Enter

To go to a site from your Favorites folder:

1. Click **Favorites** button Favorites ▾ on Web toolbar.
2. Click site name.
   - ✓ *If necessary, Word starts your Web browser to connect to the Internet and display the site.*

Exercise Directions

✓ *Use the Internet simulation provided on the CD that accompanies this book to complete this exercise.*

1. Start Word, if necessary.
2. Create a new, blank document.
3. Display the Web toolbar.
4. Open the Internet simulation provided on the CD:
   a. Click **Go**.
   b. Click **Open Hyperlink**.
   c. In the Address line type the following:
      D:/Internet/E60/whitepassrailroad.htm
      ✓ *If you've copied the Internet simulation files to your hard drive or your CD-ROM drive is a letter other than D:, substitute the correct letter for D.*
   d. Click **OK**.
      ✓ *A welcome page for the White Pass Railway opens in your browser.*
5. Use your Web browser to add the page to your Favorites folder.
6. Click the Schedule link on the Welcome page.
7. Click the General Information link.
8. Click the Top link.
9. Click the White Pass Summit Excursion link.
10. Click the Top link.
11. Save the page in Web archive format with the name TRAIN.
12. Click the Back button enough times to return to Word.
    OR
    Exit the simulation by clicking the Close button [X].
13. Open the TRAIN document in Word.
    ✓ *If the document is not listed in Word's Open dialog box, change the list to display all file types.*
14. Display the document in Print Preview. Page 1 should look similar to Illustration A.
15. Use Word to add the TRAIN document to your Favorites folder.
16. Close the document, saving all changes.
17. Disconnect from the Internet if necessary.

Illustration A

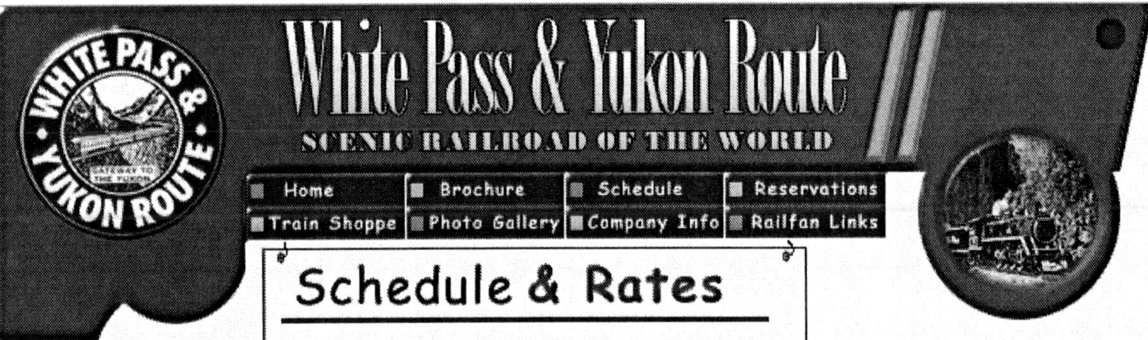

TRAIN TRIPS FOR 2001

MAIN TRACK

- White Pass Summit Excursion
- Lake Bennett Adventure
- Special Steam Excursions
- Skagway - Whitehorse Train + Bus

THINGS TO KNOW BEFORE YOU GO

- General Information
- Terms & Conditions
- MAP
- Independent & Cruise Ship Passengers

SIDE TRACK

- Chilkoot Trail Hikers Service
- Skagway to Fraser / Fraser to Skagway

QUICK PRINT
Main Schedules

White Pass Summit Rail Excursion

The most popular rail adventure! This three hour fully narrated round trip from Skagway climbs 2,865 feet in just 20 miles - an unforgettable journey!

Departures	Skagway		Adult	Child 3-12
May 7 - Sep 26	departs		roundtrip	infants free
Daily	8:30 am		$82 US	$41 US
Daily	1:00 pm		$82 US	$41 US
May 23 - Sept 5				
Tue & Wed also at	4:30 pm		$82 US	$41 US

Reservations a must.

▲Top

On Your Own

1. If you have access to the Internet, use it to explore a Web site about something that interests you. You can find the URL for most sites on advertisements, packaging, or in the yellow pages. For example, go to the Web site for your hometown, a sports team that you follow, or a writer, musician, or artist you admire.
2. When you get to a site you like, add it to your Favorites folder.
3. Save one of the pages you find as a Web archive document so you can spend more time reading it offline. Save it as OWDNET.
4. If you want, try saving it in one or more of the other available formats to see the difference between them.
5. In Word, open OWDNET or open 60OWDWEB.
6. Read the document in Word.
7. Close the document and exit Word.
8. Disconnect from the Internet, if necessary.

Exercise 61

Skills Covered:

◆ **Search the Internet** ◆ **Print Web Page Information**

◆ **Copy Data from a Web Page to a Word Document**

On the Job

Search the Internet when you do not know the URL of the Web site you need. Use Word to select a search engine that can display a list of Web sites that match the information you are looking for. When the Web page is displayed on your computer, print it for future reference or to pass along to someone else. If you don't need to print the entire page, you can copy the data you need into a Word document to save or print for future use.

Your supervisor has asked you to locate a hotel in Skagway, Alaska in case she needs to spend the night there. In this exercise, you will search the Internet for lodging in Skagway. You will print some of the information that you find, and you will copy some of the information into a Word document to save for future use.

Terms

Search engine Software available on the Internet that searches for Web sites containing the information you are looking for.

Notes

Search the Internet

- The Internet and World Wide Web contain millions of pages of information.
- If you do not know the URL for a Web site, you can use one of a number of available **search engines** to locate the site.
- Search engines prompt you to enter information, and then they display a hyperlinked list of Web sites containing that information.
- There are many different search engine Web sites available.
- Some search engines are designed for specific purposes, such as finding a business, or locating an e-mail address.
- Others are for more general use. Some general purpose search engines include AltaVista, Yahoo!, About.com, Google.com, and Ask.com.
- Your ISP might have its own search engine, it might suggest a specific search engine when you select the Search option, or it might give you a choice of search engines.
- You can also access a specific search engine site by entering its URL in the Address bar. For example, to go to the Yahoo search engine site, enter www.yahoo.com.

Search the Web with a search site such as Yahoo

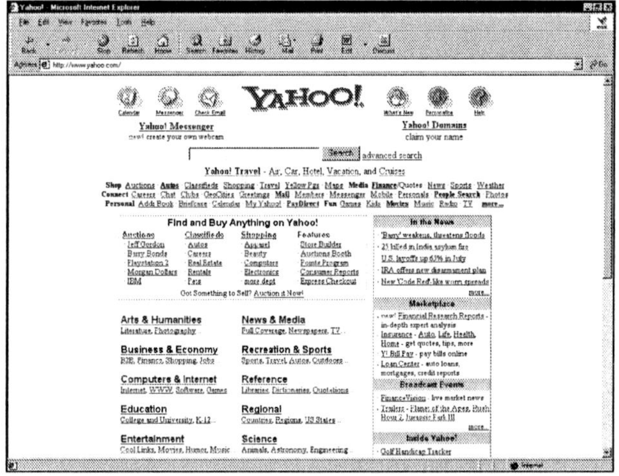

- The search results vary depending on the information you type and the search engine you use.
- For a successful search, enter specific information, such as a full company name.

Print Web Page Information

- You can print a Web page displayed in Word or displayed in your browser.
- The commands for printing a Web page are the same as for printing a regular Word document.
- Many Web sites contain graphics, such as photographs and artwork. Some printers may not be able to print the graphical content of a Web page.

Copy Data from a Web Page to a Word Document

- You can use the Copy and Paste commands to copy data from a Web page into a Word document.
- The commands may be accessed from a shortcut menu, or from the Edit menu in your Web browser.
- Remember that copying someone else's work and using it without attribution is plagiarism.
- If you use Web page data in a report or other project, you must cite the source in a footnote, bibliography, or other list of sources.
- You can copy a URL from an Address bar and paste it into a Word document. This is useful for recording a Web page address that you will need to use in a footnote or bibliography.

Procedures

Access a Search Engine Web Site

✓ *You must have an Internet connection and an account with an ISP in order to search the Internet or Web. When prompted, you must enter an ID and/or password in order to gain access.*

1. Display the Web toolbar.
2. Click **Search the Web** button.

   OR

   a. Click **Go** button .... Alt+G
   b. Click **Search the Web** .... W

   ✓ *The Search site options will vary depending on ISP.*
3. Click desired search engine.

OR

1. Display the Web toolbar.
2. Type search engine URL in Address bar.
3. Press **Enter** .... Enter

Search the Internet

1. Open search engine Web site.
2. Type search topic in Search text box.
3. Click **Search** button.

   ✓ *The name on the search button (Find It, Go Get It, etc.) will vary depending on the Search site.*
4. Click a hyperlink on the Search Results page to go to that site.

Print Web Page Information (Ctrl+P)

1. Display the desired Web page.
2. Click the **Print** button on your browser's toolbar.

   OR

   a. Click **File** .... Alt+F
   b. Click **Print** .... P
   c. Click **OK** .... Enter

Copy Data from a Web Page into a Word Document (Ctrl + C/Ctrl + V)

1. Display the desired Web page.
2. Select data to copy.
3. Right-click selection.
4. Click **Copy** C
5. Open Word document.
6. Position insertion point at desired location.
7. Right-click and click **Paste** .. P

OR

1. Display the desired Web page.
2. Select data to copy.
3. Click **Edit** .... Alt+E
4. Click **Copy** C
5. Open Word document.
6. Position insertion point at desired location.
7. Click **Edit** .... Alt+E
8. Click **Paste**. .... P

Exercise Directions

✓ *Use the Internet simulation provided on the CD that accompanies this book to complete this exercise.*

1. Start Word, if necessary.
2. Create a new blank document and name it LODGING.
3. Display the Web toolbar.
4. Open the Internet simulation provided on the CD:
   a. Click **Go**.
   b. Click **Open Hyperlink**.
   c. In the Address line type the following: **D:/Internet/E61/altavista.htm**
      ✓ *If you've copied the Internet simulation files to your hard drive or your CD-ROM drive is a letter other than D:, substitute the correct letter for D.*
   d. Click **OK**.
5. In the Search text box type **Skagway Alaska Lodging**.
   ✓ *The simulation uses the search site AltaVista. If you are using a live Internet connection instead of the simulation, the results of the search will vary depending on the search site used.*
6. Click the Search button.
7. Scroll down the search results list to locate the link for Alaska! – Adventure! – Skagway – Gold Rush Starting Point that goes to the URL www.skagway.com. Notice that the search engine lists the page name, the first few lines of text from the page, and the page's URL. Click the link.
8. Click the The Businesses link.
9. Click the link for Westmark Inn.
10. Print the page that is displayed.
11. Click the Back button.
12. Click the link for The White House.
13. After reading the page, click the Next link.
14. Select the telephone and address information at the bottom of the page and copy it to the Clipboard.
15. Click the Back button on your browser's toolbar until you return to the LODGING.DOC document.
16. On the first line of the document, type **The White House in Skagway, Alaska**, and then press Enter.
17. Paste the data into the document.
18. Click the Forward button on the Web toolbar to return to the AltaVista site, and then click the Forward button on your browser's toolbar to return to that last page you visited at The White House site.
19. Click the Next link again.
20. Select the text on the page beginning with the line above the table (**Rates based upon single/double occupancy**) and ending with the last line on the page (**Open year round. Off-season rates October through April.**), and copy the selection to the Clipboard.
21. Exit the simulation by clicking the Close button **X**.
22. Insert a new line in the LODGING document, and paste the data from the Clipboard.
23. Display the document in Print Preview. It should look similar to Illustration A.
24. Close the document, saving all changes.

Illustration A

The White House in Skagway, Alaska
Telephone: (907)983-9000
Fax: (907)983-9010
The Tronrud Family
Post Office Box 41
Skagway, Alaska 99840

Rates based upon Single/Double Occupancy

Seven Rooms	Upstairs with One Queen Sized Bed	$106
One Room	Upstairs with Two Twin Beds	$106
One Room	Larger, Downstairs with (2) Queen Sized Beds and (1) Twin Beds	$120
One Room	Larger, Downstairs, Handicapped Accessible, (1) Queen Sized Bed and (1) Double Bed	$120

For each addiditonal person, over two
(including the use of a rollaway or crib if requested) there is a charge of $10.

Features found in all rooms:

Private baths
Telephones
Cable Television
Ceiling Fans
Cozy bed decorated with a comfy quilt.

Recommended by Fodor's, Frommer's, Alaska's Best Places and Sunset magazine.

Open year round. Off-season rates October through April.

On Your Own

1. If you have access to the Internet, use the Word Web toolbar to access a search engine.
2. Search for a Web site about something of interest to you. For example, search for information about a performer, a location, or a subject.
3. Select a few sites from the search results list.
4. Add one that you like to your Favorites folder.
5. Print the Web page.
6. When you are finished, disconnect from the Internet, and exit Word.

Exercise 62

Skills Covered:

◆ **Create a Web Page Document in Word**
◆ **Use Web Layout View** ◆ **Preview a Web Page**
◆ **Open an HTML Document**

On the Job

Documents on the World Wide Web must be in HTML format. With Word, you can easily prepare documents for storage on the Web. You can save existing documents in HTML format, and you can use all of Word's features and tools to edit and format HTML documents. When you complete a document in HTML format, you can store it on a **Web server** so everyone with access to the Web can access the document.

Pete Newell, the owner of Pelican Peter's Dive Shop, has asked you to create a document that can serve as a Web page for the store's new Web site. In this exercise, you will create a new Web page document. You will also save an existing document as a Web page, and use hyperlinks to link the two to each other.

Terms

Web server A computer connected to the Internet used to store Web page documents.

HTM An extension given to files saved in HTML format.

HTML (Hypertext Markup Language) The file format used for files accessed on the World Wide Web.

Notes

Create a Web Page Document in Word

- You can create new blank Web page documents with Word.
- You can also save an existing Word document in HTML format. Word preserves most of the formatting in the new document.
- For example, some of the formatting that Word won't preserve includes headers and footers some table formatting, and some font effects.
- If existing formatting is not supported in HTML format, Word displays a message informing you that some formatting will be changed. You have the option of continuing, canceling, or displaying a Help page describing the formatting that isn't supported.
- When you save a document as a Web page, Word abbreviates the file extension to **htm**.
- If the file contains graphics elements such as bullets, lines, and pictures, Word automatically creates a folder to store the graphics files. The folder has the same name as the file, followed by an underscore and the word *files*, like this: *Filename_files.*

  ✓ *Use caution when moving or renaming the graphics file or the folder they are stored in. The graphics files are linked to the HTML document. If they are not available, the page will display without graphics elements.*

  ✓ *You learn more about using graphics in an HTML document in Exercise 63.*

The Save As Web page dialog box

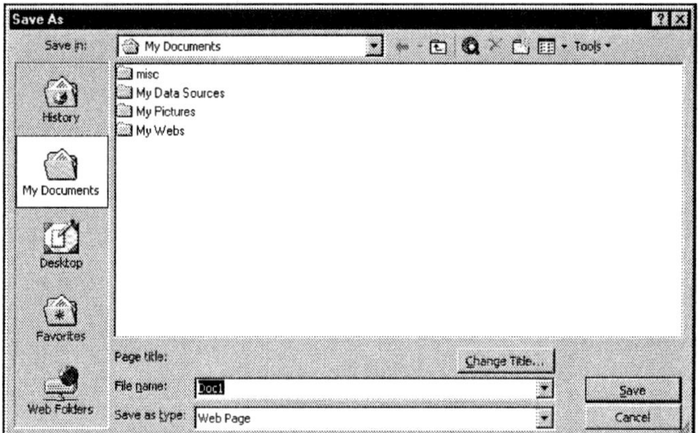

Use Web Layout View

- Web Layout view displays documents in Word as they will look on the Web.
- Word automatically switches to Web Layout view when you save a document as a Web page, when you create a new Web page document, or when you open an existing Web page document.
- You can also switch to Web Layout view using the View menu or the View buttons.
- Web Layout view lets you edit a document for viewing on-screen, instead of for printing on a page.
- Features of Web Layout view include:
  - Word wrapping to fit the window, not a page.
  - Graphics positioned as they would be in a Web browser.
  - Backgrounds (if there are any) displayed as they would be in a browser.
- Use Web Layout view to edit Word documents for use as Web pages.

Preview a Web

- Use Web Page Preview to see how a Word document will look in a Web browser.
- You can display regular Word documents or HTML documents in Web Page Preview.
- When you preview a Web page document, Word opens the document in your default browser.
- You cannot edit a document in Web Page Preview; however, you can test hyperlinks or other interactive features.

A document in Web Page Preview

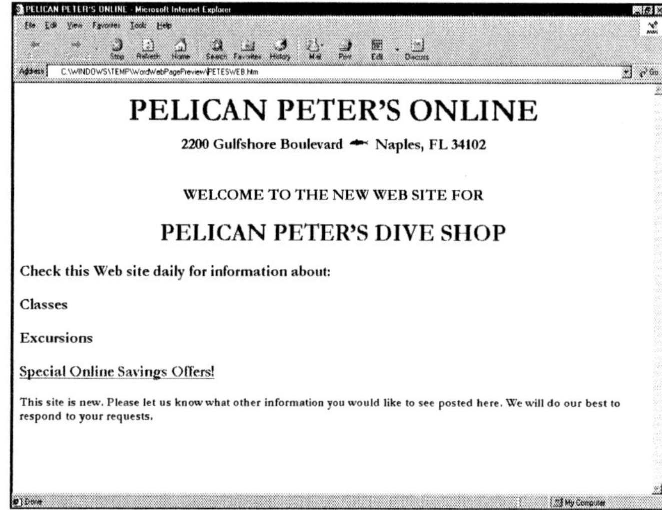

Open an HTML Document in Word

- You open an **HTML** document in Word the same way you open a regular Word document.
- You can also open MHTML documents, such as those you save using the Web Archive file type.

  ✓ *The file extension of MHTML document is .mht. Refer to Exercise 60 for more information on the Web Archive file type.*

- The document opens in Web Layout view.

  ✓ *By default, if you try to open an HTML document from Windows, the document displays in your Web browser, not in Word.*

Procedures

Create a New Blank Web Page Document

1. Click **File** .... Alt+F
2. Click **New** .... N
3. Click **Blank Web Page** [Blank Web Page] in New Document task pane.
4. Click **File** .... Alt+F
5. Click **Save as** .... A
6. Type file name.
   ✓ *If necessary, open the folder, disk, or server where the file will be stored.*
7. Click **Save** button  .... Alt+S

Save a Document as a Web Page

1. Open the document.
2. Click **File** .... Alt+F
3. Click **Save as Web Page**.... G
4. Type file name.
   ✓ *If necessary, open the folder, disk, or server where the file will be stored.*
5. Click **Save** button 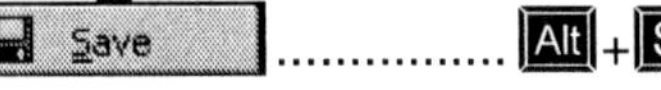 .... Alt+S
   ✓ *If Word displays a warning that some formatting features cannot be preserved, click Continue to save the document, click Cancel to cancel the save, or click Tell me more to open a Help page.*

Change to Web Layout View

1. Open Web page document in Word.
2. Click **Web Layout view** button [icon].

OR

1. Click **View** .... Alt+V
2. Click **Web Layout** .... W

Use Web Page Preview

1. Click **File**...................... Alt+F
2. Click **Web Page Preview** .... B

Close Web Page Preview

- Click **Close** button [X].

OR

1. Click **File**...................... Alt+F
2. Click **Close** C

Open an HTML Document

1. Click **File**...................... Alt+F
2. Click **Open**........................... O
3. Click file name.
   ✓ *If necessary, open the folder or disk where the file is stored.*
4. Click **Open** button ........... Alt+O

Exercise Directions

1. Start Word, if necessary.
2. Create a new blank Web page document.
3. Save the document as PETESWEB.
4. Type and format the document shown in Illustration A.
5. Check the spelling and grammar in the document.
6. Display the document in Web Page Preview. It should look similar to Illustration A.
7. Close Web Page Preview.
8. Open the file 62ONLINEAD, a version of the advertisement you created for Pelican Peter's in an earlier exercise.
9. Save the file as a Web page with the name ONLINEAD.htm.
   ✓ *Click Continue if Word warns you that some formatting may not be preserved.*
10. Press Ctrl+End to move the insertion point to the end of the document.
11. Insert a new blank line and then type the text **RETURN**.
12. Select the text **RETURN** and insert a hyperlink to the PETESWEB.htm document.
    ✓ *For a refresher on inserting hyperlinks, refer to Exercise 30.*
13. Switch to the PETERSWEB.htm document.
14. Insert a hyperlink from the text **Special Online Savings Offers!** to the ONLINEAD.htm document.
15. Test the link.
16. Test the RETURN link back to the PETESWEB document.
17. Close all open files, saving all changes.

Illustration A

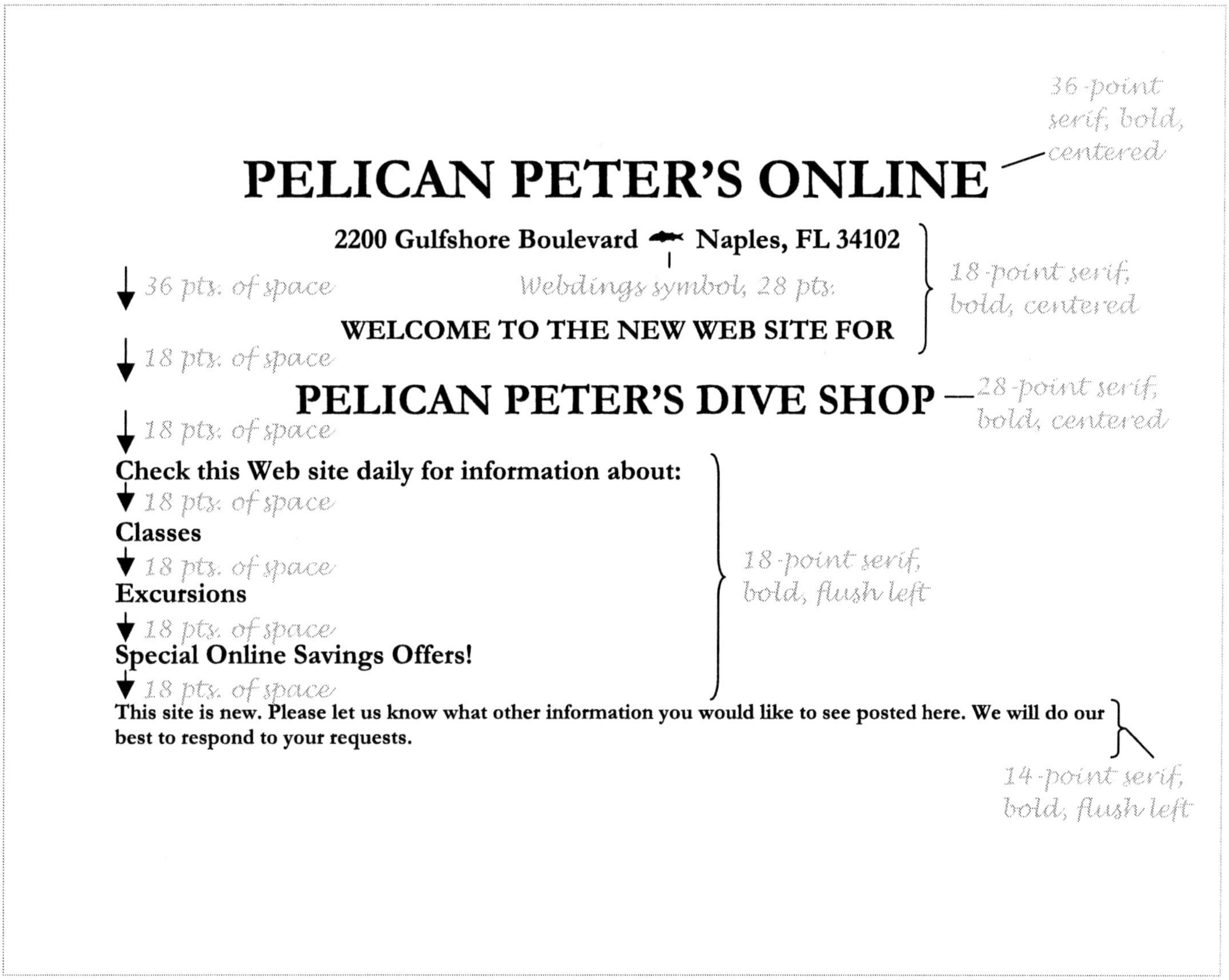

PELICAN PETER'S ONLINE
36-point serif, bold, centered

2200 Gulfshore Boulevard Naples, FL 34102
Webdings symbol, 28 pts.
36 pts. of space
WELCOME TO THE NEW WEB SITE FOR
18-point serif, bold, centered
18 pts. of space
PELICAN PETER'S DIVE SHOP
28-point serif, bold, centered
18 pts. of space
Check this Web site daily for information about:
18 pts. of space
Classes
18 pts. of space
Excursions
18 pts. of space
Special Online Savings Offers!
18 pts. of space
18-point serif, bold, flush left
This site is new. Please let us know what other information you would like to see posted here. We will do our best to respond to your requests.
14-point serif, bold, flush left

On Your Own

1. Create a new Web page document in Word.
2. Save the file as OWDMYWEB.
3. Use this document to create your own personal Web page. Think about what you want to include on your Web page. You should include your name and other information about yourself—what you like to do, who your favorite musicians and sports teams are, where you go to school, or where you work.
4. Add some other information you think will be interesting: favorite sayings, upcoming events in your life, or fun things your family or friends plan to do.
5. View the document in Web Layout view.
6. Use Web Page Preview to look at your new Web page in your browser software.
7. Close Web Page Preview.
8. Close the document, saving all changes.

Exercise 63

Skills Covered:

◆ **Use Web Page Titles** ◆ **Web Page Graphics**
◆ **Apply a Background** ◆ **Apply a Theme**

On the Job

The title of a Web page is displayed at the top of the screen in your Web browser. You can enter any title you want. You can enhance and edit HTML documents by adding elements such as a background and by applying a theme.

The owner of Pelican Peter's Dive Shop wants you to improve the appearance of the Web pages you already designed. In this exercise, you change the page titles for both pages. You apply a theme to one page and a background to the other page. You edit the hyperlinks, and then test the pages in your browser.

Terms

Graphics object A picture, chart, shape, or other element that can be inserted into a Word document.

Clip art Picture files that can be inserted into a document.

Background The color, pattern, or fill displayed on the page behind data in a document.

Fill effect A texture, shading, picture, or pattern used as a background.

Theme A collection of formatting settings applied to a document.

Web bullets Graphics files inserted as bullet markers.

Graphics lines Graphics files inserted as horizontal lines or dividers.

Notes

Use Web Page Titles

- Web page titles are displayed in the Web browser title bar.
- By default, Word uses the file name or the first line of document text as the Web page title.
- You can set or change the page title name by accessing the Set Page Title dialog box from the Save As dialog box.

Set Page Title dialog box

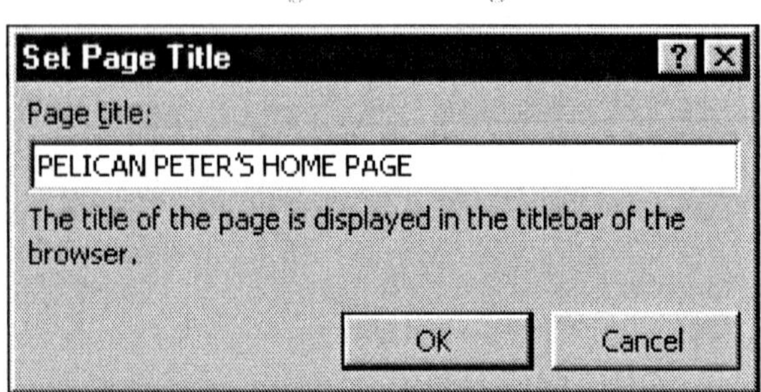

Web Page Graphics

- In order for HTML documents to display correctly on all Web browsers, many visual elements must be inserted as **graphics objects**.
- For example, horizontal lines, bullets, and even background textures are inserted as graphics objects in HTML documents.
- All graphics files that are associated with an HTML document are stored in a folder that is stored at the same location as the HTML document.
- Word creates the folder automatically when you save the file, giving it the same name as the file, followed by an underscore and the word *files*, like this: *Filename_files*.
- If the folder or the graphics files are moved, the HTML document cannot be displayed correctly.
- Graphics inserted in an HTML document are usually in .gif or .jpg file format.
- In general, .gif is used for drawings and **clip art**, including bullets and lines, and .jpg is used for photographs and background textures.
- Word comes with .gif and .jpg formatted graphics files for use in regular documents and in HTML documents.

  ✓ *For more information on working with graphics, see Lesson 13.*

Apply a Background

- By default, Word documents—including HTML documents—have a plain white **background**.
- Add visual interest or create an effect by applying a color, pattern, **fill effect**, or picture to a document background.

Fill Effects dialog box

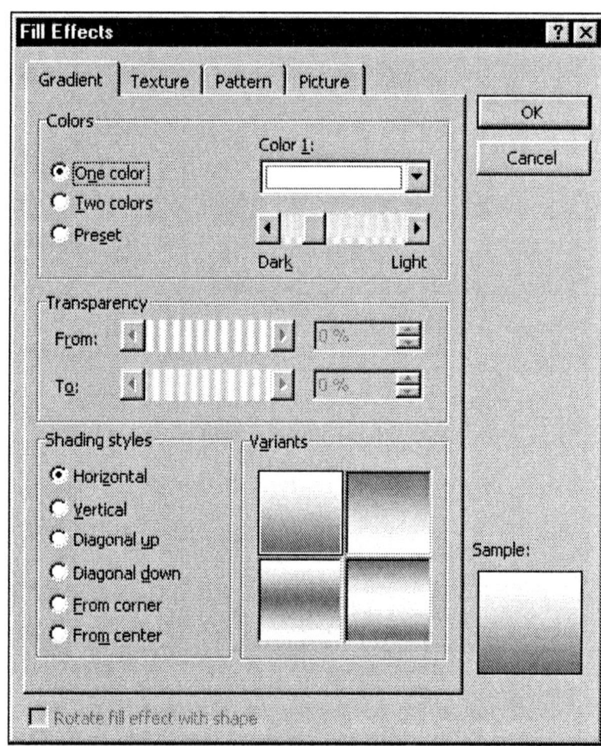

- You should coordinate backgrounds for pages in a Web site to establish continuity.

Apply a Themes

- Word comes with built-in **themes** you can use to format any Word document.
- Each theme includes a background, font formatting, and graphics elements such as **Web bullets** and **graphics lines**.
- You can select a theme to apply consistent formatting to a document.
- Themes can be used with any Word document, but they are particularly useful for formatting Web pages.

Procedures

Set a Web Page Title

1. Click **File** .... Alt+F
2. Click **Save As** .... A
3. Click **Change Title** button [Change Title...] .... Alt+C
4. Type new title.
5. Click **OK**.
6. Click **Save** button [Save] .... Alt+S

Apply a Background

1. Open file to format.
2. Click **Format**................ Alt+O
3. Click **Background**.............. K
4. Click desired color.

   OR

   a. Click **Fill Effects** .... F
   b. Click desired page tab .... Ctrl+Tab
   c. Select desired effect.
   d. Click **OK** .... Enter

Apply a Theme

1. Open file to format.
2. Click **Format**................ Alt+O
3. Click **Theme** .... H
4. Select desired **Theme** .... Alt+T, ↑↓
5. Click **OK**........................... Enter

   ✓ *Not all themes are installed automatically. If a theme you select is not installed, use the Setup disk to install it, or select a different theme.*

Exercise Directions

1. Start Word, if necessary.
2. Open the document PETESWEB.htm or open 63PETESWEB.htm.
3. Save the file as PETESWEB2.htm.
4. Change the Web Page Title to **Pelican Peter's Home Page**.
5. Apply the Citrus Punch theme.

   ✓ *If the Citrus Punch theme is not available, select a different theme.*
6. Change **Classes, Excursions**, and **Special Online Savings Offers!** into a bulleted list, using the default bullet style.
7. Apply the Heading 1 style to the first line in the document, and then center it.
8. Copy the formatting from the first line in the document to the fourth line in the document.
9. Use Web Page Preview to preview the document. It should look similar to the one in Illustration A.
10. Save and close the document.
11. In Word, open the document ONLINEAD.htm or open 63ONLINEAD.htm.
12. Save it as ONLINEAD2.
13. Change the Web Page Title to **ONLINE SAVINGS**.
14. Apply the Fish Fossil background texture to the page.

    ✓ *If you don't have this background, select another.*
15. Edit the hyperlink so it goes to the PETESWEB2 page instead of to the PETESWEB page.

    ✓ *For a refresher on hyperlinks, see exercise 30.*
16. Use Web Page Preview to preview the page.
17. While in Web Page Preview, test the link to PETESWEB2.
18. Close Web Page Preview and apply the Parchment background texture to the page.

    ✓ *If you don't have this background, select another.*
19. Preview the page again.
20. Close Web Page Preview.
21. Save the document and close it.
22. Edit the hyperlink on the PETESWEB2 page so it goes to ONLINEAD2 instead of to ONLINEAD.
23. Change to Web Page Preview.
24. Test the link.
25. Close your browser.
26. Close all open documents, saving all changes.

Illustration A

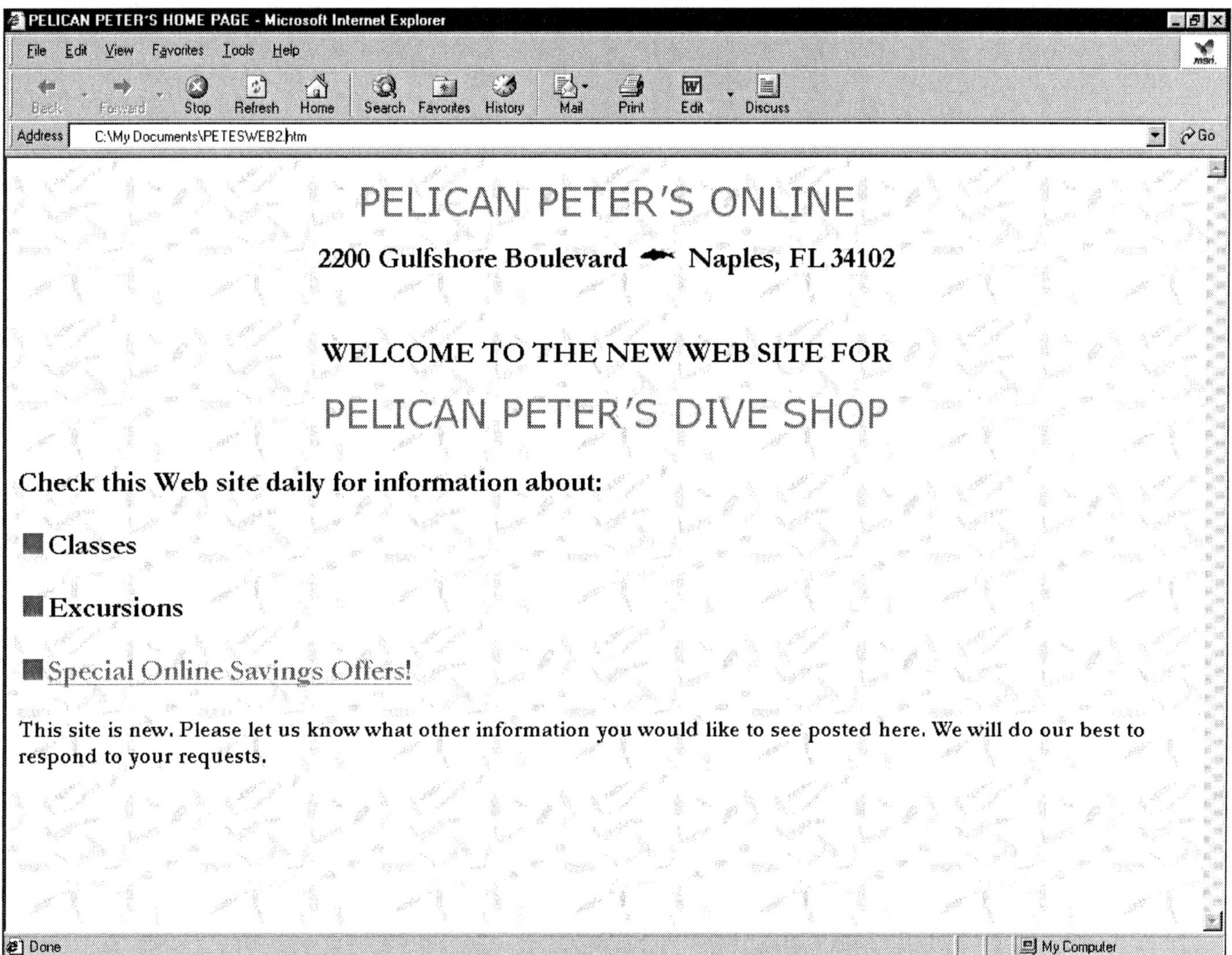

On Your Own

1. Start Word and open OWDMYWEB.htm, the Web page you created in the On Your Own section of Exercise 62, or open 63OWDMYWEB.htm.
2. Save the document as OWDMYWEB2.htm.
3. Change the Web Page title to **Your Name's Web Page**. (Substitute your own name for the text My Personal.)
4. Apply a theme.
5. If there is not already a bulleted list on your Web page, create one.
6. Try a different theme.
7. Keep trying themes until you find one you like.
8. Try changing just the background on the page.
9. If you don't like the background you apply, use Undo to remove it.
10. Use Web Page Preview to preview the document.
11. Close the document, saving all changes.

Exercise 64

Skills Covered:

◆ **Use Tables in HTML Documents** ◆ **Use Web Page Templates**
◆ **Insert a Link Bar in a Word Document**

On the Job

Use tables in an HTML document to organize and align data on a Web page. In addition to letting you set up data in columns and rows as in a regular Word document, tables let you define different areas on a page because you can format each cell differently. Use Web Page templates to create new Web Page documents that already include formatting such as fonts, styles, and bullet lists as well as tables. All you have to do is fill in the content and set up any necessary hyperlinks.

The owner of Pelican Peter's Dive Shop has asked you to design two new Web pages to link to the store's Web site. In this exercise, you will design a Web page listing upcoming diving excursions and a Web page providing SCUBA safety information. You will create the first page using a table in a Word document. You will create the second page using a Web Page template.

Terms

Template A Word document on which new documents are based. Templates include formatting settings, placeholder text, and graphics used to create the new document.

Link bar A Web page element that automatically creates buttons which can be clicked to move to specified links.

Notes

Use Tables in HTML Documents

- Tables are common features in Web page documents.
- Tables can be used in a Web page just as they are used in a regular document—to set up information in columns and rows. For example, you can use a table in a Web page that lists a schedule.
- You can also use a table in a Web page to organize the page into independent areas. Since each cell can be formatted separately, you can create visual effects that might otherwise be unavailable.
- Steps for creating, modifying, and formatting tables in HTML documents are the same as in regular Word documents.
- You can insert more than one table on a Web page. You can also insert a table within a table.

A table can be used to define areas on a Web page

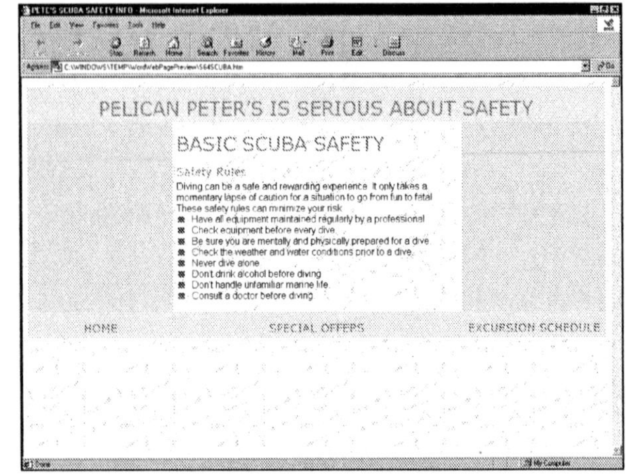

Use Web Page Templates

- Word comes with built-in **templates** for creating Web page documents.
  - ✓ *Word also includes templates for many other types of documents. You learn more about using Word's General Templates in Exercise 75.*
- Select a template to create a document in HTML format and save as a Web page.

Select a Web page template

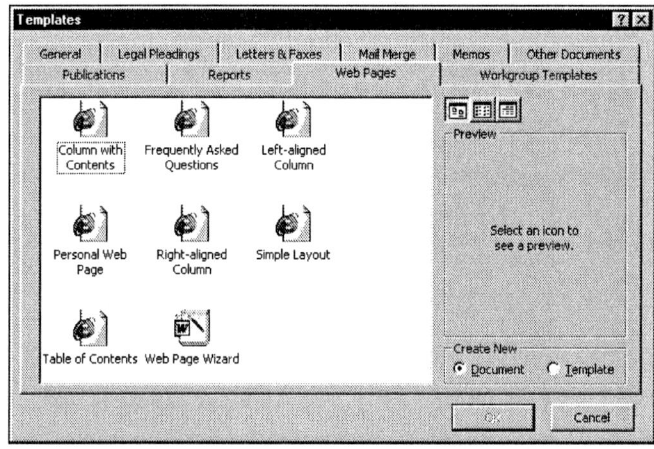

- ✓ *The Templates dialog box may vary.*
- Most Web page templates use tables to align text and graphics.
- Web page templates usually include text already formatted as hyperlinks.
- Web page templates may include sample text and graphics.
- To complete the document, you replace the sample text and graphics and edit or insert hyperlinks.

Insert a Link Bar in a Word Document

- If you save a Word document as a Web page on a Web server that has the Microsoft FrontPage Server Extensions 2002, or the SharePoint Team Services from Microsoft, you can automatically insert a **link bar**.
  - ✓ *Saving Word documents to a Web server is not covered in this book.*
- A link bar lists hyperlinked buttons that help you navigate through a Web site. You can select to insert a link bar with Back and Next buttons (for moving to the previous or next pages in a site), or you can create customized buttons.
- Once you create a link bar, you can insert it in multiple documents.
- You can select to display a link bar across the top or along the left side of the Web page.

Procedures

Create a Web Page Using a Template

1. Click **File** .... Alt+F
2. Click **New** .... N
3. Click **General Templates** [General Templates...] in the New Document task pane.
4. Click **Web Pages** tab .... Ctrl+Tab
5. Click desired template icon.
6. Click **OK** .... Enter
   - ✓ *If the document contains elements such as decorative borders that are not supported by the default Browser, Word displays a warning message. Click Continue to create the page.*
7. Replace directional text and graphics.
8. Apply formatting as needed.
9. Create hyperlinks as needed.
10. **Save** and name the document .... Ctrl+S
    - ✓ *Word saves the document in HTML format.*

Insert a Link Bar

1. Save your document as a Web page to a Web server that is running Microsoft FrontPage Server Extensions 2002 or SharePoint Team Services from Microsoft.
2. Click **Insert** .... Alt+I
3. Click **Web Component** .... W
4. Select Link Bars in the **Component type** list .... Alt+T, ↑↓
5. Select desired bar type in the **Choose a bar type** list .... Alt+H, ↑↓
6. Click **Next** .... Alt+N
7. Select desired style .... Alt+H, ↑↓
8. Click **Next** .... Alt+N
9. Select desired orientation.... ↑↓
10. Click **Finish** .... Alt+F
    - ✓ *The Link Bar Properties dialog box is displayed.*
11. Do one of the following:
    - Select an existing link bar.

    OR

    a. Click **Create New** ... Alt+C
    b. Type new link bar name
    c. Click **OK** .... Enter

d. Click **Add link** .... Alt+A

✓ *The Add to Link Bar dialog box appears.*

e. Select destination for first button on link bar.

f. In **Text to Display** box, type text to display on link bar button.

g. Click **OK** .... Enter

h. Repeat steps d through g for additional buttons.

12. Click **OK** .... Enter

✓ *To quickly access the Link Bar Properties dialog box so you can add or modify links, click the edit links link.*

Create Tables

- Refer to Lesson 7 for a review on creating tables.

Exercise Directions

1. Start Word, if necessary.
2. Create a new blank Web page document.
3. Save the document as TRIPS with the Web page title **Schedule of Diving Excursions**.
4. Apply the Citrus Punch theme to the document.
5. Type and format the document shown in Illustration A.
   a. Type the title using the Heading 1 style.
   b. Insert a table with three columns and eleven rows.
   c. Merge the cells in the first row as shown.
   d. Type the text in the table as shown.
   e. Apply a light yellow shading fill to the first row.
   f. Apply a light green shading to all remaining rows.
   g. Insert a second table with three columns and one row.
   h. Type the text in the second table as shown.
   i. Center both tables and the title on the page.
6. Check the spelling and grammar in the document.
7. Preview the document using Web Page Preview. It should look similar to illustration A.
8. Close Web Page Preview and save the document.
9. Create a new document based on the Simple Layout Web Page Template.
10. Save the document as SCUBA.htm with the Web Page title **PETE'S SCUBA SAFETY INFO**.
11. Apply the Citrus Punch theme.
12. Type and format the document shown in Illustration B.
    a. Insert a new row at the top of the table.
    b. Insert a new row at the bottom of the table.
    c. Merge the new top row into one cell.
    d. Type and format the text as shown in Illustration B, replacing or deleting the sample text as necessary.
    e. Apply a light yellow fill to the first row.
    f. Apply a light green fill to the middle cells in the left and right columns.
13. Check the spelling and grammar in the document.
14. Use Web Page Preview to preview the document. It should look similar to the one in Illustration B.
15. Close Web Page Preview.
16. Create a hyperlink from the text **EXCURSION SCHEDULE** to the TRIPS Web page.
17. Close the document, saving all changes.
18. In the TRIPS document, create a hyperlink from the text **SCUBA SAFETY** to the SCUBA Web page.
19. Save the document.
20. Test the link.
21. Test the link back to the TRIPS document.
22. Close Web Page Preview.
23. Close all open documents, saving all changes.

Illustration A

Pelican Peter's Diving Excursions

Heading 1, centered

Normal, 16 point

Diving Excursion Schedule for Six Months Beginning in January

Heading 2

Heading 3, centered

Dates	Destination	Cost
1/15 – 1/21	Aruba	$1,275.00
1/21 – 1/31	Belize	$1,895.00
2/12 – 2/20	U.S. Virgin Islands	$999.00
3/10 – 3/18	Hawaii	$1,295.00
3/20 – 3/30	Costa Rica	$1,395.00
4/10 – 4/18	Venezuela	$1,595.00
5/29 – 6/05	Cancun	$895.00
6/10 – 6/18	Cayman Islands	$1,895.00
6/21 – 6/30	Antigua	$1,150.00

Right-align

HOME	SPECIAL OFFERS	SCUBA SAFETY

Heading 3, centered

Illustration B

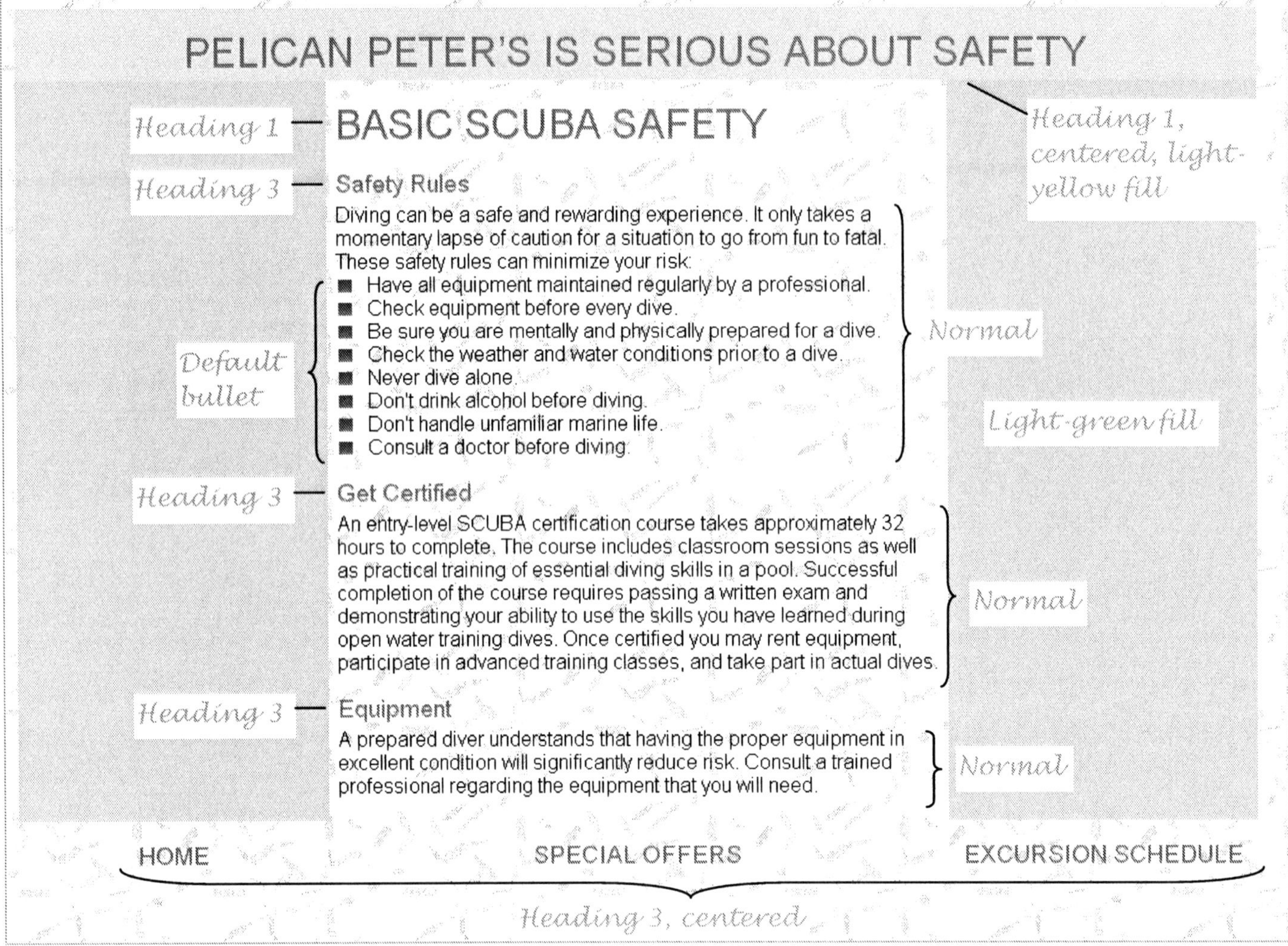

On Your Own

1. Start Word and create a new HTML document using one of the Web Page templates that includes a table.
2. Save the document with the name **OWDMYLINK**.
3. Type text to provide information about some part of your life. For example, make a page about your family, or about a club or organization to which you belong.
4. Open the document **OWDMYWEB2**, the personal home page you used in the On Your Own section of Exercise 63, or open **64OWDMYWEB2**.
5. Save the document as **OWDMYWEB3**.
6. Create hyperlinks between the **OWDMYWEB3** page and the **OWDMYLINK** page.
7. Test the links.
8. Close all open documents, saving all changes.

Exercise 65

◆ Critical Thinking

You have been hired by Fox Footwear, Inc. to develop pages to link to its Web site. The company is particularly interested in how other company's handle customer satisfaction regarding online sales. In this exercise, you will browse the Internet looking at other footwear Web sites. You will print one page and save another locally. You will create and format a Web page document based on a template, and you will save an existing document as a Web page. Finally, you will link the two Web pages.

Exercise Directions

✓ *Use the Internet simulation provided on the CD that accompanies this book to complete this exercise.*

1. Start Word, if necessary.
2. Display the Web toolbar.
3. Open the Internet simulation provided on the CD:
   a. Click **Go**.
   b. Click **Open Hyperlink**.
   c. In the Address line type the following: **D:/Internet/Ex65/yahoo.htm**
      ✓ *If you've copied the Internet simulation files to your hard drive or your CD-ROM drive is a letter other than D:, substitute the correct letter for D.*
4. Type **shoes** in the search box and click Search.
5. Scroll down the page and note the links.
6. Go back to Word.
7. If you have an Internet connection, go to the URL www.onlineshoes.com; otherwise, go to **D:/Internet/Ex65/onlineshoes.htm**.
8. Go back to Word.
9. If you have an Internet connection, go to the URL www.shoebuy.com; otherwise, go to **D:/Internet/Ex65/shoebuy.htm**.
10. Click the 30 Day Money Back Guarantee link.
11. Save the page locally in Web Archive format with the name SATISFY.
12. Click the click here link under the paragraph describing the money back guarantee policy.
13. Print the page.
14. Exit the simulation by clicking the Close button ☒.
15. Create a new Web page document in Word, based on the Column with Contents Web page template.
16. Save the file as FOXPAGE with the page title **Fox Footwear Home Page**.
17. Type and format the document shown in Illustration A, replacing or deleting the sample text as necessary.
    ✓ *To delete the picture, click it, then press Delete.*
18. Apply the Straight Edge theme to the document.
19. Check the spelling and grammar in the document.
20. Display the file in Web Page Preview. It should look similar to the one in the illustration.
21. Open the file CONTEST3 that you last used in Exercise 35, or open 65CONTEST3.
22. Save the file as a Web page with the file name CONTEST3 and the Web page title **Fox Footwear's Essay Contest**.
23. Apply the Canvas background texture to the document.
24. Insert a new blank line at the top of the document, and type the text **RETURN TO HOME PAGE**, and then press Enter.
25. Insert a hyperlink from the text **RETURN TO HOME PAGE** to the FOXPAGE document.
26. Close the document, saving all changes.
27. Insert a hyperlink from the text **Essay Contest** in the FOXPAGE document to the CONTEST3 document.
28. Test the link.
29. Test the RETURN TO HOME PAGE link.
30. Close all open documents, saving all changes.

Illustration A

About Fox Footwear's Web Site — *Heading 1*

Retail

Information

Events

Retail — *Heading 3*

Fox Footwear's Web site is a retail outlet!

Use our Web site as a convenient home shopping tool. You'll find every item we sell available here, including shoes for guys, girls, and kids. You might even find items that aren't available in bricks and mortar stores!

Our online specials change daily, so check our site frequently for the best deals of the day.

Information — *Heading 3*

Fox Footwear's Web site is educational!

This site also provides links to other sites where you'll find information about lots of related topics including the history of footwear, foot health, and footwear fashion. We even have a consultant available to answer your footwear questions.

Events — *Heading 3*

Fox Footwear's Web site is fun!
In addition to special online savings, you'll find information about contests and other promotional events that Fox Footwear is sponsoring. Learn the rules, download entry forms, or enter right online. There's always something exciting happening at Fox Footwear.

Click a link below to learn more.

Essay Contest

Lesson 11

Collaboration

Exercise 66

- Insert Comments
- Track Changes
- Customize Revision Marks
- Compare and Merge Documents
- Accept/Reject Changes

Exercise 67

- Create Multiple Versions of a Document
- Protect a Document
- Use Digital Signatures

Exercise 68

- Open Multiple Documents
- Arrange Documents On-screen
- Copy/Move Text from One Document to Another

Exercise 69

- Send E-mail from Word
- Attach a Word Document to an E-mail Message
- Send a Word Document as E-mail
- Copy Data from a Word Document into an E-mail Message

Exercise 70

- Receive E-mail Messages in Outlook or Outlook Express
- Print an E-mail Message
- Save an E-mail Attachment

Exercise 71

- Merge to an E-Mail Message

Exercise 72

- Critical Thinking

Exercise 66

Skills Covered:

◆ **Insert Comments** ◆ **Track Changes** ◆ **Customize Revision Marks** ◆ **Compare and Merge Documents** ◆ **Accept/Reject Changes**

On the Job

Insert comments in a document when you want to include a private note to the author, another reader, or to yourself, in much the same way you might attach a slip of paper to a hard copy print out. Track changes made to a document to monitor when and how edits are made. Tracking changes lets you consider revisions before incorporating them into a document. If you agree with the change, you can accept it, but if you disagree with the change you can reject it. You can track changes made by one person, or by many people, which is useful when you are collaborating on a document with others. When you compare and merge documents, differences between the two are marked like revisions.

The Director of Training at Murray Hill Marketing has asked you to revise a document listing in-house training courses. In this exercise, you will use the track changes feature while you edit the document and insert comments. You will then review the document to accept or reject the changes. Finally, you will compare the document to a version edited by a coworker. When you are satisfied with the document you will print it.

Terms

Comment A hidden note attached to a document for reference.

Comment balloon An area in the right margin in which comment text is displayed.

Reviewing pane A window where revisions and comments are displayed.

Comment mark A color-coded I-beam that marks the location in the document where a comment was inserted.

Revision marks Formatting applied to text in a document to identify where insertions, deletions, and formatting changes have been made.

Revision balloon An area in the right margin in which revisions are displayed.

Notes

The Reviewing toolbar

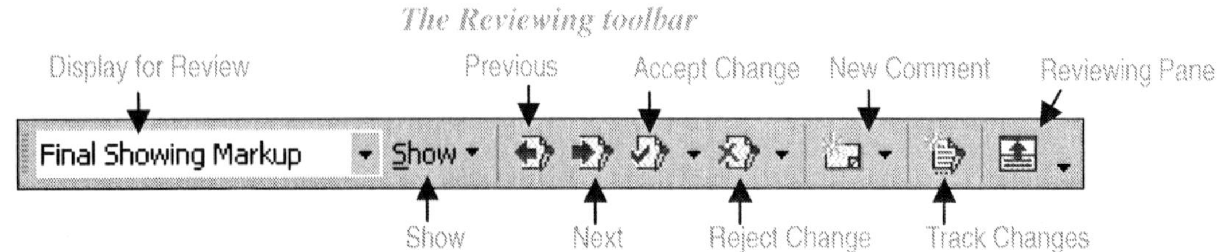

Insert Comments

- Insert **comments** to annotate text, communicate with readers, or to attach reminders or questions.
- By default, in Print Layout and Web Layout views you can type and edit comments in either the **comment balloon** or in the **Reviewing pane**. In Normal view, you must use the Reviewing pane.
- In the Reviewing pane, comments are organized according to where they occur in the document. For example, they may be listed under Main Document, or Header and Footer.
- When you create a comment, Word inserts a **comment mark**. In Print Layout and Web Layout views, the mark is connected to the comment balloon by a dashed line.
- The comment balloons are displayed in the page margin; Word automatically reduces the size of the display on-screen to accommodate the balloons.
- Both the comment mark and comment balloons are color coded by author.
- You can choose to hide or show comments on-screen.
- Comments can be printed with a document.

A comment in Print Layout view

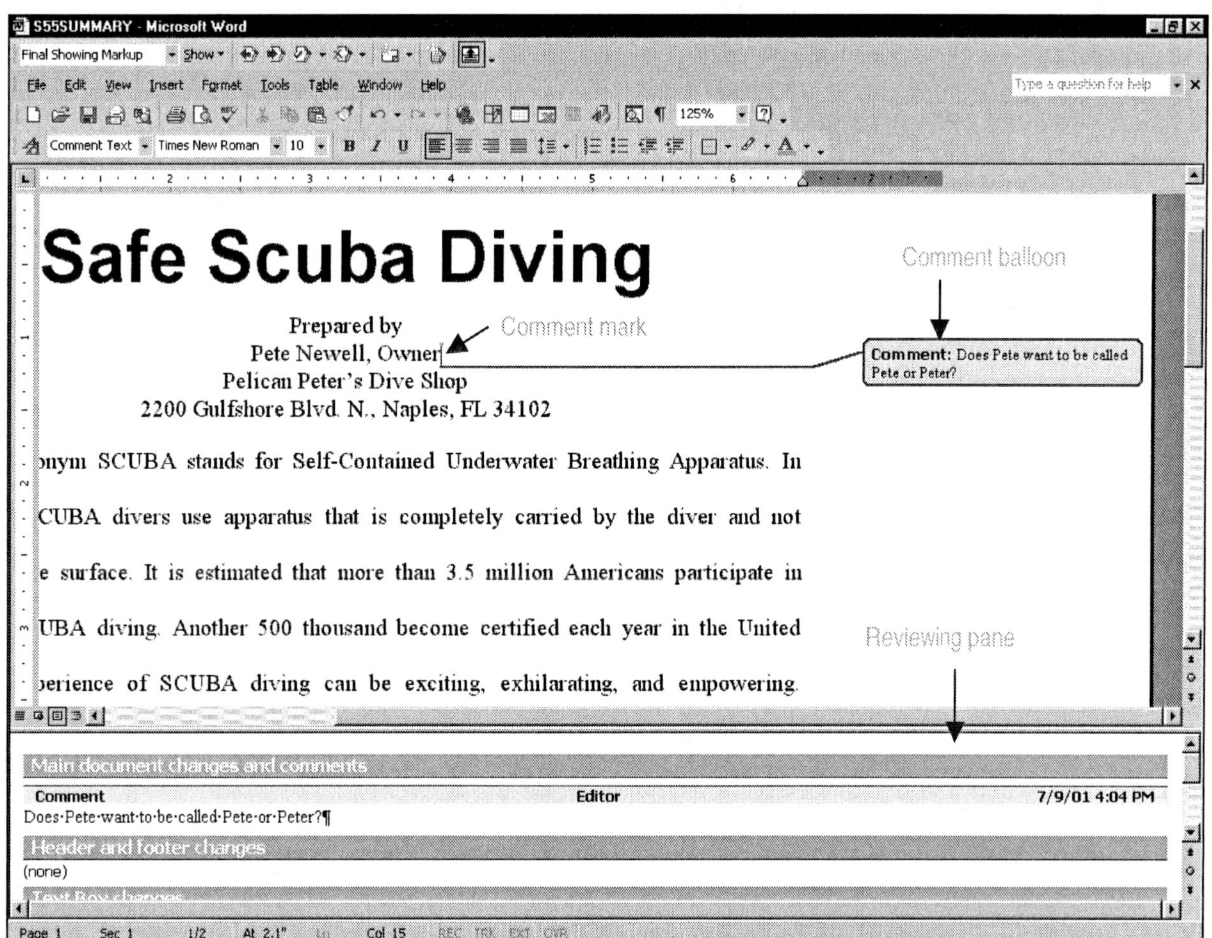

Track Changes

- Turn on Word's Track Changes feature to apply **revision marks** to all insertions, deletions, and formatting changes in a document.
- When Track Changes is active, the TRK button on the status bar is bold and Word applies revision marks as you edit a document.
- The way that revisions are marked on-screen depends on the current view and on the selected Display for Review option:
  - Final Showing Markup (default). This option displays inserted text in color with an underline, and all formatting changes are applied. In Print Layout and Web Layout views deleted text is moved into a **revision balloon** while in Normal view, deleted text is marked in color with a strikethrough effect.
  - Final. In all views, this option displays the document as it would look if all of the revisions that had been entered were incorporated in the document.
  - Original Showing Markup. This option displays deleted text in color with a strikethrough effect. In Print Layout and Web Layout views inserted text and formatting are displayed in a revision balloon, while in Normal view inserted text is marked in color with an underline.
  - Original. In all views, this option displays the document as it would look if no revisions had been made.
- Like comments, revisions are color coded by author.
- By default, Word also inserts a vertical line to the left of any changed line to indicate where revisions occur in the document.
- In any view, you can view descriptions of all revisions in the Reviewing pane.
- You can select which changes you want displayed on-screen. For example, you can display insertions and deletions, but not formatting.
- You can even set Word to show only the changes made by one reviewer at a time.

Tracking changes in Normal view

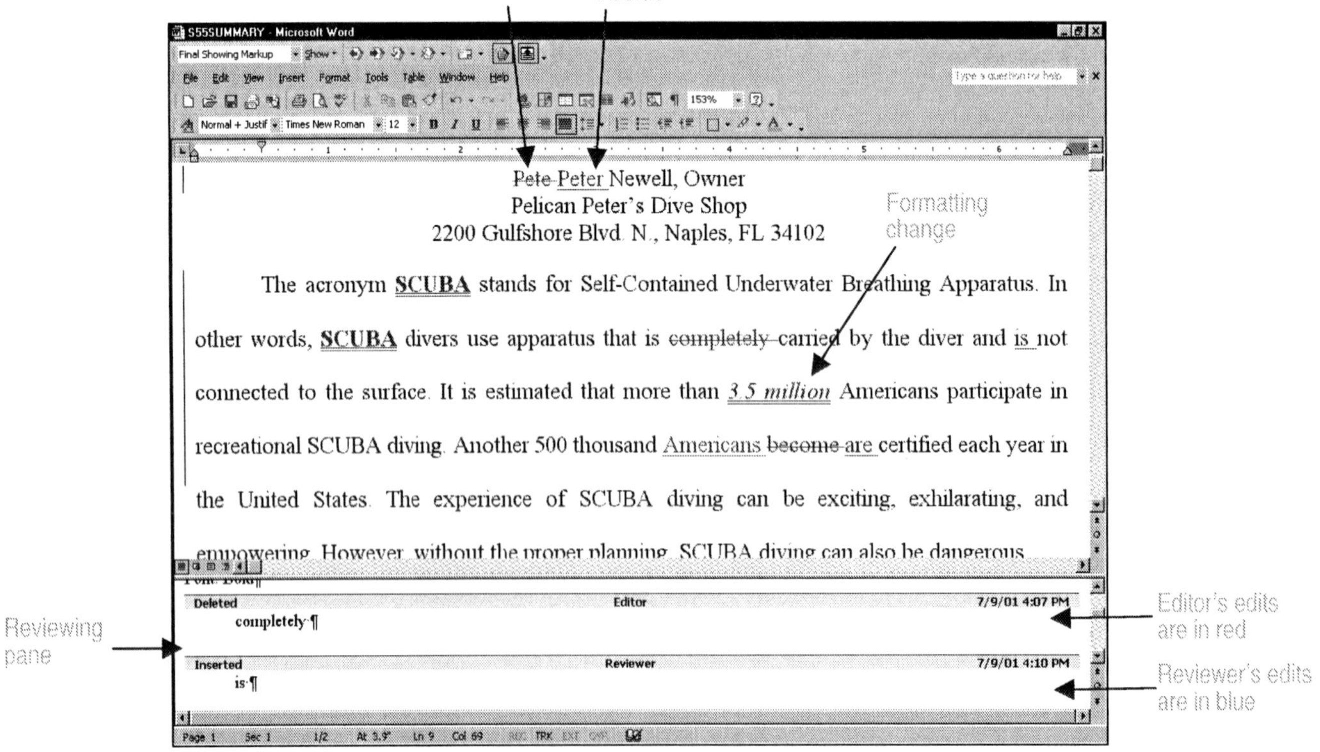

Deletion
Insertion
Formatting change
Reviewing pane
Editor's edits are in red
Reviewer's edits are in blue

Customize Revision Marks

- You can customize revision marks in the Track Changes dialog box as follows:
  - You can select the color you want to use.
  - You can select the formatting used to indicate changes. For example, you can mark formatting changes with a double-underline, or insertions with color only instead of color and an underline.
  - You can customize the location vertical bar used to mark lines that have been changed.
  - You can also customize the way balloons are displayed in a document.

Track Changes dialog box

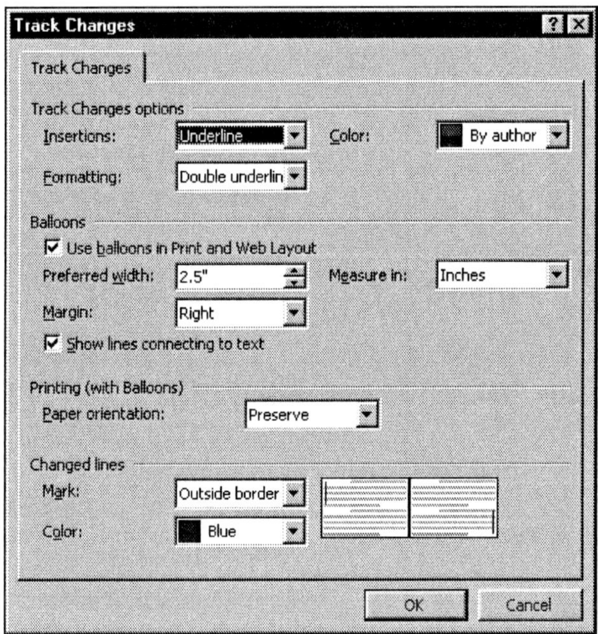

Compare and Merge Documents

- You can compare two or more documents to mark the differences between them.
- When you compare documents, Word uses revision marks to indicate where text has been inserted, deleted, or formatted.
- Comparing and merging documents is useful if you have more than one version of a document and need to see what changes have been made, if more than one person has edited a document, or if someone has edited a document without using the track changes features.
- You can merge the documents into the original document, the current document, or into a new document.

Accept/Reject Changes

- Revision marks remain stored as part of a document until the changes are either accepted or rejected.
- To incorporate edits into a document file, accept the changes.
- To cancel the edits and erase them from the file, reject the changes.
- You can also reject comments to delete them from the file.

Procedures

Display Reviewing Toolbar

1. Right-click any toolbar.

   OR

   a. Click **View** .... Alt+V

   b. Select **Toolbars** .... T

2. Click **Reviewing** ..... ↓, Enter

Display Reviewing Pane

- Click **Reviewing Pane** button on Reviewing toolbar.

OR

1. Click **Show** drop-down arrow .... Alt+S on Reviewing toolbar.
2. Click **Reviewing Pane** .... P

   ✓ *Repeat steps to hide reviewing pane.*

OR

1. Right-click **TRK** button TRK on Status bar.
2. Click **Reviewing Pane** button.

Display Balloons in Print Layout or Web Layout View

1. Click **View** .... Alt+V
2. Click **Markup** .... A

   ✓ *Repeat steps to hide balloons.*

Insert a Comment
(Alt + Ctrl + M)

1. Position insertion point where you want to insert comment.
2. Click **New Comment** button on Reviewing toolbar.

   OR

   a. Click **Insert** ... . Alt+I

   b. Click **Comment** .... M

3. Type comment text.

   ✓ *Click back in the document to continue working.*

Edit a Comment

1. Click in comment balloon.

   OR

   a. Display Reviewing pane.

   b. Scroll up or down to locate comment.

   OR

   a. Right-click commented text.

   b. Click **Edit Comment** ...... E

   OR

   a. Click **New Comment** drop-down arrow on the Reviewing toolbar.

   b. Click **Edit Comment** ..... E

2. Edit comment text.

Delete a Comment

1. Right-click comment balloon.

   OR

   Right-click comment in Reviewing pane.

2. Click **Delete Comment** .... M

OR

1. Click anywhere in comment text.
2. Click **New Comment** drop-down arrow on the Reviewing toolbar.
3. Click **Delete Comment** .... M

OR

1. Click anywhere in comment text.
2. Click **Reject Change/Delete Comment** drop-down arrow on the Reviewing toolbar.
3. Click **Reject Change/Delete Comment** .... R

Turn Track Changes On or Off
(Ctrl+Shift+E)

- Double-click **TRK** button TRK on Status bar to toggle feature on and off.

OR

- Click **Track Changes** button on Reviewing toolbar.

OR

1. Right-click **TRK** button TRK on Status bar.
2. Click **Track Changes** button.

OR

1. Click **Tools** .... Alt+T
2. Click **Track Changes** .... T

   ✓ *Repeat steps to turn feature off.*

Select a Display for Review

1. Click **Display for Review** drop-down arrow Final Showing Markup on Reviewing toolbar.
2. Click desired option: .... ↓, Enter
   - **Final Showing Markup**
   - **Final**
   - **Original Showing Markup**
   - **Original**

Compare and Merge Documents

1. Open edited document.
2. Click **Tools** .... Alt+T
3. Click **Compare and Merge Documents** .... D
4. Locate and select original document.
5. Click **Merge** drop-down arrow .... Alt+M
6. Click desired option:
   - **Merge** .... M
     to merge changes into original document.

- **Merge into current document**......C
  to merge changes into document opened in step 1.
- **Merge into new document**......N
  to merge changes into a new document.

Print Comments and Revisions (*Ctrl + P*)

1. Click **File**......Alt+F
2. Click **Print**......P
3. Click **Print what** drop-down arrow......Alt+W
4. Click **Document showing markup** to print comment and revision balloons with the document
   ✓ *If you select this option, the size of the printed document is reduced in order to accommodate the balloons on the page.*

   OR

   Click **List of markup** to print a list of comments and revisions separately
5. Click **OK**......Enter

Select Revision Display Options

1. Click **Show** drop-down arrow Show ▾ on Reviewing toolbar......Alt+S
2. Select Desired option:
   - **Comments**......C
   - **Insertions and Deletions**......I
   - **Formatting**......F

   ✓ *Repeat to select additional options.*

To select which reviewers' marks to display:

1. Click **Show** drop-down arrow Show ▾ on Reviewing toolbar......Alt+S
2. Select **Reviewers**......R
3. Click **All Reviewers**......A
   to display marks for all reviewers.

   OR

   Click desired reviewer name.

   ✓ *Repeat to select additional reviewers.*

Customize Revision Marks

1. Click **Show** drop-down arrow Show ▾ on Reviewing toolbar......Alt+S

   OR

   Right-click **TRK** button TRK on Status bar
2. Click **Options**......O
3. Select options as desired.
4. Click **OK**......Enter

OR

1. Click **Tools**......Alt+T
2. Click **Options**......O
3. Click **Track Changes** tab......Ctrl+Tab
4. Select options as desired.
5. Click **OK**......Enter

Accept/Reject Changes One by One

1. Right-click revision in document.

   OR

   Right-click revision in balloon.
2. Click **Accept Insertion** (or **Deletion**)......E

   OR

   Click **Reject Insertion** (or **Deletion**)......R

OR

1. Click **Next** button on Reviewing toolbar to browse forward from insertion point.

   OR

   Click **Previous** button to browse back from insertion point.
2. Click **Accept Change** button to incorporate highlighted change into document.

   OR

   Click **Reject Change** button to delete highlighted change from document.

Accept Changes All At Once

1. Click **Accept Change** drop-down arrow on Reviewing toolbar
2. Click **Accept All Changes Shown**......S

   OR

   Click **Accept All Changes in Document**......H

Reject Changes All At Once

1. Click **Reject Change/Delete Comment** drop-down arrow on Reviewing toolbar
2. Click **Reject All Changes Shown**......S

   OR

   Click **Reject All Changes in Document**......H

Exercise Directions

1. Start Word, if necessary.
2. Open 66NEWCLASS.
   - ✓ *This is a version of the course list document you worked with earlier in this book.*
3. Save the file as NEWCLASS.
4. Insert the comment shown in Illustration A.
5. Turn on the Track Changes feature.
6. Make sure Word is set to display comments, insertions, deletions, and formatting changes.
7. Customize the marks to show formatting changes with a double-underline and set the Changed lines color to red.
8. Switch to Normal view.
9. Make the insertions and deletions as shown in Illustration A.
10. Switch to Print Layout view.
11. Display the document as Final.
12. Display the Document as Original Showing Markup.
13. Display the Document as Final Showing Markup.
14. Print the document with the comments and changes.
15. Delete the comment.
16. Reject the changes to the names of the courses in the headings and in the course description.
17. Accept all other changes.
18. Turn off the Track Changes feature.
19. Save the changes
20. Locate and open the document 66REVIEW, save it with the name REVIEW.
    - ✓ *This is a third version of the course list document.*
21. Compare the NEWCLASS document with the REVIEW document, merging the changes into the REVIEW document.
22. Accept all changes.
23. Check the spelling and grammar in the document.
24. Print the document.
25. Close the document, saving all changes.

On Your Own

1. Open OWDRESUME, the resume you worked with earlier, or open 66OWDRESUME.
2. Save the document as OWDREV.
3. Insert at least one comment.
4. Turn on the Track Changes feature.
5. Customize revision marks.
6. Make changes to the document.
7. Save the changes.
8. Print the document with revision marks.
9. Save the document as OWDREV2.
10. Review the changes, accepting some, and rejecting others.
11. If the document is more than one page, shrink it to fit, or add a footer to the second page, including your name, a document title, and the page number.
12. Save the changes.
13. Compare the two documents.
14. Close all document without saving the changes

Illustration A

Highland Property Management Co.

575 W. Osborne Street, Phoenix, AZ 85013 602-555-4326

Training Schedule

September:

~~April~~

~~Microsoft~~ Word 1 - Basics

Insert comment: Do you think an introductory course is necessary?

This introductory course will cover the basics of using ~~Microsoft~~ MS Word to create common business documents. By the end of the course you will know how to create and print text-based documents such as letters and envelopes, and apply formatting.

October:

~~May~~

~~Microsoft~~ Word 2 - Intermediate

A continuation of the Word 1 course, this ~~introductory~~ Intermediate level class will delve into some of the more intriguing features of ~~Microsoft~~ Word. By the end of the course you will know how to conduct a mail merge, set up a document in columns, include headers and footers, and insert pictures.

November

~~June~~

~~Microsoft~~ Word 3 - Advanced

This final course in the ~~Microsoft~~ MS Word series covers the advanced features. By the end of this course you will know how to work with tables, create and modify outlines, use e-mail and Internet features in Word, and share documents with other users.

For more information call: 602-555-4326 ext. 343.

Exercise 67

Skills Covered:

◆ **Create Multiple Versions of a Document**
◆ **Protect a Document** ◆ **Use Digital Signatures**

On the Job

Word includes tools that make it easy to collaborate with others to create and generate documents. You can protect documents that you do not want others to change—and you can add digital signatures to verify the authenticity of a document. You can create multiple versions of a document so you know which one is the most up-to-date.

The Manager of Corporate Communications at Northlake Video Links wants her staff to collaborate on a new version of the company's mission statement. As the team leader for this project, she has asked you to create the first new version of the mission statement, which other members can then revise. In this exercise, you will first create a one-page report drafting the new mission statement. You will protect the document so that all changes are tracked with revision marks, and you will save multiple versions of the document. When the document is complete, you will authenticate it by attaching your own digital signature.

Terms

Workgroup A group of individuals who work together on the same projects, usually connected via a network.

Version An archived snapshot of a document saved in the same file as the original document.

Digital signature An electronic, encryption-based, secure stamp of authentication on a macro or document.

Digital certificate An attachment for a file, macro project, or e-mail message that vouches for its authenticity, provides secure encryption, or supplies a verifiable signature.

Notes

Create Multiple Versions of a Document

- Save a **version** of a file when you want to keep track of documents passed around to multiple users.
- You can manually save a version of a document at any time, or you can set Word to automatically save a version every time a document is closed.
- Saving a version creates an archive of the document, not a copy.
- Word automatically marks each version with the name of the person who saves it, the date the version was last saved, and the time the version was saved.
- You can save multiple versions of a document; all saved versions are stored in one file.

- Add comments to a saved version to help identify it. For example, you can identify an original version, a version that has been edited by someone, or a version that incorporates changes.

Word displays a list of all versions saved with a document

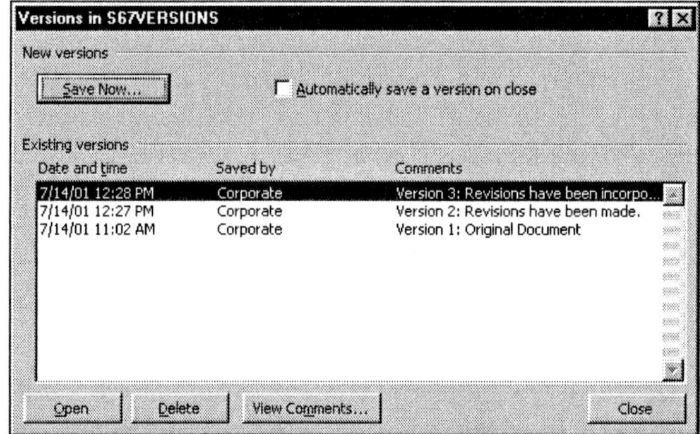

- When you display a list of saved versions, you can select to view the comments.
- You can open a saved version in a split-screen with the original file to compare the two.
- If you want to edit a saved version, you must use the Save As command to save the version as a separate file.
- When there are multiple versions of a file, Word displays the Versions icon on the Status bar.

Protect a Document

- There are three types of document protection available in Word:
  - Tracked Changes
  - Comments
  - Forms

Protect Document dialog box

- Use the Tracked Changes option to automatically display changes to a document with revision marks.
  - ✓ *Tracking changes is covered in Exercise 66.*
- Use the Comments option to allow **workgroup** members to enter comments without being able to edit document text.
  - ✓ *Using comments is covered in Exercise 66.*
- Use the Forms option to allow changes in form fields only.
  - ✓ *Forms and form fields are covered in Exercise 78.*
- To ensure that users cannot remove or change document protection, you can assign password protection as well. Only someone who enters the assigned password can change the document protection settings.

Use Digital Signatures

- You can add a **digital signature** to a Word file in order to confirm the authenticity of the file.
- Word will not save changes to a file that has a digital signature, thereby insuring that the file has not been edited since the author attached the signature.
- The signature is created using a **digital certificate**, and it certifies that the file has not been altered.
- You obtain a digital certificate from an authorized vendor or from the internal security administrator responsible for the computer system that you use.
- A list of available digital certificates is displayed in the Select Certificate dialog box.

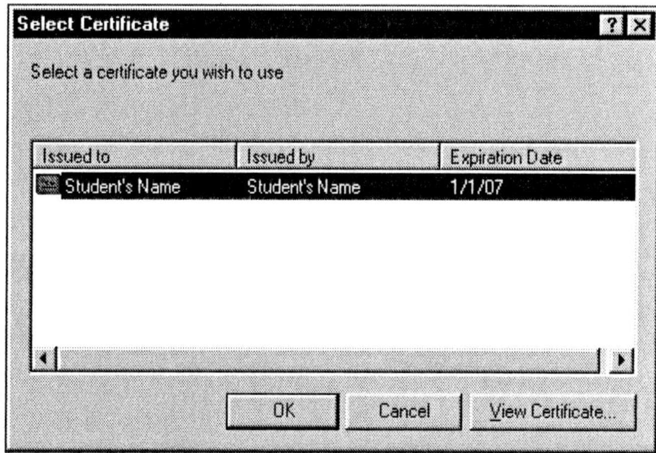

- You can also create a digital signature for yourself.
  - ✓ *Self-made digital signatures are considered unauthenticated and may trigger a security warning on some computers.*

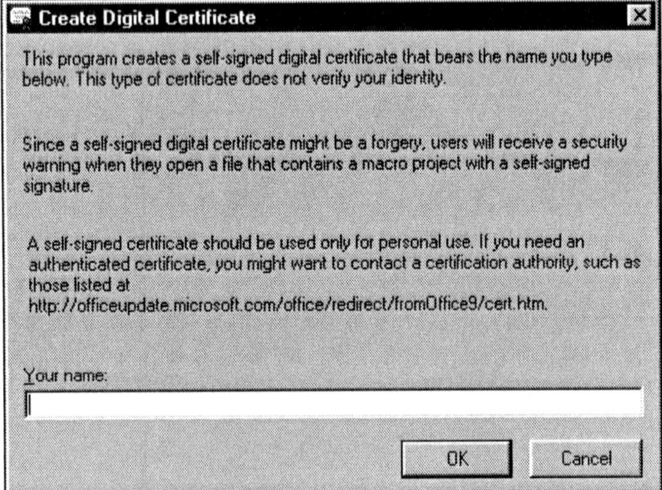

- If you try to save changes to a file that has a digital signature, Word prompts you to remove the digital signature.
- The text *(Signed)* is displayed in the title bar of a document that has a digital signature attached.
- Also, when there is a digital signature attached to a document, Word displays the Digital Signatures icon on the Status bar.

Procedures

Save a Version of a Document

1. Click **File** .... Alt+F
2. Click **Versions** .... R
3. Click **Save Now** button [Save Now...] .... Alt+S
4. Type desired comments.
5. Click **OK** .... Tab, Enter

OR

1. Click **File** .... Alt+F
2. Click **Save As** .... A
3. Click **Tools** drop-down arrow [Tools ▾] .... Alt+L
4. Click **Save Version** V

Set Word to automatically save versions:

1. Click **File** .... Alt+F
2. Click **Versions** .... R
3. Click **Automatically save a version on close** check box .... Alt+A
4. Click **Close** button [Close].

Display a list of saved versions:

1. Click **File** .... Alt+F
2. Click **Versions** .... R

Display comments for saved versions:

1. Click **File** .... Alt+F
2. Click **Versions** .... R
3. Select desired version .... ↑↓
4. Click **View Comments** button [View Comments...] .... Alt+M

Open a saved version:

1. Click **File** .... Alt+F
2. Click **Versions** .... R
3. Select desired version .... ↑, ↓
4. Click **Open** button [Open] .... Alt+O

Delete a saved version:

1. Click **File** .... Alt+F
2. Click **Versions** .... R
3. Select desired version .... ↑↓
4. Click **Delete** button [Delete] .... Alt+D
5. Click **Yes** .... Y

Protect a Document

1. Open the document to protect.
2. Click **Tools** .... Alt+T
3. Click **Protect Document** ..... P
4. Select one of the following:
   - **Tracked changes** .. Alt+T
   - **Comments** .... Alt+C
   - **Forms** .... Alt+F
5. Click **OK** .... Enter

Add password protection:

1. Open the document to protect.
2. Click **Tools** .... Alt+T
3. Click **Protect Document** ..... P
4. Select desired type of protection.
5. Click **Password** text box .... Alt+P
6. Type password.
7. Click **OK** .... Enter
8. Type password again.
9. Click **OK** .... Enter

Remove document protection:

1. Click **Tools** .... Alt+T
2. Click **Unprotect Document** .... P

✓ *If password protection has been applied, Word will prompt you to enter the correct password.*

Add a Digital Signature to a Document

1. Save document to certify.
2. Click **Tools** .... Alt+T
3. Click **Options** .... O
4. Click the **Security** tab .... Ctrl+Tab
5. Click the **Digital Signatures** button [Digital Signatures...] .... Alt+D
6. Click **Add** button [Add...] .... Alt+A
7. Select certificate to use.
8. Click **OK** .... Enter
9. Click **OK** .... Enter
10. Click **OK** .... Enter

Create Your Own Digital Certificate

1. Locate the file SelfCert.exe using Windows Explorer or My Computer.

   ✓ *The SelfCert.exe file should be located in the Program Files\Microsoft Office\Office 10 folder. If it is not, it may not be installed on your computer. Run Office Setup to install it.*

2. Double-click the **SelfCert.exe** file.
3. Type your name.
4. Click **OK** .... Enter

Exercise Directions

1. Start Word, if necessary.
2. Open the file 11MISSION, or open 67MISSION.
3. Save the new document as VERSIONS.
4. Save a version of the document with the comment: **Version 1: Original Document**.
5. Set document protection so that all changes will be displayed with revision marks.
6. Make the following edits to the document (refer to Illustration A to see the end results):
   - On a new line at the beginning of the document insert the title **Northlake Video Links Mission Statement** in the heading 1 style, centered.
   - Insert a blank line, and then type the text **Customer Satisfaction** using the heading 2 style.
   - Edit the first paragraph to read: **Northlake Video Links is committed to providing quality service to all of our clients at every level of the organization. Our ultimate goal is to hear our clients say "Thank you. That is just what we wanted."**
   - Insert a blank line, and then type the text **Employee Well-Being** using the heading 2 style.
   - Edit the second paragraph the read: **Second only to customer satisfaction is the happiness and well-being of our employees. The employees at Northlake Video are encouraged to set personal and professional goals. We respect all employees as individuals and believe that fostering a strong community within the workplace strengthens our position in the marketplace.**
   - Insert a blank line, and then type the text **Conclusion** using the heading 2 style.
   - Type the following: **At Northlake Video Links we vow to maintain the highest standards, pursue the extraordinary, and guarantee customer satisfaction. We are confident that our commitment to quality will make us leaders in our industry.**
7. Save another version of the document with the comment: **Version 2: Revisions have been made**.
8. Remove document protection.
9. Accept all changes to the document.

   ✓ *See Exercise 66 for information about accepting and rejecting revisions.*
10. Check the spelling and grammar in the document.
11. Save another version of the document with the comment: **Version 3: Revisions have been incorporated**.
12. Preview the document. It should look similar to the one in Illustration A.
13. Save all changes to the document.
14. Create your own digital certificate, using your own name.
15. Attach the digital certificate to the document as a digital signature
16. Close the document, saving all changes.

On Your Own

1. Start Word and create a new document.
2. Save the document as OWDCLUB.
3. Type three or four paragraphs describing group, club, class, or organization to which you belong.
4. Save a version of the document.
5. Protect the document so that only comments can be inserted.
6. Try to edit the document.
7. Insert two or three comments.
8. Save a version of the document
9. Change the document protection so all changes will appear with revision marks.
10. Edit the document some more.
11. Save a third version of the document.
12. Unprotect the document and incorporate the revisions.
13. Attach your digital signature to the document.
14. Close the document, saving all changes.

Illustration A

Northlake Video Links Mission Statement

Customer Satisfaction

Northlake Video Links is committed to providing quality service to all of our clients at every level of the organization. Our ultimate goal is to hear our clients say "Thank you. That is just what we wanted."

Employee Well-Being

Second only to customer satisfaction is the happiness and well-being of our employees. The employees at Northlake Video are encouraged to set personal and professional goals. We respect all employees as individuals and believe that fostering a strong community within the workplace strengthens our position in the marketplace.

Conclusion

At Northlake Video Links we vow to maintain the highest standards, pursue the extraordinary, and guarantee customer satisfaction. We are confident that our commitment to quality will make us leaders in our industry.

Exercise 68

Skills Covered:

◆ **Open Multiple Documents** ◆ **Arrange Documents On-screen**
◆ **Copy/Move Text from One Document to Another**

On the Job

Open multiple documents when you need to work with more than one document at a time. For example, if you are planning a meeting, you may need to work with an agenda and a list of attendees at the same time. You can easily copy or move text from one document to another. You can view one open document at a time, or you can arrange the documents so they are all visible on-screen.

The Director of Training at Highland Properties Management has asked you to write a memo informing all employees about the new Introduction to the Internet class that will be offered in September. In this exercise, you will create the memo, and then open the document that already contains the course description. You will arrange the documents on-screen, and then copy and move text from one document to the other.

Terms

Active document The document in which the insertion point is currently located. Commands and actions occur in the active document.

Tile Arrange windows so they do not overlap on-screen.

Notes

Open Multiple Documents

- You can open multiple Word documents at the same time.
- By default, each open document is represented by a button on the Windows taskbar.
- By default, the **active document** is displayed on-screen, while other open documents are hidden.
- Only one document can be active at a time. You can identify the active document window by the following:
  - The active document window contains the insertion point.
  - The active document window has a brighter or colored title bar than other open document windows.
  - The active document window is represented by the “pressed in” taskbar button.

Arrange Documents On-screen

- You can arrange all open documents on-screen at the same time.
- Word **tiles** up to three open documents horizontally one above the other.
- Additional documents are tiled vertically side by side.
- The more open documents there are, the smaller each document window is on-screen. Therefore, editing with more then two documents arranged on-screen is difficult.

Copy/Move Text from One Open Document to Another

- Use standard Cut, Copy, and Paste commands to copy and/or move text from one open document to another.
- If you can see both documents on-screen, use drag-and-drop-editing to copy/move text from one location to another.

✓ *Moving and copying are covered in Exercises 17 and 18.*

✓ *If you minimize a document before arranging open documents Word will not tile it with the other open documents.*

- Even when multiple documents are displayed on-screen, only one document is active.

Multiple documents tiled on-screen

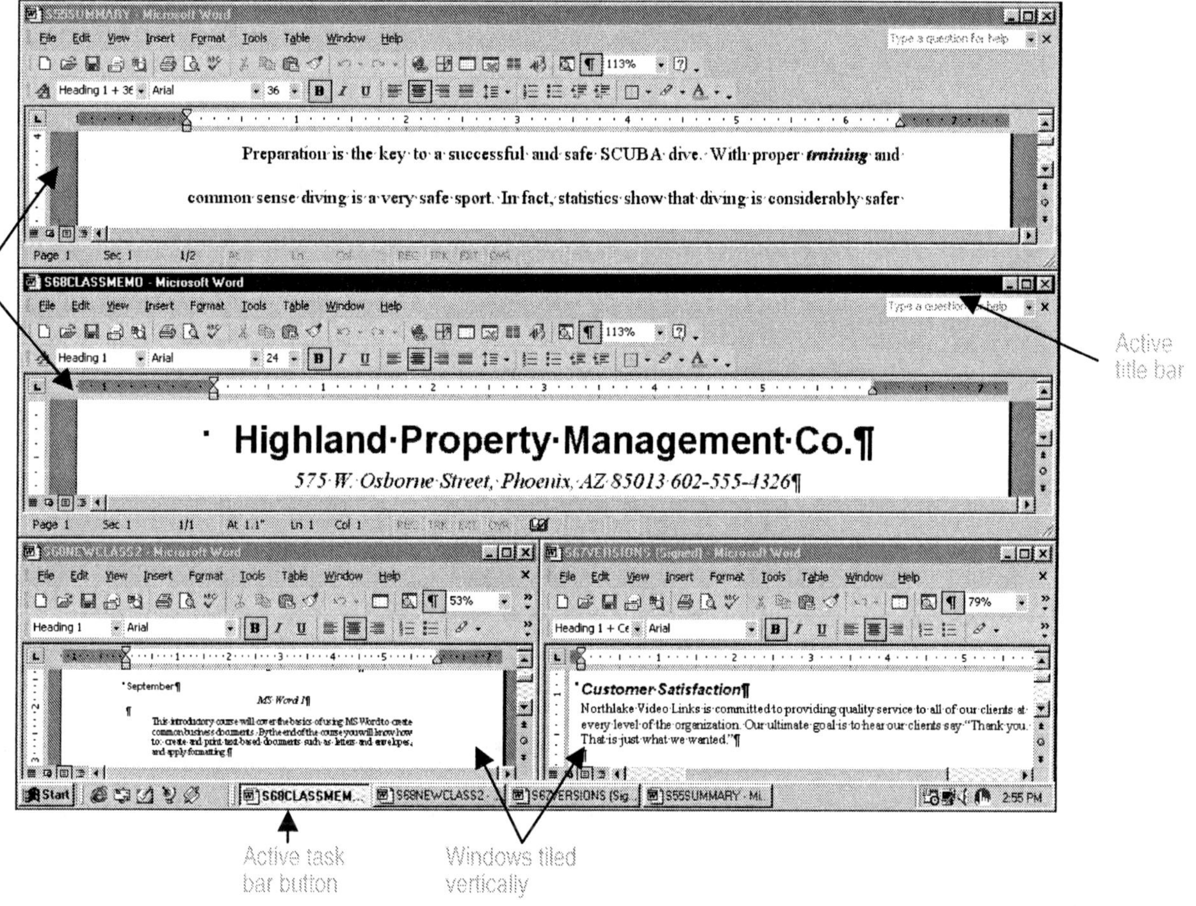

Procedures

Open Multiple Documents (Ctrl+O)

1. Open first document.
2. Open second document.
3. Continue opening documents as desired.

   ✓ *Too many open documents will strain your computer's resources.*

Open multiple documents stored in same folder:

1. Click **File** .... Alt+F
2. Click **Open** .... O
3. Click first file name.
4. Press and hold **Ctrl**.
5. Click additional file names.
6. Click **Open** button 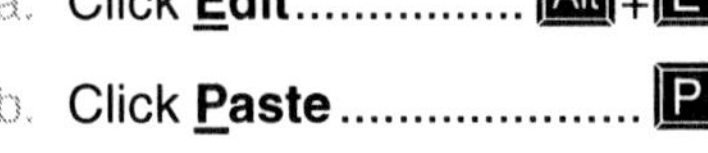 .... Enter

Arrange documents on-screen:

1. Open all documents.
2. Click **Window** .... Alt+W
3. Click **Arrange All** .... A

Display active document only:

- Click active document's **Maximize** button.

Switch among open documents:

- Click in desired document.

OR

- Press Ctrl+F6 until desired document is active.

OR

1. Click **Window**.
2. Click desired document name.

Copy Text from One Document to Another

Use Copy and Paste (Ctrl+C, Ctrl+V):

1. Select the text to copy.
2. Click **Copy** button.

   OR

   a. Click **Edit** .... Alt+E
   b. Click **Copy** C

   OR

   a. Right-click selected text.
   b. Click **Copy** C
3. Display other document and position insertion point in new location.
4. Click **Paste** button.

   OR

   a. Click **Edit** .... Alt+E
   b. Click **Paste** .... P

   OR

   a. Right-click where you wish to paste text.
   b. Click **Paste** .... P

Use drag-and-drop editing:

1. Arrange documents on-screen.
2. Select text to copy.
3. Move mouse pointer anywhere over selected text.
4. Press and hold **Ctrl** .... Ctrl
5. Drag selection to new location.
6. Release mouse button.
7. Release **Ctrl** .... Ctrl

Move Text from One Document to Another (Ctrl+X, Cltr+V)

1. Select text to move.
2. Click **Cut** button.

   OR

   a. Click **Edit** .... Alt+E
   b. Click **Cut** .... T

   OR

   a. Right-click selected text.
   b. Click **Cut** .... T
3. Display other document and position insertion point at new location.
4. Click **Paste** button.

   OR

   a. Click **Edit** .... Alt+E
   b. Click **Paste** .... P

   OR

   a. Right-click where you wish to paste text.
   b. Click **Paste** .... P

Use drag-and-drop editing to move text:

1. Arrange documents on-screen.
2. Select text to move.
3. Move mouse pointer anywhere over selected text.
4. Drag selection to new location.
5. Release mouse button when the insertion point is in new location.

Exercise Directions

1. Start Word, if necessary.
2. Create the document shown in Illustration A, or open 68CLASSMEMO.
3. Save the document as CLASSMEMO.
4. Open NEWCLASS, or open 68NEWCLASS.
5. Save the document as NEWCLASS2.
6. Arrange the documents so both are visible on-screen.
7. Copy the first two lines from the NEWCLASS2 document to the top of the CLASSMEMO document.
8. Move the last ten lines in the NEWCLASS2 document (from the heading **New in September** to the end of the document) to the end of the CLASSMEMO document.
9. Maximize the memo document. It should look similar to Illustration B.
10. Check the spelling and grammar in the document.
11. Print the document.
12. Make the NEWCLASS2 document active and maximize it.
13. Make the CLASSMEMO document active.
14. Close all documents, saving all changes.

On Your Own

1. Open OWDCLUB or open 68OWDCLUB.
2. Save the document as OWDCLUB2.
3. Open OWDREV2 or open 68OWDREV2.
4. Save the document as OWDREV3.
5. Arrange the open documents on-screen.
6. Copy your name and address from the top of the resume to the top of the other document.
7. Move the title of the CLUB2 document to the resume document.
8. Undo the move.
9. Maximize the resume document.
10. Close it, saving all changes.
11. Maximize the club document.
12. Close it, saving all changes.

Illustration A

To:	All Employees
From:	Training Department
Date:	Today's Date
Subject:	New class offering

The Highland Property Management training department is pleased to announce a new course for the fall schedule.

Illustration B

Highland Property Management Co.

575 W. Osborne Street, Phoenix, AZ 85013 602-555-4326

MEMORANDUM

To: All Employees
From: Training Department
Date: Today's Date
Subject: New class offering

The Highland Property Management training department is pleased to announce a new course for the fall schedule.

New in September

Using the Internet

Specially designed for Highland Property Management employees, this course covers the basics of getting around the Internet and World Wide Web without getting lost! You'll learn how to locate the information you need quickly and effectively, and what to do with it once you find it. Sign up now for this new and exciting offering.

For more information call the training department at: 602-555-4326 ext. 343.

Exercise 69

Skills Covered:

- Send E-mail from Word
- Attach a Word Document to an E-mail Message
- Send a Word Document as E-mail
- Copy Data from a Word Document into an E-mail Message

On the Job

E-mail is suitable for jotting quick notes such as an appointment confirmation. You can create and format e-mail messages, then send the messages via Outlook or Outlook Express directly from Word. When you need to communicate in more depth, you can attach a Word document to the message, or simply send a document as the message itself. You can exchange e-mail messages via the Internet or an intranet with anyone who has an e-mail account, including coworkers located down the hall, in a different state, or halfway around the world.

As the assistant to the marketing director at Fox Footwear, you have been compiling a list of employees willing to be judges for an essay contest. In this exercise, you will use e-mail to communicate with the marketing director about the contest. First, you will create and send a brief e-mail message about the list of judges. Then, you will follow up with a second message to which you will attach the list of prospective judges. You will then send a copy of a memo you plan to distribute to the prospective judges.

Terms

E-mail (electronic mail) A method of sending information from one computer to another across the Internet or intranet.

HTML (Hypertext Markup Language) A universal file format used for files displayed on the World Wide Web.

Internet A global network of computers.

Intranet A network of computers within a business or organization.

Mail service provider A company that maintains and controls e-mail accounts.

Outlook A personal information management program that includes e-mail features and that is included in the Microsoft Office XP suite.

Outlook Express An e-mail program that is included as part of the Microsoft Internet Explorer Web browser.

E-mail address The string of characters that identifies the name and location of an e-mail user.

To: Mail notation that indicates to whom an e-mail message is addressed.

Cc: (carbon copy) Mail notation that indicates to whom you are sending a copy of the message.

Subject The title of an e-mail message.

Message window The area in an e-mail message where the message body is typed.

Online Actively connected to the Internet.

Offline Not connected to the Internet.

Attachment A document attached to an e-mail message and sent in its original file format.

Notes

Send E-mail from Word

- You can create and send **e-mail** messages directly from Word.
- You can edit and format the messages with Word's editing and formatting features, including the spelling and grammar checkers, and AutoCorrect.
- Messages created in Word are sent in **.HTML** format so they can be read by almost all e-mail applications.
- To send e-mail messages, you must have the following:
  - A connection to the **Internet** or to an **intranet**.
  - An account with a **mail service provider**.
  - An e-mail program such as **Outlook** or **Outlook Express**.

    ✓ *To exchange e-mail, the e-mail program must be correctly configured with your e-mail account information.*
- To send an e-mail message you must know the recipient's **e-mail address**.
- E-mail messages have the following basic parts:
  - The recipient's address is entered in the **To**: text box.
  - The addresses of other people receiving copies of the message are entered in the **Cc**: text box.
  - A title for the message is entered in the **Subject** text box.
  - The body of the message is typed in the **message window**.
  - Message headers used to send a document as e-mail also have an Introduction text box, in which you can type a message to the recipient.

E-mail created and formatted in Word

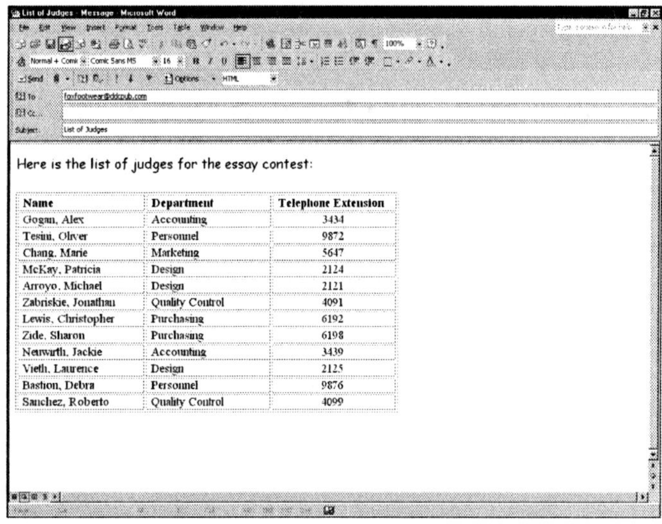

Here is the list of judges for the essay contest:

Name	Department	Telephone Extension
Gogan, Alex	Accounting	3434
Tesini, Oliver	Personnel	9872
Chang, Marie	Marketing	5647
McKay, Patricia	Design	2124
Arroyo, Michael	Design	2121
Zabriskie, Jonathan	Quality Control	4091
Lewis, Christopher	Purchasing	6192
Zide, Sharon	Purchasing	6198
Neuwirth, Jackie	Accounting	3439
Vieth, Laurence	Design	2125
Bastion, Debra	Personnel	9876
Sanchez, Roberto	Quality Control	4099

- By default, when you send the message, Word stores it in the Outbox folder in Outlook. You must start Outlook and sign in to your mail service provider in order to transmit the message.
- The Internet connection remains **online** in the background until you disconnect.

Attach a Word Document to an E-mail Message

- You can attach a Word document to an e-mail message.
- The original document remains stored on your computer, and a copy is transmitted as the **attachment**.
- An attached message is sent in its original file format.
- The message recipient can open the attached Word document on his or her computer in Word, or in another application that is compatible with Word.

Send a Word Document as E-mail

- You can send an existing Word document as an e-mail message without attaching it to another message.
- Word adds an Introduction text box to the message header when you send a Word document as e-mail. This text box gives you more room to enter information about the document.
- The original document remains stored on your computer, and a copy is transmitted as e-mail.
- The transmitted document is sent in HTML format so the recipient can open it in Outlook, Outlook Express, or in most other e-mail programs.

A Word document ready for transmission

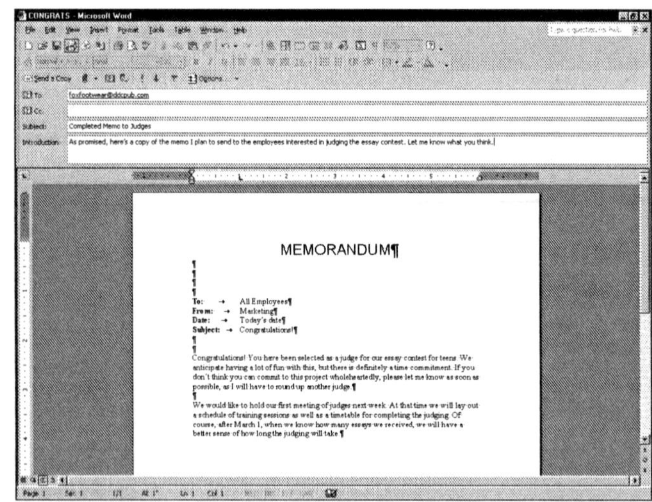

Copy Data From a Word Document into an E-mail Message

- If you don't want to send or attach an entire document, you can paste a selection from the document into the e-mail message.
- Use the Copy and Paste commands to copy the data from the Word document and paste it into the e-mail message.

Procedures

Create E-mail Message in Word

1. Click **New E-Mail Message** button.
   - ✓ *Use a ScreenTip to identify the button; it looks a lot like the E-mail button used to send a document as e-mail.*

   OR

   a. Click **File** .... Alt+F
   b. Click **New** .... N
   c. Click **Blank E-mail Message** icon in task pane.
2. Fill in **To:** information .... *type recipient's address*
3. Press **Tab** .... Tab
4. Fill in **Cc:** information .... *type additional recipients' addresses*
5. Press **Tab** .... Tab
6. Fill in **Subject** information...... *type subject title*
7. Press **Tab** .... Tab
8. Type and format message text.
9. Click **Send** button Send .... Alt+S
   - ✓ *If you change your mind about sending the message, simply click the **New E-Mail Message** button again. Word removes the message heading.*

Attach Word Document to an E-mail Message

1. Compose an e-mail message.
2. Click **Insert File** button.
3. Select file to attach.
   - ✓ *Select disk or folder from Look in drop-down list, then double-click folder name to locate file.*
4. Click **Insert** .... Alt+S
   - ✓ *Word adds a new text box to the message heading called Attach: and enters the document name.*
5. Click **Send** button  .... Alt+S

OR

1. Open or create the document to attach.
2. Click **File** .... Alt+F
3. Highlight **Send To** .... D
4. Click **Mail Recipient (as Attachment)** .... A
5. Compose e-mail message.
   - ✓ *By default, Word enters the document name in the Attach text box.*
6. Click **Send** button 

Send a Word Document as E-mail

1. Open or create document to send.
2. Click **E-mail** button.

   OR

   a. Click **File** .... Alt+F
   b. Select **Send To** .... D
   c. Click **Mail Recipient** .... M
3. Fill in **To**: information .... *type recipient's address*
4. Press **Tab** .... Tab
5. Fill in **Cc**: information .... *type additional recipients' addresses*
6. Press **Tab** .... Tab
7. Fill in Subject information .... *type subject title*

   ✓ *By default, Word enters the document name in the Subject text box. You can edit it if necessary.*
8. Press **Tab** .... Tab
9. Fill in Introduction information type introductory text.
10. Click **Send a Copy** button

    .... Alt+S

    ✓ *If you change your mind about sending the document as e-mail, simply click the* ***E-Mail*** *button again. Word removes the message heading and displays the document.*

Copy Data from a Word Document into an E-mail Message

1. Compose an e-mail message.
2. Open Word document containing data to copy.
3. Select data to copy.
4. Click **Copy** button.

   OR

   a. Click **Edit** .... Alt+E
   b. Click **Copy** C

   OR

   a. Right-click selected text.
   b. Click **Copy** C
5. Display e-mail message and position insertion point in new location.
6. Click **Paste** button .

   OR

   a. Click **Edit** .... Alt+E
   b. Click **Paste** .... P

   OR

   a. Right-click where you wish to insert text.
   b. Click **Paste** .... P

Send E-mail from Outlook

1. Click **Start** button ....
2. Click **Programs** .... P
3. Select **Microsoft Outlook**.

   ✓ *Alternatively, you may use a shortcut icon to start Outlook from the desktop or taskbar. For more information about starting applications, refer to Exercise 90.*

   ✓ *Outlook may automatically connect to your mail service provider and download new messages. Enter account name and password if prompted.*
4. Click **Send/Receive** button

   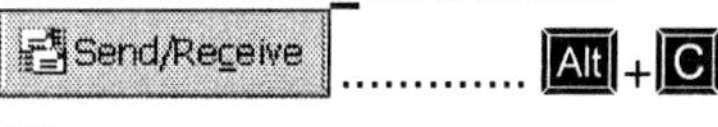
   .... Alt+C

   OR

   a. Click **Tools** .... Alt+T
   b. Select **Send/Receive** .... E
   c. Click **Send All** .... S

   ✓ *If not already online, Outlook will automatically connect to your mail service provider and send all messages. If prompted, enter your account name and password.*

Send E-mail from Outlook Express *(Ctrl+M)*

1. Click **Start** button

   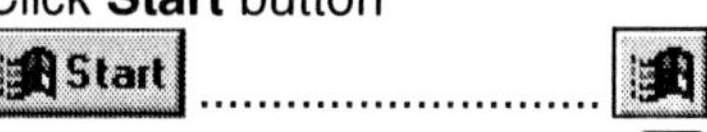
2. Click **Programs** .... P
3. Select **Outlook Express**.

   ✓ *Outlook Express may automatically connect to your mail service provider and download new messages. Enter account name and password if prompted.*
4. Click **Send and Receive** button .

   OR

   a. Click **Tools** .... Alt+T
   b. Highlight **Send and Receive** .... Alt+S
   c. Click **Send All** .... Alt+S

   ✓ *If not already online, Outlook Express will automatically connect to your mail service provider and download all messages. If prompted, enter your account name and password.*

Disconnect Outlook from Internet

1. Click **File** .... Alt+F
2. Click **Work Offline** .... K
3. Click **Yes** .... Y

Disconnect Outlook Express from Internet

1. Click **File** .... Alt+F
2. Click **Work Offline** .... W
3. Click **Yes** .... Y

Exercise Directions

✓ *If you do not have access to the Internet, you may still complete the steps in this exercise. However, when you try to send the e-mail, you will receive an error message.*

1. Start Word, if necessary.
2. Create a new blank e-mail message and compose it as follows:
   a. Enter the address: **foxfootwear@ddcpub.com**
   b. Enter the subject: **Essay Judges**
   c. Enter the message: **I just want to let you know I have just about completed the list of employees interested in judging the essay contest. As soon as I type it up, I'll send it to you. Thanks.**
3. Check the spelling and grammar in the message.
4. Send the message.
   - Enter your user name and password if prompted.
5. Open the document 69JUDGES.
6. Save the document as JUDGES and close it.
7. Open the document 69CONGRATS.
8. Save the document as CONGRATS and leave it open.
9. Create a new blank e-mail message and compose it as follows:
   a. Enter the address: **Foxfootwear@ddcpub.com**
      ✓ *Don't be surprised if Word automatically completes the address as you type it!*
   b. Enter the subject: **List of Judges**
   c. Using 14-point Arial, type the message: **I've attached the list of potential judges. Let me know if there's anyone you think we should omit. I'm working on a memo to the judges to let them know what they're in for. I'll send you a copy when it's complete. So far I've got the following:**
10. Press Enter, then copy the paragraph from the document CONGRATS and paste it on the last line of the e-mail message.
11. Attach the document JUDGES to the e-mail message. The message should look similar to the one in Illustration A.
12. Check the spelling and grammar in the message.
13. Send the message.
14. Insert the following paragraph at the end of the CONGRATS document:
    We would like to hold our first meeting of judges next week. At that time we will lay out a schedule of training sessions as well as a timetable for completing the judging. Of course, after March 1, when we know how many essays we received, we will have a better sense of how long the judging will take.
15. Check the spelling and grammar in the document.
16. Save the CONGRATS document.
17. Prepare to send the CONGRATS document as e-mail by entering the following message heading information:
    a. Enter the address: **foxfootwear@ddcpub.com**
    b. Edit the subject to: **Completed Memo to Judges**
    c. Enter the introduction: **As promised, here's a copy of the memo I plan to send to the employees interested in judging the essay contest. Let me know what you think.**
18. The message should look similar to the one in Illustration B.
19. Send the document.
20. Use Outlook or Outlook Express to send the messages.
21. Disconnect from the Internet.
22. Close all open documents, saving all changes.

Illustration A

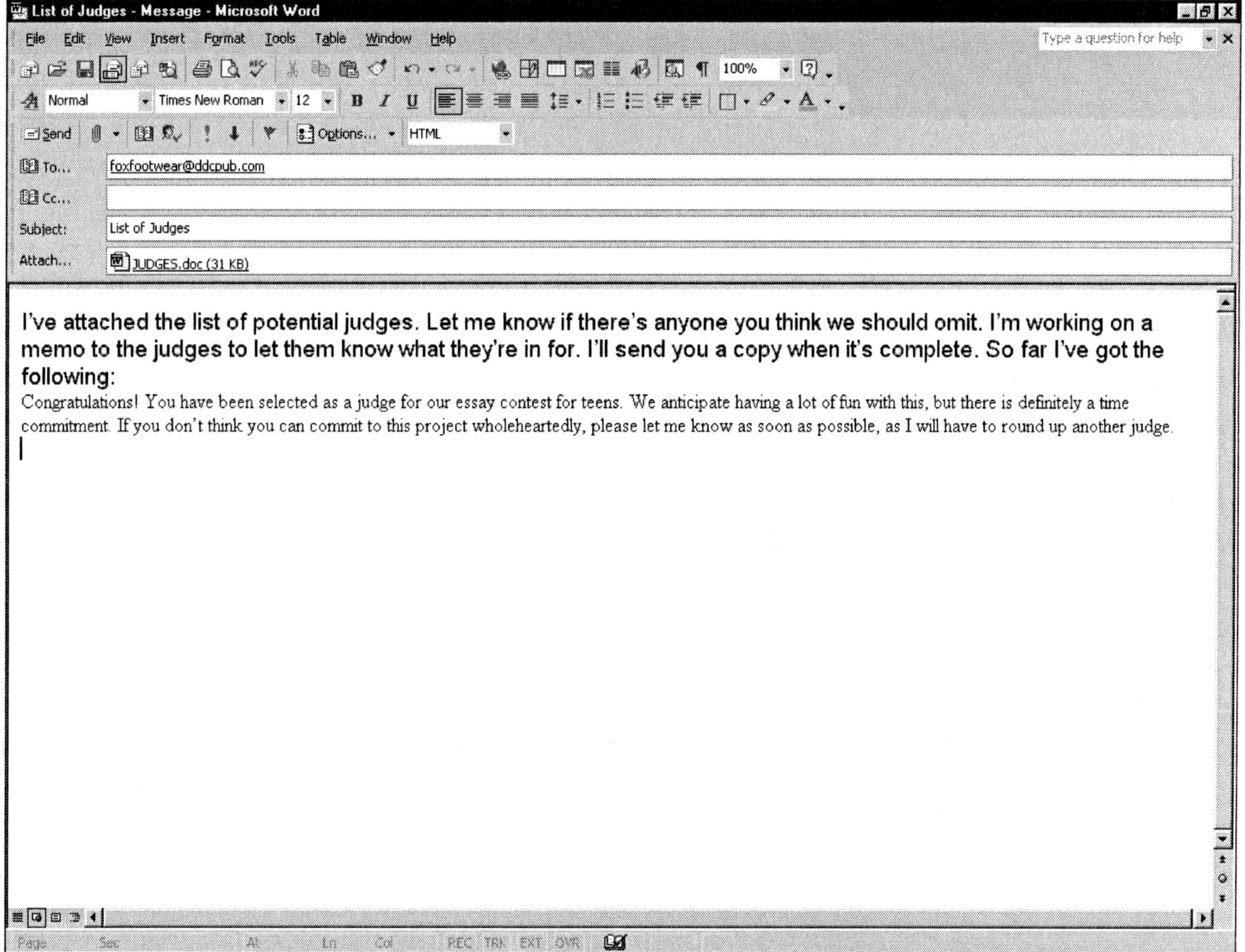

Illustration B

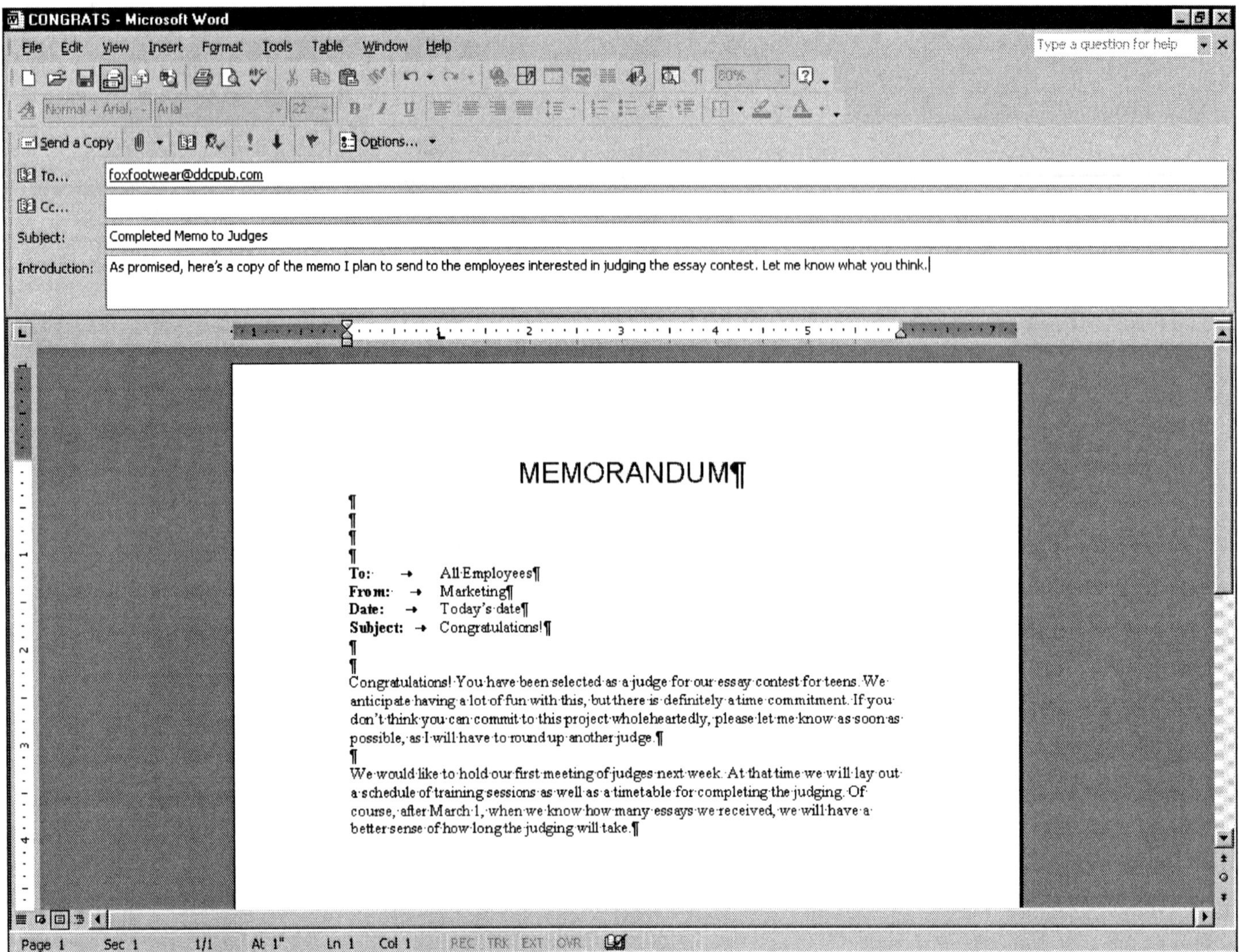

On Your Own

1. Find out and record e-mail addresses for friends, coworkers, and companies with which you do business. You can find e-mail addresses by asking around, looking on business cards or stationery, or by using the Internet to search for addresses.
2. Send an e-mail message to a friend or co-worker.
3. Create a new document and type a letter to someone else whose e-mail address you have. For example, type a letter to your boss thanking him or her for a promotion, a raise, or for time off, or type a letter to a friend or relative inviting him or her to an event.
4. Save the document as OWDEMAIL.
5. Close the document.
6. Attach the document to an e-mail message and send it.

Exercise 70

Skills Covered:

◆ **Receive E-mail Messages in Outlook or Outlook Express**
◆ **Print an E-mail Message** ◆ **Save an E-mail Attachment**

On the Job

To receive e-mail, you use an e-mail application such as Outlook or Outlook Express. You can print an e-mail message using your e-mail application, and save documents attached to e-mail messages to open in Word.

In this exercise, you will send an e-mail message to the director of training at Highland Property Management asking if there has been any interest in the new Introduction to the Internet class being offered in September.

Terms

Download Retrieve information from the Internet and store it locally on your computer.

Inbox A folder in Outlook and Outlook Express where new e-mail messages are received.

Notes

Receive E-mail Messages in Outlook or Outlook Express

- To receive electronic mail (e-mail) messages with Microsoft Outlook or Outlook Express you must have a connection to the Internet or to an intranet and an account with a mail service provider.
  - ✓ *To exchange e-mail, Outlook or Outlook Express must be correctly configured with your e-mail account information.*
- When you connect to the Internet, the e-mail application **downloads** new messages into a folder called **Inbox**.
- You can read the downloaded messages immediately, while still online, or after you disconnect and are working offline.
- Messages remain in the Inbox folder until you move them or delete them.
  - ✓ *You can use the File, Save As command to save e-mail messages in HTML or text format to open in Word.*

Print an E-mail Message

- You can use Outlook or Outlook Express to print any e-mail message.
- Your computer must be connected to a printer, and the printer must be on and loaded with paper in order to print an e-mail message.

Save an E-mail Attachment

- Documents attached to e-mail messages in Outlook or Outlook Express have a paper clip icon next to them in the Inbox.
- You can save a document attached to an e-mail message so you can open it in another application later.
- An attachment is saved in its original file format. For example, a Word document attached to an e-mail message is saved in Word document format.

- The attachment is saved with its original file name. You select the disk and/or folder where you want to store the file.

✓ *E-mail is often used to spread computer viruses, so you should use care when downloading and opening e-mail attachments. Make sure you know and trust the sender. If you are unsure, delete the message and attachment before opening, or leave it in the Inbox folder until you can verify that it does not contain a virus.*

Procedures

Receive E-mail Messages in Outlook (*F9*)

1. Click **Start** button Start .... Start
2. Click **Programs** .... P
3. Select **Microsoft Outlook**.
   - ✓ *Alternatively, you may use a shortcut icon to start Outlook from the desktop or taskbar. For more information about starting applications, refer to Exercise 90.*
   - ✓ *Outlook may automatically connect to your mail service provider and download new messages. Enter account name and password if prompted.*
4. Click **Send/Receive** button Send/Receive .. Alt+C

   OR

   a. Click **Tools** .... Alt+T
   b. Select **Send/Receive** ..... E
   c. Click **Send and Receive All** .... A

   - ✓ *If not already online, Outlook will automatically connect to your mail service provider and download all messages. If prompted, enter your account name and password.*
   - ✓ *You may read messages online, or disconnect from the Internet to read messages offline.*
5. Click **Inbox** folder in Folder list.......... Ctrl+Shift+I
6. Click message to open and read.
   - ✓ *To open the message in its own window, double-click it.*

Receive E-mail Messages in Outlook Express (*Ctrl+M*)

1. Click **Start** button Start .... Start
2. Click **Programs** .... P
3. Select **Outlook Express**.
   - ✓ *Outlook Express may automatically connect to your mail service provider and download new messages. Enter account name and password if prompted.*
4. Click **Send and Receive** button Send/Recv.

   OR

   a. Click **Tools** .... Alt+T
   b. Highlight **Send and Receive** .... Alt+S
   c. Click **Send and Receive All** .... Alt+A

   - ✓ *If not already online, Outlook Express will automatically connect to your mail service provider and download all messages. If prompted, enter your account name and password.*
   - ✓ *You may read messages online, or disconnect from Internet to read messages offline.*
5. Click **Inbox** folder .... Ctrl+Y, I, Enter
6. Click message to read.
   - ✓ *To open the message in its own window, double-click it.*

Disconnect Outlook from Internet

1. Click **File** .... Alt+F
2. Click **Work Offline** .... K
3. Click **Yes** .... Y

Disconnect Outlook Express from Internet

1. Click **File** .... Alt+F
2. Click **Work Offline** .... W
3. Click **Yes** .... Y

Print an E-mail Message (*Ctrl + P*)

1. Select message.
2. Click **File** .... Alt+F
3. Click **Print** .... P
4. Click **OK** .... Enter

Save an E-mail Attachment in Outlook

1. Select message.
2. Click **File** .... F
3. Select **Save Attachments** ... N
4. Click file name to save.
5. Select storage location (disk and/or folder) in **Save Attachment** dialog box.
6. Click **Save** button Save .... Alt+S

Save an E-mail Attachment in Outlook Express

1. Select message.
2. Click **File** .... F
3. Click **Save Attachments** V
4. Click **Browse** button Browse... .... Alt+B
5. Select storage folder
6. Click **OK** .... Enter
7. Click **Save** .... Alt+S

Exercise Directions

✓ *If you do not have access to the Internet, you may still complete the steps in this exercise. However, when you try to send the e-mail, you will receive an error message.*

1. Start Word, if necessary.
2. Compose an e-mail message as follows:
   a. Enter the address: **highlandproperty70@ddcpub.com**
   b. Enter the subject: **Intro to Net Enrollment**
   c. Enter the message: **Hi. I am assigning classroom space for the fall training classes and would like to know how much interest there is in the Intro to the Internet course. Do you have an enrollment list that you could send me? Reply by e-mail as soon as possible. Thanks.**
3. Check the spelling and grammar in the message.
4. Send the message.

   ✓ *For information on composing and sending e-mail messages, see Exercise 69.*
5. Launch or switch to your e-mail program (either Outlook or Outlook Express).
6. Send all messages.
7. Download new messages.

   ✓ *The ddcpub.com site is set to automatically return messages to you.*
8. Disconnect from the Internet if necessary
9. Find the response to your e-mail in the list of downloaded e-mail.
10. Read the response.
11. Exit your e-mail program.
12. Close the document, saving all changes.

On Your Own

1. Use Word to compose an e-mail message to someone and ask him or her to send you an e-mail message with a Word document attached to it. If you don't know anyone who can do this, send one to yourself.
2. Download the new message and save the attachment.
3. Open the attachment in Word.
4. When you are finished, close the document, saving all changes, and exit Word.

Exercise 71

Skills Covered:

◆ **Merge to an E-Mail Message**

On the Job

Use Word's mail merge feature to create and distribute customized e-mail message to a group of recipients. You can merge a message or send the merged document as an attachment.

You want to increase the enrollment in the new Introduction to the Internet class. In this exercise, you will send a message to the students who have taken other training classes to see if you can interest them in the new class.

Terms

There is no new vocabulary in this exercise.

Notes

Merge to an E-Mail Message

- You can use Word's Mail Merge Wizard to generate customized e-mail messages to send to a group of recipients.
- To create the merge, you select E-mail messages as the document type in step 1 of the wizard; the remaining steps are basically the same as for merging a form letter, directory, envelopes, or labels.

  ✓ *For a refresher on using Mail Merge, refer to the exercises in Lesson 8.*
- You type the standard text that will be the same in every message into a document, and then insert merge fields or merge blocks to customize the message.
- You can use an existing document as the message, or you can create a new document.
- You can use an existing data source file such as an Office Address List or an Outlook Contacts list, or you can create a new data source file.
- The data source file must include the e-mail address information for each recipient.
- When you complete the merge, Word generates the customized messages, and sends them to your e-mail program's Outbox.
- You can sign in to send the messages at any time.

  ✓ *Refer to Exercise 69 for information on sending e-mail.*

The merged messages in the Outlook Outbox

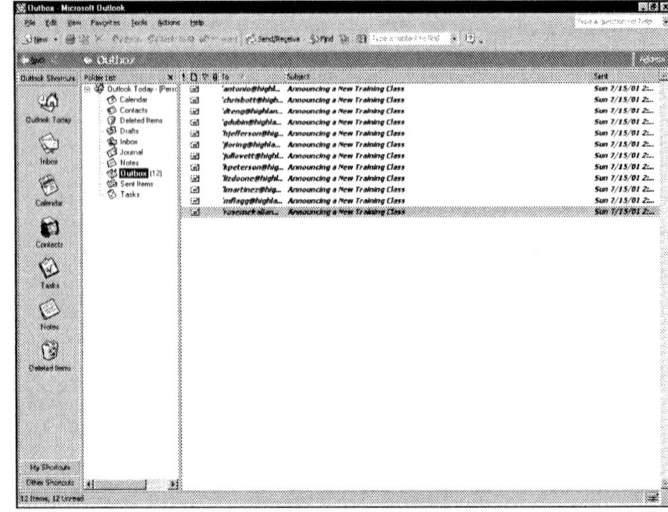

Procedures

Use the Mail Merge Wizard to Generate Customized E-mail Messages using an Existing Address List Data Source File

Select the main document:

1. Open message document.
   ✓ *This document may be blank, or it may already contain text that you want to send.*
2. Click **Tools**.................. Alt+T
3. Select **Letters and Mailings**.............................. E
4. Click **Mail Merge Wizard**..... M
5. Click the **E-mail messages** option button.
6. Click **Next: Starting document**.
7. Click the **Use the current document** option button.
8. Click **Next: Select recipients**.

Select an existing Address List data source file:

1. Click the **Use an existing list** option button.
2. Click **Browse** .
   ✓ *Word opens the Select Data Source dialog box.*
3. Locate and select the desired data source file.
4. Click **Open** button  .... Alt+O
5. Word displays the Mail Merge Recipients dialog box.
   ✓ *Word displays the Mail Merge Recipients dialog box. By default, all recipients are selected. For information on selecting specific recipients, refer to Exercise 48.*
6. Click **OK**.................. Tab, Enter
7. Click **Next: Write your e-mail message.**
   ✓ *Word displays the starting document and a list of available merge blocks.*

Create the message document:

1. Type the message, including all text and formatting as you want it to appear on each merge document.
   ✓ *If you are using an existing document, skip step 1.*
2. Insert merge blocks and/or merge fields at the appropriate locations.
3. Continue typing and formatting the message, repeating steps to insert merge fields or merge blocks at desired location(s).
4. Save the document.
5. Click **Next: Preview your e-mail messages.**
   ✓ *Word displays the first merge document.*

Preview merge documents:

1. Click the **Next recipient** button >> in the Mail Merge Wizard task pane.

   OR

   Click the **Next recipient** button on the Mail Merge toolbar.

   OR

   Click the **Previous recipient** button << in the Mail Merge Wizard task pane.

   OR

   Click the **Previous recipient** button on the Mail Merge toolbar.
2. Click **Next: Complete the merge.**

Complete the merge:

1. Click **Electronic Mail** Electronic Mail... .
   ✓ *Word displays the Merge to E-Mail dialog box.*
2. Verify that the name of the field containing e-mail addresses is entered in the **To** box ..... Alt+O, ↕, Enter
3. Click the **Subject line** box........................ Alt+S
4. Enter the subject information......................... *type*
5. Click the **Mail format** box.............................. Alt+M
6. Select desired format type......................... ↕, Enter
   - **Attachment**
   - **Plain text**
   - **HTML (default)**
7. Specify records to send.
8. Click **OK** .... Enter to complete the merge.
   ✓ *Word sends the messages to your e-mail program's outbox. Start the program and send the messages as required. Refer to Exercise 69 for information on sending e-mail.*

Exercise Directions

- ✓ *In this exercise you will use NAMES, the Office Address List file you created in Exercise 49, or the file 71NAMES. Prior to starting the exercise copy either file and save the copy as NAMES2.*
- ✓ *To copy the file, right-click the file name and select Copy. Right-click the destination folder and select Paste. Right-click the copied file name and select Rename. Type the new file name and press Enter.*

1. Start Word, if necessary.
2. Create a new blank document.
3. Save the document as MESSAGE.
4. Start the Mail Merge Wizard.
5. Select to create e-mail messages, using the current document.
6. Select to use an existing address list file as a data source document.
7. Locate and open the NAMES2 data source file.
8. Close the Mail Merge Recipients dialog box.
9. Type the message shown in Illustration A, inserting the GreetingLine merge block and the Course merge field as indicated.
10. Check the spelling and grammar in the document.
11. Preview the merged documents.
12. Complete the merge by generating all of the e-mail messages in HTML format, including the following subject line: **Announcing a New Training Class**.
13. Start your e-mail program to see if the messages are in the Outbox.
    - ✓ *The e-mail addresses are fictitious and will not work. If you try sending the messages you will receive an undeliverable message for each one.*
14. Exit your e-mail program.
15. Close all open files, saving all changes.

On Your Own

1. Find out the e-mail addresses of at least three people.
2. Create a new document in Word.
3. Save it as OWDEMERGE.
4. Use the Mail Merge Wizard to create e-mail messages.
5. Create a new data source file that includes the names and e-mail addresses. Alternatively, modify an existing data source file to include an e-mail address field.
6. Save the data source file as OWDEADDRESS.
7. Type a message, customizing it with the information in the data source file. For example, insert each person's name.
8. Generate the messages in HTML format, including a subject line appropriate to the message.
9. If you have an Internet connection, send the messages.
10. Close all open documents, saving all changes.

Illustration A

Merge field

««GreetingLine»» ← Merge block

As the assistant to the director of training here at Highland Property Management, I hope that you enjoyed the «Course» class that you took last spring. I would like to take this opportunity to invite you to join a new class that we are offering in September: Introduction to the Internet. It promises to be very exciting and informative. We are planning to limit the class size, so please let me know as soon as possible if you are interested.

Sincerely,

Your Name ← Replace with your own name

Exercise 72

◆ Critical Thinking

The designers of the Web site for Fox Footwear, Inc. have been asking for the copy they need to put on the Customer Satisfaction page. In this exercise, you will open the original document and save a version. You will protect it and send it as an attachment to a message asking for input from the legal department and the marketing department. You will open their revised copies and reject or accept the changes. You will compare the revised copies to the original, saving versions of each one. Finally, you will attach a digital signature to the final copy and send it as e-mail to the Web site designers.

Exercise Directions

1. Start Word, if necessary.
2. Open the document 72PROMISE and save it as PROMISE.
3. Insert the following comment at the word **Promise** in the title: **Is it OK to use the word promise?**
4. Save a version of the document with the comment: **Original sent to legal and marketing for input.**
5. Compose a new e-mail message as follows:
   a. Enter the address: **Foxfootwearlegal@ddcpub.com**
   b. Copy the message to: **Foxfootwearmktg@ddcpub.com**
   c. Enter the subject: **Request input**
   d. Using 14-point Arial, type the message: **I've attached a document with the text I think should go on the customer satisfaction page of the Web site. Please make changes to the document and send it back to me as soon as possible. Thanks.**
6. Attach the document PROMISE to the e-mail message. The message should look similar to the one in Illustration A.
7. Check the spelling and grammar in the message.
8. Send the message.
9. Open the document 72LEGAL and save it as LEGAL. This is a version of the document that has tracked changes.
10. Unprotect the document.
11. Accept and reject changes as follows:
    a. Delete both comments.
    b. Accept the changes in the first paragraph.
    c. Reject the changes to the first sentence of the third paragraph, but accept the remaining changes to that paragraph.
    d. Accept all remaining changes.
12. Save the document.
13. Compare the LEGAL document to the PROMISE document, merging the changes into the PROMISE document.
14. Save the changes to the PROMISE document and then save a version with the comment: **Track changes made by legal department**.
15. Open the document 72MKTG and save it as MKTG. This is another version of the document that has tracked changes.
16. Unprotect the document.
17. Accept and reject changes as follows:
    a. Delete both comments.
    b. Reject the changes in the first paragraph.
    c. Accept all remaining changes.
18. Save the document.

19. Compare the MKTG document to the PROMISE document, merging the changes into the PROMISE document.
20. Save the changes to the PROMISE document and then save a version with the comment: **Track changes made by marketing department**.
21. Arrange all three documents on-screen at the same time.
22. Save and close the MKTG and LEGAL documents.
23. Maximize the PROMISE document.
24. Delete the comment.
25. Accept all other changes.
26. Change the font size of the word **sales** in the last paragraph to 10 points.
27. Check the spelling and grammar in the document.
28. Preview the document. It should look similar to the one in Illustration B.
29. Print the document.
30. Attach your digital signature to the document.
31. Send the document as e-mail using the following message heading:
    a. Enter the address: **Foxfootwearwebdesign@ddcpub.com**
    b. Enter the subject: Customer Satisfaction Copy
    c. Enter the Introduction: **Here's the copy for the Customer Satisfaction page. Thanks.**
32. Send the document.
33. Close the document, saving all changes, and exit all open programs.

Illustration A

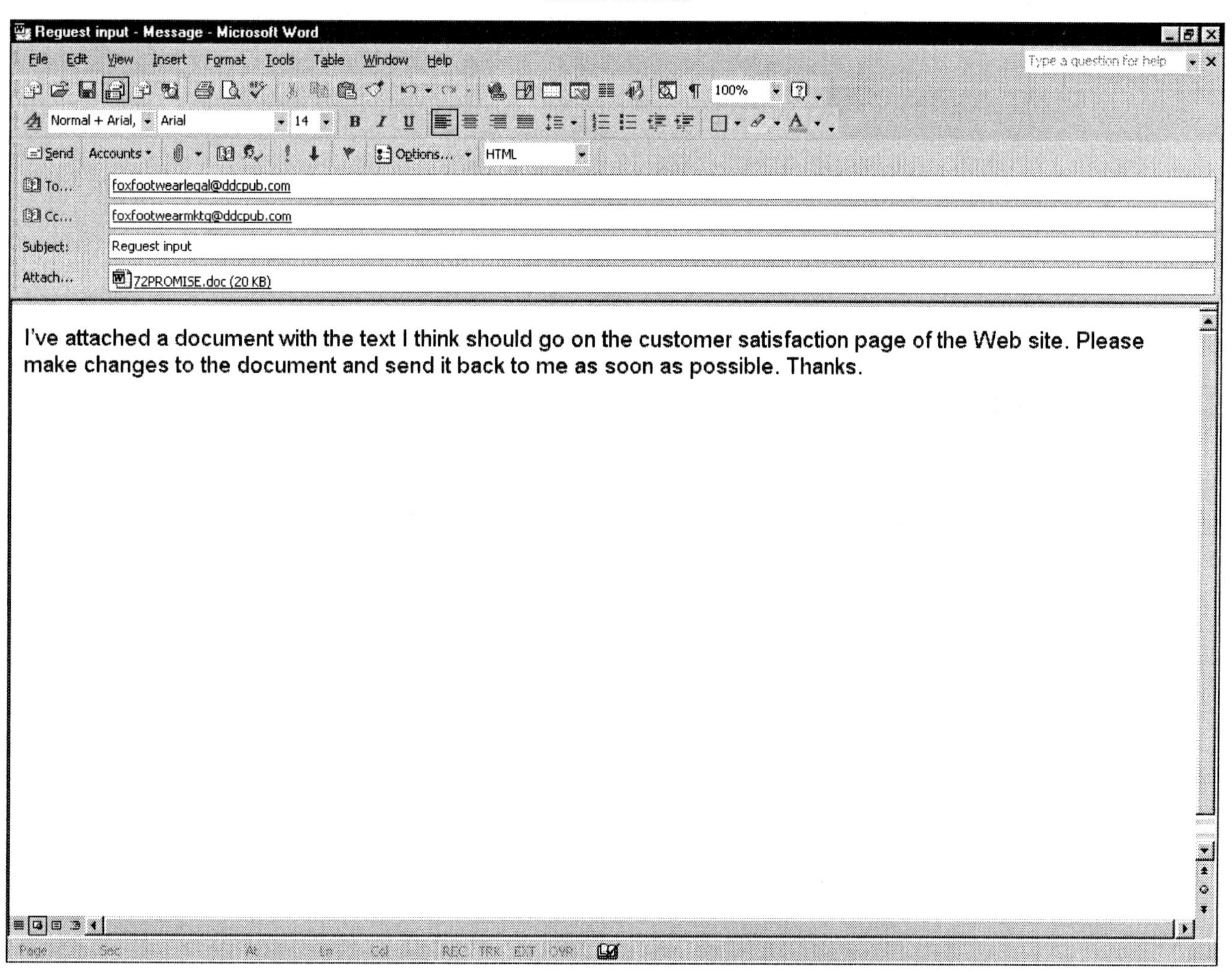

Illustration B

A Promise to Our Online Customers

Fox Footwear Online takes customer satisfaction seriously. If you are not completely satisfied, we promise to exchange the merchandise or refund your purchase price along with shipping and handling charges.

We promise to supply shoes that fit!
If the pair of shoes you receive does not fit you like a glove, we will exchange it for a pair that does.

We promise to supply shoes that compliment your appearance!
If you are not satisfied with the style or color of your shoes, we will exchange them for a pair that suits you better.

We promise to provide shoes that work as hard as you do!
If the shoes do not perform the way you expect, we will exchange them for a pair that does. For example, if you order running shoes that are heavier than expected, or if you order walking shoes that do not supply adequate support, we will exchange them.

We promise to provide shoes that last!
If the shoes do not hold up well under normal use, we will exchange them for a pair that does. Normal use is defined as everyday wear and tear according to the manufacturer's recommendation. Shoes used for purposes other than intended cannot be guaranteed.

To obtain a full refund, customer must return footwear in like-new condition within 30 days, accompanied by a copy of the original sales receipt. Exchanges due to manufacturing errors may be made at the discretion of Fox Footwear Online management.

Lesson 12

Desktop Publishing and Automation

Exercise 73
- Create Newsletter Columns
- Set Column Width
- Insert Column Breaks
- Balance Columns

Exercise 74
- Use Dropped Capitals
- Enhance a Document with Borders and Shading

Exercise 75
- Templates
- Wizards
- Save a Document as a Template
- Set Default File Location for Workgroup Templates

Exercise 76
- Insert a File in a Document
- Use AutoText

Exercise 77
- Record a Macro
- Run a Macro

Exercise 78
- Create a Form
- Insert Form Fields
- Set Form Field Options
- Fill Out a Form

Exercise 79
- Critical Thinking

Exercise 73

Skills Covered:

◆ **Create Newsletter Columns** ◆ **Set Column Width**
◆ **Insert Column Breaks** ◆ **Balance Columns**

On the Job

Designing a document with columns lets you present more information on a page, as well as create a visually interesting page. Newsletter-style columns are useful for creating documents such as newsletters, pamphlets, articles, or brochures.

Pete Newell, the owner of Pelican Peter's Dive Shop, wants to send a newsletter to customers. In this exercise, you will create a newsletter to send to people who have signed a store register.

Terms

Newsletter-style columns Columns in which text flows from the bottom of one column to the top of the next column.

Gutter The space between column margins.

Notes

Create Newsletter Columns

- By default, a Word document has one column, the width of the page from the left margin to the right margin.
- Use Word's Columns feature to divide a document into more than one **newsletter-style column**.
  - ✓ *Use tables to create side-by-side columns; use the Columns feature to create newsletter-style columns; use tabs to align data along a single line in a document.*
- You can apply column formatting to existing text or you can set column formatting before typing new text.
- You can apply column formatting to an entire document or to the current section.
- By dividing a document into sections using section breaks, you can combine different numbers of columns within a single document.
- For example, you can create a headline banner across the top of the page using one column, then insert a continuous section break and divide the remainder of the page into two or more columns.
- Multiple columns are not displayed in Normal view. Switch to Print Layout view or Print Preview to see the column formatting in a document.

Newsletter columns

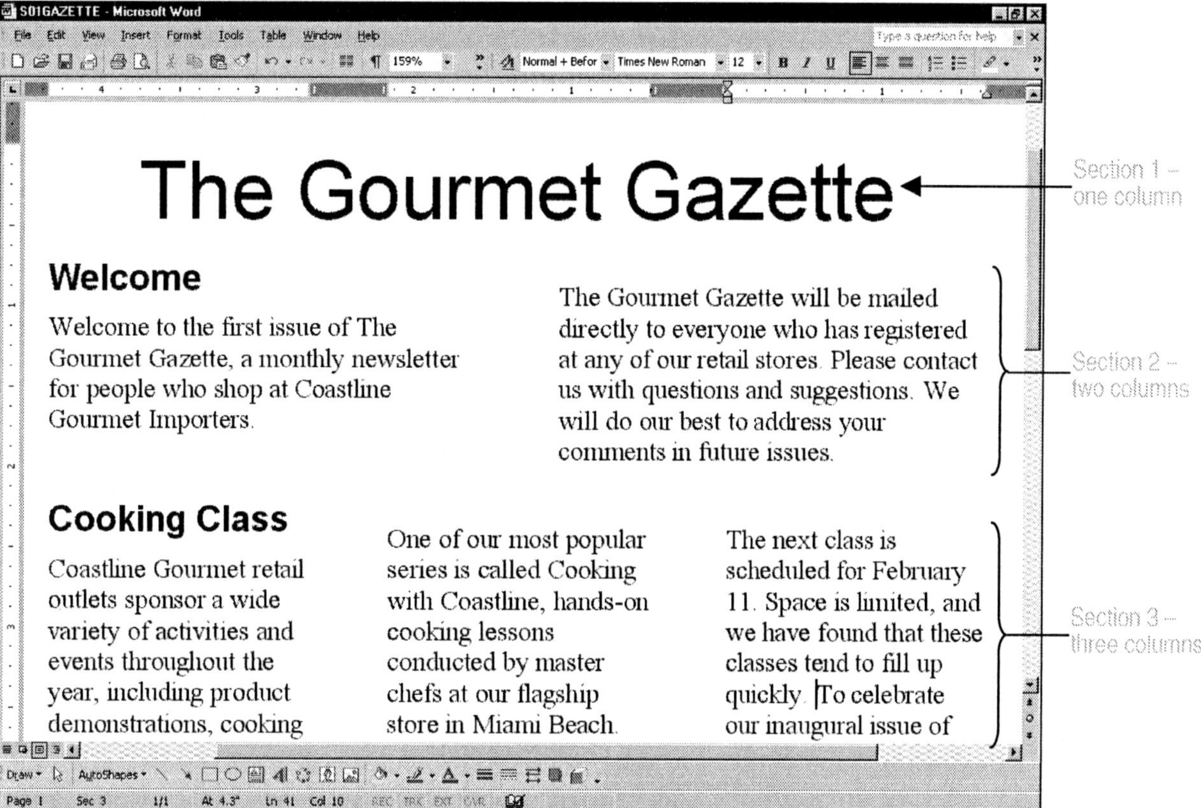

Set Column Width

- By default, Word creates columns of equal width.
- You can change the width of any column. Select from Word's five preset column width arrangements or set precise column widths.
- You can also use the Columns dialog box, or drag the column margins, to adjust the amount of space in the **gutter** between columns.

Columns dialog box

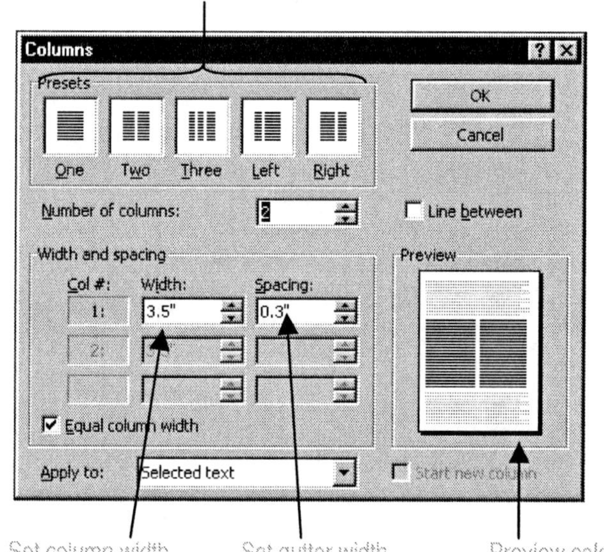

Drag column margins to adjust gutter

Mouse pointer

Dotted line shows new margin

Insert Column Breaks

- By default, text flows to the top of the next column when the current column is filled.
- Use a column break to force text to flow to the top of the next column before the current column is filled.
- Column breaks are useful for moving headings or headlines to the top of a column.

Balance Columns

- If there is not enough text to fill the last column in a document, the columns will appear uneven.

Unbalanced columns

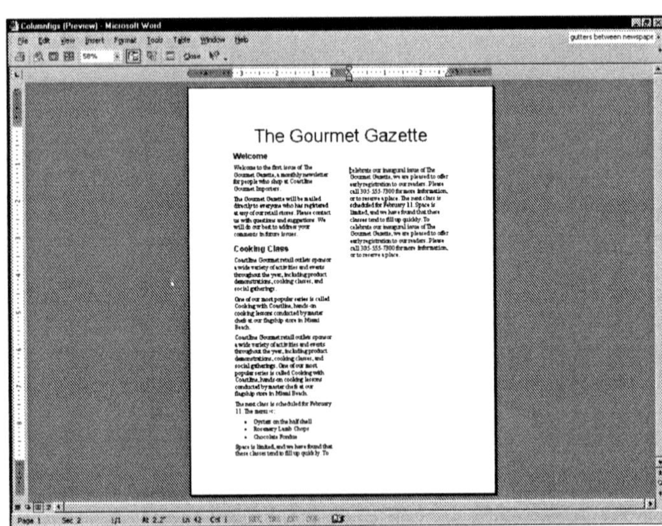

- You can balance the amount of text in multiple columns on a page by using a continuous section break.

Balanced columns

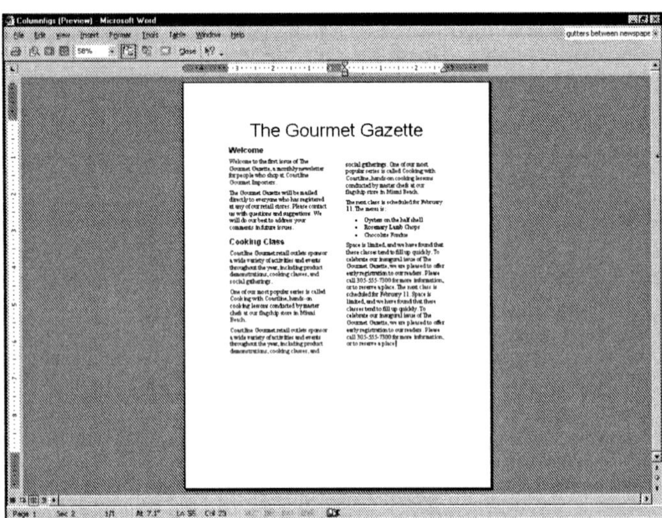

Procedures

Create Columns of Equal Width

1. Click the **Columns** button.
2. Drag across the number of columns to create.
3. Release mouse button.

OR

1. Click **Format** .... Alt+O
2. Click **Columns** C
3. Click **Number of columns** .... Alt+N
4. Type the number of columns to create.
5. Click **OK** .... Enter

Select a Preset Column Format

1. Click **Format** .... Alt+O
2. Click **Columns** C
3. Click the desired Preset option:
   - **One** .... Alt+O
   - **Two** .... Alt+W
   - **Three** .... Alt+T
   - **Left** .... Alt+L
   - **Right** .... Alt+R
4. Click **OK** .... Enter

Return to One Column Formatting

1. Click the **Columns** button.
2. Drag across one column only.
3. Release mouse button.

OR

1. Click **Format** .... Alt+O
2. Click **Columns** C
3. Click **One** .... Alt+O

   OR

   a. Click **Number of columns** .... Alt+N
   b. Type **1** 1
   c. Click **OK** .... Enter

Create Columns of Any Width

1. Click **Format** .... Alt+O
2. Click **Columns** C
3. Click **Number of columns** .... Alt+N
4. Type the number of columns to create.
5. For column 1, do the following:
   a. Type column **Width** .... Alt+I in inches.
   b. Type gutter **Spacing** .... Alt+S in inches.
6. Clear **Equal column width** check box.......... Alt+E
7. Repeat step 5 for additional columns.
8. Click **OK** .... Enter

Adjust Gutter Spacing

1. Position mouse pointer on column margin marker.
   ✓ *When positioned correctly, the ScreenTip shows either Left Margin or Right Margin.*
2. Drag left or right.

Insert Column Break

1. Position insertion point where you want the break.
2. Click **Insert** .... Alt+I
3. Click **Break** .... B
4. Click **Column break** C
5. Click **OK** .... Enter

Balance Columns

1. Position insertion point at end of last column.
2. Click **Insert** .... Alt+I
3. Click **Break** .... B
4. Click **Continuous** .... T
5. Click **OK** .... Enter

Exercise Directions

1. Start Word, if necessary.
2. Open 73THEBILL.
3. Save the file as THEBILL.
4. Format the document as follows:
   a. Center the title in 36-point sans serif.
   b. Center the company name and address (lines 2 and 3) in 12-point sans serif.
   c. Leave 12 points of space after address.
   d. Format the three headlines (**Welcome, Tour with The Pelican,** and **Recipe Showcase**) using the Heading 1 style
   e. Format all occurrences of **The Pelican's Bill** in the body of the newsletter in italics.
   f. Insert 6 points of space before and 6 points of space after all body text paragraphs in the first two articles.
   g. Format the recipe title and serving information (**Oyster Fritters** and **Yield: Six Servings**) with the Heading 2 style.
   h. Insert a right tab stop on that line to align the serving information at the 5" mark on the horizontal ruler.
   i. Apply the Heading 3 style to the text **Ingredients** and **Directions**.
   j. Format the directions as a numbered list.
5. Format the entire document into three columns of equal width.
6. Preview the document.
7. Return to one column formatting.
8. Insert a continuous section break before the headline **Welcome**.
   ✓ *There are now two sections in the document.*
9. Format the second section (from the headline **Welcome** to the end of the document) into two columns of equal width.
10. Preview the document.
11. Insert another continuous section break before the headline **Recipe Showcase**.
    ✓ *There are now three sections in the document.*
12. Insert another continuous section break before the heading **Ingredients**.
    ✓ *There are now four sections in the document.*
13. Apply one column formatting to the third section (the section containing the headline **Recipe Showcase**).
14. Format the fourth section (from the heading **Ingredients** to the end of the document) using the Left preset column arrangement.
15. Decrease the gutter spacing between the columns in the second section and the fourth section to .25".
16. Preview the document.
17. Insert a column break before the headline **Tour with the Pelican**.
    ✓ *This moves the headline to the top of the second column.*

18. Preview the document. It should look similar to the one in Illustration A.
19. Check the spelling and grammar in the document.
20. Print the document.
21. Close the document, saving all changes.

Illustration A

The Pelican's Bill

Published by Pelican Peter's Dive Shop
2200 Gulfshore Boulevard North ← Naples, FL 34102

Welcome

Welcome to the first issue of *The Pelican's Bill*, a monthly newsletter for people who shop at Pelican Peter's Dive Shop. The primary goal of this publication is to provide you with news and information about activities and events that you might find of interest. In addition, we plan to publish dive trip itineraries, class schedules, tips, product reviews, and even recipes that we think you will enjoy.

The Pelican's Bill will be mailed directly to everyone who has registered at any of our retail stores. Please contact us with questions and suggestions. We will do our best to address your comments in future issues.

Tour with the Pelican

Pelican Peter's sponsors a wide variety of activities and events throughout the year, including SCUBA certification classes, fishing and diving excursions, and kayak tours. In cooperation with the National Parks Service, we are pleased to announce that we are now booking day-long tours of the Everglades. These Everglades Adventures include a small boat trip through the mangrove islands, an air boat tour of the freshwater swamps, and a walking tour along established boardwalks.

The first tour is scheduled for March 11. Space is limited, and we have found that these tours tend to fill up quickly. To celebrate our inaugural issue of *The Pelican's Bill*, we are pleased to offer early registration to our readers. Please call 941-555-0780 for more information, or to reserve a place.

Recipe Showcase

Oyster Fritters

Yield: Six Servings

Ingredients

1 lb. oysters
1 teaspoon vinegar
1 egg
3 tablespoons flour
½ tablespoon salt
½ teaspoon baking powder
7 cups oil

Directions

1. Soak oysters in shell for a minimum of two hours, changing water as necessary.
2. Heat oil in deep fryer to 365 degrees.
3. Shell and rinse oysters.
4. Drain oysters, and add vinegar.
5. Beat in the egg, flour, salt, and baking powder.
6. Place rounded spoonfuls into fryer basket.
7. Cook for 3 – 4 minutes or until light golden brown.

On Your Own

1. Start Word and create a new document.
2. Save the document as OWDNEWS.
3. Create a newsletter about yourself.
4. Set the newsletter up so it has a one-column title at the top.
5. Divide the rest of the document into either two or three columns, and include two or three articles about things happening in your life. For example, write an article about classes you are taking, jobs you have, trips you have taken or are going to take, or movies or T.V. shows you have watched recently.
6. Try adjusting the widths of the columns.
7. Try changing the number of columns.
8. Insert column breaks as necessary.
9. Balance the columns if necessary.
10. Check the spelling and grammar in the document.
11. Print the document.
12. Close the document, saving all changes

Exercise 74

Skills Covered:

◆ **Use Dropped Capitals**

◆ **Enhance a Document with Borders and Shading**

On the Job

Dropped capital letters, borders, and shading can call attention to a single word, a line, a paragraph, or an entire page. They make a document visually appealing and interesting to the reader, so the reader will be more likely to take the time to read and remember the text.

Wayland Home Health Care Associates has asked you to create a one-page flyer to distribute to its patients. You'll use newsletter-style columns for the flyer, and you will enhance the document with dropped capitals, borders, and shading.

Terms

Dropped capital An enlarged capital letter that drops below the first line of body text in the paragraph.

Border A line placed on one or more sides of a paragraph(s), page, or text box.

Shading A color or pattern applied to a paragraph(s), page, or text box.

3D A perspective added to a border to give the appearance of three dimensions.

Shadow An effect designed to give the appearance of a shadow behind a border.

Notes

Use Dropped Capitals

- **Dropped capital** letters, called *drop caps,* are used to call attention to opening paragraphs.
- Drop caps can be placed in the margin to the left of the paragraph, or within the paragraph.
- Drop caps can be in the same font as the surrounding text or in a different font.
- Selecting a different, more decorative font can enhance the drop-cap effect.
  - ✓ *In Normal view, drop caps will not appear exactly as they will in a printed document. Use Print Layout view or Print Preview to display the drop cap correctly.*

Drop Cap dialog box

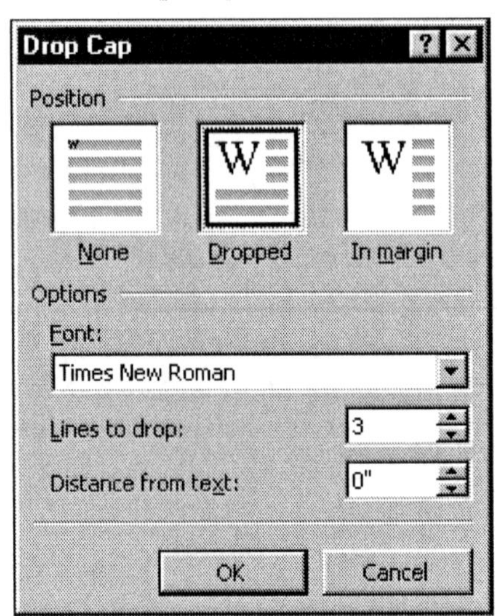

Enhance a Document with Borders and Shading

- You can apply **borders** and/or **shading** to a paragraph, selected paragraphs, or an entire page.
- Basic border and shading options are similar to those for tables, including line style, line weight (width), and line color.
- Additional border options include **3D** or **Shadow** effects.
- You can apply page borders to the whole document or to specified section(s).
- In addition to using basic border options, Word has a built-in list of artwork designed for page borders. Art borders are useful for stationery, invitations, and other informal, decorative documents.
- You can apply paragraph and page borders and shading using the Borders and Shading dialog box; you can also apply paragraph borders and shading using the Tables and Borders toolbar.
  - ✓ *Using the Tables and Borders toolbar is covered in Exercise 40.*

Borders and Shading dialog box: Borders tab

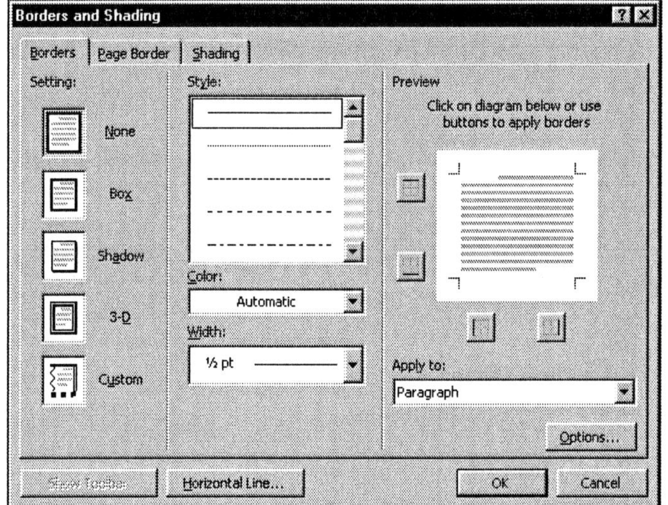

Borders and Shading dialog box: Page Border tab

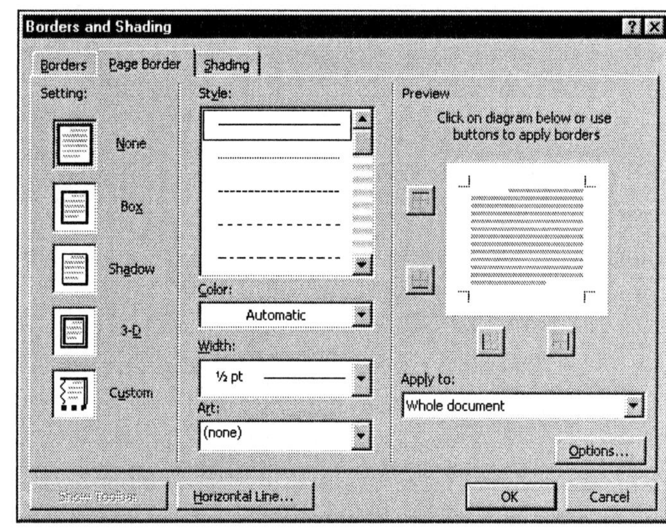

Borders and Shading dialog box: Shading tab

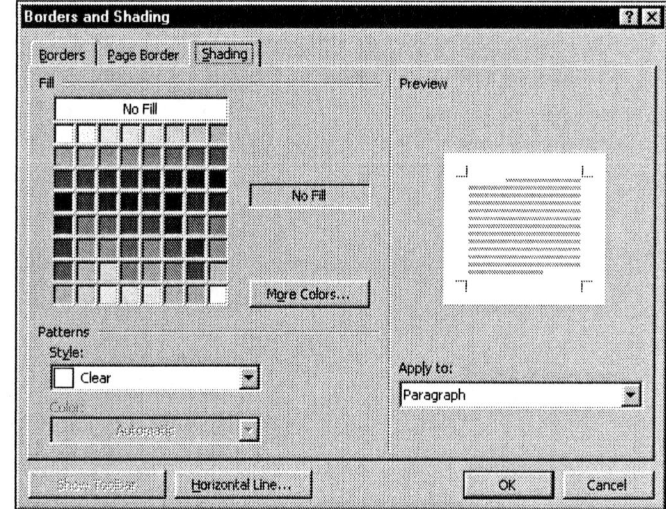

Procedures

Dropped Capital

1. Position insertion point in the paragraph.
2. Click **Format** .... Alt+O
3. Click **Drop Cap** .... D
4. Select one of the following:
   - **Dropped** .... Alt+D
   - **In margin** ...... Alt+M

   ✓ *Click None to remove an existing drop cap.*
5. If desired, do the following:
   a. Click the **Font** drop-down arrow .... Alt+F
   b. Select font to apply.
   c. Click **Lines to drop** .... Alt+L
   d. Type the number of lines to drop capital letter.

      ✓ *The default is three.*
   e. Click **Distance from text** .... Alt+X
   f. Type the distance from text to position dropped capital (in inches).

      ✓ *The default is zero.*
6. Click **OK** .... Enter

Paragraph Borders

1. Position insertion point in the paragraph.

   OR

   Select paragraphs.
2. Click **Format** .... Alt+O
3. Click **Borders and Shading** .... B
4. Click the **Borders** tab.......... B
5. Click a Setting option:
   - **Box** .... Alt+X

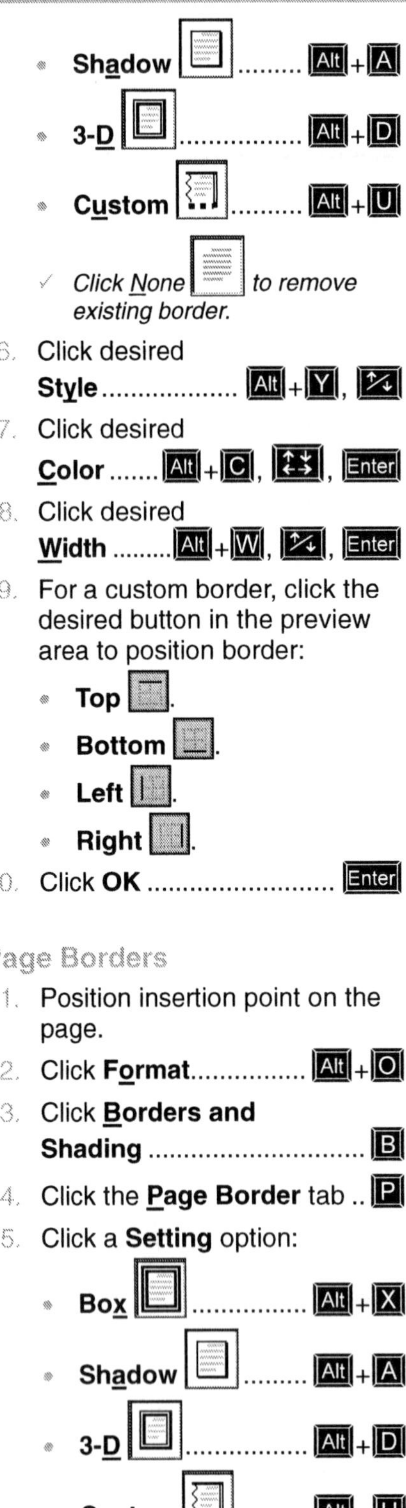

   - **Shadow** .... Alt+A
   - **3-D** .... Alt+D
   - **Custom** .... Alt+U

   ✓ *Click None to remove existing border.*
6. Click desired **Style** .... Alt+Y, ↕
7. Click desired **Color** .... Alt+C, ↕, Enter
8. Click desired **Width** .... Alt+W, ↕, Enter
9. For a custom border, click the desired button in the preview area to position border:
   - **Top**.
   - **Bottom**.
   - **Left**.
   - **Right**.
10. Click **OK** .... Enter

Page Borders

1. Position insertion point on the page.
2. Click **Format**............... Alt+O
3. Click **Borders and Shading** .... B
4. Click the **Page Border** tab .. P
5. Click a **Setting** option:
   - **Box** .... Alt+X
   - **Shadow** .... Alt+A
   - **3-D** .... Alt+D
   - **Custom** .... Alt+U

   ✓ *Click None to remove existing border.*

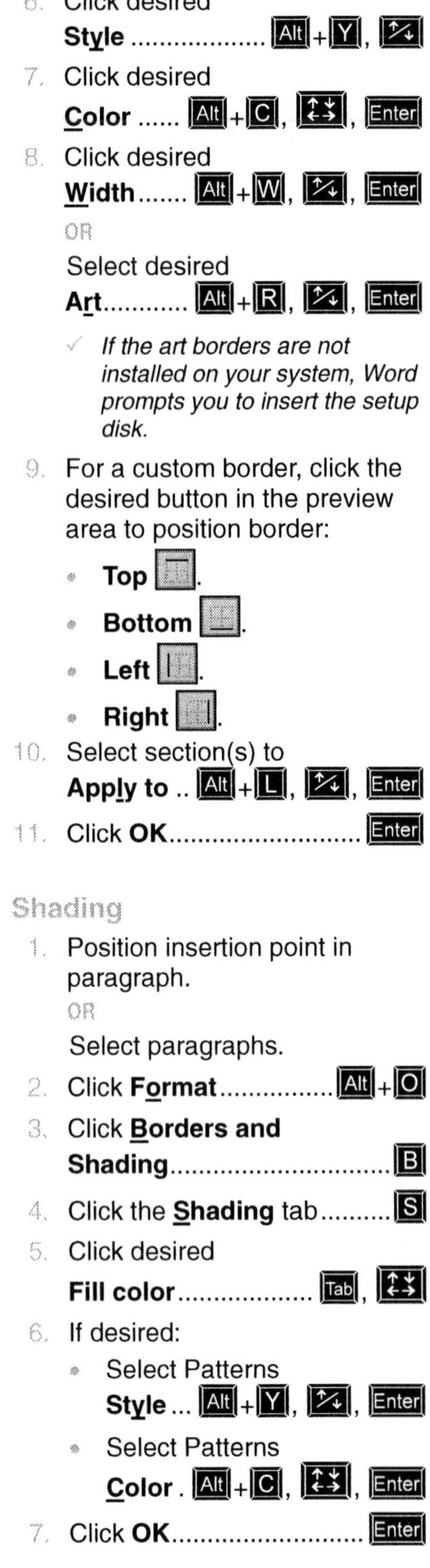

6. Click desired **Style** .... Alt+Y, ↕
7. Click desired **Color** ...... Alt+C, ↕, Enter
8. Click desired **Width**....... Alt+W, ↕, Enter

   OR

   Select desired **Art**............ Alt+R, ↕, Enter

   ✓ *If the art borders are not installed on your system, Word prompts you to insert the setup disk.*
9. For a custom border, click the desired button in the preview area to position border:
   - **Top**.
   - **Bottom**.
   - **Left**.
   - **Right**.
10. Select section(s) to **Apply to** .. Alt+L, ↕, Enter
11. Click **OK**.......................... Enter

Shading

1. Position insertion point in paragraph.

   OR

   Select paragraphs.
2. Click **Format**............... Alt+O
3. Click **Borders and Shading**.............................. B
4. Click the **Shading** tab.......... S
5. Click desired **Fill color** .... Tab, ↕
6. If desired:
   - Select Patterns **Style** ... Alt+Y, ↕, Enter
   - Select Patterns **Color** . Alt+C, ↕, Enter
7. Click **OK**.......................... Enter

Exercise Directions

1. Start Word, if necessary.
2. Open 74HEALTH.
3. Save the file as HEALTH.
4. Apply a 28-point sans serif font to line 1 (the company name).
   ✓ *This wraps the text on to two lines.*
5. Apply a 20-point sans serif font to line 3 (the address).
6. Apply formatting to leave 6 points of space after line 3.
7. On line 4, set a right tab stop flush with the right page margin (6" on the horizontal ruler). This will right-align the date, **Fall/Winter**, while leaving the text **Patient News** flush left.
8. Apply formatting to leave 12 points of space after line 4.
9. Apply the Heading 1 style to the headlines: **Caregiver's Symposium, New Associate, Expanded Office Hours,** and **Report Available**.
10. Modify the formatting of the headlines **Caregiver's Symposium** and **Report Available** so that there is no space left before.
11. Leave 6 points of space before and after all body text paragraphs.
12. Insert a continuous section break before the headline **Caregiver's Symposium**.
13. Format section 2 into three newsletter-style columns, of equal width, with .25" of gutter space between columns.
14. Insert a column break before the headline **New Associate**.
15. Apply the default dropped capital formatting to the first character under the headlines **Caregiver's Symposium, New Associate,** and **Report Available**.
16. Select the headline **Expanded Office Hours** and the paragraph following it, and apply a 1½ point solid line shadow border and a 12.5% gray shading.
17. Justify the text in the paragraph.
18. In the third article (**Report Available**), italicize every occurrence of the report title **Nutrition for the Elderly**.
19. Apply bullet list formatting to the sections listed as being included in the report (if necessary, change the paragraph formatting so there is no space before or after the bulleted items).
20. Select the bulleted list and apply a ½ point solid line outside border.
21. Display the Tables and Borders toolbar.
22. Apply the borders shown in Illustration A along the top and bottom of line 4.
    a. Select the top line style (unequal double-line with the thinner line on the bottom).
    b. Select the line weight (3 points).
    c. Select Top Border from the Border drop-down palette.
    d. Select the bottom line style (unequal double-line with the thinner line on the top).
    e. Select the line weight (3 points).
    f. Select Bottom Border from the Border drop-down palette.
23. Apply a 10% gray shading to line 4, as shown in Illustration A.
24. Apply the Stars page border (select the border from the Art drop-down list) to the entire document.
25. Check the spelling and grammar.
26. Display the document in Print Preview. It should look similar to the one in Illustration A.
27. Print the document.
28. Close the document, saving all changes.

Illustration A

WAYLAND HOME HEALTH CARE ASSOCIATES, INC.

954 St. Charles Street, St. Louis, MO 63101

Patient News — Fall/Winter

Caregiver's Symposium

On Sunday, February 14, our very own Dr. Finn Broderbund will be the featured speaker at the St. Louis Home Health Caregiver's Breakfast Symposium.

The symposium is held every year on St. Valentine's Day. It is sponsored by a consortium of home health care providers and is intended to foster awareness of the special issues faced by professional and nonprofessional caregiver's throughout the community. This year, Dr. Broderbund will speak about the types of support and training available to nonprofessional caregivers.

Tickets are still available. If you are interested in attending, call the office as soon as possible.

New Associate

Wayland Home Health Care is pleased to welcome Ms. Cynthia Ramirez, R.N.

Expanded Office Hours

As of January 1, the telephone switchboard at Wayland Home Health Care will be open until 10:30 p.m. Monday through Friday. At other times, the answering service will handle all calls.

Ms. Ramirez received her nursing degree from Framingham State College in 1991. She has extensive experience working with geriatric patients, and she specializes in rehabilitation therapy. She is fluent in English, Spanish, and Portuguese.

We know that Ms. Ramirez will be an excellent addition to our staff. Please call the office for more information.

Report Available

The associates at Wayland Home Health Care have been hard at work researching and writing *Nutrition for the Elderly*, a four-page report that we hope offers useful information.

The report takes a straight forward approach to providing information in regards to managing the nutritional needs of our senior citizens.

Nutrition for the Elderly includes the following sections:

- A Nutritional Overview
- Diet Counts
- Risk Factors
- Identifying the Elderly at Risk
- Foods to Avoid
- Solutions

The report is now available. Call the office for more information or to request a copy.

On Your Own

1. Open OWDNEWS, the newsletter document you created in the On Your Own section of Exercise 73, or open 74OWDNEWS.
2. Save the file as OWDNEWS2.
3. Apply dropped capitals to the first paragraph of each article.
4. Use borders to call attention to paragraphs. Try different effects, including different line styles, shadows, and 3-D. You might want to insert a border between the single column section and the multicolumn section.
5. Apply a page border.
6. If necessary, adjust column breaks and balance columns to improve the appearance of the newsletter.
7. Check the spelling and grammar in the document.
8. Preview the document.
9. Print the document.
10. Close the document, saving all changes.

Exercise 75

Skills Covered:

◆ **Templates** ◆ **Wizards** ◆ **Save a Document as a Template**
◆ **Set Default File Location for Workgroup Templates**

On the Job

Templates and wizards help you create similar documents efficiently—and time after time. Templates include page setup and formatting settings to insure that new documents will be uniform. In many cases they include standard text and graphics as well. Wizards are automated templates that prompt you to provide information that can be used to customize the resulting document. Because workgroups often share templates for creating documents, you can store the templates in a location that everyone can access easily.

As a representative at Optical General, Inc. you are planning a business trip to a new client. In this exercise, you will use save a document as a template, and then use it to create a memo telling the client when you will arrive. You will then use a Wizard to create a fax cover sheet, which you could use when transmitting the memo to the client.

Terms

Template A Word document on which new documents are based. Templates include formatting settings, text, and graphics used to create the new documents.

.dot extension The file extension assigned by Word to template files.

Normal.dot The default template used to create new documents in Word.

Wizard An automated template.

Workgroup A group of individuals who work together on the same projects, usually connected via a network.

Notes

Templates

- All new Word documents are based on a **template**.
- Templates include formatting settings such as margins, font, and font size.
- Some templates include boilerplate text and graphics that are part of new documents.

Memo template

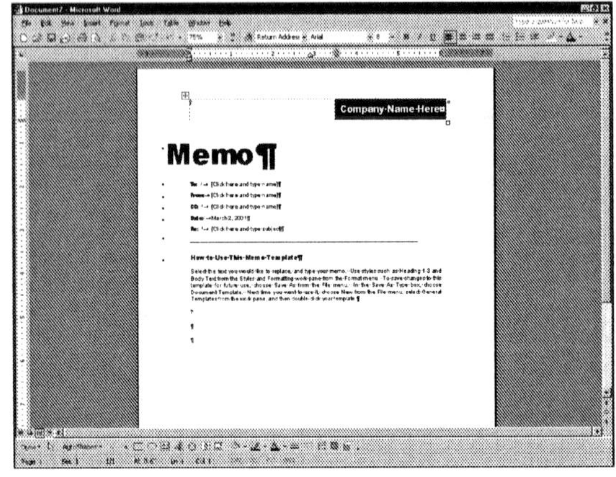

- All new documents based on the same template will have the same default formatting settings and will display any boilerplate text and graphics.
- Some templates include editing directions and sample or placeholder text for completing the document. You replace sample text, fill in missing information, and customize the document using standard editing and formatting commands.
- Word comes with built-in templates for creating common documents such as memos, letters, Web pages, and resumes.
- Built-in templates are usually available in several styles, which means different formatting settings for different situations. For example, a letter in the Professional template may be suitable for business correspondence, while the Elegant, template may be more suitable for personal correspondence.
- Document templates are stored in the Templates folder on your computer system; if they are not stored in the Templates folder they may not be available to use to create new documents.

  ✓ *Not all templates are installed by default.*
- You can preview built-in templates in the Templates dialog box.
- Recently used templates are listed in the New Documents task pane.
- Template files have a **.dot extension**. The default template for creating a blank document is called **Normal.dot**.

Templates dialog box

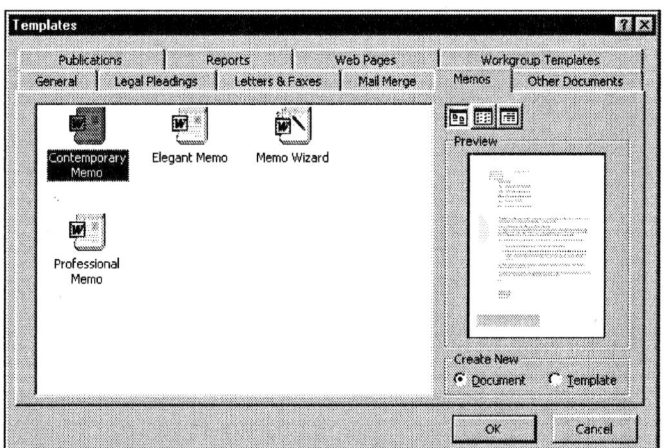

Wizards

- You can use **Wizards** to create customized new documents.
- Wizards prompt you through a series of dialog boxes to enter information that can be incorporated into the document.

  ✓ *The flowchart in the first dialog box indicates how many dialog boxes there are.*

Memo Wizard

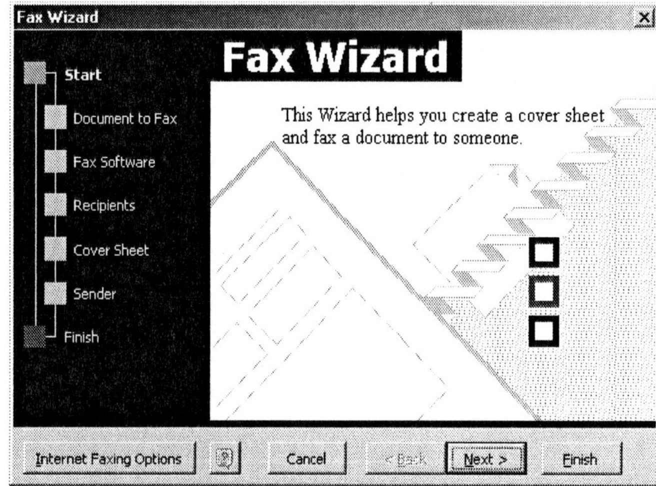

- For example, a memo Wizard might prompt you for the recipient's name and the memo subject. When Word creates the document, the recipient's name and the memo subject will be entered automatically.
- You can customize documents created with a Wizard using standard editing and formatting commands.
- Wizards are listed along with templates in the Templates dialog box; recently used Wizards are listed in the New Documents task pane.

Save a Document as a Template

- You can create your own templates that include boilerplate text as well as formatting settings.
- For example, you can create a template that includes a business letterhead, a specific font, margins, and paragraph spacing. By default, every document you create based on your template will have the same text and formatting.
- To create your own templates, simply save a document using the template file type.
- As soon as you select the Document Template file type in the Save As dialog box, Word switches to the Templates folder.

- You can create a new folder within the Templates folder to store your templates. The new folder name will be listed on a tab in the Templates dialog box, and your templates will be displayed on that tab. If you do not create a new folder, the templates will be displayed on the General tab.

Set Default File Location for Workgroup Templates

- Members of a **workgroup** are often expected to use the same templates to create new documents.
- Documents created with the same template will be consistent in layout and design.
- You can use Word to specify a folder where workgroup file templates are stored.
- The specified folder name will be displayed on a tab in the Templates dialog box, and templates stored in the folder will be listed on that tab. This makes it easy for everyone in the workgroup to find the templates they need.

Procedures

Create a Document Using a Template

1. Click **File** .... Alt+F
2. Click **New** .... N
   ✓ *The New Document task pane opens.*
3. Click **General Templates** [General Templates...]
   ✓ *If the desired template is listed in the New Document task pane, click it and skip to step 8.*
4. Click the desired tab.... Ctrl+Tab
5. Select the desired template icon.................... ↑↓←→
6. Click **OK** .... Enter
7. Replace directions and prompts with text.
8. Edit and format document as desired.
9. Name and save the document .... Ctrl+S

Create a Document Using a Wizard

1. Click **File** .... Alt+F
2. Click **New** .... N
   ✓ *The New Document task pane opens.*
3. Click **General Templates** [icon]
   ✓ *If the desired wizard is listed in the New Document task pane, click it and skip to step 8.*
4. Click the desired tab... Ctrl+Tab
5. Click the desired Wizard icon...................... ↑↓←→
6. Click **OK** .... Enter
7. Respond to prompts in dialog box.
8. Click **Next** .... Alt+N
   ✓ *Click Back to return to previous dialog box to change responses. Click Finish to create document with default settings.*
9. Repeat steps 7 and 8 until last dialog box is displayed.
10. Click **Finish** .... Alt+F
11. Edit and format document as desired.
12. Save document........... Ctrl+S

Save a Document as a Template

1. Create a new document.
2. Enter and format text as desired.
3. Set page, paragraph, and font formatting.
4. Click **File** .... Alt+F
5. Click **Save** .... S
6. Type file name .... *type*
7. Click **Save as type** box .... Alt+T
8. Click **Document Template** .... ↑↓←→, Enter
   ✓ *Word automatically switches to the Templates folder. Select the desired subfolder or create a new folder as necessary.*
9. Click **Save** button [Save] .... Alt+S

Set Default Location for Workgroup File Templates

1. Click **Tools** .... Alt+T
2. Click **Options** .... O
3. Click **File Locations** tab.............................. Ctrl+Tab
4. Select **Workgroup templates** .... ↑↓
5. Click **Modify** button [Modify...] .... Alt+M
6. Select desired folder using Look in drop-down list.
   ✓ *If necessary, create new folder using **Create New Folder** button [icon].*
7. Click **OK**.......................... Enter
8. Click **OK**.......................... Enter

Exercise Directions

1. Start Word, if necessary.
2. Open the document 75OPTICAL and save it as a template named OPTICAL, in the Workgroup Templates folder.

   ✓ *If necessary, create a new folder named Workgroup Templates in which to store the file. Make sure that the folder is stored in your Word Templates directory, for example, in the C:\Program Files\Microsoft Office\ \Templates directory. If necessary, ask your instructor for more information.*
3. Close the OPTICAL template file.
4. Set the Workgroup Templates folder as the default Workgroup template file location.
5. Create a new document based on the OPTICAL template. Note that the letterhead text is already entered in the document, because it is part of the template file.

   ✓ *The template should be displayed on the Workgroup Templates tab of the Templates dialog box. If it is not, you did not store the folder in the correct template directory.*
6. Save the new document as OPTIMEMO.
7. Type the document shown in Illustration A.
8. Check the spelling and grammar in the document.
9. Display the document in Print Preview. It should look similar to the one in Illustration A.
10. Print the document.
11. Close the document, saving all changes.
12. Use the Fax Wizard to create a fax cover sheet.
13. Complete the prompts in the Wizard dialog boxes as follows:
    - In the document to fax screen, select the option to create just a cover sheet with a note.
    - Specify that you want to print the document and send it from a separate fax machine.
    - Use the following information:

      Recipient's name: **Harold Daderian**

      Recipient's fax number: **941-555-2598**

      Use the Professional style.

      Sender: **Your Name**

      Sender's company: **Optical General, Inc.**

      Mailing address: **685 West 500 South, Salt Lake City, Utah 84101**

      Phone: **801-555-9191**

      Fax: **801-555-9292**
14. Replace all remaining sample text in the document as shown in Illustration B.

    ✓ *Double-click in the Please Reply box to insert the check mark.*
15. Save the document as FAXCOVER.
16. Check the spelling and grammar in the document.
17. Display the document in Print Preview. It should look similar to the one in Illustration B.
18. Print the document.
19. Close the document, saving all changes.

On Your Own

1. Start Word and use the Letter Wizard to create a new document.
2. In the document, type a letter to a friend or relative explaining some of the documents you have learned to create with Word.
3. Check the spelling and grammar in the document.
4. Save the document as OWDRAVE.
5. Display the document in Print Preview.
6. Print the document.
7. Use the Envelope Wizard to create an envelope for the letter.
8. Add the envelope to a new document.

   ✓ *When you add the envelope to a new document, Word inserts a blank document page.*
9. Save the document as OWDRAVE2.
10. Close the documents, saving all changes.

Illustration A

Optical General, Inc.

685 West 500 South ◉ Salt Lake City, Utah 84101

Telephone: 801-555-9191 ◉ Fax: 801-555-9292 ◉ E-mail: opgen@ddcpub.com

MEMO

To: Harold Daderian

From: Your Name

Date: Today's Date

Subject: Travel Plans

I have finalized my travel plans and will be arriving on Flight 6234 at 9:55 a.m. on Friday the 13th.

Please make the necessary arrangements to have a car meet me at the airport.

I look forward to meeting you on the 13th. If you have any questions, please contact me as soon as possible.

Illustration B

685 West 500 South
Salt Lake City, Utah 84101
Phone: 801-555-9191
Fax: 801-555-9292

Optical General, Inc.

To:	Harold Daderian	**From:**	Your Name
Fax:	941-555-2598	**Date:**	Today's Date
Phone:	941-555-2500	**Pages:**	2 (including cover)
Re:	Travel plans	**CC:**	

☐ **Urgent** ☐ **For Review** ☐ **Please Comment** ☑ **Please Reply** ☐ **Please Recycle**

•Comments: Please review this memo and respond as soon as possible.

Thanks.

Exercise 76

Skills Covered:

◆ **Insert a File in a Document** ◆ **Use AutoText**

On the Job

Insert a file into another file to save time retyping existing text. When you insert a file, the entire contents of the file become part of the current document, while the original file remains unchanged. Use AutoText to quickly insert words or phrases you type often, such as the closing to a letter.

As an administrative assistant at Fox Footwear, you want to show that you are resourceful. In this exercise, you will design a letterhead that you will save as AutoText. You can then insert it at the top of a press release you will write announcing the winners of the essay contest. You also need to include the names of the contest judges in the press release. Since you already have a document containing the names of the judges, you can simply insert it directly into the press release.

Terms

AutoText A feature of Word that lets you automatically insert a selection of stored text and graphics.

Notes

Insert a File in a Document

- You can insert one file into another file to incorporate the first file's contents into the second file.
- The entire contents are saved as part of the second file.
- The first file remains unchanged.
- Inserting a file is different from copying and pasting, because you do not have to open the file to insert it and the entire file contents are inserted—no selecting is necessary.
  - ✓ *To mark where a file is inserted into an existing document, turn on the Track Changes feature before the insertion.*

Use AutoText

- **AutoText** is part of Word's AutoCorrect feature.
  - ✓ *Using* AutoCorrect *is covered in Exercise 8.*
- AutoText eliminates repetitive typing by automatically inserting saved blocks of text or graphics.
- An unlimited amount of text or graphics may be stored in an AutoText entry.
- Word comes with a built-in list of AutoText entries, including standard letter closings and salutations.
- You can add entries to the AutoText list.
- You can delete an entry when you don't need it anymore.

The AutoText tab of the AutoCorrect dialog box

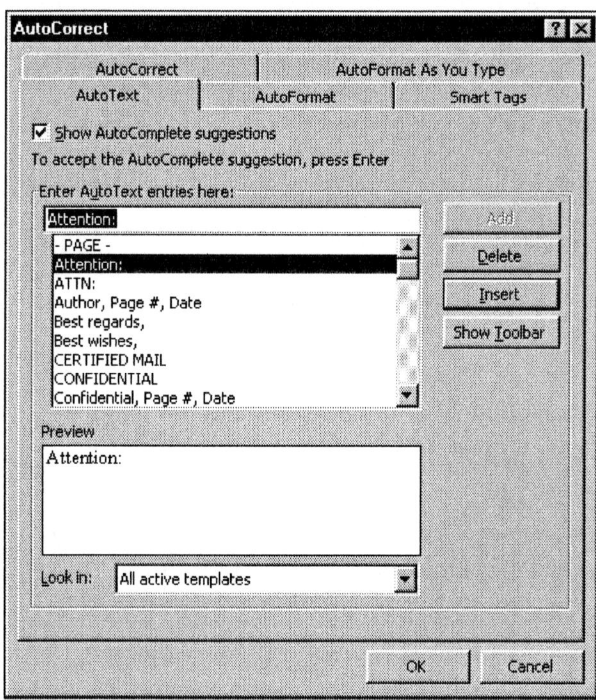

Procedures

Insert a File

1. Position the insertion point where you want file inserted.
2. Click **Insert** .... Alt+I
3. Click **File** L
4. Select file to insert..............
5. Click **Insert** button Insert .... Alt+S

Use AutoText

To create an AutoText entry *(Alt+F3)*:

1. Select text or graphics.
2. Click **Insert**. .... Alt+I
3. Select **AutoText**.................... A
4. Click **New**............................ N
5. Type the entry name.
   - ✓ *AutoText entry names can have 31 characters including spaces. Use descriptive names.*
6. Click **OK**........................... Enter

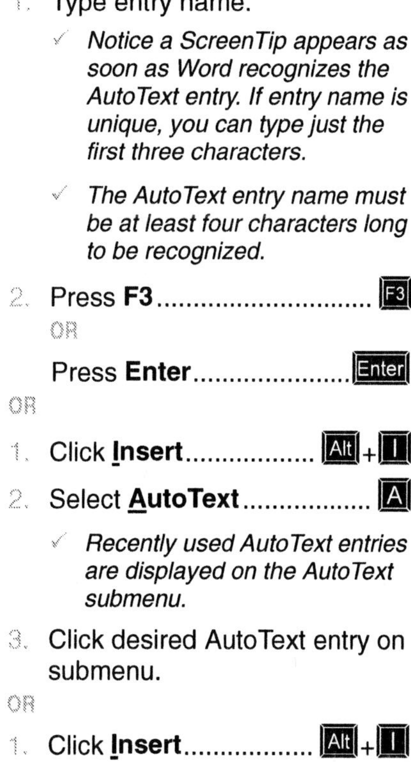

To insert an AutoText entry:

1. Type entry name.
   - ✓ *Notice a ScreenTip appears as soon as Word recognizes the AutoText entry. If entry name is unique, you can type just the first three characters.*
   - ✓ *The AutoText entry name must be at least four characters long to be recognized.*
2. Press **F3**.............................. F3

   OR

   Press **Enter**...................... Enter

OR

1. Click **Insert**.................. Alt+I
2. Select **AutoText**.................. A
   - ✓ *Recently used AutoText entries are displayed on the AutoText submenu.*
3. Click desired AutoText entry on submenu.

OR

1. Click **Insert**.................. Alt+I
2. Select **AutoText**.................. A
3. Click **AutoText** X
4. Select desired AutoText entry.
5. Click **Insert** button Insert .... Alt+I

Delete an AutoText entry:

1. Click **Insert**.................. Alt+I
2. Select **AutoText** .... A
3. Click **AutoText** X
   - ✓ *The AutoCorrect dialog box is displayed, with the AutoText tab active.*
4. Locate and select entry to delete in list of entries.
   - ✓ *You can type the entry in the text box at the top of the list to quickly scroll to it.*
5. Click **Delete** button Delete .... Alt+D
6. Click **OK** .... Enter

Exercise Directions

1. Start Word, and create a new document.
2. Design the letterhead shown in Illustration A.
   a. Type the company name in a 34-point serif font with the small caps effect (Garamond is used in the illustration), flush right.
   b. Type the address using the same font formatting in 16 points, also flush right.
   c. Type the phone numbers using the same font formatting in 10 points, also flush right.
   d. Leave 48 points of space after the last line in the letterhead.
   e. Insert a diamond shaped Wingding symbol to separate parts of the address and phone numbers.
   f. Apply a 20% gray shading behind the letterhead.
   g. Apply a triple-line border above and below the letterhead, as shown.
3. Save the letterhead as an AutoText entry named **foxhead**.
   a. Press Ctrl+A to select everything in the document.
   b. Click Insert, AutoText, New.
   c. Type the name **foxhead** in the Create AutoText dialog box.
   d. Click OK.
4. Close the document without saving any changes.
5. Open 76WINNERS.
6. Save the file as WINNERS.
7. Position the insertion point at the beginning of the document, and then insert the foxhead AutoText entry.
8. Move the insertion point to the end of the document and insert the file 76JUDGES.
9. Check the spelling and grammar in the document.
10. Display the document in Print Preview. It should look similar to the one in Illustration B.
11. Print the document.
12. Close the file, saving all changes.

On Your Own

1. Start Word, and create a new document.
2. Design a letterhead for yourself.
3. Save the letterhead as an AutoText entry with a descriptive name, such as **MYNAME**.
4. Close the document without saving the changes.
5. Create another new document.
6. Save the document as OWDMOREBIO.
7. Type a brief biography. The biography should be no more than two paragraphs, and it should be appropriate for inclusion in a document such as a yearbook, a team or club roster, or a theater program.
8. Check the spelling and grammar in the document.
9. Close the document, saving all changes.
10. Create another new document, and save it as OWDINCLUDE.
11. Type a letter to the yearbook editor or the club president or whoever is responsible for printing the collection of biographies. Leave space above the closing to insert the OWDMOREBIO document.
12. Insert the OWDMOREBIO biography into the OWDINCLUDE letter.
13. Check the spelling and grammar in the document.
14. Display the document in Print Preview.
15. Print the document.
16. Close the document, saving all changes.

Illustration A

FOX FOOTWEAR, INC.

4500 MONTGOMERY STREET • SAN FRANCISCO, CA 94111

TELEPHONE: (415) 555-6750 • FACSIMILE: (415) 555-6751 • E-MAIL: FOXFOOTWEAR@DDCPUB.COM

FOX FOOTWEAR, INC.

4500 MONTGOMERY STREET ♦ SAN FRANCISCO, CA 94111

TELEPHONE: (415) 555-6750 ♦ FACSIMILE: (415) 555-6751 ♦ E-MAIL: FOXFOOTWEAR@DDCPUB.COM

FOR IMMEDIATE RELEASE

SAN FRANCISCO, CA – Fox Footwear, Inc. is pleased to announce the winners of its second annual essay contest. The theme of the contest this year was "Put Your Best Foot Forward." Over 150 entries were received, and the judges were hard pressed to pick a winner. After much deliberation, the winners are as follows:

Grand Prize: Kristen Montegna, Silver Spring, MD
First Place: Vincent Jackson, Indianapolis, IN
Second Place: Bailey Hartmann, Atlanta, GA
Third Place: Peter King, Provo, UT

All participants received commemorative T-Shirts and discount coupons for use in any Fox Footwear retail outlet. Due to the success of the program, Fox Footwear anticipates sponsoring an essay contest every year. Information about the next contest will be made available in the fall.

List of Judges for the Second Annual Fox Footwear Essay Contest

Name	Department	Telephone Extension
Arroyo, Michael	Design	2121
Chang, Marie	Marketing	5647
Gogan, Alex	Accounting	3434
Lewis, Christopher	Purchasing	6192
McKay, Patricia	Design	2124
Neuwirth, Jackie	Accounting	3439
Tesini, Oliver	Personnel	9872
Vieth, Laurence	Design	2125
Zabriskie, Jonathan	Quality Control	4091
Zide, Sharon	Purchasing	6198

Exercise 77

Skills Covered:

◆ **Record a Macro** ◆ **Run a Macro**

On the Job

Macros let you simplify tasks that ordinarily require many keystrokes or commands such as creating a header or footer, or changing line spacing and indents for a paragraph. Once you record a macro, you can run it at any time to repeat the recorded actions. You can use macros for tasks as simple as opening and printing a document, or for more complicated tasks such as creating a new document, inserting a table, entering text, and applying an AutoFormat.

As an administrative assistant at Fox Footwear, Inc., you frequently have to format documents by changing the margins to 1" on all sides and by inserting a standard header and footer. In this exercise, you will create macros for setting the margins and creating a header and footer. You will then use the macros to format a press release.

Terms

Macro A series of commands and keystrokes that you record and save together. You can run the macro to replay the series.

Normal template A document that stores the default settings for new Word documents.

Shortcut key A combination of keys (including Alt, Ctrl, and/or Shift, and a regular keyboard key) that you assign to run a macro.

Visual Basic Editor (VBE) The programming environment used to write new VBA code or to edit existing VBA code.

Visual Basic for Applications (VBA) A macro language version of the Microsoft Visual Basic language used to program Windows applications.

Notes

Record a Macro

- Record a **macro** to automate tasks or actions that you perform frequently.
- By default, new macros are stored in the **Normal template**, so they are available for use in all new documents created with the Normal template.
- Macros can save time and help eliminate errors.
- A single macro can store an unlimited number of keystrokes or mouse actions.
- You can record mouse actions that select commands in menus and dialog boxes; however, you cannot record mouse actions that select text or position the insertion point.
- Recording a macro is similar to recording on a cassette tape. As soon as you start recording, everything you input into your computer is stored in the macro, just as everything you input into a cassette recorder is stored on a tape.

✓ *When recording a macro, the mouse pointer changes to an arrow with a cassette tape icon* .

- A macro is different from AutoText because a macro can store actions and commands as well as text and graphics.
- You can assign a **shortcut key** combination including Alt, Ctrl, and/or Shift and a regular keyboard key to a macro when you record it to use to play the macro back at any time.

Customize Keyboard dialog box

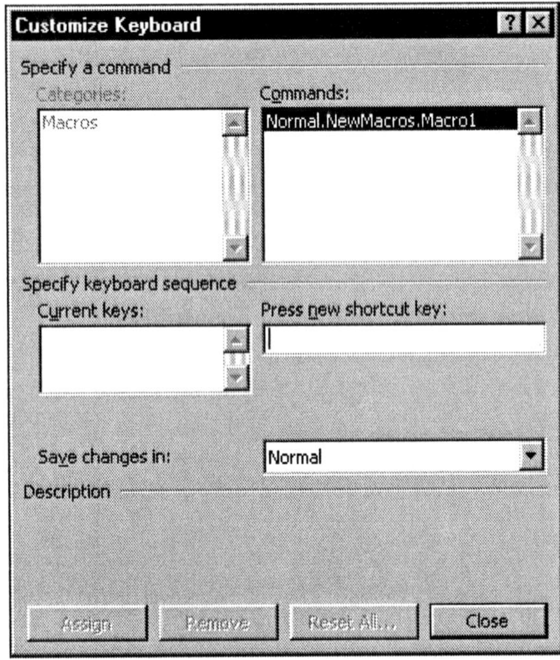

✓ *You can also create a toolbar button to assign to the macro.*

- If a macro doesn't work the way you want, you can delete it and record it again, or edit it using the **Visual Basic Editor**.
- Macros created in Word are recorded using the **Visual Basic for Applications** (VBA) programming language, but you do not need to know how to use VBA to record a macro.
- If you do know how to use VBA you can create a macro by entering code in the Visual Basic Editor (VBE).
- The VBE includes the tools you need to find syntax, logic, and run-time errors in VBA code and to fix them.
- To start the VBE from Word, click Tools, Macro, Macros, select the template or document in which you want to store the macro, type a name for the macro, and then click Create.

Run a Macro

- Once you have recorded a macro, you can run it any time you are using the template with which it is stored.
- When you run a macro, Word executes the recorded commands and actions in the current document.
- Use the key combination you assigned when you recorded the macro to run the macro.
- To perform the macro on part of a document, be sure to select the part first.

Procedures

Record a Macro

1. Position the insertion point where you want it to be when you start recording the macro.
2. Double-click **REC** button REC on the Status bar.

   OR

   a. Click **Tools** .... Alt+T
   b. Click **Macro** .... M
   c. Click **Record New Macro** .... R
3. Type a macro name.
4. Click **Description** .... Alt+D
5. Type a description of the macro.
6. Click **Keyboard**............ Alt+K
7. Press a shortcut key combination.

   ✓ *Word indicates whether the combination is unassigned or already assigned to a Word command. If you use a combination that is already assigned, the original purpose of the combination is replaced. For example, if you assign the combination Ctrl+S, you will no longer be able to use that combination to save a file.*
8. Click **Assign** .... Tab, Alt+A
9. Click **Close** button Close .... Enter
10. Perform actions to record.

To stop recording a macro:

- Click the **Stop** button ■ on the Macro Control box.

OR

1. Click **Tools**................. Alt+T
2. Click **Macro** .... M
3. Click **Stop Recording**......... R

   OR

   - Double click **REC** button REC on Status bar.

Run a Macro *(Alt+F8)*

- Press assigned key combination.

OR

1. Click **Tools** .... Alt+T
2. Select **Macro**...................... M
3. Click **Macros**....................... M
4. Click the name of macro to run .... ↑↓
5. Click **Run** button Run .... Alt+R

Delete a Macro *(Alt+F8)*

1. Click **Tools** .... Alt+T
2. Click **Macro** .... M
3. Click **Macros** .... M
4. Click the name of macro to delete.................. ↑↓
5. Click **Delete** button Delete .... Alt+D
6. Click **Yes** button Yes .... Y
7. Click **Close** button Close .... Enter

Exercise Directions

1. Start Word, if necessary.
2. In a new blank document create the following macros:
   a. Open the Record Macro dialog box.
   b. Name the macro **Margins**.
   c. Enter the description: **Sets all margins to 1"**.
   d. Assign the macro to the key combination Alt+Ctrl+G.
   e. Click Assign and then Close to begin recording the macro keystrokes.
   f. Perform the steps to set all page margins to 1".
   g. Stop recording the macro.
3. Open the Record Macro dialog box and create a second macro as follows:
   a. Name the macro **Header**.
   b. Include the description: **Creates a header and footer in Fox Footwear documents**.
   c. Assign the macro to the key combination Alt+Shift+H.
   d. Click Assign and then Close to begin recording the macro keystrokes.
   e. Create a header with the company name flush left and today's date flush right.
      ✓ *If necessary, move the right tab stop so that the date is flush with the right margin.*
   f. Create a footer with your name flush left and the word **Page** followed by a space then the page number flush right.
   g. Close the Header/Footer dialog box.
   h. Stop recording the macro.
4. Close the blank document without saving any changes.
5. Open WINNERS or open 77WINNERS.
6. Save the file as WINNERS2.
7. Run the Header macro.
8. Run the Margins macro.
9. Preview the document. It should look similar to the one in Illustration A.
10. Check the spelling and grammar in the document.
11. Print the document.
12. Close the document, saving all changes.

Illustration A

Fox Footwear, Inc. Today's Date

FOX FOOTWEAR, INC.

4500 MONTGOMERY STREET ♦ SAN FRANCISCO, CA 94111

TELEPHONE: (415) 555-6750 ♦ FACSIMILE: (415) 555-6751 ♦ E-MAIL: FOXFOOTWEAR@DDCPUB.COM

FOR IMMEDIATE RELEASE

SAN FRANCISCO, CA – Fox Footwear, Inc. is pleased to announce the winners of its second annual essay contest. The theme of the contest this year was "Put Your Best Foot Forward." Over 150 entries were received, and the judges were hard pressed to pick a winner. After much deliberation, the winners are as follows:

Grand Prize: Kristen Montegna, Silver Spring, MD
First Place: Vincent Jackson, Indianapolis, IN
Second Place: Bailey Hartmann, Atlanta, GA
Third Place: Peter King, Provo, UT

All participants received commemorative T-Shirts and discount coupons for use in any Fox Footwear retail outlet. Due to the success of the program, Fox Footwear anticipates sponsoring an essay contest every year. Information about the next contest will be made available in the fall.

List of Judges for the Second Annual Fox Footwear Essay Contest

Name	Department	Telephone Extension
Arroyo, Michael	Design	2121
Chang, Marie	Marketing	5647
Gogan, Alex	Accounting	3434
Lewis, Christopher	Purchasing	6192
McKay, Patricia	Design	2124
Neuwirth, Jackie	Accounting	3439
Tesini, Oliver	Personnel	9872
Vieth, Laurence	Design	2125
Zabriskie, Jonathan	Quality Control	4091
Zide, Sharon	Purchasing	6198

Your Name Page 1

On Your Own

1. Start Word and open OWDMOREBIO, the brief biography you created in the On Your Own section of Exercise 76, or open 77OWDMOREBIO.
2. Save the document as OWDMOREBIO2, and then close it.
3. Create a new blank document.
4. Create a new macro named **Insertbio** and assign it to a shortcut key combination, such as Shift+Alt+B.
5. Record the keystrokes for inserting the OWDMOREBIO2 file into the open document.
6. After you stop recording the macro, close the current document without saving the changes.
7. Create a new blank document and save it as OWDMACRO.
8. Type a document in which you can include your biography. You might type a letter to someone other than the person you wrote to in Exercise 76, or you might type part of a program or yearbook page.
9. At the appropriate location, use the Insertbio macro to insert the OWDMOREBIO file into the OWDMACRO document.
10. Check the spelling and grammar in the document.
11. Preview the document.
12. Print the document.
13. Close the document, saving all changes

Exercise 78

Skills Covered:

◆ **Create a Form** ◆ **Insert Form Fields**
◆ **Set Form Field Options** ◆ **Fill Out a Form**

On the Job

Use forms to collect information such as names and addresses for product registrations, data for surveys, or products and pricing for invoices or purchase orders. With Word, you can create forms that can be printed and filled out by hand, by typewriter, or with a computer printer. You can also store forms on a computer so they can be filled out on-screen.

As the manager of in-house training at Highland Property Management, you have decided to survey the employees to find out what types of training classes they are interested in. In this exercise, you will create a form that employees can fill out indicating their class preferences, time preferences, whether they have ever taken an in-house training class, and, if so, whether they were satisfied with the class. You will print the form, and, finally, you will test the form by filling it out online.

Terms

Form A document used to collect and organize information.

Protected Locked so that unauthorized changes cannot be made.

Form field A field inserted in a form document where users can enter information.

Text box form field A field inserted on a form in which users can enter data such as text and numbers.

Check box form field A rectangular box-shaped field inserted on a form for users to select or deselect.

Drop-down form field A field inserted on a form from which users can display a list and select an option.

Notes

Create a Form

- In Word, you store **forms** as template files.
- To use the form, you create a document based on the template.
- Forms are **protected** so that users can enter data in the **form fields**, but cannot change any other parts of the document.
- You can print the document and fill out the form on paper, or you can fill out the form on your computer and store it on a disk.
- You can save a new Word document as a form, or you can save an existing Word document as a form.
- In some ways, Word forms are similar to mail merge documents. They contain standard text and graphics that appear the same on every document, and they contain form fields where users can enter variable data.

Insert Form Fields

- There are three basic types of form fields:
  - **Text box form fields**
  - **Check box form fields**
  - **Drop-down form fields**
- You use the Forms toolbar to insert form fields.

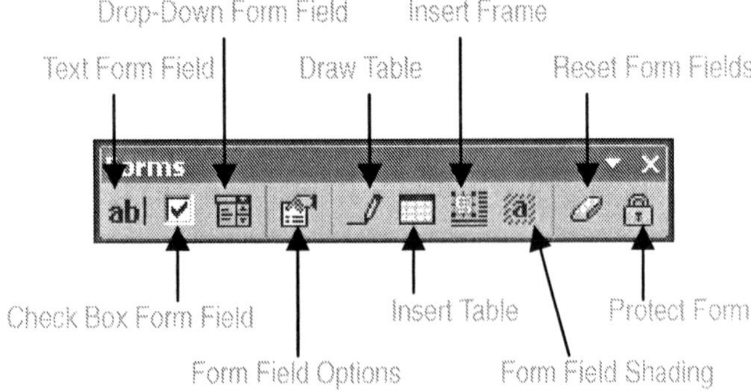

- When inserting form fields, give some consideration to the form layout. You may want to use a table or tab stops to be sure fields are aligned to look good on the page and so that it will be easy for users to fill out the form.
- When a user fills out a form online, Word moves the insertion point from form field to form field based on the order in which fields are inserted in the document. To ensure a logical order for users filling out the form, you should give some thought to the order in which you will insert the form fields.

Set Form Field Options

- By default, Word inserts form fields using basic settings. For example, text form fields are set to allow users to enter an unlimited number of text characters.
- You can customize the form field options to control the way data may be entered in the field. For example, you can set text form field options to limit users to entering valid dates, or no more than ten characters.
- You must set properties for drop-down form fields in order to enter the drop-down list items.

Fill Out a Form

- To fill out a form manually, simply print it.
- To fill out a form on-screen, create a new document based on the form template, enter data in the form fields, then save the document.
- You can leave form fields blank.

Procedures

Create a Form

1. Create a new Word document.
   OR
   Open an existing document.
2. Display Forms toolbar.
3. Type standard text that will appear on all forms.
4. Delete variable text that will not appear on all forms.
5. Insert form fields as necessary.
   ✓ *Refer to Insert Form Fields procedures at right for step-by-step instructions on inserting form fields.*
6. Click **Protect Form** button on Forms toolbar.
   OR
   a. Click **Tools** .... Alt+T
   b. Click **Protect Document** .... P
   c. Click **Forms** option button .... Alt+F
   d. Click **OK** .... Enter
7. Click **File** .... Alt+F
8. Click **Save As** .... A
9. Click **Save as type** drop-down arrow .... Alt+T
10. Select **Document Template** .... ↓, Enter
11. Select template folder where you want form template stored.
    ✓ *In the Templates dialog box, the form template will be displayed on the tab with the name of the folder where it is stored.*
12. Click **File name** .... Alt+N
13. Type desired file name.
14. Click **Save** button Save .... Alt+S
15. Click **File** .... Alt+F
16. Click **Close** C

Insert Form Fields

1. Open form template document.
2. Display Forms toolbar.
3. If necessary, click **Protect Form** button on Forms toolbar to unprotect the form.
   OR
   a. Click **Tools** .... Alt+T
   b. Click **Unprotect Document** .... P
4. Position insertion point where you want to insert first form field.
   ✓ *Remember, users will tab through form fields in the order in which form fields are inserted.*
5. Click desired button on Forms toolbar:
   - Click **Text Form Field** button abl to insert text form field.
   - Click **Check Box Form Field** button to insert check box field.
   - Click **Drop-Down Form Field** button to insert drop-down field.
6. Repeat steps 4 and 5 until all form fields are inserted.
   ✓ *You can toggle form field shading off and on using the **Form Field Shading** button on the Forms toolbar.*
7. Click **Protect Form** button on Forms toolbar.
   OR
   a. Click **Tools** .... Alt+T
   b. Click **Protect Document** .... P
   c. Click **Forms** option button .... Alt+F
   d. Click **OK** .... Enter
8. Click **Save** .... Alt+S
9. Click **Close** C

Set Form Field Properties

Text form fields:

1. Open form template document.
2. If necessary, click **Protect Form** button on Forms toolbar.
   OR
   a. Click **Tools** .... Alt+T
   b. Click **Unprotect Document** .... P
3. Click desired form field.
4. Click **Form Field Options** button on Forms toolbar.
   OR
   a. Right-click desired form field.
   b. Click **Properties** .... R
5. Select desired options as follows:
   - Select type of text allowed from **Type** drop-down list .... Alt+P, ↓, Enter
   - Enter default text to display in **Default text** text box .... Alt+E
   - Enter number of characters allowed in **Maximum length** text box .... Alt+M
   - Select format from **(Type) format** drop-down list .... Alt+F
     ✓ *Name of format text box changes depending on the type of text selected from **Type** drop-down list.*
6. Click **OK** .... Enter
7. When all changes are complete, click **Protect Form** button on Forms toolbar.
   OR
   a. Click **Tools** .... Alt+T
   b. Click **Protect Document** .... P
   c. Click **Forms** option button .... Alt+F
   d. Click **OK** .... Enter

Check box form fields:

1. Open form template document.
2. If necessary, click **Protect Form** button on Forms toolbar.

   OR

   a. Click **Tools** .... Alt+T
   b. Click **Unprotect Form** .... P
3. Click desired form field.
4. Click **Form Field Options** button on Forms toolbar.

   OR

   a. Right-click desired form field.
   b. Click **Properties** .... R
5. Set size options as follows:
   - Select **Auto** option button .... Alt+A to set size according to current font size.
   - Select **Exactly** option button .... Alt+E type text to enter desired size to specify desired size.
6. Set default value options as follows:
   - Select **Not Checked** .... Alt+K to display check box not checked by default.
   - Select **Checked** ..... Alt+D to display check box checked by default.
7. Click **OK** .... Enter
8. Click **Protect Form** button on Forms toolbar.

   OR

   a. Click **Tools** .... Alt+T
   b. Click **Protect Document** .... P
   c. Click **Forms** option button .... Alt+F
   d. Click **OK** .... Enter

Drop-down form fields:

1. Open form template document.
2. If necessary, click **Protect Form** button on Forms toolbar.

   OR

   a. Click **Tools** .... Alt+T
   b. Click **Unprotect Document** .... P
3. Click desired form field.
4. Click **Form Field Options** button on Forms toolbar.

   OR

   a. Right-click desired form field
   b. Click **Properties** .... R
5. Click **Drop-down item**: text box .... Alt+D
6. Type first option.
7. Click **Add** .... Alt+A
8. Repeat steps 5-7 until all drop-down options are entered.
9. Click **OK** .... Enter
10. Click **Protect Form** button on Forms toolbar.

    OR

    a. Click **Tools** .... Alt+T
    b. Click **Protect Document** .... P
    c. Click **Forms** option button .... Alt+F
    d. Click **OK** .... Enter

Fill Out a Form

1. Start Word.
2. Click **File** .... Alt+F
3. Click **New** .... N
4. Click **General Templates**.
5. Click tab where form template is stored .... Ctrl+Tab
6. Double-click desired form template.

   ✓ *First form field is selected.*
7. Enter data in first form field as follows:
   - Type text in text form field.
   - Click check box form field .... Space to select or deselect check box.
   - Click drop-down form field arrow, then click desired option.. Alt+↓, ↑↓, Enter
8. Press **Tab** .... Tab to move to next form field.
9. Repeat steps 6 and 7 until form is complete.

   ✓ *You do not have to enter data in every field.*
10. Click **Save** button and name document.

Exercise Directions

1. Start Word, if necessary.
2. Create a new blank document.
3. Save the document as a template with the name SURVEY.
4. Type a letterhead at the top of the document as follows (refer to illustration A):
   a. Type the company name (**Highland Property Management Co.**) on line 1, using the Heading 1 style, centered.
   b. Type the company address (**575 W. Osborne Street, Phoenix, AZ 85013**) on line 2, using the Normal style in 14 points, centered.
   c. Type the telephone information (**Telephone: 602-555-4326; Facsimile: 602-555-4327; E-mail: highlandpmc@ddcpub.com**) on line 3, using the Normal style in 10 points, centered.
   d. Leave 54 points of space after the letterhead.
5. Insert a table in the document as shown in Illustration A. Keep gridlines displayed, but do not use any borders.
   ✓ *Use the Draw table features and the Tables and Borders toolbar to create the table as shown. Cell sizes are approximate. For a refresher on drawing tables, see Exercise 40.*
6. Using a 16-point bold, serif font, type the text in the table shown in Illustration A.
7. Center the words **Yes**, **No**, and **Maybe** in their cells.
8. Check the spelling and grammar in the document.
9. Preview the document. It should look similar to Illustration A.
   ✓ *Gridlines are displayed in the illustration so you can see the size of columns and rows; they will not be displayed in Print Preview.*
10. Print the document.
11. In row 1, column 2, insert a text form field using default properties.
12. In row 2, column 2, insert another text form field, using default properties.
13. In row 3, column 2, insert a third text form field. Set the type property to *Current date*, and select the *M/D/YY* format.
14. In rows 5 and 6, insert check box form fields under the text **Yes** and **No** in columns 2 and 3.
    ✓ *Press Enter after the text in each column to position the insertion point centered on the next line in the cell.*
15. In row 7, column 2, insert a text form field.
16. In row 8, insert check box form fields under the text **Yes**, **No**, and **Maybe** in columns 2, 3, and 4.
17. In row 9, insert a drop-down form field. Enter the following three drop-down list items: **Corporate Headquarters, Local Office, Off-site Training Center**.
18. In row 10, column 2, insert a text form field.
19. Form protect the template.
20. Preview the document. It should look similar to the one in Illustration B.
21. Close the template document, saving all changes.
22. Create a new document based on the SURVEY form template.
23. Save the document as SURVEY1.
24. Fill out the form as follows:
    - Enter your name in the first text form field.
    - Enter **Marketing** in the second text form field.
    - Skip the date field, which should fill in the current date automatically.
    - Select *Yes* for whether or not you have attended in-house training classes.
    - Select *No* for whether or not you were satisfied.
    - For the reason why you were not satisfied, type that you thought the course was not challenging enough.
    - Select *Maybe* for whether or not you are interested in future classes.
    - Select *Off-site Training Center* as the location you would prefer.
    - Enter any comments you would like in the final text form field.
25. Print the document.
26. Close the document, saving all changes.

Illustration A

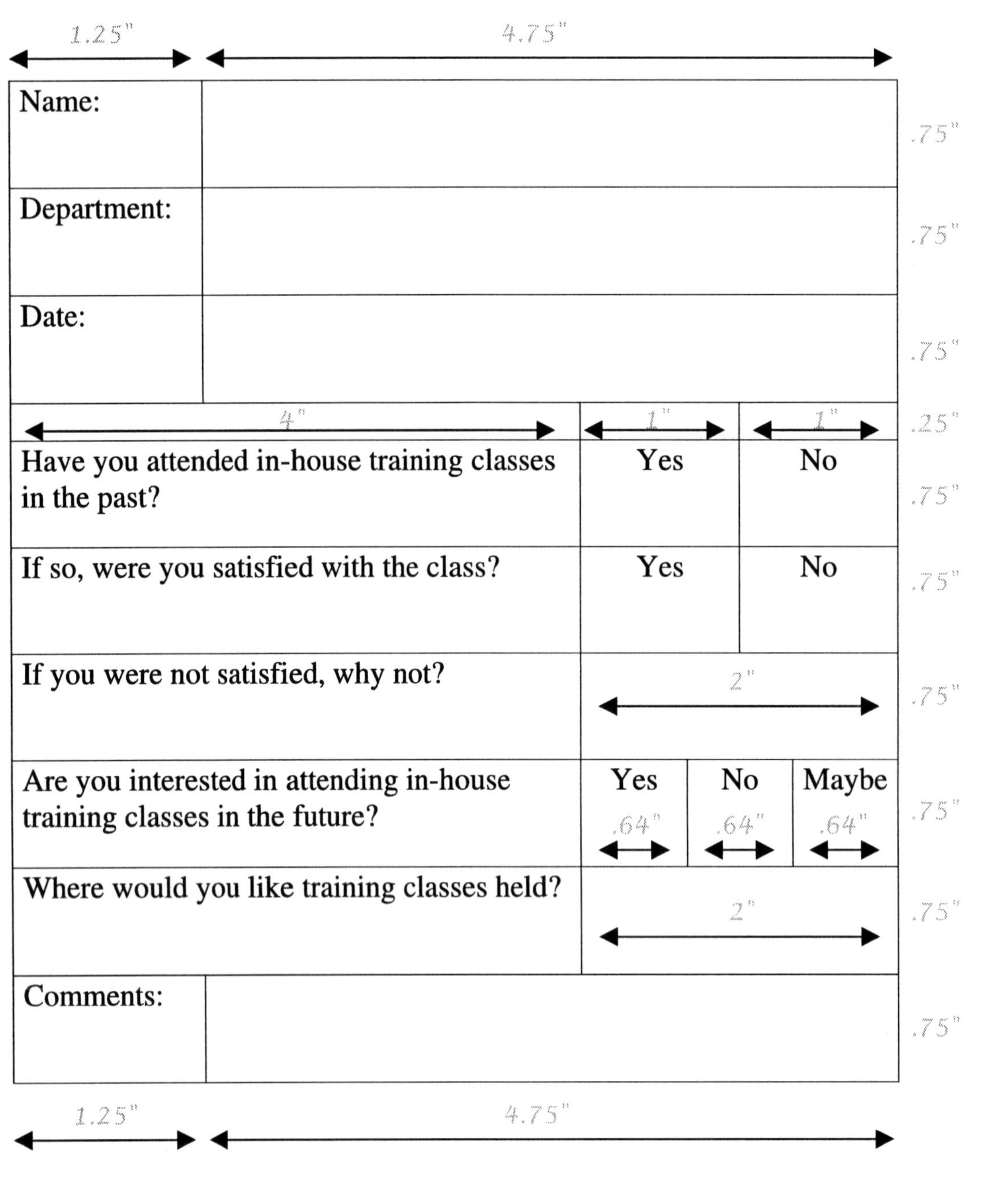

Highland Property Management Co.

575 W. Osborne Street, Phoenix, AZ 85013

Telephone: 602-555-4326; Facsimile: 602-555-4327; E-mail: highlandpmc@ddcpub.com

Name:			
Department:			
Date:			
Have you attended in-house training classes in the past?	Yes	No	
If so, were you satisfied with the class?	Yes	No	
If you were not satisfied, why not?			
Are you interested in attending in-house training classes in the future?	Yes	No	Maybe
Where would you like training classes held?			
Comments:			

Illustration B

Highland Property Management Co.

575 W. Osborne Street, Phoenix, AZ 85013

Telephone: 602-555-4326; Facsimile: 602-555-4327; E-mail: highlandpmc@ddcpub.com

Name:

Department:

Date: m/dd/yy

Have you attended in-house training classes in the past?	Yes ☐	No ☐	
If so, were you satisfied with the class?	Yes ☐	No ☐	
If you were not satisfied, why not?			
Are you interested in attending in-house training classes in the future?	Yes ☐	No ☐	Maybe ☐
Where would you like training classes held?	Corporate Headquarters		

Comments:

On Your Own

1. Think about the type of form that you could use to register members of a club or organization. The form might include fields for entered name and address information as well as fields for selecting meeting times, the best time to be reached by phone, committee selection preferences, and so on.
2. Start Word and create a new document.
3. Save the document as a template with the name OWDREGISTER.
4. Enter all of the standard text you want on your form. Use a table if it helps you line up the information neatly on the page.
5. Enter the form fields you will need on your form. Remember to enter them in the order in which you want users to fill them out.
6. Form protect the document.
7. Save the template and close it.
8. Create a new document based on the OWDREGISTER template.
9. Save the document as OWDFILLED.
10. Fill out the form.
11. Save the form, close it, and exit Word.

Exercise 79

◆ Critical Thinking

The Fox Footwear essay contest was such a success that the company has promoted you to work on it full time. In preparation for the third annual contest, you have decided to design some documents that can be used for all promotional material. In this exercise, you will create an AutoText entry with your name and new job title so you can insert it in all letters, memos, and other documents you generate. You will also design a newsletter template that you can use to issue monthly updates, and you will create a registration form. You will use the newsletter template to create the first monthly update, inserting a file that already contains some text you want to use. You will also test the registration form by filling it out on-screen.

Exercise Directions

1. Start Word, if necessary.
2. Create a new document.
3. Create an AutoText entry named **mysignature** from the following text:
   Your Name
   Contest Coordinator
   Fox Footwear, Inc.
   415-555-6750, ext. 2233
4. Once the AutoText entry is saved, delete the text from the document.
5. Record a macro that inserts a continuous section break and then divides the second section into two columns of equal width.
   - Name the new macro **Columns**.
   - Type the description: **Applies newsletter formatting**.
   - Assign the key combination Alt+C.
   - Record the necessary keystrokes, and then stop recording.
6. Close the current document without saving it.
7. Create a new blank document.
8. Save the document as a template with the name FOOTSTEP.
9. Design the template shown in Illustration A, including the blank line below the letterhead.
   ✓ *The font Tempus Sans ITC is used in the illustration. If that font is not available on your system, select a different sans serif font.*
10. Move the insertion point to the blank line at the end of the document and run the Columns macro.
11. Close the file, saving all changes.
12. Create a new document based on the FOOTSTEP template.
13. Save the file with the name MONTH1.
14. Move the insertion point to the end of the document and insert the file 79UPDATE.
15. Insert a column break before the heading **Registration Forms**.
16. Select the information about the prize winners (the paragraphs beginning **Grand Prize, First Place, Second Place,** and **Third Place**) and apply a hanging indent of 1" in order to align the information.
17. Move the insertion point to the end of the document and type: **For more information contact**, and then press Enter.
18. Insert the *mysignature* AutoText entry.
19. Check the spelling and grammar in the document.
20. Preview the document. It should look similar to Illustration B.
21. Print the document and then close it, saving all changes.
22. Create a new blank document and save it as a template with the name REGFORM.

23. Type and format the document shown in Illustration C.

    ✓ *Do not include any border lines. The grid lines are shown so you can see the cell sizes.*

    ✓ *Cell measurements are approximate.*

24. Insert form fields as follows:
    - First Name: Text field.
    - Last Name: Text field.
    - Age: Text field set to accept numbers only, in the general format (the first format in the list)
    - Contest Division: Drop-down field offering a choice of **Junior (grades 1 - 4), Middle (grades 5 - 9), Senior (grades (10 - 12)**.
    - Street Address: Text field.
    - Building or Apartment Number: Text field.
    - City: Text field.
    - State: Text field, limited to two characters.
    - Postal Code: Text field, limited to five characters and set to access numbers only, in the general format.
    - Telephone Number: text field.
    - E-mail Address: text field.
    - Yes: Check box.
    - No: Check box.

25. Form protect the document.
26. Check the spelling and grammar.
27. Preview the document. It should look similar to Illustration C, without the border lines.
28. If there are border lines in your document, remove them.
29. Print the form.
30. Close the document, saving all changes.
31. Create a new document based on the REGFORM template.
32. Save the document as MYREG.
33. Fill out the document using your own information.
34. Print the document.
35. Close the document, saving all changes.

Illustration A

FOOTSTEPS

The Monthly Update for the Fox Footwear Essay Contest

Get Ready for the 3rd Annual Essay Contest

Fox Footwear's Second Annual Essay Contest was a huge success! Entries came in from around the country, and the judges had a hard time selecting the winners. The response was so great that the company has committed to sponsoring a contest every year. A contest coordinator has been appointed (see the end of the newsletter), and a budget has been set aside.

Planning for the third annual contest is underway. The first order of business is to select a theme. Although we have some ideas, we would welcome additional suggestions. To increase participation, we intend to divide the competition into categories based on ages and grade levels. This will give more entrants the opportunity to win. We also hope to increase the prize awards.

Judge Training

Also in the works is a training plan for judges. In the interest of fairness, Fox Footwear has determined that judges cannot serve two years in a row. We hope that experienced judges will help train newcomers in their off years.

Registration Forms

Finally, we are in the process of formalizing a contest registration form. It will be made available on the company's Web site, as well as in retail outlets or by mail. Interested participants will be asked to fill out and return the form, at which time they will receive an official entry form stating the contest rules and regulations.

2nd Annual Essay Contest Winners

Grand Prize:	Kristen Montegna, Silver Spring, MD
First Place:	Vincent Jackson, Indianapolis, IN
Second Place:	Bailey Hartmann, Atlanta, GA
Third Place:	Peter King, Provo, UT

All participants received commemorative T-Shirts and discount coupons for use in any Fox Footwear retail outlet.

For more information contact:
Your Name
Contest Coordinator
Fox Footwear, Inc.
415-555-6750, ext. 2233

Illustration C

36-point sans serif

FOX FOOTWEAR, INC.

Essay Contest Registration Form

36-point sans serif

54 points of space

All text is 16 point serif

All rows are .5" high

First Name: (2")	(4")
Last Name:	
Age (as of 9/1):	
Contest Division:	Junior (grades 1 - 4)
Street Address:	
Building or Apartment Number:	

City: (.5")	(2")	State: (.75")	(.5")	Postal Code: (1.5")	(.75")

Telephone Number:	
E-mail Address:	

Have you ever entered a Fox Footwear Essay Contest Before? (4")	Yes ☐ (1")	No ☐ (1")

Index

✓ *Important note: All index references to pages 439-578 refer to the bonus lessons on the CD.*

.

.dot extension 409
.HTML 379

3

3D 402, 403
3-D effect 470

A

About Word 2002 3
Access a Search Engine Web Site 339
Access query 537
Access table 537
Activate Click and Type 34
Active document 372
Add a button to a toolbar 14
Add text to an AutoShape 451
Address list
  edit 244, 246
Address list form 230
Adjust objects 466
Adjust zoom 20
Adjustment handle 466
Advanced alignment options
  use 451
Align a table horizontally 199
Align a table on the page 198
Align an object 451
Align horizontally 48
Align vertically 135
Alt+Tab switching 498
Anchor 448
Antonyms 59
Apply cell borders 223
Arrange documents on-screen 372
Arrange multiple program windows 500
Ask a Question box 6
Attach a Word document to an e-mail message 379
Attachment 378
AutoCorrect 45, 46
  disable 47
  options 48
  use 47
Automatic format checking
  turn on 115
Automatically create a watermark from a picture 490
Automatically create a watermark from text 490
Automatically display Properties dialog box 175
AutoShape 440
AutoText
  use 414, 415
Axis 522

B

Backgrounds 346, 347, 348
Balance columns 398, 399
Balloons
  display 362
Basic search 177
Bitmap 440
Blank drawing canvas
  insert 443
Bookmark 154, 297
  create 298, 299
Border 402
Border line 186
borders 403
Bounding box 440
Break a link 511
Browse by object button 6
Browse object 297
Bullet 124
Bulleted lists 124
Business letter 65

C

Calculate in a table 216
Caps Lock 45, 46
Cascade 498
Case 86
  change 87, 88
Cc
  (carbon copy) 378
Cell 186
Cell borders and shading 222
Cells 187
Change a link's source 511
Change back to one-page preview 292
Change page number formatting 270
Change the view 41
Changes
  accept all at once 363
  accept/reject 361, 363
  reject all at once 363
Chart
  create 522, 52
  create from existing Word table data 52
  import delimited text data 52
  import worksheet Data 52
  modify 52
  set options 52
Chart object 52
Chart title 52
Check box 1
Check box form field 42
Check box form fields 42
Check Grammar 60, 6

Check spelling 60, 61
Citation 149
Click and Type 34
Clip art 346, 440, 456
Clip collection 456
Clip Organizer
  use 458, 459
Clipboard 90, 91
  delete selection 92
  paste 92
  paste selection 97
  set options 92
Close a document 34, 35
Close a menu without making a selection 13
Close programs 501
Close Web Page Preview 344
Closed AutoShape
  insert 444
Collapse 262
Column 186
Column break 398
Column heading 250
Column markers 186
Column width
  change 197
  set 397
Column width and row height 198
Columns 186
  create 398
  create any width 399
  return to one 398
  select preset format 398
Command 10
Command button 12
Comment 358
  delete 362
  edit 362
  insert 362
Comment balloon 358
Comment mark 358
Comment pane 358
Comments 359
  print 363
Compare documents 362
Compatible file types 165
Computer clock 65
Context menus 14
Contiguous 45
Control buttons 6
Control text flow 269, 271
Control Windows 20
Conventions 2, 3
Conventions used in this book 3
Copy 96
Copy an object 449, 452
Copy and paste 96, 97
Copy data from a Web page into a Word document 339
Copy data from a Word document
  into an e-mail message 380
Copy data from one office document to another 504
Copy or move text from one page to another 283
Copy text from one document to another 374
Copy/move text from one open document to another 373
Correct errors 33, 34
Correct Grammar as You Type 60, 61
Correct Spelling as You Type 59, 61
Create a chart 522
Create a directory with mail merge 251
Create a form 427
Create a master document 304, 307
Create a new blank Web page document 344
Create a new document 32, 34
Create a table 186, 188
Create a table of contents 320, 321
Create a Web page document in Word 342
Create a Web page using a template 351
Create an index 313, 314
Create bulleted list 126
Create headers/footers 276, 277
Create WordArt 482, 484
Criteria 250
Cross-reference
  insert a cross-reference 312
  update a cross-reference 314
Current file 2
Customize toolbars 119
Cut 90
Cut and paste 92, 283
  text 91

D

Data axis 521
Data label 521
Data series 521
Data source 230
Database 498
Datasheet 521
Datasheet cell 521
Default 2
Default Word window 5
Delete a hard page break 270
Delete a section break 270
Delete an object 444
Delete columns, rows, or cells 193
Delete entire table 193
Delimited 521
Delivery address 71
Demote 262
Destination file 503
Diagram 521, 525
Dialog box
  dialog box options 14
  use a dialog box 14
Different first page headers/footers 276
Different odd/even headers/footers 276
Different section headers/footers 277
Digital certificate 366
Digital Signature 366
Direct formatting 112
Directory 250
Disconnect Outlook Express from Internet 381, 386
Disconnect Outlook from Internet 381, 386
Display for Review
  select 362
Display Tables and Borders toolbar 206
Display/Hide toolbars 13
Divider 186
Document
  close a document 34

- create a new document 32
- open as read-only 164, 165
- open from Windows Explorer 165
- open from Windows 164
- preview 170
- save a new document 33
- type in a document 33

Document Close button 6
Document Map 282
Document properties 174
Document window 6
Dot extension 408
Dot leaders 313
Download 385, 462
Download clips from the Web 462
Download graphics objects from the Web 463
Drag and drop text from one page to another 292
Drag-and-drop
- copy text 96, 97

Drag-and-drop editing 90
Draw a table 205, 206
Draw closed shapes 443
Draw lines 443
Drawing canvas 440
Drawing object 440
Drawing toolbar
- display 443

Drop-down form field 425
Drop-down list box 12
Dropped capital 402

E

Edit a linked object 510
Edit and format a table in a Word document 557
Edit Embedded Objects 515
Edit Linked Object 511
Elements 3
Ellipsis 10
E-mail 378
- create in Word 380
- receive in Outlook 386
- receive in Outlook Express 386
- save attachment in Outlook 386
- save attachment in Outlook Express 386
- send from Outlook 381

E-mail address 378
E-mail attachment
- save 385

E-mail message
- print 385

Embed 515
Embed a new object 516
Embed a PowerPoint slide in a Word document 541
Embed entire file 516
Embed objects 515
Embed selected data 516
Embedding 515
End of cell markers 187
End of row markers 187
Endnote 149
- delete 151

Enter data in a table 187, 188
Enter text in Diagram or Organization Chart 525
Envelope
- create 74

Exit Word 6, 7
Expand a menu 13
Export 541
Export PowerPoint slides and notes to a Word document 541
Export PowerPoint text to a Word document 541

F

Favorites Folder 333, 334
Field 216, 230
Field code 312
Field results 312
Fields
- check box form fields 426
- drop-down form fields 426
- insert form fields 427
- text form fields 426

File
- insert 414, 415

File extension 164
File icon 164
File type 32, 33, 164
Fill 470
Fill color 471, 472
Fill effect 346
Fill out a form 426, 428
Filter 250
Filter recipients 251, 253
Find 297
Find and select text 299
Flip 466
Flip object 467
Floating object 440
Flush 45
Flyer
- create 78

Folder 32
Font 53
- sans serif 53
- script 53
- select 53, 55
- serif 53

Font color
- apply 105, 106

Font effects 104
Font face 53
Font size 53
- change 54
- select 55

Font style 53
Footer 27
Footnote 14
- delete 15
- edit 15

Footnote mark
- change 15

Footnotes 14
- insert 15

Footnotes and endnotes 15
Form 42
- create a form 42
- fill out a form 42

Form field 42
Form field options 42

Format 2
Format a one-page report 144
Format a table 187
Format diagram or organization chart 525
Format text in a table 188
Formatting
  change 127
  check 113
  clear 114, 115
  copy 108, 109
  paste options 114, 115
Formatting as You Type
  check 115
Formatting task pane
  open 114
Formatting toolbar 5
Forms 425
Formula 216
Freeform Line
  insert 444
Full block 65
Full Screen view 42, 43
Full-block business letter 65, 68
Function 216

G

Go To Bookmark 299
Graphics lines 346
Graphics object 346, 440
Gridline 186
Group and ungroup objects 476
Gutter 144, 396
  adjust spacing 399

H

Hard copy 37
Hard page break 267
Header 276
Header row 216
Help program 24
Highlight 45
Highlight formatting 108
Highlight text 108
Highlighted 46
Hotkey 10
HTM 342
HTML 154, 342, 378
Hyperlink 2, 154
  change destination 156
  insert to a different document 155
  insert to a Web Page 155
  insert to an e-mail address 156
  insert within a document 155
  remove 156
  select 156
  set Word to follow on click 156
  use 334
Hyperlink destination 154
Hyperlink source 154
Hyperlinks 24, 333
  create 154
Hyperlinks or links 23, 332

I

I-beam 2
Icon 10
Import data into a chart 523
Import delimited text data into a chart 524
Import worksheet data into a chart 524
In line 440
Inbox 385
Increment box 12
Indent text 139, 140
Indents 139
Index 313
  create an index 313, 314
  modify an index 314
Insert a cross-reference 312
Insert
  columns, rows, or cells 192, 193
  date and time 67
  diagram or organization chart 525
  form fields 427
  hard page breaks 267
  mode 86, 87
  nonprinting characters 42
  page numbers 269, 270
  section breaks 268
  text 87
Insertion point 2, 6
Insertion point movements 41, 43
Internet 2, 3, 25, 332, 378, 379
  features in Word 333, 334
Internet Basics 332
Internet Service Provider (ISP) 332
Intranet 378

K

Keyboard shortcuts 3
Keywords 174

L

Labels
  create 73
Landscape orientation 144, 145
Layer 476
Layer drawing objects 476
Layer objects and text 477
Layer objects with other objects 478
Leading 138
Legend 521
Letterhead stationery 67
Line color and styles 470
Line spacing 138
Line style 222, 470
Line weight 222
Link 509
Link bar 350
Link files 509, 511
Links 333
List
  sort 127
List box 12
Locate Data on the Internet 556

M

Macro.................419
delete.................421
record.................419, 421
run.................420, 421
stop recording.................421
Magnifier.................291
Mail merge.................230
Mail Merge toolbar.................231
Mail Merge Wizard.................232
Mail service provider.................378
Main document.................230
Make Web data available for use offline.................556
Manually create a watermark from a picture.................490
Manually create a watermark using a drawing object.................490
Margins.................144
set.................144
Master document.................304
Maximize.................17
Menu
close a menu without making a selection.................13
expand a menu.................13
open a menu with the keyboard.................13
open a menu with the mouse.................13
select a menu command.................13
shortcut menus.................14
Menu bar.................5
Menus.................10, 11
Merge.................204
Merge a Word document with an Access database.................537
Merge and split cells.................205
Merge block.................230
Merge cells.................206
Merge cells and erase table dividers.................206
Merge document.................230
Merge envelopes.................239
Merge field.................230
customize.................244, 246
Merge labels.................245
Merge to an e-mail message.................388
Merge with an existing Address list.................238
Message window.................378
Microsoft Access database.................230, 231
Microsoft Clip Organizer.................456, 458
Microsoft Graph.................521
Microsoft Word on the Web.................25
Minimize.................17
Mode buttons.................6
modem.................332
Modem.................332
Modified block.................65
Modified-block business letter
format.................74
Modify a chart.................522
Modify an index.................314
Mouse.................3
mouse pad.................4
mouse pointer.................3
Mouse Selection Shortcuts.................48
Move
and resize tables.................211
data from one office document to another.................504
floating object.................444
in-line object.................444
insertion point in a table.................187, 18
paragraph.................91, 9
table.................21
text from one page to another.................28
text in a document.................9
toolbar.................1

N

New Address list.................23
New Document task pane.................1
Newsletter-style columns.................39
Noncontiguous.................4
Nonprinting characters.................4
Normal template.................41
Normal.dot.................408, 40
Note reference mark.................14
Note text.................14
Note text
display.................15
Number formats.................21
Numbered list
create.................12

O

Object.................21
browse by.................29
Office address list.................230, 23
Office Assistant
change Office Assistant animation.................2
change Office Assistant options.................2
hide Office Assistant.................2
use Office Assistant.................2
Offline.................37
Online.................37
Open a compatible file type.................16
Open a menu with the keyboard.................1
Open a menu with the mouse.................1
Open a recently used document.................82, 8
Open a Word document from the Documents menu.................16
Open a Word document from the Open Office Document
dialog box.................16
Open an HTML document.................34
Open any stored document.................8
Open HTML document.................34
Open multiple documents.................372, 37
Open RTF file in Word.................54
Open the Basic Search task pane.................17
Option buttons.................1
Organization chart.................52
Orphan line.................26
Outline.................26
collapse/expand.................263, 26
create.................262, 26
edit.................26
number.................263, 26
Outlook.................378, 37
Outlook contact list.................230, 23
Outlook Express.................378, 37
disconnect from Internet.................38
Overtype mode.................8

P

Page borders 404
Page orientation
  landscape 145
  portrait 145
  set 145
Palette 12
Paragraph borders 404
Paragraph mark 32
Paragraph spacing 138
Paste 90
  from Clipboard 92
Personal business letter 65
Personal information manager (PIM) 499
Picture object 440
Pictures 441
Places bar 82
Portrait orientation 144, 145
Presentation graphics 498
Preview a document 37
Preview area 12
Preview multiple pages 291, 292
Print 38
  document without opening 170
  multiple files 170
  specific pages 292
  Web page information 339
  without opening document 169
Program Control icon 6
Promote 262
Proofreaders' marks 86
Protect a document 367, 369
Protected 425

Q

Query 537

R

Read-only 164
  open document as 164, 165
Receive e-mail messages in Outlook 386
Receive e-mail messages in Outlook Express 386
Recognizer 531
Record 230
Recover a file 27
Redo 32, 34
  use 33
Repeat 34
Replace 297
Replace selected text 47, 48
Resize a table 212
Resize an object 450
Restore 17
Return address 71
Return address labels
  create 74
Reviewing pane 359
Reviewing toolbar
  display 362
Revise 82
Revision balloon 358
Revision Display options
  select 363
Revision marks 358
Revision Marks
  customize 361, 363
Revisions
  print 363
Rotate 466
Rotate and flip objects 467
Rotate text 211, 212
Rotation handle 466
Row 186
Row height 197
Rows 186
Rulers 5, 42
Run multiple programs at the same time 499

S

Salutation 65, 67
Sans serif 53
Save 32
  changes 47, 48
  compatible file as a new file in Word format 165
  compatible file 165
  document as a template 409, 410
  document as a Web page 344
  document with a new name 83, 84
  e-mail attachment in Outlook Express 386
  e-mail attachment in Outlook 386
  new document 33, 35
  version of a document 369
  Web page locally 333
Scale 448
Scale an Object 450
ScreenTip 6, 11
Script 53
Scroll 3, 19, 20
Scroll bars 6
Scroll wheel 2
Search engine 338
Search for files from the Open dialog box 179
Search for files from the Search task pane 178
Search the Internet 338, 339
Section 144, 267
Section break 267
Select 45
  text 46
  using keyboard 48
  using mouse 48
Select a command from a toolbar 13
Select a menu command 13
Select cell shading 223
Select grammar style 61
Select in a table 192, 193
Select multiple objects 450
Select objects 448
Select text 46
Select with the mouse 193
Selection
  cancel 48
Selection bar 45
Send a Word document as e-mail 381
Send e-mail from Outlook 381
Send e-mail from Outlook Express 381
Send e-mail from Word 379

Serif ... 53
Set a Web page title ... 348
Set alignments within table cells ... 197
Set default file location for workgroup templates ... 410
Set form field properties ... 427
Set line spacing ... 139
Set margins ... 144
Set page orientation ... 145
Set paragraph spacing ... 139
Set tabs ... 71, 73
  in a cell ... 199
Set Word to follow hyperlink on click ... 156
Shading ... 222, 402, 404
Shadow ... 402, 403, 470
Shortcut key ... 419
Shortcut menu ... 10
Show or hide ruler ... 43
Show/Hide gridlines ... 188
Show/Hide marks ... 42, 43
Shrink to Fit
  use ... 67, 68
Single label
  create ... 74
Sizing handle ... 211, 448
Smart tags
  remove all ... 533
  save with document ... 533
  show/hide action button ... 533
  show/hide underlines ... 533
  turn off/on ... 533
  turn on/off for e-mail messages ... 533
Soft page break ... 267
Software suite ... 498
Sort ... 124, 125
Sort a list ... 127
Sort by multiple columns ... 217
Sort recipients in an Address list ... 252
Sort rows ... 217
Source file ... 503
Special characters
  find/replace ... 299
  insert ... 118, 119
Split cells ... 206
Spreadsheet ... 216, 498
Spreadsheet functions ... 216
Standard toolbar ... 5
Start multiple programs ... 501
Start Word ... 4, 7
Status bar ... 6
Style ... 112
  apply ... 114
  apply using task pane ... 114
  create ... 113, 115
  modify ... 113, 115
Style sheet ... 112
Styles ... 112
  change ... 114
  open ... 114
Subdocument ... 304
Subject ... 378, 379
Submenu ... 10
Suite ... 499
Switch among open programs ... 500
Symbol ... 118
Synonyms ... 59

T

Tab ... 71
Tab leader ... 71
Table ... 186
  align horizontally ... 199
Table anchor ... 211
Table AutoFormat ... 188
Table components ... 192
Table dividers
  erase ... 206
Table of contents ... 320
  create a table of contents ... 320, 321
  update a table of contents ... 321
Tables and Borders toolbar ... 205
Task pane ... 6
Template ... 350, 408
  about ... 408
  use to create document ... 410
Text
  find ... 298
  insert ... 88
  replace ... 299
Text box ... 12, 440, 448
Text box form field ... 425
Text effects ... 104
Text form fields ... 426
Text wrap options
  set ... 442
Themes ... 347, 348
Thesaurus ... 59
Thumbnail ... 462
Tile ... 23, 372, 498
Title bar ... 5
Titles ... 522
To: ... 378, 379
Toggle ... 10
Toolbar ... 3
  add a button to a toolbar ... 14
  display/hide toolbars ... 13
  move a toolbar ... 14
  select a command from a toolbar ... 13
Total values in a column or row ... 217
Track changes ... 360
  turn on or off ... 362
Type in a document ... 33

U

Underlines
  apply ... 10
Undo ... 32, 3
  use ... 3
Ungroup ... 47
Uniform Resource Locator (URL) ... 332, 33
Update a cross-reference ... 31
Update a table of contents ... 32
Update links ... 510, 51
Update the total ... 21
Uppercase Mode
  use ... 87, 8
URL
  go to in Word ... 33

Use
  Access database as a data source file for a Mail merge ... 538
  Answer Wizard ... 26
  Ask a Question box ... 26
  Click and Type ... 33
  copy and paste to copy text from one page to another ... 283
  dialog box ... 14
  Document Map ... 282, 283
  document properties ... 175
  drag-and-drop editing to copy text ... 292
  drag-and-drop editing to move text ... 292
  index ... 26
  keyboard ... 4, 7
  Microsoft Word Help ... 26
  mouse ... 3, 7
  Office Assistant ... 25
  tables in HTML documents ... 350
  task panes ... 13
  Thesaurus ... 60
  Web Layout view ... 344
  Web Page Preview ... 344
  Web page templates ... 351
  What's This? ... 26

V

Versions
  create multiple ... 366
Vertical alignment ... 134, 199
View buttons ... 6
Visual Basic Editor ... 419, 420

W

Watermark ... 488
Web browser ... 332
Web bullets ... 346, 347
Web Layout view ... 343
Web page ... 41, 332, 333
Web page graphics ... 347
Web Page Preview ... 343
Web page titles ... 346
Web server ... 342
Web site ... 332, 333
Web toolbar
  display ... 334
What's This? ... 25
Widow line ... 267
Widow/Orphan control ... 269
Wildcard characters ... 177
Window ... 2
Window controls
  maximize ... 17
  minimize ... 17
  restore ... 17
Wizard ... 408
  use to create document ... 410
Wizards
  template ... 409
Word Count ... 270
  view ... 271
Word processing ... 2
Word window ... 5
Word wrap ... 32
WordArt ... 482
WordArt shapes and formatting ... 483, 484
WordArt style ... 482
WordArt text ... 482, 483, 484
Work with subdocuments ... 305, 307
Workgroup ... 366, 408
World Wide Web ... 23, 25, 332
Wrap ... 211
Wrap text ... 212
Wrap text around an object ... 444

Z

Zoom
  adjust zoom ... 20
  use zoom dialog box ... 20
  zooming in ... 18
  zooming out ... 18